Understanding
Constitutional Law

Carolina Academic Press Understanding Series

Understanding
Constitutional Law

FIFTH EDITION

William D. Araiza
PROFESSOR OF LAW
BROOKLYN LAW SCHOOL

CAROLINA ACADEMIC PRESS
Durham, North Carolina

Library of Congress Cataloging-in-Publication Data

Names: Araiza, William D., author.
Title: Understanding constitutional law / by William D. Araiza.
Description: Fifth edition. | Durham, North Carolina : Carolina Academic
    Press, LLC, [2020] | Series: Understanding Series. | Includes bibliographical
    references and index.
Identifiers: LCCN 2020030659 | ISBN 9781531018702 (paperback) |
    ISBN 9781531018719 (ebook)
Subjects: LCSH: Constitutional law--United States--Cases.
Classification: LCC KF4550.Z9 R43 2020 | DDC 342.73--dc23
LC record available at https://lccn.loc.gov/2020030659

Carolina Academic Press
700 Kent Street
Durham, North Carolina 27701
Telephone (919) 489-7486
Fax (919) 493-5668
www.cap-press.com

Printed in the United States of America
2023 Printing

Contents

CONTENTS

Acknowledgments

I am honored to be taking over this book from John Attanasio and Joel Goldstein, who themselves had taken the reins from Norman Redlich and Bernard Schwartz, the co-authors of the First Edition. While this Fifth Edition reflects some reorganizing and editing in addition to the inevitable updating, the spirit of those earlier editions, and of their authors, remains in the book's basic structure and its insights. The book is surely better for that.

The task of editing a book of this size and scope necessarily requires the work of many hands, eyes, and minds. In writing the Fifth Edition I have had the benefit of extraordinary work by research assistants at Brooklyn Law School: Roger Acosta, Alexis Archer, Parker Brown, Katherine Cassirer, Derek Knight, Cody Laska, and Katherine Powell. It is no exaggeration to say that this book would not have been possible without their meticulous and creative work. I am also grateful to my friends and colleagues at Carolina Academic Press, especially Ryland Bowman, Sean Caldwell, and Linda Lacy, for giving me the chance to take on this project and for their help and encouragement along the way. Many thanks are also due to Keith Moore for excellent editing work. Of course, errors and omissions are my sole responsibility. I welcome any comments, criticisms, and suggestions, at bill.araiza@brooklaw.edu.

William D. Araiza
May, 2020

Understanding
Constitutional Law

Chapter 1

The Constitution and Constitutional Argument

§ 1.01 Introduction

Understanding constitutional law is an ambitious undertaking. The subject is complex and can be viewed from many different angles. An effort to understand the subject may appropriately consider the constitutional text, the events and arguments leading to its drafting and ratification, the principles it reflects, its operation in practice, the interaction of the various institutions it created, the rules, principles and doctrines which are known as constitutional law, and the nature and relative capabilities of the various institutions that may have occasion to interpret the Constitution.

Section 1.02 introduces the notion of a constitution, while Section 1.03 describes in broad terms the historical events leading to the ratification of our Constitution. Section 1.04 then discusses structural arrangements used to control government. Section 1.05 addresses the need for constitutional interpretation and considers the main interpretative theories applicable to constitutional law. Section 1.06 explores different types of constitutional arguments commonly employed. Section 1.07 concludes this brief introduction to the study of constitutional law.

§ 1.02 Constitutions

The word "constitution" is used in several different senses. At times, it describes the basic rules, written and unwritten, which create and control government. Alternatively, "constitution" may denote a document which contains the rules which provide the framework for government. Both senses of the word apply to the American system. Unlike the British constitution, our Constitution is a written document, which both delegates and defines governmental power and specifies limits on that power, in addition to providing for a catalogue of rights that, over the course of our history, has gradually expanded.

The Constitution's primary purpose is to create a national government, distribute powers between the national and state governments, and limit government so as to protect individual liberty. As such, constitutional government signifies an arrangement in which governmental institutions and their occupants are subject to, not superior to, law. Under American constitutional assumptions, "We the People of the United States"[1] delegated and allocated powers to the institutions the document created (most notably, the three branches of the federal government) and those whose existence it assumed (most notably, the states, which pre-existed the Constitution). A prominent feature of our Constitution is that its text can be formally changed only with great difficulty. Formal amendment requires (1) a proposal by either two-thirds of the House of Representatives and Senate or by a convention called by request of two-thirds of the state legislatures and (2) ratification by three-fourths of the States.[2] Only 27 constitutional amendments have been ratified, and ten of those came in a package shortly after the Constitution itself was adopted. In essence, the Constitution's terms are placed well outside the reach of normal political action. This may be a good thing or a bad thing, depending on one's point of view and the particular situation facing the country. The difficulty of amending the Constitution has, however, increased pressure on institutions charged with interpreting it—in particular, the Supreme Court—to adapt their interpretations to account for new circumstances that the formal amendment process has been unable to address.

The English scholar, Sir Kenneth C. Wheare, observed that "[i]f we investigate the origins of modern Constitutions, we find that, practically without exception, they were drawn up and adopted because people wished to make a fresh start, so far as the statement of their system of government was concerned."[3] The experience in the United States was no exception.

§ 1.03 Ratifying the Constitution

The Constitution represented Wheare's "fresh start"[4] after the initial period of American independence under the Articles of Confederation. The thirteen colonies had ratified the Articles in 1781. The Articles created a weak national government. States retained their sovereignty and all powers not "expressly delegated" to the United States.[5] The national government consisted of Congress; there was no executive or federal judiciary. Congress had limited power. It could not tax or regulate interstate commerce. Indeed, it could only act via the states, rather than regulating the American people directly. It is not inaccurate to describe the nation during the Articles period as a loose confederation, rather than a firmly united nation.

---

1. U.S. CONST., Preamble.
2. U.S. CONST. art. V.
3. K. C. WHEARE, MODERN CONSTITUTIONS 6 (1966).
4. *See* WHEARE, *supra* note 3.
5. Articles of Confederation, art. II.

In hindsight, it is not difficult to understand the problems the new nation experienced. Without an executive and judiciary, the national government lacked effective means to enforce federal law. "Congress simply could not make anyone, except soldiers, do anything," wrote historian Leonard Levy. "It acted on the states, not on people."[6] Some states adopted economic protectionist laws which predictably spawned retaliatory measures. These measures eroded any semblance of national economic unity and thus national unity more broadly. Shays' Rebellion in 1786–87 raised the specter of anarchy and persuaded many of the need for a stronger national government.[7] More generally, though, the nationwide deleterious economic impact of state protectionist policies triggered calls for strengthening national governmental power.

The Constitutional Convention convened in Philadelphia on May 25, 1787, to consider changes to the Articles of Confederation. The Convention consisted of representatives of 12 of the states (all except Rhode Island). Under the terms of the Articles, any change required unanimous consent. Five days later, the Convention voted to create a national government comprised of legislative, executive, and judicial branches. Thus, within a few days of gathering, the delegates decided to abandon, rather than salvage, the Articles. The vote was not unanimous; Connecticut opposed the motion, and New York was divided.[8] Under the terms of the Articles, the motion failed. But those who met in Philadelphia were no longer proceeding under the prior arrangement. Edwin M. Yoder, Jr., an astute constitutional historian, observed, "The fifty-five Framers performed radical surgery with a clearer notion of need than mandate from the constituents they represented, who in any case were not a mass electorate. They worked in the name of 'the people of the United States,' but could afford to deliberate in secret and in indifference to 'public opinion' in the modern sense."[9]

Delegates approached the Convention with different visions of the shape a new government should take. Virginia offered a plan for a strong national government which could regulate individuals. New Jersey, however, proposed a plan more hospitable to smaller states. It suggested a unicameral congress in which each state would have an equal voice and a supreme court which would be the only national court. Unsurprisingly, small states typically wanted equal representation in the legislature, whereas large states thought seats should be allocated based on population.

During the next four months, behind closed doors, the delegates reached compromises regarding their competing ideals and interests. A bicameral congress was proposed with a House of Representatives based on population and a Senate based on equal representation. Under the Madisonian Compromise, named for James Madi-

---

6. Leonard W. Levy, *Introduction: American Constitutional History, 1776–1789, in* THE FRAMING AND RATIFICATION OF THE CONSTITUTION 6 (Leonard W. Levy & Dennis S. Mahoney eds., 1987).

7. Stanley Elkins and Eric McKitrick, *The Founding Fathers: Young Men of the Revolution*, 76 POL. SCI. Q. 181 (1961).

8. CLINTON L. ROSSITER, 1787: THE GRAND CONVENTION 172 (1987).

9. EDWIN M. YODER, JR., THE HISTORICAL PRESENT: USES AND ABUSES OF THE PAST 60 (1997).

son, the delegates agreed to create a Supreme Court but to give Congress the discretion to "ordain and establish" lower federal courts.[10] The method of selecting the executive proved controversial. Some thought the President should be selected by Congress; others would have assigned the task to the people, via election. One group doubted the people had sufficient information to make the choice; the other feared legislative selection would make the President too weak and dependent on congressional favor. Repeated votes failed to resolve the issue. Ultimately, the delegates compromised. Electors chosen in each state would meet solely to choose a President and Vice President. Each state would have the number of electors equal to its representatives in Congress.

The Convention adjourned on September 17, 1787, after nearly four months of deliberation which produced a proposed new constitution signed by 39 of the delegates, including George Washington, Benjamin Franklin, James Madison, and Alexander Hamilton. Attention then turned towards securing ratification by at least nine states, as Article VII of the new Constitution required before it could go into effect.

In some states, the ratification issue was hotly contested. The ratification debate in New York triggered the writing and publication of what have become some of the most influential documents speaking to the Constitution's meaning. Between October 1787 and August 1788, some 85 essays advocating ratification of the Constitution were published in New York City newspapers, under a pseudonym, to counter strong "anti-federalist" (*i.e.,* anti-ratification) sentiment in New York. The essays were written by Alexander Hamilton, James Madison, and John Jay, the first two of whom had served as delegates to the Convention. Subsequently assembled and published as the *Federalist Papers*, the collection has a threefold significance. First, it provides insight into the subjective understanding of at least two delegates to the Convention, Madison and Hamilton, regarding the Constitution's meaning. Second, it provides some inkling of how the Constitution was understood by at least some people in New York who may have read the essays before considering whether to ratify it. Finally, it is a classic American work of political theory. The *Federalist Papers* have become widely accepted as an important and influential source of constitutional meaning. Courts frequently cite them in constitutional law cases.

Ratification came easily in some small states, but some larger states, such as Massachusetts, witnessed both close votes and suggestions for amendments, some of which were adopted soon after the national government was organized. New Hampshire became the ninth state to ratify on June 21, 1788, by a 57 to 47 vote, accompanied by twelve proposed amendments. The debates in Virginia and New York, both critical states, were contentious, and ratification prevailed by narrow margins, in June and July, 1788, respectively. North Carolina did not approve the Constitution until late 1789, and Rhode Island not until May, 1790.

The founders appreciated the fact that they had undertaken a momentous task. Alexander Hamilton wrote in the *Federalist 1*:

---

10. U.S. CONST. art. III, § 1.

It has been frequently remarked that it seems to have been reserved to the people of this country, by their conduct and example, to decide the important question, whether societies of men are really capable or not of establishing good government from reflection and choice, or whether they are forever destined to depend for their political constitutions on accident and force. If there be any truth in the remark, the crisis at which we are arrived may with propriety be regarded as the era in which that decision is to be made; and a wrong election of the part we shall act may, in this view, deserve to be considered as the general misfortune of mankind.[11]

§ 1.04 The Structural Constitution

The Constitution sought both to protect individual liberty from governmental tyranny and to provide a government effective enough to be able to respond to public needs. The Framers were well aware of the delicacy of their task. In *Federalist 51* James Madison wrote:

If men were angels, no government would be necessary. If angels were to govern men, neither external nor internal controls on government would be necessary. In framing a government which is to be administered by men over men, the great difficulty lies in this: You must first enable the government to control the governed; and in the next place oblige it to control itself.[12]

Constitutions typically employ two different strategies to restrain government from invading individual freedom. At times, constitutions design their structure to restrain government. They arrange institutions in such a manner as to divide power and introduce obstacles to governmental action. Alternatively, constitutions often contain a bill or catalogue of rights which place certain liberties beyond government's reach.

The American Constitution initially relied primarily on the first strategy. "Ambition must be made to counteract ambition," wrote Madison, again in *Federalist 51*. In other words, Madison insisted that governmental units must be set against each other, each jostling with the others for power, to ensure that no one unit become all-powerful and able to invade the people's liberties. Yet at the same time, the government must be energetic enough to act effectively.

Some Anti-Federalists insisted that only a bill of rights would assuage their concern about the Constitution creating a new, overly-powerful national government that could trample the people's liberties. Hamilton disagreed, arguing that such a bill would be "unnecessary," given the limitations already included in Article I, and even dangerous. He feared that inclusion of a bill of rights would expand governmental powers in unanticipated directions by encouraging the argument that any powers

---

11. THE FEDERALIST No. 1 (Hamilton).
12. THE FEDERALIST No. 51 (Madison).

not explicitly limited were implicitly conferred. Madison thought a bill of rights could not effectively control a majority intent on acting. In fact, at Philadelphia a proposal to add a bill of rights was unanimously defeated. (Still, the original Constitution did contain some specific safeguards of individual liberties.[13])

Others, including Madison, thought that adding a bill of rights might induce states like North Carolina and Rhode Island to join the Union. During the ratification debates across the nation, pro-ratification forces committed to introducing amendments that would constitute such a bill of rights. They kept their word. The first Congress proposed 12 amendments, ten of which were ratified by three-fourths of the state legislatures in 1791. Those amendments, as well as others adopted later, have proved the source of important rights of individuals against national or state government. Later chapters of this book explore several of those amendments.[14]

Despite the ratification of the Bill of Rights, the Constitution relied primarily on various structural devices to limit governmental power. The most significant device was the Constitution's division of power between different governmental institutions and branches. Madison explained: "In the compound republic of America, the power surrendered by the people is first divided between two distinct governments, and then the portion allotted to each subdivided among distinct and separate departments."[15] First, power was divided between Nation and State, creating the concept of federalism. Congress's powers were limited to those "herein granted"[16] in Article I, with the remainder residing with the states or the people.[17] On the other hand, the Supremacy Clause declared federal law supreme over state law and bound state officials to respect and enforce federal law even when it conflicted with state law.[18] The states also were given influence in constituting the national government. State legislatures chose each state's senators, and electors chosen in each state elected the President and Vice President.

The Constitution also divided power between the three branches of the federal government, the concept known as the Separation of Powers. Indeed, the vesting clause of each of the first three articles implied this division. Article I vested "all legislative powers herein granted" in Congress, Article II vested "the executive power" in the President, and Article III vested "the judicial power" in a Supreme Court and whatever other courts Congress might choose to create. Moreover, the Constitution

---

13. *See, e.g.,* U.S. Const. art. I, §§ 9, 10.

14. Many provisions of the Bill of Rights speak to criminal procedure. For the most part, this book does not examine those provisions. Readers are referred to books on constitutional criminal procedure for information about those amendments.

15. The Federalist No. 51 (Madison).

16. U.S. Const. art. I, § 1.

17. U.S. Const. amend. X. The Tenth Amendment is generally understood not to be the source of this understanding that states and the people retain power that has not been delegated, but rather simply as confirmation of that original understanding. *See, e.g.,* United States v. Darby, 312 U.S. 100, 124 (1941) ("The [Tenth] amendment states but a truism that all is retained [by states and the people] which has not been surrendered.").

18. U.S. Const. art. VI.

created various checks and balances between governmental institutions. The President could propose legislation,[19] but a bill could not become law unless both the House and the Senate passed it and the President signed it.[20] If the President chose to veto legislation, a two-thirds majority of each house was required to enact it.[21] Ultimately, the Court's power to review legislation to ascertain its constitutionality, which was implicit in the structure of the Constitution,[22] was recognized.[23] On the other hand, the President, with the advice and consent of the Senate, chose federal judges, and those judges (along with the President himself) were subject to impeachment and removal by Congress.

§ 1.05 Constitutional Interpretation

The Constitution is the basic source from which American government derives its authority. Nevertheless, as a relatively short document, it provides only an outline of the governmental system. In a seminal case considering how to interpret the Constitution, Chief Justice John Marshall reminded his readers that "we must never forget that it is a *constitution* we are expounding."[24] He insisted that the powers it gave the federal government had to be understood in flexible, expansive terms, in order to allow the government to adapt to changing circumstances. In 1870, Justice William Strong explained the general, expansive tenor of the Constitution's language: "We do not expect to find in a constitution minute details. It is necessarily brief and comprehensive."[25] The "nature" of a Constitution "requires that only its great outlines should be marked, its important objects designated"[26] and the rest left to be deduced.

Thus, the Constitution requires interpretation. To be sure, some clauses direct clear outcomes. For instance, the Constitution provides that no one is eligible to be President until they have reached age 35,[27] that each state gets two senators[28] and that conviction for treason must be based "on the testimony of two witnesses to the same overt act, or on confession in open court."[29] These provisions give relatively clear direction. But the meaning of other constitutional provisions is far less clear. The Fifth and Fourteenth Amendments protect against deprivations of "life, liberty or property without due process of law." Concepts like "life, liberty and property" and "due process of law" are deeply contestable. The Eighth Amendment proscribes "cruel and unusual

---

19. U.S. Const. art. II, § 3.

20. U.S. Const. art. I, § 7.

21. *Id.*

22. *See* The Federalist No. 78 (Hamilton).

23. Marbury v. Madison, 5 U.S. (1 Cranch) 137, 178–180 (1803).

24. McCulloch v. Maryland, 17 U.S. (4 Wheat.) 316, 407 (1819) (emphasis in original).

25. Legal Tender Cases, 79 U.S. (12 Wall.) 457, 532 (1871).

26. *McCulloch*, 17 U.S. at 407. *See also Legal Tender Cases*, 79 U.S. at 532 ("It prescribes outlines, leaving the filling up to be deduced from the outlines.").

27. U.S. Const. art. II, § 1, cl. 5.

28. U.S. Const. art. I, § 3, cl. 1.

29. U.S. Const. art. III, § 3, cl. 1.

punishments"; does capital punishment come within that prohibition? Does the guarantee of the Equal Protection Clause in the Fourteenth Amendment pertain to equal opportunity, equal outcomes, or something else? And what is an "establishment of religion" about which Congress cannot legislate?[30]

As the above examples illustrate, much of the Bill of Rights is notoriously open textured, but ambiguity is not limited to the Constitution's amendments. Rather, its structural provisions also raise numerous questions. What does it mean that Article I empowers Congress "[t]o regulate commerce ... among the several states"?[31] A substantial amount of litigation has addressed that question over the last century and a half. The President can appoint officers of the United States with the advice and consent of the Senate,[32] but can he remove an officer? The Constitution does not speak specifically to that not-uncommon contingency. The Constitution provides that the Chief Justice presides when the President is tried on impeachment.[33] Who presides if the Vice President is impeached? Can the Vice President, as President of the Senate,[34] preside over his own impeachment?[35] Suppose there is no Chief Justice; can someone else preside over the President's impeachment trial? If so, who? Congress can support an army[36] and provide for a navy[37] but the Constitution says nothing about an air force. Is the U.S. Air Force unconstitutional?

These examples are illustrative, not exhaustive; one can easily multiply questions to which the Constitution does not provide clear answers. The U.S. Reports and constitutional law casebooks are filled with cases addressing contested language in the Constitution. Constitutional interpretation thus becomes a necessary task of those charged with acting in accordance with the Constitution.

This realization raises the question regarding how one interprets and argues about the Constitution. The appropriate method(s) of constitutional analysis is/are controversial.[38] Some believe constitutional interpretation should focus on the text. Many text-based theories call for constitutional language to be construed consistently with its original understanding.[39] "Originalists" sometimes contend that either the drafters' or ratifiers' original intent or understanding provides the most natural meaning of the document, or furnishes the best way to limit judicial dis-

---

30. U.S. Const. amend. I.

31. U.S. Const. art. I, §8, cl. 3.

32. U.S. Const. art. II, §2, cl. 2.

33. U.S. Const. art. I, §3, cl. 6.

34. U.S. Const. art. I, §3, cl. 4.

35. For different views, see Joel K. Goldstein, *Can the Vice President Preside at His Own Impeachment Trial? A Critique of Bare Textualism*, 44 St. Louis U. L.J. 849 (2000) (no); Michael Stokes Paulsen, *Someone Should Have Told Spiro Agnew*, 14 Const. Comment. 245 (1997) (yes).

36. U.S. Const. art. I, §8, cl. 12.

37. U.S. Const. art. I, §8, cl. 13.

38. *See* Richard H. Fallon, Jr., *How to Choose a Constitutional Theory*, 87 Cal. L. Rev. 535, 541–45 (1999).

39. *See, e.g.*, Robert H. Bork, The Tempting of America: The Political Seduction of the Law (1990).

cretion, or gives appropriate respect to the work of the founding generation. More recently, many originalists have begun to argue that what matters is the document's so-called original public meaning — that is, the meaning of the actual words as would be understood by a person alive when the Constitution (or the relevant amendment in question) was ratified.

Others advocate a "living constitution." They take their inspiration in part from John Marshall's observation that the "Constitution [is] intended to endure for ages to come, and, consequently, to be adapted to the various *crises* of human affairs."[40] They advocate reading the text in accordance with contemporary, rather than original, understandings.[41] Some advocates of a "living constitution" believe legal precedent and/or ongoing practice are more important in constitutional interpretation. Thus, Professor David Strauss endorses a common law approach to constitutional interpretation. He argues:

> The common law tradition rejects the notion that law must be derived from some authoritative source and finds it instead in understandings that evolve over time. And it is the common law approach, not the approach that connects law to an authoritative text, or an authoritative decision by the Framers or by "we the people," that best explains, and best justifies, American constitutional law today.[42]

Other interpretive theories focus heavily on process. For instance, Professor John Hart Ely argued that the Constitution is primarily focused on assuring fair processes, not particular outcomes. Taking his cues from Justice Harlan Fiske Stone's famous footnote four in *United States v. Carolene Products Co.*,[43] he argued that, other than the Constitution's textually clear commands, constitutional interpretation should properly focus on ensuring that political processes are open to participation by all on a fair basis. Accordingly, he argued that courts should reserve their most careful review to government actions that impair the democratic process or that burden minority groups which had historically been shut out from that process.[44]

Others have criticized process-based theories. Professor Laurence Tribe argued, for instance, that such theories elevate one substantive value, democratic participation, beyond others, and ignore the many constitutional provisions which reflect commitments to those other values.[45] Focusing on those other values, Professor Christopher

---

40. McCulloch v. Maryland, 17 U.S. (4 Wheat.) 316, 415 (1819) (emphasis in original). *See also* Cohens v. Virginia, 19 U.S. (6 Wheat) 264, 387 (1821) ("But a constitution is framed for ages to come, and is designed to approach immortality as nearly as human institutions can approach it.").

41. *See, e.g.*, Paul Brest, *The Misconceived Quest for the Original Understanding*, 60 B.U. L. REV. 204, 209–17 (1980).

42. *See, e.g.*, David A. Strauss, *Common Law Constitutional Interpretation*, 63 U. CHI. L. REV. 877, 879 (1996).

43. 304 U.S. 144, 152 n.4 (1938).

44. JOHN HART ELY, DEMOCRACY AND DISTRUST: A THEORY OF JUDICIAL REVIEW (1980).

45. Laurence H. Tribe, *The Puzzling Persistence of Process-Based Constitutional Theories*, 59 YALE L.J. 1063 (1980).

Eisgruber argued that constitutional interpretation involves "principled argument about moral and political issues."[46]

This synopsis neither provides an exhaustive catalogue of constitutional theories nor does it comprehensively explain the theories that it mentions. Legal academic literature discusses numerous possible approaches, and those mentioned here (and others) lend themselves to lengthy and detailed discussion and critique.

The following section shifts the focus slightly. It considers different modes of constitutional argumentation, as distinct from the methodologies this section has briefly canvassed.

§ 1.06 Constitutional Argumentation

If it is difficult to agree on a prescriptive theory of constitutional interpretation, it is easier to describe the types of constitutional arguments which governmental officials and lawyers typically make. These modes of constitutional arguments can be divided into several categories.

[1] Textual Argument

The text of the Constitution is an obvious starting point for constitutional interpretation. Virtually all students of constitutional law agree that clear textual commands merit substantial deference and that even contestable provisions must be engaged rather than ignored. For example, the "liberty" protected by the Due Process Clause may be subject to different meanings, but we must at least acknowledge that that is the concept under discussion.

Textualism comports with a sense of law as a positive system of rules.[47] Moreover, textualism has a democratic character to it. The text is available to all. Citizens can, at least to some degree, interpret it in some fashion without recourse to the original records or philosophical arguments more accessible to academics. Although some see the text in originalist terms, meaning forever what it meant at ratification,[48] others believe textualism allows constitutional meaning to evolve to comport with the way in which language is understood today. As Professor Philip Bobbitt put it, "one power of textual argument is that it provides a valve through which contemporary values can be intermingled with the Constitution."[49] Finally, some defend textualism as a way to restrain judicial choice, to keep judges from introducing their own political and moral sensibilities into constitutional argument.

---

46. CHRISTOPHER L. EISGRUBER, CONSTITUTIONAL SELF-GOVERNMENT 6 (2001).

47. *See, e.g.*, ELY, *supra* note 44, at 3 (explaining basis behind textualism).

48. *See, e.g.*, South Carolina v. United States, 199 U.S. 437, 448 (1905) ("The Constitution is a written instrument. As such its meaning does not alter. That which it meant when adopted, it means now.").

49. PHILIP BOBBITT, CONSTITUTIONAL FATE 33, 36 (1982).

Textualism has its limits, however. The Constitution often fails to resolve difficult questions, because it does not speak directly or clearly to a problem that arises. For example, can the President abrogate a treaty by his own action?[50] The Constitution does not provide an explicit answer. Under the Commerce Clause, Congress can regulate commerce among the States. Suppose Congress had not regulated a particular area of commercial life. Can states regulate that matter or is the constitutional grant of power to Congress exclusive? The Constitution's text again lacks specific language answering that question. Yet as Professor Bobbitt points out, "in a Constitution of limited powers what is *not* expressed must also be interpreted."[51] Constitutional analysis must interpret textual silence, a challenge which often yields disputed conclusions.

At times, the Constitution uses language which is, in Professor Ely's phrase, "open-textured,"[52] using formulations so general and abstract that they invite interpretation. Perhaps the Eighth Amendment's ban on "cruel and unusual punishments" and the Due Process Clause's protection of "liberty" imply broad meanings that require significant interpretation. Even if we engage the text, its open-textured language may not point in only one direction. Indeed, the Ninth Amendment[53] might be viewed as a textual invitation to go beyond the Constitution in searching for protected rights.

Finally, constitutional practice often reveals that the text often does not play a crucial role. On some occasions, courts decide cases based on concepts not stated in the Constitution. The Constitution's text does not explicitly confer a general right of privacy, yet decisions prohibiting states from outlawing the use of contraceptives or acknowledging a woman's right to terminate a pregnancy rest on that concept. Even if the Equal Protection Clause provided a basis to outlaw state-sponsored school segregation, as the Court held in *Brown v. Board of Education*,[54] that clause only limits actions of the states. There is no such clause in the text that applies to the federal government. Does that mean that the federal government could operate segregated schools even though the states could not? Such an outcome would seem inconceivable. The Court avoided that result by finding, the same day as *Brown*, an equal protection component in the Due Process Clause of the Fifth Amendment.[55] But that approach created other textual anomalies. As one prominent academic has written: "In the important cases, reference to and analysis of the constitutional text plays a minor role."[56]

These criticisms do not sideline textual analysis. The text certainly does decide some issues, *e.g.*, the age of eligibility to be President. Even when it may not be

---

50. *See* Goldwater v. Carter, 444 U.S. 996 (1979).

51. Bobbitt, *supra* note 49 at 38.

52. *See generally* Ely, *supra* note 44, at 13–14.

53. U.S. Const. amend. IX ("The enumeration in the Constitution, of certain rights, shall not be construed to deny or disparage others retained by the people.").

54. 347 U.S. 483 (1954).

55. Bolling v. Sharpe, 347 U.S. 497 (1954).

56. Thomas C. Grey, *Do We Have an Unwritten Constitution?*, 27 Stan. L. Rev. 703, 707–08 (1975).

decisive, it may at least limit the terms of discussion: for example, the Eighth Amendment applies to "punishments" while the Commerce Clause allows Congress to regulate "commerce."[57] If the text restrains judges by focusing their attention on the Constitution's language, it also empowers them by suggesting they are free to reject decades of doctrine if it is inconsistent with the text.

One application of textual argument is the technique which Professor Akhil Reed Amar has labeled "intratextualism."[58] It involves using the Constitution as a dictionary to help define its recurring words and phrases by reference to their meaning elsewhere in the document. As will be seen later, John Marshall used this technique in *McCulloch v. Maryland*;[59] other cases also used it to interpret constitutional language. Yet some critique intratextualism, contending that it mistakenly attributes greater coherence to the document than appropriate, and it assumes judges have greater capacity to reach correct interpretations than they do.[60]

Because the text is often not conclusive, the judiciary has developed other modes of analysis to help give meaning to general constitutional language in specific cases. In addition to the text, several other modes of argument command widespread support.[61]

[2] Framers' Intent

At least three types of historical arguments find their way into legal and judicial statements about the Constitution. First, some view constitutional interpretation as a quest to capture and apply the intent of the Framers. These originalist arguments generally seek to discover and enforce either the intent of the drafters or ratifiers of the original Constitution or the understanding of the generation alive at that time. (Of course, for amendments originalists emphasize the intent or understandings related to the amendment in question.)

Proponents of originalism often advance one or more of several justifications for giving it strong weight. First, ratification of the Constitution was the positive act which elevated it from paper to law. It was ratified by a democratic act which required super-majoritarian support. Those who ratified it presumably understood its language to achieve certain purposes. Accordingly, those understandings are what became law.[62] Second, the founding generation was a unique collection of individuals acting

---

57. *See* Richard H. Fallon, Jr., *A Constructivist Coherence Theory of Constitutional Interpretation*, 100 Harv. L. Rev. 1189, 1196 (1987).

58. Akhil Reed Amar, *Intratextualism*, 112 Harv. L. Rev. 747 (1999).

59. 17 U.S. (4 Wheat) 316 (1819).

60. Adrian Vermeule & Ernest A. Young, *Hercules, Herbert, and Amar: The Trouble with Intratextualism*, 113 Harv. L. Rev. 730 (2000).

61. *See generally* Bobbitt, *supra* note 49; Charles A. Miller, The Supreme Court and the Uses of History 14–38 (1969).

62. *See generally* Keith E. Whittington, Constitutional Interpretation: Textual Meaning, Original Intent, and Judicial Review (1999); Antonin Scalia, A Matter of Interpretation: Federal Courts and the Law (1997).

in a time of heightened political consciousness, whose judgments therefore merit particular respect. Further, originalists argue that originalism confines the discretion allowed unelected judges. A jurist bound to apply original meaning is limited in a way that one licensed to interpret an ever-evolving Constitution is not. Finally, originalism gives the Constitution some rigor. If the Constitution is viewed as being elastic enough to accommodate changing conditions, it will stretch until it loses all ability to restrain.[63]

But originalism also encounters serious problems. First, can the intent of the Framers or ratifiers or the understanding of their generation really be fathomed? No official minutes were kept at the Constitutional Convention. Records there and at the various ratifying conventions are fragmentary. Only a fraction of what was said was preserved, and some portions of that record are cryptic. The comments of a speaker may or may not have reflected the views or rationales of the greater number who were silent or whose thoughts were not preserved. Sources like the *Federalist Papers* may tell us how Hamilton, Madison, and Jay defended constitutional provisions, but their explanations may not have reflected the sentiments of other Framers or those of ratifiers, most of whom were not familiar with these essays.

More generally, the Framers and ratifiers clearly did not anticipate or address new problems and contexts beyond their imaginations. Even when the founding generation did anticipate issues, it may be treacherous to ascribe to a group the articulated views of the few who may have spoken.[64] And it is difficult to determine with any certainty how the founding generation understood much constitutional language. In *Brown v. Board of Education*, the Court rescheduled arguments ostensibly so the parties could brief the question of the original understanding of the Fourteenth Amendment regarding school desegregation. But after many of the nation's ablest lawyers and historians labored for months to elucidate the subject, the Court concluded that the historical argument was "at best ... inconclusive."[65] Finally, it must be remembered that the framing generation severely limited political participation, with the result that those who were allowed to take part in the ratification debates constituted a small sliver of the American population, distinguished by race, sex, and property-owning status.

Recovering original intent may be particularly problematic when those doing the recovery are lawyers and judges rather than historians. Of course, even a historian's account of the past may reflect more the view of the particular historian than history itself. Yet historians, even with their limitations, are likely to be more trained in the historical craft than are lawyers and judges, and better able to transport themselves back in history to recreate what prior generations thought or understood to be the public meaning of their work. Moreover, they presumably do not approach an his-

---

63. *See, e.g.,* SCALIA, *supra* note 62, at 47.

64. *See, e.g.,* Daniel A. Farber, *The Originalism Debate: A Guide for the Perplexed*, 49 OHIO ST. L.J. 1085 (1989).

65. Brown v. Board of Educ., 347 U.S. 483, 489 (1954).

torical issue as advocates in the same way lawyers do. Perhaps even more fundamentally, transformative events—westward expansion, the Civil War, immigration, two World Wars, the Great Depression, the change from an agrarian to an industrial and now a post-industrial society, the emergence of the nation as a world superpower, the civil rights movement, and many more—have created quite a different world from the one Madison, Hamilton, and Jay knew. Should the Constitution bind contemporary people to the specific choices of those who lived two centuries ago?[66]

Finally, originalism cannot account for numerous decisions of the Supreme Court. The First Amendment has been interpreted to protect a broad "marketplace of ideas" which seems to extend far beyond the view of the founders. The Equal Protection Clause has been understood to outlaw racial segregation in schools and most sex discrimination, neither of which appeared to be a specific focus of those who ratified it. And it has been made applicable against the federal government, an interpretive move hard to defend on originalist grounds.

[3] Ongoing Practice

A second type of historical argument involves ongoing history. These arguments rest on the premise that constitutional meaning evolves to embrace changing reality. In part, the Constitution changes in response to the accepted interpretations of government officials (such as Presidents and legislators) over a period of time. It also responds to accommodate changes in social practice, technology and morality. Whereas original intent history seeks to confine judges to the constitutional meaning prevailing at the time a constitutional text was generated, ongoing history "allows the Constitution to move with the prevailing temper of the country and may therefore be considered forward-looking."[67] In part, ongoing history reflects judicial deference to the ability of members of the legislative and executive branches to interpret the Constitution. It assumes that these figures would act in accordance with the Constitution and accords significance to their behavior over time.[68]

Ongoing history may allow the Constitution to change to accommodate new circumstances or to recognize traditional practice. But how does one decide which practices are significant in changing constitutional meaning and which are not? For centuries, American society oppressed African-Americans and excluded women from certain preferred roles. The longevity of these practices would not seem a basis to accord them constitutional sanction. One escape from this quandary is to admit ongoing practice to shape the meaning of provisions respecting institutional

---

66. *See generally* STEPHEN BREYER, MAKING OUR DEMOCRACY WORK: A JUDGE'S VIEW 76–80 (2010); RICHARD H. FALLON, JR., IMPLEMENTING THE CONSTITUTION 13–14 (2001).

67. *See* MILLER, *supra* note 61, at 25.

68. A well-known example of this approach is Justice Felix Frankfurter's concurring opinion in *Youngstown Sheet & Tube v. Sawyer*, in which Justice Frankfurter answered a difficult question about presidential power by examining the history of presidential and congressional conduct on that issue. 343 U.S. 579, 610–611 (1952) (Frankfurter, J., concurring) (referring to the "gloss" that historical practice has placed on the words of the Constitution). *Youngstown* is discussed in Section 3.07[2].

practice and behavior, but not regarding those directly impacting individual liberty. Chief Justice Marshall used this approach in *McCulloch v. Maryland*. There he suggested that past practice might be appropriate in certain cases in which "the great principles of liberty are not concerned."[69] Yet, at times, justices do look to tradition to determine whether practices like homosexuality,[70] abortion[71] and assisted suicide[72] are constitutionally protected. Moreover, accepting Chief Justice Marshall's formulation does not eliminate the difficulty but simply limits it to cases dealing with structural questions. At times, the Court has found past practice suggestive of constitutional meaning on those structural questions; at other times, not. In an early case, *Stuart v. Laird*, Justice William Patterson used ongoing practice to respond to the argument that the Constitution precluded Supreme Court justices from sitting on circuit courts. He wrote:

> To this objection, which is of recent date, it is sufficient to observe, that practice and acquiescence under it for a period of several years, commencing with the organization of the judicial system, affords an irresistible answer, and has indeed fixed the construction.[73]

Less than two decades later, Chief Justice Marshall thought the earlier decisions of the executive and legislative branches in favor of a national bank suggested its constitutionality.[74] But over a century-and-a-half later, in *Immigration and Naturalization Service v. Chadha*, Chief Justice Burger, in the course of striking down so-called "legislative veto" provisions, commented that their increased appearance in federal statutes "sharpened rather than blunted"[75] the appropriate judicial scrutiny.

[4] Judicial Doctrine and Precedent

A third type of historical argument relates to judicial doctrine or precedent. These distinct, yet closely related, types of constitutional arguments use judicial formulations of the past to decide new constitutional cases. Precedent involves the use of previously decided cases to resolve later cases, either by way of analogy or as binding authority. In turn, precedent helps establish doctrine—the holdings, concepts, and tests that often assume a life of their own and become the stuff of constitutional law. Constitutional law includes many judge-made rules which are developed in caselaw, especially the decisions of the Supreme Court.

Doctrine and precedent both reflect a common law approach to constitutional law. They emphasize judicial decisions and the principles they articulate. To be sure,

---

69. McCulloch v. Maryland, 17 U.S. 316, 401 (1819).
70. *See, e.g.*, Bowers v. Hardwick, 478 U.S. 186 (1986), *overruled by* Lawrence v. Texas, 539 U.S. 558 (2003).
71. *See, e.g.*, Roe v. Wade, 410 U.S. 113 (1973).
72. *See, e.g.*, Washington v. Glucksberg, 521 U.S. 702 (1997).
73. Stuart v. Laird, 5 U.S. (1 Cranch) 299, 309 (1803).
74. *McCulloch*, 17 U.S. at 401.
75. 462 U.S. 919, 944 (1983).

as Justice Oliver Wendell Holmes observed, "General propositions do not decide concrete cases."[76] While his admonition most clearly states a limitation on doctrine,
precedent, too, does not always precisely speak to the diverse situations new cases
present.

Reliance on precedent enjoys some clear advantages. It preserves judicial resources,
adds certainty and stability to constitutional law, links current decisions to those of
the past, and limits judicial discretion.[77] Yet some question why doctrine and precedent
should receive such deference. After all, if our allegiance is to the Constitution, then
why should a past court's decision on what the Constitution means assume the authority
of the document itself? In the early twentieth century, a group of scholars called "legal
realists" pointed out that judges have policy preferences and suggested that their decisions may mask those preferences as law. Why should later generations honor and
perpetuate the work of jurists motivated by potentially outdated policy concerns?

Stare decisis, the practice of following precedent, is practiced in constitutional adjudication, although not with the same rigor as in statutory cases. Justice Louis Brandeis explained:

> *Stare decisis* is usually the wise policy, because in most matters it is more im-
> portant that the applicable rule of law be settled than that it be settled right....
> But in cases involving the Federal Constitution, where corrections through
> legislative action is practically impossible, this Court has often overruled its
> earlier decisions. The Court bows to the lessons of experience and the force
> of better reasoning, recognizing that the process of trial and error, so fruitful
> in the physical sciences, is appropriate also in the judicial function.[78]

Thus, at times, the Court explicitly or implicitly abandons or overrules pernicious
or anachronistic precedents or doctrine, as it did in *Brown* when it rejected the notion
from *Plessy v. Ferguson*[79] that "separate but equal" race segregation was consistent
with the Fourteenth Amendment.

Nevertheless, *stare decisis* has force even in constitutional cases. Thus, in *Planned
Parenthood of Southeastern Pennsylvania v. Casey,* the Court affirmed the "central
holding"[80] of *Roe v. Wade,*[81] which recognized a woman's constitutional right to terminate a pregnancy, even though three justices jointly authoring the lead opinion
repeatedly suggested that they (or some of them) may have had misgivings about *Roe*
as an original matter. In *Casey,* Justices O'Connor, Kennedy and Souter suggested
that whether *stare decisis* should apply should turn upon several criteria: Was the
earlier rule workable? Had it engendered substantial reliance? Had "related principles
of law ... so far developed as to have left the old rule no more than a remnant of

---

76. Lochner v. New York, 198 U.S. 45, 75 (1905) (Holmes, J. dissenting).
77. *See generally* Geoffrey R. Stone, *Precedent, the Amendment Process, and Evolution in Constitutional Doctrine,* 11 HARV. J.L. & PUB. POL'Y 67, 70 (1988).
78. Burnet v. Coronado Oil & Gas Co., 285 U.S. 393, 406–08 (1932) (Brandeis, J., dissenting).
79. 163 U.S. 537 (1896).
80. 505 U.S. 833, 879 (1992).
81. 410 U.S. 113 (1973).

abandoned doctrine?" Had facts changed so much "to have robbed the old rule of significant application or justification?"[82] Because *Roe* was so controversial, that bloc of justices added that to "overrule under fire"[83] would subvert the Court's legitimacy as an impartial arbiter of law; thus, the very fact that *Roe* was so deeply controversial gave the Court an additional reason to reaffirm it.

Yet since *Casey*, the Court has not always applied these tests in determining whether to apply or abandon an earlier doctrine. For example, in *Lawrence v. Texas*,[84] the Court overruled *Bowers v. Hardwick*[85] without assessing the earlier case against all the *Casey* principles.

[5] Structural Arguments

In addition to historical arguments, constitutional interpretation often relies on structural argument — that is, inferences from the structures and relationships built into the Constitution.[86] Such arguments rely on concepts implicit in the Constitution's architecture to interpret the document. Thus, constitutional concepts such as federalism, separation of powers, checks and balances, the rule of law, and democratic accountability emerge from constitutional structures, although those terms do not themselves appear in the Constitution.

Structural reasoning is linked to the text, because it draws general conclusions based upon the text. It differs from textual argument, because it draws meaning not from any particular clause but from the relationships between, and the principles that emerge from, various clauses. Structural reasoning features prominently in some of Chief Justice John Marshall's seminal opinions, including *Marbury v. Madison*[87] and *McCulloch v. Maryland*.[88] Thus, in *Marbury*, he concluded that the Constitution is paramount law, that Congress's powers are limited, and that citizens with rights must have remedies, all drawn from basic concepts relating to constitutionalism and rule of law. In *McCulloch*, he cited the structural idea that constitutions are created to succeed and that, accordingly, Congress can exercise means necessary to accomplish its enumerated ends. Proponents of such reasoning argue that it is more likely to yield practical outcomes than other forms of legal reasoning.

Yet critics find structural arguments elusive and malleable. To identify federalism or separation of powers as a constitutional concept does not provide very precise guidance in resolving specific cases. Thus, rather than restraining judges, structural reasoning may give them license to reach results they wish to reach. Moreover, struc-

---

82. *Casey*, 505 U.S. at 855.
83. *Id.* at 867.
84. 539 U.S. 558 (2003).
85. 478 U.S. 186 (1986).
86. *See generally* CHARLES L. BLACK, JR., STRUCTURE AND RELATIONSHIP IN CONSTITUTIONAL LAW (1969).
87. 5 U.S. (1 Cranch) 137 (1803).
88. 17 U.S. (4 Wheat.) 316 (1819).

tural argumentation generally seems better suited for questions involving the relationships between different institutions of government; it is thus less useful for protecting individual rights, although occasionally, such argument appears in individual rights cases.[89]

[6] Consequential Arguments

Prudential or consequentialist arguments proceed from the assumption that constitutional interpretation should consider likely outcomes. Thus, in *McCulloch v. Maryland*, Chief Justice Marshall justified the Court's conclusion that Congress had the power to create a national bank by considering the difficulties that would exist if Congress lacked that power. Prudential arguments may, at times, lead the Court to decline deciding a case in order to avoid institutional harm.[90] Or it may lead in the opposite direction. For example, in *Bolling v. Sharpe*, the companion case to *Brown v. Board of Education* dealing with federal school segregation (in Washington, D.C.), Chief Justice Warren wrote that "[i]n view of our decision that the Constitution prohibits the states from maintaining racially segregated public schools, it would be unthinkable that the same Constitution would impose lesser a duty on the Federal Government."[91]

Consequential arguments, however, may require the Court to speculate about the practical results of possible decisions it might reach. Considering outcomes might strike some critics as policy-oriented, not law-oriented, and involve courts in legislating, not adjudicating. Beyond exceeding judges' formal authority, such policy-based reasoning triggers a consequentialist objection of its own: namely, that judges have no special qualifications to perform such policy-making competently.

[7] Ethical Argument

At times, courts and lawyers invoke ethical or value arguments. These assertions seek to vindicate what is deemed moral, just, or desirable. The open-ended language of the Constitution often seems to invite such arguments, for example, when the Court is asked to define "liberty" or "equal protection." On other occasions, ethical arguments are invoked when other arguments seem inconclusive. As Professor Ronald Dworkin writes, "The moral reading proposes that we all—judges, lawyers, citizens—interpret and apply these abstract clauses on the understanding that they invoke moral principles about political decency and justice."[92]

However, as one can probably immediately imagine, moral argumentation has its critics. Some attack it as contestable, since different people will reach different results

---

89. *See, e.g.*, Griswold v. Connecticut, 381 U.S. 479 (1965) (using structural reasoning to find a constitutional right to privacy).

90. *See, e.g.*, ALEXANDER BICKEL, THE LEAST DANGEROUS BRANCH (1962).

91. 347 U.S. 497, 500 (1954).

92. RONALD DWORKIN, FREEDOM'S LAW: THE MORAL READING OF THE AMERICAN CONSTITUTION 2 (1996).

from moral reasoning. As such, some view moral argument as representing an effort to incorporate personal sentiments into constitutional law. Moreover, introducing moral argument into constitutional interpretation may diminish the role of elected decisionmakers. Some argue that elected officials, not unelected judges, best reflect the people's moral convictions.[93]

[8] Sociological Evidence

Courts sometimes use social facts as a basis for deciding constitutional cases. The so-called Brandeis brief, offered in *Muller v. Oregon*,[94] pioneered this approach.[95] Rather than devote his brief to a discussion of legal precedents, then-attorney (and later Justice) Louis Brandeis submitted a brief in *Muller*, defending the constitutionality of an Oregon law imposing working hours limitations on women, which focused almost entirely on presenting sociological data to show the reasonableness of the conclusions the Oregon legislature had reached. Attorneys challenging school desegregation in the 1950s employed extensive psychological and sociological evidence to support their ultimately successful claim that racially segregated education violated equal protection because of its impact on African-American children.[96] More recently, in a Michigan affirmative action case, the Court relied on evidence regarding the beneficial effects of affirmative action programs in college admissions.[97]

As common-sense as it might seem for courts to base their decisions, at least in part, on social reality, sociological argumentation raises problems. When presented in briefs, rather than offered in evidence, there may not be effective opportunity to impeach the evidence and offer rebuttal.[98] Moreover, its use may make legal principles turn on sociological data and accordingly remain vulnerable to a change in sociological knowledge or understanding. For example, Justice Clarence Thomas has derided sociological claims supporting affirmative action programs as passing "fads" that make the law deeply unstable.[99] Regardless of what one might think about that particular argument, the fact that yesterday's accepted sociological truth might be tomorrow's discarded relic raises concerns about constitutional decisionmaking that relies on such support.

[9] Comparative Constitutional Argument

Finally, some justices have recently argued that the practices and experiences of other constitutional democracies furnish a basis for reaching decisions on American

---

93. *See generally* Michael W. McConnell, *The Importance of Humility in Judicial Review: A Comment on Ronald Dworkin's "Moral Reading" of the Constitution*, 65 Fordham L. Rev. 1269 (1997).

94. 208 U.S. 412 (1908).

95. Alpheus T. Mason, Brandeis: A Free Man's Life (1946).

96. *See* Brown v. Board of Education, 347 U.S. 483, 494 n. 11 (1954) (discussing that evidence).

97. *See* Grutter v. Bollinger, 539 U.S. 306, 330 (2003).

98. Paul A. Freund, The Supreme Court of the United States 151 (1961).

99. *See Grutter*, 539 U.S. at 350 (Thomas, J., concurring in part and dissenting in part).

constitutional law. In cases dealing with assisted suicide,[100] sexual orientation,[101] and affirmative action,[102] some justices have cited the ways other countries handle these issues in resolving American constitutional law issues. Although this type of argument appears most often in cases involving constitutional rights, it has also appeared in cases dealing with constitutional structure.[103] Not all embrace the use of comparative constitutional law in interpreting our Constitution. In fact, its use has become very controversial with originalists. For example, Justice Scalia has suggested that the American Constitution should be interpreted without reference to experiences abroad.[104]

§ 1.07 Conclusion

The previous discussion has implicitly assumed that courts and lawyers have a special role in constitutional argument. Indeed, much constitutional argumentation is performed by judges and lawyers. But this does not mean that only lawyers and judges can engage in constitutional debate. Over the last two decades, a theory known as "popular constitutionalism" has arisen, which argues, in essence, that the American people have a legitimate and important role in determining the Constitution's meaning, not through the formal procedures of litigation and adjudication but through political debate and the resulting legislative action and even social evolution.[105] At times this book will note the political and social backdrop to the subjects and the cases it discusses. More generally, one should always remember that the Supreme Court, and even more so other government actors, are aware, to a greater or lesser degree, of larger political and social trends. It would be naïve to think that those larger forces play no role in the development of the legal doctrine this book discusses.

The following chapter will introduce and explore the institution of judicial review, which recognizes the important judicial role in interpreting the Constitution. The judiciary is the primary source of constitutional law, although it is by no means the only institution that shapes constitutional meaning. The President[106] and members of the executive and legislative branches[107] also take oaths to enforce the Constitution, an obligation which arguably allows them to interpret it. Indeed, Presidents Thomas

---

100. *See* Washington v. Glucksberg, 521 U.S. 702, 718 n.16 (1997).

101. *See* Lawrence v. Texas, 539 U.S. 558, 572–73 (2003).

102. *See Grutter*, 539 U.S. at 344 (Ginsburg, J., concurring).

103. *See, e.g.*, Printz v. United States, 521 U.S. 898, 976–78 (1997) (Breyer, J., dissenting).

104. For an example of the justices debating the appropriateness of using foreign law, compare Roper v. Simmons, 543 U.S. 551, 622–628 (2005) (Scalia, J., dissenting) (taking issue with the use of foreign law in an Eighth Amendment case), with *id.* at 604–605 (2005) (O'Connor, J., dissenting) (agreeing with Justice Scalia on the proper result in the case but disagreeing with his refusal to consider foreign law).

105. *See, e.g.*, LARRY KRAMER, THE PEOPLE THEMSELVES: POPULAR CONSTITUTIONALISM AND JUDICIAL REVIEW (2004).

106. U.S. CONST. art. II, § 1, cl. 8.

107. U.S. CONST. art. VI, cl. 3.

Jefferson, Andrew Jackson, Abraham Lincoln, and Franklin D. Roosevelt among others suggested at times that they had some independent authority to interpret the Constitution. Indeed, judicial decisions to uphold the constitutionality of legislative and executive action based on deference to those branches rest in part on a view that those branches have at least some authority to interpret the Constitution.

Officials in the executive and legislative branches interpret the Constitution in the regular course of their duties.[108] When, for instance, the House of Representatives considered impeaching Presidents Richard Nixon, Bill Clinton, and Donald Trump, it had to interpret the Impeachment Clause to determine whether the acts alleged constituted "high crimes and misdemeanors."[109] Congress sometimes considers constitutional arguments in legislating in other contexts as well. For instance, Senator Thomas F. Eagleton argued and voted against the War Powers Resolution in 1973 because he concluded that the measure unconstitutionally gave the President some of Congress's power to declare war.[110] When the bill passed nonetheless, President Nixon vetoed it, because he thought it unconstitutionally encroached on the President's power.[111] In each case, their interpretation was based on their reading of the Constitution and their assessment of other constitutional materials.

Neither Senator Eagleton's nor President Nixon's actions were unprecedented. On the contrary, members of the executive and legislative branches often consider constitutional arguments for or against proposed actions. At times, courts recognize that one of the political branches has a superior right or competence to interpret a particular part of the Constitution. On other occasions, the Court adopts, or is influenced by, the constitutional views of the executive or legislative branches. Indeed, at times, the text appears to give Congress a clear role in at least considering what the Constitution means, for example, when the Fourteenth Amendment gives Congress the power to "enforce" the provisions of that amendment. Even without such an explicit reference to constitutional interpretation or enforcement, one would expect Congress (and the President) to consider whether actions they are contemplating are constitutional. And, of course, "We the People" retain a large role in interpreting the Constitution, through the political choices we make that reflect our understanding of the Constitution's text and values.

<hr>

108. *See generally* Louis Fisher, Constitutional Dialogues: Interpretation as Political Process (1988).

109. U.S. Const. art. II, §4.

110. Thomas F. Eagleton, War and Presidential Power 163 (1974).

111. Richard M. Nixon, Veto of the War Powers Resolution (Oct. 24, 1973), *in* Public Papers of the Presidents: Richard Nixon 1973, at 311 (1975).

Chapter 2

The Courts and Judicial Review

§ 2.01 Introduction

Any effort to understand American Constitutional law must quickly encounter the institution of judicial review. It is, of course, as Chief Justice John Marshall suggested, a Constitution being expounded, and accordingly the Constitution itself is the touchstone of constitutional law. But it is hard to discuss constitutional law without coming to grips with judicial review—the power of the federal courts to review legislation to determine whether it is consistent with the Constitution.

The very concept of judicial review invites questions. What authorizes courts to exercise this power? What is its scope? How can one reconcile judicial review with principles of democratic accountability so basic to our system? Do courts alone interpret the Constitution or is that task shared with other branches? What, if any, restraints exist on the federal judiciary when they perform this function?

This chapter addresses these subjects. It begins, in Section 2.02, by discussing *Marbury v. Madison*, the foundational case for many principles of American constitutional law. Section 2.03 examines the principle, firmly established in *Marbury*, that federal courts and the Supreme Court in particular have the power of judicial review—that is, the power to strike down laws that violate the Constitution. Section 2.04 considers the status and jurisdiction of the Supreme Court, while Section 2.05 considers the analogous questions as applied to the lower federal courts. Section 2.06 discusses limits on congressional control over the federal courts, while Section 2.07 focuses in particular on Congress's power to create non-Article III adjudicators—so-called Article I courts. Section 2.08 concludes by considering the justiciability doctrines (standing, timing issues, and the political question doctrine) that limit the authority of federal courts to decide a case, even when they otherwise have jurisdiction.

§ 2.02 *Marbury v. Madison*

Marbury v. Madison[1] is a foundational case in American constitutional law. It articulated or suggested many central principles of that enterprise. Four, perhaps, are

---

1. Marbury v. Madison, 5 U.S. (1 Cranch) 137 (1803).

most critical. First, it enunciated the basic structural idea that our government is based upon the rule of law. Second, it pronounced that the Constitution is paramount law such that any inconsistent statute is invalid. Third, it held that ours is a system of limited government. Finally, it held that the judiciary has the power of judicial review.

[1] Historical Context

Marbury arose at a historically fraught time, and that context is important in understanding the case. The 1800 presidential election produced a victory for the Democratic-Republicans and Vice President Thomas Jefferson and a defeat for the Federalists and President John Adams. The Federalists' loss of the White House and Congress brought the nation's first partisan transition of governmental control. During the closing months of Federalist control,[2] the party sought to establish a bastion of power in the third branch of government, the judiciary. In early 1801, Congress enacted a statute that reduced the Supreme Court from six justices to five, eliminated justices' obligation to "ride circuit" and hear cases around the country, and created sixteen new circuit judges. These reforms provided clear political benefits to the Federalists. Reducing the size of the Court would deny Jefferson an appointment when the first vacancy appeared, while staffing the new circuit judgeships with Federalists both provided patronage for a party about to leave office and promised to entrench Federalist control of the judiciary. Yet the changes also had certain salutary purposes. If the Supreme Court justices no longer had to ride circuit, they could function as a powerful national court to balance the work of the other branches. Creating circuit judges relieved the justices of this burdensome duty and, along with the additional judges, made the judiciary more efficient.

Two weeks later, with only one week before Adams' term ended, Congress enacted a second statute, which allowed the President to appoint 42 justices of the peace for the District of Columbia. In the closing days of his administration, President Adams appointed various Federalist loyalists, including William Marbury, to these newly-created judicial positions. However, some of the official justice of the peace commissions were not delivered to their intended recipients by the end of the Adams Administration. Upon taking office, Jefferson directed that the remaining commissions, including Marbury's, not be delivered. Marbury sought a writ of mandamus from the Supreme Court, directing Jefferson's Secretary of State, James Madison, to deliver his commission.[3] In a great irony of American history — and one that could have had significant consequences — John Marshall, who was appointed Chief Justice in early 1801, continued to serve as Secretary State for a period of time after ascending to the Court. As a result, he was directly involved in the failure to deliver Marbury's commission.

---

2. Prior to the adoption of the Twentieth Amendment in 1933, presidential terms began and ended on March 4.

3. The case came to the Supreme Court in 1803. Marbury had filed suit in December, 1801 but the new, Jefferson-allied Congress had abolished the June and December 1802 terms of the Court.

[2] The Opinion

It was against this background that *Marbury* came to the Court. The case presented Marshall with a clear problem. Marbury's petition asked the Court to order Madison to deliver the commission, thereby reversing President Jefferson's contrary direction. If the Court granted Marbury's petition and ordered Madison to deliver the commission, it would risk a potentially humiliating confrontation with the executive branch, given Jefferson's warning that he would direct Madison to ignore such an order. Losing such a confrontation would likely have meant permanently relegating the judiciary, including the Supreme Court, to a decidedly inferior position relative to the executive branch. On the other hand, if the Court denied Marbury's petition as beyond its power, it would appear to have acquiesced to the reality of its impotence.

Marshall resolved this conundrum through an ingenious opinion which avoided the confrontation with Jefferson which the Court could not afford, while nonetheless establishing important principles that strengthened its hand. Ultimately, Marshall ruled that the Court lacked jurisdiction over Marbury's case because the statute under which Marbury proceeded was unconstitutional. As Professor Robert G. McCloskey concluded, "The decision is a masterwork of indirection, a brilliant example of Marshall's capacity to sidestep danger while seeming to court it, to advance in one direction while his opponents are looking in another."[4]

Marshall began his opinion by concluding that Marbury was entitled to the commission.[5] According to Marshall, Marbury's appointment was complete once signed and sealed, with the delivery failure merely a formality. Thus, by law, Marbury was entitled to the four-year term the judgeship provided. Since he was appointed for a fixed term, his appointment was irrevocable and conferred on him a vested property right. By withholding the commission, Madison was violating the law.

Marshall then turned to a second question: whether law gave Marbury a legal remedy for the violation of his legal right. Marshall's response articulated the basic American principle of the rule of law: "The very essence of civil liberty certainly consists in the right of every individual to claim the protection of the laws, whenever he receives an injury."[6]

But did this grand principle mean that the "supreme executive" was answerable in court for the conduct of his job? Marshall essentially responded, "sometimes yes and sometimes no," depending on what he called "the nature of" the complained-of executive action. He explained that, in the exercise of "political powers," the President and his subordinates had "discretion" for which the President was "accountable only to his country in his political character, and to his own conscience." For these acts,

---

4. Robert G. McCloskey, The American Supreme Court 40 (1960).

5. Much useful scholarship has been written about *Marbury*. See, for instance, William E. Nelson, *Marbury v. Madison*: The Origins and Legacy of Judicial Review (2000), and William W. Van Alstyne, *A Critical Guide to* Marbury v. Madison, 1969 Duke L.J. 1.

6. *Marbury*, 5 U.S. at 163.

the President and administration were not answerable judicially, but rather only politically. But he continued that where executive officials were assigned duties in which
they are "directed peremptorily to perform certain acts" on which "the rights of individuals are dependent," they are "amenable to the laws" and cannot disregard such
"vested rights of others."[7]

Accordingly, Marshall articulated a framework for determining whether executive
acts are judicially reviewable. Under that framework, where an executive official acts
in an area where the President has "constitutional or legal discretion," his or her acts
are political and not subject to judicial scrutiny. By contrast, where law assigns the
executive a duty on which "individual rights depend,"[8] an individual who suffers
injury from the breach of that legal duty has a remedy in court. In concluding that
the executive branch was judicially answerable for violations of legal rights, Marshall
articulated, albeit in *dicta*, an important component of the rule of law. His analysis
of this issue has been highly influential in understanding the role of courts in reviewing
presidential actions. In addition, it has provided the foundation for the political question doctrine, as explained later in this chapter.[9]

Applying this reasoning to the case before him, Marshall concluded that, since
Marbury was appointed for a term of years and had a legal right to the commission,
he had a vested right, not one over which the executive enjoyed any discretion. Thus,
Marbury's claim was one courts could consider. Moreover, the Secretary of State was
an officer to whom a court could issue a writ of mandamus under the terms of Section
13 of the Judiciary Act of 1789, the jurisdictional statute under which Marbury was
proceeding.

These two conclusions outlined in the first parts of the opinion — that Marbury
was entitled to his commission and the executive was amenable to suit in such circumstances — would suggest that the Court was headed for a fateful collision with
the executive branch. But the Court escaped the confrontation with Jefferson and
Madison by veering off on a surprising, yet historic, detour.

Having disposed of the merits of the case — again, however, only in *dicta* —
Marshall turned to the question of the Court's jurisdiction.[10] Marbury had initiated
his case in the Supreme Court under the authority of Section 13 of the Judiciary
Act of 1789. Marshall construed that provision as purporting to provide the Court
with jurisdiction to issue writs of mandamus in situations such as Marbury's. That
interpretation, however, raised the question whether such a grant of original ju-

---

7. *Id.* at 165–166.
8. *Id.* at 166.
9. *See* Section 2.08[5].
10. Marshall's decision to opine on the merits of the case before reaching the jurisdiction question
is one of the oddities of the opinion, for which he has been criticized. It is a standard judicial principle
that courts concluding that they lack jurisdiction should state that conclusion first and refrain from
reaching the merits. Marshall did the opposite — he reached the merits issue only to conclude eventually
that the Court lacked jurisdiction. As discussed later in the text, however, it was this ordering of the
issues that allowed Marshall to escape the trap in which he otherwise found himself.

risdiction by Congress to the Supreme Court was consistent with the Constitution — in particular, with Article III's relatively precise specification of the Court's original jurisdiction.[11]

Before turning to that constitutional analysis, however, note that Marshall did not have to read Section 13 as purporting to grant the Court additional, "mandamus jurisdiction." Instead, he could have read that provision as simply providing the Court with the additional tool of mandamus when it already had jurisdiction, or, perhaps, providing "jurisdiction" to issue writs of mandamus when acting as an appellate court, rather than an original one. Those interpretations would still have led Marbury to lose the case, but had Marshall adopted one of them, Marbury would have lost simply because he misread Section 13, not because Section 13 was unconstitutional. Such a reading would have been at least plausible — after all, the Judiciary Act of 1789 was enacted by the first Congress, which included a great many of the Constitution's drafters. One would think they would be careful not to violate Article III in such an obvious way. Moreover, it is generally accepted that courts, if presented the choice between a statutory interpretation that raises a serious constitutional issue and one that did not, should adopt the interpretation that avoids the constitutional issue. Marshall did the exact opposite — another anomaly in the case. However, his decision to read Section 13 as he did allowed him to establish the power of judicial review.

Thus, despite strong reasons to do otherwise, Marshall interpreted Section 13 as purporting to increase the Court's original jurisdiction, thus triggering the question whether such an addition was consistent with Article III's specification of that jurisdiction. He decided that it was not consistent with Article III. Marshall reasoned that Article III granted the Court original jurisdiction in only two types of cases — those "affecting ambassadors, other public ministers and consuls, and those in which a state shall be a party."[12] In all other cases Article III identified as coming within the federal judicial power generally, the Court's jurisdiction was appellate. Marbury's claim fell into neither category of original jurisdiction and thus Section 13 was unconstitutional unless Congress could expand the Court's original jurisdiction beyond what Article III specified. Marshall rejected this possibility. He argued that a holding that Congress could increase the Court's original jurisdiction would render meaningless Article III's specification of that jurisdiction.[13]

To be sure, while Marshall's constitutional analysis was certainly reasonable, it was not the only one available. The Constitution might simply have stated an initial allocation between the Court's original and appellate jurisdiction, but an allocation subject to redistribution. Instead of Marshall's inference that the Constitution would not have allocated cases to these categories if such redistribution were permitted, an alternative conclusion would suggest that the Constitution allowed a different division,

---

11. Marbury brought his suit as an original matter in the Supreme Court, rather than as an appeal from a lower court ruling.

12. U.S. Const. art. III, § 2, cl. 2.

13. *Marbury*, 5 U.S. at 174.

but unless one was made, the initial allocation stood as stated. In other words, the two types of cases in the Court's original jurisdiction could have been understood as reflecting simply a starting point, subject to change.

Indeed, the Appellate Jurisdiction Clause (often referred to as the Exceptions Clause) conferred appellate jurisdiction over other cases "with such Exceptions, and under such Regulations as the Congress shall make."[14] This clause might support authorizing Congress to alter the initial allocation of jurisdiction to the Supreme Court. On the other hand, the lack of an "exceptions" clause in connection with the Original Jurisdiction Clause might support Marshall's view that no expansion of the Court's original jurisdiction was allowed. On this theory, the Exceptions Clause could be read to permit reductions of the Court's appellate jurisdiction, but not expansions of its original jurisdiction. Most fundamentally, in light of this ambiguity, the respect due a coordinate branch of government perhaps should have led Marshall to adopt a reading that would have made his understanding of Section 13[15] constitutional, as an expression of the idea that courts should strike down only laws that are unambiguously unconstitutional.[16] Nevertheless, while Marshall's interpretation of Article III was contestable, it was not frivolous.[17]

Regardless of these ambiguities, Marshall concluded that the Constitution imposed a ceiling, not a floor, on the Court's original jurisdiction. Thus, to the extent Section 13 sought to expand the Court's original jurisdiction, it violated the Constitution. The Court could only issue a mandamus in Marbury's case incident to its appellate jurisdiction. But Marbury's case did not implicate the Court's appellate jurisdiction since it asked the Court to direct the writ to the executive branch rather than to review a lower court proceeding.

Marshall's decision that Section 13 conflicted with Article III raised a central issue in the case: whether a statute "repugnant to the Constitution" was nonetheless the law of the land. He concluded that it was not. He observed that, in creating the Constitution, the people exercised their sovereign right to create a government and establish limits on it. If Congress could legislate beyond the bounds the Constitution set, Congress would not be limited.[18] The fact that Congress had duly enacted Section 13 was not dispositive.

In arguing that the Constitution was paramount, Marshall relied primarily on structural arguments—that is, arguments inferred from the Constitution's design and the principles underlying it. However, toward the end of the opinion, Marshall invoked the Supremacy Clause as a textual reinforcement to his conclusion. He pointed

---

14. U.S. Const. art. III, §2, cl. 2.

15. Again, recall that Marshall's reading of Section 13 itself was not the only one available, and, indeed, was perhaps a strained interpretation.

16. The foundational statement of this call for extreme judicial deference is James B. Thayer, *The Origin and Scope of the American Doctrine of Constitutional Law*, 7 Harv. L. Rev. 129 (1893).

17. *See* The Federalist No. 81 (Hamilton) (describing the Supreme Court's original jurisdiction as limited to two types of cases).

18. *Marbury*, 5 U.S. at 176–77.

out that the Supremacy Clause listed the Constitution before mentioning laws and treaties, and only gave effect to laws made in pursuance of the Constitution.[19] He argued that this point confirmed the preeminent status of the Constitution.

Marshall's reliance on the Supremacy Clause to demonstrate the primacy of the Constitution was not entirely convincing. The statement that the Constitution and all federal statutes made "in pursuance thereof" are supreme law is subject to at least two readings. "In pursuance thereof" could mean "consistent with" as Marshall argued, thereby suggesting that the only valid statutes were those in accord with the Constitution. Alternatively, it could have a chronological meaning, separating those statutes passed before the Constitution (which were not supreme laws) from those passed later (which were). Under that interpretation, the Supremacy Clause would not seem to elevate the Constitution above federal statutes.

Nevertheless, Marshall's conclusion *was* supported by the structural principle that the Constitution imposed limits on government. Without a principle of constitutional preeminence, the only checks on government would be those the democratic process imposed. Moreover, the disparity between the onerous requirements Article V imposed for amending the Constitution and the more modest requirements of enacting a mere statute suggests the superior authority of the Constitution. Further, the Exceptions Clause itself implies that the Constitution trumps statutory law. If Congress could override the Constitution by passing statutes, there would be no need to authorize Congress to change the Court's appellate jurisdiction as the Exceptions Clause did.[20] Indeed, in the *Federalist Papers*, Alexander Hamilton had written that, when a conflict arose between the Constitution and a statute, the statute had to give way.[21]

All this analysis raised a final issue: the power of judicial review. The idea that the Constitution was supreme did not compel the conclusion that the Court had the power to decide when a statute clashed with the Constitution. One could instead take the position that a congressional decision to enact a statute reflected that body's authority to decide for itself whether that legislation was constitutional. Marshall, however, argued that courts were not bound to enforce legislative acts, like Section 13, that were "repugnant to the Constitution."[22] "It is emphatically the province and duty of the judicial department to say what the law is," wrote Marshall in *Marbury*'s most quoted passage.[23] The traditional function of the judge was to decide cases, a task that required interpreting and applying the relevant law. That function required courts to decide which law to apply when two laws conflicted in a way relevant to the outcome of the case. In such cases, that imperative required courts to give effect to the superior law. Thus, when a statute conflicted with the Constitution, the judicial task of deciding cases required the Court to refuse to give effect to—that is, to strike down—such a statute.

---

19. *Id.* at 180.

20. *See* John Harrison, *The Constitutional Origins and Implications of Judicial Review*, 84 Va. L. Rev. 333, 347 (1998).

21. The Federalist No. 81 (Hamilton).

22. *Marbury*, 5 U.S. at 180.

23. *Id.* at 177.

Marshall invoked several specific clauses of the Constitution to support his point. He defended the power of judicial review by pointing out that Article III extended the "judicial power" to "all cases arising under the Constitution."[24] That jurisdictional grant implied that the Court should consider the Constitution in deciding a case. Chief Justice Marshall also pointed out that judges take an oath to support the Constitution which implied that they may interpret it.[25]

These arguments may not be as conclusive as Marshall suggested. The jurisdictional grant could be just that — a grant of power to decide a certain category of cases without suggesting that the Court had power to declare that the legislature had acted unlawfully. Moreover, the judicial oath argument begged the question, since legislators and presidents also take an oath to support the Constitution. At any rate, the Oath Clause at most directs officials to enforce the Constitution. That duty would include enforcing whatever guidance the Constitution provided regarding who interprets the Constitution. But the direction to courts (among others) to enforce the Constitution does not necessarily suggest that courts are its authoritative interpreter.

This final portion of Marshall's opinion asserted three fundamental principles of American constitutional law: ours is a government of limited power, the Constitution is paramount law, and the Court has a power, in a proper case, to examine whether a legislative act is consistent with the Constitution. At times, Marshall skipped from point to point, blurring the distinctions between the three concepts. He no doubt sought to emphasize the relationship between the various ideas and to strengthen each argument by associating each of them with the others.

[3] *Marbury*'s Significance

Marbury established foundational principles regarding our system of government. Marshall's arguments articulated the basic commitment to the rule of law which subjected government to limits. *Marbury* illustrated that principle through Marshall's conclusion, albeit in *dicta*, that the President had violated the law by refusing to give Marbury his commission. Yet he also signaled that concept by his refusal to allow Congress to expand the Court's original jurisdiction. To be sure, this decision was strategic. Presumably, Marshall preferred not to have jurisdiction so he could avoid a confrontation with Jefferson. Yet it also signaled the Court's unwillingness to assume a power which it did not believe the Constitution gave it. This posture was rich in symbolism for it communicated the judiciary's adherence to the rule of law even when that commitment ostensibly cost it jurisdictional authority. In so doing, the Court, through Marshall's brilliance, solidified its claim to more significant powers: the power to enforce executive branch adherence to law and the power of judicial review.

Again, though, recall the price in terms of good judicial practice that Marshall had to pay in order to achieve these goals. He likely should have recused himself from

---

24. *Id.* at 178.
25. *Id.* at 180.

the case, given his personal involvement in the facts out of which the case arose. He also should have reached the jurisdictional issue first, which would have obviated the need to reach the merits question about the amenability of the executive branch to a court order. And he quite possibly should have read Section 13 in a way that entirely avoided having to find that statute unconstitutional. But any one of these steps would have deprived him of the chance to make the foundational statement that we now understand *Marbury* to be.

§ 2.03 Judicial Review

[1] Constitutional Arguments

The power of judicial review is a central feature of our constitutional system. Considerable evidence suggested the Framers intended to lodge such a power in the federal courts.[26] One could also infer it from the Constitution's history, text and structure. Written constitutions had developed from the colonial commitment to limited government. Those documents could succeed only if treated as fundamental law, a concept which suggested judicial enforcement of their provisions.

Judicial review helps make constitutional provisions legally enforceable rules rather than just hortatory expressions of maxims of political morality. Absent legal machinery to enforce the Constitution, its limitations would depend entirely on the democratic process, which might result in political temptations to aggrandize government power and oppress minorities. To be sure, giving that role to the federal judiciary also runs a risk, since it, too, may abuse its power. Still, the Constitution gives federal judges life tenure and salary protection to insulate them from majoritarian pressures. They would seem to have greater incentive to enforce constitutional boundaries. Of course, the judiciary may be inclined, consciously or unconsciously, to favor its own institutional interests. But possessed of neither the purse nor the sword, it is the "least dangerous" branch[27] and thus is least likely to encroach on the turf of other branches or suppress individual freedoms. Regardless of its merits, judicial review has come to be a firmly-entrenched institution of American government. Absent a doctrinal revolution, it is hard to see the doctrine coming under serious attack as a general matter.

[2] Later Formulations of Judicial Review

Since *Marbury*, the Court has frequently invoked its role as constitutional interpreter. Although the Court did not declare another federal law unconstitutional until

---

26. *See generally* Bernard Schwartz, A History of the Supreme Court 22–24, 41–43 (1993); Alexander M. Bickel, The Least Dangerous Branch: The Supreme Court at the Bar of Politics 15–16 (1962).

27. *See* The Federalist No. 78 (Hamilton).

1857,[28] at different stages of our history it has deployed that power more frequently. Particularly when its authority has been challenged, the Court has asserted its power in strong language.

An important example of the Court's assertion of this power is *Cooper v. Aaron*.[29] In *Cooper*, the Court confronted a claim by a southern school district that it was not formally bound by the holding in *Brown v. Board of Education*[30] striking down racial segregation of public school students. The district's claim was simple, but far-reaching: as a non-party to *Brown*, the district was not bound by the judgment in that case. Of course, *Brown* was still precedent, and any district that was sued for segregating would lose, with the court relying on *Brown*. But the prospect of forcing African-American plaintiffs to sue each and every segregating district across the nation would slow the progress of school desegregation, and severely impair the authority of *Brown* as the Court's authoritative statement that segregation was unconstitutional.

The Court responded to this defiance by invoking *Marbury* for a very broad proposition. According to *Cooper*, *Marbury*:

> declared the basic principle that the federal judiciary is supreme in the exposition of the law of the Constitution, and that principle has ever since been respected by this Court and the Country as a permanent and indispensable feature of our constitutional system. It follows that the interpretation of the Fourteenth Amendment in the *Brown* case is the supreme law of the land, and Art. VI of the Constitution makes it of binding effect on the States "any Thing in the Constitution or Laws of any State to the Contrary notwithstanding."[31]

Note that this statement quite arguably goes beyond *Marbury*'s explanation of judicial review, to embrace a view that has become known as "judicial supremacy." Recall that *Marbury*'s defense of judicial review relied heavily on the simple fact that, as part of its duty to adjudicate cases, courts would on occasion encounter conflicting laws, and thus would have to decide which law to apply. On this understanding, judicial review—the power to strike down a statute as inconsistent with the Constitution— says nothing about the Court's special or supreme status as interpreter of the Constitution. By contrast, *Cooper* states that, not only is the Constitution the supreme law of the land, but so is the Court's interpretation of the Constitution—presumably, regardless of what any other branch might think about that interpretation.

The *Cooper* idea is controversial. On the one hand, accepting the school district's argument in *Cooper* would severely hamper the ability of the Court to establish the meaning of the Constitution across the nation. If a case, such as *Brown*, formally

---

28. *See* Dred Scott v. Sanford, 60 U.S. 393 (1857). *Dred Scott*, discussed in Section 10.04[1], was and remains highly criticized. It is a testament to *Marbury*'s staying power that the institution of judicial review with which it became closely associated survived the attack on this second instance of the Court's use of that power.

29. 358 U.S. 1 (1958).

30. 349 U.S. 294 (1954).

31. 358 U.S. 1, 18 (1958) (quoting U.S. CONST. art. VI).

only bound the parties to the case, then vindication of any right or principle the Court might announce would depend on subsequent litigation against government defendants across the country. That process could seriously impair the status of constitutional rights found by the Court. On the other hand, the idea seems to denigrate the status of Congress and the President as co-equal branches, each able to make constitutional determinations within the legitimate sphere of its own conduct (*e.g.*, considering whether to enact a statute some have attacked as unconstitutional, or to pardon someone convicted of a crime the President believes is unconstitutional). The appropriate role for the political branches in constitutional interpretation is discussed in Section 2.03[3].

In *Marbury*, Marshall's use of judicial review allowed him to sidestep a confrontation with the Executive. By 1974, when the Court decided *United States v. Nixon*,[32] the concept was sufficiently robust for the Court to deploy it to order President Richard M. Nixon to disclose communications which revealed his criminal complicity in the Watergate scandal. The Court unanimously rejected Nixon's claim that he, not it, had power to interpret the Constitution regarding access to presidential documents. It relied on *Marbury* to support its claim. To be sure, Nixon's political weakness limited his ability to contest the Court's claim. Yet his ultimate compliance with the Court's order, even when it was clear that compliance would unleash political forces that would force him to resign, spoke volumes regarding the status of judicial review. The Court's stature as the ultimate arbiter of constitutional meaning again became clear in 2000, when the Court decided *Bush v. Gore*,[33] the case that effectively decided the presidential election of 2000. The loser in that litigation, Al Gore, responded by conceding the election rather than insisting on further action by either Congress or the electoral authorities in Florida, the contested state.

Marshall took occasion to reassert the Court's power of judicial review during his tenure on the Court. Yet he did not preside over another case striking down a congressional statute.[34] Indeed, he suggested that the power of judicial review should rarely be used to invalidate a law:

> The question, whether a law be void for its repugnancy to the constitution, is, at all times, a question of much delicacy, which ought seldom, if ever, to be decided in the affirmative, in a doubtful case.... The opposition between the constitution and the law should be such that the judge feels a clear and strong conviction of their incompatibility with each other.[35]

Thus, while the power of judicial review is firmly established today, critics of any particular Court decision striking down a law often charge the Court with overstepping the power Marshall established in *Marbury*.

---

32. 418 U.S. 683 (1974).
33. 531 U.S. 98 (2000).
34. *See* note 28 and text accompanying, *supra*.
35. Fletcher v. Peck, 10 U.S. (6 Cranch) 87, 128 (1810).

[3] Is the Court the Sole or Ultimate Interpreter of the Constitution?

To be sure, other officials also have responsibilities to interpret the Constitution, and at times, various presidents, members of Congress and state officials have asserted such a prerogative. In vetoing a law, an earlier version of which the Court had previously upheld as constitutional, President Andrew Jackson said:

> It is as much the duty of the House of Representatives, of the Senate, and of the President to decide upon the constitutionality of any bill or resolution which may be presented to them for passage or approval as it is of the supreme judges when it may be brought before them for judicial decision.... The authority of the Supreme Court must not, therefore be permitted to control the Congress or Executive when acting in their legislative capacities, but to have only such influence as the force of their reasoning may deserve.[36]

Other Presidents have sounded similar themes.[37] These claims are controversial. Still, some scholars argue that, in addition to the judiciary, other branches must also interpret the Constitution. Relatedly, some question the idea that the Court is the ultimate interpreter.[38]

Although not totally free of ambiguity, much of *Marbury* is consistent with a robust interpretive role for other institutions. Recall the discussion of *Cooper v. Aaron*, in the previous sub-section. That discussion at least suggested the possibility that other branches shared interpretive authority with the Court, since *Marbury* can be read as claiming simply the power to review statutes as they arise in cases before the Court, not as making the Court the exclusive or ultimate constitutional voice. If *Marbury* is understood as establishing simply a power of judicial review of statutes that arise in cases before courts but not claiming for the Court the status of the sole or final arbiter of all constitutional questions, the necessary conflict between *Marbury* and declarations such as Andrew Jackson's, above, is less severe.

Alternatively, *Marbury* might stand for the proposition that the Court is the final constitutional interpreter regarding some, but not all, constitutional questions. Constitutional issues which arise in some contexts are left to other branches to interpret. Thus, during the Nixon, Clinton, and Trump impeachment proceedings, members

---

36. Andrew Jackson Veto Message (July 10, 1832), *in* MESSAGES AND PAPERS OF THE PRESIDENTS 1145 (1897).

37. *See, e.g.*, Abraham Lincoln, First Inaugural Address (Mar 4, 1861), in Don E. Fehrenbacher, ed., ABRAHAM LINCOLN: SPEECHES AND WRITINGS, 1859–1865 215, 221 (Library of America 1989) ("I do not forget the position assumed by some that constitutional questions are to be decided by the Supreme Court, nor do I deny that such decisions must be binding in any case upon the parties to a suit as to the object of that suit, while they are also entitled to very high respect and consideration in all parallel cases by all other departments of the Government.... At the same time, the candid citizen must confess that if the policy of the Government upon vital questions affecting the whole people is to be irrevocably fixed by decisions of the Supreme Court, the instant they are made in ordinary litigation between parties in personal actions the people will have ceased to be their own rulers, having to that extent practically resigned their Government into the hands of that eminent tribunal.").

38. *See, e.g.*, MARK TUSHNET, TAKING THE CONSTITUTION AWAY FROM THE COURTS (1999); LOUIS FISHER, CONSTITUTIONAL DIALOGUES: INTERPRETATION AS POLITICAL PROCESS (1988); Neal Devins & Louis Fisher, *Judicial Exclusivity and Political Instability*, 84 VA. L. REV. 83 (1998); Michael Stokes Paulsen, *The Most Dangerous Branch: Executive Power to Say What the Law Is*, 83 GEO. L.J. 217 (1994).

of Congress had to interpret the Constitution's phrase, "high crimes and misdemeanors" to determine whether the acts charged were impeachable. Similarly, a president might decide to issue a veto or pardon based on constitutional grounds.

Yet there is some sense in which many believe that the Court occupies a special role as constitutional interpreter. Constitutional law helps coordinate disparate views of multiple actors, something that cannot occur if each can perpetually resist decisions he does not like.[39] Some institution must perform this function, and the Court is deemed best suited for this role. Lacking the purse and sword and a democratic mandate, and possessed of life tenure and salary protection, federal judges may be the least likely to abuse such a power. More theoretically, to the extent adjudication involves the declaration of foundational constitutional principles, the training judges receive in principled argumentation and reasoned decision-making may equip them well for that role.[40] In practice, the Court's constitutional decisions receive substantial, though not complete, deference as the final word.

In *Marbury*, the Court reviewed, and held unconstitutional, an act of Congress. Critical as the power to review Congress's acts has been, it represents only part, and not the most important part, of the doctrine of judicial review. The Court did not strike down another act of Congress during the remainder of Marshall's tenure as Chief Justice. It did, however, in a number of notable cases, address the constitutionality of state legislative acts. The power to review the validity of *state* action is probably more important if the Constitution is to survive as supreme law throughout the land. As Justice Oliver Wendell Holmes later put it, "I do not think the United States would come to an end if we lost our power to declare an Act of Congress void. I do think the Union would be imperiled if we could not make that declaration as to the laws of the several States."[41]

In one sense, judicial review of state legislation rests on the same foundations as those *Marbury* laid out in the context of judicial review of federal laws. But one difference will require examination later in this book. In cases from the early nineteenth century, state courts (and litigants who had won their cases in front of a state court) argued that U.S. Supreme Court review of state high court decisions that involved the constitutionality of a federal law violated the sovereignty that states retained under the Constitution. The Court rejected those arguments. The seminal case on that point, *Martin v. Hunter's Lessee*, is discussed later in this Chapter.[42]

[4] The Judiciary and the Political Branches

In order to insulate federal courts from majoritarian control, the Framers attached two attributes to federal judges. They provided that Article III judges would enjoy lifetime tenure during "good behavior" and that their salary could not be reduced.[43]

---

39. Larry Alexander & Frederick Schauer, *On Extrajudicial Constitutional Interpretation*, 110 HARV. L. REV. 1359 (1997).

40. *See, e.g.*, ALEXANDER BICKEL, THE LEAST DANGEROUS BRANCH: THE SUPREME COURT AT THE BAR OF POLITICS (1962).

41. OLIVER WENDELL HOLMES, COLLECTED LEGAL PAPERS 295–96 (1920).

42. *See* Section 2.05; *see also* Section 4.05 (also briefly discussing *Martin*).

43. U.S. CONST. art. III, § 1.

The Framers thought these protections necessary to secure an independent judiciary that could enforce individual rights in the face of majoritarian pressure.[44] Thus, Hamilton thought life tenure during good behavior was an "excellent barrier to the encroachments and oppressions of the representative body." It was "the best expedient which can be devised in any government to secure a steady, upright, and impartial administration of the laws."[45] Judicial independence would "guard the Constitution and the rights of individuals."[46] Similarly, the Framers thought salary protection a sound way of safeguarding judicial independence.[47]

Although life tenure and compensation protection insulate federal judges from some political pressures, they are not wholly independent. The Constitution provides that federal judges are nominated by the President and appointed only with the advice and consent of the Senate.[48] The political nature of the selection and confirmation process guarantees that political considerations influence the composition of the federal judiciary, including the Supreme Court, where the stakes are greatest.[49] Judges are also subject to impeachment, trial and removal for treason, bribery and other high crimes and misdemeanors, although this remedy is rarely invoked.

Courts depend in part on executive enforcement to give effect to their judgments. Recall that John Marshall presumably worried over how Jefferson and Madison would respond if served a writ of mandamus issued by the Court. Other examples in history reveal similar concerns about executive willingness to enforce court orders. Nevertheless, executive officials nearly always at least make a showing of complying with a court order. As discussed earlier in this chapter, even President Richard Nixon obeyed a Court order that he produce tapes of incriminating conversations which traced his participation in the Watergate scandal. He complied with that order even though he likely knew that publication of these conversations would hasten the end of his presidency (as it did).

The judiciary is also dependent on the legislative branch. The extent of the dependence becomes clear from the language of Article III: "The judicial Power of the United States shall be vested in one supreme Court, and in such inferior Courts as the Congress may from time to time ordain and establish...." This provision mandates a Supreme Court but gives Congress discretion regarding whether to "or-

---

44. *See, e.g.,* THE FEDERALIST Nos. 78, 79 (Hamilton).

45. *Id.* No. 78 (Hamilton).

46. *Id.*

47. *Id.* No. 79 ("a power over a man's subsistence amounts to a power over his will"). However, Congress can impose non-discriminatory taxes, such as income taxes, on federal judges. *See United States v. Hatter,* 532 U.S. 557, 571 (2001) ("the Compensation Clause does not forbid Congress to enact a law imposing a nondiscriminatory tax (including an increase in rates or a change in conditions) upon judges, whether those judges were appointed before or after the tax law in question was enacted or took effect").

48. U.S. CONST. art. II, § 2, cl. 2.

49. *See generally* HENRY J. ABRAHAM, JUSTICES, PRESIDENTS, SENATORS: A HISTORY OF U.S. SUPREME COURT APPOINTMENTS FROM WASHINGTON TO BUSH II (5th ed. 2005); Joel K. Goldstein, *Choosing Justices: How Presidents Decide,* 26 J.L. & POL. 425 (2011).

dain and establish" lower federal courts. This approach reflected the so-called Madisonian Compromise, which James Madison brokered between those Framers who wanted the Constitution to create lower federal courts and those who preferred to entrust state courts with the duty to handle virtually all litigation. As such, lower federal courts owe their existence to Congress, which established them by statute. Over the course of our history, on several occasions, Congress has extensively reorganized the federal courts.

Similarly, the jurisdiction of the federal courts, with the exception of the original jurisdiction of the Supreme Court, depends largely on Congress's choices, subject to the outer limits the Constitution allows. Congress also can control the Supreme Court's appellate jurisdiction based on the Exceptions Clause, which confers appellate jurisdiction on the Court over specified cases "with such Exceptions, and under such Regulations as the Congress shall make."[50] Finally, the Necessary and Proper Clause[51] allows Congress to pass other laws regarding jurisdiction in federal and state courts over various types of cases. The (narrow and largely speculative) limits on congressional power to alter the jurisdiction of the federal courts is discussed later in this chapter.[52]

§ 2.04 The Supreme Court

[1] The Supreme Court's Status and Structure

The Constitution itself established the Supreme Court.[53] But it says nothing about the size of that Court, a subject Congress has addressed by statute. The Court's size has ranged from six initially to five, to seven, to nine, to ten, to seven again, and finally in 1869 to the present size of nine. Congress can also control the Court's organization and functioning. Indeed, in 1801, Congress changed the Court's terms so that it did not sit for fourteen months. Congress also can prescribe procedural and other rules for the Court.[54] For example, Congress initially assigned the justices to the various circuits it created, an assignment that required them to preside over trials. Still, the constitutional basis of the Supreme Court limits congressional authority. The Supreme Court has functioned as a continuing governmental institution since February 2, 1790, and its existence is constitutionally guaranteed.

The Constitution does not impose any age, residency, citizenship or occupational requirements for Supreme Court Justices. Every justice to date has been a lawyer, but that reflects practice, not a legal requirement.

---

50. U.S. Const. art. III, § 2, cl. 2.

51. *Id.* art. I, § 8, cl. 18.

52. *See* Section 2.05.

53. U.S. Const. art. III, § 1 ("The judicial Power of the United States, shall be vested in one supreme Court....").

54. *See* Wayman v. Southard, 23 U.S. (10 Wheat.) 1 (1825).

[2] The Supreme Court's Jurisdiction

The Constitution accords different treatment to the Supreme Court's original and appellate jurisdiction. Article III expressly specifies its original jurisdiction, extending it to cases involving ambassadors and those involving states.[55] Professor Akhil Reed Amar suggests that geographic considerations helped explain the placement of these two categories. Foreign envoys would likely reside in the nation's capital so they should be sued there. States could be represented there, too, by their senators.[56] As construed in *Marbury*, Congress lacks the power to revise that jurisdiction, and that jurisdiction can be exercised without legislative action.[57] In practice, it accounts for a tiny portion of the Court's work.

Congress has, however, made the Court's original jurisdiction concurrent with jurisdiction in lower federal courts or state courts with respect to most cases within it. Thus, the Court's original jurisdiction is exclusive regarding "all controversies between two or more states"[58] but not regarding cases to which ambassadors and other foreign envoys are parties, controversies between the United States and a state, and actions by a state against citizens of another state or aliens.[59]

The Constitution treats the Supreme Court's appellate jurisdiction differently. Article III makes the Court's appellate jurisdiction subject to such "Exceptions" and "Regulations" as Congress may prescribe.[60] Under the Exceptions Clause, the Supreme Court's appellate jurisdiction extends to the cases and controversies over which Article III grants federal court jurisdiction generally, less the categories of the Court's original jurisdiction, subject to Congress's power to divest it of that appellate jurisdiction.[61]

The Supreme Court's appellate jurisdiction is "strictly speaking, conferred by the Constitution."[62] Thus, the Judiciary Act of 1789, which among other things organized the Supreme Court, did not actually confer appellate jurisdiction on the Supreme Court. Rather, according to Chief Justice Marshall, when the first Congress enacted that statute it intended to make exceptions to the appellate jurisdiction of the Supreme Court in giving effect to Article III.[63] Since Marshall's time, Congress's grant of appellate jurisdiction has been understood as implicitly denying jurisdiction in cases not mentioned.[64]

---

55. Marbury v. Madison, 5 U.S. (1 Cranch) 137, 174–76 (1803).

56. Akhil Reed Amar, *Marbury, Section 13, and the Original Jurisdiction of the Supreme Court*, 56 U. Chi. L. Rev. 443, 463–78 (1989).

57. *See* California v. Arizona, 440 U.S. 59, 65 (1979); Kentucky v. Dennison, 65 U.S. (24 How.) 66, 98 (1861).

58. 28 U.S.C. § 1251(a).

59. 28 U.S.C. § 1251(b).

60. U.S. Const. art. III, §2, cl. 2.

61. The Francis Wright, 105 U.S. 381, 385 (1882); Durousseau v. United States, 10 U.S. (6 Cranch) 307, 314 (1810).

62. *Ex parte* McCardle, 74 U.S. 506, 512–13 (1869).

63. *See Durousseau*, 10 U.S. at 314.

64. *See Ex parte* McCardle, 74 U.S. at 513.

The crucial question relates to the extent of congressional control over the Supreme Court's appellate jurisdiction. How far may Congress go in limiting that jurisdiction via the Exceptions Clause? Could it divest from the Court's appellate jurisdiction all cases other than, say, admiralty cases? Could it completely divest the Supreme Court of any appellate jurisdiction, or appellate jurisdiction over some hot-button issue such as abortion rights cases?[65] Some argue that the Exceptions Clause gives Congress such plenary power.

Yet it might be argued that the text of Article III refutes any claim that Congress possesses such plenary control. On this theory, an "exception" is just that; the term presupposes some substantial core that remains. It might seem inconceivable that the Constitution intended to vest in Congress authority to nullify the practical exercise of the judicial power. More likely, this argument might run, the purpose was to authorize exceptions and regulations consistent with the essential function of the Supreme Court in the constitutional system.[66] The Framers created a three-part government with a system of checks and balances to safeguard liberty. Congress could undermine that structure if it could dispense with the judiciary.

Indeed, such a possibility seems at war with basic structural principles in *Marbury*—the concepts of limited government, rule of law, and judicial review. If Congress has broad power to limit lower courts, the role of the Supreme Court, especially in its appellate role, becomes all the more critical. If Congress could abolish lower federal courts under the Ordain and Establish Clause[67] and also slash the Supreme Court's appellate jurisdiction under the Exceptions Clause, Congress could reduce a coordinate department to irrelevance and erode the judicial check on unconstitutional governmental action.

Those who argue for broad congressional power over the Court's appellate jurisdiction cite *Ex parte McCardle*[68] for support. In *McCardle*, a Mississippi newspaper editor who had been arrested under the Reconstruction Acts and held for trial by military commission petitioned for a writ of habeas corpus. A lower court denied the writ and McCardle appealed to the Supreme Court under an 1867 statute which authorized appeals to the Court from circuit court decisions in such cases.

---

65. Note that a stripping statute of the latter sort would simply freeze in place lower court opinions and previous Supreme Court opinions on that hot-button topic. However, at least in terms of lower court opinions, Congress conceivably could strip the Supreme Court of appellate jurisdiction over those cases while at the same time stripping lower federal courts of all jurisdiction over such cases, as part of Congress's general control over the lower federal courts. Such a move would freeze in place current Supreme Court law, while potentially allowing state courts to continue to apply that law in cases plaintiffs brought in those courts.

66. RICHARD H. FALLON, JR. ET AL., HART AND WECHSLER'S THE FEDERAL COURTS AND THE FEDERAL SYSTEM 1364–65 (5th ed. 2003).

67. U.S. CONST. art. III, § 1 ("The judicial Power of the United States, shall be vested in one Supreme Court, and in such inferior courts as the Congress may from time to time ordain and establish."). Congress's power over the lower federal courts is discussed below, in Section 2.05.

68. 74 U.S. (7 Wall.) 506 (1869).

The Court unanimously decided that it had subject matter jurisdiction,[69] heard arguments on the merits, and took the matter under advisement. Many feared the Court would invalidate military rule in the South after the Civil War, and thus call into doubt the entire project of reconstructing southern governments. To avoid such a result, Congress repealed the 1867 statute to the extent it authorized appeal to the Supreme Court from circuit court judgments in habeas corpus cases, and prohibited the Court from acting on appeals that had been or might be taken. The Court then heard argument regarding Congress's authority to remove its jurisdiction over a case already submitted on the merits.

Addressing that issue, the Court, speaking through Chief Justice Chase, wrote that "The first question necessarily is that of jurisdiction," for if jurisdiction had been removed, "it is useless, if not improper, to enter into any discussion of other questions."[70] The *McCardle* Court unanimously acknowledged congressional power over its appellate jurisdiction based upon the Exceptions Clause. The repealing act plainly withdrew jurisdiction over the appeal. The Court decreed itself precluded from questioning Congress's intent in doing so. The appeal, therefore, was dismissed even though the repealing Act was clearly designed simply to prevent a merits decision with which Congress might have disagreed.

McCardle was far-reaching. The Court upheld a law Congress passed to prevent the Court from reviewing the constitutionality of a statute. Still, the Court did not hold that Congress could validly oust it of all appellate jurisdiction over habeas corpus cases. The repealing act at issue lacked that extreme effect. At the very end of its opinion, the Court went out of its way to assert that the 1868 jurisdiction stripping act only removed jurisdiction over appeals under the 1867 Act; "jurisdiction which was previously exercised" (*i.e.*, under the Judiciary Act of 1789) was not affected. Indeed, a few months later, *Ex parte Yerger*[71] held that after *Ex parte McCardle* the Supreme Court could still review lower court habeas denials by petitions in the Supreme Court properly brought under the 1789 Act.[72]

If the *McCardle* statute had tried to deny the Supreme Court all jurisdiction in habeas corpus cases, it would have encountered another problem. The Habeas Corpus Clause provides that "The Privilege of the Writ of Habeas Corpus shall not be suspended, unless when in cases of Rebellion or Invasion the public safety may require it."[73] The Clause thus seems to contemplate the availability of a habeas corpus writ from some court, unless Congress acts explicitly to suspend the writ. More recent decisions of the Court seem to recognize some constitutional right to the writ,[74]

---

69. *See Ex parte* McCardle, 73 U.S. (6 Wall.) 318 (1868).

70. *Ex parte McCardle*, 74 U.S. (7 Wall.) at 512. Compare the Court's approach to that in *Marbury* where jurisdiction issues were addressed last.

71. 75 U.S. (8 Wall.) 85, 104–06 (1868).

72. This distinction was explained further in a more recent case, *Felker v. Turpin*, 518 U.S. 651, 660–661 (1996).

73. U.S. Const. art. I, §9, cl. 2.

74. *See, e.g.*, Immigration and Naturalization Service v. St. Cyr, 533 U.S. 289 (2001).

subject to congressional suspension in dire circumstances. To the extent a constitutional right to habeas review exists, Congress's ability to restrict it, absent circumstances the Suspension Clause addresses, would be limited. The example of Congress's ability to limit the Court's authority to issue writs of habeas corpus illustrates the intricate balance between the seeming limitless power of Congress over federal courts' jurisdiction and the role of those courts in our tripartite federal system.

That intricate balance surfaced just a few years after *McCardle* and *Yerger*. In *United States v. Klein*,[75] the Supreme Court recognized that congressional power over jurisdiction is subject to limits. In *Klein*, the administrator of an estate sought to recover compensation for property confiscated by the Union Army during the Civil War, under a federal statute that permitted such claims provided the claimant was loyal to the United States. The Court had previously held that a presidential pardon for war-time activities constituted proof of loyalty.[76] While *Klein* was pending, however, Congress enacted legislation to the effect that a pardon could not be used to prove loyalty, and in fact demonstrated the opposite, and deprived the Court of jurisdiction in any such case predicated on a pardon. (The statute was phrased in jurisdictional terms, thus making *Klein* relevant to the present discussion.) The *Klein* Court held that the statute was not a proper exercise of the Exceptions Clause, because Congress did not "intend to withhold appellate jurisdiction except as a means to an end" — that is, to deny to presidential pardons the effect the Court said they had.[77]

Klein is a confusing case and its meaning is controversial. It may hold that, despite congressional authority to make exceptions and regulations, Congress cannot manipulate jurisdiction to dictate to the Supreme Court the result in a particular case.[78] Alternatively, it may mean simply that Congress cannot make exceptions to the Court's appellate jurisdiction which violate some other constitutional limitation. In any event, *Klein* suggests that the Constitution imposes some limits on Congress's ability to control the Court's appellate jurisdiction. However, despite having several opportunities to do so, the Court has not used *Klein* to strike down other jurisdiction stripping laws.[79]

§ 2.05 Congressional Control over Lower Federal Courts

The lower federal courts lack the precise constitutional foundation possessed by the Supreme Court, although it is clear that Congress has the authority to create

---

75. 80 U.S. (13 Wall.) 128 (1872).

76. United States v. Padelford, 76 U.S. (9 Wall.) 531 (1869).

77. *Klein*, 80 U.S. at 145.

78. The result-dictation aspect of *Klein* is also implicated by another provision of the statute *Klein* struck down, and is discussed later, in Section 2.06.

79. Howard M. Wasserman, *The Irrepressible Myth of Klein*, 79 U. CIN. L. REV. 53 (2011). *See also* Patchak v. Zinke, 138 S. Ct. 897 (2018) (rejecting a *Klein* attack on a jurisdiction-stripping statute).

them. Article III refers to them only in general terms, when it states that judicial power shall be vested in the Supreme Court and "in such inferior Courts as the Congress may from time to time ordain and establish."[80] The Ordain and Establish Clause suggests that the Constitution left Congress free to establish inferior courts or not, as it thought appropriate.[81] Quite clearly, the Constitution contemplated that "cases within the judicial cognizance of the United States not only might but would arise in the state courts in the exercise of their ordinary jurisdiction."[82] Moreover, the Supremacy Clause bound state judges to recognize federal law as supreme, a requirement which would have been unnecessary if they were not expected to decide at least some cases involving federal law.

Of course, the fact that some federal cases could originate in state court does not prove that federal courts were optional. Indeed, some have questioned whether Congress has unlimited discretion regarding the existence of lower federal courts. In *Martin v. Hunter's Lessee*, Justice Story, for instance, argued that the language of Article III "is manifestly designed to be mandatory upon the legislature."[83] He relied on language in Article III that the judicial power "shall be vested" to conclude that the Constitution obligated Congress to vest all judicial power set out in Article III. Accordingly, Congress was obliged to create at least some inferior federal courts.[84]

Justice Story's view has not prevailed. On the contrary, the law has recognized that Congress enjoys significant discretion to create or abolish inferior federal courts.[85] Others make more modest claims, suggesting, for instance, that lower federal courts must exist to hear at least those matters not within the jurisdiction of the state courts or the original jurisdiction of the Supreme Court. Absent lower federal courts with at least that jurisdiction, some rights would lack judicial remedies, a violation of *Marbury*'s rule of law principle.

It may seem inefficient for a federal judicial system to operate alongside the state courts. Yet the existence of federal courts with competence over matters specified in Article III serves some basic objects of the Constitution. Justice Story articulated these basic principles in *Martin v. Hunter's Lessee*.[86] Federal courts play a critical role in preserving the supremacy of federal law. A federal judiciary is needed to interpret

---

80. U.S. Const. art. III, cl. 1, § 1.

81. *See* Lockerty v. Phillips, 319 U.S. 182, 187 (1943). *See also* Palmore v. United States, 411 U.S. 389, 401 (1973) ("Congress ... was not constitutionally required to create inferior Art. III courts").

82. Martin v. Hunter's Lessee, 14 U.S. (1 Wheat.) 304, 340 (1816).

83. *Id.* at 328.

84. Moreover, Article III's grant of nine categories of cases and controversies over which Article III courts have jurisdiction, by beginning each grant with either "all cases" or "controversies," at least is consistent with a view that federal court jurisdiction over the "all cases" categories is mandatory. *See, e.g.*, Akhil Amar, *A Neo-Federalist View of Article III: Separating the Two Tiers of Federal Jurisdiction*, 65 B.U. L. Rev. 205 (1985).

85. *See* Palmore v. United States, 411 U.S. 389, 401–402 (1973); Glidden Co. v. Zdanok, 370 U.S. 530, 561 (1962).

86. 14 U.S. (1 Wheat.) 304 (1816).

and apply the laws of the Union and to compel obedience to them. Also, Justice Story suggested that federal courts might be necessary to vindicate national interests over conflicting local interests that state courts might on occasion favor or be perceived to favor. In some instances, federal courts were needed to provide an impartial tribunal. Other cases might raise issues "touching the safety, peace, and sovereignty of the nation" which would justify federal jurisdiction. Moreover, federal courts are needed to assure that federal law is interpreted uniformly across the nation.[87] Still, these goals could be met simply by having one United States Supreme Court with power to review state court decisions implicating federal law — the question at issue in *Martin*.

Article III establishes the jurisdiction of the federal courts by laying out nine categories of "cases" and "controversies" to which their jurisdiction extends.[88] In practice, however, Congress has never given lower federal courts the full range of jurisdiction Article III would allow. As just one of many examples, it limits diversity jurisdiction to cases involving a certain dollar amount in controversy. Indeed, even though a federal court system was created in large part to vindicate federal rights, Congress did not give the lower federal courts federal question jurisdiction until 1875.[89]

Despite the seemingly wide breadth of Congress's discretion to prescribe the jurisdiction of the lower federal courts it creates, the Court has never confronted a case in which Congress has completely deprived the federal courts of jurisdiction over a type of case, *e.g.*, abortion, school prayer, or busing, that has engendered controversial judicial rulings. No decision specifically addresses that question because Congress to date has not passed such legislation. Thus, it is not at all clear that Congress could restrict federal court jurisdiction to eliminate all opportunity to enforce constitutional rights in federal court. To do so would contravene the *Marbury* principle that the rule of law requires judicial remedies for violations of rights.[90] The Due Process Clause of the Fifth Amendment might provide an additional restriction on Congress's power to strip federal court jurisdiction, since such stripping would severely limit or even eliminate the ability to seek judicial redress for violations of constitutional rights, and thus might be seen as violating the underlying right itself. Again reprising the

---

87. *Id.* at 347–48.

88. *See* U.S. CONST. art. III § 2 ("The judicial Power [of the United States] shall extend to all Cases, in Law and Equity, arising under this Constitution, the Laws of the United States, and Treaties made, or which shall be made, under their Authority; — to all Cases affecting Ambassadors, other public Ministers and Consuls; — to all Cases of admiralty and maritime Jurisdiction; — to Controversies to which the United States shall be a Party; — to Controversies between two or more States; — between a State and Citizens of another State; — between Citizens of different States; — between Citizens of the same State claiming Lands under Grants of different States, and between a State, or the Citizens thereof, and foreign States, Citizens or Subjects.").

89. 1 Stat. 73, 77 (1789); *Palmore*, 411 U.S. at 401.

90. *See* Marbury v. Madison, 5 U.S. (1 Cranch) 137, 163 (1803). *Cf.* Guam v. Olsen, 431 U.S. 195, 204 (1977) (statute that denied litigants access to Article III courts "might present constitutional questions").

idea of the structural role federal courts play in our system, it is at least arguable that congressional authority to prescribe federal court jurisdiction must preserve those courts' essential function of vindicating constitutional rights.

§ 2.06 Other Constitutional Limits on Congressional Control over Federal Courts

Separation of powers principles may also limit Congress's discretion to impose other constraints on the federal courts. For example, an early Supreme Court case held invalid a statute that empowered the executive branch to review and revise judicial decisions.[91] Much more recently, in 1995, the Court struck down a statute that authorized federal courts to reinstate cases that had already proceeded to final judgment. The Court in *Plaut v. Spendthrift Farm*[92] held that the Article III power to decide cases implied that, once conclusively and finally decided, those cases were not subject to a congressional mandate that they be reopened. The power to decide a case was the power to resolve it. Thus, while the Court acknowledged that Congress could change the underlying substantive law while a case was pending and require courts in that case to apply the new law, Congress could not require federal courts to reopen cases once they had reached final judgment.

A further separation of powers limitation on Congress's control over the federal courts flows from *United States v. Klein*,[93] discussed earlier in this chapter.[94] In addition to its jurisdiction-stripping feature, discussed earlier, the statute at issue in *Klein* also required courts hearing cases in which a plaintiff relied on a pardon for proof of his loyalty to the Union to treat a pardon as "'conclusive evidence ... that the claimant did give aid to the rebellion.'"[95] Beyond rejecting the statute's jurisdiction-stripping provision, *Klein* also held that this evidentiary provision was unconstitutional because it "prescribe[d] a rule of decision"[96] for federal courts to follow.

This holding has caused a great deal of confusion, since "prescribing a rule of decision" is what Congress does every time it enacts a statute that regulates conduct (for example, criminalizing armed bank robbery) — and, indeed, defines the conduct (for example, defining "armed" to include situations where the robber is not actually armed but misleads victims into thinking he is). Since *Klein*, the Court has never relied on this "rule of decision" language to strike down a law, and, indeed, has upheld a number

---

91. Hayburn's Case, 2 U.S. (2 Dall.) 409 (1792).
92. Plaut v. Spendthrift Farm, Inc., 514 U.S. 211, 240 (1995).
93. 80 U.S. 128 (1872).
94. *See* Section 2.04.
95. 80 U.S. at 143–144 (quoting statute).
96. *Id.* at 146.

of statutes against challenges based on this language.[97] Nevertheless, no aspect of *Klein* has ever been overruled, and thus, the "rule of decision" prohibition remains, despite difficult questions about its application and even its underlying coherence.

§ 2.07 Non-Article III Adjudication

Congress may affect judicial conduct not only by restricting the jurisdiction of Article III courts but also by assigning some work within their competence to federal tribunals, including those housed in administrative agencies, that do not have the Article III safeguards of life tenure and salary protection. Congress might do so for a variety of reasons. In some instances, it might prefer to avoid establishing additional life tenured judgeships to preserve flexibility. Alternatively, administrative agencies might provide a more efficient means of adjudicating certain disputes, as they would be staffed by adjudicators more knowledgeable about the particular subject of the litigation and the overall regulatory scheme under which those disputes arise. Still, this power poses some danger. Unless regulated, this legislative power could subvert the basic constitutional separation of powers and checks and balances by allowing Congress to bypass Article III courts without having to rely on state courts.

Congress's power to create non-Article III courts flows from its enumerated powers in Article I (for example, its power to regulate interstate commerce) combined with the Necessary and Proper Clause. Chief Justice Marshall recognized the legitimacy of so-called legislative courts or Article I courts, which he concluded rested on certain legislative powers granted to Congress.[98] Thus, for example, the Court held that the Necessary and Proper Clause, combined with Congress's power over military forces,[99] confers power to establish non-Article III military tribunals. Similarly, that Clause, combined with Congress's power to govern territories[100] allows it to establish territorial courts.[101] These are only examples: the wide variety of regulatory powers Congress possesses under Article I, when combined with the Necessary and Proper Clause, gives Congress broad authority to establish such "Article I courts" to adjudicate a wide variety of disputes.

Many of these Article I courts adjudicate civil disputes between citizens and the federal government. The Court first articulated the doctrine governing the constitutionality of Article I adjudication of such disputes in the 1856 case *Murray's Lessee v. Hoboken Land & Improvement Co.*, where it said:

---

97. *See, e.g.*, Patchak v. Zinke, 138 S. Ct. 897 (2018); Bank Markazi v. Peterson, 136 S. Ct. 1310 (2016); Robertson v. Seattle Audubon Society, 503 U.S. 429 (1992); *see also* Pennsylvania v. Wheeling & Belmont Bridge Co., 18 How. 421 (1856) (pre-*Klein* case rejecting an analogous challenge).

98. American Insurance Co. v. Canter, 26 U.S. (1 Pet.) 511 (1828).

99. *See* U.S. CONST. art. I, § 8, cl. 14.

100. U.S. CONST. art. IV, § 3, cl. 2.

101. *See Canter, supra.* note 98.

there are matters, involving public rights, which may be presented in such form that the judicial power is capable of acting on them, and which are susceptible of judicial determination, but which Congress may or may not bring within the cognizance of the Courts of the United States, as it may deem proper.[102]

The "public rights" mentioned in *Murray's Lessee* encompass a range of categories. The paradigmatic public rights are "claims against the United States" for "money, land or other things."[103] (Consider, for example, a taxpayer's claim for an income tax refund, an importer's claim for a refund of customs duties paid to the United States, the claim by a holder of a government license for a renewal of that license, or an alien's claim for legal status.) Presumably, the doctrine of sovereign immunity insulates the United States from liability on such claims absent congressional consent.[104] An important theory underlying the constitutionality of Article I court adjudication of such public rights is that Congress could condition that consent on trial of such claims in an Article I court.

In *Northern PipeLine Construction Co. v. Marathon Pipe Line Co.*,[105] the Court addressed the question of what adjudicatory authority Congress could delegate to such Article I tribunals. In the Bankruptcy Reform Act of 1978 Congress had given bankruptcy judges, who did not enjoy life tenure, jurisdiction over some types of controversies that would otherwise reside in Article III courts. *Northern Pipeline* raised the question whether such Article I courts could decide questions based on the bankrupt party's state-created common law rights.

The Court struck down the grant to the Article I court of such Article III jurisdiction, which would normally fall under Article III's grant of diversity jurisdiction. The *Northern PipeLine* plurality opinion interpreted Article III literally, subject to some historical exceptions (for example, territorial and military courts). It invoked the public rights/private rights dichotomy as the hinge on which delegation of adjudicatory authority to Article I tribunals turned. The opinion conceded that Congress could create agencies to adjudicate "public rights," *i.e.*, disputes between the government and others. However, it concluded that Article I courts could not adjudicate disputes between individuals that involve only "private rights," which are normally defined as rights between two private parties and especially those based on state common law.

This issue has more than semantic consequence. If Article I tribunals may adjudicate only matters of public rights, the practice of administrative agencies adjudicating a range of cases between private parties is constitutionally suspect. *Northern PipeLine* thus threatened to undo a significant part of the Article I court structure that had arisen over time, and in particular since the proliferation during and after the New

---

102. 59 U.S. (18 How.) 272, 284 (1856).
103. *Ex parte* Bakelite Corp., 279 U.S. 438, 452 (1929).
104. *Id. See also* Northern PipeLine Co. v. Marathon Pipe Line Co., 458 U.S. 50, 67 (1982).
105. 458 U.S. 50 (1982).

Deal of federal administrative agencies (including Article I courts housed within those agencies).

But *Northern PipeLine* was only a plurality decision. Three years later, the Court revisited the issue of whether Article I courts could decide private rights disputes in *Thomas v. Union Carbide Agricultural Products Co.*[106] There, it reviewed a statute requiring binding arbitration of private claims for compensation owing to another private party's use of data submitted for pesticide registration. Essentially, a federal pesticide control law required marketers of pesticides to provide safety data, but also allowed subsequent marketers of similar products to rely on the data submitted by an earlier applicant. The law called for arbitration of any disputes arising out of the first marketer's claim that the second marketer owed it money for the use of its data.

This Article I adjudication provision was attacked on the ground that it involved adjudication of "private rights" that, under *Northern Pipeline*, must be committed to an Article III court. The Court rejected that argument. According to Justice O'Connor's majority opinion, the public rights/private rights dichotomy did not provide "a bright-line test for determining the requirements of Article III."[107] Justice O'Connor wrote that Congress could, for a valid legislative purpose, create a private right "so closely integrated into a public regulatory scheme as to be a matter appropriate for agency resolution."[108] The Court thus rejected *Northern Pipeline*'s bright-line rule forbidding an Article I court from adjudicating something that looked like a private right.

One year after *Thomas*, the Court considered, in *Commodities Futures Trading Commission v. Schor*, whether the Commodity Futures Trading Commission, an Article I tribunal, could adjudicate state common-law counterclaims between private persons — that is, private rights — as a matter of ancillary or pendent jurisdiction related to the statutory claims over which the Article I court had jurisdiction.[109] Again writing for a majority, Justice O'Connor repeated *Thomas*'s rejection of a formalistic approach and articulated a balancing test in which no single factor was decisive, "with an eye to the practical effect that the congressional action will have on the constitutionally assigned role of the federal judiciary":

> Among the factors upon which we have focused are the extent to which the essential attributes of judicial power are reserved to Article III courts, and, conversely, the extent to which the non-Article III forum exercises the range of jurisdiction and powers normally vested only in Article III courts, the origins and importance of the right to be adjudicated, and the concerns that drove Congress to depart from the requirements of Article III.[110]

Applying these factors, Justice O'Connor found that the Article I court did not share enough of those "essential attributes" to call the legislative scheme into doubt.

---

106. 473 U.S. 568 (1985).
107. *Id.* at 586.
108. *Id.* at 593–94.
109. 478 U.S. 833 (1986).
110. *Id.* at 851.

She also observed that Congress intended to create an adjudication scheme that was quicker and simpler than litigation in an Article III court, and one that was conducted by experts in the subject-matter of those lawsuits (commodities transactions). She conceded that the common law counterclaim at issue was a private right, and that private rights normally should be litigated by Article III courts. However, she concluded that that was just one factor in the balancing test, and that the other factors outweighed the constitutional concerns triggered by that particular grant of jurisdiction to the Article I court.

Justice Brennan, joined by Justice Marshall, dissented. Adhering to the views he expressed in *Northern PipeLine*, Justice Brennan insisted that the private nature of the common law counterclaim at issue meant that Congress could not place adjudication of that right in an Article I court. He worried that the Court's balancing approach allowed Congress to eviscerate Article III courts, since he suggested that in any particular case, the balance might come out in favor of allowing Article I adjudication but that, over the long-run, such decisions could result in a vastly-weakened Article III judiciary. For that reason, he urged that the private/public rights issue remain the decisive question in answering most Article I adjudication issues.[111]

More recently, the Court has sent confusing messages about the private rights doctrine and the constitutional status of Article I courts more generally. In the 2011 case *Stern v. Marshall*, it held that Congress could not confer power on an Article I bankruptcy court to enter a final judgment on a state law counterclaim involving a bankrupt party.[112] Writing for five justices, Chief Justice Roberts wrote that allowing Congress to take such claims away from Article III courts would transform Article III "from the guardian of individual liberty and separation of powers we have long recognized into mere wishful thinking."[113] The Court distinguished *Schor* on the ground that the Article I court in that case was part of a larger administrative apparatus implementing a comprehensive regulatory scheme, a fact that either justified the Article I court in adjudicating a private right or perhaps even justified describing that right as a public right. By contrast, the bankruptcy court in *Stern* was a standalone entity whose only purpose was adjudicating; in that case, the Court suggested, the nature of the right as a private one should play a more decisive role in evaluating (and invalidating) the scheme. Justice Breyer, dissenting for four justices, called for what he described as "a more pragmatic approach to the constitutional question,"[114] one informed by cases such as *Schor*.

In 2015, the Court gave a narrow interpretation to *Stern*, and provided more jurisdictional latitude for bankruptcy courts and, by extension, other Article I tribunals. In *Wellness International Network v. Sharif*,[115] the Court allowed a bank-

---

111. Justice Brennan accepted historically-grounded exceptions to this rule, such as military and territorial courts.

112. 564 U.S. 462 (2011).

113. *Id.* at 495.

114. *Id.* at 510 (Breyer J., dissenting).

115. 575 U.S. 665 (2015).

ruptcy court to decide a claim relevant to the bankrupt party's estate. Speaking for the most part for six justices,[116] Justice Sotomayor relied heavily on the parties' supposed consent to adjudication of the issue by a bankruptcy court; based on that consent, she distinguished *Stern*. Writing for three dissenters, Chief Justice Roberts conceded that an exception identified in *Stern* allowed a bankruptcy court to adjudicate the question at issue in *Sharif*. But he took issue with the majority's heavily reliance on the parties' consent as the relevant factor. He argued that that reliance mis-read *Stern* and allowed Congress to undermine the authority of the Article III judiciary by delegating the adjudication of traditional common law-like legal issues to Article I tribunals.

§ 2.08 Justiciability Doctrines

[1] An Overview of Justiciability

Justiciability doctrines address, in general terms, the criteria for the sort of disputes federal courts can adjudicate. Federal courts must confine their power of review to cases warranting the judicial function. The Constitution delegated to federal courts "the judicial Power of the United States" which, under Article III, extends only to nine categories of "Cases" and "Controversies." Thus, federal courts may only entertain complaints which meet the Article III requirement of alleging an actual "case" or "controversy."

The various justiciability doctrines generally respond to three separate concerns. "Standing" addresses the "who" question—is the litigant before the Court the right party to invoke its jurisdiction? The "when" question—is the question ready for judicial attention, or, conversely, has its time passed?—is addressed, respectively, by the doctrines of ripeness and mootness. The Advisory Opinion doctrine, in a sense, cuts across both standing and timing issues. Finally, the political question doctrine evaluates the "what" grounds; that is, it considers whether certain topics are beyond judicial competence regardless of who raises them or when they are brought to court.

Justiciability doctrines arise in part from the Constitution, either from the "case or controversy" requirement with respect to the "who" and "when" questions or from particular constitutional commitments of decision-making authority to other branches of government in the case of the political question doctrine.[117] Structural principles of separation of powers and checks and balances also provide further justification for these doctrines. In other instances, prudential, rather than constitutional, concerns provide the rationale. In such latter cases, although the Court has constitutional power to hear a matter, it deems it prudent not to exercise it.

---

116. Justice Alito did not join all of the majority opinion.

117. For a careful consideration of the question whether the political question doctrine implicates, or by contrast is distinct from, Article III's case or controversy requirement, see RICHARD FREER & EDWARD COOPER, 13C FED. PRAC. & PROC. JURIS. § 3534.3 (Charles Alan Wright) (3d ed. 2005) ("Political Questions—Relation to Other Justiciability Doctrines").

Many of the justiciability doctrines are implicit in *Marbury v. Madison*. In *Marbury*, Marshall repeatedly tied judicial intervention to protection of rights[118] and related the power of judicial review to the need to decide the case or controversy in front of the court.[119] These doctrines implicate all of the justiciability doctrines.[120]

The justiciability doctrines provide some comfort against fears of a judiciary eager to expand its own space and enhance its own power. At the same time, courts sometimes invoke them to serve the judiciary's particular instrumental purposes. They reflect the belief that courts should confine themselves to deciding matters presented in an adversary context which enhance judicial resolution and "furnish ... a safeguard against premature or ill-advised decisions in the constitutional field."[121] Justiciability doctrines also facilitate efficient and effective judicial decisions by making sure courts are presented with a full record of factual and legal materials on which to rule, rather than, for example, a sparse or non-existent record in the case of a lawsuit that is not yet ripe. They also serve as a filter to protect courts' dockets from being overburdened by too many cases. Finally, they respond to fairness concerns by limiting judicial intervention to instances of real disputes between aggrieved parties.

The justiciability doctrines are constitutional and prudential requirements applicable in federal courts only.[122] This fact may create problems when a state court adjudicates a case on the merits in a situation where a federal court would dismiss the action as nonjusticiable. For example, in *Doremus v. Board of Education*,[123] taxpayers challenged under the Establishment Clause a New Jersey statute providing for reading of the Old Testament in public schools. The highest state court upheld the statute on the merits. The taxpayers appealed to the Supreme Court, only to have their appeal dismissed for lack of standing to sue. The dismissal of the federal appeal on justiciability grounds left the statute and the state court opinion in place, since federal court standing limits did not apply to New Jersey courts.

[2] Advisory Opinions

The Supreme Court has construed the "Case" or "Controversy" requirement to preclude federal courts from giving advice to other departments outside of formal cases or controversies. Indeed, when George Washington sought an advisory opinion on questions of international law in 1793, the first Court politely declined, in a letter

---

118. *Marbury*, 5 U.S. at 162–64, 167, 177.

119. *Id.* at 177–78.

120. *See* Henry P. Monaghan, *Constitutional Adjudication: The Who and When*, 82 YALE L.J. 1363, 1365 (1973).

121. PAUL A. FREUND, THE SUPREME COURT OF THE UNITED STATES: ITS BUSINESS, PURPOSES, AND PERFORMANCE 17 (1961).

122. Of course, state judiciaries and/or constitutions may feature analogous doctrines or limitations.

123. 342 U.S. 429 (1952).

from the Chief Justice to the President.[124] The Court invoked the structural principle of checks and balances and its status as a court of last resort as "considerations" mitigating against an extrajudicial reply. Moreover, it pointed out that Article II gave the President power only to require opinions from heads of executive departments, not from the federal courts.[125]

Over a century later, the Court considered another variant on another branch's request for an advisory opinion. *Muskrat v. United States*[126] considered a lawsuit challenging a federal law redistributing Native American lands. The plaintiff was one of several individuals Congress had authorized to challenge the law to test its constitutionality; however, there was no showing that the plaintiff was in fact injured by the law. The Court refused to rule on the merits of the lawsuit. It concluded that the case presented no true "case" or "controversy" since the United States had no interest adverse to the claimants[127] but had essentially arranged the lawsuit to determine the constitutionality of federal legislation. Echoing *Marbury*'s justification for asserting the power of judicial review, the Court stated that that power "is not given to it as a body with revisory power over the action of Congress, but because the rights of the litigants in justiciable controversies require the Court to choose between the fundamental law and a law purporting to be enacted within constitutional authority, but in fact beyond the power delegated to the Legislative branch of the Government."[128]

Half a century after *Muskrat*, in *Chicago & Southern Air Lines, Inc. v. Waterman S.S. Corp.*,[129] the Court dismissed a petition which asked it to review an order of the Civil Aeronautics Board which was subject to subsequent review by the President. The Court held that the statutory scheme improperly put the federal courts in the business of rendering advisory opinions. In doing so, the Court, speaking through Justice Jackson, explained the fundamental nature of such an opinion. He wrote: "It has ... been the firm and unvarying practice of Constitutional Courts to render no judgments not binding and conclusive on the parties and none that are subject to later review or alteration by administrative action."[130]

Few criticize the Court's refusal to render advisory opinions.[131] Decisions unaccompanied by a true case suffer from being divorced from the reality of actual facts. Advisory opinions are consequently bound to speak in an unreal, abstract tone not

---

124. Letter from Chief Justice Jay (Aug. 8, 1793), *in* Bernard Schwartz, A Basic History of the U.S. Supreme Court 97–98 (1968).

125. U.S. Const. art. II, § 2, cl. 1 ("The President ... may require the Opinion, in writing, of the Principal officer in each of the executive Departments, upon any subject relating to the Duties of their respective offices.").

126. 219 U.S. 346 (1911).

127. *Id.* at 361.

128. *Ibid.*

129. 333 U.S. 103 (1948).

130. *Id.* at 113–14.

131. While the cases discussed in the text were not feigned in the sense that the plaintiffs and defendants colluded to create a lawsuit where no real dispute existed, the Court has connected the ban on advisory opinions with an analogous ban on deciding such collusive cases. *See, e.g.,* United States

conducive to effective judicial decision-making. The absence of concrete facts may also deprive the Court of opportunities to avoid constitutional decisions or to decide cases narrowly, based (literally) on the facts of the given case. Still, despite these compelling justifications, advisory opinions are not totally foreign to the American experience. State courts are not governed by Article III's case or controversy requirement, and a number of state courts are authorized to render advisory opinions.

[3] Standing

[a] Constitutional Requirements

Recall that standing asks the "who" question — who is a proper plaintiff to sue in federal court? To have standing to sue, a plaintiff must have a direct personal interest in the governmental act she challenges: unless she is hurt personally, she is seeking only an abstract judgment on the validity of the act. It is critical, although sometimes challenging, to distinguish between a plaintiff's standing and the merits of her claim. A party may have standing to assert a claim on which she is not entitled to prevail. Standing simply means that the party has the right to assert the claim in federal court, not that her claim has merit.

The Supreme Court has articulated three standing requirements as the "irreducible constitutional minimum."[132] First, the plaintiff must allege past or imminent injury to her. Second, the defendant's conduct must have caused the harm. Finally, a favorable court ruling must be able to redress the injury.[133] These requirements are thus shorthanded as "injury," "causation," and "redressability."

At times, standing turns upon a plaintiff's ability to allege facts sufficiently specific to demonstrate injury. For example, in *Sierra Club v. Morton*,[134] the Court found that the Sierra Club lacked standing to challenge construction of a ski resort since it failed to allege that any of its members had used the area and would thus be injured by the project. Similarly, in *Lujan v. Defenders of Wildlife*,[135] the Court found that another environmental group lacked standing because its members alleged only vague intentions to visit an area to view endangered species that were allegedly threatened by the challenged government action.

The injuries in the cases above — the inability to hike in a forest and to observe an endangered species — may seem intuitive. Indeed, other injuries, such as those to one's physical integrity (*e.g.*, getting punched) or one's other common law-protected interests (*e.g.*, injury to your real property or chattel) might seem even more straightforward. But beyond these types of harms, Article III "injury" extends farther, to in-

---

v. Johnson, 319 U.S. 302, 305 (1943) (describing the suit it dismissed as "collusive because it is not in any real sense adversary").

132. Lujan v. Defenders of Wildlife, 504 U.S. 555, 560 (1992).

133. *Id.* at 560–61.

134. 405 U.S. 727 (1972).

135. 504 U.S. 555 (1992).

clude injury to interests that a legislature might choose to bestow on an individual or group of persons.

Consider *Havens Realty v. Coleman*.[136] *Havens* featured a claim that a defendant had provided false information about the availability of rental housing, based on the race of the prospective tenant. The plaintiffs in *Havens* were "testers" — employees of a housing rights organization who pretended to be looking for rental housing, and who, paired as a white and a Black tester, presented equivalent qualifications, seeking to uncover landlords who favored one applicant over another based on the applicant's race. When a Black tester was told that housing in a given apartment building was not available, even though the equally-qualified white tester was offered housing, the Black tester sued. The Court held that federal fair housing statutes provided all Americans with a right to truthful information about housing availability. Thus, the Court concluded that the Black tester had established Article III injury, based on the alleged deprivation of that statutorily-granted right to truthful housing information.

Causation presents its own difficulties. For example, in *Allen v. Wright*,[137] parents challenging an IRS failure to deny tax exemptions to racially segregated schools demonstrated injury in their children's diminished ability to be educated in a racially integrated school, but could not show that the injury was caused by the IRS's decision. Rather, the Court concluded that the number of such schools was uncertain and the impact of the IRS action on the plaintiffs' children's education prospects was speculative. In an analogous case, indigent plaintiffs failed to establish standing to challenge an IRS ruling that relaxed requirements that non-profit hospitals provide free medical care.[138] The plaintiffs had been harmed by the lack of free medical care, but they could not trace the harm to the IRS action that made it easier for hospitals to deny free care while maintaining their tax-exempt status. Addressing the causation issue, the Court questioned whether it was really the IRS's decision that caused the hospitals to deny the care, or rather, whether the expense of providing such care would have led the hospitals to deny the care regardless of any IRS tax exemption policy.

Cases such as these illustrate that causation is "substantially more difficult to establish" when the plaintiff himself is not the target of challenged government action.[139] To state the matter bluntly: if the challenged action operates directly on the plaintiffs, then causation is easier to establish. But if the action operates on a third party, who in turn acts on a plaintiff, then causation will be "substantially more difficult to establish."

Finally, the plaintiff must prove *redressability* in order to establish standing. Often, redressability is the mirror image of causation. Thus, in the indigent medical care case described above, the Court's doubt whether the IRS's policy caused the plaintiffs'

---

136. 455 U.S. 363 (1982).
137. 468 U.S. 737 (1984).
138. Simon v. E. Ky. Welfare Rights Org., 426 U.S. 26 (1976).
139. *Allen*, 468 U.S. at 562; *see also Defenders of Wildlife*, 504 U.S. at 562.

injury similarly led the Court to question whether an injunction requiring the IRS to change its policy would redress that injury. Sometimes the relationship between causation and redressability is more indirect. For example, in *Linda R.S. v. Richard D.*,[140] an unwed mother was held to lack standing to seek to require Texas to prosecute her child's father for non-support. The Court reasoned that, even if the mother's suit succeeded and Texas, thus ordered to prosecute, convicted the offender, that result would not redress her injury (*i.e.*, lack of support) but only result in jailing the father. Cases such as these make clear that redressability, just like causation, will be difficult to establish if the challenged government conduct acts not upon the plaintiffs themselves, but upon third parties.

[b] Prudential Requirements

In addition to the constitutional requirements derived from Article III's "case" or "controversy" language, the Court has imposed various prudential standing requirements. These prudential principles, like the constitutional requirements, reflect the Court's concern for the judiciary's appropriate role in a democracy. But unlike the constitutional requirements, Congress can modify or override prudential considerations, and courts themselves can make exceptions to them. The prudential standing requirements include the limitations on third party standing, the zone of interests test, and, according to some authority, the rule against standing based on a generalized grievance.

[i] Third Party Standing

Even when a plaintiff satisfies the Article III standing requirements, federal courts hesitate to reach the merits of disputes when the plaintiff asserts the legal rights of absent third parties. Several considerations account for this reluctance. The right-holder may prefer not to litigate her rights in the manner or in the court chosen by the plaintiff. Moreover, a court may believe the issues will be more rigorously presented or will benefit from a richer factual context if litigated by an actual right-holder. Finally, declining to adjudicate a legal rights claim raised by a third party may render it unnecessary for a court to decide that claim, if the right-holder never chooses to litigate it herself.

Warth v. Seldin[141] illustrates the basic principle. *Warth* considered a constitutional challenge to a community's allegedly exclusionary zoning rules. One of the plaintiffs was a group of residents of a neighboring community. Those residents argued that they had Article III standing because the defendant community's alleged exclusion of low-income persons meant that such persons would likely live in the plaintiffs' own community, thus increasing demands for social services that would require raising the plaintiffs' taxes. While the Court doubted the taxpayers' Article III standing on causation grounds,[142] the Court further concluded that they were not proper plain-

---

140. Linda R.S. v. Richard D., 410 U.S. 614 (1973).
141. 422 U.S. 490 (1975).
142. *See id.* at 509 ("Apart from the conjectural nature of the asserted injury, the line of causation between [the defendant] Penfield's actions and such injury is not apparent from the complaint. What-

tiffs because they were asserting the legal claims of third parties — *i.e.*, their legal claim was that other persons (the would-be residents of the exclusionary community) were being denied their constitutional rights.

Courts will sometimes make an exception to this rule against litigating the rights of absent third parties if (1) the litigant has a close relationship with the person whose right he seeks to assert and (2) "some genuine obstacle" impedes the third party's assertion of his rights. For example, in *Singleton v. Wulff*,[143] the Court allowed doctors who performed abortions to sue to assert the legal rights of women whose abortion rights were allegedly being unconstitutionally infringed by a state law that restricted payments for certain types of abortions. The doctors had Article III standing because, if they prevailed, they would be compensated for abortions they performed. The Court also allowed the doctors to assert the legal rights of their women patients, on the ground that the doctors had a special and close relationship with their patients. (On this point, compare the residents of the neighboring community in *Warth*, who were really nothing more than accidental allies of the would-be residents/right-holders.)

The *Singleton* Court concluded that the closeness of the doctor-patient relationship would render the doctors effective advocates of the women's legal interests. It also observed that those women might encounter difficulties in asserting their own rights, given the potential stigma of being a named plaintiff in a case seeking to vindicate a right to an abortion. The Court also noted that, because pregnancies naturally end after nine months, women seeking abortions usually had to seek judicial relief in some representative capacity, either via a class action or by seeking an exception to the rule that the ending of a plaintiff's direct interest in a case normally moots that case.[144] Since those latter solutions involved some sort of indirect representation of the right-holder's interest, the Court did not see a serious problem in allowing that indirect representation to be accomplished by the doctors.

In addition to courts, Congress also can make an exception to the prudential rule against third-party standing. Recall again *Havens Realty v. Coleman*, discussed earlier.[145] In that case, a Black "housing tester" was held to have suffered Article III injury due to the denial of his statutorily-granted right to truthful housing information. His colleague, the white tester, did not suffer that injury, since he was not given untruthful information. Nevertheless, the Court held that both testers were at least theoretically able to assert a different Article III injury — the injury of not being able to live in an integrated community, due to the defendant's provision of untruthful housing information to minority apartment seekers. The Court recognized that such a standing claim involved the white tester asserting the legal interests of others — that is, the

---

ever may occur in Penfield, the injury complained of — increases in taxation — results only from decisions made by the appropriate Rochester authorities [*i.e.*, the authorities in the taxpayers' own community], who are not parties to this case.").

143. 428 U.S. 106 (1976).

144. Mootness is discussed in the next sub-section 2.08[4][b].

145. 455 U.S. 363 (1982). *See* Section 2.08[3][a].

white tester had his own injury (the inability to live in an integrated community), but that injury arose from the defendant's invasion of other parties' legal rights to truthful housing information. The Court nevertheless allowed this assertion of third parties' rights to go forward,[146] on the ground that, in enacting the Fair Housing Act, Congress had sought to expand standing to the very limits allowed by Article III. That congressional choice thus wiped away any standing restrictions that were merely prudential in nature.

[ii] Zone of Interests

The zone of interests test requires that a plaintiff's grievance be within the zone of interests protected by the statute or constitutional provision invoked by the plaintiff. Thus, in *Bennett v. Spear*,[147] the Court held that certain ranchers challenging government action were within the zone of interests of the Endangered Species Act (ESA), the statute they alleged was being violated. The ranchers objected to government action withholding water from their irrigation district to preserve certain endangered species. The Court held that, by providing in the ESA that "any person may commence a civil suit,"[148] Congress expanded the zone of interests to include not only environmentalists but also those injured by the species preservation action.

The zone of interest test was developed in the specialized context of judicial review of administrative agency action under the Administrative Procedure Act (APA), the statute that governs such judicial review. However, in subsequent cases, the Court has applied the test beyond the APA context.[149]

[iii] Generalized Grievances and Citizen Standing

The Court has also insisted that a plaintiff's injury be particularized to him, rather than constituting a "generalized grievance" shared by many persons. Although the generalized grievance principle initially was described as "prudential,"[150] the Court more recently has vacillated on the question whether that principle is of constitutional or merely prudential status.[151] In *Federal Election Commission v. Akins*, the Court suggested that the generalized grievance disqualification only applies when the harm is

---

146. The Court recognized the potential implausibility that one defendant's actions could have impaired the plaintiffs' right to live an integrated community throughout the entire city. Nevertheless, it remanded the case to the lower court in order to allow the plaintiffs to attempt to make more definite allegations on that point.

147. 520 U.S. 154 (1997).

148. *Id.* at 164.

149. *See id.* at 163; *see also* Jonathan Siegel, *Zone of Interests*, 92 GEO. L.J. 317, 328 (2004).

150. Warth v. Seldin, 422 U.S. 490, 499 (1975).

151. *See* Lujan v. Defenders of Wildlife, 504 U.S. 555, 575–576 (1992) (suggesting its constitutional stature); Akins v. Federal Election Comm'n, 524 U.S. 11, 23 (1998) ("Whether styled as a constitutional or prudential limit on standing, the Court has sometimes determined that where large numbers of Americans suffer alike, the political process, rather than the judicial process, may provide the more appropriate remedy for a widely shared grievance.").

not only "widely shared" but is also "abstract and indefinite."[152] Thus, for example, plaintiffs in a mass tort case do not state a generalized grievance, because each plaintiff is the victim of particularized and concrete harm (for example, a physical injury that is unique to her). By contrast, a generally held interest in having the government follow the Constitution or some other law, without more specific injury to the individual plaintiff, would not be allowable to establish standing.

Instances where a litigant asserts standing as a citizen present the classic case of a generalized grievance. The Court has rejected the idea that citizenship confers standing to require the government to follow or enforce the law. Thus, in *Schlesinger v. Reservists Committee to Stop the War*,[153] citizens lacked standing to sue to prevent members of Congress from serving in the military reserves under the Incompatibility Clause.[154] The Court observed that the plaintiffs' grievance was generalized and common to all; allowing a citizen to sue on that basis alone would violate basic principles of separation of powers. In *Lujan v. Defenders of Wildlife*, the Court concluded that such citizen standing would effectively transfer the power to enforce the law from the Article II executive branch to the Article III judiciary.[155]

Note, however, that sometimes Congress includes in statutes provisions that allow "any citizen" or "any person" to sue.[156] As explained immediately above, such "citizen suit" provisions do not provide the interest the deprivation of which would constitute standing, if the grievance thereby created is considered to be "generalized." But this is not to say that citizen-suit provisions have no effect. Rather, as discussed earlier in *Havens Realty v. Coleman*,[157] such provisions have the effect of wiping away any prudential limitations on standing, for example, the requirement that a plaintiff assert his own legal rights.

Nevertheless, the citizen suit cases illustrate a central dilemma in our system. The refusal to recognize citizen standing may create some cases in which no private citizen can sue to enforce a constitutional provision. On the other hand, if the Court permitted citizens to bring such suits, little would remain of the standing requirement. The resolution may reside in a realization that some constitutional issues must be left to the political process. The executive or legislative branches, or the electorate, not the courts, may have the final word regarding such issues.

---

152. 524 U.S. 11, 23 (1998).

153. 418 U.S. 208 (1974).

154. U.S. Const. art. 1 §6, cl. 2 ("No Senator or Representative shall, during the time for which he was elected, be appointed to any civil office under the Authority of the United States, which shall have been created, or the emoluments whereof shall have been increased during such time; and no person holding any office under the United States, shall be a member of either House during his continuance in office.").

155. *See* 504 U.S. 555, 571–578 (1992).

156. *See, e.g.*, Bennett v. Spear, 520 U.S. 154 (1997) (considering such a "citizen suit" provision that was part of the Endangered Species Act).

157. 455 U.S. 363 (1982). *Havens* is discussed above, in the sub-section dealing with the prudential bar on a plaintiff asserting a third party's legal rights. *See* Section 2.08[3][b][i].

[c] Taxpayer Standing

A closely-related variant of citizen standing is taxpayer standing, which speaks to the ability or, usually, the inability, of a plaintiff to challenge a government spending decision based on her capacity as a taxpayer. Does her status as a taxpayer confer standing to challenge the law? In *Frothingham v. Mellon*,[158] the Court said no. In that case, the plaintiff, in her capacity as a taxpayer, challenged a federal statute that appropriated money to be apportioned among the states. She based her standing claim on her allegation that the appropriations would increase future taxation.

The Supreme Court dismissed the case, holding that the plaintiff, in her capacity as a federal taxpayer, did not have standing to challenge a federal law. It concluded that a taxpayer's interest was too minute and remote to justify standing. Moreover, a taxpayer suing simply in that capacity has no personal interest in the challenged statute. Consequently, a taxpayer suing in that capacity fails to allege the type of direct injury required for standing. Undoubtedly, the *Frothingham* Court feared that allowing any taxpayer to raise constitutional issues even if she lacked a unique personal interest would open the floodgates of constitutional law litigation. Regardless of how real this threat is, the general prohibition on taxpayer standing is an accepted part of standing doctrine.

Strictly applied, *Frothingham* would render some legislation immune from constitutional attack. For example, if Congress made grants to religious schools in violation of the First Amendment, *Frothingham* would preclude judicial review. To avoid that result, the Court modified the *Frothingham* rule in *Flast v. Cohen*,[159] where it upheld a federal taxpayer's standing to challenge congressional expenditures as violating the Establishment Clause of the First Amendment. The Court attempted to limit its exception to taxpayer standing by requiring, among other things, that the taxpayer must demonstrate that the challenged expenditure "exceeds specific constitutional limitations" (*e.g.*, the Establishment Clause) on the taxing and spending power.[160]

Flast may have been driven by the particular problem of the Establishment Clause, which is understood specifically to restrict government payments to religious institutions.[161] At any rate, its exception to the general rule against taxpayer standing has not been given a wide interpretation. The Court has refused to extend *Flast* beyond the Establishment Clause.[162] Indeed, in a series of cases starting in the 1980s and con-

---

158. 262 U.S. 447 (1923).

159. 392 U.S. 83 (1968).

160. *Id.* at 102–03. The Court also required that "the taxpayer must establish a logical link between that status and the type of legislative enactment attacked." *Id.* at 102. Thus, the taxpayer would have to allege a congressional exercise of its power under the Taxing and Spending Clause of Article I, rather than incidental expenditures of taxpayer funds under a general regulatory statute. *See ibid.*

161. For a more detailed examination of the Establishment Clause, see Chapter 12.

162. *See, e.g.*, DaimlerChrysler Corp. v. Cuno, 547 U.S. 332, 346 (2006) (refusing to apply the *Flast* exception to a suit by taxpayers challenging a state tax under the dormant Commerce Clause).

tinuing into more recent years, it has refused to apply *Flast* in particular Establishment Clause contexts.[163]

Like citizen standing cases, taxpayer standing cases present a paradox. On the one hand, recognizing a taxpayer's right to sue would raise the specter the *Frothingham* Court likely feared of taxpayers suing any federal program they happened to dislike, without having any direct interest at stake in the litigation. On the other hand, constitutional limitations such as the Establishment Clause are understood, at least in part, as prohibitions on some types of government expenditures. If taxpayers were not allowed to challenge such expenditures, it would be hard to know who else would have the right to sue. This paradox illustrates the tangled relationship between the merits of certain constitutional claims and the seemingly distinct (but in fact related) question of who has standing to raise such claims.[164]

[4] Timing Doctrines

In addition to featuring the "right" plaintiff, constitutionally valid "cases and controversies" must come at the "right" time. The Supreme Court has recognized two temporal limitations on cases and controversies. First, when commenced, a lawsuit must be "ripe." Second, during the course of the lawsuit, a lawsuit must not become "moot." These timing doctrines are closely related to standing doctrine, in that they all seek to ensure the existence of an adversarial "case" or "controversy," with the timing doctrines seeking to ensure that that adversarialness exists both at the commencement of the suit and throughout its life.[165] This sub-section considers ripeness and mootness in turn.

[a] Ripeness

Courts cannot consider constitutional issues prematurely. Ripeness thus responds to a separation of powers concern by postponing judicial intervention until it is clear a dispute exists that can and should be resolved by a court. As such, it serves the adversary system by deferring litigation until a dispute has developed sufficiently. In constitutional cases and other cases challenging the validity of government action,

---

163. *See* Valley Forge v. Americans United, 454 U.S. 464 (1982); Hein v. Freedom From Religion Foundation, 551 U.S. 587 (2007); Arizona Christian School Tuition Organization v. Winn, 563 U.S. 125 (2011).

164. Another example of this tangled relationship arises yet again in the Establishment Clause, in the context of the constitutionality of government religious displays. In *American Legion v. American Humanist Ass'n*, Justice Gorsuch's concurring opinion argued against a theory that found such displays unconstitutional if they offended a non-believer, in part on the ground that such a theory, by allowing persons to sue merely if they were offended by the display, violated Article III's standing requirements. 139 S. Ct. 2067, 2098 (2019) (Gorsuch, J., concurring in the judgment). The Establishment Clause is discussed in Chapter 12.

165. *See, e.g.*, Arizonans for Official English v. Arizona, 520 U.S. 43, 68 n. 22 (1997) ("Mootness has been described as 'the doctrine of standing set in a time frame: The requisite personal interest that must exist at the commencement of the litigation (standing) must continue throughout its existence (mootness).'").

ripeness also minimizes the instances in which courts must determine the validity of another branch's acts. More generally, it avoids the prospect of courts issuing advisory opinions.

As stated in the leading modern ripeness case, *Abbott Laboratories v. Gardner*, ripeness involves a dual inquiry into whether the issue in question is fit for judicial review when the plaintiff sues and the hardships that would ensue if judicial review was delayed.[166] Fitness for review turns on whether the claim—and thus the court's analysis—relies on facts that are still contingent or, by contrast, whether the facts have sufficiently developed to render the legal question susceptible to a definitive answer. This "fitness" factor is generally thought to be based in Article III's case or controversy mandate, since it speaks to whether the case is one that can be resolved by the court at the current time, or, contrarily, whether a decision at the current time would have practical impact only if certain still-contingent facts eventually arose. As such, this factor has a clear connection to the prohibition on federal courts issuing advisory opinions. By contrast, the balance of the hardships factor is probably best thought of as a prudential one, rather than a constitutional one, perhaps somewhat akin to the equitable considerations courts consider when deciding whether to issue preliminary injunctions and other equitable relief.

The significance of this difference is that Congress may, if it wishes, determine that some suits should be heard earlier than a court would otherwise decide is appropriate, if Congress's decision relates to the hardship factor, as opposed to the Article III-grounded fitness factor. Congress often makes such determinations in the realm of administrative action, when Congress allows early challenges to regulatory action, to allow both the agency and regulated parties to discover sooner rather than later whether the challenged agency action is legal. As long as the reviewing court is convinced that the constitutional "fitness" prong of ripeness is satisfied, it will give effect to Congress's decision to override any prudential considerations for delaying review. One can very roughly analogize this sort of dynamic to the one in which congressional inclusion of a "citizen suit" provision in a statute overrides any prudential (but not Article III) limitations on standing that a court would otherwise impose.[167]

Fitness for review turns in large part on the extent to which resolution of an issue hinges on its facts. For example, in *Abbott Laboratories* itself, the Court concluded that the issue was fit for judicial resolution because it presented a pure legal question—the legality of an agency regulation requiring changes in drug labeling. The matter was straightforward: did federal food and drug law authorize the regulation? Thus, even though the plaintiffs sued soon after the regulation was promulgated, there was no need for the development of any facts, since none were needed for the Court to decide the issue.

Hardship often turns on the practicalities of the particular situation. For example, in *Abbott Laboratories*, the Court acknowledged that the drug manufacturers faced

166. 387 U.S. 136, 149 (1967).
167. For a discussion of this effect of broad congressional grants to sue, see Section 2.08[3][b][i].

a difficult situation in the wake of the agency's new labeling regulation: they could either comply with the regulation and thus lose significant money by having to destroy existing labels, or they could defy the regulation and run the risk of the Food and Drug Administration (FDA) accusing them of selling unsafe drugs (which included mislabeled drugs). By contrast, the Court found little hardship in having a court immediately consider the manufacturers' challenge. Indeed, as suggested above, Congress has often realized that such "pre-enforcement challenges" help not just regulated parties but the government, by providing a swift answer to the question of the legality of the government's conduct.

A case decided the same day as *Abbott Laboratories* provides another application of this two-part, fitness and hardship test. In *Toilet Goods Assn v. Gardner*,[168] the Court found unripe a challenge to another FDA regulation, this one authorizing the FDA to suspend marketing licenses for pharmaceutical products if the manufacturer refused to allow government inspectors into the factory where the products were made. The regulation was promulgated pursuant to the agency's authority to promulgate regulations "for the efficient enforcement" of the food and drug laws.[169]

In finding the challenge unripe, the Court explained that the issue was not fit for resolution because it was not yet clear how the regulation furthered the "efficient enforcement" of the food and drug laws. In other words, it was not yet clear how the regulation would help resolve enforcement problems the agency might encounter — and it would not become clear until the agency had actually tried to visit a factory, been turned away, and in turn suspended the manufacturer's license. Similarly, the plaintiffs had not shown any hardship because their conduct was not being immediately impacted — after all, the agency might never seek to visit a factory, and even if it did, it was not clear how it would respond to being turned away.

By contrast, the regulation in *Abbott Laboratories* was both fit for review immediately (because it presented a pure question of law unaffected by any contingent facts) and satisfied the hardship prong (because the companies faced an immediate obligation to destroy their current labelling stock). Indeed, if the manufacturers' suit in *Abbott Laboratories* was held unripe, they only way they could have gotten judicial review of the regulation would have been to use the labels and thus violate the law, and defend against the prosecution on the ground that the regulation was invalid. The Court clearly believed that that option imposed too much hardship on the manufacturers, especially given what it called the "sensitive industry"[170] in which they were engaged.

Poe v. Ullman[171] raised another aspect of ripeness: whether a party can bring a pre-enforcement challenge to a statute that is never enforced. *Poe* involved a challenge to a state law prohibiting the use of contraceptives. The Supreme Court found the

---

168. 387 U.S. 158 (1967).
169. *Id.* at 161.
170. *Abbott Laboratories*, 387 U.S. at 153.
171. 367 U.S. 497 (1961).

challenge unripe, relying heavily on the fact the state had only enforced the law once in the last 80 years, in a case that it described as a "test case."[172] Thus, even though the law imposed criminal penalties, the Court concluded that fear of enforcement under these circumstances was "chimerical."[173]

Only seven years later, the Court took a very different approach to the fact of state non-enforcement of a challenged law. In *Epperson v. Arkansas*,[174] the Court reached the merits of a challenge to an Arkansas law that required the teaching of creationism, even though it had never been enforced in the over forty years it had been on the books. In a marked contrast to its approach in *Poe*, the Court, speaking through Justice Fortas, wrote: "There is no record of any prosecutions in Arkansas under its statute. It is possible that the statute is presently more of a curiosity than a vital fact of life.... Nevertheless, the present case was brought, the appeal as of right is properly here, and it is our duty to decide the issues presented."[175]

One can understand *Poe*'s reluctance to decide a controversial issue such as the constitutionality of an anti-contraception law when the law has not been enforced for decades. Nevertheless, *Epperson*'s quick and decisive resolution of the ripeness issue responds to the reality that the very existence of a criminal law[176] chills conduct, since it remains a tool for a prosecutor to use should she see fit.

[b] Mootness

Like ripeness, mootness addresses a timing question. But whereas ripeness asks whether the suit is ready for review, mootness considers whether the case or controversy has disappeared. The mootness doctrine filters out cases that were once live cases or controversies but no longer are.[177]

A prominent example of mootness is *DeFunis v. Odegaard*.[178] In *DeFunis*, a plaintiff claimed a state university law school had not admitted him due to his race. The trial court granted an injunction ordering the plaintiff's admission. By the time the Supreme Court heard argument, the plaintiff was in his final quarter of law school and the university said it would allow him to graduate regardless of the outcome of the litigation. Accordingly, the Court deemed the case moot.

The Court has recognized an exception to the mootnesss doctrine when the underlying dispute is "capable of repetition, yet evading review."[179] This exception requires that (1) the challenged action be too short in duration to be fully litigated before its cessation or expiration, and (2) "there was a reasonable expectation that the *same*

---

172. *Id.* at 501.
173. *Id.* at 508.
174. 393 U.S. 97 (1968).
175. *Id.* at 101–102.
176. The law in *Epperson* carried criminal penalties.
177. *See supra* note 165.
178. 416 U.S. 312 (1974).
179. Kremens v. Bartley, 431 U.S. 119, 133 (1977).

complaining party would be subjected to the same action again."[180] Abortion challenges illustrate this concept. Because pregnancies terminate on their own accord after nine months, a woman asserting a right to abortion will almost always find her claim to have been mooted by the time her case works its way up the appellate system. Thus, as the Court explained in *Roe v. Wade*, judicial review of such claims would be effectively denied absent some modification of mootness doctrine.[181] Pregnancy thus provides a classic occasion for a conclusion of non-mootness; a rigid concept of mootness would mean that cases involving pregnancy would always evade review.

Normally, a defendant "giving up," and stopping the complained-of conduct will moot a case. However, courts also make an exception to this rule when the defendant fails to demonstrate that it will not simply resume that activity at some future point. In such cases, courts suspect that the surrender constitutes strategic conduct designed to dispose of the lawsuit while leaving the defendant "free to return to his old ways."[182] Thus, such a case will be dismissed as moot only if defendant can demonstrate the lack of a "reasonable expectation" of the wrong recurring. The Court has called that burden "a heavy one."[183]

A case may, however, be rendered moot where the losing party appealing its loss ceases operation. In *City News and Novelty, Inc. v. City of Waukesha*,[184] the Court dismissed as moot an adult entertainment business's appeal from a state court judgment upholding a city's action against it, after that business ceased operations. The Court contrasted that situation to a superficially-analogous one in *City of Erie v. Pap's AM*,[185] where the adult business had *won* in the lower court and then sought to declare the city's appeal moot because the business had ceased operation. The Court rejected the latter request, since the city, which had lost in the lower court, would have suffered a continuing injury from the lower court judgment striking down its adult business regulation ordinance. By contrast, the Court said in *City News*, the appealing party "left the fray as a loser, not a winner,"[186] thus, in the Court's view, rendering the appeal moot when it ceased operations.

[5] The Political Question Doctrine

The political question doctrine places certain questions outside the bounds of judicial decision, based on the subject matter involved. The name of this doctrine may stem from *Marbury v. Madison*, where Chief Justice Marshall spoke of certain "[q]uestions, in their nature political."[187] Marshall introduced the concept to distinguish

---

180. SEC v. Sloan, 436 U.S. 103, 109 (1978) (emphasis in original).
181. *See* 410 U.S. 113, 125 (1973).
182. United States v. W.T. Grant Co., 345 U.S. 629, 632 (1953).
183. *Id.* at 633.
184. 531 U.S. 278 (2001).
185. 529 U.S. 277 (2000).
186. *City News*, 531 U.S. at 284.
187. 5 U.S. (1 Cranch) 137, 170 (1803).

issues where the President or executive officers had unlimited discretion, not subject to judicial scrutiny, from those involving rights, the deprivation of which a court could remedy. The political question doctrine as now practiced extends beyond that narrow boundary, but it remains grounded in Marshall's distinction between discretion and legal duty.

At the outset, it is helpful to clarify a misconception the term may create. The political question doctrine does not withdraw from judicial review all matters with political overtones. On the contrary, courts frequently decide such matters. Courts regularly decide legal questions that are also highly controversial politically, on matters including abortion,[188] affirmative action,[189] and even the outcome of elections and the fate of presidencies.[190] Yet those political consequences alone did not make the cases "political questions." Rather, political questions are those which are committed to, or more appropriately decided by, a political branch rather than the judiciary.

It is also worth noting at the outset that the political question doctrine relates to concerns about the separation of powers, not federalism. Thus, it involves the relationship between the federal judiciary and the other branches of the national government, not that between the federal courts and state government.[191]

In *Baker v. Carr*,[192] the Court articulated six situations which, if existing, would tend toward a case being held to involve a political question: (1) "A textually demonstrable constitutional commitment of [an] issue to a coordinate political department"; (2) "a lack of judicially discoverable and manageable standards for resolving it"; (3) "the impossibility of deciding [the case] without an initial policy determination of a kind clearly for nonjudicial discretion"; (4) a court's inability to resolve an issue without expressing disrespect for a coordinate branch; (5) "an unusual need" to defer to a prior political decision; and (6) "the potentiality of embarrassment from multifarious pronouncements by various departments on one question."[193] In *Vieth v. Jubelirer*, Justice Scalia, for himself and three others, observed that the six *Baker v. Carr* tests "are probably listed in descending order of both importance and certainty."[194] Consider the first three *Baker* factors. One can understand all three of them as speaking to whether the Court has the authority to speak the law in that case. Thus, if the Constitution's text grants decision-making power to another branch or if there are no judicially-manageable standards available to decide the case, one might naturally conclude that the issue is not one for courts to decide. Similarly, if resolution of the

---

188. *See* Roe v. Wade, 410 U.S. 113 (1973).

189. *See, e.g.*, Grutter v. Bollinger, 539 U.S. 306 (2003).

190. *See, e.g.*, Bush v. Gore, 531 U.S. 98 (2000) (effectively deciding the 2000 presidential election); United States v. Nixon, 418 U.S. 683 (1974) (requiring President Nixon to turn over tape recordings that were likely to lead to his impeachment).

191. Baker v. Carr, 369 U.S. 186, 210 (1962).

192. 369 U.S. 186 (1962).

193. *Id.* at 217.

194. 541 U.S. 267, 278 (2004) (plurality opinion).

issue requires a policy, rather than a legal judgment, then one can again readily conclude that the issue is not one for courts to resolve.

By contrast, the final three *Baker* factors speak less to judicial *authority*, and more to judicial *prudence*—that is, whether it is simply a bad idea for a court to decide that case. One can easily conclude that that it might be a bad idea for a court to decide a case if a judicial decision would show unusual disrespect for a coordinate branch, if there was an unusual need for adherence to the prior decision by the other branch, or if a judicial decision risked "embarrassing" the government. Indeed, just like the first three *Baker* factors are all closely related in their reference to court's authority to speak, so too the final three are related in their reference to the prudential aspects of the political question doctrine.

Following on Justice Scalia's statement, one might agree that the first three factors, in their reference to judicial authority, are weightier than the final three. One might also agree that, of those first three, an actual textual commitment of the issue to another branch may be the clearest sign of a political question, followed, in turn, by the lack of standards available to a court and, finally, a need for an antecedent policy determination before a court could resolve any legal questions.

All six situations need not be present for the court to find a political question. Indeed, they rarely are. On the other hand, some strands may on occasion reinforce each other. Thus, Chief Justice Rehnquist observed that "the lack of judicially manageable standards may strengthen the conclusion that there is a textually demonstrable commitment to a coordinate branch."[195] Although the Court often invokes one or more of these criteria in political question cases, they provide principles to consult rather than hard-and-fast rules. The political question doctrine is, perhaps more than many other constitutional law concepts, more art than science.

Luther v. Borden,[196] a classic early political question case, involved a dispute regarding the identity of the lawful government of Rhode Island. The incumbent government had declared participation in certain elections to be unlawful. Thereafter, Sheriff Borden entered the home of election commissioner Luther to seek evidence of who had voted in the proscribed election. Luther sued for trespass, while Borden claimed that his behavior was legitimate government action. Luther, however, argued that the government Borden served violated the Constitution's Guarantee Clause.[197]

The Court ducked this difficult and fraught question. It claimed that the case raised a political question because "Under [the Guarantee Clause] it rests with Congress to decide what government is the established one in a State."[198] The Guarantee Clause

---

195. Nixon v. United States, 506 U.S. 224, 228–29 (1993).

196. 48 U.S. (7 How.) 1 (1849).

197. U.S. CONST. art. IV, §4 ("The United States shall guarantee to every State in this Union a Republican Form of Government, and shall protect each of them against Invasion; and on Application of the Legislature, or of the Executive (when the Legislature cannot be convened) against domestic Violence.").

198. *Luther*, 48 U.S. at 42.

does not textually commit this power to Congress. Rather, it provides that "*The United States* shall guarantee to every State in this Union a Republican Form of Government."[199] But Chief Justice Taney reasoned that Congress implicitly makes the decision whether to recognize a state government as legitimate when it decides whether to seat the representatives and senators that government sends to Washington, D.C.

In *Nixon v. United States*,[200] a federal judge sought judicial review of the Senate's action in convicting and removing him from office after he was impeached by the House of Representatives. Judge Nixon challenged a Senate rule under which he was tried because it allowed a committee of the Senate, rather than the whole body, to hear witnesses. Nixon claimed that such fact-finding by committee approach violated the Constitution's grant of power to try impeachments to "the Senate" (rather than a committee thereof).

The Court held that Nixon's challenge raised a nonjusticiable political question. Speaking for the majority, Chief Justice Rehnquist argued that the Constitution committed that issue to the Senate by providing the Senate "shall have the sole Power to try all Impeachments."[201] He argued that the use of "sole" effectively precluded judicial review by providing a textual commitment of that question to the Senate. The Court also concluded that "try" was ambiguous and accordingly provided the Court no judicially manageable standard to apply. A concurring opinion disagreed, offering an alternative explanation of the Constitution's use of "sole" that saw that word as emphasizing the separate roles of the House and Senate in impeachment proceedings, especially since the only other time the Constitution uses "sole" is in the House Impeachment Clause.[202] That concurrence, by Justice White, also observed that the Constitution included many ambiguous terms that the Court nevertheless applied in the course of deciding cases.[203]

Although the Court invoked these strands from *Baker*'s classic statement of the elements of a political question, another justification for the Court's result were three structural arguments it advanced. First, because judges might later preside over criminal proceedings of previously impeached officials, judicial review of impeachment might create a real or perceived conflict of interest. Second, impeachment is an important check on judicial conduct that would be lost if courts could review and control the implementation of that check. Finally, judicial review would interfere with the need to resolve with finality the right of an individual to hold office. The interference could have serious consequences, especially following a presidential impeachment and removal, if, for example, a President were convicted and removed from office, only to later win a court decision that the Senate conviction was procedurally improper.

---

199. U.S. Const. art. IV, §4 (emphasis added).
200. 506 U.S. 224 (1993).
201. U.S. Const. art. I, §3, cl. 6.
202. U.S. Const. art. I, §2, cl. 5.
203. *See Nixon*, 506 U.S. at 239 (White, J., concurring in the judgment).

The political question doctrine has had its greatest scope in issues touching on foreign affairs. Thus, in *Chicago & Southern Air Lines v. Waterman S.S. Co.*, Justice Jackson argued that once the President approved an agency's orders regarding foreign air transportation, "the final orders embody Presidential discretion as to political matters beyond the competence of the courts to adjudicate."[204] Similarly, in *Goldwater v. Carter*, a case involving a senator's challenge to a president's decision to abrogate a treaty without the Senate's agreement, a four-justice plurality found the case to constitute a political question "because it involves the authority of the President in the conduct of our country's foreign relations and the extent to which the Senate or the Congress is authorized to negate the action of the President."[205]

The plurality's view in *Goldwater* reflects a frequent inclination in cases dealing with foreign affairs, but nevertheless was controversial. Justice Powell denied that the case presented a political question. He argued that the Constitution made no textual commitment of the issue to the President, since the text was silent regarding who could abrogate treaties. The text did address the making of treaties — it requires the President to get the advice and consent of two-thirds of the Senate — and the status of treaties — they are the supreme law of the land. Justice Powell argued that these provisions implied the President lacked unilateral authority of the sort he asserted in *Goldwater*. Thus, he concluded that the extent of the President's asserted power was susceptible to judicial resolution. Justice Brennan argued that the political question doctrine precluded courts from reviewing the foreign policy decisions of branches authorized to make them, but did not apply to "the *antecedent* question whether a particular branch has been constitutionally designated as the repository of political decisionmaking power."[206]

Given the plurality's statement in *Goldwater*, it is not surprising that the political question doctrine has been applied to questions involving recognition of foreign governments,[207] relating to sovereignty over a given area,[208] involving the diplomatic status of foreign representatives,[209] regarding the existence of a state of war or belligerency,[210] and the relation of the United States to any conflict.[211] The doctrine has also applied to issues involving military force, including questions involving employment of the armed forces abroad[212] and relating to the commencement and duration

---

204. 333 U.S. 103, 114 (1948).

205. 444 U.S. 996, 1002 (1979) (Rehnquist, J., concurring).

206. *Id.* at 1007 (Brennan, J., dissenting).

207. United States v. Belmont, 301 U.S. 324, 330 (1937).

208. *See* Williams v. Suffolk Ins. Co., 38 U.S. (13 Pet.) 415, 422 (1839); Foster v. Neilson, 27 U.S. (2 Pet.) 253, 306–07 (1829).

209. *See In re* Baiz, 135 U.S. 403 (1890).

210. *See* The Three Friends, 166 U.S. 1, 63 (1897); The Divina Pastora, 17 U.S. (4 Wheat.) 52, 63–64 (1819).

211. *See* United States v. Palmer, 16 U.S. (3 Wheat.) 610, 634–35 (1818).

212. *See* Johnson v. Eisentrager, 339 U.S. 763, 789 (1950); Durand v. Hollins, 8 F. Cas. 111 (4 Blatchf. 451) (C.C.S.D.N.Y. 1860). *But compare* Holtzman v. Schlesinger, 414 U.S. 1304, 1311 (1973) (suggesting a growing body of lower court opinion at the time that such questions are justiciable).

of a war in which the United States is engaged.[213] However, *Baker* cautioned against automatically labelling of all foreign relations issues as political questions.[214]

The political question doctrine also applies to some cases dealing with domestic affairs. These include questions relating to the constitutional guaranty of a republican form of government,[215] involving the constitutional guaranty against domestic violence,[216] concerning the organization and procedure of the legislative department,[217] relating to whether laws have been validly enacted,[218] and concerning the procedure followed in impeachment proceedings.[219] The Supreme Court has also removed some such issues from the political question category. For example, in *Powell v. McCormack*,[220] the Court held that the judiciary could review whether a member of Congress who met the Constitution's requirements for membership could nevertheless be excluded by a congressional vote.

In one sense, the political question doctrine constitutes something of an exception or affront to *Marbury*'s principle of judicial power to review government conduct. But the conflict is more apparent than real. Recall *Marbury*'s recognition of a zone of executive discretion, where no legal duty required the executive to take a particular action. In cases involving such discretion, Marshall conceded that such questions should be understood as having been committed to the political branches' decision. Implicitly, the lack of judicially accessible legal standards governing such discretionary decisions and the primacy of policy, rather than legal, considerations in such cases justified courts in standing aside. Of course, these factors ultimately found their way into the analysis in *Baker v. Carr*.

---

213. *See* Ludecke v. Watkins, 335 U.S. 160, 168–70 (1948); The Protector, 79 U.S. (12 Wall.) 700 (1871).

214. *See* 369 U.S. at 211 ("There are sweeping statements to the effect that all questions touching foreign relations are political questions.... Yet it is error to suppose that every case or controversy which touches foreign relations lies beyond judicial cognizance.").

215. *See* Ohio *ex rel.* Bryant v. Akron Park Dist., 281 U.S. 74 (1930); Pacific States Tel. & Tel. Co. v. Oregon, 223 U.S. 118 (1912); Minor v. Happersett, 88 U.S. (21 Wall.) 162 (1874); Luther v. Borden, 48 U.S. (7 How.) 1 (1849).

216. *See Luther, supra.*; Martin v. Mott, 25 U.S. (12 Wheat.) 19 (1827).

217. *See* Barry v. United States *ex rel.* Cunningham, 279 U.S. 597 (1929); United States v. Ballin, 144 U.S. 1 (1892).

218. *See* Field v. Clark, 143 U.S. 649 (1892). The same is true of a constitutional amendment. *See* Coleman v. Miller, 307 U.S. 433 (1939).

219. *See* Nixon v. United States, 506 U.S. 224 (1993).

220. 395 U.S. 486 (1969).

Chapter 3

Executive Power and the Separation between Executive and Congressional Power

§ 3.01 Introduction

A fundamental aim of American constitutionalism is to disperse governmental power between different institutions, so as to prevent the accumulation of power in one set of hands — a state of affairs the Framers feared as conducive to tyranny. One way in which the Constitution accomplishes this dispersal is to allocate certain powers to the federal government and other powers to the states — what we call federalism. Federalism is introduced and explained in more detail in the next chapter of the book. Another way in which the Constitution disperses power is to take the powers granted to the national government and divide them up between the judicial, legislative, and executive branches. This structure is referred to as the separation of powers. Chapter 2 already considered the powers of one branch of the national government — the judiciary — and how those powers related to those of the other two branches. This chapter introduces into the analysis Congress and, especially, the executive branch — the presidency.

Like federalism, the separation of powers doctrine is not expressly provided for in the Constitution. It is, however, a fundamental structural concept implicit in the Constitution, as a conclusion logically following from the creation of the three branches. As the Court stated nearly a century ago, "It may be stated then, as a general rule inherent in the American constitutional system, that ... the Legislature cannot exercise either executive or judicial power; the executive cannot exercise either legislative or judicial power; the judiciary cannot exercise either executive or legislative power."[1] This statement reveals an important point: even though this chapter will focus mainly on presidential power and its relationship to congressional power, that relationship is not the only one relevant to the separation of powers. Rather, issues involving how the federal courts relate to Congress and the President — including illustrations of those relationships in Chapter 2 — are also part of our body of separation of powers law.

---

1. Springer v. Philippine Islands, 277 U.S. 189, 201–202 (1928).

The "general rule" referred to above—that no branch can exercise powers allotted to another—must accommodate exceptions. Indeed, the term "separation of powers" is something of a misnomer. As the political scientist Richard Neustadt pointed out, "The Constitutional Convention of 1787 is supposed to have created a government of 'separate powers.' It did nothing of the sort. Rather, it created a government of separated institutions *sharing* powers."[2] As Justice Louis Brandeis stated, "The separation of the powers of government did not make each branch completely autonomous. It left each in some measure dependent upon the others, as it left to each power to exercise, in some respects, functions in their nature executive, legislative and judicial."[3]

Some of this interdependence flows from the related concept of checks and balances, the metaphor which captures the extent to which the federal branches exercise power and control over each other. Yet that interdependence also reflects a degree of accommodation and compromise which is necessary for government to operate. As Chief Justice Burger explained, "In designing the structure of our Government and dividing and allocating the sovereign power among three co-equal branches, the Framers of the Constitution sought to provide a comprehensive system, but the separate powers were not intended to operate with absolute independence."[4]

The tension implicit in these ideas between separated and independent but still interconnected and mutually dependent branches flows through separation of powers cases. As this chapter will illustrate, separation of powers doctrine exists in an uneasy space between what will be referred to as a "formalistic" insistence on bright lines and clear divisions between the branches, and a more "functionalist" approach which recognizes the blurriness of the boundaries separating the branches. This tension reflects the twin, although often conflicting goals the Framers had when designing the national government. On the one hand, they wanted to create a government that was not so capable of centralizing power that it would be able to risk the people's liberties. On the other, they of course wanted to create a government that was sufficiently energetic and capable to govern effectively. Squaring that circle—creating a national government that is powerful and capable of swift action—but not *too* powerful—has proven to be one of the enduring challenges of our constitutional system.

Before discussing the details of the separation of powers, this chapter begins by discussing the presidency. Chapter 2 discussed the federal courts. A later chapter will discuss Congress as an institution. But the presidency is in some ways the least intuitively knowable branch. We might have intuitions of what a court is and does, and similarly might intuitively know what a legislature is and does. But what is an "executive" branch? As this chapter will begin by illustrating, the modern American presidency is an amalgam of discrete, textually-based powers and broad, inherent powers. After considering that institution, this chapter then considers the relationship of that branch to Congress and the federal courts.

---

2. Richard E. Neustadt, Presidential Power and the Modern Presidents: The Politics of Leadership from Roosevelt to Reagan 29 (1990) (emphasis in original).

3. Myers v. United States, 272 U.S. 52, 291 (1926) (Brandeis, J., dissenting).

4. United States v. Nixon, 418 U.S. 683, 707 (1974).

This chapter addresses those subjects. After Section 3.02 introduces the Presidency, Section 3.03 explains the process by which the President is elected. Sections 3.04 and 3.05 discuss the President's role as, respectively, a legislator and a law enforcer. Section 3.06 considers the Constitution's statements about removal of the President, either permanently or due to a temporary disability.

Subsequent sections describe in more detail the President's role in formulating and implementing policy. After a general introduction in Section 3.07, Section 3.08 considers the particular doctrines governing the President's ability, with the assistance of executive agencies, to carry out federal domestic policy. Sections 3.09 and 3.10 shift the focus abroad, to consider the President's powers with regard to foreign affairs and war, respectively. Section 3.11 concludes by considering the President's relationship to the courts and, in particular, the question of his immunity from litigation.

§ 3.02 The Presidency

The provisions of Article II regarding the executive branch are, in several respects, unique. Whereas Article I creates and empowers a bicameral legislature consisting of hundreds of equal players, and Article III authorizes a multi-member Supreme Court and potentially a large number of inferior courts, Article II lodges all executive power in a single leader. Moreover, some provisions of Article II are among the most general in the Constitution, leaving the precise authority granted somewhat obscure. Consider these grants of power: "The executive Power shall be vested in a President.... The President shall be Commander-in-Chief of the Army and Navy ... he shall take Care that the Laws be faithfully executed."[5] The generality may have traced to difficulties the Framers encountered in creating the executive. As Alexander Hamilton wrote, "There is hardly any part of the system which could have been attended with greater difficulty in the arrangement of it than [the executive branch]."[6]

These two features, a single executive leader and open-ended grants of power, have enabled the presidency to grow in power during the twentieth century. To be sure, other developments have encouraged this evolution, such as the expanded international role of the United States, the growth of the administrative state, and the rise of both mass media and a two-party system, with one party always informally (but unmistakably) led by the President. Against this backdrop, the presidency has emerged as a focal point of American political life.[7]

---

5. U.S. Const. art. II § 1, cl. 1; § 2, cl. 1; § 2, cl. 3.

6. The Federalist No. 67 (Hamilton).

7. *See e.g., Youngstown Sheet & Tube v. Sawyer*, 343 U.S. 579, 653 (1952) (Jackson, J., concurring) ("Executive power has the advantage of concentration in a single head in whose choice the whole Nation has a part, making him the focus of public hopes and expectations. In drama, magnitude and finality his decisions so far overshadow any others that almost alone he fills the public eye and ear. No other personality in public life can begin to compete with him in access to the public mind through modern methods of communications.").

The Framers were committed to a concept of an energetic executive. But they also believed it imperative to harness that energy so it would serve, not imperil, the ends of good government. The effort to preserve the accountability of a powerful executive has posed a critical challenge for the nation since at least the end of World War II.

§ 3.03 Election

In contrast to the general treatment it accords presidential powers and duties, Article II, as superseded in part by the Twelfth Amendment, describes in some detail the mechanism for electing the President. Under it, the President is chosen by presidential electors the states "appoint" for this purpose. The question of how to choose the President vexed and divided the Framers. Some proposed direct election by the people; others, deeming the people uninformed, advocated some form of legislative election.[8] Yet such a plan, James Madison and others pointed out, might lead to legislative domination of the executive, thereby eroding the separation of powers doctrine intended to help guard against government tyranny. Ultimately, the Framers struck a compromise. Electors chosen in each state would elect the President and Vice President. Each state would have a number of electoral votes equal to its representation in the house and senate, yet the electors would not be, indeed could not be, members of Congress.[9]

By the fourth presidential election, in 1800, this system had begun to break down. As originally designed, each elector cast two votes for President with the winner, provided he won a majority, being President and the runner up, Vice President. The Framers did not, however, anticipate the formation of national political parties coalescing around one presidential candidate.[10] In 1800, Thomas Jefferson and Aaron Burr ran as a ticket with the former intended for the Presidency. Since all of their party's electors voted for each, however, they ended in an electoral vote deadlock which threw the decision into the House of Representatives under the contingent election plan. Although Jefferson was ultimately elected, the episode led to the Twelfth Amendment, which was ratified in 1804. It preserved the Electoral College system but abandoned the single election, creating instead separate elections for President and Vice President.[11]

---

8. DEBATES IN THE FEDERAL CONVENTION OF 1787 REPORTED BY JAMES MADISON, 40–42, 267–69 (Galliard Hunt & James B. Scott eds., 1920).

9. This system thus reinforced the three-fifths compromise that counted slaves as three-fifths of a person for purposes of a state's representation in the House of Representatives. For more discussion of that compromise, see Section 10.04[1].

10. *See* RICHARD HOFSTADTER, THE IDEA OF A PARTY SYSTEM (1969).

11. For more information about the election of 1800 and its relationship to the Twelfth Amendment, see Brian Kalt, *Of Death and Deadlocks: Section 4 of the Twentieth Amendment*, 54 HARV. J. LEG. 101, 106–107 (2017).

The Electoral College system gives states broad discretion in deciding how to choose electors. As the Court wrote in *Bush v. Gore*, the case that decided the 2000 election, "The individual citizen has no federal constitutional right to vote for electors for the President of the United States unless and until the state legislature chooses a statewide election as the means to implement its power to appoint members of the Electoral College."[12] Of course, today it is overwhelmingly accepted that a state's voters select that state's electors by voting for the candidate to whom those electors are pledged. It is close to inconceivable that a state could attempt to take that choice away.[13]

Another issue, which could have had actual electoral consequences, revolves around Article II's provision that "[e]ach state shall appoint [presidential electors], in such Manner as the *Legislature* thereof may direct."[14] In *Bush v. Gore*,[15] Governor George W. Bush argued that this language delegated the method of appointment to the Florida legislature. Accordingly, he contended, the Florida Supreme Court invaded the authority the Constitution delegated to the Florida legislature when it reviewed the state's methods for ascertaining individual votes.

Although the Court did not accept this argument, ruling for Governor Bush on other grounds, Chief Justice Rehnquist, joined by Justices Scalia and Thomas, essentially endorsed the Bush conclusion. Relying on dicta from *McPherson v. Blacker*,[16] the concurring justices viewed the constitutional provisions as one of the "few exceptional cases in which the Constitution imposes a duty or confers a power on a particular branch of a State's government."[17] However, six justices did not accept this position, and four explicitly rejected it. Justice Stevens, writing for three justices, argued that the Constitution takes state legislatures "as they come—as creatures born of, and constrained by, their state constitutions."[18] Accordingly, the Florida legislature was subject to state judicial review. Justice Souter, writing for himself and the three justices who joined Justice Stevens' opinion, thought the Florida Supreme Court decision fell "within the bounds of reasonable interpretation."[19]

---

12. 531 U.S. 98, 104 (2000).

13. In recent years, questions have arisen about whether an elector pledged to vote for a particular candidate can be punished by a state for reneging on that commitment and casting her vote for someone else. Although this has not happened often, and never in a way that has changed the outcome of an election, the problem of so-called faithless electors has remained a nagging one. In 2020, the Court unanimously held that a state may enforce an elector's pledge to cast her vote for her party's nominee. Chiafalo v. Washington, 140 S. Ct. 2316 (2020).

14. U.S. Const. art. II, § 1, cl. 2 (emphasis added).

15. 531 U.S. 98 (2000).

16. 146 U.S. 1 (1892).

17. *Bush*, 531 U.S. at 112.

18. *Id.* at 123 (Stevens, J., dissenting).

19. *Id.* at 131 (Souter, J., dissenting).

Whereas the Constitution conditioned eligibility to be President on age (35), length of residency of the United States (14 years), and status as a "natural born citizen," the Twenty-Second Amendment, added after Franklin D. Roosevelt was elected for four terms, added an additional limitation: no person could be elected more than twice or, having served more than two years of someone else's term, more than once. Could someone who was barred from seeking another term as President run for Vice President? The Twenty-Second Amendment does not bar such a candidacy, but the Twelfth Amendment seems to make eligibility to be Vice President turn on the same factors as those for President. The Twentieth Amendment made January 20th the beginning and ending date for presidential and vice-presidential terms.

§ 3.04 The President as Legislative Leader

[1] Constitutional Basis for Legislative Role

Modern presidents have assumed a leadership role in legislation. Although this legislative authority is often attributed to political evolution, it is also work the Constitution suggests. The Constitution requires the President occasionally to report to Congress on the State of the Union and to "recommend to their Consideration such Measures as he shall judge necessary and expedient."[20] The State of the Union and Recommendation Clauses "envision the President as an active participant in the embryonic stages of law making."[21] In certain extraordinary situations, the President may continue or adjourn Congress. And as the Vice President has become associated with the executive branch,[22] his privilege of casting a tie-breaking vote in the Senate as a practical matter gives the President slightly more power in the upper body on the rare occasion that the Senate is deadlocked 50–50. But the most significant legislative role the Constitution vests in the President is contained in Article I, not Article II. It is the veto power.

[2] Veto Power

The veto power, located in the Presentment Clause of Article I,[23] is essentially a legislative power, since it implicates the President in the law-making process. Although the Framers probably conceived the veto as a means to protect against legislative encroachments on the executive and perhaps against unconstitutional measures generally,[24] it has long been recognized that the President may veto a bill for any reason. The veto allows the President to interpose a formidable obstacle to legislation and

---

20. U.S. Const. art. I, § 7.
21. Vasan Kesavan & J. Gregory Sidak, *The Legislator-in-Chief*, 44 Wm. & Mary L. Rev. 1, 63 (2002).
22. *See* Joel K. Goldstein, *The New Constitutional Vice Presidency*, 30 Wake Forest L. Rev. 505 (1995).
23. U.S. Const. art. I, § 7, cl. 2.
24. The Federalist No. 73 (Hamilton).

provides the President with substantial leverage in the legislative process. For Congress to override a presidential veto, it must muster a two-thirds vote of each House, a formidable task, especially given the President's leadership of one of the major political parties represented in Congress.

The President may elect to neither sign nor veto the bill, in which case the inaction is treated as a failure to object, and the bill becomes law. The President has ten days from presentation of bills to approve or veto. However, if "Congress by their adjournment prevent ... [r]eturn" of a vetoed bill, the bill does not become law unless the President signs it.[25] In other words, the normal default rule (a bill passed by both houses becomes law unless vetoed) is inverted, creating the so-called "pocket veto" rule.

The President may not veto only part of an enacted bill. The Supreme Court applied the Presentment Clause to strike down the Line Item Veto Act (LIVA) in *Clinton v. City of New York*.[26] LIVA, which Congress had passed in 1996, authorized the President, following specified procedures, to cancel three particular types of provisions that had been signed into law. Under LIVA, Congress could pass a disapproval bill to nullify any such cancellation, subject, of course, to the President's constitutional veto power.

Although President Clinton properly followed LIVA's procedures in cancelling an item of new spending and a limited tax benefit, the Court, on a 6–3 vote, ruled that those actions went beyond the Chief Executive's constitutional power. The Court, speaking through Justice Stevens, reasoned that the Constitution gave the President a role in enacting statutes but was "silent on the subject of unilateral Presidential action that either repeals or amends parts of duly enacted statutes."[27] Justice Stevens' reading of the historical materials suggested that the founders intended that the President accept or reject a bill in its entirety, a conclusion that caused him to construe the Constitution's silence as an "express prohibition" of LIVA.

The dissenters implicitly accepted the majority's conclusion that the Constitution's silence precluded Congress from authorizing the President to amend or repeal a statute. But as they saw it, LIVA conferred no such thing. Rather, it simply gave the President power to refrain from spending certain authorized amounts, a power that judicial doctrine and historical practice made clear were constitutional. Accordingly, the President had "simply executed a power" properly conferred by Congress.

§ 3.05 Law Enforcement

[1] The Constitutional Duty to Execute the Laws

The Constitution imposes on the President the duty to "take Care that the Laws be faithfully executed."[28] The Take Care Clause confers perhaps the President's most

---

25. U.S. Const. art. I, § 7, cl. 2.
26. 524 U.S. 417 (1998).
27. *Id.* at 439.
28. U.S. Const. art. II, § 3, cl. 3.

basic responsibility, one that informs the President's other activities. Yet the Clause raises as many questions as it resolves. Must the President simply enforce congressional statutes? May the President choose not to enforce an act the President deems unconstitutional? To what extent may other branches participate in law execution?

Although the Constitution often uses "Laws" to mean statutes, it is clear that the President must enforce the Constitution as well.[29] The President's Oath Clause reinforces this responsibility, committing the President not only to "faithfully execute" the presidential office but also to "preserve, protect and defend the Constitution of the United States."[30] The President's duty to enforce the Constitution as well as other laws should not be controversial so long as no conflict appears between them. The more difficult question involves the extent of the President's power or duty to interpret the Constitution to determine whether any such conflict exists.

A traditional view compels the President to give effect to judicial or legislative judgments of constitutionality. Under this view, the President enforces measures deemed constitutional by the judicial and legislative branches, regardless of personal misgivings.[31] In other contexts, such as the veto and pardon power, the President is generally understood to be free to act on his own constitutional views. The traditional view has been questioned, however, and some commentators have argued that the Constitution's grant of executive powers would allow a President to decline to enforce a law the President personally believes is unconstitutional.[32] At times, presidents will append so-called "signing statements" to bills that they sign into law, explaining any constitutional objections they have to a bill and sometimes suggesting that the objectionable provision will not be enforced.[33]

[2] The Power to Pardon

The power "to grant Reprieves and Pardons" allows the President to mitigate the effect of the enforcement of some laws. The pardon power is broad. It extends to "Offenses against the United States, except in Cases of Impeachment."[34] This description does impose some limits. It only applies to offenses against federal, not state law. As such, it even extends to treason since "in seasons of insurrection or rebellion, there are often critical moments when a well-timed offer of pardon to the insurgents

---

29. *See, e.g.,* In re Neagle, 135 U.S. 1 (1890) (implying this obligation).

30. U.S. Const. art. II, § 1, cl. 8.

31. For a broader discussion of this issue from the perspective of the judicial power, see Section 2.03.

32. *See, e.g.,* Michael Stokes Paulsen, *The Most Dangerous Branch: Executive Power to Say What the Law Is,* 83 Geo. L.J. 217 (1994); Michael Stokes Paulsen, *The Merryman Power and the Dilemma of Autonomous Executive Branch Interpretation,* 15 Cardozo L. Rev. 81 (1993); Edwin Meese III, *The Law of the Constitution,* 61 Tul. L. Rev. 979 (1987).

33. *See, e.g.,* Zivotofsky v. Clinton, 566 U.S. 189, 192 (2012) (providing one example of such a signing statement and suggestion of non-enforcement).

34. U.S. Const. art. II, § 2.

or rebels may restore the tranquility of the commonwealth. . . ."[35] Finally, it applies to criminal, but not civil, matters.[36] The President need not wait until after conviction and sentence to exercise the power. A pardon may be granted at any time after an offense has been committed, either before legal proceedings commence, during their pendency, or after conviction and judgment.[37] In a notable example, President Gerald Ford pardoned his predecessor, Richard Nixon, for any offenses the latter may have committed against the United States while he was in office, even though no prosecutions against him had commenced.

Ex parte Garland[38] addressed the effect of a pardon. An 1865 statute required that any person who wanted to practice law in a federal court swear that he had never fought against the United States or aided its enemies. Garland, a former Confederate official, sought to appear before the Supreme Court without taking the oath. He argued that President Andrew Johnson had given him a "full pardon for all offenses committed by his participation, direct or implied, in the Rebellion." The Court ruled that the pardon relieved him from the duty to take the oath. The pardon restored his civil rights and made him as innocent as if the offense had never been committed. "[It] makes him as it were, a new man, and gives him a new credit and capacity."[39]

Congress's power to legislate regarding pardons is limited. In *United States v. Klein,*[40] the Court invalidated a statute making proof of loyalty necessary to recover property abandoned by the owner and then later sold by the government during the Civil War. The law explicitly provided that acceptance of a presidential pardon would constitute proof of disloyalty, thus precluding any recovery. At least part of the Court's rationale in invalidating the law rested on the perceived congressional interference with the President's pardon power.[41] But the pardoning power is not wholly beyond legislative reach. Congress may, under the Necessary and Proper Clause, legislate regarding pardons in a manner which does not infringe upon presidential authority.[42] Moreover, Congress may pass acts of general amnesty,[43] which is a legitimate exercise of legislative power because it prescribes a general rule to govern future cases.

---

35. THE FEDERALIST No. 74 (Hamilton).

36. *See Ex parte* Grossman, 267 U.S. 87, 121–22 (1925) (President can pardon criminal but not civil contempt.).

37. *Ex parte* Garland, 71 U.S. (4 Wall.) 333, 380 (1867).

38. 71 U.S. (4 Wall.) 333 (1867).

39. *Id.* at 380–81.

40. 80 U.S. 128 (1871).

41. Other aspects of the Court's analysis in *Klein* are discussed in Section 2.04[2].

42. Congress may give the Secretary of the Treasury power to remit penalties and forfeitures, which does not in any way abridge the President's power to remit. *See, e.g.,* The Laura, 114 U.S. 411, 416–17 (1885); *Ex parte* United States, 242 U.S. 27, 52 (1916) (Congress may empower federal judges to suspend original sentences); United States v. Benz, 282 U.S. 304 (1931) (Congress can empower judges to reduce sentences to time served).

43. *See, e.g.,* Brown v. Walker, 161 U.S. 591 (1896) (upholding a statute providing immunity from prosecution for persons testifying before federal agencies).

Although the President's power to pardon is broad, it presumably is not without limit. It is doubtful, for instance, that the Constitution would tolerate a self-pardon.[44] Such an action would offend the structural principle against an individual judging her own case.

§ 3.06 Succession, Disability, and Impeachment

[1] Vice Presidential Succession and Disability

Presidential succession and inability has presented one of the vexing problems in American history. When President William Henry Harrison died in 1841, barely one month into his term, Vice President John Tyler took the presidential oath and insisted he was President, not simply Vice President acting as President, as many believed. This controversy traced to a textual ambiguity. Article II, Section 1, Clause 6 provides that in case of removal, death, resignation, or inability of the President "to discharge the powers and duties of the said office, the same shall devolve on the Vice President...." If "the same" was the "said office" Tyler was right; if it referred simply to "the powers and duties" of the office, Tyler assumed the authority and responsibility of the office but not the position itself. In any event, the Tyler precedent was followed on each of the seven other occasions when a President died in office.[45] The Twenty-Fifth Amendment, ratified in 1967, expressly provides that on the removal, death, or resignation of the President, "the Vice President shall become President."

The Twenty-Fifth Amendment also recognized the transformation of the American Vice Presidency into an executive position of importance.[46] Section Two provides a mechanism to fill a vice-presidential vacancy by presidential nomination, subject to confirmation by each House of Congress. This provision enabled the Federal Government to avoid problems that might have arisen with the resignation in 1973 and 1974 of both the Vice President and the President. On the resignation of Vice President Agnew in October 1973, President Nixon nominated Gerald R. Ford as Vice President and, in accordance with the Amendment, Ford took office once confirmed by a majority vote of both Houses of Congress. When Nixon resigned as President in August 1974, Ford succeeded to the Presidency and nominated Nelson Rockefeller as Vice President. He, too, was confirmed by the vote of the two Houses. Ford and Rockefeller were accepted as legitimate leaders, since they had secured their positions under the Twenty-Fifth Amendment's express provisions.[47]

---

44. *See* Brian C. Kalt, *Pardon Me?: The Constitutional Case Against Presidential Self-Pardons*, 106 YALE L.J. 779 (1996).

45. *See generally* JOHN D. FEERICK, FROM FALLING HANDS (1965).

46. *See generally* Joel K. Goldstein, *The New Constitutional Vice Presidency*, 30 WAKE FOREST L. REV. 505 (1995).

47. *See* JOHN D. FEERICK, THE TWENTY-FIFTH AMENDMENT: ITS COMPLETE HISTORY AND APPLICATIONS 117–90 (1992); JOEL K. GOLDSTEIN, THE MODERN AMERICAN VICE PRESIDENCY: THE TRANS-

The Twenty-Fifth Amendment recognizes that the President may be disabled from performing presidential functions by causes short of death. It provides a method for determining when presidential disability exists, thereby addressing one of the principal gaps in the Constitution. The Amendment makes clear that, in the event of a disability that renders the President unable to discharge the powers and duties of the office, the Vice President becomes Acting President until the disability is removed. Thus, the Constitution now provides for administration of the executive power when the President becomes incapacitated.

In July 1985, President Reagan transferred power to Vice President George Bush for several hours while the President underwent surgery under anesthesia. Although Reagan claimed he was not using Section Three of the Amendment, he followed its procedures exactly, and it afforded the only basis to make the transfer. In 2002, President George W. Bush briefly transferred power to Vice President Richard Cheney while the President underwent a medical procedure. He did so again in 2007 under similar circumstances.

The Twenty-Fifth Amendment addresses who decides the existence of presidential disability. The Amendment recognizes that the President personally possesses the power to declare disability. It also empowers the Vice President and a majority of the Cabinet or of such other body as Congress may by law provide to declare that the President is unable to fulfill the powers and duties of the office. Congress is empowered to decide the issue only in case of dispute between the President and the officers designated.

[2] Impeachment

Generally, presidential impeachment has been a theoretical possibility, not a realistic prospect. For the first 185 years of our history, only one president, Andrew Johnson, was impeached. The impeachment proceedings against President Nixon in 1974, President Clinton in 1998–99, and President Trump in 2018–2019 have changed that perception. They focused attention on the constitutional provision governing removal of federal officers. That brief provision raises several legal issues. First, who may be impeached? Article II limits impeachment to the President, Vice President, and "all Civil Officers of the United States."[48] Congresspersons are not officers of the United States within the meaning of the Impeachment Clause and accordingly are not included.[49] Other federal civil officers are subject to impeachment. Resignation does not immunize an officer from impeachment as a constitutional matter, although practically speaking it may take much of the momentum out of the effort. An impeachment proceeding may result in removal from office and disqualification from holding further office.[50]

FORMATION OF A POLITICAL INSTITUTION 228–48 (1982); John D. Feerick, *Presidential Succession and Inability: Before and After the Twenty-Fifth Amendment*, 79 FORDHAM L. REV. 907 (2010); Joel K. Goldstein, *Taking from the Twenty-Fifth Amendment: Lessons in Ensuring Presidential Continuity*, 79 FORDHAM L. REV. 959 (2010).

48. U.S. CONST. art. II, §4.

49. This is not a unanimous view. For a different view, see RAOUL BERGER, IMPEACHMENT: THE CONSTITUTIONAL PROBLEMS 214–23 (1973).

50. U.S. CONST. art. I, §3, cl. 7.

A second important question is what offenses are impeachable. The Impeachment Clause authorizes impeachment for "Treason, Bribery, or other high Crimes and Misdemeanors."[51] The meaning of this term is highly contested. Most, though not all, scholars believe that it does not require the commission of an otherwise-punishable crime; conversely, most scholars do not believe that any such crime (*e.g.*, speeding) would be sufficiently serious as to be an impeachable offense. During the Framers' debates, it was suggested that "maladministration" should be added as an impeachable offense, but this was rejected, apparently on the theory that it would make the President liable to removal simply on the basis of serious policy disagreements with Congress. At the same time, persons including Alexander Hamilton argued that impeachable offenses included "public offenses" which "proceed from the misconduct of public men" and "relate chiefly to injuries done immediately to the society itself."[52] Since such a question is almost assuredly a non-justiciable political question, the answer will likely arise from congressional practice, rather than authoritative judicial interpretation.

Historically, most impeachment proceedings have targeted federal judges.[53] A broad conception of impeachable offenses has prevailed with respect to them. Some have been impeached for behavior inconsistent with their office. For instance, Judge John Pickering in 1803 and Judge Mark Delahay were impeached for intoxication on the bench. Justice Samuel Chase was impeached in 1804 for allegedly letting his political views color his conduct of trials as a circuit judge. Other judges have been impeached for using their office for an improper purpose. Federal judges hold office during "good Behaviour,"[54] which may account for the broader interpretation of the class of conduct subject to impeachment.

The impeachment proceeding against President Nixon reflected the view that criminal conduct was not a prerequisite for impeachment of an executive officer. The House Judiciary Committee adopted three articles of impeachment which charged both indictable offenses and abuses of executive power. President Clinton was impeached for perjury and obstruction of justice. President Trump was impeached for "abuse of power" and "obstruction of Congress" (the latter article growing out of his refusal to turn over particular documents and allow particular officials to testify in the House's impeachment inquiry).[55]

---

51. U.S. CONST. art. II, § 4.

52. THE FEDERALIST No. 65 (Hamilton). The impeachment of President Andrew Johnson in 1868 proceeded upon the theory that impeachment need not depend on an indictable offense. The articles against Johnson alleged no indictable offense, but were based on his failure to execute certain laws and his public utterances attacking Congress. Johnson's defense insisted an indictable offense was the prerequisite for impeachment. Johnson escaped removal by a single vote in the Senate.

53. *See* CASS SUNSTEIN, IMPEACHMENT: A CITIZEN'S GUIDE Ch. 6 (2017) (listing the impeachments voted on by the House of Representatives up to the date of publication).

54. U.S. CONST. art. III, § 1.

55. H.R. 755 (Dec. 18, 2019).

§ 3.07 Theories of Presidential Power

[1] Historical Background

For over 200 years, constitutional scholars have debated the bounds of presidential power. The vesting clause that begins Article II provides that "The executive power shall be vested in a President of the United States." One might view the Vesting Clause as simply naming the executive and establishing its unitary character, but not conferring additional powers. Others, such as Alexander Hamilton, have viewed the Vesting Clause as a source of broader, "inherent" executive powers.[56]

The scope of the Executive Vesting Clause has remained a topic of heated judicial and scholarly debate. Justice Robert H. Jackson rejected the Hamiltonian position. He regarded the Clause as simply "an allocation to the presidential office of the generic powers thereafter stated."[57] If the Vesting Clause conferred broad powers on the Chief Executive, the subsequent specific grants—the Commander-in-Chief Clause, Take Care Clause, Pardon Power—would have been superfluous, he reasoned. Thus, under Justice Jackson's view, the Vesting Clause essentially identifies the officer who holds the powers and duties set forth in the rest of Article II.

As illustrated by the example of Alexander Hamilton, not all agree with the Jackson position. For example, two legal scholars have written that "The Executive Power Clause actually does what it says it does, *i.e.*, it vests (or grants) a power over law execution in the President, and it vests that power in him alone."[58] Their elaborate argument draws heavily from inferences from the constitutional text. They noted that the Judicial Vesting Clause in Article III is a "general grant of power to the federal judiciary," thus arguing that "it makes sense to read the analogously worded Vesting Clause of Article II" as a "*general* grant of power."[59] They argued that their reading does not render the rest of Article II superfluous, as Justice Jackson suggested. Instead, they suggested that redundancy may have virtue.[60]

Theodore Roosevelt also embraced the broad Hamiltonian view. Roosevelt conceived of the President as "a steward of the people," who could "do anything that the needs of the Nation demanded unless such action was forbidden by the Constitution

---

56. In defending President Washington's 1793 Proclamation of Neutrality, Hamilton noted the difference between the language of Article I conferring "[a]ll legislative Powers herein granted" on Congress and that of Article II vesting "[t]he executive Power" in the President. He argued that the different modes of expression suggest that the authority vested in the President is not limited to the specific enumerations in Article II. 15 THE PAPERS OF ALEXANDER HAMILTON 396 (Harold C. Syrett ed., 1969).

57. Youngstown Sheet & Tube Co. v. Sawyer, 343 U.S. 579, 641 (1952) (Jackson, J., concurring).

58. Steven G. Calabresi & Saikrishna B. Prakash, *The President's Power to Execute the Laws*, 104 YALE L.J. 541, 549 (1994).

59. *Id.* at 571 (emphasis added).

60. *Id.* at 577 ("[Redundancy] may be used to add emphasis, or it may be employed out of an abundance of caution, lest anyone miss the significance of the message....").

or by the laws."[61] His conception of the Presidency has influenced many later Presidents, but not his successor, William Howard Taft. Taft, who later served as Chief Justice of the Supreme Court, asserted that the President was confined to expressly delegated powers rather than possessing any "undefined residuum of power."[62]

These competing views illustrate the conflicting constitutional attitudes towards executive power throughout American history. This debate has produced no clear prevailing view. In 1952, Justice Jackson noted "the poverty of really useful and unambiguous authority applicable to concrete problems of executive power as they actually present themselves." He continued. "A century and a half of partisan debate and scholarly speculation yields no net result but only supplies more or less apt quotations from respected sources on each side of any question. They largely cancel each other."[63]

[2] *Youngstown Sheet & Tube*

Youngstown Sheet & Tube v. Sawyer[64] presented the occasion for the judiciary's most extensive consideration of inherent presidential power. *Youngstown* involved President Truman's order to his Secretary of Commerce to seize the nation's steel mills to avert a strike that threatened production of war materiel during the Korean War. Lacking statutory authorization to seize the mills, Truman relied instead on inherent constitutional power to seize a critical industry to prevent a production stoppage during a time of national emergency.

By a 6–3 vote, the Supreme Court rejected Truman's position. In the majority opinion, Justice Black reasoned that since no act of Congress authorized the President to seize the mills, his power, if any, must come from the Constitution. The Constitution did not expressly delegate such power to the President, and Justice Black did not find such a power "implied from the aggregate" of the President's constitutional powers. The Commander-in-Chief Clause authorized the President to direct the military forces but did not license him to invade private property in the domestic economy. The Take Care[65] and Vesting Clauses[66] at most made the President a law-enforcer, not a "lawmaker." Justice Black concluded that, in acting as he had, President Truman had arrogated to himself the powers of the legislative branch: he had announced a policy to be the policy of the United States Government, had promulgated it, and had directed subordinates to carry it out. Given these legislative characteristics of the President's action, he concluded that that action had to emanate from Congress. Justice Black also rejected the idea that past practice had validated the President's action.

---

61. THEODORE ROOSEVELT, AN AUTOBIOGRAPHY 388 (1913).

62. WILLIAM HOWARD TAFT, OUR CHIEF MAGISTRATE AND HIS POWERS 140 (1925).

63. Youngstown Steel & Tube Co. v. Sawyer, 343 U.S. at 634–35 (Jackson, J., concurring).

64. 343 U.S. 579 (1952).

65. U.S. CONST. art. II, § 3 (The President "shall take Care that the Laws be faithfully executed.").

66. U.S. CONST. art. II, § 1 ("The executive Power shall be vested in a President of the United States of America").

Justice Black's rather formalistic opinion divided governmental power into distinct spheres (*i.e.*, legislative, executive, and judicial) based on a textual analysis of Article II. In his view, neither practice nor exigencies could alter the constitutional scheme to confer the power President Truman exercised. Nevertheless, Justice Black's view did not correspond to the real world of American governance by the middle of the twentieth century: by then, executive branch administrative agencies were already beginning to promulgate broad regulations based on loose delegations of congressional power[67] — or, in other words, they were already producing output that Justice Black insisted could only emanate from Congress. Thus, while his view had the virtue of simplicity and clarity, it ignored the reality of American government as it had developed by 1952.

Justice Black's majority opinion lost some of its significance, since other justices who joined it also wrote separate opinions which diverged somewhat from the Court's opinion. Justice Frankfurter shared Justice Black's conclusion that the seizure was unconstitutional, but he reached that result through a different path. According to Justice Frankfurter, the issue did not turn on a comprehensive survey of the President's Article II powers. Rather, Justice Frankfurter found Congress's actions decisive. When Congress substantially amended federal labor law in 1947, it had considered giving the President the authority to seize productive facilities to resolve labor disputes in times of emergency, but ultimately declined to do so. Congress's decision was important to Justice Frankfurter's analysis, because it came freighted with what he called a "gloss" of historical practice which had established a pattern: throughout American history, the general practice had been for presidents to seize productive facilities in times of emergency only with congressional authorization. In essence, Congress and the President had established a set of understandings — a "gloss" — on the Constitution's vague allocations of power over the history of their interactions. That gloss cut against the President's claim of power in *Youngstown*.

Justice Jackson joined Justice Black's opinion but also wrote a separate concurrence. Indeed, his concurrence has proven the most significant opinion in the case. Before joining the Court, Robert Jackson had confronted many problems dealing with the scope of presidential power, as a close adviser to President Franklin Roosevelt and as Attorney General in his administration.[68] His opinion provides an often-cited analysis of situations involving exercises of presidential power.[69] Justice Jackson identified three separate categories of presidential action with different legal consequences:

---

67. The principle forbidding Congress from delegating "legislative" power to the executive branch (or elsewhere) is discussed later in this chapter, in Section 3.08[2].

68. *See* ROBERT H. JACKSON, THAT MAN: AN INSIDER'S PORTRAIT OF FRANKLIN D. ROOSEVELT 75–110 (John Q. Barrett ed., 2003).

69. For examples of cases in which individual justices or a Court majority applied Justice Jackson's analysis, see Zivotofsky v. Kerry, 576 U.S. 1 (2015); Hamdan v. Rumsfeld, 548 U.S. 557 (2006); Medellin v. Texas, 552 U.S. 491 (2008); Dames & Moore v. Regan, 453 U.S. 654 (2979). Several of these cases are discussed later in this Chapter.

1. When the President acts pursuant to an express or implied authorization of Congress, his authority is at its maximum, for it includes all that he possesses in his own right plus all that Congress can delegate. In these circumstances, and in these only, may he be said (for what it may be worth), to personify the federal sovereignty. If his act is held unconstitutional under these circumstances, it usually means that the Federal Government as an undivided whole lacks power. A seizure executed by the President pursuant to an Act of Congress would be supported by the strongest of presumptions and the widest latitude of judicial interpretation, and the burden of persuasion would rest heavily upon any who might attack it.

2. When the President acts in absence of either a congressional grant or denial of authority, he can only rely upon his own independent powers, but there is a zone of twilight in which he and Congress may have concurrent authority, or in which its distribution is uncertain. Therefore, congressional inertia, indifference or quiescence may sometimes, at least as a practical matter, enable, if not invite, measures on independent presidential responsibility. In this area, any actual test of power is likely to depend on the imperatives of events and contemporary imponderables rather than on abstract theories of law.

3. When the President takes measures incompatible with the expressed or implied will of Congress, his power is at its lowest ebb, for then he can rely only upon his own constitutional powers minus any constitutional powers of Congress over the matter. Courts can sustain exclusive Presidential control in such a case only by disabling the Congress from acting upon the subject. Presidential claim to a power at once so conclusive and preclusive must be scrutinized with caution, for what is at stake is the equilibrium established by our constitutional system.[70]

Justice Jackson thought Truman's action presented a category three situation. Referring to the same labor statute Justice Frankfurter had discussed, Jackson concluded that Congress had "not left seizure of private property an open field but ha[d] covered it by ... statutory policies inconsistent with this seizure...."[71] Thus, Truman's action was subject to "the severe tests" of the third category "where it can be supported only by any remainder of executive power after subtraction of such powers as Congress may have over the subject."[72] He refused to find in favor of presidential power against the strict requirements of category three. Importantly, he noted the power of the contemporary presidency (as it existed in 1952), with the President being able to command public and media attention like no other government official and also leading one of the two main political parties.[73] Given those built-advantages, Jackson ex-

---

70. 343 U.S. at 635–638 (Jackson, J., concurring).
71. *Id.* at 639.
72. *Id.* at 640.
73. *See id.* at 653–654.

pressed reluctance to give expansive readings to the core Article II powers that served as the only authority for presidential action in a category three situation.[74]

Justice Jackson's opinion has been *Youngstown*'s most enduring legacy.[75] This chapter will discuss several of the subsequent cases that have relied on his opinion.[76] For now, however, note that Jackson's opinion, while highly responsive to the realities of the relationship between the President and Congress, gives very little guidance for determining the scope of presidential powers in a category two situation. Indeed, it gives little guidance for how to determine into which category a particular situation falls.

More generally, Jackson's concurrence can be understood as reflecting what is sometimes called a "functionalist" approach to the separation of powers. Functionalist approaches seek to answer separation of powers questions not by reference to rigid demarcations between the powers of the different branches, but instead by tests that recognize the interdependence between the branches and the fact that branches may share certain functions or powers. For example, Jackson's category two implies that certain powers may be shared by Congress and the President, rather than belonging exclusively to one or the other.

This functional approach can be contrasted with a more rigid or formalistic approach, as exemplified by Justice Black's majority opinion. A formalist approach answers separation of powers questions by reasoning that seeks to place every federal governmental power firmly in one branch to the exclusion of others. As exemplified by Justice Black's opinion in *Youngstown*, such an approach has the virtue of simplicity and clarity: by defining the President's action as inherently legislative, it became easy for Black to conclude that such actions could emanate only from Congress, the legislative branch. On the other hand, this approach gains those virtues at the expense of abstracting out from reality, often in ways that are deeply unrealistic. By contrast, Justice Jackson's shared powers approach reflects the reality that some actions — for example, the promulgation of broad rules of conduct — could emanate either from Congress (if it enacted a statute mandating those rules) or from the executive branch (if it promulgated an administrative regulation based on broadly-worded statutory authority). But his approach purchases that realism at the expense of a marked lack of precision and clarity in application. The separation of powers cases in this chapter

---

74. *See id.* at 653 & 654 (Jackson, J., concurring) ("As to whether there is imperative necessity for [the inherent emergency powers claimed by President Truman], it is relevant to note the gap that exists between the President's paper powers and his real powers. The Constitution does not disclose the measure of the actual controls wielded by the modern presidential office.... I cannot be brought to believe that this country will suffer if the Court refuses further to aggrandize the presidential office, already so potent and so relatively immune from judicial review, at the expense of Congress.").

75. There was a dissent in this case, written by Chief Justice Vinson and joined by two other justices. *See id.* at 667. His dissent focused on the magnitude of the national security threat posed by a steel strike, the history of presidential initiatives of this sort, the lack of any statute forbidding such action, and the fact that President Truman immediately informed Congress of his action and pledged to abide by any decision it might make.

76. *See* note 69, *supra*.

will illustrate both of these approaches, as the Court has never conclusively adopted one or the other.[77]

§ 3.08 The President, Congress, and the Setting of Domestic Policy

[1] Introduction

Today, the federal government regulates a vast swath of American life, from food safety to labor standards to securities markets and many, many other important topics. The authority of the federal government to regulate in these areas poses questions of federalism, which are discussed in Chapters 4–6. But this regulatory authority poses important separation of powers questions, also. Assuming federal regulatory authority over a given area, the question arises how specific Congress must be in its regulatory choices. Complex regulatory issues require expert administrators, usually (but not always) housed in the executive branch, to implement Congress's choices. When does such implementation by the executive branch cross the line into unconstitutional legislative action? The next sub-section considers that question and explains the broad discretion Congress has to "delegate" important implementation issues to administrative agencies. The subsequent sub-section examines the constitutionality of the "legislative veto," a device Congress has inserted into many statutes as a way of retaining control over how agencies wield the power Congress has delegated to them.

The final sub-section considers a matter just as important as these: the staffing of the administrative agencies that perform this critical implementation work. It considers the fate of Presidents' claims over the years that Article II's grant of "the executive power" to the President, and its mandate that the President "take Care that the Laws be faithfully executed,"[78] give the President broad power to select the top officials charged with implementing, or "executing" the laws that Congress has enacted.

[2] Delegation of Legislative Power

Article I begins by vesting in Congress "all legislative powers herein granted."[79] The Article I Vesting Clause at least implies that Congress, as the recipient of these

---

77. These approaches were also illustrated in some of the material on the judicial power in Chapter 2. For example, one can see the Article I courts analysis performed by the majority in *Commodities Futures Trading Comm'n v. Schor*, 478 U.S. 833 (1986), as reflecting a more functional, or balancing, approach, while Justice Brennan's dissent in that case reflected a more bright-line, formalistic approach.

78. U.S. CONST. art. I § 1; art. II § 3.

79. U.S. CONST. art. I, § 1.

powers from "We the People,"[80] lacks the power to delegate (or, more precisely, re-delegate) those powers to other institutions, including other branches of the federal government. This reasoning constitutes the foundation of the non-delegation doctrine — the doctrine that limits Congress's ability to delegate its legislative power to the administrative agencies that have grown so greatly in size and prominence since the start of the twentieth century.

The Court has considered non-delegation claims from the earliest years of the Republic.[81] But for over a century, it had always upheld such laws, recognizing that Congress could direct agencies or the President to act if they found certain conditions to be satisfied.[82] Until 1928, the Court had used a variety of formulas to describe how precise Congress's direction to the agency had to be in order for that direction to not constitute delegation of legislative power. That year, the Court wrote in *J.W. Hampton v. United States* that, in order to survive non-delegation review, a statute had to contain an "intelligible principle" that provided sufficient guidance for the agency to execute Congress's wishes.[83]

Until 1935, no law had been struck down as exceeding Congress's power to delegate such authority. In that year, the Court issued two opinions striking down the National Industrial Recovery Act (NIRA), a statute enacted in the early years of Franklin Roosevelt's New Deal program, which gave the President wide-ranging power to set the terms by which firms in individual industries were to compete. But, with one possible exception,[84] since 1935 the Court has not used the non-delegation doctrine to strike down a law. Instead, it has upheld major legislation delegating broad authority to administrative agencies.[85] This is not to say that the non-delegation doctrine is a nullity. Often, when faced with a very broad statute, the Court will give that statute

---

80. U.S. CONST. Preamble.

81. *See, e.g.,* The Brig Aurora, 11 U.S. (7 Cranch) 382 (1813) (upholding, against a non-delegation challenge, a law authorizing the President to lift trade embargoes against Britain and France if he determined that those nations had stopped interfering with American shipping, on the ground that the law merely authorized his action if he found certain conditions to exist).

82. *See, e.g.,* Field v. Clark, 143 U.S. 649 (1892) (upholding a law authorizing the President to impose tariffs on imports when he found the "fact" that the exporting nation had imposed "unequal and unreasonable" tariffs on American goods).

83. 276 U.S. 394, 409 (1928).

84. *See* Carter v. Carter Coal, 298 U.S. 238 (1936). In *Carter Coal*, the Court used non-delegation language as part of its argument for striking down a federal law. However, some commentators have understood that analysis, which involved a congressional delegation of power to a private entity rather than a government agency, as focusing more on due process concerns. *See, e.g.,* Alexander Volokh, *The New Private Regulation Skepticism: Due Process, Non-Delegation, and Antitrust Challenges*, 37 HARV. J. L. & PUB. POL'Y 931, 973–980 (2014) (suggesting the due process reading).

85. *See, e.g.,* Whitman v. American Trucking Ass'n, 531 U.S. 457, 472 (2001) (upholding Congress's grant of authority to the Environmental Protection Agency to promulgate air quality standards "which ... allowing an adequate margin of safety, are requisite to protect the public health"); National Broadcasting Co. v. United States, 319 U.S. 190, 224 (1943) (upholding Congress's grant of authority to regulate radio broadcasters "in the public interest").

a narrow reading, sometimes explaining that the failure to read the statute narrowly would pose a non-delegation concern.[86]

The non-delegation doctrine is controversial. The standard critique of broad delegations holds that Congress, as the elected representatives of the American people, should make the hard choices many regulatory issues pose.[87] On the other hand, defenders of broad delegations argue that the complexity of modern regulatory issues requires broad congressional delegations of power to administrative agencies who are more expert and able to focus more of their energy on the details of such difficult regulatory problems. Indeed, some commentators go further and argue that the procedures administrative agencies must follow before promulgating regulations actually make those agencies more democratic than the legislative process.[88]

In recent years, some justices have indicated an interest in revisiting the Court's approval of broad delegations. In *Gundy v. United States*,[89] the Court upheld against a non-delegation challenge a grant of seemingly standardless discretion to the Attorney General to promulgate registration and notification requirements sex offenders had to satisfy upon being released from prison. Four justices took the conventional approach of construing that seemingly broad power to in fact include limits, and on that basis rejected the non-delegation claim. But three justices (Justice Gorsuch, joined by Chief Justice Roberts and Justice Thomas) dissented, arguing for a narrower understanding of what the non-delegation doctrine allowed Congress to do. Crucially, Justice Alito agreed with the majority's result, but indicated a possible willingness to reconsider the Court's approach to non-delegation issues. Justice Kavanaugh, the ninth justice, had not yet taken his seat when *Gundy* was argued. However, in a subsequent opinion speaking only for himself, he also indicated a willingness to reconsider the non-delegation doctrine.[90] Thus, this area of the law may well be ripe for change.

[3] The Legislative Veto

The "legislative veto" represents Congress's effort retain some control over decisions it has otherwise delegated to an administrative agency. In essence, legislative veto provisions authorize one or both houses of Congress or some subset (*e.g.*, a committee) to disapprove of an action an agency has taken when implementing a statute, in which case the action would have no effect, having been legislatively "vetoed." Legislative vetoes first appeared in the 1930s, when Congress began delegating broad swaths of

---

86. *See, e.g.*, Indus. Union Dept, AFL-CIO v. American Petroleum Inst., 448 U.S. 607, 646 (1980) (plurality opinion) (giving such a narrowing construction to a workplace safety law because a broader reading of the law would trigger a non-delegation issue).

87. *See, e.g.*, *Industrial Union*, 448 U.S. at 687 (Rehnquist, J., concurring) (arguing that, in the challenged statute, Congress had not made the "hard choices" between worker safety and costs).

88. *See, e.g.*, JERRY MASHAW, REASONED ADMINISTRATION AND DEMOCRATIC LEGITIMACY (2018).

89. 139 S. Ct. 2116 (2019).

90. Paul v. United States, 140 S. Ct. 342 (2019) (Kavanaugh, J.). *Paul* was a denial of *certiorari*, with which Justice Kavanaugh agreed, while nevertheless indicating his willingness in a future case to reconsider the non-delegation doctrine.

power to administrative agencies as part of the New Deal. Their use multiplied in the 1970s. By 1983, some 200 statutes included versions of legislative vetoes.[91]

The legislative veto provision at issue in *Immigration and Naturalization Service v. Chadha*[92] was typical. The Immigration and Naturalization Act (INA) made certain categories of aliens subject to deportation, but also delegated to the Attorney General the authority to suspend an alien's deportation if he found certain criteria (such as the alien's hardship were he to be deported) to be satisfied. However, the INA also allowed either house of Congress to reject, or "veto," any suspension decision the Attorney General made. When the House of Representatives vetoed the Attorney General's decision to suspend the deportation of several aliens, including Mr. Chadha's, Chadha sued, challenging the constitutionality of the legislative veto.

Eight justices agreed that the legislative veto in Chadha's case was unconstitutional. In an opinion for seven of those justices, Chief Justice Burger held all legislative vetoes unconstitutional. The Court concluded that the formal lawmaking requirements of bicameralism and presentment[93] applied to any legislation. The legislative veto was legislation, because its effect was to alter "the legal rights, duties, and relations of persons, including the Attorney General, Executive Branch officials and Chadha, all outside the legislative branch."[94] Hence, the house's veto of the Attorney General's suspension decisions constituted legislation that, because it failed the bicameralism and presentment requirements, fell short of Article I's procedural requirements for lawmaking. Justice Powell concurred in the judgment, on the narrower ground that the House's decision to reject the suspension decisions for several named individuals came too close to adjudication — a function the Constitution reserved to the courts.

Justice White dissented. In contrast to Chief Justice Burger's formalist opinion which emphasized text and bright line rules, Justice White urged a more flexible approach which focused on the way in which legislative vetoes really operated. He viewed the Court's decision as "of surpassing importance" because it struck down more than 200 statutory provisions.[95] Far from being a device by which Congress aggrandized its power, Justice White argued that the legislative veto allowed Congress to delegate power to the executive while retaining a modicum of authority to review and, if desired, disapprove of, how the executive was using that delegated power. The innovation enabled government to adapt to demands of a changing world without imperiling the basic distribution of government power.

The majority opinion in *Chadha* illustrates a formalist approach to the separation of powers. As Justice White's dissent points out, the Court's decision that all "lawmaking" must be shared by Congress and the President "ignores that legislative au-

---

91. *See* INS v. Chadha, 462 U.S. 919, 967 (1983) (White, J., dissenting).

92. 462 U.S 919 (1983).

93. *See* U.S. CONST. art. 1, §7. Bicameralism refers to the requirement that both the House and Senate agree to a bill before it can become law, while presentment refers to the requirement that any bill that is passed be presented to the President for his signature or veto.

94. *Id.* at 952.

95. *Id.* at 967 (White, J., dissenting).

thority is routinely delegated to the Executive branch, to the independent regulatory agencies, and to private individuals and groups."[96] Justice White suggested that if Congress could accomplish such delegations, it ought to be able to reserve for itself a degree of oversight through a legislative veto. If congressional action under the legislative veto is "lawmaking" that Congress and the President must share precisely as Article I states, why doesn't administrative rule-making, which the technique attempts to control, also have to conform to the constitutional formalities?

To be sure, Chief Justice Burger had an answer to the question posed above. In a footnote to his majority opinion,[97] he acknowledged the argument that the Attorney General's suspension decisions themselves did not have to go through bicameralism and presentment. However, citing Justice Black's formalist opinion in *Youngstown*, he argued that, essentially, the Attorney General's action was by definition not legislative (and thus did not have to go through Article I's requirements for lawmaking). He added that the Attorney General's decision-making was limited by the terms of the statute (the INA) under which he was acting, and that, if that statute gave him truly legislative power, the non-delegation doctrine would step in and prohibit that delegation. Of course, this answer meets the objection only if the Court is serious about enforcing the non-delegation doctrine. While there may be movement in that direction today, in 1983, the non-delegation doctrine was generally considered if not moribund then at least a very weak restriction on congressional authority.

In his *Chadha* opinion, Chief Justice Burger displayed an antipathy to a functional approach to constitutional interpretations. He insisted that the fact that a legislative veto might be "efficient, convenient and useful in facilitating functions of government" would not matter if it violated the Constitution. Moreover, the frequency with which Congress inserted legislative vetoes "sharpened rather than blunted" judicial scrutiny.[98] Thus, in his view, a long history of congressional and presidential accommodation on this practice was not persuasive.

Interestingly, notwithstanding *Chadha*, Congress continues to insert legislative veto provisions in new statutes. Constitutional scholar Louis Fisher reported that, by 1999, more than 400 new legislative vetoes had been enacted, many vesting control in various congressional committees.[99] More generally, one should not assume that the apparent demise of the legislative veto deprives Congress of any controls over how agencies operate and the decisions they make. Appointments of key agency officials must be approved by the Senate, and they must appear before congressional committees at some point. Congress must also approve agency budgets. Moreover, informal influence networks permeate the administrative process, including networks in which key congresspersons, committees, and even staffers have significant informal sway over how agencies operate.

---

96. *Id.* at 984.
97. *Id.* at 953 n. 16 (majority opinion).
98. *Id.* at 944–46.
99. *See* LOUIS FISHER, AMERICAN CONSTITUTIONAL LAW 248–50 (3d ed. 1999).

Nevertheless, *Chadha*'s strike-down of the legislative veto (despite Congress's continued appetite for inserting those provisions in statutes) did restrict congressional power in an important way. But perhaps the most important general lesson to take away from *Chadha* is the Court's continued vacillation between formalist and functional approaches to separation of powers issues.

[4] Staffing the Bureaucracy

[a] Introduction

Given the broad policy-making discretion the non-delegation doctrine allows Congress to delegate and the lack of formal congressional controls on delegated power with the demise of the legislative veto, it becomes a very important matter who has the power to name and remove high-ranking officials. The first sub-section below considers the power to appoint such officials, while the second considers the power to remove them. While the constitutional text speaks only to the first of these issues, both of them have been the subject of complex and contentious Supreme Court opinions.

[b] The Appointment Power

As with many other constitutional arrangements, the appointing power divides functions between different institutions. The Constitution separates the power to create offices from the right to appoint to them. The Constitution empowers Congress to create "offices," an easy implication of the Necessary and Proper Clause.[100] But Congress lacks power to appoint persons to fill the offices it creates. The denial of this power to Congress is consistent with the Framers' rejection of parliamentary government and their commitment to separate institutions checking and balancing each other.

The Constitution subdivides officers into two classes: "officers" (which can be thought of as principal officers) and inferior officers. The Appointments Clause of Article II provides as follows:

> ... [The President] shall nominate, and by and with the Advice and Consent of the Senate, shall appoint Ambassadors, other public Ministers and Consuls, Judges of the supreme Court, and all other Officers of the United States, whose Appointments are not herein otherwise provided for, and which shall be established by Law: but the Congress may by Law vest the Appointment of such inferior Officers, as they think proper, in the President alone, in the Courts of Law, or in the Heads of Departments.[101]

Thus, the President nominates and, with the advice and consent of the Senate, appoints officers of the United States. These procedures apply to appointment of those officers who will serve as the most important officials in the bureaucracy, and

---

100. U. S. CONST. art. I, §8, cl. 18. The Necessary and Proper Clause is discussed in Section 5.03.
101. U.S. CONST. art. II, §2, cl. 2.

often the President's most important associates (which have become known as "principal officers"), as well as to those who will constitute the judiciary. Traditionally, the Senate defers to the President to a much greater degree with respect to cabinet appointments than it does regarding judicial nominees, especially those to the Supreme Court or appellate courts.

The Appointments Clause also speaks to a lesser class of officer. It states that Congress may vest the appointment of "such inferior Officers as they think proper" in either the President, the courts, or "the Heads of Departments." Under the Constitution, all federal officers are either (1) "officers" who must be appointed by the President and confirmed by the Senate or (2) "inferior Officers" whose appointments Congress may vest in (a) the President, (b) the courts, or (c) department heads. Of course, the federal government also employs mere employees — the letter carrier, the window clerk at the Social Security office, or the janitor at a federal office building. Those persons are not mentioned in the Constitution, but it is clear that such employees need not be appointed by the President or any other high-ranking official.[102]

Returning to the distinction between principal and inferior officers, the text of Article II makes clear that the President enjoys the Article II authority to appoint the former, but is only one of several persons or institutions in which Congress can place the appointment of the latter. This distinction has raised difficult questions about the nature of particular officers as either "principal" or "inferior." As the Court recognized in one of the seminal cases dealing with this issue, "[t]he line between 'inferior' and 'principal' officers is ... far from clear."[103]

That case was *Morrison v. Olson*.[104] *Morrison* considered the constitutionality of the independent counsel provisions of the Ethics in Government Act of 1978. The law provided, in part, for the appointment of an independent counsel to investigate and prosecute certain high officials of the executive branch. The law arose out of the Watergate scandal of the 1970s, and in particular President Nixon's firing of the special counsel who had been appointed before this statute had been enacted. The experience with that firing convinced Congress that such independent counsels needed insulation from the very White House they would be charged with investigating. The law provided that insulation both at the hiring and the firing stages. This sub-section considers *Morrison's* discussion of the hiring issue.

Under the statute, if the Attorney General receives information he deems sufficient to justify a preliminary investigation into the matter, he must perform such an investigation. Unless that investigation finds no "reasonable grounds" to believe that further investigation is warranted, he must request a "Special Division" of the federal judiciary (essentially, a panel of federal judges selected for this purpose) to appoint a special counsel. Thus, it was this Special Division of Article III judges who appointed

---

102. *See* Buckley v. Valeo, 424 U.S. 1, 126 n.162 (1976) (discussing the status of federal "employees").

103. Morrison v. Olson, 487 U.S. 654, 671 (1988).

104. *Ibid.*

the counsel. Given the language quoted earlier from Article II's Appointments Clause, it would be constitutional for the Special Division to have this power if the counsel was an inferior officer. But if she was a principal officer, Article II required that the appointment be made by the President himself.

In *Morrison*, the Court identified no bright line test to decide the question but instead held that the independent counsel was an inferior officer based on the following factors: (1) she was subject to removal by a higher executive official, here the Attorney General, for sufficient cause; (2) she was empowered to perform only certain limited duties; (3) she had limited investigatory jurisdiction and (4) the office of the independent counsel had limited tenure.[105]

The Court subsequently recognized that *Morrison* does not set forth the exclusive or definitive criteria for distinguishing superior from inferior officers.[106] Moreover, the definition the Court later advanced seemed at least potentially inconsistent with *Morrison*'s conclusion that the independent counsel was an inferior officer. In *Edmond v. United States*, Justice Scalia (who dissented in *Morrison*) wrote for the majority that:

> Generally speaking, the term "inferior officer" connotes a relationship with some higher ranking officer or officers below the President: Whether one is an "inferior" officer depends on whether he has a superior.... [I]n the context of a Clause designed to preserve political accountability relative to important Government assignments, we think it evident that "inferior officers" are officers whose work is directed and supervised at some level by others who were appointed by Presidential nomination with the advice and consent of the Senate.[107]

A lower court recognized the tension between the approaches taken in these two cases.[108]

In addition to the President and the "Heads of Departments," Congress may also vest the power to appoint an inferior officer in "the Courts of Law,"[109] and that power may, in appropriate cases, extend to interbranch appointment—that is, an appointment of officials who would be located in another branch. That would, however, be improper if such an "interbranch" appointment would impact the functioning of an-

---

105. *Id.* at 671–72.

106. Edmond v. United States, 520 U.S. 651, 661 (1997).

107. *Id.* at 662–63.

108. *See* U.S. v. Libby, 429 F. Supp. 2d 27, 37 (D.D.C. 2006) ("there appears to be some tension between [*Morrison* and *Edmond*] because they do not rely on identical factors").

109. Article I courts, too, may appoint inferior officers. Thus, the Court has held that Congress could allow the Chief Judge of the United States Tax Court to appoint special trial judges without violating the Appointments Clause, because, as used in that clause, "Court of law" was not limited to Article III courts. Freytag v. Commissioner of Internal Revenue, 501 U.S. 868 (1991). Four justices who concurred viewed the Tax Court as a department, not a court of law.

Freytag also held that tax court judges were inferior officers. In 2018, the Court held that Article I administrative law judges located in the Securities and Exchange Commission were also inferior officers. Lucia v. SEC, 138 S. Ct. 2044 (2018).

other branch or "if there was some 'incongruity' between the functions normally performed by the courts and the performance of their duty to appoint."[110]

In *Morrison*, the Court confronted a claim that allowing a panel of Article III judges (the Special Division) to appoint a prosecutor violated this principle. It rejected the argument, noting that courts sometimes appointed litigators and also noting that the independent counsel law forbade members of the Special Division from hearing cases involving the independent counsel. Similarly, in *Mistretta v. United States*,[111] the Court rejected the argument that a statute creating a commission to establish a federal criminal sentencing structure could not constitutionally include federal judges. Writing for the eight-justice majority, Justice Blackmun cited Justice Jackson's concurrence in *Youngstown* for the proposition that some federal governmental functions crossed the boundary lines between different branches and thus could be shared.[112]

Congress, however, cannot give itself the power to designate the persons to staff the offices it creates. In *Buckley v. Valeo*,[113] the Court struck down the method Congress had provided to select members of the Federal Election Commission, under which certain members were to be appointed by legislative leaders (in addition to those the President would name), subject to confirmation by a majority vote of both Houses. This provision violated the Appointments Clause of Article II, which made no provision for congressional appointment of such an officer. Thus, any appointee exercising significant authority pursuant to the laws of the United States is an officer of the United States (whether principal or inferior) and must be appointed as prescribed by Article II, which excludes Congress from any such appointing power other than the Senate's role in advising and consenting to the appointment of principal officers. Congress may, however, appoint officials who assist Congress specifically, such as the congressional Sergeant-At-Arms.

[c] The Removal Power

The removal power is crucial to preserving presidential control over the executive branch. Although Presidents rarely use it, the very existence of the power helps make executive branch officials responsive to the President. The President's power to dismiss an officer at pleasure makes it costly for office holders to resist the President's will and thus helps make the President accountable for activities of the executive branch.

To be sure, the Constitution does not explicitly confer any such removal power on the President. This silence, coupled with the impeachment power, might indicate that only congressional removal was contemplated. But in an early decision, which became known as the "Decision of 1789," Congress provided that the President could

---

110. *Morrison*, 487 U.S. at 676.
111. 488 U.S. 361 (1989).
112. *See id.* at 386.
113. 424 U.S. 1 (1976).

remove the head of the newly created Department of Foreign Affairs.[114] This decision recognized presidential authority to remove department heads and accordingly provided an important constitutional gloss.[115]

Important structural principles support giving the President removal power. If the President is to lead and be held accountable for the executive branch, the President must control its principal agents. Accordingly, some removal power is inferred from the Vesting and Take Care Clauses. Nevertheless, questions have arisen about the scope of the President's Article II removal authority.

Myers v. United States[116] considered a statute providing that postmasters "may be removed by the President with the advice and consent of the Senate." After President Woodrow Wilson unilaterally removed a postmaster named Myers, Myers sued, and the Court ruled the statute invalid. According to Chief Justice (and former President) William Howard Taft, the power to remove officers is "an incident of the power to appoint them, and is in its nature an executive power."[117] According to his opinion, the Constitution's silence regarding removal, coupled with the Take Care Clause, suggested the President had the power to remove.[118]

Myers spoke broadly, suggesting that the Constitution gives the President unlimited power to remove all officers, other than judges, whom the President has appointed. Nine years later, the Court severely limited *Myers*'s broader implications. In *Humphrey's Executor v. United States*,[119] the Court upheld a statutory limitation on the President's authority to remove a commissioner of the Federal Trade Commission (FTC), who his predecessor had appointed. In his dismissal notice, the President wrote that "the aims and purposes of the Administration with respect to the work of the Commission can be carried out most effectively with personnel of my own selection." Yet the statute accorded members of the FTC a seven-year term and limited presidential removal power to "inefficiency, neglect of duty, or malfeasance in office."[120]

In *Humphrey's Executor*, the Court upheld that limitation on presidential dismissal authority. Writing for the Court, Justice Sutherland rejected *Myers*' suggestion of an

---

114. *See* David Currie, The Constitution in Congress, 1789–1801, at 37–41 (1997).

115. *See Myers v. United States, 272 U.S. 52, 114 (1926); Ex parte* Hennen, 38 U.S. 225, 258–59 (1839). The Tenure of Office Act of 1867 forbade the removal of department heads without consent of the Senate. Its passage precipitated a constitutional crisis when President Andrew Johnson resisted it and was impeached (but not removed). That statute later came to be seen an invalid infringement upon the President's power. *See Myers*, 272 U.S. at 167–68, 176.

116. 272 U.S. 52 (1926).

117. *Id.* at 161. *See also Ex parte* Hennen, 38 U.S. at 259 (power of removal is incident to appointment power).

118. Three justices dissented. Justice McReynolds, who had been Wilson's Attorney General, thought no removal power could be inferred absent clear constitutional language. Justice Brandeis thought senatorial approval of removals established a past practice which shaped constitutional meaning. Justice Holmes emphasized the power Congress had over the underlying office in reaching his conclusion about Congress's power to limit the President's removal authority over the office's occupant.

119. 295 U.S. 602 (1935).

120. *Id.* at 618–619.

unlimited presidential power to remove officials. He reasoned that *Myers* applied to "purely executive officers," who carried out the President's duty to execute the laws. But the President's constitutional removal power was limited when it came to members of quasi-legislative or quasi-adjudicative agencies, with the result that, for the heads of such agencies (such as the FTC), Congress can, if it wishes, limit the President's removal power.

The Court further developed this distinction in *Wiener v. United States*.[121] *Wiener* involved President Dwight Eisenhower's dismissal of his predecessor's appointee to a war claims commission. Although Congress had not made any specification for the removal of a commissioner beyond setting the commission's expiration date, the Court held that the President lacked the authority to remove a member of the commission for reasons of simple policy disagreement. In so holding, the Court relied heavily on the nature of the adjudicatory functions the commission performed, and thus followed the approach set forth in *Humphrey's Executor*.

Morrison v. Olson[122] narrowed the President's removal power even further. Congress had provided that the Attorney General could only remove an independent counsel for cause, a limitation inspired by President Nixon's firing of the special prosecutor named during the Watergate scandal (which predated the statute at issue in *Morrison* but also served as the law's impetus). Unlike the statute at issue in *Myers* and in another case, *Bowsher v. Synar*,[123] Congress did not reserve for itself any role in removal. Nor did it eliminate all presidential removal power; rather, it simply limited it to "good cause." On the other hand, the Court conceded that the special prosecutor, unlike the officials in *Humphrey's Executor* and *Wiener*, performed executive functions. While the other features of the statute might support its constitutionality under then-current doctrine, the executive nature of the work the prosecutor performed strongly suggested that the limitation on the President's removal power was unconstitutional.

Nevertheless, the Court held that Article II did not require absolute presidential removal authority over the independent counsel. Writing for seven justices,[124] Chief Justice Rehnquist downplayed the language in *Humphrey's Executor* and *Wiener* which focused on whether the officer subject to removal was exercising quasi-legislative or quasi-judicial as opposed to purely executive functions. Instead, the Court held that Congress may limit the President's freedom to dismiss certain executive officials so long as such restrictions do not "impede" the President's ability to fulfill the constitutional duties of the office. As such, the Court seemed to suggest a balancing test based on the circumstances of each individual case.[125]

---

121. 357 U.S. 349 (1958).

122. 487 U.S. 654 (1988).

123. 478 U.S. 714 (1986). In *Bowsher*, Congress attempted to retain for itself the power to remove the Comptroller General, an official who was given authority to take executive-like action regarding federal spending. The Court held that such congressional involvement was unconstitutional.

124. Justice Scalia dissented, while Justice Kennedy did not participate in the case.

125. *Morrison*, 487 U.S. at 689 & 691 (1988) ("We undoubtedly did rely on the terms 'quasi-legislative' and 'quasi-judicial' to distinguish the officials involved in *Humphreys' Executor* and *Wiener*

In 2010, in a sharply divided decision, the Supreme Court held unconstitutional an agency structure in which the heads of a department (the commissioners of the Securities and Exchange Commission) who the President could only remove for good cause could themselves only remove for good cause the members of a commission housed within the department.[126] Essentially, this structure created a double insulation of the commission members from presidential control: the members could be removed by the heads of the SEC only for good cause, while the heads of the SEC themselves could be removed by the President only for good cause.

In the opinion for a five-justice majority in *Free Enterprise Fund v. Public Company Accounting Oversight Board*,[127] Chief Justice Roberts wrote that this dual insulation violated Article II's Vesting and Take Care Clauses. Although the Court had upheld "limited restrictions" on the President's removal power, the Chief Justice's opinion said that the structure's two levels of protection "transforms" that power and deprives the President of the ability to discharge duties for which he is accountable. Thus, for the majority, two levels of good cause-type insulation from presidential removal was constitutionally different from the one level upheld in *Morrison*. Justice Breyer's dissent argued that the Court had typically examined such restrictions by looking at how they would actually impact the agency's functioning. He also argued that the Court should be more deferential to congressional and presidential judgments regarding the optimal structure for administrative agencies. The debate in *Free Enterprise Fund* again reflects the ongoing struggle between justices favoring a more formalist approach to the separation of powers and those more committed to a functional approach.[128]

---

from those in *Myers*, but our present considered view is that the determination of whether the Constitution allows Congress to impose a 'good cause'-type restriction on the President's power to remove an official cannot be made to turn on whether or not that official is classified as 'purely executive.' ... We do not mean to suggest that an analysis of the functions served by the officials at issue is irrelevant. But the real question is whether the removal restrictions are of such a nature that they impede the President's ability to perform his constitutional duty, and the functions of the officials in question must be analyzed in that light.").

126. Free Enterprise Fund v. Public Company Accounting Oversight Board, 561 U.S. 477 (2010).

127. *Ibid.*

128. That debate has continued. In 2020, the Court struck down, as violating the separation of powers, the structure of the Consumer Financial Protection Bureau (CFPB). The CFPB was set up as an independent agency, whose head was removable by the president only for good cause. However, unlike other independent agencies whose heads enjoyed similar removal immunity, the CFPB was led not by a multi-member board, but instead by one person. The Court held that this structure violated the separation of powers, by vesting too much unaccountable power in the single head of the agency. The five-justice majority, speaking through Chief Justice Roberts, distinguished *Humphrey's Executor* on the ground that that case involved an agency headed by a multi-person body. It also distinguished *Morrison* on the ground that that case involved an inferior officer, while the head of the CFPB was understood to be a principal officer. The dissent reprised many of the arguments made by the dissent in *Free Enterprise Fund*, in particular about Congress's broad power to structure agencies as it saw fit, subject only to *Morrison*'s rule that any removal immunity not impede the President's power to carry out his Article II responsibilities. Seila Law LLC v. CFPB, 140 S.Ct. 2183 (2020).

§ 3.09 Foreign Affairs

[1] The Leading Role of the President

The Constitution does not explicitly speak of a "foreign affairs power." However, it divides between Congress and the President the individual powers that implicate foreign affairs. The President is Commander-in-Chief of the Army and Navy[129] and is "empowered" to receive Ambassadors and other public Ministers,[130] a duty which has broader implications than literally receiving ambassadors.[131] On the other hand, the Senate's advice and consent is required to confirm ambassadors and ratify treaties,[132] and Congress has the power to raise and regulate armies and navies,[133] regulate foreign commerce,[134] define and punish international maritime crimes,[135] and declare war.[136]

Despite this division of responsibilities, the President has assumed the paramount role in foreign affairs, particularly in recent times. This development has resulted from both executive action and congressional abdication.[137] In the modern era, ambitious claims of presidential dominance in foreign policy trace to the Court's 1936 decision in *United States v. Curtiss-Wright Export Corporation*.[138] The defendant in *Curtiss-Wright* was indicted for selling 15 machine guns to Bolivia in violation of a congressional resolution delegating to the President the power to prohibit certain arms sales and a related presidential proclamation.

The issue before the Court was the propriety of the delegation to the President. Although the Court had recently struck down delegations of domestic power,[139] it concluded that Congress had more latitude to extend authority to the executive in foreign affairs. In support of that conclusion, the Court articulated a sweeping theory of presidential dominance in foreign matters. Justice Sutherland's argument began with the premise that the Constitution does not limit the federal givernment's foreign affairs authority as it does its domestic regulatory powers. Before the Constitution, the nation existed and exercised powers of "external sovereignty," and these powers were independent of the Constitution. Thus, the power to engage in foreign affairs was an inherent attribute of sovereignty. Turning to the presidential role, the Court spoke expansively:

---

129. U.S. Const. art. II, §2, cl. 1.

130. U.S. Const. art. II, §3.

131. *See* Zivotofsky v. Kerry, 576 U.S. 1 (2015) (relying on the Reception Clause to invalidate a federal statute allowing parents of child born in Jerusalem to request that the child's passport mark the child as being born in "Israel").

132. U.S. Const. art. II, §2, cl. 2.

133. U.S. Const. art. I, §8, cl. 11–15.

134. U.S. Const. art. I, §8, cl. 3.

135. U.S. Const. art. I, §8, cl. 10.

136. U.S. Const. art. I, §8, cl. 12–14.

137. *See* Louis Fisher, *Congressional Abdication: War and Spending Power*, 43 St. Louis U. L.J. 931 (1999).

138. 299 U.S. 304 (1936).

139. *See* Section 3.08[2] (discussing those cases).

In this vast external realm, with its important, complicated, delicate and manifold problems, the President alone has the power to speak or listen as a representative of the nation.... It is important to bear in mind that we are here dealing not alone with an authority vested in the President by an exertion of legislative power, but with such an authority plus the very delicate, plenary and exclusive power of the President as the sole organ of the federal government in the field of international relations—a power which does not require as a basis for its exercise an act of Congress, but which, of course, like every other governmental power, must be exercised in subordination to the applicable provisions of the Constitution.[140]

In addition to various textual provisions, the Court advanced two related justifications for constitutional deference to the President in foreign affairs: first, the President needed considerable discretion in foreign affairs to avoid "embarrassment," and second, the President had knowledge and expertise which would probably not be shared by others.[141]

Curtiss-Wright holds simply that Congress may delegate broad foreign affairs authority to the President—recall that the President had acted pursuant to a congressional resolution delegating him authority. Nevertheless, the Court's expansive *dicta* has been invoked to support presidential claims of foreign powers autonomy even absent any delegation from Congress. Scholars have criticized this aggressive reliance on *Curtiss-Wright*.[142] In 2015, in a case discussed in the next sub-section, the Court suggested that it might retreat from that *Curtiss-Wright*'s broad statement of executive power over foreign affairs.[143] Still, the pull of such power claims is undeniable, given the President's unique access to diplomatic and intelligence information and the prestige of the office abroad.

[2] The Recognition Power

In the aftermath of *Curtiss-Wright*, some broad lines emerged delineating presidential authority over foreign affairs. The President has constitutional power to conduct external relations and guide diplomacy. He represents the nation in dealing with foreign nations, a status implied from his position as head of the executive branch, which alone possesses the tools to conduct effective diplomacy and foreign policy. That status also flows from Article II's grants of particular powers, including the power to "appoint Ambassadors, other public Ministers and Consuls"[144] and "receive

---

140. 299 U.S. at 319–20.

141. *See id.* at 320 (noting both of these concerns).

142. *See, e.g.*, Louis Fisher, *The Staying Power of Erroneous Dicta: From* Curtiss-Wright *to* Zivotofsky, 31 Const. Comm. 149 (2016).

143. *See* Zivotofsky v. Kerry, 576 U.S. 1 (2015).

144. U.S. Const. art. II, §2, cl. 2.

Ambassadors and other public Ministers."[145] These provisions empower the President to conduct diplomatic relations with foreign nations.

Hamilton described the power to "receive Ambassadors" as "more a matter of dignity than of authority."[146] Yet it endows the President with exclusive authority to determine which governments to recognize. In receiving a foreign ambassador (and sending our own), the President identifies a country's lawful government, a decision that can have important foreign and domestic consequences. Whether to recognize a foreign government is a non-justiciable political question,[147] given the obvious embarrassment that would occur if a court's recognition of a nation conflicted with a presidential decision. However, this should not be understood as a broad rule that all cases implicating the Reception Clause were political questions. In 2012, the Court decided the opposite, rejecting that proposition.[148]

In 2015, in the second visit to the Supreme Court of the case referred to immediately above, the Court relied on the Reception Clause to strike down a federal law that sought to govern how the U.S. Government treated the status of Jerusalem (a question that has for many years posed a difficult diplomatic question). The statute in question required the State Department to mark a child's birthplace as "Israel" if a U.S. citizen was born in Jerusalem and his parents requested that birthplace identification. After the law was enacted, the State Department refused such a request made by parents whose child was born in Jerusalem, citing its policy of reserving the final status of Jerusalem pending Middle East peace talks. The parents sued.

The Court in *Zivotofksy v. Kerry*[149] held the statute to be unconstitutional congressional interference with the President's Article II powers. The Court relied heavily on the Reception Clause, reasoning that, at the founding, a decision to recognize an ambassador was tantamount to recognizing the sovereignty of the nation sending that representative. It also argued that decisions such as these required that the nation speak with one voice. The Court conceded that congressional opposition to the executive's Jerusalem policy placed the executive action within Justice Jackson's third *Youngstown* category, where the President's power was at its lowest, since Congress had clearly manifested a different policy preference than the President. Nevertheless, the Court concluded that the President had core Article II authority to refuse to implement the policy reflected in the statute, despite Congress's clear disagreement with presidential policy.[150]

---

145. U.S. Const. art. II, § 3.

146. THE FEDERALIST No. 69 (Hamilton).

147. United States v. Belmont, 301 U.S. 324, 330 (1937); Jones v. United States, 137 U.S. 202, 212 (1890). For a more recent statement, see Baker v. Carr, 369 U.S. 186, 211–12 (1962).

148. Zivotofsky v. Clinton, 566 U.S. 189 (2012). The Court later ruled in favor of the President's Article II authority to make the decision at issue in that case. *See* Zivotofsky v. Kerry, 576 U.S. 1 (2015).

149. 576 U.S. 1 (2015).

150. *Youngstown*, and Justice Jackson's influential concurrence, are discussed in Section 3.07[2].

[3] Presidential Authority to Enter into Executive Agreements

Presidents have long made executive agreements with other countries which, though not treaties in the constitutional sense, are binding obligations of the United States. Executive agreements can be divided into three main kinds: those concluded (1) pursuant to treaty, (2) pursuant to statute, and (3) by the executive alone, without any legislative authorization. Executive agreements pursuant to treaty enjoy the force of the authorizing treaty, provided they are within its scope. Although the Constitution does not expressly mention congressionally-authorized executive agreements, they have been accepted in practice and constitute part of the law of the land. As such, they supersede inconsistent prior federal law and state law. They have been held not to improperly delegate legislative power to the President.[151]

Executive agreements made without legislative authorization depend upon the President possessing independent constitutional authority to act. Presidents typically identify four sources of constitutional authority: (1) the Vesting Clause, (2) the Reception Clause, (3) the Commander-in-Chief Clause, and (4) the Take Care Clause. Whether made with or without legislative authority, executive agreements within the President's authority to enter into are binding international obligations, and have the status equal to a treaty.[152]

In 1981, President Jimmy Carter signed a series of executive orders as part of an agreement with Iran to release Americans held hostage after the 1979 Iranian Revolution. In *Dames & Moore v. Regan*,[153] the Court considered a constitutional challenge to the President's authority to issue those orders. In response to the hostage-taking, President Carter had frozen all Iranian government assets located in the United States. Ultimately, the United States and Iran agreed that in return for the hostages' release, the United States would terminate legal proceedings against Iran pending in American courts and would "nullify all attachments and judgments obtained therein, [and] prohibit all further litigation based on such claims."[154] The United States would also transfer such claims to a new Iran-United States Claims Tribunal for binding arbitration, with arbitral awards being funded by the frozen assets, which were also transferred to the tribunal.

The petitioner in *Dames & Moore* had sued Iran in federal court prior to the agreement, claiming more than $3 million from an Iranian governmental entity. The court had ordered the attachment of Iranian property to secure any judgment the petitioner won. After the court complied with the President's executive orders and vacated those attachments, the petitioner sued, claiming that those orders "were unconstitutional to the extent they adversely affect petitioner's final judgment ... its execution of that judgment ... its prejudgment attachments, and its ability to continue to litigate."[155]

---

151. J. W. Hampton, Jr. & Co. v. United States, 276 U.S. 394, 411 (1928); Field v. Clark 143 U.S. 649, 693 (1892).

152. *See* United States v. Pink, 315 U.S. 203, 230 (1942).

153. 453 U.S. 654 (1981).

154. *Id.* at 665.

155. *Id.* at 667.

A unanimous Court, speaking through Justice Rehnquist, rejected the petitioner's contentions and reaffirmed the President's power to enter into executive agreements settling such claims even though they essentially nullified a court judgment and its enforcement. No federal statute explicitly authorized the President to suspend private claims pending in American courts. The Court found, however, that Congress had in the past implicitly accepted the President's authority to engage in such activity. This past practice raised a presumption of congressional consent. Thus, the Court believed it was confronted with a situation in Justice Jackson's first category, *i.e.*, in which the President acts with congressional consent.

In addition to reflecting a full-throated embrace of Jackson's approach in *Youngstown*,[156] *Dames & Moore* also illustrates the malleability of that approach. The evidence justifying categorizing *Dames & Moore* as a *Youngstown* category 1 situation is, at best, ambivalent. The Court's ability to characterize past congressional acquiescence in and authorization for presidential resolution of previous analogous situations as creating a category 1 situation reflects that approach's lack of precision and predictability. The foreign affairs character of the issue in *Dames & Moore* likely influenced the Court's willingness to strain to find congressional approval of the President's conduct. When combined with the inherent imprecision of Jackson's approach, the foreign affairs overlay in cases such as *Dames & Moore* strongly suggests that applications of Jackson's three category approach to foreign affairs questions will continue to create vague, rather than clear, constitutional boundaries.

§ 3.10 The President and the Use of Military Force

[1] The President's Commander-in-Chief Power

Although the text of the Constitution seems to give Congress the upper hand in defense matters—at least seven clauses of Article I give it defense responsibilities[157]—the President has emerged as the dominant figure in military and defense matters. The President's sole constitutional duty in this respect is to serve as "Commander-in-Chief of the Army and Navy of the United States" and the state militias.[158] This textual reed has sufficed to support broad authority, which has in turn generated scholarly controversy.[159]

---

156. It may or may not be coincidence that the author of *Dames & Moore*, Justice William Rehnquist, clerked for Justice Jackson during the term in which *Youngstown* was decided, and is widely thought to have influenced, if not played a larger role in, Justice Jackson's development of his three-category approach.

157. U.S. CONST. art. I, §8, cl. 1, cl. 11–16.

158. U.S. CONST. art. II, §2, cl. 1.

159. *See, e.g.*, LOUIS FISHER, PRESIDENTIAL WAR POWER (1995).

Article II, in declaring the President Commander-in-Chief of the armed forces, makes the President the highest officer in the military, as well as the civilian, establishment. The President is not simply a ceremonial chief; the Constitution puts the armed forces directly under presidential command,[160] in order to preserve civilian control of the military. Yet the Commander-in-Chief Clause also implies some limits on that authority. Alexander Hamilton stressed the respect in which the President's military authority was "much inferior" to that of the King of England. He wrote that the President's authority would "amount to nothing more than the supreme command and direction of the military and naval forces, as first general and admiral of the Confederacy," in contrast to which the King could also raise and regulate his own forces and declare his own wars.[161] Hamilton's distinction suggests that at least some Framers were sensitive to the importance of dividing responsibility for military matters.

The President, as Commander-in-Chief, has authority to play a role in military strategy. He may, as Abraham Lincoln did, intrude directly in command matters. Like Franklin Roosevelt, the President may map the strategy of global conflict. The President may even, as Woodrow Wilson did, place American forces under foreign command. The President normally delegates actual command to military officers but is not required to do so. Rather, he may assume personal command in the field, as George Washington did in accompanying troops to suppress the Whisky Rebellion in 1794. President Truman himself decided to drop the atomic bomb on Japan in 1945. In more recent years, it has been the President who has decided to launch limited strikes, such as with drones and cruise missiles, on foreign targets.

The President's power is clearest when he acts to repel attack. Indeed, at the Constitutional Convention, an earlier draft of the Constitution gave Congress power "to make war"; the verb was changed to "declare" to remove any inhibitions against presidential action to defend against attack. This issue arose after President Lincoln blockaded Southern ports after the Confederacy attacked Fort Sumter in 1861. The Court agreed that the President "is not only authorized but bound to resist force by force" without awaiting legislative approval.[162]

The Commander-in-Chief's use of the armed forces has largely escaped judicial control. Cases have held the President not legally accountable for using troops to address an emergency. For instance, *Martin v. Mott*[163] upheld a presidential order calling the militia into service during the War of 1812. The Court concluded that only the President could decide whether and when to call up the militia. Executive military action has received even greater deference from the other branches since World War II. The concept of "repelling sudden attacks," which had furnished latitude in the

---

160. Youngstown Sheet & Tube Co. v. Sawyer, 343 U.S. 579, 614 (1952) (Jackson, J., concurring).
161. THE FEDERALIST No. 69 (Hamilton).
162. The Prize Cases, 67 U.S. (2 Black) 635, 668 (1863) (upholding President Lincoln's blockade of South after the attack on Fort Sumter).
163. 25 U.S. (12 Wheat.) 19, 30–31 (1827).

past, expanded to encompass actions abroad to protect American property, personnel, or interests. With the onset of the Cold War after 1945, presidential uses of military force only increased, justified by the asserted threat posed by the Soviet Union. While some of these actions rested on congressional authorization short of full-blown declarations of war, others did not.

During the Vietnam War, some questioned whether the judiciary should deem cases regarding presidential use of armed forces as political questions. Despite "a respectable and growing body of lower court opinion" that cases challenging presidential war-making in Vietnam presented justiciable controversies,[164] the Supreme Court continued to treat the issue as a political question,[165] although sometimes over vigorous dissents. Regardless of those decisions—or perhaps because of them—as dissatisfaction with the Vietnam War increased in the early 1970s, Congress acted to reassert its war-making prerogative by enacting the War Powers Resolution of 1973.

[2] The War Powers Resolution

Congress's most significant power in the war field is its power to declare war. However, the near-disappearance of the practice of formally declaring wars[166] and Congress's desire to reassert its constitutional power (spurred by the growing unpopularity of the Vietnam War) led Congress to enact the War Powers Resolution (WPR), over President Nixon's veto, in 1973. The WPR[167] regulates presidential power to employ the armed forces abroad. It responds not just to the dissatisfaction with the Vietnam War, but more generally to the realization that, in the modern era, formal declarations of war had declined to the point of disappearance. It provides that, absent a declaration of war, the President, "in every possible instance,"[168] shall consult with Congress before introducing armed forces into hostilities or foreign territory, and must, in any event, report to Congress within 48 hours of doing so.[169] The operation must end within 60 days of the required report unless Congress declares war or specifically authorizes military force.[170] The 60-day period may be extended no more than 30 days if the President certifies to Congress that unavoidable military necessity respecting the safety of the armed forces requires their continued use in connection with their prompt removal. Congress may refuse to support the President during the initial 60 to 90-day period or may thereafter terminate the action by concurrent resolution.

---

164. Holtzman v. Schlesinger, 414 U.S. 1304, 1311 (1973) (Marshall, J.).

165. Orlando v. Laird, 404 U.S. 869 (1971); Mora v. McNamara, 389 U.S. 934 (1967).

166. For example, the United States has not formally declared war on any nation since World War II, despite fighting, in the pre-War Powers Resolution era, major conflicts in Korea and Vietnam and, in the post-WPR era, major conflicts in Iraq (twice) and Afghanistan.

167. 50 U.S.C. § 1541–1548.

168. *Id.* § 3, 50 U.S.C. § 1542.

169. *Id.* § 4, 50 U.S.C. § 1543.

170. *Id.* § 5(b), 50 U.S.C. § 1544(b).

President Nixon denounced the WPR as an unconstitutional infringement upon the powers Article II vests in the President. In practice, Presidents have usually failed to comply with it, in particular the pre-hostilities consultation requirement, unless the anticipated hostilities threaten to rise to the level of a major conflict with significant American casualties. Three such anticipated conflicts — the two Iraq wars and the war in Afghanistan — were preceded by congressional debates and the passage of authorizations for the use of military force. But because most uses of U.S. forces today involve very short-term, discrete operations, such as cruise missile or drone attacks, U.S. involvement often ends long before the 60-day withdrawal limit approaches. Even when the President has sought and received pre-hostilities congressional authorization to begin a war, he has often insisted that the decision to seek that authority did not imply any concession that the WPR was constitutional.[171]

While President Nixon and his successors have deemed the WPR an intrusion on presidential powers, others identify other constitutional problems. One might question whether Congress can delegate power to make war for 60 days without a congressional declaration. If not, the War Powers Act might violate Congress's, rather than the President's, power. Moreover, the concurrent resolution procedure would seem to run afoul of the Court's decision in *Immigration and Naturalization Service v. Chadha* invalidating the legislative veto.[172] On the other hand, the fact that the power to declare war is one of the few Article I, Section 8 powers that does not require presidential approval[173] suggests that perhaps authorizations to initiate wars do not fall within *Chadha*'s requirement of bicameralism and presentment.

[3] Military Justice

Presidential power generally swells in war-time, as military exigency is often used to justify unusual domestic measures. The Civil War tested the resiliency of the Constitution and provided the occasion for the exercise of broad presidential emergency powers in several areas, including military justice.

In response to the crisis of the Civil War, President Lincoln took a number of actions which normally would have required legislation. He blockaded Southern ports,

---

171. *See, e.g., Statement by President George Bush upon Signing H.J. Res. 77*, 27 WEEKLY COMPILATION OF PRESIDENTIAL DOCUMENTS 48 (January 21, 1991) (presidential signing statement accompanying the signing of the authorization to commence the first Iraq war, stating the President's position that his decision to sign the authorization did not constitute agreement that the WPR was constitutional).

172. 462 U.S. 919 (1983). *Chadha* and the legislative veto more generally are discussed in Section 3.08[3].

173. *See* William Trainor, *Fame, the Founding, and the Power to Declare War*, 82 CORNELL L. REV. 695, 724 (1997) ("relevant evidence strongly indicates that the predominant view was that the President did not have the power to veto declarations of war."). One hopes that this remains a theoretical question: the prospect of the nation declaring war against the opposition of the President presents so many difficulties (*e.g.*, what if the President refuses to engage U.S. military forces, or immediately surrenders) that one would expect this scenario never to arise.

extended the term of military enlistment, increased the size of the military, and disbursed public moneys to private citizens to purchase arms and supplies. He also suspended the writ of habeas corpus. Quite clearly, the privilege of the writ of habeas corpus can be suspended only under certain dire circumstances. The constitutional text,[174] which forbids suspension save in such occasions, implies that when those conditions arise, the privilege may temporarily give way. The more difficult issue relates to who has the power of suspension. The placement of the clause in Art. I §9 as a limitation on the powers of Congress would seem to imply that the Constitution vests that power, in its restricted form, with Congress. Indeed, Congress eventually authorized the President to suspend the writ, but not until 1863. But Lincoln had acted to suspend the writ two years earlier, in 1861. He prevailed in a tense confrontation with Chief Justice Roger Taney, who had granted a habeas writ on behalf of an arrested secessionist but who was unable to prevent the military commander from refusing to release the individual.

Military commissions, as a substitute for civilian courts, have a long pedigree in American practice. They were used under a variety of circumstances during the war with Mexico, the Civil War, and World War II. Supreme Court decisions authorize their use to try alleged war criminals[175] as well as civilians alleged to have committed criminal offenses in occupied areas.[176] Some decisions authorize their use on enemy territory where American civil courts do not operate.[177] The more difficult question involves the propriety of military tribunals within the United States. The two leading decisions, *Ex Parte Milligan*[178] and *Ex Parte Quirin*,[179] seem to point in different directions.

In *Ex Parte Milligan*, the Court held that a military tribunal could not try an American citizen charged with conspiracy to aid the confederacy while civil courts were open and functioning. During World War II, however, the Court in *Ex Parte Quirin* upheld the power of a military tribunal to try eight German saboteurs captured in the United States, one of whom was an American citizen. Because the saboteurs had discarded their military uniforms upon disembarking from a German submarine, the indictment charged them with violating the law of war. The Court found that Congress had authorized use of military commissions to try such offenses. Thus, *Ex Parte Quirin* did not require the Court to reach the question of whether the President had unilateral power to convene military tribunals. Military tribunals could be used to try "unlawful combatants," *e.g.*, enemy combatants without uniforms, including the American citizen defendant. The Court distinguished *Ex Parte Milligan* on the

174. U.S. CONST. art. I, §9, cl. 2 ("The Privilege of the Writ of Habeas Corpus shall not be suspended, unless when in Cases of Rebellion or Invasion the public Safety may require it.").
175. *See, e.g.*, Application of Yamashita, 327 U.S. 1 (1946).
176. *See, e.g.*, Madsen v. Kinsella, 343 U.S. 341 (1952).
177. *See, e.g., id.*
178. 71 U.S. (4 Wall.) 2 (1866).
179. 317 U.S. 1 (1942).

ground that Milligan was not an unlawful belligerent, and limited the older case to its facts.

These cases gained new prominence in the aftermath of the September 11, 2001, terror attacks. Very soon after those attacks, Congress authorized military force against the regimes, organizations, and persons who helped plan them. Shortly thereafter, the United States began military operations against the al-Qaeda organization that conducted the attacks and the regime in Afghanistan that provided it a safe haven.

The major constitutional issue that has arisen out of the Afghan war has been the constitutional status of enemy combatants housed at the U.S. military base in Guantanamo Bay, Cuba. In *Hamdi v. Rumsfeld*,[180] the Court provided a fractured answer to the question of what an American citizen's rights were when he was accused of making war against the United States. Hamdi was an American citizen captured in Afghanistan, but he claimed, in a petition for habeas corpus, that he had not entered the fight against U.S. forces. A plurality opinion found that the post-September 11 Authorization for Use of Military Force (AUMF)[181] gave the government the legal authority to detain him for the duration of the conflict. The Court acknowledged the existence of a previously enacted federal law that authorized federal detention of U.S. citizens only upon explicit congressional authorization. However, Justice O'Connor's plurality opinion found such authorization in the Afghanistan AUMF.

Justice Souter, joined by Justice Ginsburg, disagreed, finding the AUMF insufficiently precise to serve as such authority. However, he joined with the plurality in a judgment requiring that U.S. citizen-detainees be given a hearing at which they could attempt to show their innocence. Justice Scalia, joined by Justice Stevens, dissented, arguing that because Hamdi was an American citizen, he either had to be released immediately or Congress had to act to suspend the writ of habeas corpus (which it had not). Justice Thomas dissented on a radically different ground. He argued that Article II gave the President nearly unreviewable authority to determine whether a person was an enemy combatant, and on that basis to detain him.

Later detainee cases dealt with non-citizen detainees.[182] Those cases culminated with the Court's 5–4 holding in *Boumediene v. Bush*[183] giving detainees located within a *de facto* U.S. jurisdiction[184] the right to seek habeas corpus relief for their detentions. Both Justice Kennedy's majority opinion and Justice Scalia's dissent looked to the history underlying the Suspension Clause and found no case where a noncitizen held

---

180. 542 U.S. 507 (2003).
181. 115 Stat. 224.
182. Rasul v. Bush, 542 U.S. 466 (2004); Hamdan v. Rumsfeld, 548 U.S. 557 (2006).
183. 553 U.S. 723 (2008).
184. The detainee in *Boumediene* was held at Guantanamo Bay, Cuba, a territory that was formally under Cuban sovereignty but was occupied by the United States under a long term lease.

outside the Crown's sovereignty had invoked habeas relief. But whereas Justice Scalia thought that finding dispositive, Justice Kennedy did not, in part because he questioned the assumptions that the historical record was complete or that it answered the questions before it, since eighteenth century courts may not have faced situations similar to that before the Court. Justice Kennedy's opinion rested on the premise that questions about the territorial and substantive scope of the Constitution's individual rights protections should turn on objective factors (such as the extent of U.S. control over the territory in question) and practical concerns (such as the ease or difficulty in producing prisoners for habeas hearings), rather than formalistic questions such as whether the United States enjoys *de jure* sovereignty over a given territory.

Boumediene opened up a wide set of questions about the content of the habeas procedures for the hearings the majority opinion mandated. To date, the Court has not granted review on any case that would allow it to opine on those issues.

§ 3.11 Presidential Litigation Immunities

[1] The President as Defendant

In *Marbury v. Madison*,[185] the Court suggested that, at times, the executive branch could be held accountable in court for its conduct, but on other occasions, it enjoyed immunity. In essence, if executive conduct allegedly violated an individual's rights, a court could assert jurisdiction over even the Secretary of State. By contrast, if the executive enjoyed what Chief Justice Marshall called "discretion," the Court could not consider the matter. *Marbury*, of course, involved James Madison as the defendant, not President Thomas Jefferson. It therefore did not reach the question of whether the President himself could be sued. Later cases have considered that question.

Mississippi v. Johnson[186] involved an action against President Andrew Johnson to enjoin him from enforcing Reconstruction legislation on the ground that it was unconstitutional. Based on the separation of powers doctrine, the Court decided such an action could not be maintained. The Court stated: "The Congress is the legislative department of the government; the President is the executive department. Neither can be restrained in its action by the judicial department."[187] Although the Court clearly held that it lacked power to enjoin the President from executing a law alleged to be unconstitutional, it did not go so far as to say that the President could never be sued. More recently, the Court indicated that, "in general," a federal court lacks jurisdiction to enjoin the President regarding performance of official duties.[188]

---

185. 5 U.S. (1 Cranch) 137 (1803).
186. 71 U.S. (4 Wall.) 475 (1867).
187. *Id.* at 500.
188. Franklin v. Massachusetts, 505 U.S. 788, 802–03 (1992). Only four members of the Court joined that part of the opinion, but Justice Scalia made clear his agreement with this view. *See id.* at 827 (Scalia, J., concurring in part and concurring in the judgment).

Even if correct, the lack of judicial power to enjoin the President does not mean that presidential action is unreviewable; rather, the legality of Presidential action can ordinarily be examined in a suit to enjoin those charged with enforcing the President's order.[189] For example, in *Youngstown Sheet & Tube v. Sawyer*,[190] the steel companies tested the validity of President Truman's order in an action against Secretary of Commerce Sawyer, the President's instrument for the execution of the seizure order. In the extraordinary case where only an order directed against the President will prove effective, *United States v. Nixon*[191] holds that the President may be sued in a federal court and ordered to produce presidential documents under certain circumstances.[192]

[2] Executive Privileges and Immunities

In recent years, the question of executive privilege has generated increased interest. The President has claimed the power to withhold information when he deems disclosure contrary to the public interest. Most notably, during the Watergate scandal, President Richard Nixon asserted the right to withhold from courts evidence crucial to a pending criminal prosecution. The Court rejected Nixon's assertion in *United States v. Nixon*.[193] The Court refused to quash a subpoena to the President issued on the motion of the Watergate Special Prosecutor, directing the President to produce certain tape recordings and documents relating to his conversations with aides, which were needed as evidence in criminal prosecutions.

To be sure, the *Nixon* Court recognized a presumptive privilege for presidential communications based on the President's expectation of confidentiality of his conversations and correspondence, in order to ensure that he received candid advice that would not be later disclosed. However, that privilege was qualified, not absolute. The Court concluded that a claim of privilege based only on the generalized interest in confidentiality could not prevail over the demonstrated specific need for evidence in a pending criminal trial. The Court indicated that a different result might follow from a claimed need to protect military, diplomatic, or national security secrets. But *Nixon* featured no such claim. Similarly, the Court suggested that the President's claims would have greater weight against disclosure in a civil case or congressional proceeding.[194]

---

189. *Id.* at 828 (Scalia, J., concurring in part and concurring in the judgment).

190. 343 U.S. 579 (1952).

191. 418 U.S. 683 (1974).

192. *But see Franklin*, 505 U.S. at 826 (Scalia, J., concurring in part and concurring in the judgment) (distinguishing *Nixon* on the ground that "the order upheld there merely required the President to provide information relevant to an ongoing criminal prosecution, which is what any citizen might do; it did not require him to exercise the 'executive Power' in a judicially prescribed fashion").

193. 418 U.S. 683 (1974). The Court's decision was unanimous with Justice Rehnquist not participating.

194. *Id.* at 712 n.19.

In *Nixon v. Administrator of General Services*, the Court held that executive privilege survived a particular President's term.[195] Nonetheless, it held that former President Nixon was not entitled to an absolute bar to the disclosure of his papers and effects that Congress had mandated in a statute. A practice of making presidential papers available in libraries had existed. The Court concluded that review by archivists and later public disclosure of Nixon's papers would not interfere with a President's interest in receiving confidential advice.

What about civil liability? In *Nixon v. Fitzgerald*,[196] the Court held that the President is immune from civil suits for damages caused by official acts. Fitzgerald, a Pentagon employee, had sued President Nixon and various White House aides for allegedly eliminating his job to retaliate against him for his whistle-blowing activities. Although an eight-justice majority had held the same day as *Fitzgerald* that other executive officials had only a qualified immunity from civil liability for official acts,[197] in *Nixon v. Fitzgerald*, a five-justice majority concluded that the President enjoys absolute immunity from damage actions based on official acts. The Court reasoned that litigation would distract the President from his Article II duties, and the prospect of personal liability might interfere with official decision-making.

Fifteen years later, *Clinton v. Jones*[198] held that this immunity does not extend to suits for damages arising out of events that occurred before the President took office. *Jones* arose in the context of a civil suit brought against President Bill Clinton based on his alleged conduct before he took office. President Clinton did not claim absolute immunity for such conduct—rather, he claimed simply the right to have the litigation deferred until after he left office. The Court rejected such a general right to defer, expressing skepticism that such litigation would so consume the President's time as to make him unable to perform his constitutional duties. However, it did observe that a trial court could on a case-by-case basis issue orders deferring aspects of such litigation in deference to the President's need to attend to those duties. Whether modern political developments call into the question the Court's assumptions about the burdensomeness of such private litigation is something that remains to be conclusively determined. Notably, however, in his concurring opinion in *Jones* Justice Breyer observed that Congress was always free to create any immunity it thought appropriate.

In *Cheney v. United States District Court*,[199] the Court sounded more deferential to the President and Vice President than it had in *Clinton v. Jones*. *Cheney* arose in the context of a civil suit against a variety of persons, including the Vice President, related to their official duties, which led to the issuance of a discovery order encompassing the Vice President. The Court acknowledged courts' need to "give recognition

---

195. 433 U.S. 425, 449 (1977).

196. 457 U.S. 731 (1982).

197. Harlow v. Fitzgerald, 457 U.S. 800, 818 (1982) (officials are immune from civil liability if the conduct "does not violate clearly established statutory or constitutional rights of which a reasonable person would have known").

198. 520 U.S. 681 (1997).

199. 542 U.S. 367 (2004).

to the paramount necessity of protecting the Executive Branch from vexatious litigation that might distract it from the energetic performance of its constitutional duties."[200] The Court left open the possibility, however, that the lower courts could shape appropriate discovery orders which would allow the case to proceed against the Vice President and other close presidential advisors without unduly impairing the performance of the highest officials in the executive branch.

---

200. *Id.* at 382.

Chapter 4

The Federal System: Introduction and Basic Concepts

§ 4.01 Introduction

The federal system allocates power between the national and state governments. Although the Constitution does not use the word "federalism," the concept represents one of the important structural ideas implicit in the document. Judicial review of state legislation and state court decisions allows the federal judiciary to police state action. When federal legislative power grows to occupy a larger sphere of regulatory activity, it displaces state power. Finally, the Constitution's grant to Americans of important rights against state conduct places both the federal courts and Congress in the position of overseeing states' relationships with their own citizens.[1] On the other hand, despite these assertions of federal power, states retain a great deal of residual sovereign authority. In recent decades, the Supreme Court has been carefully attuned to protecting that authority.

This chapter provides a summary of the main features of our federal system. After it does so, subsequent chapters consider particular federal and state powers that implicate the federal-state relationship. Later chapters consider constitutional rights that Americans enjoy as against their states. While those later chapters focus on the substance of those rights, rather than structure *per se*, the existence of federal rights against state action again reveals the federal-state balance in action.

"Federalism was our Nation's own discovery," Justice Anthony Kennedy observed.[2] Yet defining that discovery has been a continuing source of controversy. More than a half century ago, Professor Edward Corwin identified the following features as intrinsic to American federalism: (1) a union of autonomous states; (2) the division of powers between the federal government and the states; (3) the direct operation

---

1. Congress's role in this oversight flows from the provisions in many constitutional rights amendments, starting with the Thirteenth Amendment, authorizing Congress to enforce those amendments. The scope of this congressional enforcement power is discussed in Chapter 13.

2. United States Term Limits, Inc. v. Thornton, 514 U.S. 779, 838 (1995) (Kennedy, J., concurring).

of each government, within its assigned sphere, on persons within its territorial limits; (4) the provision of each government with the complete apparatus of law enforcement; and (5) federal supremacy over any conflicting assertion of state power.[3] The intervening years have witnessed a further shift of power from state to nation and have added some gloss to Professor Corwin's formulation. Nonetheless, it continues to state some basic features of American federalism. With one exception, his formulation provides the outline for most this chapter, in Sections 4.02 through 4.05.[4] After considering his formulation, Sections 4.06 and 4.07 discuss the states' reserved powers and the theory that federalism questions are best answered by recourse to consideration of the proper workings of the national and state political processes. Section 4.08 concludes this Chapter by considering the advantages and drawbacks of a federal system.

§ 4.02 A Union of Previously Autonomous States

The Constitution brought previously autonomous states together into one union. The Constitution was formed, Chief Justice Marshall argued in *McCulloch v. Maryland*,[5] by action by the people, not the state governments. To be sure, the delegates to the constitutional convention were chosen by the state legislatures and the proposal it produced was ultimately submitted to delegates meeting in the states—"where else should they have assembled?"[6] Marshall asked rhetorically. But he insisted that the fact that the people met to act in states did not make their action any less that of the whole American people.

The Constitution brought together a voluntary union of autonomous governments, previously linked only by the loose bonds of the Articles of Confederation. When considering the proper scope of federal power relative to the states, it is important to remember that the Constitution was established, and the Articles of Confederation jettisoned, to escape a regime in which state sovereignty and a weak central government produced a dysfunctional system.

Nevertheless, the implications of *McCulloch*'s analysis remain contested. In 1995, the Court split 5–4 on a foundational question of how best to read the founding moment. The issue in *U.S. Term Limits v. Thornton*[7] was whether a state could impose

---

3. *See* Edward S. Corwin, The Constitution of the United States of America: Analysis and Interpretation xi–xii (1953).

4. Professor Corwin's fourth principle—the provision of each level of government with its own law enforcement apparatus—is discussed more generally throughout this chapter.

5. 17 U.S. (4 Wheat.) 316 (1819).

6. *Id.* at 403.

7. 514 U.S. 779 (1995).

additional eligibility requirements (in that case, term limits) on national representatives selected from that state. If one believes, as the majority did, that Congress was a body representing the whole American people, then no one state could interpose its own additional qualifications for membership in that fundamentally national body. But if one believed, as the dissenters did, that Congress represented not the whole American people as a mass, but instead the American people as a set of distinct set of state-level polities, then presumably, any state could add whatever additional requirements it wished on the representatives it sent to Congress.

Thus, Justice Stevens' majority laid heavy stress on its description of the founding as a moment where the people of the entire nation replaced a confederation of sovereign states with a national government whose representatives in Congress owed allegiance to the entire American people. Such a description of Congress was incompatible with the ability of one state to alter the qualifications for service in that body. By contrast, Justice Thomas' dissent argued that the Constitution arose from the people coming together as citizens of different states, rather than as one united American polity. He described the Congress as, literally, a congress of representatives from various states, rather than a congress of the whole American people chosen via the states. Thus, under his view, any state had an inherent right to set any qualifications it wanted for its representatives, as long as those qualifications did not conflict with those set forth in the Constitution itself.

Even under the view of *McCulloch* that prevailed in *U.S. Term Limits*, the states are not "mere political subdivisions of the United States."[8] Rather, they occupy a special position in our constitutional system and may exercise powers the Constitution does not vest in Congress or deny them.[9] The Constitution did not produce "[a]n entire consolidation of the States into one complete national sovereignty."[10] Rather, under our system, states retained a degree of sovereignty. They are represented as states in the Senate; their senators were initially chosen by the state legislatures,[11] and no state could lose its equal representation in the Senate without its consent. In addition, as discussed in subsequent sub-sections, the constitutional system assumes that powers not granted to the federal government are retained by the states, an assumption codified in the Tenth Amendment. At the same time, the Constitution divested states of many attributes of sovereignty. The limitations on state power set forth in Article I, § 10, coupled with the Supremacy Clause, suggest some limits the new union placed on state sovereignty. The Civil War Amendments later imposed further restraints.

---

8. New York v. United States, 505 U.S. 144, 188 (1992).

9. *See* Garcia v. San Antonio Metro. Transit Auth., 469 U.S. 528, 547 (1985).

10. The Federalist No. 32 (Hamilton).

11. This feature was changed by the Seventeenth Amendment, which provided for popular election of the Senate.

"[S]tate sovereignty is, [however,] a ghost that refused to remain in repose."[12] Throughout our history, states have claimed a degree of sovereignty that has brought them into conflict with federal mandates of different sorts, whether legislative, judicial, or executive. Underlying many challenges to federal authority has been the implicit (or explicit) argument that the claimed federal power unconstitutionally trenches on the sovereign prerogatives retained by states within a system in which ultimate federal supremacy must be reconciled with a meaningful level of residual state sovereignty.

§ 4.03 Division of Power between the Federal and State Governments

The federal system divides power between the nation and the states. In his concurring opinion in *U.S. Term Limits v. Thornton*, Justice Kennedy wrote that "[t]he Framers split the atom of sovereignty."[13] The federal government possesses those powers the Constitution delegates to it either explicitly or implicitly. The States retain authority not granted to the nation or retained by the people. The Constitution's text discloses this division. Congress is given only the legislative powers "herein granted,"[14] not all legislative power. Moreover, the enumeration of eighteen categories of legislative power in Article I suggests other authority not conferred. Finally, the Tenth Amendment reminds readers that some power is not given to the federal government.

To a great extent, the boundaries of the division were left to future generations to demarcate. Although the Articles of Confederation had limited the Federal Government to those powers "expressly delegated" to it,[15] the Framers had repeatedly declined to include such a limitation in the Constitution,[16] a point Chief Justice Marshall thought significant in *McCulloch v. Maryland*.[17] The Constitution clearly contemplated that the federal government would have some body of implied powers which might impact state regulatory authority. Nonetheless, the States retained a separate basis of power. As Alexander Hamilton wrote in *The Federalist*:

> An entire consolidation of the States into one complete national sovereignty would imply an entire subordination of the parts; and whatever powers might remain in them would be altogether dependent on the general will. But as the plan of the convention aims only at a partial union or consolidation, the State governments would clearly retain all the rights of sovereignty which

---

12. Bernard Schwartz, National League of Cities v. Usery — *The Commerce Power and State Sovereignty Redivivus*, 46 Fordham L. Rev. 1115 (1978).

13. *U.S. Term Limits*, 514 U.S. at 838 (Kennedy, J., concurring).

14. U.S. Const. art. I, § 1.

15. Articles of Confederation, 1777, art. II.

16. 5 The Founders Constitution 403–04 (Philip Kurland & Ralph Lerner eds., 1988).

17. 17 U.S. at 406 ("But there is no phrase in the [Constitution] which, like the articles of confederation, excludes incidental or implied powers; and which requires that everything granted shall be expressly and minutely described.").

they before had, and which were not, by that act, *exclusively* delegated to the United States.[18]

§ 4.04 Direct Federal Government Operation on Citizens

The federal system featured the direct operation of both state and federal governments, within their assigned spheres, on all persons and property within their respective territorial limits. In other words, both levels of government have the authority directly to regulate private persons subject to their jurisdiction. This attribute enhanced the status of the national government, as compared to the Articles period, during which the central government only had the authority to regulate the states, who alone had the power to regulate the citizenry. The Constitution's grant of direct regulatory power to the federal government thus allowed that government to vindicate its regulatory choices without depending on state cooperation.

To be sure, the federal government is a government of enumerated powers—that is, the federal government only enjoys the regulatory powers the Constitution gives it. Of course, those powers are quite broad, and have been construed generously for most of the last 100 years. Nevertheless, an important corollary of the enumerated powers limitation on the federal government is that states retain the residual sovereign power that the Constitution does not vest in the federal government. This residual power is often termed the "police power," although the scope of that power extends far beyond traditional law enforcement activities, to encompass the broad power to regulate for the general health and safety of society. This power thus allows states to provide many essential governmental functions. States provide public education, fire and police protection, sanitation, public health, and parks and recreation, among other services. States may regulate their local economies through laws addressing banking, insurance, public utilities, local transportation, and various occupations and professions. Finally, much law enforcement is performed locally.

Note, though, that many of these functions could conceivably come within one of the enumerated powers delegated to the federal government. For example, regulation of sanitation may impact interstate commerce, and thus implicate federal power, to the extent the operations of waste haulers affect interstate commerce. Even more obviously, state regulation of local economic activity, such as banking or transportation services, could implicate interstate commerce and thus come within Congress's regulatory power. When a given subject of regulation comes within both federal and state regulatory jurisdictions, difficult issues of federalism arise. Sometimes the local nature of an issue may influence whether Congress possesses that regulatory authority at all under its power to regulate interstate commerce. Chapter 6, which

18. THE FEDERALIST No. 32 (Hamilton) (emphasis in original).

considers the scope of Congress's power over interstate commerce, examines the significance of the local nature of an activity to the question whether Congress enjoys regulatory power over that activity. However, issues of shared control over such issues are mainly addressed by a concept called the dormant Commerce Clause, which discussed in Chapter 7.

§ 4.05 Federal Supremacy

Separate levels of government make disputes inevitable. Often, those disputes take the form of conflicting federal and state laws. The Supremacy Clause of Article VI decisively resolves such conflicts in favor of the federal government. Federal law, within its allotted sphere, is supreme throughout the nation. States cannot impede or control those laws.[19]

Chief Justice Marshall interpreted the Supremacy Clause to carry essentially two meanings: (1) states may not interfere with the federal government; and (2) constitutionally valid federal action prevails over inconsistent state action. Both of these ideas play critical roles in the federal-state relationship.

McCulloch v. Maryland[20] expressed the first idea. In *McCulloch*, Maryland had taxed the Bank of the United States, a federal instrumentality. The Court, speaking through Chief Justice Marshall, held the Maryland tax unconstitutional, on the ground that it allowed a state to control an instrumentality (the Bank) established by the national government. Because nothing would limit the degree of taxation Maryland could impose if the tax were upheld, Marshall reasoned that upholding the tax would effectively give a state the power to destroy a federal institution and frustrate the federal goals that motivated its creation. To be sure, at the end of the opinion, Marshall suggested that Maryland could impose on the bank a more generally-applicable tax — for example, a tax on the real estate on which the bank sat, which would be imposed equally on all other similarly-situated real estate in the state. But taxes that singled out the federal instrumentality would not be allowed.

U.S. Term Limits v. Thornton,[21] discussed earlier in this Chapter, reflects another aspect of this same idea. Recall that in that case, the Court rejected a state's attempt to impose an additional qualification (term limits) on the state's congressional representatives. An important part of the majority's analysis centered on its argument that Congress was a nationally-scoped institution representing the American people as an entirety, rather than a collection of representatives each from his or her own state. Given this description, the Court reasoned that one state's imposition of ad-

---

19. U.S. CONST. art. VI ("This constitution, and the Laws of the United States which shall be made in Pursuance thereof; and all Treaties made, or which shall be made, under the Authority of the United States, shall be the supreme Law of the Land.").

20. 17 U.S. 316 (1819).

21. 514 U.S. 779 (1995).

ditional qualifications would disturb the connection between Congress and the entirety of the American people.

A concept related to this first understanding of the Supremacy Clause deals with federal courts and federal law. Recall from Chapter 2 that in *Martin v. Hunter's Lessee*,[22] the Court upheld provisions of the Judiciary Act of 1789 that gave the U.S. Supreme Court the power to reverse decisions made by state supreme courts when they involved a federal law. *Martin* implicitly expressed concern that a contrary ruling—that is, a ruling that a state supreme court's interpretation of federal law was immune from review by the U.S. Supreme Court—would result in a system in which federal rights would rest on state courts. As with the situations in *McCulloch* and *U.S. Term Limits*, this situation would place the federal government in a subordinate position relative to the states, since federal rights would be at the mercy of state courts. Chief Justice Marshall did not participate in *Martin*. However, he made the same point, even more explicitly, in an opinion he wrote several years later, in *Cohens v. Virginia*. In *Cohens*, he wrote for the Court rejecting what amounted to Virginia's reiteration of the argument it had unsuccessfully raised in *Martin*.[23]

The second concept animating the Supremacy Clause is illustrated by *Gibbons v. Ogden*.[24] In *Gibbons*, the Court upheld, as a valid federal regulation of interstate commerce, a federal law that granted sailors licenses to sail up and down the U.S. coastline. This aspect of *Gibbons*, which furnished the foundation for today's broad congressional power under the Interstate Commerce Clause, is discussed in Chapter 6. But the decision to uphold the federal coasting license brought federal law into conflict with New York law, which had granted an individual a monopoly right to ply the waters between two particular ports. That conflict required Chief Justice Marshall to conclude that a valid federal law, such as the coasting license, trumped, or "preempted" conflicting state law, such as the New York-granted monopoly in *Gibbons*. The preemptive effect of federal law flowed from the Supremacy Clause. The details of preemption doctrine—that is, the principles that guide courts in determining whether in fact a conflict between federal and state law exists such that the state law must give way—are discussed in Chapter 7.

---

22. 14 U.S. (1 Wheat.) 304 (1816).

23. 19 U.S. 264, 385 (1821) ("The mischievous consequences of the construction contended for on the part of Virginia are also entitled to great consideration. It would prostrate, it has been said, the [federal] government and its laws at the feet of every State in the Union. And would not this be its effect? What power of the government could be executed by its own means in any State disposed to resist its execution by a course of legislation? The laws must be executed by individuals acting within the several States. If these individuals may be exposed to penalties, and if the Courts of the Union cannot correct the judgments by which these penalties may be enforced, the course of the [federal] government may be at any time arrested by the will of one of its members. Each member will possess a veto on the will of the whole.").

24. 22 U.S. (9 Wheat.) 1 (1824).

Article VI underscores federal supremacy in two additional ways. The remaining part of the Supremacy Clause mandates that state judges are bound by federal law even when that federal law conflicts with their state constitution or state laws.[25] Moreover, the Oath Clause commits officers of the state executive and judicial branches and members of state legislatures to support the Constitution.[26]

§ 4.06 Reserved Powers

The Supremacy Clause, combined with the powers Article I vests in Congress, enables the nation to limit and override much state government conduct. Defenders of a more expansive view of states' autonomy often invoke the Tenth Amendment as a source of countervailing state power. It provides: "The powers not delegated to the United States by the Constitution, nor prohibited by it to the States, are reserved to the States respectively, or to the people."[27] The text of the Tenth Amendment offers little help in solving concrete constitutional issues. It does confirm that all power is not given to the federal government. Yet the Tenth Amendment seems to contemplate a three-part division of governmental power—among the federal government, state governments, and the people. Although it makes clear that the federal government cannot exercise all power, it provides no criteria to distinguish between the powers reserved to the states and those reserved to the people.

Perceptions of the Tenth Amendment have fluctuated over time and vary among different commentators and judges. One view sees it as reinforcing, but not adding to, the proposition that the federal government has simply those powers the Constitution delegates to it. The Tenth Amendment was added to the Constitution to allay fears that the new government might seek to exercise powers not granted. Under this view, the Tenth Amendment does not on its own accord curtail federal authority. As the Court stated in a unanimous opinion in 1941 in *United States v. Darby*: "The amendment states but a truism that all is retained which has not been surrendered."[28]

Another view understands the Tenth Amendment as a significant restraint on federal activity. In *New York v. United States*, for instance, Justice O'Connor suggested that the Tenth Amendment's protection for state sovereignty may act as a substantive limit on what the federal government is authorized to do:

> In some cases the Court has inquired whether an Act of Congress is authorized by one of the powers delegated to Congress in Article I of the Constitution. See *McCulloch v. Maryland*. In other cases the Court has sought to determine whether an Act of Congress invades the province of state sovereignty reserved by the Tenth Amendment. In a case like these, involving the division of authority between federal and state governments, the two inquiries

---

25. U.S. Const. art. VI, cl. 2.
26. U.S. Const. art. VI, cl. 3.
27. U.S. Const. amend. X.
28. 312 U.S. 100, 124 (1941).

are mirror images of each other. If a power is delegated to Congress in the Constitution, the Tenth Amendment expressly disclaims any reservation of that power to the States; if a power is an attribute of state sovereignty reserved by the Tenth Amendment, it is necessarily a power the Constitution has not conferred on Congress.[29]

The force and effect of the Tenth Amendment has waxed and waned over the course of the nation's history. The Commerce Clause materials and the materials on federal regulation of the states will trace this ebb and flow.

§ 4.07 Federalism and the Political Process

Rather than attempting to identify particular regulatory areas that are forbidden to the federal government (and thus reserved to the states), the Supreme Court has sometimes concluded that such issues are best decided by recourse to the national political process. At times, the Court has found that such arguments counsel for, or against, claims of national or state regulatory authority. Alternatively, sometimes such arguments are used to suggest that states must seek their federalism-based protection from federal action in the political process, rather than from courts.

Chief Justice John Marshall invoked political process arguments in *McCulloch* in support of his conclusion that Maryland could not tax the national bank. The only security against an abuse of the power to tax, Marshall argued, was "found in the structure of the government itself"—that is, the fact that a legislature taxes its constituents who retain the power to turn legislators out of office if the taxes (or other regulation) are inappropriately onerous.[30] This legitimating check did not exist, however, when a state sought to tax an instrumentality of the federal government, since the federal entity was not represented in state government. Marshall explained that, just as the people of one state would not trust those of another state with a power to control even the most insignificant function of the first state's government, so, too, the people of the United States would never trust those of any individual state with this power over it. He wrote: "In the legislature of the Union alone, are all represented. The legislature of the Union alone, therefore, can be trusted by the people with the power of controlling measures which concern all, in the confidence that it will not be abused."[31]

In an influential article, Professor Herbert Wechsler argued in 1954 that "the national political process in the United States—and especially the role of the states in the composition and selection of the central government—is intrinsically well adapted to retarding or restraining new intrusions by the center on the domain of the states."[32]

---

29. New York v. United States, 505 U.S. 144, 155–56 (1992).

30. McCulloch v. Maryland, 17 U.S. 316, 428 (1819).

31. *Id.* at 431.

32. Herbert Wechsler, *The Political Safeguards of Federalism: The Role of the States in the Composition and Selection of the National Government,"* 54 Colum. L. Rev. 543, 558 (1954).

Professor Wechsler noted that electors chosen by each state elect the President and that each state sends to Congress two Senators and a number of Representatives. Based on factors such as those, which he viewed as providing states with ample political power in the national government, he argued that Congress, not the Court, has "ultimate authority for managing our federalism."[33] Indeed, echoing Marshall in *McCulloch*, he added that the main role the Framers saw for judicial review in federalism disputes "was the maintenance of national supremacy against nullification or usurpation by the individual states, the national government having no part in their composition or councils."[34] Professor Weschler thought the Court was "on weakest ground when it opposes its interpretation of the Constitution to that of Congress in the interest of the states...."[35] Professor Wechsler's analysis came to be known as "the political safeguards of federalism."

In *Garcia v. San Antonio Metropolitan Transit Authority*, the Court essentially adopted Professor Wechsler's analysis. It found that "the principal means chosen by the Framers to ensure the role of the States in the federal system lies in the structure of the Federal Government itself."[36] In *Garcia*, the Court rejected the idea that the Tenth Amendment provides any judicially enforceable standards to protect states from generally applicable federal regulations. (The challenged law in *Garcia* subjected state-operated transit systems, like all major employers, public and private, to federal minimum wage and maximum working hour laws.) In adopting the political safeguards analysis, the Court argued that the lack of judicial enforcement of federalism norms would not leave the states vulnerable. Rather, it concluded, the political system would afford them substantial protection, given that it was representatives of states that composed that system. Justice Blackmun concluded:

> In short, the Framers chose to rely on a federal system in which special restraints on federal power over the States inhered principally in the workings of the National Government itself, rather than in discrete limitations on the objects of federal authority. State sovereign interests, then, are more properly protected by procedural safeguards inherent in the structure of the federal system than by judicially created limitations on federal power.[37]

Justice Blackmun's claim was controversial. In dissent, Justice Powell argued that the political process afforded insufficient protection for the states. He argued that congresspersons become part of the federal government and lose any inclination to limit their own power in order to protect state prerogatives. At any rate, he noted that both representatives and senators are selected not by states themselves but by the people of each state. He also dismissed the role of the Electoral College in rendering the President the representatives of the states themselves, rather than the people of

---

33. *Id.* at 560.
34. *Id.* at 559.
35. *Id.*
36. Garcia v. San Antonio Metropolitan Transit Authority, 469 U.S. 528, 550 (1985).
37. *Id.* at 552.

each state. Chief Justice Rehnquist and Justice O'Connor also each wrote a dissenting opinion to reiterate many of these same points.

Political process arguments are not deployed exclusively to allow federal power at the expense of the states. In *New York v. United States*,[38] Justice O'Connor used political process reasoning to support the Court's holding that the federal government could not compel states to regulate in particular ways. As a result of such federal mandates, she wrote, "the accountability of both state and federal officials is diminished."[39] Citizens may become confused regarding the source of unpopular regulation and blame local, instead of federal, officials for the state regulation that was in fact mandated by Congress. Repeating this general idea, in *Printz v. United States*, Justice Scalia wrote: "The Constitution ... contemplates that a State's government will represent and remain accountable to its own citizens."[40]

At times, political process arguments may push justices into seemingly inconsistent positions. In *U.S. Term Limits*, Justice Stevens argued for the majority that states could not impose additional qualifications on Senators and Representatives because these officials were chosen by the people, not by the states, and represent the people, not the states. In the federal government, "representatives owe primary allegiance not to the people of a State, but to the people of the Nation."[41] Yet Justice Stevens had joined Justice Blackmun's *Garcia* opinion which characterized Senators and Representatives as representatives of the states that sent them, not of the nation. By the same token, the *Term Limits* dissenters viewed members of Congress as representatives of the states which selected them. Chief Justice Rehnquist and Justice O'Connor joined this dissent, although a decade earlier, they had joined Justice Powell's dissent in *Garcia*, which argued that congresspersons acted as members of the federal government rather than as representatives of the states that elected them.

§ 4.08 The Advantages and Disadvantages of a Federal System

The characteristics which Professor Corwin identified, and which are identified in the introduction to this Chapter, suggest some of the advantages commonly associated with federalism. The vertical division between governing units helps prevent concentration of power. As such, federalism is seen as a means to prevent government tyranny and to promote individual liberty, similar to the hoped-for dynamic created by the separation of powers at the national level. Federalism also helps government operate more efficiently by allocating functions to the unit best equipped to discharge them. On this theory, the national government is empowered to handle matters which

---

38. 505 U.S. 144 (1992).
39. *Id.* at 168.
40. 521 U.S. 898, 920 (1997).
41. 514 U.S. 779, 803 (1995).

require a uniform approach, whereas state governments regulate matters where local knowledge or diversity of treatment are valued.

Three other theoretical advantages of federalism perhaps receive less emphasis but are worth noting. The presence of multiple governments presents opportunities for experimentation with little risk to the whole. Justice Louis Brandeis famously observed: "It is one of the happy incidents of the federal system that a single courageous state may, if its citizens choose, serve as a laboratory; and try novel social and economic experiments without risk to the rest of the country."[42] Presumably, successful experiments may be adopted elsewhere, whereas failed approaches may be avoided. Justice Brandeis's "laboratories of democracy" concept has become one of the enduring metaphors in federalism discourse.

Federalism also allows for diverse arrangements which may be attractive to different groups. Minorities of different types may exit one community to find sanctuary in a more hospitable one. Finally, federalism affords more opportunities for individuals to join in civic life. As such, it may facilitate political and civic participation with a range of democratic benefits. As an offshoot of that final dynamic, federalism may also provide occasions for minorities to find a voice in governing matters which may impact national as well as local politics.[43]

On the other hand, federalism exacts a price. Most notably, the division of sovereign authority among different levels of government risks creating disorganization and triggering blame-shifting if things go wrong. Those phenomena are particularly costly when the nation confronts a crisis that requires fast, decisive, coordinated action. For example, the coronavirus pandemic of 2020 exposed the problems that can occur when states and the federal government disagree about the responsibility for leading particular initiatives and, indeed, about the substantive direction government policy should take. Even in more normal times, federal and state disagreement on a given issue—for example, the recreational use of marijuana—can cause confusion and uncertainty if a state takes one position and the federal government takes another. Political scientists and policymakers have given substantial thought to how to fine-tune the federal-state balance so as to minimize these problems, while maximizing the undeniable benefits that arise from a federal system. Some of their insights are reflected in the Court's federalism doctrines.

The basic concepts introduced in this Chapter influence the federalism doctrines the next few chapters will cover (as well as the federal court/state court review issue already presented in Chapter 2). Chapter 5 will consider federal regulatory powers in general. The following chapter, Chapter 6, will consider perhaps the most important of those powers—the power to regulate interstate commerce. The history of Commerce Clause jurisprudence features a great deal of anxiety about the possibility that an overly-broad definition of "interstate commerce"—a definition that has expanded

---

42. New State Ice Co. v. Liebmann, 285 U.S. 262, 311 (1932) (Brandeis, J., dissenting).
43. *See generally* Heather K. Gerken, *Foreword: Federalism All the Way Down,* 124 HARV. L. REV. 4, 6 (2010).

over our history as technology and business developments have led to a much more tightly integrated national economy—would result in Congress having the power to regulate virtually anything, a result some might consider inconsistent with the spirit of the Tenth Amendment.

Chapter 7 deals with residual state regulatory powers, and their limits. That chapter is mainly concerned with the so-called dormant Commerce Clause. The idea behind this principle is that the Commerce Clause, which gives Congress the power to regulate interstate commerce, has a negative, or "dormant" facet that prohibits states from regulating interstate commerce even if Congress has not acted. The dormant Commerce Clause idea thus reflects a balancing between the commerce power that Article I gives to Congress and the residual police powers that states retain. That chapter also considers the doctrine—called "preemption"—that seeks to determine when Congress intends that federal regulation displace, or "preempt" state regulation on that topic via the Supremacy Clause. It also considers Article IV's Privileges and Immunities Clause, which requires states to treat out-of-staters equally for purposes of many important rights.

Finally, Chapter 8 considers federal regulation, not of private parties, but of the states themselves. This regulation can take several forms. It might take the form of federal judicial orders aimed at state defendants. Such judicial action threatens to run afoul of the Eleventh Amendment, which, as Chapter 8 will explain, limits federal judicial remedies against states. Or it could take the form of legislation requiring states to act in certain ways as either economic actors (*e.g.*, as employers, which Congress might force to pay a minimum wage) or as sovereign entities (*e.g.*, as lawmakers or law enforcers). Finally, it could take the form of congressional inducements to states, for example, by offering money to states on the condition that states take certain actions. As Chapter 8 will explain, all these measures raise concerns that are grounded in federalism.

The balance of this book considers individual rights. But federalism plays an important, if often-unstated, role in the Court's interpretation of those rights. Because these are federal constitutional rights applicable to the states, a broad reading of these rights impinges on states' regulatory prerogatives. Thus, individual rights issues impact the federal-state balance, even if that consideration does not always appear on the face of the Court's decisions interpreting those rights.

Chapter 5

Congress and Congressional Powers

§ 5.01 Introduction

The Constitution assigns a great deal of importance to congressional power. Article I, which establishes Congress and sets out its powers, is longer than the articles creating the Executive and Judiciary combined. Article I begins by providing that "All legislative Powers herein granted shall be vested in a Congress." This Vesting Clause[1] is significant in at least two respects. First, it purports to grant to Congress *all* legislative powers it bestows. That language suggests that no other branch participates in the legislative process. But this is a false impression. The President participates in the Treaty Power,[2] is required to give Congress information about the state of the union and make legislative recommendations,[3] and is authorized to veto legislation,[4] all provisions that involve him in legislation.

Article I's Vesting Clause also signals the conceptually-limited nature of legislative power. Not "all legislative powers" are vested, but rather, only those "herein granted."[5] The "herein granted" language constitutes a limitation that appears in Article I's grant of legislative powers but not in the parallel clauses in Articles II and III. As we will see, this limitation plays an important role in challenges to federal laws based on claims that Congress has exceeded its Article I powers. Congressional authority is thus limited to those powers granted, even though, as a practical matter, the allowable subjects of federal legislation today comprise a massive and massively important array of topics.

This chapter addresses some of Congress's most significant powers. Section 5.02 begins by discussing the structure of Congress as an institution. Section 5.03 then considers the Necessary and Proper Clause, which has come to be understood as an

---

1. Similar vesting clauses introduce Articles II and III, pertaining, respectively, to "the executive power" and "the judicial power."

2. U.S. Const. art. II, § 2, cl. 2.

3. U.S. Const. art. II, § 3.

4. U.S. Const. art. I, § 7.

5. Article I later enumerates the subject-matters on which Congress can legislate. U.S. Const. art. I, §§ 7, 8. Amendments ratified later in our history have provided further topics on which Congress may legislate.

important source of congressional power.[6] Sections 5.04 through 5.06 then discuss, in turn, the General Welfare Clause and the taxing and spending powers it modifies. Those powers, and the General Welfare Clause to which they are appended, combine to give Congress enormous power over Americans' daily lives. Section 5.07 considers Congress's other fiscal powers, while Section 5.08 examines some of Article I's grants of regulatory power over domestic affairs. Sections 5.09 and 5.10 discuss, respectively, Congress's power over citizenship and naturalization and its power to advise and consent to treaties.[7]

Article I is not the only source of congressional power. The Constitution gives Congress the power to "enforce" many of the amendments to the Constitution. This book considers Congress's power to enforce the Thirteenth Amendment (abolishing slavery), the Fourteenth Amendment (prohibiting states from denying due process, equal protection, and the privileges and immunities of federal citizenship), and the Fifteenth Amendment (prohibiting racial discrimination in voting). Because it is difficult to understand those powers without understanding those amendments themselves, the book defers discussion of these enforcement powers until after it presents the Fourteenth Amendment itself.[8]

This discussion is still incomplete, however. The most important regulatory power Article I gives Congress is the power to regulate interstate commerce. That topic requires its own extended presentation, which this book provides in Chapter 6.

§ 5.02 The Structure of Congress

[1] Composition and Election

Congress consists of two houses, the Senate and House of Representatives, in which together are vested "[a]ll legislative powers ... granted"[9] in Article I. Article I defines the terms of each: members of the House are chosen for two year terms, while Senators are chosen for six-year terms[10] with one-third chosen every two years.[11] Each state has two Senators, while Representatives are allocated to states based on

---

6. Justice Scalia once implied the importance the Necessary and Proper Clause has taken on when he referred to it as "the last, best hope of those who defend *ultra vires* congressional action." Printz v. United States, 521 U.S. 898, 923 (1997). But he himself relied on that Clause. *See* Gonzalez v. Raich, 545 U.S. 1, 33 (2005) (Scalia, J., concurring in the judgment) (arguing that laws that regulate local activities that substantially affect interstate commerce are constitutional because they rest on the Necessary and Proper Clause, and finding the law in question to be constitutional on that basis).

7. Congress's power to declare war is considered in Section 3.10, given its co-mingling with the President's power as commander-in-chief of the armed forces.

8. *See* Chapter 13.

9. U.S. Const. art. I, § 1.

10. U.S. Const. art. I, § 2, cl. 1; § 3, cl. 1; amend. XVII.

11. U.S. Const. art. I, § 3, cl. 1.

population.[12] The bicameral legislature represented one of the critical compromises between the large and small states. The large states wanted representation based on population, while the small states insisted on equal state representation. The bicameral compromise with one house following each approach resolved that impasse. Representatives and senators are elected "by the People."[13] The Constitution confers a right of qualified voters "to cast their ballots and have them counted at congressional elections."[14] The Supreme Court has interpreted the words "by the People" to mean that, to the extent practicable, "one [person's] vote in a congressional election is to be worth as much as another's."[15] Thus, states must draw congressional districts so all voters in a state have substantially the same voice in electing their representatives.[16]

Initially, state legislatures elected Senators,[17] a process that was changed by constitutional amendment in 1913, when the Seventeenth Amendment mandated popular election of senators. That Amendment also provides for special elections to fill Senate vacancies and allows the state legislature to empower the Governor to fill vacancies pending special elections.

[2] Qualifications

The Constitution sets the qualifications for representatives and Senators. Senators must be at least 30 years and have been a U.S. citizen for nine years, while representatives must be at least 25 years old and have been citizens for seven years. Both senators and representatives must be inhabitants of the state they represent when elected.[18]

The House or Senate may not exclude someone who meets the specified qualifications. In *Powell v. McCormack*,[19] the Court reviewed action by the House in refusing to seat Representative Adam Clayton Powell in 1967 based on his alleged financial improprieties. Although the Constitution makes each house "the Judge of the Elections, Returns and Qualifications of its own members,"[20] the Court concluded that those "Qualifications" are limited to the three set out above. To be sure, each house may punish its members "for disorderly Behaviour" and expel them by a two-thirds vote.[21] However, *Powell* concluded that Congress could not refuse to seat a duly elected representative who met the Constitution's age, citizenship, and residency qualifications.

---

12. U.S. Const. art. I, § 2, cl. 1, 3; § 3, cl. 1.
13. U.S. Const. art. I, § 2, cl. 1; amend. XVII.
14. United States v. Classic, 313 U.S. 299, 315 (1941).
15. Wesberry v. Sanders, 376 U.S. 1, 7–8 (1964).
16. *Id.*; Kirkpatrick v. Preisler, 394 U.S. 526, 531 (1969). It is not constitutionally-mandated that House members represent individual districts. Rather, Congress made that choice by statute in 1842. Apportionment Act of 1842, ch. 47, § 2, 5 Stat. 491.
17. U.S. Const. art. I, § 3, cl. 1.
18. U.S. Const. art. I, § 2, cl. 2; § 3, cl. 2.
19. 395 U.S. 486 (1969).
20. U.S. Const. art. 1, § 5, cl. 1.
21. U.S. Const. art. I, § 5, cl. 2.

A quarter of a century after *Powell*, in *U.S. Term Limits v. Thornton*,[22] the Court held that the states, just like Congress itself, were prohibited from adding additional qualifications; thus, the Court struck down Arkansas's attempt to impose term limits on federal legislators. The Court reached that conclusion partly based on a textual argument. The respective Qualifications Clauses do not state that the qualifications listed are, or are not, exclusive. But just as the Court concluded in *Marbury* that the enumeration of two categories of cases in the Court's original jurisdiction signaled exclusivity, the Court implicitly concluded that the Qualifications Clauses, by setting some qualifications, implicitly disallowed the imposition of additional ones. The Court also deployed structural arguments. It argued that basic principle of democracy suggests citizens should be accorded maximum latitude in choosing their representatives. Moreover, it concluded that members of the House and Senate are representatives and servants of the Nation, not of the constituency that sends them. The Court reasoned that allowing individual states to impose additional qualifications on national representatives would allow them to obstruct the relationship between those representatives and the whole nation.[23]

Justice Thomas' dissent for four justices viewed the Qualifications Clauses as setting a constitutional floor, rather than a ceiling. On his view, the power to set additional qualifications was reserved to states by the Tenth Amendment. The majority rejected that argument, countering that the Amendment could only reserve powers states initially possessed; prior to the creation of the federal government, they had no power to add qualifications for federal officers, since those officers (and the federal government itself) did not exist.

The Article I Elections Clause gives states power to regulate the "times, places and manner of holding elections for Senators and Representatives" subject to Congress's authority to "make or alter such Regulations except as to the Places of choosing Senators."[24] This provision confers on the states "broad power" regarding *procedural* matters relating to congressional elections; it does not, however, license them to dictate electoral outcomes or favor a class of candidates. Thus, in *Cook v. Gralike*,[25] the Court struck down a Missouri law requiring the identification on the ballot of any candidate who failed to act in certain specified ways to advance a term limits amendment. Congress is not limited to regulating general elections; its power "includes the authority to regulate primary elections when ... they are a step in the exercise by the people of their choice of representatives in Congress."[26] The state's power includes providing for a recount under specified circumstances; a recount does not usurp Congress's power to judge elections and returns.[27]

---

22. 514 U.S. 779, 783 (1995). *See generally* Kathleen M. Sullivan, *Dueling Sovereignties*: U.S. Term Limits, Inc. v. Thornton, 109 HARV. L. REV. 78 (1995).

23. This aspect of *U.S. Term Limits* is discussed in more detail in Section 4.02.

24. U.S. CONST. art. I, §4, cl. 1.

25. Cook v. Gralike, 531 U.S. 510, 523–26 (2001).

26. United States v. Classic, 313 U.S. 299, 317 (1941).

27. Roudebush v. Hartke, 405 U.S. 15, 25–26 (1972).

[3] Lawmaking Procedures

The Constitution prescribes certain procedures Congress must follow when legislating. In order for a bill to become "a law," it must pass the House and Senate in identical form (bicameralism) and be "presented" to the President for signature or veto (presentment).[28] The Constitution does not use the word "veto," referring instead to the President's prerogative to "return a bill" to the originating chamber with "his objections."[29] Congress can then enact the bill only with a two-thirds majority in each house.

Although the Court has upheld delegations of quasi-legislative power to administrative agencies, it has not allowed Congress to deviate from bicameralism and presentment. For instance, during the last two-thirds of the twentieth century, Congress began to attach "legislative veto" provisions to measures authorizing the executive branch or administrative agencies to regulate. These veto provisions took different forms but generally allowed Congress as a whole, one house, or one committee, to reverse an executive or administrative action. Such legislative vetoes were struck down in *Immigration and Naturalization Service v. Chadha*.[30] *Chadha* was examined in Chapter 3's discussion of the separation of powers between Congress and the President.[31]

On occasions, the Constitution assigns different duties to the two houses of Congress. Thus, only the Senate has a role in giving advice and consenting to treaties and to appointment of officers the President nominates. The House has the sole power to impeach, whereas the Senate has the sole power to try impeachments. Both the House and Senate must approve revenue bills like other legislation. Yet all bills for the raising of revenue must "originate" in the House, although the Senate may "propose or concur with amendments."[32]

[4] Legislative Immunity

The Speech or Debate Clause[33] assures Congress wide freedom of speech, debate, and deliberation in the legislative process.[34] It protects congressional independence against "prosecution by an unfriendly executive and conviction by a hostile judiciary."[35] The main purpose of the Clause is to allow Congress to legislate without fear of criminal prosecution. The Clause is "read broadly, to include not only 'words spoken in

---

28. U.S. Const. art. I. §7, cl. 2.

29. *Id.*

30. 462 U.S. 919 (1983).

31. *See* Section 3.08[3].

32. U.S. Const. art. I, §7; *see* Flint v. Stone Tracy Co., 220 U.S. 107, 142–43 (1911).

33. U.S. Const. art. I, §6, cl. 1 ("[The Senators and Representatives] shall in all Cases, except Treason, Felony and Breach of the Peace, be privileged from Arrest during their Attendance at the Session of their respective Houses, and in going to and returning from the same; and for any Speech or Debate in either House, they shall not be questioned in any other Place.").

34. Gravel v. United States, 408 U.S. 606, 616 (1972).

35. United States v. Johnson, 383 U.S. 169, 179 (1966).

debate,' but anything 'generally done in a session of [Congress] by one of its members in relation to the business before it.'"[36] Thus, the Speech or Debate Clause confers legislative immunity for, among other activities, written reports and votes in Congress,[37] the investigative work of congressional committees,[38] and the placing of classified documents in the official public record.[39] Thus, the Clause precluded a prosecution based upon inquiries into the motivations and language of a Congressperson's speech on the House floor.[40] It does not insulate a member of Congress from scrutiny by the house in which they serve or by their electorate.

The Clause does not generally immunize members of Congress from criminal prosecution relating to all acts they regularly perform. In *United States v. Brewster*,[41] the Supreme Court overturned a district court dismissal of the government's indictment of a former senator for bribery. The Court distinguished between "purely legislative activities" protected by the Speech or Debate Clause and "political" activities the Clause does not protect.[42] The Clause's privilege extends only to what is necessary to preserve the integrity of the legislative process—a limitation, the Court held, which excludes the bribe-taking with which the Senator was charged. For that reason, the Speech or Debate Clause provided him no protection from the prosecution.

Gravel v. United States[43] implicated not only the Speech or Debate Clause at the end of Article I, Section 6, clause 1, but the Privilege from Arrest Clause which precedes it. Congressman Gravel read from the classified "Pentagon Papers" during a subcommittee meeting, placed the 47-volume study in the public record, and arranged for its private republication. The government subpoenaed Gravel's congressional aide to testify before a grand jury investigating the private republication. Gravel intervened, claiming that the Speech or Debate Clause privilege applied to the private republication of the Pentagon Papers and protected his aide as well as himself.

The Court held that the Privilege from Arrest Clause exempts members of Congress from arrest in civil cases only.[44] The narrow scope of that privilege reflects "the judgment that legislators ought not to stand above the law they create but ought generally

---

36. *Id.* at 179 (quoting Kilbourn v. Thompson, 103 U.S. 168, 204 (1880)).

37. *Kilbourn*, 103 U.S. at 204.

38. Eastland v. U.S. Servicemen's Fund, 421 U.S. 491, 504 (1975); Tenney v. Brandhove, 341 U.S. 367, 377 (1951).

39. *Gravel*, 408 U.S. at 615–16.

40. *Johnson*, 383 U.S. at 184–85.

41. 408 U.S. 501 (1972).

42. *Id.* at 512. "Political" activities include a "wide range of legitimate 'errands' performed for constituents, the making of appointments with Government agencies, assistance in securing Government contracts, preparing … 'news letters' to constituents, news releases, and speeches delivered outside the Congress." *Id.*

43. 408 U.S. 606 (1972).

44. *Id.* at 614. The Court explained that, during the founding era, arrests in civil cases were still common. *See ibid.*

to be bound by it as are ordinary persons."[45] Members are not exempt from service, the obligations of subpoena, or "from testifying at trials or grand jury proceedings involving third-party crimes where the questions do not require testimony about or impugn a legislative act."[46] The Speech or Debate Clause protected Senator Gravel from "question[ing] in any other Place for any speech or debate in either House."[47] However, it did not protect him from prosecution for the private republication of the Pentagon Papers, activity "in no way essential to the deliberations of the Senate."[48] Because of the Senator's lack of protection for that latter conduct, his aide was similarly unshielded, even though the Court observed that the Clause's protections as a general matter extend equally to a congressperson's aide.

§ 5.03 Implied Congressional Powers under the Necessary and Proper Clause

Article I, Section 8 sets forth Congress's regulatory powers. After providing a list of discrete powers (for example, to regulate interstate commerce and enact bankruptcy laws), Section 8 ends by giving Congress the power "To make all Laws which shall be necessary and proper for carrying into Execution the foregoing Powers, and all other Powers vested by this Constitution in the Government of the United States, or in any Department or Officer thereof."[49] The Necessary and Proper Clause has become an important source of congressional power to enact laws that relate to, but are not explicitly encompassed by, the more discrete powers given to Congress in Article I and elsewhere in the Constitution.

In *McCulloch v. Maryland*,[50] Chief Justice Marshall established the fundamental meaning and importance of the Necessary and Proper Clause. *McCulloch* considered the constitutionality of the Bank of the United States, an institution Congress created as a depository for federal funds and a source of bank notes. The Constitution did not expressly authorize the federal government to establish a national bank. However, it did confer the power to impose and collect taxes, to borrow money, to regulate commerce, to declare war, and to support armies and navies, all of which a national bank would facilitate. Moreover, the first Congress had created a bank. Its charter had not been renewed. After the War of 1812, Congress re-established it.

Marshall began his opinion by arguing that the historical experience with, and the acquiescence to, the Bank after long debate created a presumption in favor of its constitutionality. In essence, Marshall argued that historical practice can shape consti-

---

45. *Id.* at 615.
46. *Id.* at 622.
47. *Id.* at 615.
48. *Id.* at 625.
49. U.S. CONST. art. I, § 8, cl. 18.
50. 17 U.S. (4 Wheat.) 316 (1819). On *McCulloch* generally, see MARK. R. KILLENBECK, M'CULLOCH V. MARYLAND: SECURING A NATION (2006).

tutional meaning. The argument was certainly a respectable one that other justices have adopted.[51] Marshall thought the arguments based on ongoing practice were relevant and persuasive but not essential; they were not advanced "under the impression, that, were the question entirely new, the law would be found irreconcilable with the Constitution."[52]

Marshall preferred to rely on a more general and ambitious theory of congressional power. He used textual arguments to bolster his claim that the Constitution gave Congress implied, as well as enumerated, powers. Unlike the Articles of Confederation, the Constitution did not limit Congress to powers "expressly" granted. Moreover, Article I, Section 9 contained some limitations on powers not expressly granted to Congress. Marshall asked his readers why the Constitution would include such limitations on Congress if Congress lacked implied powers that might otherwise transgress Section 9's limits? But Marshall's primary argument came from the Constitution's structure. No one could expect a Constitution to specify all the specific powers and means to implement those powers that it conferred, he argued. To do so, the Constitution "would partake of the prolixity of a legal code." The people would not understand such a document, Marshall argued, an implicit expression of his view of its democratic character. He then added to his opinion a statement that has since become canonical: "we must never forget that it is a *constitution* we are expounding."[53] By this statement, Marshall argued that the Constitution should be construed in a way to allow the government it created to succeed and to respond to future needs, not to create obstacles destined to frustrate it at each turn.

In *McCulloch*, John Marshall argued that the enumeration of the major powers, set forth in Article I, Section 8, implied the existence of those needed to carry them out:

> But it may with great reason be contended, that a government, entrusted with such ample powers, on the due execution of which the happiness and prosperity of the nation so vitally depends, must also be intrusted with ample means for their execution. The power being given, it is the interest of the nation to facilitate its execution.[54]

This was a compelling structural argument with logical plausibility. Moreover, it seemed consistent with the Framers' likely intent. Just as Hamilton's *Federalist 78* supported Marshall's conclusions regarding judicial review in *Marbury*, so, too did Madison's *Federalist 44* provide originalist support for Marshall's doctrine of implied powers in *McCulloch*. Even had the Constitution not contained the Necessary and Proper Clause, wrote Madison, "there can be no doubt that all the particular powers requisite as means of executing the general powers would have resulted to the gov-

---

51. *See, e.g.,* Dames & Moore v. Regan, 453 U.S. 654, 686 (1981); Youngstown Sheet & Tube Co. v. Sawyer, 343 U.S. 579, 610–11 (1952) (Frankfurter, J., concurring); United States v. Midwest Oil Co., 236 U.S. 459, 474 (1915).

52. *McCulloch,* 17 U.S. at 402.

53. *Id.* at 407 (emphasis in original).

54. *McCulloch,* 17 U.S. at 408; *see also* THE FEDERALIST No. 44 (Madison).

ernment by unavoidable implication." Madison thought it basic that "wherever the end is required, the means are authorized; wherever a general power to do a thing is given, every particular power necessary for doing it is included."[55] To take a simple example used by Marshall himself, the power Section 8 granted Congress "[t]o establish Post Offices and post Roads"[56] implied the power to punish postal theft.[57]

After articulating his theory as an implication of the Constitution's structure,[58] Marshall proceeded to connect it to the Necessary and Proper Clause. *McCulloch* rejected the view that the Necessary and Proper Clause conferred on Congress power only to pass laws that were "absolutely necessary." By authorizing it to make "necessary" laws, the Constitution could not have meant to confine Congress to those laws that were indispensable. Elsewhere the Constitution used the phrase "absolutely necessary." Thus, he argued, "necessary" must impose a less exacting standard which must be broadly construed.

Nor was "necessary" a limitation on Congress's power, as Maryland argued, especially because the Clause was listed with the grants of powers in Section 8, not the limits set forth in Section 9. Using language that again has become foundational, he wrote, "Let the end be legitimate, let it be within the scope of the Constitution, and all means which are appropriate, which are plainly adapted to that end, which are not prohibited, but consist with the letter and spirit of the Constitution are constitutional."[59]

Marshall's construction enabled the Necessary and Proper Clause to become an important source of federal legislative authority. Later Supreme Court opinions have repeated his formulation. Thus, in *The Legal Tender Cases*, Justice Strong argued that "in the judgment of those who adopted the Constitution, there were powers created by it, neither expressly specified nor deducible from any one specified power, or ancillary to it alone, but which grew out of the aggregate of powers conferred upon the government, or out of the sovereignty instituted."[60] Similarly, in *Ex parte Yarborough*, Justice Miller explained that constitutional interpretation must embrace the doctrine "universally applied" to written instruments, "that what is implied is as much a part of the instrument as what is expressed."[61] This principle is necessarily applied to constitutional interpretation, Justice Miller wrote, "by reason of the inherent inability to put into words all derivative powers,"[62] a difficulty the Constitution recognized by including the Necessary and Proper Clause.

The clause has stretched many powers of the federal government. Of course, it does not authorize Congress to do anything which is "necessary and proper." Rather,

---

55. THE FEDERALIST No. 44 (Madison); *see also* THE FEDERALIST No. 33 (Hamilton).

56. U.S. CONST. art. I, § 8, cl. 7.

57. *McCulloch*, 17 U.S. at 385.

58. *See* CHARLES L. BLACK, JR., STRUCTURE AND RELATIONSHIP IN CONSTITUTIONAL LAW, 22–33 (1969).

59. *McCulloch*, 17 U.S. (4 Wheat.) at 421.

60. 79 U.S. (12 Wall.) 457, 535 (1870).

61. 110 U.S. 651, 658 (1884).

62. *Ibid.*

the license to legislate extends only to laws necessary and proper "for carrying into execution" other powers set out in the Constitution. Thus, legislation grounded on the clause must also relate to some other constitutional provision. But those provisions are not limited to the Article I, Section 8 list of congressional powers. Instead, it relates to "the foregoing powers" (*i.e.*, Article I powers) as well as to "all other powers vested by this Constitution in the Government of the United States, or in any Department or officer thereof." In other words, the clause does not simply confer additional congressional power with respect to other grants of power to Congress. It confers power on Congress to legislate to give effect to every other power in the Constitution. Thus, the authority of Congress under the clause includes power to pass laws to carry out treaties,[63] to organize a department of government,[64] to collect revenue,[65] to acquire property by eminent domain,[66] to make treasury notes legal tender,[67] to create corporations,[68] to exclude and deport aliens,[69] to pass banking laws,[70] to determine marine law,[71] to regulate the civil service,[72] to address foreign affairs,[73] to build the Capitol and White House,[74] to protect voters from intimidation,[75] and to enact the Federal Criminal Code.[76]

The Supreme Court reiterated the breadth of the Necessary and Proper Clause in *United States v. Comstock*,[77] when it upheld Congress's power to enact a statute authorizing the civil commitment of mentally ill, sexually dangerous federal prisoners after their criminal sentences ended. The Court rejected Justice Thomas's argument in dissent that the Necessary and Proper Clause only allows Congress to pursue means which directly execute an enumerated power.

Embracing a broader conception of the Necessary and Proper Clause, Justice Breyer's majority opinion rested its conclusion on five factors, considered together. The Court reasoned that the Necessary and Proper Clause conferred a broad power which allowed Congress to pursue means which were connected by a chain of reasoning to any enumerated power. The Constitution grants few enumerated powers to create federal crimes (counterfeiting, treason, piracies and felonies on the high seas) yet Congress has criminalized much conduct (*e.g.*, mail theft and fraud) as a

---

63. *See* Neely v. Henkel, 180 U.S. 109, 121 (1901).

64. *See* Boske v. Comingore, 177 U.S. 459 (1900).

65. *See* Murray v. Hoboken Land & Improvement Co., 59 U.S. (13 How.) 272, 281 (1856).

66. *See* Kohl v. United States, 91 U.S. (1 Otto) 367 (1875).

67. *See* Legal Tender Cases, 79 U.S. (12 Wall.) 457 (1871).

68. *See* McCulloch, 17 U.S. (4 Wheat.) 316 (1819).

69. *See* Fong Yue Ting v. United States, 149 U.S. 698 (1893).

70. *See* Franklin Nat. Bank of Franklin Square v. People of New York, 347 U.S. 373 (1954).

71. *See* Swanson v. Marra Bros., 328 U.S. 1 (1946).

72. *See* White v. Berry, 171 U.S. 366 (1898).

73. *See* Kennedy v. Mendoza-Martinez, 372 U.S. 144 (1963).

74. *See* Legal Tender Cases, 79 U.S. at 535.

75. *See* Ex parte Yarbrough, 110 U.S. 651 (1884).

76. *See* Logan v. United States, 144 U.S. 263, 283–84 (1892); United States v. Hall, 98 U.S. 343 (1879); United States v. Fox, 95 U.S. 670 (1878).

77. 560 U.S. 126 (2010).

means to enforce various enumerated powers (*e.g.*, to establish a system of post roads and regulate interstate commerce). Having done so, it may also use the Necessary and Proper Clause to establish a federal prison system, regulate its administration and adopt other criminal laws to protect against threats to it as means reasonably related to those ends.

Continuing, the Court pointed out that a long history of governmental conduct offered precedents for the civil commitment statute at issue, and concluded that this ongoing history was suggestive, though not conclusive, of the statute's constitutionality. Moreover, Congress was acting in an area where the federal government had a responsibility as custodian of federal prisoners. The statute also accounted for state interests by requiring that the Department of Justice contact the state which would have jurisdiction over the prisoner and surrender him or her to that state if it prefers to accept responsibility. Finally, Justice Breyer observed that the statute was not too remote from an enumerated power, nor was it too sweeping. The combination of these (sometimes vague) factors established the constitutionality of the statute. Given that vagueness, *Comstock* left many questions regarding how broadly it will apply these five considerations in future cases.

In 2012, a five-justice majority rejected the Necessary and Proper Clause as a constitutional justification for the Affordable Care Act's (ACA's) requirement that most Americans purchase health insurance.[78] Writing for himself only, Chief Justice Roberts concluded that it was not "necessary" or "proper" for Congress to create the predicate for the use of its commerce regulation power by requiring persons to participate in interstate commerce (by requiring them to purchase insurance). In other words, because, in his view, Congress can only "regulate" commerce that already exists, it was not necessary and proper to that regulatory power to require that persons enter into commerce by requiring them to purchase insurance. Justice Scalia, writing for himself and three other justices, reached the same conclusion by reasoning that there were other ways for Congress to reach its regulatory goals, and because, in his view, accepting the government's Necessary and Proper Clause argument would allow government to regulate anything.[79]

The ACA case may ultimately become viewed as an outlier, given the statute's unusual provision requiring persons to purchase a product. Beyond that unusual circumstance, the Necessary and Proper Clause remains a source of broad congressional power. To be sure, the expansive uses of the Necessary and Proper Clause does have its critics. As noted earlier, Justice Scalia once dismissed over-reliance on the Clause by describing it as "the last, best hope of those who defend *ultra vires* congressional action."[80] He thus argued that a law executing the Commerce Clause which infringed

---

78. National Federation of Ind. Bus. v. Sebelius, 567 U.S. 519 (2012).

79. *Id.* at 654–55 (Scalia, J., dissenting). His opinion was characterized as a dissent because, while a majority of the Court agreed with him that the Commerce and Necessary and Proper Clauses did not authorize the ACA's individual mandate, a majority also agreed that the mandate was constitutional as a tax.

80. Printz v. United States, 521 U.S. 898, 923 (1997).

on state sovereignty was not a *"proper"* law.[81] Nonetheless, the Necessary and Proper Clause has proven a powerful source of national power when appended to the Commerce Clause, a topic discussed in the next chapter, or when coupled with other clauses.

§ 5.04 Legislation to Provide for "The General Welfare"

Although the Constitution expressly uses the term "general welfare" in the Tax and Spend Clause,[82] the Constitution accords the federal government no blanket police power to promote public welfare. Article I, Section 8 begins by providing that: "The Congress shall have Power to lay and collect Taxes, Duties, Imposts and Excises, to pay the Debts and provide for the common Defence and general Welfare of the United States."[83] Despite some contrary contentions, the generally-accepted view is that this clause does not delegate blanket authority to the federal government to promote the general welfare, a position which would render the rest of Section 8 superfluous. On this view, the General Welfare Clause is not an independent grant of power, but a qualification of the taxing and spending powers.

The founders did not agree on how the clause qualified those powers. James Madison thought the taxing and spending power was confined to the enumerated fields the Constitution committed to Congress.[84] Thus, on Madison's view, Congress could tax and spend only to implement the particularized grants of legislative power in the rest of Section 8 (for example, the power to regulate interstate commerce). Disagreeing, Alexander Hamilton thought the General Welfare Clause provided additional power not limited by the scope of other enumerated powers. He thought Congress could tax and spend as appropriate to advance the general welfare.[85] In *United States v. Butler*,[86] the Supreme Court endorsed Hamilton's view. It concluded: "While, therefore, the power to tax is not unlimited, its confines are set in the clause which confers it, and not in those of section 8 which bestow and define the legislative powers of the Congress. It results that the power of Congress to authorize expenditure of public moneys for public purposes is not limited by the direct grants of legislative power found in the Constitution."[87]

Thus, Congress can tax and spend for the general welfare of the United States.[88] In conjunction with the Necessary and Proper Clause,[89] the General Welfare Clause,

---

81. *Id.* at 923–24 (emphasis in original).
82. U.S. Const. art. I., § 8, cl. 1.
83. *Ibid.*
84. *See* The Federalist No. 41 (Madison).
85. *See* The Federalist No. 34 (Hamilton).
86. 297 U.S. 1 (1936).
87. *Id.* at 66.
88. *See* Buckley v. Valeo, 424 U.S. 1, 90 (1976).
89. *See id.*

though only a qualification of the taxing and spending power, confers generous authority.

§ 5.05 The Taxing Power

[1] The Breadth of the Power to Tax

The Constitution gives the federal government a broad power to tax for all national purposes. Indeed, the founders appreciated that allowing government to tax many objects would have several advantages. For example, it would distribute the taxation burden across industries and across states.[90]

To be sure, Congress may exercise this authority only to "provide for the common Defense and general Welfare." But, as suggested in the previous section, these purposes impose slight if any limits at all; indeed, the Court has described the general welfare provision as a grant of power, not a limitation on it.[91] Thus, the constitutional text provides a broad taxing power. Congress, not the courts, determines whether a given exercise of the tax power will promote the general welfare, and courts will overturn Congress's conclusion only in an extreme case.[92] The Court has consistently refused to pass on the "reasonableness" of a tax otherwise within the power of Congress.[93] Further, "general welfare" is not a static concept but one which changes to accommodate historical events.[94]

Although the Constitution provides that "direct Taxes shall be apportioned among the several States ... according to their respective Numbers,"[95] this provision has imposed little restraint on Congress's power.[96] The Court essentially limited direct taxes to those on real property and capitation[97] and accordingly left Congress broad latitude to impose "indirect taxes."[98] Although the Court declared a federal income tax unconstitutional in a 5–4 decision in *Pollock v. Farmers' Loan & Trust Co.*,[99] the decision seemed based in part on the conclusion that the income tax impacted real property and thus was a direct tax which needed to be apportioned. In any event, the Sixteenth

---

90. *See* THE FEDERALIST No. 35 (Hamilton).

91. *See Buckley*, 424 U.S. at 90.

92. *See* Helvering v. Davis, 301 U.S. 619 640 (1937) ("The discretion belongs to Congress, unless the choice is clearly wrong, a display of arbitrary power, not an exercise of judgment.").

93. *See* Pittsburgh v. Alco Parking Corp., 417 U.S. 369, 373 (1974).

94. *Helvering*, 301 U.S. at 641.

95. U.S. CONST. art. I., § 2.

96. *See also* U.S. CONST. art. I, § 9 ("No Capitation or other direct, Tax shall be laid unless in Proportion to the Census.").

97. *See* Veazie Bank v. Fenno, 75 U.S. (8 Wall.) 533, 544 (1869). A capitation tax, sometimes called a "head tax," is a tax imposed on a person in an amount regardless of the person's income, wealth, or any other characteristic.

98. *See, e.g., id.* (tax on state bank notes was indirect); Springer v. United States, 102 U.S. 586 (1881) (Civil War Income Tax imposed indirect tax); Hylton v. United States, 3 U.S. (3 Dall.) 171 (1796) (tax on carriages was indirect).

99. 157 U.S. 429 (1895).

Amendment overturned *Pollock* in 1913.[100] The direct tax prohibition seems to have theoretical significance at most,[101] unless perhaps Congress imposes a national tax on real property.

[2] The Purposes of Taxation

Governments tax primarily to obtain revenue to fund government spending. Yet taxation inevitably has economic and regulatory consequences. Significantly, the Constitution's text does not restrict the taxing power to revenue generation. Rather, Congress may tax to promote the general welfare. "[T]he power to tax," John Marshall famously observed, "involves the power to destroy."[102] But it may produce other results, too. "It is not only the power to destroy, but it is also the power to keep alive."[103] Taxation to preserve has been relatively uncontroversial. Congress initially used the taxing power to impose tariffs to protect American industry from foreign competition. It still uses the taxing power for that purpose.

Taxation also provides a means to regulate. A tax might suppress an undesirable activity by raising the cost of engaging in it. For example, in *McCray v. United States*,[104] the Court rejected the proposition that it might strike down a tax formally within Congress's power based on legislative motive. In *McCray*, Congress had imposed a steeper tax on margarine colored to resemble butter than on uncolored margarine. The tax was challenged as an impermissible attempt to control the manufacture of margarine, a matter beyond the commerce power as then construed. The Court dismissed the argument. Congress's power depended on what authority the Constitution conferred, not on "the consequence arising from the exercise of the lawful authority."[105] The tax raised revenue, and accordingly, it was within Congress's power. Neither Congress's purpose nor the measure's effect altered the analysis.

McCray left open the possibility that the Court might intervene in case of an extreme abuse of the taxing power, "where it was plain to the judicial mind that the power had been called into play, not for revenue, but solely for the purpose of destroying rights which could not be rightfully destroyed consistently with the principles of freedom and justice upon which the Constitution rests."[106] The *Child Labor Tax Case*[107] posed the problem whether the taxing power allowed Congress to reach an activity otherwise beyond its regulatory power. The Court had invalidated as exceeding Congress's Commerce Clause power a federal law barring from interstate commerce

---

100. That amendment states: "The Congress shall have power to lay and collect taxes on incomes, from whatever source derived, without apportionment among the several States, and without regard to any census or enumeration."

101. *See* Flint v. Stone Tracy Co., 220 U.S. 107 (1911).

102. McCulloch v. Maryland, 17 U.S. (4 Wheat) 316, 431 (1819).

103. Nicol v. Ames, 173 U.S. 509, 515 (1899).

104. 195 U.S. 27 (1904).

105. *Id.* at 59.

106. *Id.* at 64.

107. Bailey v. Drexel Furniture Co., 259 U.S. 20 (1922).

products made by child labor.[108] Congress then taxed the profits earned by companies that employed children. The legislative intent was no mystery: Congress sought to use its taxing power to accomplish what it could not achieve under the Commerce Clause. The Court found the tax invalid. Writing for the Court, Chief Justice Taft reasoned that the regulatory motive was apparent on the very face of the statute; it did not require supposition.

United States v. Butler[109] applied the *Child Labor Tax* approach. The Agricultural Adjustment Act of 1933 used incentives to restrict farm production. It taxed agricultural commodities and distributed the proceeds to farmers who decreased production. This exercise was intended to regulate agricultural production, a matter then deemed, like manufacturing in the *Child Labor Tax* case, beyond Congress's regulatory power. The Court held the tax unconstitutional. Because Congress could not, under then prevailing Commerce Clause decisions, directly regulate agricultural production, it thus could not regulate such production under the guise of exercising the taxing power. The tax was void, not because it was not a tax for the general welfare,[110] but because an improper motive inspired it.

The Court has since repudiated the limitation *Butler* imposed on the taxing power. Instead, it has embraced the *McCray* approach of deferring to Congress. For example, in *Sonzinsky v. United States*,[111] the Court upheld excise taxes imposed on dealers, manufacturers and importers of firearms. On its face, the law was "only a taxing measure" and the fact that it might deter some commerce in firearms did not invalidate that feature. "Every tax is in some measure regulatory," wrote Justice Stone. "To some extent it interposes an economic impediment to the activity taxed as compared with others not taxed. But a tax is not any the less a tax because it has a regulatory effect."[112] In support of that conclusion, the Court noted that the tax did in fact raise revenue.[113]

Thirteen years later, the Court articulated the principle even more expansively in *United States v. Sanchez.*[114] A tax is not invalid "merely because it regulates, discourages, or even definitely deters the activities taxed," even though it generates little revenue and treats raising revenue as a secondary purpose at best.[115]

In 2012, the Court upheld the Affordable Care Act's (ACA's) requirement that most Americans purchase health insurance.[116] While only four justices would have upheld the so-called "individual mandate" as a regulation of interstate commerce, a

---

108. Hammer v. Dagenhart, 247 U.S. 251 (1918).

109. 297 U.S. 1 (1936).

110. Recall from earlier in this Chapter that it was the *Butler* Court that decided that the taxing and spending powers were independent from the regulatory powers provided Congress elsewhere in Article I, Section 8.

111. 300 U.S. 506 (1937).

112. *Id.* at 513.

113. *See id.* at 514 n. 1.

114. 340 U.S. 42 (1950).

115. *Id. at 44.*

116. National Federation of Ind. Business v. Sebelius, 567 U.S. 519 (2012).

majority of five (those same four justices plus Chief Justice Roberts) upheld it as a tax, since a person's failure to purchase insurance triggered what the Court called a tax on that decision. Writing for that majority, Chief Justice Roberts explained that the tax was not so high that it denied persons a realistic choice whether to forego insurance and choose to pay the tax, it applied even to unintentional failures to comply with the individual mandate, as taxes often do (but as regulations do less often), and it was collected by the Internal Revenue Service just like any other tax.

Though broad, the tax power may not be exercised in violation of constitutional rights. Thus, Congress may not impose a tax on newspapers alone in violation of the First Amendment[117] or use the taxing power to compel self-incrimination barred by the Fifth Amendment.[118]

§ 5.06 The Spending Power

The same clause that confers the power to tax also conveys the power to spend. It provides that "The Congress shall have power ... to pay the debts and provide for the common defense and general welfare of the United States...." As with the taxing power discussed in the previous section, Congress is accorded broad discretion to decide which expenditures will promote the general welfare.[119]

United States v. Butler,[120] discussed in the two prior sections, construed the Spending Clause as well as the Taxing Clause. It held that the spending power, just like the taxing power, was not limited to the purposes set out in Article I's specific grants of legislative power, but rather extended beyond those grants so long as exercised to provide for the general welfare. In so doing, the Court again adopted the Hamiltonian approach to the taxing and spending power, rather than the approach Madison advocated. But the Court cautioned that Congress must pursue "matters of national as distinguished from local, welfare."[121] It thus invalidated a federal expenditure for a "local" end that Congress could not directly attain. The spending scheme was unconstitutional because its purpose was to regulate agricultural production, a "local" end prohibited to Congress under the then-prevailing interpretation of Congress's power under the Interstate Commerce Clause.

---

117. *See* Grosjean v. American Press Co., 297 U.S. 233 (1936).

118. *See* Marchetti v. United States, 390 U.S. 39 (1968) (finding a violation of the right against self-incrimination when a tax was imposed on an illegal activity, thus trapping persons into either paying the tax and thereby incriminating themselves or not paying it and exposing themselves to prosecution for tax avoidance).

119. Buckley v. Valeo, 424 U.S. 1, 90 (1976); South Dakota v. Dole, 483 U.S. 203, 207 (1987) ("In considering whether a particular expenditure is intended to serve general public purposes, courts should defer substantially to the judgment of Congress."); Helvering v. Davis, 301 U.S. 619, 640 (1937).

120. 297 U.S. 1 (1936).

121. *Id.* at 67.

The Court has subsequently rejected *Butler*'s limitation on the spending power, just as it has rejected its analogous limitation on the taxing power. Thus, courts will not closely examine a taxing or a spending measure to ferret out an improper purpose.[122] Funds disbursed to advance Congress's vision of the general welfare are not suspect simply because they act in an area Congress cannot regulate directly. Thus, for example, Congress may condition expenditures on terms it sets in order to attain regulatory goals.[123]

The federal government often uses its Spending Clause power to distribute money to states. A separate question, based on state sovereignty, is raised when Congress attaches conditions on states' receipt of federal funds. This aspect of the spending power is discussed in Chapter 8.

§ 5.07 Congress' Other Fiscal Powers

Congress' other fiscal powers rest on its powers to borrow[124] and to coin money.[125] These grants, combined with the implied powers from the Necessary and Proper Clause, give Congress the fiscal powers generally associated with sovereignty.[126] *McCulloch* held that the fiscal powers of Congress include the authority to charter banks with the right to issue circulating notes. *McCulloch*'s logic gave Congress sweeping authority over currency. The Court relied on *McCulloch* in approving other federal measures relating to the banking system.[127]

Controversy arose, however, over the federal government's power to make its notes legal tender, a question the Supreme Court addressed in connection with the "greenbacks" issued during the Civil War (the precursors to our modern currency). The relevant statute made those Treasury notes legal tender at face value. The *Legal Tender Cases*[128] held that the nation's fiscal powers included authority to issue paper money as legal tender. The power to coin money included authority to make Treasury notes legal tender to carry into execution the government's powers. In so ruling, the Court overturned a divided decision of the prior year, in part due to changes in court personnel.[129]

---

122. *Cf.* South Dakota v. Dole, 483 U.S. 203, 207 (1987) (Court should defer to Congress regarding the propriety of an expenditure).

123. *See* Lau v. Nichols, 414 U.S. 563, 569 (1974).

124. U.S. Const. art. I, § 8, cl. 2 ("The Congress shall have power ... to borrow money on the credit of the United States.").

125. *Id.*; U.S. Const. art. I, § 8, cl. 5 ("The Congress shall have power ... to coin money, regulate the value thereof, and of foreign coin.").

126. *See* The Legal Tender Cases, 110 U.S. 421, 447 (1884) (sovereignty); Norman v. Baltimore & O.R. Co., 294 U.S. 240, 303 (1935) (inclusion of Necessary and Proper Clause into the analysis).

127. *See, e.g.*, Farmers' & Mechanics' Nat'l Bank v. Dearing, 91 U.S. 29, 33 (1875); First Nat'l Bank v. Fellows, 244 U.S. 416 (1917); Smith v. Kansas City Title & Trust Co., 255 U.S. 180 (1921).

128. 79 U.S. 457 (1871), *overruling* Hepburn v. Griswold, 75 U.S. (8 Wall.) 603 (1870).

129. *See Hepburn*, 75 U.S. at 637–39 (striking down portions of the Legal Tender Acts).

The Constitution gives Congress authority to "regulate the Value" of currency.[130] Beyond merely setting the face value of money, Congress can also regulate the value of the monetary unit by varying its gold content. *Norman v. Baltimore & O. R. Co.*[131] arose from congressional and executive action reducing the gold content of the dollar. That action also abrogated any "gold clauses" in private contracts calling for payment in gold. The holder of a bond with an interest coupon payable in gold, issued before the gold content of the dollar was lowered, sued for payment in gold or for its equivalent in legal tender. The Court held the payee must accept the devalued dollars. Congress may determine what constitutes valid money and fix its value. Congress could also alter rights from private contracts, such as the gold clauses. Pursuant to its power to regulate currency, Congress cannot, however, use this power to vary the terms of its own obligations. In *Perry v. United States*,[132] the Court held that Congress could not abrogate gold clauses in federal government contracts.

§ 5.08 Other Domestic Regulatory Powers

Article I, Section 8, along with other parts of the Constitution, provides Congress with a variety of other significant legislative powers, only some of which are discussed here. The power to establish "uniform Laws on the subject of Bankruptcies"[133] has allowed Congress to enact a comprehensive bankruptcy code and create bankruptcy courts, to ensure that debtors and creditors are not trapped in a patchwork system of inconsistent state laws and potentially conflicting judgments arising out of the fortuity of the location of creditors, debtors, or the debtor's assets. The requirement that such laws be "uniform" has been construed to require simply that such laws operate equally on every creditor and debtor. Thus, for example, a special bankruptcy statute made applicable to railroads in particular parts of the nation did not fail the uniformity requirement simply because it applied only to firms in particular regions, since it treated equally all debtors and creditors of the targeted railroads.[134]

Clause 9 of Article I, Section 8 authorizes Congress to enact patent and copyright laws.[135] It too has been given a broad construction. Most notably, even though the clause speaks of granting patent and copyright rights "for limited Times," in 2003, the Court upheld a law that, in addition to providing longer terms for new copyrights, extended to the same length copyrights that had already been issued.[136] In upholding

---

130. U.S. Const. art. I, § 8, cl. 5.

131. 294 U.S. 240 (1935).

132. 294 U.S. 330 (1935).

133. U.S. Const. art. I, § 8, cl. 4.

134. *See* Blanchette v. Conn. Gen. Ins. Corp., 419 U.S. 102, 159–160 (1974).

135. U.S. Const. art. I, § 8, cl. 8 (giving Congress the power "To promote the Progress of Science and useful Arts, by securing for limited Times to Authors and Inventors the exclusive Right to their respective Writings and Discoveries.").

136. Eldred v. Ashcroft, 537 U.S. 186 (2003).

that law, the Court stated that Congress need only act rationally in extending such periods, an inquiry on which the Court must "defer substantially" to Congress.[137]

A third important domestic power is found not in Article I, but in Article IV, Section 3. Clause 2 of that section provides Congress with the power "to dispose of and make all needful Rules and Regulations respecting the Territory or other Property belonging to the United States." In *Kleppe v. New Mexico*,[138] the Court gave the Property Clause a broad reading. It stated that "the Clause, in broad terms, gives Congress the power to determine what are 'needful' rules 'respecting' the public lands. And while the furthest reaches of the power granted by the Property Clause have not yet been definitively resolved, we have repeatedly observed that the power over the public land thus entrusted to Congress is without limitations."[139]

A final important domestic power granted Congress is the power to enforce constitutional rights. Starting with the Reconstruction Amendments (the Thirteenth through the Fifteenth), Congress has often inserted into constitutional rights amendments a provision authorizing itself to "enforce" those amendments. This book will consider Congress's power to enforce the Reconstruction Amendments. That discussion is deferred until after the substance of the most important of those amendments, the Fourteenth, is discussed.[140]

This brief tour of the federal bankruptcy, patent and copyright, and property powers cannot, of course, provide a comprehensive guide to Congress's powers. But it should illustrate that, as a very general matter, Congress enjoys broad leeway when legislating within the scope of the subject-matters addressed by the Constitution's grants of legislative powers.

§ 5.09 Citizenship and Naturalization

Congress possesses significant powers relating to citizenship. The Fourteenth Amendment makes citizenship depend solely on place of birth or the fact of naturalization. Such persons are citizens of the nation and of the states in which they live.[141] Congress cannot alter the constitutional effect of birth within the United States.[142]

Nevertheless, the Constitution gives Congress the power over naturalization.[143] This power is quite broad. For example, while the Constitution itself does not confer

---

137. *Id.* at 204.

138. 426 U.S. 529 (1976).

139. *Id.* at 539.

140. Congress's power to enforce these amendments is discussed in Chapter 13.

141. *See* U.S. CONST. amend. XIV, § 1 ("All persons born or naturalized in the United States, and subject to the jurisdiction thereof, are citizens of the United States and of the state wherein they reside.").

142. *See* United States v. Wong Kim Ark, 169 U.S. 649, 703 (1898).

143. *See* U.S. CONST. art. I, § 8, cl. 4 ("The Congress shall have Power ... [t]o establish a uniform Rule of Naturalization.").

citizenship on children of American citizens born abroad, Congress, under its naturalization power, has provided for the citizenship of such children.[144] The cases construing the Naturalization Clause emphasize the broad congressional discretion to fix the conditions on which naturalization is to be granted or withheld.[145] The Naturalization Clause empowers Congress to prescribe the rules under which aliens may secure citizenship.[146] In addition to setting general rules governing naturalization, Congress may grant citizenship to named individuals by special act or provide for collective naturalization.[147] Congress may adopt such methods for naturalizing aliens as it chooses. Under the Constitution, a naturalized citizen enjoys the same privilege of citizenship as the native except regarding eligibility to high office. As the Court said in *Knauer v. United States*, "Citizenship obtained through naturalization is not a second-class citizenship."[148]

The Constitution does, however, limit Congress's ability to *remove* citizenship from naturalized citizens. In *Schneider v. Rusk*,[149] the Court struck down a statute providing that a naturalized citizen forfeited citizenship if she resided for three years in her country of birth. The discriminatory statute curtailed naturalized citizens' rights to live abroad in a way permitted to other citizens. Absent expatriation by voluntary renunciation, Congress lacks power to remove citizenship. In *Afroyim v. Rusk*,[150] an American citizen was refused a passport on the ground that he had lost his citizenship by voting in a foreign election. The Court ruled that Congress lacked authority to expatriate someone who voted in a foreign election because such voting may not constitute a voluntary relinquishment of citizenship.

§ 5.10 The Treaty Power

The power to make treaties is a significant, though unique, aspect of legislative authority. The Constitution assigns the treaty power to the President and Senate and places it in Article II, not Article I. Article II gives the President the "Power, by and

---

144. *See* 8 U.S.C. § 1401(c), (d), (g) (1994).

145. *See* Mathews v. Diaz, 426 U.S. 67, 79–80 (1976); Schneiderman v. United States, 320 U.S. 118, 131 (1943).

146. *See* Fiallo v. Bell, 430 U.S. 787, 792 (1977).

147. Thus, Congress provided for the collective citizenship of citizens of Hawaii when that territory was annexed. Collective naturalization can also be exercised with regard to particular classes. Indians were not considered citizens until Congress provided by statute that native born Indians should be citizens at birth. *See also* Contzen v. United States, 179 U.S. 191, 193 (1900) (observing that it was not disputed that the annexation of Texas automatically converted citizens of the Republic of Texas into citizens of the United States); Boyd v. Nebraska, 143 U.S. 135, 162 (1892) (observing that many statutes and treaties had made tribes of Native Americans U.S. citizens). Collective naturalization may also be provided for by treaty providing for cession of territory to this country. *See Boyd*, 143 U.S. at 164.

148. 328 U.S. 654, 658 (1946).

149. 377 U.S. 163 (1964).

150. 387 U.S. 253 (1967). *See also* Trop v. Dulles, 356 U.S. 86 (1958) (loss of citizenship may not be imposed for desertion from armed forces).

with the Advice and Consent of the Senate, to make Treaties, provided two thirds of the Senators present concur."[151] Although the normal legislative requirements of bi-cameralism and presentment do not apply, the treaty power is a legislative power because the Supremacy Clause expressly makes treaties (along with the Constitution and federal laws) "the supreme Law of the Land." Unless a treaty makes clear that it is not self-executing,[152] once ratified, it becomes part of our law equal in status to a federal statute.[153]

As part of "the supreme Law of the Land," a treaty overrides conflicting state laws. For example, in *Ware v. Hylton*,[154] the Court held that the Treaty of Peace with Britain prevailed over state law regarding debts Americans owed British subjects. However, a treaty does not necessarily override a conflicting federal statute. Article VI assigns "Laws of the United States," and treaties equal status as part of "the supreme Law of the Land." The Court will attempt to construe a treaty and federal statute on the same subject to give effect to both when it may do so "without violating the language of either."[155] Where such construction proves impossible, the most recently enacted one controls.[156]

The treaty power is conferred without any explicit limitations.[157] Although no treaty has been held unconstitutional, a treaty is subject to basic constitutional limitations,[158] notwithstanding the contrary implication in *Missouri v. Holland*.[159] Previous to *Holland*, a federal statute regulating the shooting of migratory birds had been held unconstitutional.[160] A subsequent treaty with Great Britain regulated shooting seasons in the United States and Canada, and provided that the countries would ask their legislatures to implement the treaty. Subsequently, Congress did so. This law was challenged as violating the Tenth Amendment, the same grounds that proved fatal to the earlier regulatory law.

The Court upheld the statute, concluding that the earlier decisions holding the regulatory law unconstitutional did not govern the scope of the treaty power. The Court gave several reasons for its decision. Statutes are the supreme law only when made in pursuance of the Constitution, while treaties have that status when made under the authority of the United States—a distinction Justice Holmes, writing for

---

151. U.S. Const. art. II, §2, cl. 2.

152. A non-self-executing treaty is one that calls for legislation to make it effective.

153. For an example of a court's analysis of whether a treaty is in fact self-executing, see *Medellin v. Texas*, 552 U.S. 491 (2008) (concluding that the treaty in question was not self-executing and thus had no preclusive effect on conflicting state law).

154. 3 U.S. (3 Dall.) 199 (1796).

155. Whitney v. Robertson, 124 U.S. 190, 194 (1888).

156. *See* Cook v. United States, 288 U.S. 102, 118–20 (1933); The Cherokee Tobacco, 78 U.S. (11 Wall.) 616, 621 (1871).

157. *See* Asakura v. Seattle, 265 U.S. 332, 341 (1924).

158. *Id.; see Cherokee Tobacco*, 78 U.S. at 616, 620–21.

159. 252 U.S. 416 (1920).

160. *See* United States v. McCullagh, 221 F. 288 (D. Kan. 1915); United States v. Shauver, 214 F.154 (E.D. Ark. 1914).

the Court, seemed to imply suggested a broader scope for the treaty power.[161] The Constitution imposed no textual limit on the treaty power; Justice Holmes wrote that no "invisible radiation from the general terms of the Tenth Amendment" could apply where "a national interest of very nearly the first magnitude"[162] was involved. Thus, the federal law, which was originally beyond Congress's power, was valid when enacted to give effect to a treaty. This implies the treaty power may accomplish what Congress could not achieve alone.

The Supreme Court recognized that the Constitution limits treaties in *Reid v. Covert*.[163] Under a federal statute, an American civilian residing on a military base in England with her soldier-husband was tried by court-martial for murder. Under an executive agreement with Great Britain, American military courts exercised jurisdiction over servicemen and their dependents located there. The Court rejected the government's argument that the agreement authorized Congress to subject American citizens subject to trial by military court. According to Justice Black, however, "no agreement with a foreign nation can confer power on the Congress ... free from the restraints of the Constitution."[164] *Reid* suggested that the treaty power is subject to the Constitution's substantive limitations. It would be anomalous if the federal government could circumvent constitutional restrictions by concluding treaties with a foreign country and thereby assume powers the Constitution otherwise withheld. To be sure, just that result would seem to have flowed from the broad language in *Missouri v. Holland*. In *Reid*, Justice Black's plurality opinion attempted to distinguish *Holland* by focusing on the Tenth Amendment nature of the alleged limitation power on the treaty power that *Holland* rejected.[165]

In *Bond v. United States*,[166] the Court, again against the backdrop of a possible Tenth Amendment objection, gave a limited reading to a federal law enacted in order to implement a treaty. The treaty governed chemical weapons, and the implementing statute forbade any person to knowingly "possess or use ... any chemical weapon."[167] In *Bond*, the federal government used this statute to prosecute a person who had deposited a small amount of a minor chemical on the doorknob of the home of a romantic rival. Without construing the scope of the treaty power, the Court held that

---

161. *See* Missouri v. Holland, 252 U.S. 416, 433 (1920) ("Acts of Congress are the supreme law of the land only when made in pursuance of the Constitution, while treaties are declared to be so when made under the authority of the United States. It is open to question whether the authority of the United States means more than the formal acts prescribed to make the convention. We do not mean to imply that there are no qualifications to the treaty-making power; but they must be ascertained in a different way.").

162. *Id.* at 434, 435.

163. 354 U.S. 1 (1957).

164. *Id.* at 16. *See also* De Geofroy v. Riggs, 133 U.S. 258 (1890) (same).

165. *See Reid*, 354 U.S. at 18 ("[T]he treaty involved [in *Holland*] was not inconsistent with any specific provision of the Constitution. The Court [in *Holland*] was concerned with the Tenth Amendment which reserves to the States or the people all power not delegated to the National Government.").

166. 572 U.S. 844 (2014).

167. 18 U.S.C. §229(a)(1).

the statute did not cover the conduct alleged, given how far it was from the treaty's concern with large-scale and political uses of chemical weapons.

Although two-thirds of the Senate must advise and consent to a treaty for it to become law, it is not clear that rescission or abrogation of a treaty needs Senate participation. In *Goldwater v. Carter*,[168] Senator Barry Goldwater challenged President Jimmy Carter's action in abrogating the United States' treaty with Taiwan. He argued that rescission required two-thirds support in the Senate. The Court deemed the issue nonjusticiable, with some justices viewing it as a political question,[169] and others as unripe.[170] The justiciability aspect of *Goldwater* is discussed earlier in this book.[171]

168. 444 U.S. 996 (1979).

169. *See id.* at 1002 (Rehnquist, J., joined by Burger, C.J. and Stewart, and Stevens, JJ., concurring in the judgment).

170. *See id.* at 997 (Powell, J., concurring).

171. *See* Section 2.08[5].

Chapter 6

The Commerce Clause

§ 6.01 Introduction

The Commerce Clause[1] confers one of the most important powers of the federal government. It is the source of many regulatory laws Congress enacts, including environmental, securities, labor, and many civil rights laws, in addition to more straightforward regulation of interstate commercial transactions.

Proceeding chronologically, this chapter traces the historical development of the Commerce Clause. It begins with the era marked by Chief Justice Marshall's foundational opinions on the subject (Section 6.02) and then progresses through the late nineteenth century, a period marked by latent stresses triggered by Marshall's understanding (Section 6.03), the period from the late nineteenth century through 1937, during which the Court embraced a more limited congressional power (Section 6.04), and the nearly sixty years between 1937 and 1995, when the Commerce Clause appeared virtually limitless (Section 6.05). Section 6.06 then considers a seminal Commerce Clause case decided in 1995, *United States v. Lopez*,[2] before ending with the modern, post-*Lopez* era, during which the Court has taken modest steps to rein in that power (Section 6.07). The significance and correctness of the Court's recent interpretations of the Commerce Clause constitutes a major open question in contemporary constitutional law, as noted and considered by Section 6.08's conclusion.

§ 6.02 Marshall's Conception

The Commerce Clause was added to the Constitution to remedy a serious defect of the Articles of Confederation.[3] Under the Articles, Congress lacked power to regulate foreign commerce and commerce among the states. Thus, when Britain closed its ports to American shipping in the 1780s, the United States was powerless to retaliate in a uniform way.[4] An additional serious problem was states' tendency to impose bar-

---

1. U.S. Const. art. I, § 8, cl. 3 (giving Congress the power "to regulate commerce … among the several states").
2. 514 U.S. 549 (1995).
3. The Federalist No. 42 (Madison).
4. *See* Jack N. Rakove, Original Meanings: Politics and Ideas in the Making of the Constitution 26–27 (1996).

riers to trade with other states, a phenomenon that impeded the growth of the nation as a single economic unit.[5] These problems were thought to be among the main factors motivating leading American statesmen to propose a new national governmental structure to replace the one established by the Articles.

The Commerce Clause provided the fix. It provided, in deceptively simple language, that Congress shall have power "To regulate Commerce with foreign Nations, and among the several States, and with the Indian Tribes."[6] The first clause is often known as the Foreign Commerce Clause and the last, the Indian Commerce Clause. The intermediate provision is generally referred to as either the Interstate Commerce Clause or simply, reflecting its centrality, the Commerce Clause. It has both provided Congress authority for much federal regulation and been the source of substantial judicial controversy over the last two centuries.

Gibbons v. Ogden[7] provided the Court its first opportunity to expound on the Commerce Clause. New York had granted Robert Fulton, the inventor of the steamboat, the exclusive right to navigate steam-propelled vessels in New York waters. Ogden had secured a license from Fulton to operate steamboats on the Hudson River between New York and New Jersey. Gibbons, however, obtained a congressionally-authorized license to operate steamboats up and down the eastern seaboard. On the authority of that federal license, he began his own steamboat line between New York and New Jersey, thus violating the New York-granted monopoly. Ogden secured an injunction in a New York court to restrain Gibbons from operating within New York waters. Gibbons appealed to the Supreme Court.

The argument turned in large part on the scope of the federal commerce power. Chief Justice John Marshall used the occasion for a full-scale discussion of the commerce power. He provided a broad interpretation. First, he rejected Ogden's argument that commerce equated to mere traffic in (*i.e.*, buying and selling) commodities. Marshall concluded instead that the term covered all commercial intercourse — a conception extensive enough to include all business dealings, including navigation. He argued that the text compelled that conclusion, since the plain meaning of "commerce" as understood by "all America" included navigation. Indeed, he said, "one of the primary objects" of the Constitution was to allow the federal government to regulate commerce, including navigation. Accepting Ogden's interpretation would defeat a central purpose implicit in the structure of the Constitution.[8]

Marshall embraced a similarly expansive interpretation of the term "regulate." He viewed the power to regulate as the plenary power to control. It thus included both the power to prescribe limits and the power to determine what shall remain unrestrained. "This power," wrote Marshall, "is complete in itself, may be exercised to its utmost extent, and acknowledges no limitations, other than are prescribed in the

---

5. THE FEDERALIST No. 42 (Madison).
6. U.S. CONST. art. I, §8, cl. 3.
7. 22 U.S. (9 Wheat.) 1 (1824).
8. *Id.* at 190.

constitution."[9] He insisted that any limits on that power would have to flow from the political process—that is, the American people supporting more limited, rather than more expansive, federal regulation—rather than from narrow interpretations of the constitutional grant itself.[10]

Marshall also construed the meaning of "among the several States"—*i.e.*, the scope of the commerce subject to Congress's regulatory power. Marshall appreciated that the Commerce Clause did not state that "Congress shall have power to regulate commerce." The enumeration of three types of commerce (foreign, interstate, and Indian) which Congress could regulate suggested some class of commerce which was withheld from congressional authority. Marshall reasoned that the Constitution withheld from congressional control "the exclusively internal commerce of a State." But this did not mean that congressional power stopped at the state line. Rather, "among" meant "intermingled with." As such, "commerce among the several states" included commerce in the interior of states—for example, interstate trading expeditions that penetrated into the interior of a state. On the other hand, the clause did not authorize congressional regulation of "that commerce, which is completely internal, which is carried on between man and man in a State, or between different parts of the same State, and which does not extend to or affect other States." As Marshall explained:

> The genius and character of the whole [*i.e.*, national] government seem to be, that its action is to be applied to all the external concerns of the nation, and to those internal concerns which affect the States generally; but not to those which are completely within a particular State, which do not affect other States, and with which it is not necessary to interfere, for the purpose of executing some of the general powers of the government.[11]

Marshall drew no rigid line between the commerce over which Congress has authority and the "completely internal" commerce of the states. Rather, his approach was more flexible. As he saw it, the word *among* in the Commerce Clause "may very properly be restricted to that commerce which concerns more States than one."[12]

Marshall's analysis thus suggested a broad view of commerce. As the explanation above indicates, his test was not contingent on movement across state lines. Rather, he concluded that the clause applied to commerce which affected more than one state. Consider again the category of commercial acts he conceded was withheld from congressional regulatory authority: those "which are completely within a particular State, which do not affect other States, and with which it is not necessary to interfere, for the purpose of executing some of the general powers of the government."[13] It is

---

9. *Id.* at 196.

10. *Id.* at 197 ("The wisdom and the discretion of Congress, their identity with the people, and the influence which their constituents possess at elections, are, in this, as in many other instances, ... the sole restraints on which they have relied, to secure them from its abuse. They are the restraints on which the people must often rely solely, in all representative governments.").

11. *Id.* at 194, 195.

12. *Id.* at 194.

13. *Id.* at 195.

easy to underestimate the novelty of Marshall's approach, given how accustomed we are to the federal government legislating over a wide domain of seemingly local activities, for example, the wages a locally-owned store must pay its employees. Yet Marshall's conception of the Commerce Clause as conferring more than simply the power to remove state-imposed tariffs at interstate boundaries was controversial in his day.[14]

Of course, much of Marshall's discussion was *dicta*. The facts of the case clearly involved transportation from one state to another. No esoteric consideration of what it meant to "affect" or "concern" another state was needed since the case addressed federal and state power over commercial intercourse that was clearly interstate. Regardless, *Gibbons*' broad language set the stage for the further development of the Commerce Clause. Still, despite that broad language courts, perhaps pressed by the imperatives of the cases in front of them, sometimes read that language narrowly.

§ 6.03 The Commerce Clause in the Mid-Nineteenth Century

Despite the breadth of the power *Gibbons* conferred on Congress through its expansive interpretation of the Commerce Clause, there was relatively little federal regulation of the economy until the late nineteenth century. To be sure, Congress did engage in some regulation, but states remained the primary regulators of the marketplace in mid-nineteenth century America.

This state of affairs caused constitutional difficulties because of another aspect of *Gibbons*. After deciding that federal power authorized Congress to grant Gibbons his coasting license, Marshall had to determine the effect of that federal license in light of the conflicting state-law granted monopoly to Fulton (later partially transferred to Ogden). This should have been an easy decision: because the Supremacy Clause of Article VI makes federal law supreme over any inconsistent state law, the state-law granted monopoly had to give way to Gibbons' federal license. While Marshall eventually reached that result, he speculated (as he often did in his opinions) about matters that were not necessary to the decision in the case. In particular, he strongly suggested, although he did not formally decide, that the federal power to regulate interstate commerce was *exclusive*. While he later retreated from that suggestion,[15] the idea that the power to regulate interstate commerce was exclusive ended up creating problems for courts later in the century.

Why? Exactly because states were the primary regulators of the marketplace throughout most of the nineteenth century. That fact created a situation in which businesses who opposed such regulation could argue that the state regulatory law

---

14. *See* ARCHIBALD COX, THE COURT AND THE CONSTITUTION 85–89 (1987); BERNARD SCHWARTZ, A HISTORY OF THE SUPREME COURT 47–49 (1993).

15. Willson v. Black-Bird Creek Marsh Co., 27 U.S. (2 Pet.) 245 (1829).

was invalid because it regulated interstate commerce, conduct which *Gibbons' dicta* suggested was exclusively regulable by Congress. Thus, the exclusivity idea Marshall flirted with in *Gibbons* threatened to call into doubt the constitutionality of much state regulation, during an era when states were the main regulators of the economy and when the idea of Congress regulating local activities such as agriculture or mining was still alien to most Americans.

The Court responded to this threat by denying that much of what states were regulating was in fact interstate commerce. Consider one example. In *Kidd v. Pearson*,[16] the Court confronted a claim that an Iowa statute prohibiting most manufacturing of liquor, even if that liquor was intended for the interstate marketplace, constituted an illegitimate attempt by the state to regulate interstate commerce. Claims like this put the Court in a bind. On the one hand, if it upheld the Iowa law as a valid local regulation for the health and morals of the community, it would be calling into doubt the *Gibbons* idea that the power to regulate interstate commerce rested exclusively with Congress. On the other, if it agreed with the challenger that the law represented an unconstitutional attempt by Iowa to regulate interstate commerce, then it would be establishing a broad precedent that states lacked power to regulate activities such as manufacturing and agriculture whenever such local activity satisfied Marshall's broad definition of federally-regulable commerce. Such a precedent would threaten to revolutionize American government, by transferring from the states to Congress the power to regulate local activities that had previously been thought to be within states' regulatory authority. Indeed, while the Court did not mention it explicitly, such a result was likely viewed as conflicting with the Tenth Amendment's guarantee that powers not delegated to the federal government remained with the states, since during this time, that guarantee was thought to imply that states retained regulatory power over some set of activities not encompassed in Article I's grants to Congress.

Faced with this unpleasant choice, the Court in *Kidd* simply stated that manufacturing (and agriculture and mining) by definition did not constitute interstate commerce. The Court was explicit about its reasoning:

> If it be held that the term [regulation of interstate commerce] includes the regulation of all such manufactures as are intended to be the subject of commercial transactions in the future, it is impossible to deny that it would also include all productive industries that contemplate the same thing. The result would be that congress would be invested, *to the exclusion of the states*, with the power to regulate, not only manufacture, but also agriculture, horticulture, stock-raising, domestic fisheries, mining — in short, every branch of human industry. For is there one of them that does not contemplate, more or less clearly, an interstate or foreign market? Does not the wheat-grower of the northwest, and the cotton-planter of the south, plant, cultivate, and harvest his crop with an eye on the prices at Liverpool, New York, and Chicago? The power being vested in congress *and denied to the states*, it would

---

16. 128 U.S. 1 (1888).

follow as an inevitable result that the duty would devolve on congress to regulate all of these delicate, multiform, and vital interests — interests which in
their nature are, and must be, local in all the details of their successful management....

The Court continued:

> ... It is true that [the Iowa law's] ... effects may reach beyond the state, by
> lessening the amount of intoxicating liquors exported. But it does not follow
> that, because the products of a domestic manufacture may ultimately become
> the subjects of interstate commerce, at the pleasure of the manufacturer, the
> legislation of the state respecting such manufacture is an attempted exercise
> of the power to regulate commerce exclusively conferred upon congress.[17]

Thus, cases such as *Kidd* succeeded in preserving a realm of state regulatory authority. But they did so by constricting the definition of interstate commerce. Before
long, the federal government would begin more actively regulating the national economy. But when it did, the distinctions between local and interstate commerce drawn
in *Kidd* returned, now with the effect of impeding federal regulatory power rather
than empowering state regulatory power.

§6.04 The Commerce Clause in the First Third of the Twentieth Century

[1] The *E.C. Knight* Formal Approach

Under the pressure of industrialization and the Progressive Movement, Congress
began to use its regulatory power more aggressively toward the end of the nineteenth
century. It enacted the Interstate Commerce Act, which regulated railroad rates, in
1887, and the first major federal antitrust law, the Sherman Act, in 1890. In addition
to regulating clearly interstate matters, such laws often regulated more local conduct,
based on that conduct's ultimate effect on interstate commerce. But such assertions
of federal power did not go unchallenged.

Although *Kidd v. Pearson* involved state regulatory power, its doctrine influenced
the decision in *United States v. E.C. Knight Co.*,[18] the first important prosecution under
the Sherman Anti-Trust Act. The defendant in *E.C. Knight* had obtained a virtual
monopoly over the manufacture of refined sugar, which the government alleged violated the Sherman Act. The Supreme Court, however, held that the Commerce
Clause did not extend to allowing an application of federal antitrust law to such mo-
nopolization of manufacturing capacity.

E.C. Knight invoked three formal distinctions to confine the commerce power more
narrowly than the language in *Gibbons* would suggest. First, it distinguished between

---

17. *Kidd*, 28 U.S. at 21–23 (emphasis added).
18. 156 U.S. 1 (1895).

production (which Congress could not regulate) and commerce (which it could). "Commerce," stated the *E.C. Knight* Court, "succeeds to manufacture, and is not a part of it."[19] The same could be, and was, said of other productive industries.[20] These activities, though central to the nation's economy, were deemed beyond congressional power.

Second, *E.C. Knight* hinted at a distinction between direct and indirect effects. The Court did not deny that "the power to control the manufacture of a given thing" *affected* commerce, a criterion suggested by Chief Justice Marshall's *dicta* in *Gibbons*. But it discounted that effect as "secondary" rather than "primary," and as incidental and indirect. Congress could regulate activity that affected commerce directly, but not that which impacted it only indirectly. Thus, on this theory, federal power turned not on the magnitude of the regulated activity's impact on commerce but on the logical relationship between that activity and commerce.

Finally, the Court recognized a distinction between interstate activity (which Congress could regulate) and local activity (which it could not). The Court explained the implications of this distinction by returning to Marshall's suggestion in *Gibbons* that the power to regulate interstate commerce (however that term was defined) was exclusively vested in the federal government. Echoing its analysis several years earlier in *Kidd*, the Court stated in *E.C. Knight*: "Slight reflection will show that, if the national power extends to all contracts and combinations in ... productive industries, whose ultimate result may affect external commerce, comparatively little of business operations and affairs would be left for state control."[21] The concern, then, was that if interstate commerce was understood to include manufacturing and other productive industries and if the power to regulate such commerce was exclusively vested in the federal government, then, as a simple logical syllogism, states would be deprived of any authority to regulate manufacturing, mining, agriculture, and other such industries.

This reasoning reflected the doctrine sometime called "dual federalism" — that is, the idea that the federal and state governments operated in mutually exclusive spheres, with one, and only one, level of government authorized to regulate a given industry or type of activity. Given this understanding, the Court in cases such as *Kidd* and *E.C. Knight* set about the task of drawing lines dividing federal and state regulatory authority. Moreover, that task was thought to require that some regulatory realms be reserved for state regulations, lest the traditional federal-state balance be upset and the Tenth Amendment (which, after all, seemed to reserve some regulatory authority to states) be rendered a nullity. In short, the Court thought bright lines needed to be drawn to prevent federal power from obliterating all state regulatory authority.

---

19. *Id.* at 12.

20. *See* Coe v. Errol, 116 U.S. 517 (1886) (lumbering); United States v. Butler, 297 U.S. 1 (1936) (agriculture); Oliver Iron Co. v. Lord, 262 U.S. 172 (1923) (mining); Champlin Refining Co. v. Corporation Comm'n, 286 U.S. 210 (1932) (oil production); Utah Power & Light Co. v. Pfost, 286 U.S. 165 (1932) (generation of electric power).

21. *E.C. Knight Co.*, 156 U.S. at 16.

E.C. Knight is often viewed as a triumph of "laissez-faire conservatism."[22] This characterization may be overstated. The formalistic distinctions the Court drew do not mean it sought to protect vast economic power from regulation. Indeed, the states possessed an array of legal devices to police economic behavior.[23] Nevertheless, the national character of the large-scale monopolies that had arisen by the late nineteenth century, and, indeed, the national character of much business activity by that time, rendered states less able to serve as effective regulators of a marketplace that had become national, and even global. Indeed, recall that in *Kidd*, the Court recognized that planters and farmers planned their crops based on national and global market conditions.

E.C. Knight, like *Kidd*, adopted a much different approach than that suggested in *Gibbons*. Its formal approach linked categories of activity (manufacturing or commerce), with authorized regulators (the states or Congress, respectively). It emphasized the logical connection between a regulation and activity (*i.e.*, its direct or indirect effect) rather than the magnitude of the activity's impact on commerce. The *E.C. Knight* formal approach relied on these boundary lines to define activities Congress could and could not regulate under the Commerce Clause. The result was the mechanical separation of "manufacturing" from "commerce," without regard to their economic continuity or interdependence. Manufacturing was "purely local" activity beyond the reach of the Commerce Clause. Analogously, local activity that had demonstrable effects on interstate commerce (recall "the planter" described in *Kidd*, who planted his crops "with an eye on the prices at Liverpool, New York, and Chicago") were nevertheless immune from federal regulation if those effects were merely indirect, regardless of how obvious or large those effects were.

[2] Other Doctrinal Strands

Several other strands of Commerce Clause jurisprudence developed contemporaneously with *E.C. Knight*. Some of these buttressed the Court's general suspicion of broad federal regulation, while others cut in the opposite direction.

In the *Shreveport Rate Case*,[24] the Court upheld congressional authority to regulate intrastate rail rates that discriminated against interstate rail carriers. The Court reasoned that Congress could regulate intrastate rail activity that had a close and substantial relationship to interstate rail traffic — for example, to protect interstate traffic from unfair local competition. Thus, in *Shreveport*, the Court expressed concern that state regulation of intrastate rail rates could discriminate in favor of intrastate commerce (by making it cheaper) at the expense of interstate commerce. For that reason, the Court upheld federal regulation of purely intrastate rail rates. While this theory

---

22. *See* ARNOLD M. PAUL, CONSERVATIVE CRISIS AND THE RULE OF LAW: ATTITUDES OF BAR AND BENCH, 1887–1895, at 181 (1976).

23. *See* Charles W. McCurdy, *The Knight Sugar Decision of 1895 and the Modernization of American Corporation Law*, 1869–1903, 53 BUS. HIST. REV. 304, 305–06 (1979).

24. Houston, E. & W. Tex. Ry. Co. v. United States, 234 U.S. 342 (1914).

would seem to allow for broader federal regulation than suggested by cases such as *E.C. Knight*, the quintessentially interstate context of railroad shipping perhaps limited the applicability of the *Shreveport* doctrine and thus the risk it posed to more limited theories of federal regulatory power.

In *Swift & Co. v. United States*,[25] the Court adopted a different approach, but one which also cut in favor of broader federal regulatory power. *Swift* involved a federal antitrust lawsuit alleging price fixing by meat dealers in stockyards. The defendants described their activity as local and thus beyond Congress's power. In upholding the lawsuit, Justice Holmes articulated the "current of commerce" or "stream of commerce" doctrine:

> When cattle are sent for sale from a place in one State, with the expectation that they will end their transit, after purchase, in another, and when in effect they do so, with only the interruption necessary to find a purchaser at the stock yards, and when this is a typical, constantly recurring course, the current thus existing is a current of commerce among the States, and the purchase of the cattle is a part and incident of such commerce.[26]

The current of commerce doctrine was potentially subversive of the dual federalism that governed Commerce Clause jurisprudence. The prospect that the federal government could regulate any conduct within the flow, or current, of interstate commerce threatened to wash away conceptual dams like the direct/indirect and production/commerce distinctions.

Another doctrinal approach led in the opposite direction. In *Hammer v. Dagenhart*,[27] the Court struck down a federal prohibition on the interstate shipment of goods made with child labor employed under particular conditions. Note that the law did not explicitly regulate manufacturing—rather, it regulated the interstate shipment of particular manufactured products. One might have thought this to be an easy case for federal power, even during this period when that power was construed more narrowly. Nevertheless, in *Hammer*, a five-justice majority struck the law down. Justice Day, writing for the Court, worried that the law was aimed at regulating manufacturing, by denying access to interstate commerce to goods manufactured in non-compliance with federal standards. The Court distinguished earlier cases that upheld such denials on the ground that in those cases, the prohibited items (such as lottery tickets and unsafe food) were themselves harmful. *Hammer* therefore erected a new limitation on federal power, one that operated even when the federal law on its face regulated interstate commerce.

[3] Early New Deal Cases

The consequence of the Court's restricted conception of commerce became apparent when the Court reviewed legislation enacted to remedy the economic crisis

---

25. 196 U.S. 375 (1905).
26. *Id.* at 398–99.
27. 247 U.S. 251 (1918).

of the 1930s. In *A.L.A. Schechter Poultry Corp. v. United States*,[28] the Court considered the constitutionality of minimum wage and maximum working-hour provisions promulgated pursuant to the National Industrial Recovery Act (NIRA) and applied to a Brooklyn poultry dealer. The dealer purchased poultry that had moved interstate, slaughtered it, and sold it locally. The Court unanimously held that Congress had exceeded its power. According to the Court, the dealer was engaged in distribution, not commerce, and its activity had at most an indirect, not direct, effect on commerce. Nor could the current of commerce doctrine justify applying the regulations to the dealer, because the interstate flow had permanently stopped at the dealer's Brooklyn poultry yard. Accordingly, the regulated activity was local, not national.

Schechter was a difficult case for the government, involving as it did a small enterprise at the very end of the interstate current. But in *Carter v. Carter Coal Co.*,[29] the Supreme Court reviewed a federal law regulating prices in the coal industry and prescribing minimum wage and maximum hour conditions for coal miners. The law was an important regulation of a nationally-scoped industry; as such, the stakes in *Carter Coal* were quite high. In declaring this law, especially its labor provisions, invalid, the Court relied on the formalistic categories from *E.C. Knight* consistent with a narrow view of commerce.[30]

According to the Court, mining, like manufacturing, was not commerce. The labor provisions of the law affected production, not commerce. It was irrelevant to the Court that labor practices in the coal industry affected interstate commerce (for example, by increasing the risks of miner strikes that would halt production and thus interstate shipments of coal), because such effects were not sufficiently "direct." As Justice Sutherland, speaking for the Court, explained: "The distinction between a direct and an indirect effect turns, not upon the magnitude of either the cause or the effect, but entirely upon the manner in which the effect has been brought about."[31] Thus, the direct/indirect effects test turned on logical relation, not empirical measurement. Nor could the current of commerce theory rescue the law's regulation of labor relations involving miners, because the interstate current had not yet begun at the coal production stage where the regulation applied. As the Court stated, employer-employee relations in production "is a purely local activity"[32] for the states, not the nation, to regulate.

The Court's interpretation of commerce severely hampered Congress's attempts to revive the nation's depressed economy. Immunization of manufacturing, mining, agriculture, and other productive industries from federal regulation under the Commerce Clause substantially narrowed the economic sectors Congress could regulate

---

28. 295 U.S. 495 (1935). For an account of *Schechter Poultry*, see PETER H. IRONS, THE NEW DEAL LAWYERS 86–107 (1982).

29. 298 U.S. 238 (1936).

30. The Court invalidated the price fixing provisions on the grounds that they were not severable from the labor conditions. *Id.* at 315–16.

31. *Id.* at 308.

32. *Id.* at 304.

and assist. The grim economic background made lack of federal power conspicuous. With the economy failing throughout the 1930s, the call for national action was clear.

Carter Coal considered these concerns irrelevant. The Court insisted that there was no federal power to regulate production, regardless of the size of the industry or the magnitude of the problems involved. Magnitude had no bearing on the existence of federal power; so far as the effect on commerce was concerned, there was no difference between the mining of one ton or one million tons of coal, because production was purely local. Thus, Congress could not address the production crisis crippling the country.

Dissenting in *Carter Coal*, Justice Cardozo recognized this dilemma when he considered the law's regulation of coal prices. Although mining and agriculture "are not interstate commerce considered by themselves," he recognized that their relationship to commerce "may be such that for the protection of the one there is need to regulate the other."[33] In his view, the direct/indirect distinction was inadequate.[34] Degree mattered. Instead of the logical, but unworkable, direct-indirect dichotomy, Cardozo suggested asking whether the relevant connection was "so close and intimate and obvious," as to support federal power. He thus sought to transform the old logic-based categories into an empirical approach. Justice Cardozo also hinted at moving away from the rule-bound approach and toward *ad hoc*, case-by-case adjudication. "Always the setting of the facts is to be viewed if one would know the closeness of the tie."[35]

§ 6.05 The Commerce Clause from 1937–1995

[1] *Jones and Laughlin* and the Turn toward Greater Federal Power

Carter Coal was a closely-divided decision.[36] Within a year, in another closely-divided opinion, the Court's attitude toward the Commerce Clause changed. In *NLRB v. Jones & Laughlin Steel Corp.*,[37] the Court considered the constitutionality of the National Labor Relations Act of 1935 (NLRA), as applied to labor relations at a large steel mill operated by a massive, vertically-integrated corporation. The NLRA guaranteed employees' right to organize collectively and prohibited employers from interfering with that right or from refusing to bargain with employees' unions.

---

33. *Id.* at 327 (Cardozo, J., dissenting). Justices Brandeis and Stone joined the dissent; Chief Justice Hughes concurred in the majority opinion but thought the price regulation provisions were within Congress's power. Justice Cardozo did not reach the wage and hour regulations, because he viewed the challenge as premature.

34. *Id.* ("But a great principle of constitutional law is not susceptible of comprehensive statement in an adjective.").

35. *Id.* at 328.

36. *See* note 33, *supra*.

37. 301 U.S. 1 (1937).

In *Jones & Laughlin*, the Court departed from the restrictive approach to the meaning of commerce. Writing for the five-justice majority, Chief Justice Hughes regarded the fact that the employees were engaged in production as not determinative, because the production plainly affected interstate commerce. Given the company's vertically-integrated activities, which stretched from mining ore and shipping it to the plant, converting it into steel, shipping the products to wholesale and retail sales centers, and ultimately selling it, it ignored reality to dismiss the effects of labor unrest at the mill, which the Court characterized as the heart of this multi-state process.[38] Thus, the Court inched away from the direct/indirect nomenclature, suggesting that the pertinent question was whether the effect was sufficiently "close and intimate" or "close and substantial." As Chief Justice Hughes wrote:

> Although activities may be intrastate in character when separately considered, if they have such a close and substantial relation to interstate commerce that their control is essential or appropriate to protect that commerce from burdens and obstructions, Congress cannot be denied the power to exercise that control.[39]

Jones & Laughlin challenged the approach to Commerce Clause cases that animated decisions like *Carter Coal*. In direct contradiction to *Carter Coal*, *Jones & Laughlin* held that production could be subject to congressional regulation. *Carter Coal* had found immaterial the evils that had induced Congress to act and their effect on interstate commerce, discounting extensive empirical effects as merely indirect. By contrast, when *Jones & Laughlin* recognized the toll that industrial strife in a large manufacturing facility would impose on interstate commerce, it refused to dismiss this effect as only indirect.

More generally, *Jones & Laughlin* suggested a new judicial approach to Commerce Clause cases. In cases such as *E.C. Knight, Schechter Poultry*, and *Carter Coal*, the Court had resorted to formal rules — production vs. commerce, direct vs. indirect, and local vs. national — to assess the constitutionality of federal regulation. In *Jones & Laughlin*, the Court suggested it would henceforth proceed on a case-by-case basis. The judicial role would remain substantial. In particular, the Court committed to continuing to police the distinction "between what is national and what is local in the activities of commerce," a distinction it described as "vital to the maintenance of our federal system."[40] But that review would turn on *ad hoc*, empirically-grounded analysis rather than on formalistic bright-line rules.

That *ad hoc* approach would very soon turn decisively in favor of congressional power. *Jones & Laughlin* involved an industrial giant whose activities substantially impacted interstate commerce. But the very day it decided *Jones & Laughlin*, the Court relied on that decision to uphold federal regulatory authority over the labor

---

38. *Id.* at 41 ("In view of respondent's far-flung activities, it is idle to say that the effect on interstate commerce would be indirect or remote.").

39. *Id. at 37.*

40. *Id.* at 30.

relations at the manufacturing plant operated by the largest American manufacturer of commercial trailers.[41] Again on that same day, the Court relied on *Jones & Laughlin* to uphold the NLRA's application to a small manufacturing concern that produced less than one half of one percent of the clothing made in the country and employed only 800 workers.[42] The interruption of such a business would hardly imperil much commerce, but the Court stressed the interstate flow of raw materials and finished goods of which the manufacturer was a part. Despite the manufacturer's small size, the Court ruled that the reasoning in *Jones & Laughlin* authorized federal regulation.

Despite the significance of the changes *Jones & Laughlin* wrought, the opinion was still a careful one. The Court acknowledged both the Tenth Amendment and the need to distinguish between national and local activities. Indeed, it did not so much reject the direct/indirect effects test as apply that test with a more practical, empirical eye. Nevertheless, that practical focus, when coupled with the Court's new emphasis on the (empirical) substantiality of the effects the regulated activity had on interstate commerce, promised a much more generous standard of judicial review when Congress regulated the economy.

Two years later, in *NLRB v. Fainblatt*, the Court explicitly held that application of the Commerce Clause did not depend on the volume of commerce affected.[43] Fainblatt, though only a small clothing manufacturer, was within Congress's regulatory reach even though its contribution to interstate commerce was relatively small. The Court also observed both that Fainblatt was a link in an interstate chain stretching from the mills that produced the fabric to the retailers who sold the items to consumers, and also that some industries, such as the garment industry, were comprised of many small firms that in the aggregate accounted for a great deal of commerce.

Why did the Court change its attitude in 1937? The conventional view attributes the decision in *Jones & Laughlin* as influenced by President Franklin Roosevelt's court packing plan. Frustrated by the Court's decisions holding New Deal legislation unconstitutional, Roosevelt, after his overwhelming 1936 re-election victory, proposed creating a new seat on the Supreme Court for every justice who reached 70 years of age, a formula which would have allowed him immediately to add six justices to the Court. Roosevelt claimed the measure was needed to allow the Court to operate efficiently. Ultimately, the plan failed, but in the interim, the Court upheld some New Deal measures with Justice Owen Roberts allegedly abandoning his frequent opposition to them as a response to the Court packing plan. More recent scholarship casts doubt on this theory, suggesting that the Court was already primed on its own to move toward embracing a broader Commerce Clause power.[44] It is also worth noting that *Jones & Laughlin* was a cautious opinion that followed in the broader sweep of the

---

41. NLRB v. Fruehauf Trailer Co., 301 U.S. 49 (1937).
42. NLRB v. Friedman-Harry Marks Clothing Co., 301 U.S. 58 (1937).
43. 306 U.S. 601, 606 (1939).
44. *See* Barry Cushman, *Rethinking the New Deal Court*, 80 Va. L. Rev. 201 (1994).

Court's pre-Court Packing Plan jurisprudence, even if that opinion pushed the boundaries of that older doctrine.[45]

[2] *Darby* and *Wickard*

Despite the undeniable practical changes it worked on Commerce Clause doctrine, *Jones & Laughlin* was a cautious opinion, continuing to apply traditional Commerce Clause concepts, albeit in a way more hospitable to federal power. The Court began decisively repudiating those concepts in 1941 and 1942. That process commenced in *United States v. Darby*,[46] a unanimous 1941 opinion that upheld a federal law prohibiting both the interstate shipment of goods manufactured with labor that was paid less than the federal minimum wage, and also prohibiting the production of goods for the interstate market when those goods were manufactured with such labor.

In upholding both of these provisions,[47] the *Darby* Court held that Congress could regulate productive activity that had a substantial effect on commerce. It began with the provision prohibiting the interstate shipment of goods produced not in accordance with federal labor standards. The Court upheld that provision by overruling *Hammer v. Dagenhart*,[48] and thus validating near-complete federal authority to regulate the interstate shipment of goods. In so doing it relied on the broad language from *Gibbons* about the plenary nature of the Commerce Clause power. According to *Darby*, that nature of the power meant that courts could not inquire into what Congress intended to accomplish when regulating interstate commerce, as long as that intent was vindicated through a regulation of interstate commerce. The Court also rejected *Hammer's* focus on whether the item excluded from interstate commerce was itself harmful.

The Court then turned to the prohibition on the manufacture of goods for the interstate market with labor that was not compensated pursuant to federal standards. This was a more difficult question, since it forced the Court to confront the manufacturing/commerce distinction it had followed since the late nineteenth century.[49] Justice Stone began this part of his analysis by again citing *Gibbons*, this time for the proposition that the Commerce Clause power "extends to those activities intrastate which so affect interstate commerce or the exercise of the power of Congress over it

---

45. *See* Barry Cushman, *A Stream of Legal Consciousness: The Current of Commerce Doctrine From Swift To Jones & Laughlin*, 61 FORDHAM L. REV. 105 (1992) (making this argument and arguing that the real change in Commerce Clause doctrine occurred in 1941 and 1942). The next sub-section of this Chapter explains the critical Commerce Clause cases decided in those two years.

46. 312 U.S. 100 (1941).

47. The Court also upheld record-keeping requirements that sought to ensure compliance with these wage requirements.

48. 247 U.S. 251 (1918). *Hammer* is discussed in Section 6.04[2].

49. Immediately after posing this question Justice Stone cited *McCulloch v. Maryland*, 17 U.S. (4 Wheat.) 316 (1819), thus suggesting the foundation of this power in a combination of the Commerce Clause and the Necessary and Proper Clause. The latter clause is discussed in Section 5.03.

as to make regulation of them appropriate means to the attainment of a legitimate end, the exercise of the granted power of Congress to regulate interstate commerce."[50]

At this point, Justice Stone turned to the exclusivity issue that had troubled the Court since *Gibbons*. Recall that much pre-1937 Commerce Clause caselaw had worried that acknowledging federal Commerce Clause authority to regulate manufacturing would necessarily divest states of any authority to regulate it, given *Gibbons'* suggestion that the commerce power was exclusively vested in the federal government. In resolving that issue, Justice Stone sketched out a vision that ultimately allowed both states and the federal government to have power to regulate local activities that might affect interstate commerce. He wrote: "In the absence of Congressional legislation on the subject state laws which are not regulations of the commerce itself or its instrumentalities are not forbidden even though they affect interstate commerce."[51] Doctrinal rules governing this shared regulatory authority over such activities eventually blossomed into the modern dormant Commerce Clause, discussed in the next Chapter of this book.

Turning to the question of the second provision's constitutionality, Justice Stone found it valid for two reasons. First, he concluded that it was valid as a means to ensure the effectiveness of the first provision's exclusion of such goods from interstate commerce. In other words, to ensure the effectiveness of that regulation of interstate commerce, Congress could choose to regulate a local activity, such as the manufacturing of goods that Congress wished to exclude from the interstate market. Second, he concluded that the provision's prohibition on manufacturing served to prevent the unfair competition in interstate commerce that would arise if goods manufactured on those sub-standard terms were able to compete with goods produced through fairer labor relations.

Justice Stone concluded his Commerce Clause analysis by discounting the substantive impact of the Tenth Amendment. He rejected the argument, sometimes made in earlier cases, that that amendment had a substantive content—*i.e.*, that it required that some set of regulatory areas remain within states' exclusive control.[52] Rejecting that understanding, he wrote:

> The amendment states but a truism that all is retained which has not been surrendered. There is nothing in the history of its adoption to suggest that it was more than declaratory of the relationship between the national and state governments as it had been established by the Constitution before the amendment or that its purpose was other than to allay fears that the new national government might seek to exercise powers not granted, and that

---

50. *Darby*, 312 U.S. at 118.

51. *Id.* at 119.

52. *See, e.g.*, Hammer v. Dagenhart, 247 U.S. 251, 273–74 (1918) ("The grant of power of Congress over the subject of interstate commerce was to enable it to regulate such commerce, and not to give it authority to control the states in their exercise of the police power over local trade and manufacture. The grant of authority over a purely federal matter was not intended to destroy the local power always existing and carefully reserved to the states in the Tenth Amendment to the Constitution.").

the states might not be able to exercise fully their reserved powers. From the beginning and for many years the amendment has been construed as not depriving the national government of authority to resort to all means for the exercise of a granted power which are appropriate and plainly adapted to the permitted end.[53]

Thus, *Darby* took great steps toward rejecting the structure that had constrained the federal commerce power between the late nineteenth century and *Jones & Laughlin* in 1937. Two 1942 decisions reflected further concessions of power to Congress to regulate local activities. *United States v. Wrightwood Dairy Co.*[54] upheld application of federal regulation of the price of milk produced and sold intrastate. The intrastate milk competed with milk transported interstate. Failure to regulate the intrastate milk would affect the price of, and commerce in, interstate milk. Accordingly, the Commerce Clause authorized Congress to regulate that local commerce in order to make more effective its regulation of its interstate competitor.

In some ways, *Wrightwood Dairy* presents a straightforward case for federal regulation. As early as the 1914 *Shreveport Rate Case*,[55] the Court had upheld federal regulation of intrastate commerce that competed with interstate commerce, as a way of allowing Congress to protect that interstate commerce. But *Shreveport* dealt with railroad transportation — a quintessentially commercial activity. By contrast, *Wrightwood* dealt with production — an activity that until 1937 had been considered a purely local activity, whatever its effects on interstate commerce. Nevertheless, in upholding federal regulation of intrastate activities, the *Wrightwood* Court was able to rely on *Gibbons'* and *McCulloch's* broad statement of federal power, when Justice Stone wrote that "The commerce power ... extends to those activities intrastate which so affect interstate commerce, or the exertion of the power of Congress over it, as to make regulation of them appropriate means to the attainment of a legitimate end, the effective execution of the granted power to regulate interstate commerce."[56]

Wickard v. Filburn[57] endorsed far greater regulation of local activities, although it relied essentially on the same theory as that in *Wrightwood* and *Darby*. *Wickard* dealt with the Agricultural Adjustment Act of 1938. Under that law, participation in a federal crop marketing program required the farmer to agree to plant only the volume of crops the federal agency allocated him. Filburn, a farmer, was penalized for producing more wheat than his allotted quota. He claimed Congress could not regulate the excess crop he planted, because he intended to keep that excess on his farm, for his own needs. The Court disagreed.

---

53. *Darby*, 312 U.S. at 124.
54. 315 U.S. 110 (1942).
55. Houston, E. & W. Tex. Ry. Co. v. United States, 234 U.S. 342 (1914) (Shreveport Rate Case). This case is discussed in Section 6.04[2].
56. *Wrightwood*, 315 U.S. at 119. This language may sound familiar, as it largely repeats what Justice Stone, the author of *Wrightwood*, wrote the year before in *Darby*.
57. 317 U.S. 111 (1942).

Wickard consolidated and contributed several important strands to Commerce Clause doctrine. First, it explicitly rejected the old formal distinctions between production and commerce and between direct and indirect effects, which had been deemphasized, but never repudiated, since *Jones & Laughlin*.[58] Even if Filburn's activity was "local" and not itself commerce, Congress was empowered to regulate it when it exerts "a substantial economic effect on interstate commerce."[59]

Second, *Wickard* made clear that individual instances of the regulated intrastate activity need not themselves have the required substantial effect on interstate commerce. Rather, Congress could reach local activities with trivial effects on commerce if the cumulative effect of such activities, when aggregated, was substantial. As Justice Rehnquist explained four decades later:

> [I]n *Wickard v. Filburn* ... the Court expanded the scope of the Commerce Clause to include the regulation of acts which taken alone might not have a substantial economic effect on interstate commerce, such as a wheat farmer's own production, but which might reasonably be deemed nationally significant in their cumulative effect, such as altering the supply-and-demand relationships in the interstate commodity market.[60]

Since home-grown, home-consumed product may affect the price and market conditions for wheat, Congress could regulate it. The theory was that when the farmer grew the wheat he needed for his own use, he did not have to go out into the market to purchase it, thus depressing prices. The Court explained: "Home-grown wheat in this sense competes with wheat in commerce."[61] Alternatively, if the price of wheat rose, possessors of home-grown wheat might decide to market it, which would reduce the market price and thus impact the interstate market by raising supply and depressing prices.

Finally, *Wickard* included language that eventually ripened into the idea that Congress did not have to definitively prove that, in the aggregate, the regulated activity substantially affected interstate commerce. In *Wickard*, the Court wrote that "This record leaves us in no doubt that Congress may properly have considered that wheat consumed on the farm where grown if wholly outside the scheme of regulation would have a substantial effect in defeating and obstructing its purpose to stimulate trade therein at increased prices."[62] Eventually, this deference (the crediting of the fact that "Congress may properly have considered" that certain conduct might have a certain effect) became understood as requiring only that Congress have a rational basis for

---

58. *See id.* at 120 ("We believe ... that questions of the power of Congress are not to be decided by reference to any formula which would give controlling force to nomenclature such as 'production' and 'indirect' and foreclose consideration of the actual effects of the activity in question upon interstate commerce.").

59. *Id.* at 125.

60. Hodel v. Virginia Surface Mining Ass'n, 452 U.S. 264, 308 (1981) (Rehnquist, J., concurring).

61. *Wickard*, 317 U.S. at 128.

62. *Id.* at 128–29.

believing that, in the aggregate, the regulated activity substantially affected interstate commerce.[63]

Clearly, *Wickard* left little, if any, activity totally immune from federal regulatory authority. The substantial effects requirement, when modified by the aggregation principle and the requirement of only a rational basis, seemingly excludes nothing from the scope of the commerce power, given the deeply interconnected economy characterizing modern America. A child's neighborhood lemonade stand could come within Congress's reach because a rational basis would exist for concluding that transactions at such a stand, when aggregated with similar enterprises elsewhere, have the requisite effect on interstate commerce. Indeed, similar support would exist for congressional regulation of decisions to grow lemons in one' backyard, since such decisions, if aggregated, would likely depress the market price for lemons. Perhaps in Marshall's time, one could envision transactions that, even if aggregated, did not have this sort of effect, given the isolated nature of much American economic activity.[64] But not today. Eventually, the prospect that applying *Wickard* to its logical limit would mean that Congress could regulate anything led the Court to again search for limits to the commerce power.

[3] The Commerce Clause at Its Height

Darby and *Wickard* ushered in an era in which nearly any activity could be regulated by Congress under its Commerce Clause power. Given the nationally (and, indeed, globally) integrated economy that had developed by the middle of the twentieth century, a development that only accelerated after 1945, it was easy for any federal regulation to satisfy the Court's substantial effects test, especially when applied with the aggregation and rational basis glosses from *Wickard*.

During this period, crime was a major area in which Congress took a more active regulatory role. The Court easily upheld federal criminal laws. *Perez v. United States*[65] illustrates this phenomenon. A federal statute making "loan sharking" a crime was applied to a New York City "loan shark" who had threatened violence to collect money lent to a local butcher. The Court held that Congress could criminalize the defendant's local activity because there was "a tie-in between local loan sharks and interstate crime."[66] Congressional hearings and reports demonstrated that loan sharking fur-

---

63. *See, e.g.,* Gonzalez v. Raich, 545 U.S. 1, 22 (2005) ("In assessing the scope of Congress's authority under the Commerce Clause, we stress that the task before us is a modest one. We need not determine whether respondents' activities, taken in the aggregate, substantially affect interstate commerce in fact, but only whether a 'rational basis' exists for so concluding.").

64. *Compare* Gibbons v. Ogden, 22 U.S. (9 Wheat.) 1, 195 (1824) ("The genius and character of the whole government seem to be, that its action is to be applied to all the external concerns of the nation, and to those internal concerns which affect the States generally; but not to those which are completely within a particular State, which do not affect other States, and with which it is not necessary to interfere, for the purpose of executing some of the general powers of the government. The completely internal commerce of a State, then, may be considered as reserved for the State itself.").

65. 402 U.S. 146 (1971).

66. *Id.* at 155.

nished organized crime with much of its revenue. In a solitary dissent, Justice Stewart argued that no rational basis showed "that loan sharking is an activity with interstate attributes that distinguish it in some substantial respect from other local crime."[67] Nevertheless, *Perez* allowed Congress to reach even local loan sharking as a means of choking off interstate organized crime.

Civil rights was another area in which Congress became more active, especially with the onset of the Civil Rights Movement in the 1950s. In 1964, Congress enacted a foundational civil rights statute, the Civil Rights Act of 1964. A key provision (Title II) entitles all persons to equal access to any public accommodation without racial or religious discrimination. The Act covers inns, hotels, motels, restaurants, and cafeterias if their "operations affect commerce." The fundamental object of the 1964 Civil Rights Act was to address the moral and dignitary harms of discriminatory denials of access to public accommodations. While Congress considered grounding the public accommodations provision on other constitutional grants of authority, most notably its power to enforce the Equal Protection Clause of the Fourteenth Amendment, Congress ultimately enacted the law based primarily on its commerce power.

Heart of Atlanta Motel v. United States[68] and *Katzenbach v. McClung*[69] considered whether the Commerce Clause supported application of the Civil Rights Act to, respectively, a motel that mostly served out-of-state guests and a restaurant that imported from other states much of the food it served. In both cases a unanimous Court upheld application of the law based on the Commerce Clause. In *Heart of Atlanta*, the Court noted that Congress did not need to make formal findings connecting the regulated conduct to interstate commerce; nevertheless, it acknowledged the evidence Congress collected indicating that discrimination in public accommodations impaired interstate commerce by making it harder for racial minorities to travel interstate. As applied to the motel in *Heart of Atlanta*, which was located near an interstate highway and advertised in national magazines, the Court had no difficulty concluding that the Commerce Clause supported application of that law to the hotel.

As applied to the restaurant in *McClung*, the Court noted that in the previous year the restaurant had bought approximately $150,000 in food, of which approximately $70,000 consisted of meat that had originated in other states. In addition to discouraging interstate travel (and thus commerce), the Court in *McClung* also observed that the restaurant's discrimination and the discrimination of other restaurants like it led to less food being served and thus less interstate commerce in those food supplies. To the Court, these factors easily justified upholding the law.

Cases such as *Perez*, *Heart of Atlanta*, and *McClung* were not outliers. To the contrary, between 1937 and 1995 the Court did not strike down any law as exceeding the commerce power. To be sure, during this era, the Court did find that other federalism limits prohibited Congress from using the commerce power to regulate state

---

67. *Id.* at 157 (Stewart, J., dissenting).
68. 379 U.S. 241 (1964).
69. 379 U.S. 294 (1964).

governments.[70] Moreover, scattered dissents and concurring opinions in Commerce Clause cases reflected at least some level of judicial unease at Congress's most aggressive uses of the commerce power.[71] But until 1995, these limits and these qualms did not find expression in opinions limiting Congress's power to use the commerce power to regulate almost any private party activity it wished.

§ 6.06 *Lopez*: Another Turning Point?

The expansion of the Commerce Clause stopped, at least temporarily, in *United States v. Lopez*.[72] In *Lopez*, the Court ruled, for the first time in nearly 60 years, that a federal statute exceeded Congress's power under the Commerce Clause. *Lopez* considered a federal law that criminalized possessing a gun in or near a school. In a 5–4 decision, the Court found that law to exceed the commerce power.

Chief Justice Rehnquist's majority opinion identified three broad categories of activities that Congress may regulate under the commerce power: (1) the use of the channels of interstate commerce (for example, the interstate shipment of stolen goods); (2) protection of the instrumentalities of interstate commerce or persons or things in interstate commerce (for example, the destruction of an airplane or the theft of goods being shipped);[73] and (3) intrastate activities that substantially affect interstate commerce. The statute in *Lopez* could only be upheld under the third category, as it regulated neither a channel nor an instrumentality of interstate commerce.

The Court concluded that its prior cases upholding regulation under that third prong had all dealt with economic or commercial activity. By contrast, the Court observed, the law at issue in *Lopez* was "a criminal statute that by its terms has nothing to do with 'commerce' or any sort of economic enterprise, however broadly one might define those terms."[74] If a federal law sought to regulate non-economic activity under the substantial effects prong, *Lopez* required that (1) the regulation constitute "an essential part of a larger regulation of economic activity, in which the regulatory scheme could be undercut unless the intrastate activity were regulated" or (2) the statute contain a "jurisdictional element"—that is, a limit on its applicability to items or activities

---

70. *See, e.g.*, National League of Cities v. Usery, 426 U.S. 833 (1976). *National League of Cities* is discussed in Section 8.02.

71. *See, e.g.*, Perez v. United States, 402 U.S. 146, 157 (1971) (Stewart, J., dissenting); *Heart of Atlanta*, 379 U.S. at 275 (Black, J., concurring) ("I recognize ... that some isolated and remote lunchroom which sells only to local people and buys almost all its supplies in the locality may possibly be beyond the reach of the power of Congress to regulate commerce....").

72. 514 U.S. 549 (1995).

73. Both of these examples are taken from *Perez*, 402 U.S. at 150.

74. *Lopez*, 514 U.S. at 561. Strikingly, the lower court opinion in *Lopez* noted that the student had agreed to bring the gun into the school in exchange for $40. United States v. Lopez, 2 F.3d 1342, 1345 (5th Cir. 1993).

that affect or are connected with interstate commerce. The Court also suggested that congressional findings establishing the activity's connection to interstate commerce would assist the Court in evaluating whether that connection existed.[75] The statute featured none of these.

The Court also rejected the government's arguments that possessing a gun in a school impaired the educational process and thus impaired the nation's future economic competitiveness, and that crime more generally imposed costs that were spread throughout the economy. In rejecting those justifications for the law, the Court observed that they had no limits — that is, they would allow the regulation of essentially anything, since anything (*e.g.*, the divorce of a student's parents) might affect their education and since any crime-imposed costs filtered throughout the nation. On that point, Chief Justice Rehnquist observed that crime and education were matters traditionally regulated by the states but susceptible to federal regulation under the government's argument. He thus implied that the status of a regulated activity as one traditionally regulated by states was relevant to the Commerce Clause inquiry.

Lopez appeared to work three changes in prior law. First, the Court clarified that a valid federal regulation of a local activity had to *substantially* affect interstate commerce, rather than simply *affecting* it in some way.[76] Second, it raised the scrutiny level that would be applied to regulations of non-economic activity justified under the substantial effects prong. The opinion suggested that only regulation of economic activity would be subject to the deferential review sketched out in *Wickard*. Perhaps most fundamentally, *Lopez* suggested that the nature of Congress's powers as enumerated necessarily required that some conduct remain beyond congressional regulatory authority. Nevertheless, it is important to note that the Court went out of its way to make clear that it was not overruling any of its earlier, post-*Jones & Laughlin* precedents.

In Justice Kennedy's concurrence, joined by Justice O'Connor, he wrote that the history of the Court's Commerce Clause jurisprudence had taught the lesson "that the Court as an institution and the legal system as a whole have an immense stake in the stability of our Commerce Clause jurisprudence as it has evolved to this point."[77] Similarly, Justices Kennedy and O'Connor were unwilling to return to the formalistic

---

75. *See Lopez*, 514 U.S. at 561–63. Note that the "jurisdictional element" prong, if satisfied, arguably shifts the constitutional basis for congressional action away from the substantial effects prong and toward the channels or instrumentalities prong. Note further that in a later case, the Court appeared to deemphasize the probative value of congressional findings. *See* United States v. Morrison, 529 U.S. 598 (2000). *Morrison* is discussed in Section 6.07.

76. *See* 514 U.S. at 559 ("[O]ur case law has not been clear whether an activity must 'affect' or 'substantially affect' interstate commerce in order to be within Congress's power to regulate it under the Commerce Clause. We conclude, consistent with the great weight of our case law, that the proper test requires an analysis of whether the regulated activity 'substantially affects' interstate commerce.").

77. *Id.* at 574 (Kennedy, J., concurring).

distinctions grounding cases such as *E.C. Knight* and *Carter Coal*; they specifically criticized "the imprecision of content-based boundaries used without more to define the limits of the Commerce Clause."[78] Still, they seemed anxious to apply the structural principles of federalism to strike a new balance. In particular, they suggested greater scrutiny for federal statutes that intrude on areas of "traditional state concern"[79] like education and street crime.

Lopez left much ambiguity. The reliance on "economic" or commercial activity seemed in some respects to risk problems similar to those that doomed its formalistic ancestors, the production/commerce and direct/indirect distinctions. (Indeed, Justice Souter's dissent found a resemblance between it and the direct/indirect effects idea.) On the other hand, if, home-grown, home-consumed wheat (*Wickard*), loan-sharking (*Perez*), and the discriminatory conduct of a local restaurant in a small town (*McClung*) remained within Congress's reach, *Lopez* appeared to impose only modest restraints on federal power. In particular, both the majority opinion and Kennedy concurrence invoked *Jones & Laughlin* favorably, and both opinions seemed to exemplify the "practical conception of the commerce power" that Justice Kennedy explicitly endorsed.[80] Nevertheless, *Lopez* embarked the Court on a path of a greater level of scrutiny of Commerce Clause legislation than the Court had pursued since the 1930s.

§ 6.07 The Commerce Clause since *Lopez*

Five years after *Lopez*, the Court again held unconstitutional federal legislation grounded in part on the Commerce Clause. In *United States v. Morrison*,[81] the Court struck down a portion of the Violence Against Women Act, in a 5–4 decision reflecting the exact division of justices as in *Lopez* and in other federalism decisions of previous years.[82] In *Morrison*, a female college student sued a fellow student and another defendant for damages under the federal civil remedy VAWA afforded for victims of gender-based violence, after the defendants allegedly assaulted her.

Again writing for the majority, Chief Justice Rehnquist found that VAWA failed the test set forth in *Lopez*. The statute regulated non-economic activity, it lacked the "jurisdictional element" that *Lopez* suggested might nevertheless validate a regulation of non-economic activity, and, more generally, the connection between the regulated activity and interstate commerce was attenuated. However, unlike the statute in *Lopez*, VAWA contained findings connecting the regulated activity (gender-motivated vio-

---

78. *Id.* at 574.
79. *Id.* at 580, 583.
80. *Id.* at 572–73.
81. 529 U.S. 598 (2000).
82. *See, e.g.*, Printz v. United States, 521 U.S. 989 (1997) (prohibiting federal commandeering of state law enforcement); Seminole Tribe v. Florida, 517 U.S. 44 (1996) (holding that Congress lacks power under the Commerce Clause to hold states liable for damages and other retrospective relief). *Printz* and *Seminole Tribe* are discussed in Chapter 8.

lence) to interstate commerce. But *Morrison* concluded that such findings were not enough to uphold a statute like VAWA, since a reliance on findings would allow Congress to regulate based on an attenuated connection between the conduct being regulated and interstate commerce. Upholding a law based on findings documenting such an attenuated connection, the Court warned, would "completely obliterate the Constitution's distinction between national and local authority."[83]

Morrison's reasoning raised several important questions. First, one might have read *Lopez* as articulating a rigid rule that trivial effects on interstate commerce could be aggregated only if they involved economic activity. In *Morrison*, however, the Court went out of its way to state that it had not "adopted a categorical rule against aggregating the effects of any noneconomic activity."[84] This warning raised questions about when a court could aggregate such effects and when it could not. Second, the Court's refusal to uphold VAWA based on Congress's findings, and, indeed, its citation of *Marbury v. Madison* for the proposition that the judiciary is "the ultimate expositor of the constitutional text"[85] suggested a new willingness to scrutinize the bases for congressional action. In that sense, *Morrison* had implications not simply for federalism, but also for the separation of powers.[86]

Substantively, *Morrison's* discussion of the "attenuated effects" upon commerce of regulation of certain types of activities resembled *Lopez* in its echoes of the direct/indirect effects analysis characteristic of the pre-1937 cases. More generally, and again echoing *Lopez*, the Court seemed intent on drawing distinctions between national matters which Congress could reach and local matters reserved for the states, an enterprise the dissenters viewed as fundamentally one for the political process. *Morrison* viewed some areas as being within the traditional ambit of state government, including "noneconomic violent criminal conduct" not directed against interstate commerce, as well as family law and unspecified "other areas of traditional state regulation."[87] In that sense, one can again sense an echo of the Court's pre-1937 Commerce Clause jurisprudence.

The Court's 2005 decision in *Gonzales v. Raich*[88] suggested that *Lopez* and *Morrison* might ultimately accomplish only modest restrictions on Congress's Commerce Clause power. In *Raich*, the Court held, 6–3, that Congress had power to prohibit the local cultivation and use of marijuana for medical purposes. The Court distinguished *Lopez* and *Morrison* and relied heavily on *Wickard* to uphold the challenged federal legislation. The core of the *Raich* majority consisted of the four *Lopez/Morrison* dis-

---

83. *Id.* at 615.

84. *Id.* at 613.

85. *Id.* at 617 n.7.

86. For a similarly strong statement of judicial authority to police both the separation of powers and the federal-state balance, see City of Boerne v. Flores, 521 U.S. 507 (1997), decided only three years before *Morrison*. *City of Boerne*, which struck down a federal law defended as enforcing the Fourteenth Amendment, is discussed in Section 13.02.

87. *Morrison*, 529 U.S. at 615–17.

88. 545 U.S. 1 (2005).

senters (Justices Stevens, Souter, Ginsburg and Breyer), who were joined by Justice Kennedy. Justice Scalia concurred in the result.

Raich arose when Californians, in compliance with a state law legalizing some medical uses of marijuana, used marijuana that they either grew or received free of charge from caregivers. Federal law enforcement officers, acting pursuant to the federal Controlled Substances Act (CSA), confiscated and destroyed one of the patient's cannabis plants. The plaintiffs raised a carefully limited challenge to the federal law. Rather than attack it facially, they made the more limited claim that "the CSA's categorical prohibition of the manufacture and possession of marijuana as applied to the intrastate manufacture and possession of marijuana for medical purposes pursuant to California law exceeds Congress's authority under the Commerce Clause."[89]

The Court had little trouble upholding application of the CSA to the plaintiffs' particular facts. It did so, ostensibly, within the boundaries earlier cases had established. According to Justice Stevens' majority opinion, *Raich* differed from *Lopez* and *Morrison* in several crucial ways. First, those cases raised facial challenges to the constitutionality of a statute. By contrast, the plaintiffs in *Raich* sought "to excise individual applications of a concededly valid statutory scheme." The Court called this distinction "pivotal," since where federal power extended to a regulated class of activities, courts could not exempt individual applications as trivial.[90] Thus, ironically, the more limited nature of the challenge in *Raich*, and the plaintiffs' (probably necessary) concession that the CSA was generally valid, worked to undermine their claim.

Second, the CSA's prohibition on drug possession was an integral part of the statute's larger and more comprehensive regulation of the production, distribution, and possession of illicit drugs. This distinguished the CSA from the Gun Free School Zones Act struck down in *Lopez*, which was "a single-subject statute" that did not regulate economic activity or activity connected to interstate commerce.[91] Finally, whereas the statutes struck down in *Lopez* and *Morrison* did not regulate economic activity, the CSA did. To reach this latter conclusion, however, the Court had to define "economic" activity quite broadly, quoting a dictionary definition of "economics" as "the production, distribution, and consumption of commodities."[92] Dissenting, Justice O'Connor complained that the Court's definition was so broad that almost anything could come under it, thus placing almost all Commerce Clause-based regulation in the category of regulation of economic activity subject only to the very deferential review associated with *Wickard*.[93]

Raich also concluded that application of the law to the plaintiffs' conduct fit within the category of valid federal regulation characterized by regulation of intrastate activity that is an " 'essential part of a larger regulation of economic activity, in which the

---

89. *Id.* at 15.
90. *Id.* at 23.
91. *Id.*
92. *Id.* at 25.
93. *See id.* at 49–50 (O'Connor, J., dissenting).

regulatory scheme could be undercut unless the intrastate activity were regulated.' "[94] As suggested by this latter rationale, it was not entirely clear whether the Commerce Clause alone sufficed to support the result in *Raich* or whether the Commerce Clause needed the support of the Necessary and Proper Clause to do so. Indeed, this is a question that applies to much of the Court's post-1937 Commerce Clause jurisprudence, since much of that jurisprudence addressed federal regulation of activities that were not themselves interstate commerce but rather "merely" substantially affected interstate commerce.[95] At times, Justice Stevens framed the question in terms of the Necessary and Proper Clause.[96] Other portions of the opinion suggested the Commerce Clause alone was sufficient.[97]

Justice Scalia concurred with the Court's holding but based his analysis solely on the Necessary and Proper Clause ground.[98] Justice Scalia articulated a narrower conception of the commerce power than did the other justices in the majority. Whereas the commerce power clearly extends to federal laws regulating instrumentalities and channels of commerce, he argued that it does not authorize regulation of intrastate activities which substantially affect, but are not themselves part of, interstate commerce. He concluded that Congress can reach these activities only through the Necessary and Proper Clause, in conjunction with the Commerce Clause.

Justice Scalia accordingly saw the Commerce Clause as cutting a narrower swath than did the others in the *Raich* majority. Standing alone, it does not allow Congress to reach intrastate transactions, even intrastate transactions that substantially affect interstate commerce. Instead, he argued, it is only the Necessary and Proper Clause which allows that later sort of regulation. However, he also concluded that the Necessary and Proper Clause allows Congress to reach not just economic activities that substantially affect commerce but also local activity that is "a necessary part of a more general regulation of intrastate commerce" even if that local activity does not itself substantially affect commerce.[99] Given this understanding of the Necessary and Proper Clause, Justice Scalia found it easy to uphold federal regulation of local possession of illicit drugs, even if that possession did not substantially affect interstate commerce and even if that possession is not economic activity, because that federal regulation was essential to the broader federal effort to stamp out interstate commerce in those drugs.

Justice O'Connor agreed with Justice Scalia that the power to regulate activities with a substantial connection to intrastate commerce stems from a combination of

---

94. *Raich*, 545 U.S. at 24–25 (quoting *Lopez*, 514 U.S. at 561).

95. *See, e.g.*, United States v. Darby, 312 U.S. 100, 118–119 (1941) (upholding federal regulation of the production of goods destined for the interstate market on the theory that that regulation satisfied the *McCulloch v. Maryland* standard for legislation based on the Necessary and Proper Clause).

96. *See, e.g.*, *Raich*, 545 U.S. at 5, 22.

97. *See, e.g.*, *id.* at 19 (holding that the regulations in *Wickard* and *Raich* fell "squarely within Congress's commerce power because production of the commodity meant for home consumption, be it wheat or marijuana, has a substantial effect on supply and demand in the national market for that commodity.").

98. *Id. at 34* (Scalia, J., concurring in the judgment).

99. *See id.* at 37.

the Commerce and Necessary and Proper Clauses.[100] She contended, however, that Congress cannot immunize from judicial scrutiny federal regulation of local activity by packaging that regulation in a comprehensive statute. Indeed, she disparaged this theory for upholding federal power in *Raich* as simply providing "a drafting guide" to Congress for how it could ensure that future regulation of local activity could survive Commerce Clause scrutiny. Thus, the majority's approach, Justice O'Connor wrote, reduced *Lopez* to a case requiring Congress to follow certain procedures when it regulates local activity but one which affords no meaningful substantive protection to state regulatory power.[101] Justice O'Connor complained that the majority ignored the extent to which "the principle of state sovereignty embodied in the Tenth Amendment"[102] limits the Necessary and Proper Clause.

Justice Thomas, although joining Justice O'Connor's dissent, would have gone further in limiting federal power. Under the "traditional" meaning of commerce which he attributed to the Framers, the Commerce Clause could not justify regulating the intrastate, noncommercial activity at issue in *Raich*. Although the Necessary and Proper Clause presented a closer question, Justice Thomas concluded that the CSA, to the extent it imposed an intrastate ban, was not "necessary" since it was not "plainly adapted" to regulating interstate commerce in marijuana,[103] nor was it "proper" since "Congress has encroached on States' traditional police powers to define the criminal law and to protect the health, safety, and welfare of their citizens." Unlike the rest of the Court, Justice Thomas rejected the "substantial effects" test as "malleable" and unrooted in the Constitution.[104]

Raich seems to reclaim for Congress at least some of the ground which *Lopez* and *Morrison* took away. *Lopez* and *Morrison* signaled a higher degree of judicial scrutiny for Commerce Clause regulation of intrastate activity. Justice Stevens' majority opinion assigned the Court a much more "modest" role in Commence Clause cases. He repeatedly applied a "rational basis" test, under which the Court's charge is not to determine whether the regulated intrastate activity substantially affects commerce but whether Congress had a rational basis to so conclude. And again, the majority's broad definition of economic activity would seem to provide Congress with expansive power, subject only to the deferential scrutiny *Wickard* (and *Lopez*) set forth for federal regulation of "economic activity."

Thus, *Raich* did seem to signal a significant setback for the Rehnquist Court's federalism revolution. Nevertheless, the Court's next—and, to date, final—major encounter with the Commerce Clause again suggested narrower federal power. In

---

100. *Id.* at 43 (O'Connor, J., joined by Rehnquist, C.J. and Thomas, J., dissenting).

101. *See id.* at 46 ("If the Court is right, then *Lopez* stands for nothing more than a drafting guide: Congress should have described the relevant crime as 'transfer or possession of a firearm anywhere in the nation'—thus including commercial and noncommercial activity, and clearly encompassing some activity with assuredly substantial effect on interstate commerce.").

102. *Id.* at 52.

103. *Id.* at 61 (Thomas, J., dissenting).

104. *Id.* at 66, 67.

National Federation of Independent Business v. Sebelius,[105] the Court considered challenges to several provisions of the Affordable Care Act (ACA), including, most relevantly, the "individual mandate"—that is, the requirement that most Americans purchase health insurance.

While a narrow five-justice majority upheld the individual mandate, the only majority for that conclusion rested on Congress's power to tax—that is, the Court's decision on this point rested on characterizing the mandate as a tax on Americans that did not purchase insurance. (The ACA imposed a charge on Americans who failed to obtain insurance.)[106] But only four justices accepted the government's argument that the individual mandate was a constitutional regulation of the interstate health insurance market. Instead, a five-justice majority, speaking through several separate opinions, concluded that the ACA's individual mandate was not a valid regulation of interstate commerce, because it compelled persons to participate in that commerce (by purchasing insurance), rather that regulating pre-existing individual decisions to engage in such commerce. According to one of these opinions, by Chief Justice Roberts, construing the Commerce Clause to authorize Congress to compel persons to engage in interstate commerce would mark a novel and large expansion of Congress's powers, one not intended by the Framers when they gave Congress the power to "regulate" interstate commerce. Largely on the same reasoning, that five-justice majority refused to uphold the ACA's individual mandate under the Necessary and Proper Clause.

It is hard to know what broader effect *National Federation* will have on the interstate commerce power. Congress rarely compels persons to engage in commerce that does not already exist. Indeed, in defending the individual mandate at the Court, the federal government insisted that health insurance was unique in that, even if people did not already have it, it was statistically very likely that the vast majority of Americans would engage with the healthcare system at some point. The Court rejected that argument, but the very uniqueness of that subject-matter may render relatively unimportant *National Federation*'s distinction between "compelling" and "regulating" interstate commerce. On the other hand, if *National Federation* presages a more general impatience with broad assertions of federal regulatory power, then the Court may embrace other, more widely-applicable, limitations on that power. The unsteady history of the Court's attitude toward the Commerce Clause in the quarter-century since *Lopez* suggests that this area remains susceptible to continued change.

§ 6.08 Concluding Observations about the Commerce Clause

During the latter two-thirds of the twentieth century, and especially since *Darby* and *Wickard*, the Court recognized a broad congressional power to regulate pursuant

---

105. 567 U.S. 519 (2012).
106. This aspect of *National Federation* is discussed in Section 5.05[2].

to the Commerce Clause. Although *Lopez* and *Morrison* evidenced some disposition by a bare majority of the Court to narrow that power, *Raich* suggested that those cases may not impose serious limitations on Congress's power. *National Federation* may or may not suggest that the Court is interested in resuming the *Lopez/Morrison* campaign.

As discussed in the context of *Darby*, *Lopez*, and *Raich*, the Commerce Clause sometimes benefits from its association with the Necessary and Proper Clause. *Dicta* in *Lopez* recognized that Congress could reach non-economic activities as means reasonably adapted to implement comprehensive economic regulatory schemes, and, among other cases, *Darby* (before *Lopez*) and *Raich* (after *Lopez*) illustrate instances in which the Court has upheld legislation which rested on the Commerce and Necessary and Proper Clauses working in tandem. Indeed, in his concurrence in *Raich*, Justice Scalia recognized that the latter clause allowed Congress to regulate even non-economic local activities as a necessary part of a general regulation of interstate commerce.[107]

The proper scope of the Commerce Clause presents very difficult questions for students, lawyers, judges, scholars, policy-makers, and, ultimately, American citizens more generally. On the one hand, in a nationally- and globally-integrated marketplace, it is simply undeniable that local activities, when aggregated with others of similar types, can substantially affect interstate (or foreign) commerce. Combining that reality with Chief Justice Marshall's broad interpretation of the Commerce Clause in *Gibbons*, it is easy to understand why majorities in cases such as *Darby*, *Wickard*, and *Raich* and the dissenters in *Lopez* and *Morrison* argued for such broad federal power.

On the other hand, there is at least intuitive attractiveness to the idea that the grant of power to Congress to regulate interstate commerce presupposes something *not* granted it—something truly local. Indeed, Marshall himself recognized the force of this concept in *Gibbons*. Of course, one could say that the federal government is indeed a government of enumerated, and thus limited powers, while still conceding that, as an empirical matter in the modern world, the Commerce Power allows Congress to regulate essentially anything. Thus, perhaps Marshall could assume that some class of activities would necessarily remain regulable only by states only because he lived in an era in which that conclusion flowed from the principles he set forth in *Gibbons*.

Ultimately, one's views about the proper reach of the Commerce Clause may turn on one's methodological approach to constitutional interpretation more generally. For example, one might attempt to answer the Commerce Clause question by referring to what persons in the framing period expected would be the results that would flow from the words they ratified. Of course, such an approach would ignore technological and social developments that arguably rendered those "original expected applications"[108] irrelevant today. Other approaches—such as a purely original meaning ap-

---

107. *Raich*, 545 U.S. at 37 (Scalia, J., concurring in the judgment).

108. *See, e.g.*, Jack M. Balkin, *Original Meaning and Constitutional Redemption*, 24 CONST. COMMENT. 427 (2007) (discussing this concept).

proach, or a self-consciously living constitution approach—may or may not yield different answers to this question.[109] To the extent the Court is unwilling to defer to the national political process and whatever regulation that process produces, the Court will likely have to confront Commerce Clause questions by considering foundational questions about interpretive methodology.

---

109. The results under an original meaning approach are by no means obvious. For example, Professor Jack Balkin has argued that Justice Thomas and some originalist scholars have mis-portrayed the Commerce Clause as having been expanded beyond its original meaning. On the contrary, he argues that the original meaning of the Commerce Clause, when both its text and structural purpose are considered, was to allow the national government to regulate a broad array of intercourse where a national approach was needed because individual states could not regulate a problem or address the spillover effects between states or collective action problems that concerned multiple states. Jack M. Balkin, *Commerce*, 109 MICH. L. REV. 1 (2010). Other scholars heatedly disagree with this understanding of the original meaning of the Commerce Clause. *See, e.g.*, Randy E. Barnett, *New Evidence of the Original Meaning of the Commerce Clause*, 55 ARK. L. REV. 847 (2003); Randy E. Barnett, *The Original Meaning of the Commerce Clause*, 68 U. CHI. L. REV. 101 (2001); Robert G. Natelson & David Kopel, *Commerce in the Commerce Clause: A Response to Jack Balkin*, 109 MICH. L. REV. FIRST IMPRESSIONS 55 (2010).

Chapter 7

Commerce and the States: The Dormant Commerce Clause, Federal Preemption, and the Privileges and Immunities Clause

§ 7.01 Introduction

Under their police power, the states regulate a substantial part of everyday life. But as the Commerce Clause has been interpreted more expansively, the potential for conflict between federal and state regulation increases. When legislating under its Commerce Clause authority, Congress can, of course, displace state regulation by enacting laws that supersede, or (as this chapter explains) "preempt" state law. Suppose, however, Congress has left an area unregulated, yet state legislation impacts commerce. Does the Constitution inhibit such state regulation on the grounds that Congress, not the states, has power to regulate interstate commerce?

Answering that question in the affirmative, the Court has concluded that the Commerce Clause has a negative, or "dormant" aspect, as well as a positive one. In other words, the Clause not only confers authority on Congress to legislate over a wide area and in the course of doing so to preempt conflicting state law, but it also restricts state power by its negative implication. This negative implication—what has become known as the "dormant" Commerce Clause—means that the Constitution may invalidate state laws that impact interstate commerce even when Congress has been silent. Put differently, even when Congress has not acted, the dormant Commerce Clause sometimes operates to invalidate state legislation. As will be explained, state legislation may be held invalid under the dormant Commerce Clause if it discriminates against or unduly burdens interstate commerce.

This chapter begins by discussing the dormant Commerce Clause. After discussing the purposes and constitutional arguments regarding the dormant Commerce Clause in Section 7.02, Section 7.03 then considers the historical evolution of the concept, beginning with classic cases of the Marshall Court, continuing with a discussion of an important case from the middle of the nineteenth century, then cases from the late 19th and early 20th centuries, and the eventual move towards a balancing approach. The chapter then outlines the modern approach in Section 7.04. Section 7.05

identifies a particular rationale that sometimes is influential in deciding dormant commerce cases, one turning on concerns about a state's political processes, before Section 7.06 considers exceptions to the dormant Commerce Clause.

The chapter then examines Congress's ability to enact legislation that preempts state laws, in Section 7.07. It is uncontroversial that Congress, when acting appropriately under its Article I powers, can preempt state regulation. Thus, preemption jurisprudence focuses on statutory interpretation—that is, it considers whether and under what circumstances a federal statute will be deemed to have preempted state law. Even though this jurisprudence is more about statutory interpretation than constitutional law *per se*, how the Court goes about that statutory interpretation remains heavily influenced by constitutional considerations.

This chapter concludes in Section 7.08 by discussing a provision related to the dormant Commerce Clause, Article IV's Privileges and Immunities Clause.[1] The Privileges and Immunities Clause imposes similar restrictions on state regulations that impact out-of-staters. However, important differences differentiate those two clauses.

§ 7.02 The Purpose of the Dormant Commerce Clause

One of the foundational—indeed, arguably *the* foundational—reason for the 1787 constitutional convention was to create a national government that could enforce a national economic policy. The hope was that such a government, wielding a national commercial power, would unite the states economically and end the destructive trade wars and individual state economic policies that had inhibited the growth of the American economy and made the nation an unreliable participant in international trade. Absent the Commerce Clause, each state could ban the products of other states or inhibit their importation. The Constitution sought to end such economic isolation.

The Commerce Clause advances two fundamental national purposes implicit in the Constitution. First, it helps maintain a national economic union unfettered by state-imposed barriers to interstate commerce. Justice Jackson articulated this economic rationale in *H.P. Hood & Sons, Inc. v. Du Mond*, where he wrote:

> This principle that our economic unit is the Nation, which alone has the gamut of powers necessary to control of the economy, including the vital power of erecting customs barriers against foreign competition, has as its corollary that the states are not separable economic units.... Our system, fostered by the Commerce Clause, is that every farmer and every craftsman

---

1. The Article IV Privileges and Immunities Clause should not be confused with the Fourteenth Amendment's Privileges or Immunities Clause. This latter clause is discussed in Section 9.01[2]; while it sounds quite similar to its Article IV cousin, the Fourteenth Amendment clause is distinct.

shall be encouraged to produce by the certainty that he will have free access to every market in the Nation....[2]

The Commerce Clause thus creates a "national 'common market'"[3] which the states cannot destroy by advancing their own economic interests at the expense of the nation's.

The Commerce Clause also has a political rationale. It helps foster national political cohesion by inhibiting states from imposing reciprocal barriers that would divide rather than unite. As such, it reflects a commitment to the proposition that the states must, in Justice Cardozo's formulation, "sink or swim together" since "in the long run prosperity and salvation are in union and not division."[4]

The Commerce Clause empowers Congress to legislate to achieve these objectives. But what if Congress remains silent? Are the states free to regulate in areas that may impact interstate commerce if Congress has, by its silence, left certain space within its regulatory domain empty?

The Constitution's text is silent on the question. The Commerce Clause provides that "Congress shall have power ... to regulate Commerce ... among the several states."[5] Thus, it neither authorizes the states to regulate interstate commerce, nor does it prohibit them from doing so.[6] To be sure, the Constitution's grant of that power to Congress might be read as implicitly denying it to the states. On the other hand, in other instances, the Constitution does not treat its grants to Congress as precluding analogous state action. For instance, Article I, Section 8 empowers Congress to coin money, but this provision alone apparently does not implicitly restrict the states from taking the same action. If it did, Article I, Section 10 would not need to expressly prohibit states from engaging in that same conduct. The Framers included express prohibitions against state action in some areas but did not specifically forbid state regulations of commerce.[7] Thus, arguably, the states may regulate commerce without restriction, as long as their regulations do not conflict with federal statutes.

Neither textual argument has prevailed. The Court has recognized that, absent conflicting federal law, the states retain "a residuum of power ... to make laws governing matters of local concern which nevertheless in some measure affect interstate commerce or even, to some extent, regulate it."[8] Yet the Court has long relied on the Commerce Clause, fortified by the Supremacy Clause, to infer a judicial power to enforce a negative or "dormant" Commerce Clause. Thus, for most of our history, the Commerce Clause has been deemed to feature both an affirmative grant of power to Congress to regulate commerce and a negative aspect limiting states' intrusions into that sphere.

---

2. 336 U.S. 525, 537–539 (1949).

3. Hunt v. Washington State Apple Adver. Comm'n, 432 U.S. 333, 350 (1977).

4. Baldwin v. G.A.F. Seelig, Inc., 294 U.S. 511, 523 (1935).

5. U.S. CONST. art. I, §8, cl. 3.

6. *See Hood & Sons*, 336 U.S. at 535 (The Constitution "does not say what the states may or may not do in the absence of congressional action").

7. *See* The License Cases, 46 U.S. (5 How.) 504, 579 (1847).

8. Southern Pacific Co. v. Arizona, 325 U.S. 761, 767 (1945).

Although the constitutional text does not compel a dormant aspect to the Commerce Clause, other constitutional arguments lend it some support. First, some argue that the Framers intended to preclude states from obstructing commerce to and from other states. The Articles of Confederation failed due largely to the government's inability to remedy the states' divisive and parochial trade policies. The deleterious impact of such state policies during the Articles period and the Framers' desire to suppress them suggest that the Constitution's grant of federal power to regulate interstate commerce included this negative or dormant component. A counter-argument is that that the Framers intended simply to give Congress, via its commerce regulatory power, rather than the Court, via a dormant commerce principle, the power to override state regulation. In that case, congressional inaction might be understood as a willingness to tolerate the state measure.

Second, the dormant Commerce Clause is defended as a means of fostering national unity. The dormant Commerce Clause is consistent with the Constitution's commitment to the national unity which is implicit in its structure. Third, an economic argument supports the concept: simply put, a national free market promotes efficiency. Finally, a political process argument supports the dormant Commerce Clause. This theory maintains that there is something undemocratic about a state burdening outsiders (or external commerce) which go unrepresented in the state's legislative processes. Indeed, Chief Justice John Marshall made this argument in *McCulloch v. Maryland* when the Court ruled that the Constitution forbade Maryland from imposing the taxes it wished to levy on the Bank of the United States.[9]

The affirmative grant to Congress to regulate interstate commerce and the negative implications of that grant differ in two other significant ways. The extent of the restraints the Commerce Clause imposes on the states "appear nowhere in the words of the Commerce Clause, but have emerged gradually in the decisions of [the Supreme] Court giving effect to its basic purpose."[10] The Commerce Clause is essentially a delegation of power to Congress; since the late 1930s, the courts have largely, though not completely, deferred to congressional decisions regarding how to use that power.[11] The dormant Commerce Clause, by contrast, empowers the federal judiciary in the first instance, by giving courts the power to strike down state laws even when Congress has not acted. The phenomenon that triggers dormant Commerce Clause analysis is state regulation in the face of congressional silence, which leads a private entity to challenge that state regulation.

Second, the consequences of judicial intervention in the two situations are quite different. When a court finds that a federal statute exceeds Congress's power under the Commerce Clause, it rules the measure unconstitutional, thus foreclosing similar federal legislation. When the Court finds that a state statute offends the dormant Commerce Clause, the Court similarly strikes down the offending state measure. But

---

9. 17 U.S. (4 Wheat.) 316 (1819). This aspect of *McCulloch* is discussed in Section 4.05.

10. Philadelphia v. New Jersey, 437 U.S. 617, 623 (1978).

11. The evolution of the Court's Commerce Clause jurisprudence is discussed in Chapter 6.

the latter type of strike-down is subject to overturning by Congress. The point here is straightforward but powerful: if a court — even the Supreme Court — strikes down a state law as violating the dormant Commerce Clause, Congress can reverse that result the very next day by enacting legislation authorizing that state legislation. (The dynamic works in the other direction, as well: if a court *upholds* a state law as not violating the dormant Commerce Clause, Congress can reverse *that* result the very next day by enacting a law preempting such state regulation.) Put differently, the durability of judicial work under the dormant Commerce Clause is contingent on congressional approval or acquiescence: Congress can either endorse the court's work by letting the judicial decision stand, or it can override it by enacting legislation. The contingency of judicial decisions under the dormant Commerce Clause raises significant questions about the legitimacy of judicial review of state laws under that doctrine.

At the outset, it is important to focus on the circumstances when dormant or negative Commerce Clause analysis becomes relevant. There are two crucial preconditions. First, the area the state has regulated must fall within the domain of the federal commerce power. This precondition is almost inevitable, given the breadth of the modern federal commerce power even after *Lopez* and *Morrison* slightly contracted that breadth.[12] Nevertheless, the point is important to make: if a state law regulates in an area that Congress does not have the power to regulate, the dormant Commerce Clause simply does not apply. Second, if the state regulation falls within the federal commerce power, the question then arises whether the state measure conflicts with any statute Congress has enacted. If so, the state statute fails under the Supremacy Clause via a preemption analysis, and dormant commerce analysis becomes irrelevant. Dormant Commerce Clause scrutiny arises only when the state statute affects commerce and the federal government has not acted to preempt that state law.

§ 7.03 The Historical Evolution of the Dormant Commerce Principle

[1] Chief Justice Marshall's Views

Chief Justice John Marshall considered the possibility of a negative or dormant Commerce Clause in *Gibbons v. Ogden*.[13] In *Gibbons*, the Court concluded that the federal coasting license in question was a valid exercise of Congress's power to regulate interstate commerce. Thus, to use modern terminology, the (valid) federal law preempted the New York law granting Ogden a monopoly for the steamboat route in question.

---

12. United States v. Lopez, 514 U.S. 549 (1995); United States v Morrison, 529 U.S. 598 (2000). In both of those cases, the Court struck down federal legislation as exceeding the federal commerce power. *Lopez* and *Morrison* are discussed in Chapter 6.

13. 22 U.S. (9 Wheat.) 1 (1824). *Gibbons* is discussed in more detail in Chapter 6.

Despite the issue being settled by what we would today call preemption analysis, Marshall nevertheless engaged the question whether the federal commerce power was exclusive — that is, whether New York could have enacted its monopoly law even if the conflicting federal law had never been enacted. Marshall saw merit to the argument that the Commerce Clause precluded the states from regulating commerce. "There is great force in this argument, and the Court is not satisfied that it has been refuted,"[14] he wrote. But *Gibbons* did not require him to decide that issue, since Congress had in fact enacted a law that conflicted with, and thus preempted, the New York law.

Still, Marshall offered his thoughts about that question. Although he suggested that states might be disabled from regulating interstate commerce since that was a power given Congress, he did not ignore the concern that some peripheral impact on commerce might bar a state from acting under its police power. In considering that question, he distinguished between the *power* being exercised and the *subject matter* of the power. In essence, Marshall seemed to be thinking that states might not be able to regulate interstate commerce *per se*, but could nevertheless achieve the same effect by invoking their general police powers to regulate for the public good.[15] To illustrate this idea, consider a state's power to require that port facilities be kept clean and tidy. Such a law could be seen as a regulation of interstate commerce, since a clean port would make interstate commerce easier and more efficient. But that law could also be understood as a local police power regulation, designed for the health and safety of the local population.

Marshall thought states could not seek to regulate commerce, but could act under their police power even though their laws affected commerce. Thus, in *Willson v. Black Bird Creek Marsh Co.*,[16] he wrote a Court opinion upholding a state's power to construct a dam across a navigable creek as a proper exercise of state police power (because of the health benefits that would accrue from the dam's effect in draining a swamp), although Congress presumably could have regulated construction of the dam under the Commerce Clause because of its effect on interstate commerce. He wrote that the state statute, under the circumstances, was not "repugnant" to Congress's commerce power "in its dormant state."[17]

[2] *Cooley v. Board of Wardens*

In 1852, the Supreme Court issued an important opinion addressing the scope of state authority to regulate matters affecting interstate commerce. *Cooley v. Board of Wardens*[18] considered a Pennsylvania law requiring vessels to use a local pilot in the

---

14. *Id.* at 209.

15. *See id.* at 209–210 (recognizing the possibility that a state police power law might conflict with a federal regulation of interstate commerce).

16. 27 U.S. (2 Pet.) 245 (1829).

17. *Id.* at 252.

18. 53 U.S. (12 How.) 299 (1852).

Port of Philadelphia or pay a fine. No federal statute governed the subject.[19] Accordingly, the case posed the question of the extent of state power over commerce in the face of congressional silence.

The Pennsylvania pilotage law was challenged on the ground that the Commerce Clause gave Congress exclusive authority to regulate commerce. Although the Court might have treated the Pennsylvania law as an exercise of its police power, not a commercial regulation, and thus avoided the issue, it chose not to take that course. The Court recognized that the Commerce Clause covered navigation and that the Pennsylvania statute thus regulated commerce within the scope of Congress's power. But it rejected the contention that Congress's power was always exclusive. Instead, *Cooley* adopted an intermediate approach, concluding that whether congressional power was exclusive varied with the circumstances.

According to the Court, the decisive circumstance was the nature of the "subjects" the challenged law regulated. According to the Court, some subjects required a uniform national rule, while others needed diverse state-by-state treatment in order to accommodate local conditions. The Court explained: "Whatever subjects of this power are in their nature national, or admit only of one uniform system, or plan of regulation, may justly be said to be of such a nature as to require exclusive legislation by Congress."[20] By contrast, state law could reach subjects where national uniformity was unnecessary or positively detrimental (as it might be when differing local conditions demanded different rules). The Court ruled that Pennsylvania's pilotage requirement regulated in an area that did not need a uniform rule, given the different conditions existing in different ports and thus the varying needs to insist on a local pilot.

Cooley's approach was problematic. Most importantly, the Court failed to offer criteria to distinguish between situations requiring national uniformity and those that could tolerate varying state regulation. Thus, courts after *Cooley* often used those labels to reach conclusions for judgments the bases for which were not always clear. The approach also seemed to tolerate protectionist state measures, in conflict with the Framers' goal of prohibiting such barriers to interstate commerce. Nevertheless, the *Cooley* national/local dichotomy survived into the twentieth century.

[3] The Direct/Indirect Effects Test

The Court applied the *Cooley* test to a variety of state regulations. *Munn v. Illinois* upheld state authority to set storage rates charged by owners of grain silos in interstate commerce.[21] The Court noted that the warehouses were located and did their business

---

19. A federal statute existed, but did not affect the result. Accordingly, the Court treated the case as one in which Congress had been silent.

20. *Id.* at 319.

21. 94 U.S. (4 Otto) 113 (1877). *Munn* is also known for its discussion whether the Due Process Clause imposed limits on state regulation of business. This aspect of *Munn* is discussed in Chapter 9.02[1].

in Illinois. "Their regulation is a thing of domestic concern,"[22] concluded the Court, confirming its local, rather than national character. A companion case held that states could also regulate railroad rates. The road in question, like the warehouse in *Munn*, was "situated within the limits of a single State" and accordingly "its regulation is a matter of domestic concern."[23] A decade later, however, the Court invoked the national/local distinction to hold invalid a state statute regulating rates for interstate rail transportation. Speaking for the Court, Justice Miller wrote that interstate rate regulation was a subject of "general and national character," which required uniformity.[24]

In contrast to railroad *rates*, the Court tolerated greater diversity on matters relating to railroad *safety*. Believing that safety requirements should address local conditions, the Supreme Court upheld state statutes applicable to interstate trains that prohibited the use of stoves or furnaces to heat passenger cars,[25] ordered the elimination of dangerous grade crossings,[26] governed train speed,[27] and prescribed the manner in which interstate trains must approach various structures and intersections.[28] In one of these cases, the Court described such regulations as "eminently local in their character."[29] In other cases, the Court concluded that they were not "directed against interstate commerce"[30] but protected personal safety.[31]

In a series of cases[32] culminating in *DiSanto v. Pennsylvania*,[33] the Court articulated an alternative to *Cooley*, one based on whether a state regulated interstate commerce directly or indirectly. In *DiSanto*, a state justified its law requiring a state license to sell tickets to travel abroad as necessary to prevent fraud. The Court rejected this rationale, because the measure directly regulated interstate commerce. This mechanical direct/indirect effects test was short-lived; as Justice Harlan Fiske Stone argued in his *DiSanto* dissent, it was uncertain in application and ignored the often-critical matters of degree.[34] But, as the railroad cases discussed above suggested by their differing analyses of railroad rate and railroad safety regulations, the *Cooley* approach was not

22. *Id.* at 135.
23. Chicago, B. & Q. R. Co. v. Iowa, 94 U.S. (4 Otto) 155, 163 (1877).
24. Wabash, St. Louis & Pacific Railway v. Illinois, 118 U.S. 557, 577 (1886).
25. *See* New York, N.H. & H. R. Co. v. New York, 165 U.S. 628 (1897).
26. *See* Erie R.R. Co. v. Board of Public Util. Comm'rs, 254 U.S. 394 (1921).
27. *See* Erb v. Morasch, 177 U.S. 584 (1900).
28. *See* Crutcher v. Kentucky, 141 U.S. 47, 61 (1891). *But see* Seaboard Air Line Ry. Co. v. Blackwell, 244 U.S. 310 (1917) (striking down a state law requiring trains to slow at crossings with the effect of causing 124 stops in 123 miles).
29. *Crutcher*, 141 U.S. at 61.
30. *New York*, 165 U.S. at 632.
31. *Erie*, 254 U.S. at 410.
32. *See, e.g.*, Smith v. Alabama, 124 U.S. 465, 482 (1888) (upholding a state law described as affecting interstate commerce "only indirectly, incidentally, and remotely"); Southern Ry. Co. v. King, 217 U.S. 524, 531 (1910); Silz v. Hesterberg, 211 U.S. 31, 40–41 (1908). *See generally* James W. Ely, Jr., *"The Railroad System Has Burst Through State Limits": Railroads and Interstate Commerce, 1830–1920*, 55 ARK. L. REV. 933 (2003).
33. 273 U.S. 34 (1927).
34. *See id.* at 44 (Stone, J., dissenting).

much better. Ultimately, the Court distanced itself from such an approach, adopting instead a balancing test.

[4] Towards the Modern Approach

In two opinions written by Justice Stone, the Court began to sketch out what would become the modern approach to the dormant Commerce Clause. In 1938, the Court in *South Carolina v. Barnwell Brothers*[35] upheld a South Carolina law that imposed weight and width limits on trucks using the state's highways. In doing so the Court accorded significant deference to the legislature's judgment about the road-deterioration problems caused by large trucks.

Justice Stone explained that deference in part by referring to the fundamentally local character of highways.[36] But he also noted that the South Carolina law was non-discriminatory, in that it equally burdened both out-of-staters and in-staters. In an important footnote, he explained that such deference was inappropriate when the legislature discriminated against out-of-staters, because in that case, "legislative action is not likely to be subjected to those political restraints which are normally exerted on legislation where it affects adversely some interests within the state."[37] In other words, if the legislature only burdened persons outside of the state, a court could not trust the state's political process to ensure that the state was in fact acting for a legitimate public health or safety purpose — *i.e.*, it could not trust that the law was in fact a police power regulation. Rather, when the legislature discriminated against outsiders, it might be appropriate for courts to suspect a legislative purpose simply to harm outsiders or interstate commerce — something the dormant Commerce Clause was intended to prevent. As explained below, the modern rule subjects state laws to particularly stringent dormant Commerce Clause scrutiny when the law is held to discriminate against interstate commerce.

Barnwell's political process reasoning is deeply resonant and reflects insights that go well beyond the dormant Commerce Clause. For example, Justice Stone himself employed similar insights when suggesting that discrimination against "discrete and insular minorities" might reflect dysfunction in the political process that justifies more careful judicial scrutiny.[38] Indeed, Chief Justice Marshall suggested something

---

35. 303 U.S. 177 (1938).

36. *See id.* at 187 ("Few subjects of state regulation are so peculiarly of local concern as is the use of state highways.").

37. *See id.* at 184 n.2 ("State regulations affecting interstate commerce, whose purpose or effect is to gain for those within the state an advantage at the expense of those without, or to burden those out of the state without any corresponding advantage to those within, have been thought to impinge upon the constitutional prohibition [against states regulating interstate commerce] even though Congress has not acted. Underlying the stated rule has been the thought, often expressed in judicial opinion, that when the regulation is of such a character that its burden falls principally upon those without the state, legislative action is not likely to be subjected to those political restraints which are normally exerted on legislation where it affects adversely some interests within the state.").

38. *See* United States v. Carolene Products, 304 U.S. 144, 152 n. 4 (1938). *Carolene Products* is discussed in Section 10.01[2].

quite analogous when, in *McCulloch v. Maryland*, he concluded that the State of Maryland lacked the constitutional authority to impose taxes on the Bank of the United States, except insofar as it taxed aspects of the Bank that were shared with in-state entities (*e.g.*, a generally-applicable tax on all bank deposits).[39] As will become apparent, however, this political process analysis is not without its problems in the dormant Commerce Clause context.[40]

Seven years after *Barnwell Brothers*, in *Southern Pacific Co. v. Arizona*,[41] the Court used a balancing test to conclude that at least some railroad safety regulation demanded national uniformity. Arizona prohibited operation of trains longer than 14 passenger or 70 freight cars. The law was defended as a safety measure to reduce accidents caused by long trains. In sharp contrast to the Court's attitude in *Barnwell Brothers*, the Court in *Southern Pacific*, speaking through now-Chief Justice Stone, was openly skeptical of the Arizona law's safety benefits. The Court also remarked on the burden the law placed on interstate train traffic, noting that the practicalities of train operations in 1945 meant that the Arizona law required the breaking up of longer trains into shorter ones as far east as El Paso, Texas and as far west as Los Angeles. It also noted that the burden imposed by the Arizona law fell almost exclusively on interstate, rather than domestic, traffic, in light of the fact that "[i]n Arizona, approximately 93% of the freight traffic and 95% of the passenger traffic is interstate."[42] Finally, the Court distinguished *Barnwell Brothers* on the ground that states had "far more extensive control"[43] over highways than they did over trains.

Southern Pacific identified a number of factors that would become relevant to modern dormant Commerce Clause analysis. One could understand the Arizona law as having regulatory effects outside of its borders. Such extraterritorial regulation has sometimes been described as *per se* violating the dormant Commerce Clause,[44] although some scholars have described those statements as lacking a firm doctrinal foundation.[45] One can also note the fact that the Arizona law seemed to discriminate against interstate commerce, to the extent it regulated conduct (the operation of trains) that was nearly exclusively carried out as part of interstate, rather than domestic, commerce. Nevertheless, the Court's own language in *Southern Pacific* sug-

---

39. McCulloch v. Maryland, 17 U.S. (4 Wheat.) 316 (1819). This aspect of *McCulloch* is discussed in Section 4.05.

40. *See* Section 7.05.

41. 325 U.S. 761 (1945).

42. *Id.* at 771.

43. *Id.* at 783.

44. *See, e.g.* Healy v. Beer Institute, 491 U.S. 324, 332 (1989) (citing "our established view that a state law that has the practical effect of regulating commerce occurring wholly outside that State's borders is invalid under the Commerce Clause.").

45. *See, e.g.*, David Driesen, *Must States Discriminate Against Their Own Producers Under the Dormant Commerce Clause?*, 54 HOUSTON L. REV. 1, 20–29 (2016).

gests that the real reason the Court struck down the law was because it imposed serious burdens on interstate commerce that were not commensurate with the local safety benefits the law purported to provide.[46]

In 1945, the doctrinal categories we can identify in dormant Commerce Clause doctrine did not exist with the same rigidity they do today. Thus, Chief Justice Stone might have had all these factors in mind when he reached his conclusion about the balance between the need for a national train length rule and the state's prerogative to regulate for local safety. As the next section explains, the modern rule accounts for these factors through a two-step doctrinal structure that turns heavily on whether the law in question discriminates against interstate commerce.[47]

§ 7.04 The Modern Approach

In recent decades, the Court has adopted an approach to dormant Commerce Clause cases that incorporates a variation of the *Southern Pacific* balancing test. Although the discussion below does not account for all the decisions in this area, it summarizes the Court's most significant jurisprudence.

The Court begins by asking whether a state statute discriminates on its face or in its purpose or effect against out-of-staters or interstate commerce. If it does, the state law is subjected to stringent scrutiny and is likely to be found unconstitutional.[48] On the other hand, if the law does not discriminate but, instead, regulates interstate and domestic commerce evenhandedly, imposing only an incidental impact on interstate commerce, courts will apply a more lenient balancing test that weighs the state's interest against the burden the law imposes on interstate commerce. A discriminatory statute is presumptively invalid, but a non-discriminatory law is likely to be upheld unless the burden on commerce greatly outweighs the law's legitimate local benefits.[49]

---

46. *See, e.g.,* 325 U.S. at 783–784 ("Here examination of all the relevant factors makes it plain that the state interest is outweighed by the interest of the nation in an adequate, economical and efficient railway transportation service, which must prevail.").

47. Even today, though, justices question whether the distinction between the tests applicable to even-handed and discriminatory state legislation is as rigid as the doctrinal rules might suggest. *See, e.g.,* C.A. Carbone, Inc. v. Town of Clarkstown, 511 U.S. 383, 423 (1994) (Souter, J., dissenting) ("The analysis [used in cases of non-discriminatory state legislation] is similar to, but softer around the edges than, the test we employ in cases of overt discrimination.").

48. *See* Philadelphia v. New Jersey, 437 U.S. 617 (1978). This test is often referred to as strict scrutiny. However, one should take care when using this term, as the Court uses it in other contexts — in particular, in equal protection and substantive due process analysis — to mean something slightly different.

49. *See* Pike v. Bruce Church, Inc., 397 U.S. 137, 142 (1970) (setting forth this test and stating that a non-discriminatory law will be struck down only if the burdens it imposes on interstate commerce are "clearly excessive in relation to the putative local benefits").

[1] Discriminatory Laws

The dormant Commerce Clause seeks fundamentally to prohibit states from regulating in ways that discriminate against out-of-state competition. This principle is simple to apply when a state law discloses its protectionist character on its face. State laws that seek to accomplish such simple economic protectionism are *per se* invalid.[50] *Hood & Sons v. Du Mond*[51] illustrates the Court's scrutiny when a state seeks to protects its domestic industry against out-of-state competition. In *Hood*, New York refused to license a Massachusetts milk distributor to open a facility from which it would ship milk to the Boston market, fearing loss of needed supply to the local market. Speaking for the Court, Justice Jackson strongly suggested that such a protectionist motivation (*i.e.*, to protect local supplies by excluding those who would export it) was *per se* invalid: "This Court has not only recognized th[e] disability of the state to isolate its own economy as a basis for striking down parochial legislative policies designed to do so, but it has recognized the incapacity of the state to protect its own inhabitants from competition as a reason for sustaining particular exercises of the commerce power of Congress to reach matters in which states were so disabled."[52]

But often (indeed, usually), when a state employs regulatory power to discriminate against interstate commerce, it does not confess to such an inadmissible objective. Instead, it hides the true motive behind some pretext (*e.g.*, that its action is based on the need for highway safety or to protect its inhabitants against infected products).[53] A court must then detect and expose the subterfuge. To do so, the court typically employs a "least restrictive alternative" approach. In essence, a state law held to be discriminatory in its purpose or effect can survive only if the state can show it acted for a legitimate purpose *and* had no alternative means for achieving that purpose that was less burdensome on interstate commerce. If the statute lacks this close fit

---

50. *See* C & A Carbone, Inc. v. Clarkstown, 511 U.S. 383 (1994); City of Philadelphia v. New Jersey, 437 U.S. 617 (1978).

51. 336 U.S. 525 (1949).

52. *Id.* at 538.

53. The Court has rejected the argument that ensuring the prosperity of the people of the state constitutes a legitimate health and safety objective. *See* Baldwin v. G.A.F. Seelig, 294 U.S. 511, 522–523 (1935) ("The argument is pressed upon us ... that the end to be served by the Milk Control Act is something more than the economic welfare of the farmers or of any other class or classes. The end to be served is the maintenance of a regular and adequate supply of pure and wholesome milk; the supply being put in jeopardy when the farmers of the state are unable to earn a living income. Price security, we are told, is only a special form of sanitary security; the economic motive is secondary and subordinate; the state intervenes to make its inhabitants healthy, and not to make them rich.... This would be to eat up the rule under the guise of an exception. Economic welfare is always related to health, for there can be no health if men are starving. Let such an exception be admitted, and all that a state will have to do in times of stress and strain is to say that its farmers and merchants and workmen must be protected against competition from without, lest they go upon the poor relief lists or perish altogether. To give entrance to that excuse would be to invite a speedy end of our national solidarity. The Constitution was framed under the dominion of a political philosophy less parochial in range. It was framed upon the theory that the peoples of the several states must sink or swim together, and that in the long run prosperity and salvation are in union and not division.").

between purpose and means, the suspicion arises that the true motivation was in fact the simple protectionism that the statute accomplished, rather than the health and safety purpose asserted by the state. This test imposes a heavy burden on the state to justify its legislature's conduct.

Dean Milk Co. v. Madison[54] exemplifies this judicial scrutiny. *Dean Milk* involved a Madison, Wisconsin, ordinance that made it unlawful to sell milk unless pasteurized and bottled within five miles from the town center. The ordinance also required that milk production facilities wishing to sell in Madison obtain a city permit after an inspection, but relieved city inspectors from any obligation to travel more than 25 miles from the city center to conduct any such inspection. The law effectively excluded milk from the plaintiff's pasteurization plants in Illinois, less than 100 miles away.

The Court found that the ordinance discriminated against interstate commerce.[55] The claim that the ordinance was a health measure did not insulate it from careful scrutiny, given the discriminatory means it employed to accomplish those asserted goals. Applying that careful scrutiny, the Court concluded that regulatory alternatives, such as relying on safety ratings obtained by officials where the plants were located or simply requiring far-off plants to reimburse city inspectors for travel costs, could have served local health interests with less discriminatory impact on interstate commerce. The Court placed the burden on the state (or in this case, the city) to justify discriminatory measures both in terms of local benefits flowing from them and the unavailability of nondiscriminatory alternatives adequate to protect the asserted local interests.[56]

State statutes also may be found discriminatory if they prevent outsiders from access to a state's products. In *Hughes v. Oklahoma*,[57] the Court struck down a state law that forbade transporting minnows out of state. Since the law discriminated on its face, Oklahoma had to justify it based on the legitimate purpose/least restrictive alternative test. Although its stated purpose, conserving minnows, was legitimate, the state had sought to promote it by discriminating against interstate commerce in the item rather than adopting alternatives (*e.g.*, limiting all removal of minnows from state waters) which would have distributed the burden equally between interstate and domestic commerce.

Discriminatory state laws almost invariably fail to survive the type of scrutiny performed in *Dean Milk* and *Hughes*. But this is not an absolute rule, as the Court

---

54. 340 U.S. 349 (1951).

55. The fact that the ordinance also discriminated against milk from elsewhere in Wisconsin is irrelevant, since the body enacting the ordinance was the city, which was effectively protecting its own businesses. *See also* Fort Gratiot Sanitary Landfill, Inc. v. Michigan Dep't of Natural Resources, 504 U.S. 353, 361 (1992) ("[O]ur prior cases teach that a State (or one of its political subdivisions) may not avoid the strictures of the Commerce Clause by curtailing the movement of articles of commerce through subdivisions of the State, rather than through the State itself.").

56. *See* Hunt v. Washington State Apple Adver. Comm'n, 432 U.S. 333, 353 (1977) (citing *Dean Milk*, among other cases, for this proposition).

57. 441 U.S. 322 (1979).

demonstrated in 1986. *Maine v. Taylor*[58] considered a Maine statute that banned the importation into Maine of live baitfish from other states. The Maine law facially discriminated against interstate commerce; indeed, as a prohibition on imports from other states, it was a particularly severe form of discrimination. Nevertheless, the Court upheld the law, concluding that Maine had a legitimate state purpose — protecting the state's fragile marine ecology from the parasites out-of-state baitfish carried — and had no nondiscriminatory alternative. In response to arguments that the state could have developed testing or other less discriminatory means of protecting its legitimate interests, the Court held that Maine was not required "to develop new and unproven means of protection at an uncertain cost."[59]

The cases up to now have involved state laws that discriminate on their face. However, even facially neutral laws may be characterized as discriminatory and thus trigger strict scrutiny. The analysis of when a facially neutral law is in fact discriminatory can at times be subtle.

Consider first *Minnesota v. Clover Leaf Creamery Co.*[60] In *Clover Leaf*, the Court concluded that a Minnesota statute banning the sale of milk in plastic disposable containers but allowing it in paper containers was in fact non-discriminatory. The Court acknowledged that Minnesota's plywood industry stood to benefit from the law while the plastics industry that suffered was located outside the state. Yet the Court was not troubled by that impact. The Court noted that the statute continued to allow the use of some plastic-based products, such as recyclable or returnable plastic containers. At any rate, the fact that some in-state businesses benefitted was insufficient to establish a discriminatory effect, since some out-of-state plywood businesses also benefitted. The Court also observed that most of the challengers to the law were in-state businesses: citing *Barnwell Brothers*, the Court stated that "[t]he existence of major in-state interests adversely affected by the Act is a powerful safeguard against legislative abuse."[61] The Court thus suggested that such in-state burdened entities served as political surrogates for the out-of-state plastic container manufacturers. While this may seem intuitively sensible, it should not be forgotten that a state legislature could attempt to take advantage of this idea by enacting a law that burdens minor or powerless in-state interests and thereby claim that the law was in fact even-handed and thus merited only relatively deferential dormant Commerce Clause scrutiny.

Other cases pose more difficult issues. *Hunt v. Washington State Apple Advertising Commission*[62] involved a North Carolina statute requiring that apples sold in closed containers in the state could only display United States Department of Agriculture quality grades. Other grade certificates were banned and had to be removed from the outside of the containers. Washington State, the nation's largest apple producer,

---

58. 477 U.S. 131 (1986).
59. *Id.* at 147.
60. 449 U.S. 456 (1981).
61. *Id.* at 473 n.17.
62. 432 U.S. 333 (1977).

challenged the statute, as it precluded Washington from attaching its own certificates attesting to its more rigorous grading system—a system that benefitted its apple growers in marketing their products.

The North Carolina law did not discriminate on its face, since it applied to both North Carolina and imported apples. It did, however, discriminate in its effect, since it would strip Washington apples of the competitive advantage they otherwise enjoyed by virtue of their rigorous inspection system. The trial record contained evidence that North Carolina enacted the statute for a discriminatory motive. But the Court found it unnecessary to rely on that proof. Instead, based on the discriminatory effect, it concluded that "the burden falls on the State to justify [the discrimination] both in terms of the local benefits flowing from the statute and the unavailability of nondiscriminatory alternatives adequate to preserve the local interests at stake."[63]

In *C.A. Carbone v. Town of Clarkstown*,[64] the Court confronted a different question relevant to the discrimination issue. *Carbone* considered a Clarkstown, New York, ordinance that required that all solid waste be processed at a facility designated by the city. The ordinance clearly favored the designated facility, which would enjoy the legally-mandated trash processing business. Because the favored business was located in Clarkstown, the Court concluded that the ordinance was discriminatory. It thus applied strict scrutiny, which it found the ordinance failed.

Other justices disagreed with the majority's conclusion about discrimination. Justices O'Connor and Souter both wrote opinions that argued that, since the ordinance disfavored *other* Clarkstown-based businesses in addition to out-of-town businesses, the ordinance could not be understood as discriminatory as the dormant Commerce Clause used that term. Indeed, they noted that the very plaintiff challenging the ordinance was itself a Clarkstown-based business.[65]

Clarkstown suggests that not every law that burdens both local and out-of-jurisdictions will be held to be even-handed. At the other extreme, the Court has also made clear that not every facially neutral state law that disadvantages some out-of-state interest will be considered discriminatory. In *Exxon Corp. v. Governor of Maryland*,[66] the Court upheld a Maryland statute that prohibited petroleum producers or refiners from operating a retail gas station in Maryland. The producers and refiners required to divest themselves of their Maryland gas stations were entirely out-of-staters. In a 7–1 decision, the Court found no dormant Commerce Clause violation, and, indeed, no discrimination. Although some interstate companies were excluded, other interstate marketers (who neither produced nor refined petroleum) were not. The Act thus did not entirely exclude interstate dealers or burden their conduct of business, nor did it treat in-state and out-of-state retailers differently. The Court rea-

---

63. *Id.* at 353.

64. 511 U.S. 383 (1994).

65. Nevertheless, Justice O'Connor voted to strike down the law, concluding that it failed the balancing test used for non-discriminatory laws. Justice Souter voted to uphold it, after applying that same test.

66. 437 U.S. 117 (1978).

soned that the dormant Commerce Clause "protects the interstate market, not particular interstate firms, from prohibitive or burdensome regulations."[67] The absence of in-state burdened parties did not doom the state statute under these circumstances.

Hunt and *Exxon* were decided within a year of each other by the same Court. Yet only Justice Blackmun thought both laws were invalid. If their divergent results can be harmonized, it would probably be on the ground suggested by the *Exxon* Court in a footnote:

> If the effect of a state regulation is to cause local goods to constitute a larger share, and goods with an out-of-state source to constitute a smaller share, of the total sales in the market—as in *Hunt* and *Dean Milk*—the regulation may have a discriminatory effect on interstate commerce. But the Maryland statute has no impact on the relative proportions of local and out-of-state goods sold in Maryland and, indeed, no demonstrable effect whatsoever on the interstate flow of goods. The sales by independent retailers [who benefitted by the Maryland law] are just as much a part of the flow of interstate commerce as the sales made by the refiner-operated stations [which had to be sold off by their refiner-owners].[68]

In essence, the Court concluded that the statute was not discriminatory, because interstate commerce in gasoline continued to flow as it had before, albeit under different market structures. This analysis suggests an underlying truth about the dormant Commerce Clause: as much as the political process reasoning set forth in *Barnwell Brothers* suggested a concern with discrimination against *out-of-staters*, the ultimate concern of the dormant Commerce Clause is with discrimination against *interstate commerce*.[69]

[2] The *Pike* Balancing Test

When the Court finds that a state law regulates in an even-handed, non-discriminatory way, it employs a balancing test that compares the local health and safety benefits the law provides against the burdens the law imposes on interstate commerce. The Court stated the test in 1970 in *Pike v. Bruce Church, Inc.*: "Where the statute regulates even-handedly to effectuate a legitimate local public interest, and its effects on interstate commerce are only incidental, it will be upheld unless the burden imposed on such commerce is clearly excessive in relation to the putative local benefits."[70] This review has come to be known as "*Pike* balancing."

---

67. *Id.* at 127–28.

68. *Id.* at 126 n.16.

69. Indeed, one can harmonize this idea with the Constitution's structure more generally by recognizing that Article IV's Privileges and Immunities Clause *does* concern itself with discrimination against out-of-staters. The Article IV Privileges and Immunities Clause is considered later in this chapter.

70. 397 U.S. 137, 142 (1970).

As suggested by *Pike*'s "clearly excessive" language, *Pike* balancing favors upholding non-discriminatory state laws. To be sure, on occasion, the Court will find that a state law fails that balancing. In one notable example, *Bendix Autolite v. Midwesco Enterprises*,[71] the Court struck down an Ohio law that tolled the state's statute of limitations for any lawsuit commenced against an out-of-state entity that did not appoint an in-state agent for service of process, an action that would serve as consent to the general jurisdiction of Ohio courts. Speaking through Justice Kennedy, the Court observed that it could have struck down the law as one that discriminated against interstate commerce. But instead, the Court analyzed it as an even-handed statute, and concluded that "its legitimate sphere of regulation is not much advanced by the statute while interstate commerce is subject to substantial restraints." It concluded that the burden the law imposed on out-of-state corporations was "significant," while, on the other side of the balance, "[t]he ability to execute service of process on foreign corporations and entities is an important factor to consider."[72] After balancing those considerations, the Court concluded that the Ohio law imposed "an unreasonable burden on commerce."[73]

The *Pike* test has its critics. In *Bendix*, for example, Justice Scalia criticized its balancing methodology as incoherent—indeed, as not even "balancing" in the classic sense—famously remarking that *Pike* balancing "is more like judging whether a particular line is longer than a particular rock is heavy."[74] Others have criticized *Pike* balancing as amounting to judicial second-guessing of the importance of state interests legislatures seek to promote.[75] On the other hand, laws that impose serious burdens on interstate commerce do impair the integrity of the nation as a single economic unit, and thus seem to violate the principle that animated the Framers' decision to vest Congress with the power to regulate interstate commerce (the power that, of course, serves as the foundation for the dormant Commerce Clause).

This threat surfaced in *Bibb v. Navajo Freight Lines*.[76] *Bibb* considered an Illinois law requiring that trucks use a particular type of rear fender mud flap (called a "contour" flap) and prohibiting a different mud flap (called a "straight" mud flap) which was allowed in forty-five states and required in one state. The Court conceded that the law was non-discriminatory: trucks engaged in both local and interstate commerce were subject to the same rule. Nevertheless, the Court concluded that the Illinois law unreasonably burdened commerce while producing little safety benefit. It expressed concern that interstate trucks crossing into Illinois would have to stop at the border, replace their straight mud flaps with contour mud flaps, and reverse that operation

---

71. 486 U.S. 888 (1988).

72. *Id.* at 891, 893.

73. *Id.* at 895.

74. *Id.* at 897 (Scalia, J., concurring in the judgment).

75. *See, e.g.*, Michael T. Fatale, *Common Sense: Implicit Constitutional Limitations on Congressional Preemptions of State Tax*, 2012 MICH. ST. L. REV. 41, 62 & 62 n.106 (noting this critique).

76. 359 U.S. 520 (1959).

when they exited the state. One can perhaps understand concerns that cases such as *Bibb* reflect illegitimate judicial second-guessing of state legislative determinations on matters such as highway safety. But one can also understand the concern that laws such as the Illinois mud flap law, even if non-discriminatory, impose unacceptable burdens on interstate commerce.[77] As a counter to that latter argument, however, one must remember that Congress always retains the power to preempt any laws that do in fact threaten the nation's economic unity. That congressional power is discussed later in this chapter.

§ 7.05 The Political Process Rationale

The concern about state regulations of commerce relates in part to the tendency of groups to favor their own interests at the expense of others. If unchecked by some restraining umpire, a state legislature may benefit its constituents and burden non-citizens. Indeed, it is important to recall that it was exactly this dynamic that led the Framers to give Congress the power to regulate interstate commerce.

As noted earlier, the Court in the 1938 *Barnwell Brothers* case suggested that when state legislation distributes benefits and burdens impartially inside and outside the state, the Court may conclude that the state's political process has functioned fairly, and that out-of-state interests have been represented by in-state surrogates. However, when state legislation distributes the gains from a program to in-state interests and externalizes the costs, the state's political process may not have considered fairly non-residents' interests. Accordingly, the *Barnwell Brothers* Court concluded, more careful judicial scrutiny is appropriate in that latter situation.

A 1994 case both illustrates both this rationale but also its limitations. In *West Lynn Creamery, Inc. v. Healy*,[78] the Court struck down a Massachusetts regulation that assessed a tax on all fluid milk sold to Massachusetts retailers (two-thirds of which was produced out-of-state) and then distributed the proceeds as a subsidy to Massachusetts dairy farms. The tax was non-discriminatory, while subsidies are not considered problematic under the dormant Commerce Clause.[79] However, perhaps

---

77. In two subsequent cases, the Court struck down laws limiting the size of trucks, on the ground that they failed *Pike* balancing both because of the laws' trivial safety benefits and the burden those laws imposed on interstate commerce. *See* Kassel v. Consolidated Freightways Corp., 450 U.S. 662 (1981); Raymond Motor Transp., Inc. v. Rice, 434 U.S. 429 (1978). However, language in both of these opinions also reflects concern that the laws may have in some ways been discriminatory. *See Kassel*, 450 U.S. at 676 ("Iowa's scheme, although generally banning large [trucks] from the State, nevertheless has several exemptions that secure to Iowans many of the benefits of large trucks while shunting to neighboring States many of the costs associated with their use."); *Raymond*, 434 U.S. at 446–447 (describing the discrimination possibility as "[o]ne other consideration, although not decisive").

78. 512 U.S. 186 (1994).

79. *See* New Energy Co. v. Limbach, 486 U.S. 269 (1988). The reasons for the constitutionality of subsidies under the dormant Commerce Clause are complex, but include the impracticality of determining what would constitute an unconstitutional subsidy—for example, would a state's decision

ironically, the combination of the evenhanded tax and in-state subsidy had a pernicious, unconstitutional effect:

> When a nondiscriminatory tax is coupled with a subsidy to one of the groups hurt by the tax, a State's political processes can no longer be relied upon to prevent legislative abuse, because one of the in-state interests which would otherwise lobby against the tax has been mollified by the subsidy.[80]

In other words, the in-state group one would normally think of as the opponent of the tax—the in-state dairy interests—would not oppose the Massachusetts scheme because they would get their money back via the subsidy. Indeed, they would not only get their own money back, but they would get more than what they paid in, since they would also share in the tax revenue collected from out-of-state dairy interests (who of course would not share in the subsidy).

But weren't consumers an in-state losing group, the existence of which would suggest a well-functioning state political process? After all, the unrefunded tax paid by out-of-state producers raised the retail price of milk in Massachusetts. The Court rejected the argument that consumers constituted an in-state interest burdened by the law, reasoning that the price increase would be so small that consumers would likely not notice it. Note that this analysis required the Court to make predictions about consumer behavior, hardly a matter on which the justices could be expected to be experts. But note something more fundamental. A state's tariff on goods from another state is a paradigmatic dormant Commerce Clause violation: it is likely that such tariffs constituted the most blatant form of the economic protectionism the Framers sought to prevent when they gave Congress the power to regulate interstate commerce. But in-state consumers *always* pay the price for tariffs. If that is true, then under *Barnwell Brothers*-style political process analysis, tariffs should be generally acceptable, given the existence of in-state interests that might oppose the law.

In *West Lynn Creamery*, Chief Justice Rehnquist criticized the entire project of using political process analysis to decide dormant Commerce Clause cases, writing: "Analysis of interest group participation in the political process may serve many useful purposes, but serving as a basis for interpreting the dormant Commerce Clause is not one of them."[81] Regardless of whether his wholesale rejection of such analysis is sound, one can at least see how, if taken to its logical conclusion, such analysis raises serious concerns about its workability and even its logical coherence.

---

to build high-quality highways or maintain high-quality schools producing highly-skilled workers unconstitutionally subsidize in-state industry? Following on the political process theory this section discusses, it has also been suggested that subsidies might trigger opposition from in-state taxpayers, and thus create a group of in-state losing interests that justify characterizing the law as even-handed. *See* Dan Coenen, *Business Subsidies and the Dormant Commerce Clause*, 107 YALE L.J. 965, 985 n.112 (1998) (citing sources suggesting this dynamic).

80. 512 U.S. at 200.

81. *Id.* at 215 (Rehnquist, C.J., dissenting).

§ 7.06 Exceptions to the Dormant Commerce Clause

[1] The Market Participant Exception

Courts have recognized certain exceptions to the dormant Commerce Clause, under which states are allowed to favor in-state interests or burden interstate commerce. Some are judge-crafted exceptions that require no action by any other branch of government. First, if a state acts as a market participant rather than as a regulator, the dormant Commerce Clause does not apply and the state may favor its own citizens. The market participant exception applies when a state operates a business or purchases or sells goods or services or otherwise acts in a proprietary capacity. The exception rests in part on the word "regulate" in the Commerce Clause. This language is deemed to impose restraints on state regulation of commerce, not participation in it.

The market participant exception originated in *Hughes v. Alexandria Scrap Corp.*[82] In order to dispose of abandoned automobiles, Maryland adopted a program whereby it would pay bounties to auto demolition firms for every Maryland-registered auto a firm demolished, as a way of encouraging those firms to demolish rather than stockpile such vehicles. As amended, the statutory scheme required out-of-state firms seeking bounties to submit more extensive documentation than firms that operated a demolition facility in Maryland. The Court upheld that discrimination, concluding that the state was acting as a market participant, seeking to bid up the price of auto hulks by paying bounties for their destruction. Such conduct established the state as a participant in the market rather than a regulator. In that role, it was free to favor its own processors.

Reeves, Inc. v. Stake[83] also illustrates the principle. South Dakota owned and operated a cement plant. During a supply shortage, it decided to supply South Dakota customers before furnishing cement to others. When an out-of-state concrete distributor challenged the preference, the Court upheld the state's action, relying on the state's role as a participant in the market that should be able to choose its customers just like any private merchant can.

The market participant exception does not insulate a state when it seeks to regulate as well as participate in the market. Thus, in *South-Central Timber Development, Inc. v. Wunnicke,*[84] the Court struck down an Alaska law that required those who bought government-owned timber to process it in-state. A plurality concluded that Alaska could favor its own in selling the timber, but could not seek to regulate the downstream conduct of its customers.

In addition to the somewhat strained textual argument relying on Article I's use of the word "regulate" and omission of the word "participate," the market participant

---

82. 426 U.S. 794 (1976).
83. 447 U.S. 429 (1980).
84. 467 U.S. 82 (1984) (plurality opinion).

exception rests on other justifications.[85] Historically, the Commerce Clause grew out of concerns relating to the effect of states' discrimination with regard to transactions between private parties, not when the state was a buyer or seller of goods or services.[86] Further, the Court has come to conclude that if a state engages in the market, it should be able to act like other entrepreneurs who may, if they wish, favor some customers over others.[87] This latter instinct may reflect a view that a state discriminating as a market participant simply does not trigger the same foundational concerns about protectionism as a state discriminating as a regulator.

[2] Additional Exceptions

In recent years, the Court has suggested that governmental discharge of traditional sovereign responsibilities might excuse what would otherwise be dormant Commerce Clause violations. In *United Haulers Assn., Inc. v. Oneida-Herkimer Solid Waste Management Authority*,[88] the Court considered an ordinance requiring that trash haulers deliver solid waste to a publicly owned processing plant. Recall that 13 years earlier, in 1994, the Court in *C.A. Carbone v. Town of Clarkstown* had struck down a very similar "flow control" ordinance.[89] Unlike in *Carbone*, however, in *United Haulers* the favored entity was government-owned. A majority upheld the law, concluding that the government was discharging a traditional governmental function and accordingly was immune from normal dormant Commerce Clause restrictions. Writing for the Court, in an opinion joined by Justices Scalia, Souter, Ginsburg and Breyer, Chief Justice Roberts explained:

> Laws favoring local government ... may be directed toward any number of legitimate goals unrelated to protectionism. Here the flow control ordinances enable the Counties to pursue particular policies with respect to the handling and treatment of waste generated in the Counties, while allocating the costs of those policies on citizens and businesses according to the volume of waste they generate.

> The contrary approach of treating public and private entities the same under the dormant Commerce Clause would lead to unprecedented and unbounded interference by the courts with state and local government. The dormant Commerce Clause is not a roving license for federal courts to decide what activities are appropriate for state and local government to undertake, and what activities must be the province of private market competition.[90]

---

85. *See generally* Dan T. Coenen, *Untangling the Market-Participant Exemption to the Dormant Commerce Clause*, 88 MICH. L. REV. 395 (1989).
86. *See Reeves*, 447 U.S. at 437.
87. *See id.* at 438–39.
88. 550 U.S. 330 (2007).
89. 511 U.S. 383 (1994). *Carbone* is discussed in Section 7.04.
90. *United Haulers*, 550 U.S. at 343.

Dissenting, Justices Alito, Stevens and Kennedy found the case indistinguishable from *Carbone.* They rejected the majority's conclusion that the public nature of the facility in question distinguished it in a meaningful way from the analogous facility in *Carbone* which, according to the dissenters, was only nominally private.

The following year, in *Department of Revenue v. Davis*,[91] the Court extended the analysis in *United Haulers* to a Kentucky income tax statute which exempted from state tax municipal bond interest from Kentucky-issued municipal bonds, but not bonds issued by other states. Justice Souter explained that *United Haulers'* rationale — that "a government function is not susceptible to standard dormant Commerce Clause scrutiny owing to its likely motivation by legitimate objectives distinct from the simple economic protectionism the Clause abhors" — applied "with even greater force to laws favoring a State's municipal bonds, given that the issuance of debt securities to pay for public projects is a quintessentially public function" deeply rooted in historical practice.[92] The Court thus upheld the differential state taxation scheme.

[3] Congressional Consent

An important feature of the dormant Commerce Clause is that Congress has the final say in determining the validity of state laws that affect interstate commerce. It can use that power either to preempt such state laws (even if the Court has found them valid under the dormant Commerce Clause) or to authorize such laws (even if the Court has found them to violate the dormant Commerce Clause).

Congress has used this power to sanction state laws prohibiting the sale of liquor. In *Leisy v. Hardin*, the Court had held that states may not prohibit the sale of liquor in its original package shipped from another state "in the absence of congressional permission."[93] The implication was that congressional assent might legitimate the state law. Following the *Leisy* dictum, Congress quickly permitted state prohibition laws to apply to sales of imported liquors in their original packages as if the liquor had been produced in the state. The Court upheld the federal statute in *In re Rahrer.*[94]

These cases create a seemingly anomalous situation. If the Constitution forbids certain state action, how can Congress validate that action? The Supreme Court addressed that issue in *Prudential Insurance Co. v. Benjamin*.[95] Two years earlier, the Court had held that insurance was commerce which Congress could regulate.[96] In response, Congress passed a statute pursuant to its commerce power which authorized states to regulate insurance. This law was challenged as an improper extension of state power over interstate commerce. The Court disagreed. It held that congressional

---

91. 553 U.S. 328 (2008).
92. *Id.* at 341–342.
93. 135 U.S. 100, 124 (1890).
94. 140 U.S. 545 (1891).
95. 328 U.S. 408 (1946).
96. *See* United States v. South-Eastern Underwriters Ass'n, 322 U.S. 533 (1944).

consent could validate a state law which absent such consent would violate the dormant Commerce Clause.[97]

These cases serve as a reminder of the nature of the dormant Commerce Clause. The Commerce Clause is primarily a grant of power to Congress to regulate interstate commerce. The power to regulate includes the right to prescribe that commerce shall be subject to relevant state regulations. Accordingly, Congress may consent to state laws governing commerce, even if the Court might find those laws to impose inappropriately large burdens on interstate commerce. Put differently, the dormant Commerce Clause might be seen as reflecting a constitutional presumption that, absent federal legislation, the Constitution inhibits state legislation imposing undue burdens on interstate commerce. The Court polices that legislation with its judicially-developed strict scrutiny and *Pike* balancing tests. But once Congress acts to authorize state regulation, the constitutional presumption is rebutted. As the Court explained: "When Congress so chooses, state actions that it plainly authorizes are invulnerable to constitutional attack under the Commerce Clause."[98] However, such state actions are still subject to attack on other grounds, for example, as violating the Equal Protection Clause.[99]

§ 7.07 Federal Preemption

Regardless of a state law's validity under the dormant Commerce Clause or any other constitutional restriction on state action, Congress may exclude state regulation by enacting a federal law that displaces or "preempts" state regulation in that area. A valid congressional provision is the supreme law of the land that, under the Supremacy Clause, supersedes any incompatible state law. Determining whether a federal law preempts a state law involves a matter of statutory interpretation. That interpretive exercise seeks to determine whether Congress intended to preempt state law.[100]

Preemption cases fall into a set of categories and sub-categories. At its most basic, a federal law may explicitly preempt state law, or do so implicitly. In turn, a federal law may implicitly preempt state law either by occupying the entire regulatory field (so-called field preemption) or if the state law conflicts with the federal law (so-called conflict preemption). Finally, conflict preemption can exist in one of two circumstances: first, when it is physically impossible for a regulated party to comply with

---

97. *See also* Western and Southern Life Ins. Co. v. State Bd. of Equalization of California, 451 U.S. 648 (1981) (upholding a state discriminatory tax on out-of-state insurance companies because a federal law had removed any Commerce Clause restriction); Northeast Bancorp, Inc. v. Board of Governors, 472 U.S. 159 (1985) (upholding state laws discriminating against some out-of-state holding companies based on congressional consent).

98. Northeast Bancorp., Inc. v. Board of Governors, 472 U.S. 159, 174 (1985). *See* Metropolitan Life Ins. Co. v. Ward, 470 U.S. 869 (1985).

99. *See Ward, supra.*

100. *See, e.g.,* Medtronic Inc. v. Lohr, 518 U.S. 470, 485 (1996) ("the purpose of Congress is the ultimate touchstone in every pre-emption case").

both the federal law and the state law; and second, if the state law would frustrate the achievement of the federal law's objectives. This discussion follows this basic structure, and then adds a final consideration that overlays the entire topic.

Express preemption follows from a congressional statement prohibiting regulation except by the federal government. One might think that express preemption requires actual language speaking to preemption. However, this is not necessarily the case. Justice Kennedy explained this seeming anomaly in his partial concurrence in *Gade v. National Solid Waste Management Association*:

> Though most statutes creating express pre-emption contain an explicit state-ment to that effect, ... we have never required any particular magic words in our express pre-emption cases. Our task in all pre-emption cases is to en-force the clear and manifest purpose of Congress. We have held, in express pre-emption cases, that Congress's intent must be divined from the language, structure, and purposes of the statute as a whole.[101]

Gade considered whether a federal workplace safety law preempted Illinois workplace safety standards that went further than the federal ones. Justice Kennedy found express preemption of the state law in a provision of the federal law that read as follows:

> Any State which, at any time, desires to assume responsibility for development and enforcement therein of occupational safety and health standards relating to any occupational safety or health issue with respect to which a Federal standard has been promulgated ... shall submit [to the federal government] a State plan for the development of such standards and their enforcement.[102]

This provision never explicitly says that state law safety standards were preempted, but it did require that states wishing to regulate a workplace safety issue that federal regulations already touched obtain federal approval for the state standard. Justice Kennedy read this provision as expressly preempting state standards that had not been submitted for federal approval.

A finding of explicit preemption does not necessarily settle the entire preemption question. Rather, a court may still need to determine the scope of that preemption. For example, in *Cipollone v. Liggett Group*,[103] the Court considered a situation in which Congress had included preemption provisions in the federal law regarding warnings on cigarette packs. The issue was whether those provisions preempted a state common law action for damages. The Court held that one of the federal laws did not preempt state common law actions but did preempt state legislation mandating particular warnings. Speaking through Justice Stevens, the Court relied in large part on the precise wording of the federal preemption provisions.

Field preemption refers to a situation in which Congress has enacted a regulatory program "sufficiently comprehensive to make reasonable the inference that Congress

---

101. 505 U.S. 88, 112 (1992).
102. 29 U.S.C. §667(b).
103. 505 U.S. 504 (1992).

left no room for supplementary state regulation."[104] Field preemption often presents difficult issues, because it requires courts both to identify the relevant "field" and to determine whether congressional regulation of that field is in fact so comprehensive as to justify a conclusion of field preemption. An illustrative case of field preemption is *City of Burbank v. Lockheed Air Terminal*.[105] In *City of Burbank*, the Court found that a city noise control ordinance limiting takeoff times at an airport was preempted by federal aviation law. The Court noted the pervasive nature of federal control over aircraft noise issues and airplane traffic more generally, and worried that upholding such local laws would create a patchwork regulatory regime of the sort Congress did not intend.

Recall that conflict preemption comes in two varieties. "Physical impossibility" conflict between a federal and state law presents a relatively easy situation. In most cases, it is fairly straightforward to ask if a regulated party could possibly comply with both the federal law and the state law that the federal law allegedly preempts. For example, a federal law might limit the information that a medicine label can contain, perhaps to guard against consumer confusion arising from the proliferation of label information that Congress considers irrelevant. If a state law affirmatively requires that an additional piece of information appear on such labels, a pharmaceutical manufacturer simply cannot comply with both laws. In this situation, the state law would be preempted on a physical impossibility theory.

The other branch of conflict preemption, which asks whether the state law would frustrate federal objections, is not as straightforward. For example, in *Gade*, the plurality concluded that allowing state workplace safety laws not pre-approved by the federal government would frustrate the federal objective of subjecting workplaces to one and only one set of regulations—whether federal or state. In his concurring opinion, Justice Kennedy criticized this approach, expressing concern that a "free wheeling judicial inquiry into whether a state statute is in tension with federal objectives would undercut the principle that it is Congress rather than the courts that pre-empts state law."[106] His concern was that this type of preemption analysis gives courts a great deal of authority to determine what exactly Congress intended to achieve with the federal law, and whether those goals would be impaired by the allegedly-preempted state law. He worried that this inquiry would involve the court in policy-making that was the business of legislators, not judges.

Underlying all these preemption categories is a so-called "presumption against preemption." This principle presumes that Congress did not intend to preempt the historic police powers of the states; thus, this presumption is normally thought to apply only when the subject-matter of the allegedly-preempted law is traditionally one regulated by states rather than the federal government.[107] This presumption is thought to respect

---

104. California Sav. & Loan Ass'n v. Guerra, 479 U.S. 272, 281 (1987).

105. 411 U.S. 624 (1973).

106. *Gade*, 505 U.S. at 111 (Kennedy, J., concurring in part and concurring in the judgment).

107. At times, the applicability of the presumption is stated even more broadly. *See, e.g., Medtronic*, 518 U.S. at 485 ("[B]ecause the States are independent sovereigns in our federal system, we have long

the historic role of states as the primary regulators on traditional health and safety matters. Scholars have also suggested that the presumption assists states in marshalling their political resources to oppose any federal regulatory initiative that might impair their own regulatory authority, since the statutory clarity required to overcome the presumption against preemption would also put states on notice that Congress was considering divesting them of some of their regulatory authority.[108]

In recent years, some justices have insisted that the presumption against preemption does not apply in express preemption cases.[109] The theory behind this argument is that express preemption issues require the Court simply to read the statute and reach the best interpretation, unencumbered by any presumption that the statute does or does not preempt.

Interpreting complex regulatory schemes is by itself a difficult enterprise. When one attempts that task while also applying vague considerations such as those underlying field or federal-objective frustration preemption, to which is added an equally vague presumption against preemption, one can understand why preemption cases can be so challenging.

§ 7.08 Interstate Privileges and Immunities

Like the dormant Commerce Clause, Article IV's and Immunities Clause[110] reflects an interstate non-discrimination ideal that demonstrates the Framers' concerns with ensuring national unity. Thus, unsurprisingly, that Clause shares important similarities with the dormant Commerce Clause. But they are not the same, and the Privileges and Immunities Clause requires its own consideration.

That Clause states that "[t]he citizens of each state shall be entitled to all Privileges and Immunities of citizens in the several states."[111] It descends from a somewhat sim-

---

presumed that Congress does not cavalierly pre-empt state-law causes of action. In all pre-emption cases, and particularly in those in which Congress has legislated ... in a field which the States have traditionally occupied, we start with the assumption that the historic police powers of the States were not to be superseded by the Federal Act unless that was the clear and manifest purpose of Congress."). But other opinions have insisted that the presumption "is not triggered when the State regulates in an area where there has been a history of significant federal presence." U.S. v. Locke, 529 U.S. 89, 108 (2000).

108. See, e.g., Jack Goldsmith, Statutory Foreign Affairs Preemption, 2000 S. Ct. Rev. 175, 185 ("On [the political process] view, the presumption pushes Congress to carefully consider the federal-state balance of power when making legislation. Or, relatedly, the presumption gives the states notice of impending preemptive legislation and facilitates their efforts to marshal resources against the legislation.").

109. See, e.g., Altria Group v. Good, 555 U.S. 70 (2008) (Thomas, J., joined by Roberts, C.J., and Scalia and Alito, JJ.).

110. One should not confuse this clause with a very similar sounding clause appearing in the Fourteenth Amendment. That latter clause is examined later in this book. See Chapter 9.01[2].

111. U.S. Const. art. IV § 2, cl. 1.

ilarly worded (but much longer) version in the Articles of Confederation.[112] The Clause does not create the rights it calls privileges and immunities, nor does it control states' authority over their own citizens' rights. Instead, its purpose was "to help fuse into one Nation a collection of independent, sovereign States"[113] by ensuring that every state provide to the citizens of every other state the "privileges" and "immunities" it provides to its own citizens. As the Court explained in 1873, it declares "to the several States, that whatever those rights, as you grant or establish them to your own citizens, or as you limit or qualify, or impose restrictions on their exercise, the same, neither more nor less, shall be the measure of the rights of citizens of other States within your jurisdiction."[114] As Justice Kennedy wrote, "our Founders, in their wisdom, thought it important to our sense of nationhood that each State be required to make a genuine effort to treat nonresidents on an equal basis with residents."[115]

The preceding should suggest that the dormant Commerce Clause and Privileges and Immunities Clause share some common ground. They do — however, important differences exist in their reach.[116] First, unlike the dormant Commerce Clause, the Privileges and Immunities Clause extends only to individual "citizens." Thus, it does not protect aliens or corporations. Second, whereas the dormant Commerce Clause addresses laws that target or regulate commerce, a restriction that might or might not focus on a law's effects on out-of-staters,[117] the Privileges and Immunities Clause explicitly targets discrimination against out-of-staters. Third, the Privileges and Immunities Clause only protects what its name suggests — "privileges" and "immunities." Finally, the various exceptions to the dormant Commerce Clause, such as congressional consent to state regulation and the market participant doctrine, do not apply to the Privileges and Immunities Clause.

The threshold question under the Privileges and Immunities Clause is whether the state action jeopardizes some privilege or immunity. The Court has confined the clause's scope to activity "sufficiently basic to the livelihood of the Nation" and to

---

112. ART. OF CONF., art. IV, cl. 1 ("The better to secure and perpetuate mutual friendship and intercourse among the people of the different states in this union, the free inhabitants of each of these states, paupers, vagabonds and fugitives from Justice excepted, shall be entitled to all privileges and immunities of free citizens in the several states; and the people of each state shall have free ingress and regress to and from any other state, and shall enjoy therein all the privileges of trade and commerce, subject to the same duties, impositions and restrictions as the inhabitants thereof respectively, provided that such restrictions shall not extend so far as to prevent the removal of property imported into any state, to any other State of which the Owner is an inhabitant; provided also that no imposition, duties or restriction shall be laid by any state, on the property of the united states, or either of them.").

113. Toomer v. Witsell, 334 U.S. 385, 395 (1948).

114. Slaughter-House Cases, 83 U.S. (16 Wall.) 36, 77 (1873).

115. Barnard v. Thorstenn, 489 U.S. 546, 559 (1989).

116. *See generally* Brannon P. Denning, *Why the Privileges and Immunities Clause of Article IV Cannot Replace the Dormant Commerce Clause Doctrine*, 88 MINN. L. REV. 384 (2003).

117. *Compare* South Carolina v. Barnwell Brothers, 303 U.S. 177, 196 n.2 (1938) (focusing dormant Commerce Clause scrutiny on laws affecting out-of-state interests), *with* Exxon v. Governor of Maryland, 437 U.S. 117 (1978) (upholding a law against a dormant Commerce Clause challenge because it did not impact the amount of commerce flowing over state lines, despite its disproportionate impact on out-of-state firms).

matters "bearing on the vitality of the Nation as a single entity."[118] These phrases hardly allow for clear application. In *Corfield v. Coryell*, an opinion written by a Supreme Court Justice while sitting as a circuit judge, Justice Bushrod Washington defined the term as referring to those rights "which are, in their nature, fundamental; which belong, of right, to the citizens of all free governments; and which have, at all times, been enjoyed by the citizens of the several states." He continued:

> What these fundamental principles are, it would perhaps be more tedious than difficult to enumerate. They may, however, be all comprehended under the following general heads: Protection by the government; the enjoyment of life and liberty, with the right to acquire and possess property of every kind, and to pursue and obtain happiness and safety; subject nevertheless to such restraints as the government may justly prescribe for the general good of the whole. The right of a citizen of one state to pass through, or to reside in any other state, for purposes of trade, agriculture, professional pursuits, or otherwise; to claim the benefit of the writ of habeas corpus; to institute and maintain actions of any kind in the courts of the state; to take, hold and dispose of property, either real or personal; and an exemption from higher taxes or impositions than are paid by the other citizens of the state; may be mentioned as some of the particular privileges and immunities of citizens, which are clearly embraced by the general description of privileges deemed to be fundamental: to which may be added, the elective franchise, as regulated and established by the laws or constitution of the state in which it is to be exercised. These, and many others which might be mentioned, are strictly speaking, privileges and immunities....[119]

Privileges and immunities include basic constitutional rights. Thus, a State could not forbid out-of-staters from worshipping or engaging in political speech. The clause also protects the right of out-of-state women to obtain an abortion. Of course, the clause is not necessary for such claims, given that those rights could be vindicated by the Due Process Clause, which incorporates most Bill of Rights provisions.[120] But in the abortion case of *Doe v. Bolton*, the Court went further, to include as a privilege or immunity the right to obtain medical services out-of-state.[121]

Most cases under the clause deal with the right to engage in economic pursuits. Clearly, the right to pursue a trade is a "privilege." Thus, a state may not bar an otherwise qualified nonresident from admission to the state bar.[122] Similarly, the Court has held that a state law regulating commercial shrimp fishing may not impose a license fee of $2,500 for each shrimp boat owned by a nonresident while charging

---

118. Supreme Court of Virginia v. Friedman, 487 U.S. 59, 64–65 (1988) (quoting Baldwin v. Fish & Game Comm'n of Montana, 436 U.S. 371, 382 (1978)).
119. Corfield v. Coryell, 6 F. Cas. 546, 551–552 (C.C.E.D. Pa. 1823).
120. Incorporation is discussed later in this book. *See* Section 9.03.
121. *See* Doe v. Bolton, 410 U.S. 179, 200 (1973).
122. *See* Supreme Court of New Hampshire v. Piper, 470 U.S. 274 (1985).

residents only $25.[123] On the other hand, recreational hunting activity does not rank as a privilege or immunity.[124]

Determining that a state discriminates against out-of-staters with respect to a privilege or immunity does not end the inquiry. A restriction that discriminates against citizens of other states is invalid unless "(i) there is a substantial reason for the difference in treatment; and (ii) the discrimination practiced against nonresidents bears a substantial relationship to the State's objective."[125]

An illustrative application of this test is *Supreme Court of New Hampshire v. Piper*.[126] In *Piper*, the Court used the Privileges and Immunities Clause to strike down a New Hampshire requirement that lawyers could not be admitted to that state's bar unless they resided within the state. The Court held that the ability to practice law was a "privilege" protected by the clause, rejecting the state's argument that lawyers were officers of the court and thus that the state could constitutionally insist that they be part of the state's political community. The state then offered several reasons for its discrimination: ensuring that lawyers were likely to become and remain familiar with local bar rules, to behave ethically, to be available for court appearances, and to do *pro bono* and other volunteer work in the state.[127] The Court found no evidence supporting the state's contentions that nonresident lawyers would not be familiar with local rules or would not behave ethically. It did recognize the problem with availability, although it doubted that most lawyers who took the trouble to take the bar exam and qualify for admission to the state bar would live far away. But even conceding the possibility of a problem, the Court concluded that that interest could be served through more narrowly-tailored means. Similarly, the Court was skeptical of the state's final justification, suggesting that most lawyers who joined a state's bar would do their share of volunteer work. *Piper* illustrates that the scrutiny a court performs when a law infringes on an out-of-stater's "privileges" or "immunities" is significant.

---

123. *See* Toomer v. Witsell, 334 U.S. 385 (1948).
124. *See* Baldwin v. Fish & Game Comm'n, 436 U.S. 371 (1978).
125. *Piper*, 470 U.S. at 284.
126. 470 U.S. 274 (1985).
127. *See id.* at 285.

Chapter 8

Federal Regulation of the States

§ 8.01 Introduction

The previous several chapters have considered the federalism implications of congressional and state regulation of private parties. Distinct federalism issues arise when one level of government attempts to regulate the other. This chapter considers the limitations on federal power to regulate states.[1]

At first glance, such power appears firmly grounded in various provisions of the Constitution. Consider that Article I vests in Congress the power to regulate interstate commerce, a power that would seem to include situations when states engage in interstate commerce (for example, when a state operates a railroad or ferry boat system). Similarly, Article III vests in the federal courts the power to hear cases involving states, a power that presumably would include the power to issue judgments requiring that liable state defendants pay damages or comply with federal court injunctions. Third, the Spending Clause authorizes Congress to spend for the "general Welfare of the United States."[2] This power would presumably allow Congress to allocate money to states on the condition that states act in particular ways. Finally, Section 1 of the Fourteenth Amendment is a catalogue of rights Americans enjoy against their states. Section 5 authorizes Congress to "enforce" those provisions, a grant of power that clearly contemplates federal regulation of state conduct.

These examples—illustrative, not comprehensive—suggest the inherent logic of a federal power to regulate states. However, as explained below, textual provisions such as the Tenth and Eleventh Amendments, and the implications that flow from those texts, and from the Constitution's structure more generally, have been understood to limit some of those powers.

The Tenth Amendment, enacted as part of the first set of amendments that came to be known as the Bill of Rights, provides that "The powers not delegated to the United States by the Constitution, nor prohibited by it to the states, are reserved to the states respectively, or to the people."[3] At times the Court has treated the Tenth

---

1. One section of this chapter, on inter-governmental tax immunities, also considers one aspect of the mirror image question—that is, the extent to which states are immune from federal taxing power. *See* Section 8.04.

2. U.S. Const. art. I, § 8, cl. 1.

3. U.S. Const. amend. X.

Amendment as simply a restatement of the limited nature of federal power, lacking any substantive force of its own.[4] At other times, the Court has viewed it as a guarantee that states retain a substantive realm of regulatory authority and sovereignty.[5]

The Eleventh Amendment deals with states' sovereign immunity from lawsuits in federal court. It reads as follows: "The judicial power of the United States shall not be construed to extend to any suit in law or equity, commenced or prosecuted against one of the United States by citizens of another state, or by citizens or subjects of any foreign state." The first to be ratified after the Bill of Rights, the Eleventh Amendment was triggered by the Supreme Court's decision in *Chisholm v. Georgia*,[6] in which the Court held that it had the authority to hear a lawsuit against a state brought by its out-of-state creditors. One might read the text of the Amendment as simply overruling that decision — that is, as providing that federal courts' diversity jurisdiction does not extend to cases involving state defendants. But, despite protests, the Court has come to read it as standing for a much broader principle, precluding federal court lawsuits against states based on federal law.

Section 8.02 begins by considering federal power to regulate states in states' capacities as economic actors — for example, as polluters or employers or participants in securities markets. Section 8.03 considers federal power to regulate states not in that general capacity just discussed, but rather, in states' uniquely sovereign capacity as lawmakers, law enforcers, and adjudicators. Section 8.04 examines the thorny question of inter-governmental tax immunities (running in both directions — that is, federal immunity from state taxation and state immunity from federal taxation). Section 8.05 examines Congress's powers to attach conditions on spending grants to states. Section 8.06 considers the intricate constitutional doctrine governing when federal courts (and, in one case, state courts) can adjudicate claims against state governments that do not consent to be sued.

§ 8.02 Federal Regulation of States as Economic Actors

It is well-settled that the Commerce Clause gives Congress the power to regulate economic activities that substantially affect interstate commerce.[7] Often, though, such regulations of commerce involve states, given the reality that states perform a variety of functions that affect commerce, such as employing persons, issuing secu-

---

4. *See, e.g.*, United States v. Darby, 312 U.S. 100, 124 (1941) ("The [Tenth] amendment states but a truism that all is retained [by states and the people] which has not been surrendered.").

5. *See generally* Chapter 6 (tracing this concept in the history of the Court's Commerce Clause jurisprudence).

6. 2 U.S. (2 Dall.) 419 (1793).

7. *See generally* Chapter 6.

rities, or operating transportation systems. The Court has vacillated on whether federal regulation of such state-operated activities exceeds Congress's powers or violates the Tenth Amendment, or some combination of the two.

In *Maryland v. Wirtz*,[8] the Court upheld federal wage regulation as applied to a state hospital. Relying on precedent,[9] the Court held that any state sovereignty interests underlying resistance to that regulation did not suffice to defeat federal regulatory power. Speaking for the Court, Justice Harlan wrote:

> In the first place, it is clear that the Federal Government, when acting within a delegated power, may override countervailing state interests whether these be described as 'governmental' or 'proprietary' in character.... But while the commerce power has limits, valid general regulations of commerce do not cease to be regulations of commerce because a State is involved. If a State is engaging in economic activities that are validly regulated by the Federal Government when engaged in by private persons, the State too may be forced to conform its activities to federal regulation.[10]

To be sure, even during this period, the Court acknowledged the Tenth Amendment. For example, in *Fry v. United States*,[11] the Court rejected a claim that applying a federal law to state employees intruded on state sovereignty. Towards the end of his opinion, however, Justice Thurgood Marshall added a footnote to respond to petitioners' claims based on the Tenth Amendment. In summarily rejecting their argument, the Court acknowledged that the Tenth Amendment was "not without significance." It "expressly declares the constitutional policy that Congress may not exercise power in a fashion that impairs the States' integrity or their ability to function effectively in a federal system." However, the footnote concluded, "Despite the extravagant claims on this score made by some *amici*, we are convinced that the wage restriction regulations constituted no such drastic invasion of state sovereignty."[12]

The following year, however, in a 5–4 decision, the Court in *National League of Cities v. Usery*[13] recognized the Tenth Amendment as "an express declaration" of limitations on the power of Congress to regulate the states as states. Although the Court invoked the Tenth Amendment, it did not develop it in much detail. It cited the *Fry* footnote in support of the proposition that "our federal system of government imposes definite limits upon the authority of Congress to regulate the activities of the States as States by means of the commerce power."[14] The Court did not otherwise mention the Amendment, and Justice Rehnquist stated the Court's holding as placing the chal-

---

8. 392 U.S. 183 (1968).

9. *See id.* at 197 (citing United States v. California, 297 U.S. 175 (1936)).

10. *Id.* at 195, 196–197.

11. 421 U.S. 542 (1975).

12. *Id.* at 547 n.7.

13. 426 U.S. 833 (1976).

14. *Id.* at 842.

lenged provisions outside the authority the Commerce Clause conferred. More specifically, the Court held that, to the extent the challenged federal provisions regulating states "operate to directly displace the States' freedom to structure integral operations in areas of traditional governmental functions, they are not within the authority granted Congress by [the Commerce Clause]."[15] Based on this analysis, the Court invalidated application of federal employment law to classes of state government employees that satisfied the Court's definition of traditional governmental functions.

National League of Cities inaugurated an era in which the Court and lower courts struggled to determine what constituted a "traditional [state] governmental function" that Congress was forbidden to regulate. Nine years later, the Court abandoned this project. In *Garcia v. San Antonio Metropolitan Transit Authority,*[16] the Court overruled *National League of Cities.* In addition to remarking on the difficulty lower courts had experienced in distinguishing "traditional governmental functions" immune from federal regulation from other governmental functions that were susceptible to such regulation, the Court also concluded that the protection accorded states in the Constitution rested in the political process, which the Court observed accorded states a prominent role. That role, in turn, allowed states to defend themselves by simply defeating or limiting in the legislative process the scope of proposed federal legislation regulating states.[17]

The majority spilt little ink on dismissing the Tenth Amendment—indeed Justice Powell, dissenting, complained that the Court made "only a single passing reference"[18] to it. By ignoring it, however, the Court spoke volumes. Justice Powell thought the Tenth Amendment "was adopted specifically to ensure that the important role promised the States by the proponents of the Constitution was realized."[19] In her dissent, Justice O'Connor sketched out a more robust role for the Tenth Amendment. She complained that the Court had violated "[t]he *spirit* of the Tenth Amendment" which promised "that the States will retain their integrity in a system in which the laws of the United States are nevertheless supreme."[20]

Despite *Garcia's* 5–4 split on an issue that had sharply divided the justices over the previous two decades, and, indeed, despite the predictions from two of the dissents that the Court would eventually reconsider this issue,[21] the Court has not revisited *Garcia.* However, as noted in the next section, the Court has explored limits on federal regulation of the states in a closely-related context.

---

15. *Ibid.*

16. 469 U.S. 528 (1985).

17. For further discussion of the role of political process analysis in federalism cases, see Section 4.07.

18. *Id.* at 560 (Powell, J., dissenting).

19. *Id.* at 568.

20. *Id.* at 585 (O'Connor, J., dissenting) (emphasis in original).

21. *See id.* at 580 (Rehnquist, J., dissenting); *id.* at 589 (O'Connor, J., dissenting).

§ 8.03 Federal Regulation of the States as Sovereign Actors: The Anti-Commandeering Principle

Garcia made clear that Congress could regulate states in their capacity as participants in the national economy. However, seven years later, the Count embraced a limitation on federal regulation that was similar to, but more limited than, the *National League of Cities* rule that *Garcia* rejected.

In *New York v. United States*,[22] the Court struck down a federal law that forced any state that missed a federal deadline for resolving issues surrounding disposal of radioactive waste to assume ownership and possession of the waste and become liable for damages suffered by failure to do so. Writing for six justices, Justice O'Connor acknowledged that Congress undeniably has power under the Commerce Clause to address the problem of radioactive waste by "requiring or prohibiting certain acts." It lacked power, however, "to compel the States to require or prohibit those acts."[23] The Court concluded that the law's "take title" provision gave the states a "choice" between two unconstitutionally coercive alternatives: either accept ownership of private waste within its borders (which the Court rejected as "a congressionally compelled subsidy"[24] for producers of such waste) or regulate according to Congress's instructions. Congress could not compel the states to take either course, so the choice between the two options was really no choice at all.

The Court's analysis focused on the second of the two options the law offered states—the option to legislate a statewide solution to the problem. The Court described that option as an invalid attempt to "commandeer" states into federal service.[25] Relying on structural notions of federalism suggested by the Tenth Amendment, the Court concluded that state governments are not regional offices or agencies of the federal government, subject to its direction. Justice O'Connor also invoked a political process rationale in support of the majority's conclusion. She raised the specter of the federal government forcing the state to act in a particular way, with voters then misperceiving the resulting state government action as reflecting the preferences of the state officials and holding them accountable for it, even though the state's action had been taken only under federal compulsion.

The Court was careful to distinguish, and approve, other regulatory techniques which Congress used in other parts of the waste disposal statute. Congress could authorize states with disposal sites to tax radioactive waste from other states and then use a portion of the revenue to reward states complying with the federal program.

---

22. 505 U.S. 144 (1992).

23. *Id.* at 166.

24. *Id.* at 175.

25. *Id.* at 188 ("The Federal Government may not compel the States to enact or administer a federal regulatory program.").

The Commerce, Taxing and Spending powers authorized such an approach.[26] (In particular, such authorization constitutes an example of Congress allowing states to discriminate against interstate commerce.[27]) More generally, since Congress could regulate the subject itself, it could give the states the option of regulating according to federal standards, if it so wished, or, if it chose not to, leaving private parties in the state susceptible to federal regulation.

Justice White wrote a vigorous dissent for three justices in which he castigated what he described as the Court's formalistic approach.[28] He proposed a more flexible approach to federalism issues similar in some respects to the flexibility he urged regarding separation of powers issues.[29] Justice White also noted that state officials had worked with Congress to draft the provisions the Court condemned as unconstitutional commandeering. But Justice O'Connor replied that the involvement of state officials was irrelevant, noting that state officials might have their own incentives to have Congress command them to act, since such a command would absolve those officials of the accountability to which they would otherwise be subject.

Five years after *New York*, *Printz v. United States*[30] applied *New York* to strike down a provision of a federal gun control law that required local law enforcement officers to perform background checks on prospective handgun purchasers. The law, in effect, compelled state officers to help administer a federal regulatory scheme. Writing for the Court, Justice Scalia rejected the idea that the federal government had the authority to require state law enforcement officers to enforce federal law.

New York and *Printz* thus prohibited commandeering of, respectively, state legislative and law enforcement functions. However, in *Printz*, the Court expressly distinguished a 1947 case, *Testa v. Katt*,[31] that upheld a federal law requiring state *courts* to hear certain federal law causes of action. Such a law arguably commandeers state judiciaries, just as the laws in *New York* and *Printz* commandeered other branches of state government. Nevertheless, in *Printz*, the Court concluded that such federal direction to state courts was legitimate, reasoning that Article VI's Supremacy Clause explicitly provides that state court judges are bound by federal law.[32] The dissent in *Printz* challenged this analysis, arguing that *Testa* stood for a broader proposition that conflicted with the holding in *Printz*.[33] Regardless of that disagreement, the law today prohibits commandeering of state legislatures and state law enforcement officers, but not the sort of commandeering of state judges upheld in *Testa*.

---

26. *Id.* at 171–72.

27. *See* Section 7.06[3] (discussing this federal authority).

28. His opinion was styled as a partial concurrence because he agreed with the Court's decision to uphold other aspects of the challenged law. Justice Stevens joined Justice White's opinion but also wrote a separate partial concurrence that reached the same conclusions as Justice White.

29. *See* INS v. Chadha, 462 U.S. 919, 967 (1983) (White, J., dissenting). *Chadha*, and Justice White's dissent, is, discussed in Section 3.08[3].

30. 521 U.S. 898 (1997).

31. 330 U.S. 386 (1947).

32. *See id.* at 928–929 (distinguishing *Testa*).

33. *See id.* at 967–969 (Stevens, J., dissenting).

But this rule does not resolve sticky questions of when a federal law does in fact commandeer state government and when, instead, it merely regulates states in their capacity as economic actors, as allowed by *Garcia v. San Antonio Metropolitan Transit Authority*,[34] discussed in the prior section. In *Reno v. Condon*[35] the Court made clear that the commandeering principle does not obliterate all federal power to regulate state officials. The Drivers Privacy Protection Act of 1994 (DPPA) regulates the disclosure and resale of personal information from state driver's licenses, an activity in which many states were engaged. *Reno* rejected South Carolina's commandeering challenge to that law. The Court distinguished the commandeering cases on the ground that:

> the DPPA does not require the States in their sovereign capacity to regulate their own citizens. The DPPA regulates the States as the owners of data bases. It does not require the South Carolina Legislature to enact any laws or regulations, and it does not require state officials to assist in the enforcement of federal statutes regulating private individuals.[36]

While superficially appealing, the line *Reno* draws between unconstitutional commandeering and constitutional regulation of states as economic actors is not a completely clear one. For example, one could at least arguably conclude that a federal law requiring states to pay its law enforcement workers the federal minimum wage "require[s] the States in their sovereign capacity [for example, as operator of a state highway patrol] to regulate their own citizens" [the patrol officers] in a particular way. One might be able to reason to a conclusion that the situation presented in the *Garcia* line of cases is analytically distinct from the situation presented in the commandeering cases. Nevertheless, one might still wonder whether the distinction, or the political process reasoning that partially underlies the commandeering cases, is sufficient to draw a constitutional line between the *Garcia* line and the commandeering line.

In 2018, the Court blurred the line between the anti-commandeering doctrine and another federalism principle—the rule that, under the Supremacy Clause, Congress can preempt any conflicting state law. In *Murphy v. National Collegiate Athletic Association*,[37] the Court struck down a federal law forbidding states from allowing sports betting. Among other carve-outs and exceptions, the law gave New Jersey one year to decide to authorize sports betting in Atlantic City. It failed to do so, but later had a change of heart and attempted to authorize it. When the NCAA sued, the state argued that the federal law was unconstitutional, because it commandeered New Jersey's legislature by forbidding it (after the one year period) from acting to allow sports betting.

The Supreme Court unanimously agreed with New Jersey. Writing for the Court, Justice Alito explained that the federal law was not garden-variety federal preemption

34. 469 U.S. 528 (1985).
35. 528 U.S. 141 (2000).
36. *Id.* at 151.
37. 138 S. Ct. 1461 (2018).

of state law, because the federal law did not give any private person any federal right to do anything (for example, to engage in sports betting). Rather, the law simply regulated state legislatures, by forbidding *them* from acting—that is, from enacting a law authorizing sports betting. In particular, the Court in *Murphy* distinguished the federal law at issue from those that prevent states from regulating in a certain field that Congress wishes to be unregulated, since that latter type of law gives private persons a federal right—a right to be free of state regulation. By contrast, the sports betting law struck down in *Murphy* conferred no federal right on any person to engage in sports betting. Rather, it simply prevented states from allowing it.

Murphy is a difficult case to understand. Even if one accepts its distinction between federal laws giving persons a right do something (and thus preempting state regulation) and federal laws preventing state authorizations to do something, one might still wonder why the political accountability justifications for the anti-commandeering rule operate only with regard to the second type of law rather than the first. After all, in both cases, a state legislature can simply point to the federal law and say to the state's citizenry, in effect, "we would like to do something but the federal government has tied our hands." If the resulting lack of political accountability is constitutionally fatal to a commandeering law, why shouldn't it be fatal to a garden-variety federal law that preempts conflicting state law?

Regardless of whether one is able to find a meaningful distinction here, it is clear that, at the very least, the anti-commandeering principle sets uneasily at the edge of federal authority to regulate states as economic actors (established by *Garcia*) and federal authority to preempt conflicting state law.

§ 8.04 Intergovernmental Taxation

McCulloch v. Maryland[38] made clear that the Constitution precludes states from directly taxing the federal government. As Chief Justice Marshall saw it, the power to tax constitutes the power to destroy. Thus, if a state could tax a federal entity, it could essentially destroy it and thereby impair the operation of the federal government. The Court thus concluded that the Bank must be immune from the type of state taxation Maryland sought to impose.

As the Court explained much later, "The one constant here ... is simple enough to express: a State may not, consistent with the Supremacy Clause, ... lay a tax directly upon the United States."[39] *McCulloch* justified this principle not simply on the text of the Supremacy Clause. Rather, as discussed earlier in this book,[40] Chief Justice Marshall relied heavily on structural ideas about democracy—in particular, the lack of a built-in political check when a state taxes an out-of-state entity.

---

38. 17 U.S. (4 Wheat.) 316 (1819).
39. United States v. New Mexico, 455 U.S. 720, 733 (1982).
40. *See* Section 4.07.

Yet *McCulloch*'s analysis was difficult to apply, given the myriad ways in which states may tax and the equally myriad ways in which a federal instrumentality may be present in a state. Tax immunity exists only "when the levy falls on the United States itself, or on an agency or instrumentality so closely connected to the Government that the two cannot realistically be viewed as separate entities, at least insofar as the activity being taxed is concerned."[41] Federal tax immunity only applies if the tax falls on a body that is part of, or owned by, the federal government.

Thus, in *United States v. New Mexico*,[42] the Court held that private contractors who were managing federal atomic laboratories were not immune from New Mexico's nondiscriminatory sales, receipts, and use taxes. Tax immunity did not exist simply because the federal government was affected by the tax on contractors or bore its burden. Nor were the contractors immune because they bought property for the federal government or because the tax fell on its earnings. Tax immunity did not follow from the contractors' agency relationship with the federal government. Instead, in order to enjoy federal tax immunity, a private taxpayer must be incorporated into the federal government structure.

In *New Mexico*, the contractors were not "constituent parts" of the federal government but instead had a relationship with it "for limited and carefully defined purposes."[43] Accordingly, the contractors were not immune from the state's receipts and use taxes. The sales tax posed a closer question, since a purchasing agent might be so associated with the government as to lack any independent role. The Court had so concluded in an earlier case,[44] but the Court found that case distinguishable. In that earlier case, the purchase orders identified the government as the purchaser, the contractor was not liable for the price, and it had no independent authority to order. Here, the contractors bought items in their own name.[45]

McCulloch long supported a broad doctrine of tax immunity, which prevented a state from taxing the salary paid a federal officer.[46] No more. Federal officials have no immunity from nondiscriminatory state taxes imposed on all members of the community.[47] The Government is not burdened if its employees, like other citizens, must pay taxes to state overnments.[48] Congress may, however, accord immunity beyond that implied from the Constitution. It may, for instance, exempt government contractors from state taxation.[49]

---

41. *New Mexico*, 455 U.S. at 735. *See also* Arizona Dep't of Revenue v. Blaze Construction Co., 526 U.S. 32 (1999).

42. 455 U.S. 720 (1982).

43. *Id.* at 740–41.

44. Kern-Limerick, Inc. v. Scurlock, 347 U.S. 110 (1954).

45. *See also* Arizona Dep't. of Revenue v. Blaze Const. Co., 526 U.S. 32 (1999) (reaffirming this approach).

46. *See* Dobbins v. Commissioners of Erie County, 41 U.S. (16 Pet.) 435 (1842).

47. *See* Graves v. New York ex rel. O'Keefe, 306 U.S. 466 (1939).

48. *See* New York v. United States, 326 U.S. 572, 578 (1946).

49. United States v. New Mexico, 455 U.S. at 744; *see also* Arizona Dep't. of Revenue v. Blaze Constr. Co., 526 U.S. 32 (1999).

Does immunity from intergovernmental taxation run in both directions, such that states are also immune from federal taxation? *McCulloch v. Maryland*[50] may have implicitly suggested a reciprocal doctrine of intergovernmental tax immunity protecting both states and the federal government.[51] After all, just as federal agencies could be destroyed by state taxation, state entities would be vulnerable to federal taxation. *Collector v. Day*[52] held the salary of a state officer not subject to federal taxation. Because the Court then viewed a tax on income as a tax on its source, this holding reflected a symmetrical treatment of state and federal tax immunity.

The Court has since abandoned the theory that a tax on income is a tax on its source; as a consequence, it overruled *Day* and its progeny.[53] State employees and private persons who deal with the states no longer enjoy federal tax immunity, even though the taxation may burden the states concerned. An economic burden alone cannot support a claim of state immunity.[54]

§ 8.05 Conditional Federal Spending Grants to States

As noted in the general discussion of the Taxing and Spending Power,[55] the federal government, like any sovereign, can use its fiscal powers to accomplish regulatory goals. Congress's ability to do that is subject to special limits when the recipient of federal spending is a state and the federal spending comes with conditions that the recipient state must satisfy in order to receive the money.

The Court established the basic principles In *South Dakota v. Dole*.[56] *Dole* upheld a federal law that reduced the amount of federal highway funds distributed to states that allowed persons under 21 to purchase alcohol. The Court set forth several requirements for such conditional federal grants to states. First, the spending must be for "the general welfare." The Court stated that Congress's judgment on this question would receive substantial deference. Second, the Court imposed what is known as a "clear-statement rule" on the conditions Congress imposes — that is, the conditions Congress imposes must be unambiguous. Such a requirement ensures that states are acting knowingly when they accept the funds. Moreover, in a way akin to the presumption against preemption, a clear statement rule puts states on notice that Con-

---

50. 17 U.S. (4 Wheat.) 316 (1819).

51. *See* New York v. United States, 326 U.S. 572, 576 (1946) ("the fear that one government may cripple or obstruct the operations of the other early led to the assumption that there was a reciprocal immunity of the instrumentalities of each from taxation by the other").

52. 78 U.S. (11 Wall.) 113 (1871).

53. *See* Graves v. New York ex rel. O'Keefe, 306 U.S. 466 (1939) (overruling *Day*).

54. *See* Massachusetts v. United States, 435 U.S. 444, 461 (1978); *see also* South Carolina v. Baker, 485 U.S. 505 (1985) (rejecting a constitutional immunity from federal taxation on the interest earned by a state-issued bond, and overruling *Pollock v. Farmers' Loan & Trust Co.*, 157 U.S. 429 (1895)).

55. *See* Sections 5.04–5.06.

56. 483 U.S. 203 (1987).

gress is considering imposing conditions on a spending grant, so that, if they wish, they can mobilize political opposition to the conditions.[57]

Third, the conditions must relate to the federal interest in the particular national program being funded. Finally, the spending power may not be used to induce the states to engage in unconstitutional activities. (Thus, for example, under this last restriction, a grant of federal funds conditioned on racially discriminatory state action would be an unconstitutional exercise of the spending power.) Toward the end of the opinion, the Court implied without elaboration an additional requirement that such conditions not be coercive — i.e., the condition must leave a realistic opportunity for the state to decline the money. As explained below, this last, implied limitation played a large role in the Court's Spending Clause analysis striking down part of the Affordable Care Act in 2012.

Applying these criteria, the Court in *South Dakota* upheld the highway spending condition. Highway spending promoted the general welfare, and the drinking age condition was clearly expressed in the statute. While the Court suggested that it might consider a tighter "relatedness" requirement in the future, it concluded that the state/plaintiff had not argued for such a tighter requirement in the case before the Court,[58] and it found the condition to satisfy the looser requirement the Court applied. Nor did the condition induce the state to act unconstitutionally. To be sure, the condition did induce the state to regulate according to Congress's preferences in the area of alcohol consumption, a field where the Twenty-First Amendment reserves significant regulatory authority to the states. But the Court concluded that this sort of inducement was not what it meant by Congress inducing "unconstitutional" state action of the sort intended by its fourth criterion. Finally, the Court observed that the percentage of highway funds at stake if the state declined to accept the condition was not so great as to render the condition coercive.[59]

In *National Federation of Independent Business v. Sebelius*, the Court struck down the component of the Affordable Care Act that expanded the federal Medicaid program.[60] Medicaid is a joint federal-state program that provides health insurance for poor persons. States voluntarily choose to participate in the program, and all of them have; when they participate, the federal government pays a significant percentage of the costs. The Affordable Care Act included an offer to states to pay initially 100% and eventually 90% of the additional costs if states greatly expanded eligibility for Medicaid. However, if states declined the offer, the statute withdrew all federal Medicaid funding from that state.

---

57. *Cf.* Section 7.07 (discussing how the presumption against preemption operates in the national political process in an analogous way to clear statement rules of this type).

58. *See* 483 U.S. at 208 n.3.

59. *See id.* at 207–212 (discussing and applying these factors).

60. 567 U.S. 519 (2012). The Court's treatment of the main component that was challenged — the requirement that most Americans purchase health insurance — is discussed in Sections 5.05[2] and 6.07.

A seven-justice majority of the Court struck down that provision, concluding that it unconstitutionally coerced states into expanding Medicaid. Writing for a three-justice lead opinion on this question, Chief Justice Roberts described the conditional withdrawal of all federal Medicaid funding to states declining the program expansion as "a gun to the head" rather than as an offer of a true choice. It reached that conclusion after noting the large percentage of state budgets that were devoted to Medicaid (which Chief Justice Roberts described as up to 20% of an average state's budget) and the large proportion of that funding that came from the federal government (which he described as ranging from 50–83%). Given the size of each state's Medicaid program relative to overall state spending, and the critical role federal funding played in each state's program, he concluded that the threat to withdraw all federal Medicaid funding if a state did not expand eligibility was so coercive as to deprive states of a true choice. Four other justices agreed that the Medicaid expansion provision was unconstitutionally coercive.[61]

Of course, distinguishing between a true choice and "a gun to the head" is exceptionally difficult. Perhaps more importantly, as the dissenters on this issue pointed out, that determination requires more of a policy, rather than a legal, judgment.[62] Regardless of one's view on this question, *National Federation* gives the Court a tool it can use in the future if it wishes to apply more stringent review to a federal conditional spending program.

§ 8.06 Litigating Against a State: Eleventh and Tenth Amendment Limitations

A final constitutional limit on federal regulation of states limits both Congress and the federal courts: the power, respectively, to legislate and to enforce litigation remedies against state government defendants. The doctrine of state sovereign immunity limits courts' ability to entertain lawsuits against states. The doctrine does not apply when the United States sues a state or when one state sues another. In either of those instances, states are deemed to have waived any immunity by ratifying the Constitution. Moreover, the doctrine does not apply when a plaintiff sues a subdivision of a state, such as a city. But these caveats still leave significant scope for a state to assert sovereign immunity. In recent years, the Court has issued a number of opinions recognizing such immunity in a variety of contexts.

---

61. *See id.* at 671–691 (Scalia, J., dissenting). This opinion was labelled as a dissent, probably because it reflected those justices' disagreement with the Court's conclusion about the constitutionally of the statute's mandate that individuals purchase insurance. *See* Section 5.05[2] (discussing the Court's decision upholding the individual mandate as a tax).

62. *See id.* at 642–645 (Ginsburg, J., dissenting).

The Constitution speaks most directly to this subject in the Eleventh Amendment, which reads as follows: "The Judicial power of the United States shall not be construed to extend to any suit in law or equity, commenced or prosecuted against one of the United States by Citizens of another State, or by Citizens or Subjects of any Foreign State." While the text of the Eleventh Amendment appears to speak to diversity cases, prohibiting in federal court a citizen of State A from suing State B, it has been construed to prevent Congress from using its Article I power to create federal question causes of action against non-consenting states, including when the plaintiff is a citizen of the state she is suing.

The Eleventh Amendment does not speak to cases brought in state court. However, the end of this section discusses a case from 1999, *Alden v. Maine*,[63] in which the Court found that the *Tenth* Amendment imposes the same limits on suits against non-consenting states in state court that the Eleventh Amendment imposes on suits brought in federal court. This immunity applies even when Congress uses its Article I powers to create federal causes of action that can be heard in state court.

The Eleventh Amendment responded to *Chisholm v. Georgia*,[64] in which the Court, on a 4–1 vote, held it had jurisdiction to decide a case brought by citizens of South Carolina against the State of Georgia, seeking to recover Revolutionary War debts incurred by the state. The justices (who had participated in the drafting of the Constitution, and thus of Article III) reasoned that Article III conferred federal jurisdiction over "controversies ... between a State and citizens of another State," which would seem to cover the matter, unless it applied only when the state was a plaintiff. But the Court's original jurisdiction applied to cases "in which a state shall be party," a broader formulation that arguably suggested a State could sue or be sued in federal court.

Regardless of the correctness of the Court's decision,[65] *Chisholm* triggered a movement to limit such lawsuits, which culminated in the Eleventh Amendment. Although the text of the Amendment simply appeared to address the diversity situation of *Chisholm*, the case to which it was ratified as a response, almost a century later the Court construed it to have broader meaning. In *Hans v. Louisiana*[66] the Court held that the Amendment codified a broader principle of sovereign immunity that precluded suits in federal court against a state even by its own citizens.

Despite the Eleventh Amendment, during the twentieth century two strands of cases eventually emerged that offered ways for private parties to avoid the state sovereign immunity bar and sue non-consenting states.

---

63. 527 U.S. 706 (1999).
64. 2 U.S. (2 Dall.) 419 (1793).
65. *See* THE FEDERALIST No. 81 (Hamilton) (suggesting one Framer's view that non-consenting states could not be sued in federal court).
66. 134 U.S. 1 (1890).

[1] *Ex parte Young*

One method employed a legal fiction the Court embraced early in the twentieth century. In *Ex parte Young*,[67] the Court held that a suit against a state official alleging he was violating federal law was not a suit against the state barred by the Eleventh Amendment. The theory was that, because a state official lacked authority to violate federal law, a lawsuit of this sort operated only against the official as a private individual, not as a representative of the state. In other words, under a *Young* suit, the state official who is the nominal defendant in such a lawsuit is deemed to have been "stripped" of his official status by virtue of his non-compliance with federal law, with the result that the lawsuit was deemed not one against the state.

A moment's reflection should make clear that this stripping theory is a legal fiction: since the only way a government institution can act is through its officials, it makes little realistic sense to say that a state official that happens to violate federal law is thereby deemed no longer acting as a state official. Indeed, the irony grows when one realizes that many such *Young* causes of action involve alleged violations of the Fourteenth Amendment. Since that amendment prohibits "states" from doing certain things (*e.g.*, violating equal protection), how can a plaintiff claim that certain state action violates that amendment, but then argue that sovereign immunity does not apply because the person doing the acting (the state official) is not really acting as a state official? Justice Powell, writing a majority opinion in 1984, described this as the "well-recognized irony" of the *Young* stripping theory.[68]

Perhaps for that reason, or perhaps because of opposition to any chipping away at state sovereign immunity, some justices have been inclined to give *Young* a narrow reading. In *Edelman v. Jordan*,[69] the Court limited the availability of *Young* relief to prospective relief, such as an injunction, rather than to any relief that required the direct payment of money to the plaintiff (even if the payment was styled in equitable terms, such as, in *Edelman*, "equitable restitution"[70]). The theory—as fictional as *Young* itself—was that injunctive relief "merely" required the official to take certain actions, and thus could be understood as running against the official himself rather than the state. For example, a Fourteenth Amendment claim alleging that a state prison had inadequate medical resources might trigger a court injunction mandating the warden to provide better facilities. Of course, those facilities would be paid for by the state; thus, even this relief would, in a real way, impact the state.[71] Nevertheless, the Court, attempting to cabin *Young*'s reach, limited it to prospective relief that did not require direct payment of money awards.

---

67. 209 U.S. 123 (1908).

68. *See* Pennhurst State School and Hospital v. Halderman, 465 U.S. 89, 105 (1984).

69. 415 U.S. 651 (1974).

70. *Id.* at 668.

71. *See, e.g., id.* at 680–82 (Douglas, J., dissenting) (making this point). *But see id.* at 667 (majority opinion) (conceding that "the difference between the type of relief barred by the Eleventh Amendment and that permitted under *Ex parte Young* will not in many instances be that between day and night").

A decade after *Edelman*, the Court imposed another limitation on *Young*. In *Pennhurst State School and Hospital v. Halderman*,[72] the Court ruled that *Young* relief was not available when the lawsuit alleged violations of state, rather than federal law. *Pennhurst* involved litigation against a state hospital that involved a variety of state and federal law claims. The Court, in a five-justice opinion written by Justice Powell, reasoned that the entire justification for *Young* relief was the need to balance Eleventh Amendment state sovereign immunity with the need to find a way for persons to use federal law not just as a shield against unconstitutional state action, but as a sword — that is, allowing persons to be plaintiffs, rather than just defendants, in cases involving state action that violates federal law. Of course, as Justice Powell recognized, that imperative disappears when the claim in question involves not federal law, but state law. By contrast, the dissenters argued for a fuller application of *Young*'s stripping theory — in this case, to both federal and state claims — on the ground that it was consistent with prior practice, for example, in English decisions on which the theory was arguably based.[73]

Since 1984, the Court has imposed two additional limits on *Young* relief. In 1996 the Court, in *Seminole Tribe of Florida v. Florida*,[74] heard a tribe's challenge to a state's alleged violation of the federal law that governed gaming on native reservations. The tribe's main argument for avoiding state sovereign immunity was that the federal gaming statute abrogated that immunity. The Court rejected that argument, which will be presented below.

The tribe's second argument revolved around *Young*. In addition to suing the state itself, the tribe also sued the governor, asking for an injunction requiring him to comply with the statute's procedures for resolving disputes when a state and a tribe disagreed about tribal gaming. The Court also rejected that argument. It concluded that Congress, by enacting the gaming statute's dispute resolution scheme, had inserted a "detailed remedial scheme" into the statute. That decision, the Court argued, evinced Congress's desire to preclude injunctive relief on a *Young* theory.[75]

A year after *Seminole Tribe*, in *Idaho v. Coeur d'Alene Tribe*,[76] the Court further limited *Ex parte Young*, although in confusing fashion. It held that the Eleventh Amendment barred an action by a native tribe in Idaho for a declaratory judgment establishing ownership of certain submerged land it claimed it owned under a federal treaty. The bar applied not just to the suit against the state, but also to the *Young* action against state officials which sought to prohibit them from acting in violation of the tribe's rights in the land.

---

72. 465 U.S. 89 (1984).

73. *See, e.g.*, Vicki Jackson, Seminole Tribe, *The Eleventh Amendment, and the Potential Evisceration of* Ex parte Young, 72 N.Y.U. L. REV. 495, 511 (1997) (considering *Young*'s English roots).

74. 517 U.S. 44 (1996).

75. *Id.* at 74–75. To be sure, the Court had already concluded that Congress exceeded its Article I powers when it enacted that dispute resolution scheme. But even though invalid, that scheme, to the Court, reflected Congress's desire to preclude *Young* relief.

76. 521 U.S. 261 (1997).

In a part of the opinion speaking for five justices, Justice Kennedy affirmed "the continuing validity of the *Young* doctrine" but noted questions regarding "its proper scope and application."[77] Justice Kennedy, now joined only by Chief Justice Rehnquist, thought *Young* generally applies in two instances: first, "where there is no state forum available to vindicate federal interests"; and second, "when the case calls for the interpretation of federal law."[78] But even in those cases, he insisted that courts must engage in "careful balancing and accommodation of state interests when determining whether the *Young* exception applies in a given case."[79] Applying these principles and now again speaking for a majority, Justice Kennedy observed that the case involved "the functional equivalent of a quiet title action which implicates special sovereignty interests." The Tribe could not bring a quiet title action against the state; therefore it could not achieve "the functional equivalent" by a suit against state officers.[80]

Writing for herself and two colleagues, Justice O'Connor concurred in the result but rejected Justice Kennedy's approach to *Young*. The case, she wrote, was:

> unlike a typical *Young* action.... The *Young* doctrine rests on the premise that a suit against a state official to enjoin an ongoing violation of federal law is not a suit against the State. Where a plaintiff seeks to divest the State of all regulatory power over submerged lands — in effect, to invoke a federal court's jurisdiction to quiet title to sovereign lands — it simply cannot be said that the suit is not a suit against the State. I would not narrow our *Young* doctrine, but I would not extend it to reach this case.[81]

In her view, *Young* continues to provide a vehicle for relief against an "ongoing violation of federal law" when plaintiff seeks "prospective rather than retrospective" relief.[82] Justice O'Connor simply would have held that, despite styling the request as one for an injunction, the lawsuit was in reality one that ran against the state in its sovereign capacity. Four dissenters, speaking through Justice Souter, would have held that the tribe had adequately alleged a *Young* claim, given the nature of the relief requested (an injunction) and the target of that requested relief (a state official).

The Court subsequently clarified the status of the *Ex parte Young* doctrine by adopting Justice O'Connor's approach. Citing her concurrence in *Coeur d'Alene*, Justice Scalia wrote for the Court several years later:

> In determining whether the doctrine of *Ex Parte Young* avoids an Eleventh Amendment bar to suit, a court need only conduct a straightforward inquiry into whether the complaint alleges an ongoing violation of federal law and seeks relief properly characterized as prospective.[83]

---

77. *Id.* at 269.
78. *Id.* at 270, 274.
79. *Id.* at 278.
80. *Id.* at 281.
81. *Id.* at 296–97 (O'Connor, J., concurring in part and concurring in the judgment).
82. *Id.* at 294.
83. Verizon Maryland Inv. v. Public Service Commission of Maryland, 535 U.S. 635, 645 (2002).

[2] State Waiver and Congressional Abrogation

In addition to *Ex parte Young*, the Court has also offered another pathway for private litigants seeking to sue non-consenting states. In 1976, the Court held in *Fitzpatrick v. Bitzer*[84] that when Congress legislates pursuant to its power to enforce the Fourteenth Amendment, it is authorized to abrogate states' Eleventh Amendment sovereign immunity and make states liable for retrospective relief.[85] The Court reasoned that the Fourteenth Amendment, by both coming later in time than the Eleventh, and including explicit limitations on state conduct, constitutes a limitation on Eleventh Amendment immunity. It further reasoned that the states consented to that limitation when they ratified the Fourteenth Amendment, and essentially waived that component of their sovereign immunity. When Congress legislates pursuant to this power, any abrogation of state sovereign immunity must appear clearly on the face of the statute. But Congress had the authority to enact such an abrogation.

Thirteen years later, in *Pennsylvania v. Union Gas Co.*,[86] the Court extended the reasoning of *Fitzpatrick* to include the Commerce Clause as a source of congressional authority to abrogate state sovereign immunity. Writing for a plurality of four justices, Justice Brennan reasoned that the Commerce Clause, through its negative, or dormant, implications restricted state regulatory prerogatives just like the Fourteenth Amendment did.[87] Of course, the Commerce Clause came before, not after, the Eleventh Amendment, and thus the chronological analysis the Court engaged in in *Fitzpatrick* did not fit this situation exactly. But Justice Brennan had an answer for that. He observed that, while the Eleventh Amendment by its terms only immunized states from lawsuits brought by citizens of *different* states, the Court in *Hans v. Louisiana*[88] had held that the amendment merely codified the pre-existing common law of state sovereign immunity. Thus, he argued, Article I really did come after Eleventh Amendment immunity, since that immunity, according to *Hans*, had always existed, with the amendment simply making it official.

In addition to drawing a heated dissent from four justices, Justice Brennan's analysis also drew only a half-hearted fifth vote from Justice White, who wrote that he disagreed with much of the plurality's reasoning.[89] Thus, *Union Gas* was an unstable precedent, since, on the day it was decided, five justices announced their dissatisfaction with the plurality's analysis.

This instability prompted the Court to revisit *Union Gas* in *Seminole Tribe of Florida v. Florida*.[90] The law at issue in *Seminole Tribe*, enacted under Article I's Indian Com-

---

84. 427 U.S. 445 (1976).
85. The substantive scope of this enforcement power is discussed in Chapter 13.
86. 491 U.S. 1 (1989).
87. The dormant Commerce Clause is discussed in Chapter 7.
88. 134 U.S. 1 (1890).
89. *Union Gas*, 491 U.S. at 56–57 (White, J., concurring in the judgment in part and dissenting in part).
90. 517 U.S. 44 (1996).

merce Clause,[91] obligated states to negotiate in good faith with native tribes when a tribe wanted to institute gaming on reservation lands, and authorized a tribe to sue a state in federal court to compel performance of that duty to negotiate.

The Court in a 5–4 decision severely limited Congress's ability to enact Article I-based statutes abrogating states' sovereign immunity in federal court. Chief Justice Rehnquist's majority opinion reasoned that the Eleventh Amendment expresses a constitutional principle that state sovereign immunity limits the federal courts' Article III jurisdiction. The Court held that the Indian Commerce Clause does not grant Congress power to oust the states' sovereign immunity, as it attempted to do in the gaming statute. Thus, the tribe's suit against Florida had to be dismissed. But more importantly, *Seminole Tribe* overruled *Union Gas*, and held that the vastly more-important Interstate Commerce Clause also did not authorize congressional abrogation of state sovereign immunity.

The Court further extended the doctrine of state sovereign immunity in *Federal Maritime Commission v. South Carolina State Ports Authority*.[92] In a 5–4 decision, the Court held that state sovereign immunity applies to lawsuits not just in Article III courts but also in Article I courts, such as those housed in federal administrative agencies.[93] After its requests to berth a ship were denied by a state port authority, a private party filed a complaint with a federal agency, the Federal Maritime Commission (FMC), seeking compensatory and injunctive relief against the state. Justice Thomas, writing for the Court, reaffirmed that "the sovereign immunity enjoyed by the States extends beyond the literal text of the Eleventh Amendment" and that the Framers did not intend the states to be subject to proceedings which were "anomalous and unheard of when the Constitution was adopted."[94] Noting the "strong similarities between FMC proceedings and civil litigation," the Court concluded that "the affront to a State's dignity does not lessen when an adjudication takes place in an administrative tribunal as opposed to an Article III court."[95]

Although *Seminole Tribe*'s language limiting Congress's Article I power to abrogate states' sovereign immunity seemed to apply to *any* Article I power, the Court subsequently recognized one Article I power that does allow Congress to abrogate that immunity. In *Central Virginia Community College v. Katz*, a five-justice majority rejected the sovereign immunity defense advanced by state agencies in the context of federal bankruptcy proceedings.[96] The Court emphasized the particular importance of ensuring that bankruptcy dispositions be uniform across the nation, and thus the importance of involving interested state parties in bankruptcy proceedings. It also noted

---

91. "The Congress shall have Power ... To regulate Commerce ... with the Indian Tribes." Article I, § 8.

92. 535 U.S. 743 (2002).

93. Congress's ability to create such federal administrative tribunals, sometimes known as Article I courts, is discussed in Section 2.07.

94. 535 U.S. at 754, 755.

95. *Id.* at 760.

96. 546 U.S. 356, 359 (2006).

that bankruptcy proceedings were *in rem*, rather than *in personam*, a fact that, for the Court, mitigated the sovereign immunity implications of subjecting states to bankruptcy litigation.

On the same day in 1999, the Court decided three cases that expanded the scope of state sovereign immunity in different ways. The cases were all decided by 5–4 majorities—indeed, the line-up of justices in each case was exactly the same—and they all drew vigorous dissents.

One of these cases addressed the question of waiver. Sovereign immunity does not bar lawsuits a state consents to defend. States sometimes waive their sovereign immunity in particular types of cases, often in response to in-state political pressure from groups that enjoy federal rights against their state that they would wish to vindicate in federal court. But such waivers must be express. In one of the 1999 cases, the Court eliminated the possibility that a state can *implicitly* or constructively consent to be sued. In *College Savings Bank v. Florida Prepaid Postsecondary Education Expense Board*,[97] the plaintiff sought to sue Florida under a federal fair-trade law for allegedly making false claims regarding a financial vehicle sold by the state. The plaintiff claimed in part that Florida had constructively waived any sovereign immunity by engaging in economic activity that Congress made clear would subject it to suit.

The Court rejected that argument, and in so doing overruled the constructive waiver doctrine established in a 1964 case, *Parden v. Terminal Railway of the Alabama State Docks Department*.[98] In *Parden*, the Court had held that a state waived its Eleventh Amendment immunity by operating a railroad in interstate commerce. Congress had "conditioned the right to operate a railroad in interstate commerce upon amenability to suit in federal court."[99] The Court held that by operating such a railroad, Alabama had constructively consented to suit. Although the four *Parden* dissenters thought waiver should not be inferred absent a clearer congressional statement of intent, all nine members of the *Parden* Court thought Congress had power "to condition a state's permit to engage in [federally regulated commercial conduct] on a waiver of the State's sovereign immunity from suits arising out of such business."[100] Nevertheless, a series of decisions had eroded the doctrine.[101] In *College Savings Bank*, the Court declined "to salvage any remnant" of the constructive waiver doctrine.[102]

Although *Seminole Tribe* precluded Congress from abrogating state sovereign immunity by legislating pursuant to its Article I powers, it did not disturb the rule that it could do so under its power to enforce the Fourteenth Amendment. The second of the two 1999 cases limited that possibility. In *Florida Prepaid Postsecondary Education Expense Board v. College Savings Bank*, the Court struck down Congress's abrogation of state sovereign immunity for patent infringement claims, because the

97. 527 U.S. 666 (1999).

98. 377 U.S. 184 (1964).

99. *Id.* at 192.

100. *Id.* at 198 (White, J., dissenting for four justices).

101. *See generally* Linda Mullinex et al., Understanding Federal Courts and Jurisdiction 517 (1998).

102. *College Savings Bank*, 527 U.S. at 680.

legislation did not seek to remedy a history of "widespread and persisting deprivation of [Fourteenth Amendment] constitutional rights."[103] Thus, the Court held that the abrogation statute exceeded Congress's power to enforce the Fourteenth Amendment. The modern Court's approach to Fourteenth Amendment enforcement issues is explored in Chapter 13. It is important to understand those cases, and the limits they impose on Congress's enforcement power, given the importance of that power as a vehicle for Congress to abrogate state sovereign immunity.

The decisions above all dealt with state sovereign immunity in *federal* court (and, in one case, in a federal Article I court). However, in the third of the 1999 cases, *Alden v Maine*,[104] the Court held that Congress cannot use its Article I powers to subject a non-consenting state to a private party lawsuit for damages in *state* court. Of course, *Alden* could not rely on the Eleventh Amendment, which spoke of states' immunity from *federal* court litigation. However, it concluded that the Tenth Amendment's implications for state sovereignty mandated the same limitations on state court lawsuits as applied in federal court lawsuits via the Eleventh Amendment. Those limitations also included the same exceptions to state sovereign immunity—for example, the ability of the federal government or other states to sue the non-consenting state, and the ability of private parties to sue in a proper *Ex parte Young* suit. In other words, *Alden* essentially recreated the Court's Eleventh Amendment rules as a matter of interpreting the Tenth Amendment.

State sovereign immunity is one of the most controversial topics in modern constitutional law. Those who disagree with the Court's modern jurisprudence on that issue often criticize the very idea of state sovereign immunity as a royalist anachronism unsuited to a republic in which the people, not the government, are sovereign.[105] They also point out that the language of the Eleventh Amendment by its terms seems to prohibit only the sort of diversity jurisdiction case, such as *Chisholm v. Georgia*, that had triggered the Amendment's drafting. These commentators thus decry the Court's imposition of a state sovereign immunity bar to lawsuits alleging violations of federal law—that is, lawsuits falling under Article III courts' "federal question" jurisdiction. On the other hand, defenders of the Court's approach rely heavily on the 1890 decision in *Hans v. Louisiana*, which found in the Amendment the confirmation of a longstanding, broader sovereign immunity principle than the one suggested by its actual language. They also point to the odd litigation results that would result under a narrow reading of the Amendment, if a citizen of one state, unable to sue a different state because of the Amendment's language, simply sold or transferred her claim to a citizen of the defendant state, who could then, under that narrow read-

---

103. 527 U.S. 627, 645 (1999).

104. 527 U.S. 706 (1999).

105. *See, e.g.*, Okla. Tax Comm'n v. Citizen Band Potawatomi Indian Tribe, 498 U.S. 505, 514 (1991) (Stevens, J., concurring) ("The doctrine of sovereign immunity is founded upon an anachronistic fiction. In my opinion all Governments—federal, state, and tribal—should generally be accountable for their illegal conduct.").

ing, freely sue that state.

Perhaps most importantly, the divide over state sovereign immunity flows from fundamentally different understandings of the federal-state balance. Those favoring more robust state sovereignty immunities point to states' sovereign status and insist that encroachments on that sovereignty be as limited as possible. Those on the other side of the divide critique the entire idea of sovereign immunity, but also rely heavily on the fact that federal laws are supreme and thus override any state-based sovereign interests. This latter understanding would fit neatly into an understanding of the Eleventh Amendment as limited simply to diversity cases, since an immunity for states limited to such cases would not impair the superior status of federal law. By contrast, adherents of more robust state sovereign immunity believe that federal supremacy simply does not supersede a state's sovereign prerogative not to be sued against its will.[106]

---

106. *See, e.g.*, Seminole Tribe of Florida v. Florida, 517 U.S. 44, 72 (1996) ("In overruling *Union Gas* today, we reconfirm that the background principle of state sovereign immunity embodied in the Eleventh Amendment is not so ephemeral as to dissipate when the subject of the suit is an area, like the regulation of Indian commerce, that is under the exclusive control of the Federal Government. Even when the Constitution vests in Congress complete law-making authority over a particular area, the Eleventh Amendment prevents congressional authorization of suits by private parties against unconsenting States.").

Chapter 9

Liberty and Property: The Due Process, Takings and Contracts Clauses

The Constitution's structural provisions, discussed in previous chapters of the book, were designed to protect individual rights by preventing the concentration of government power. Such protection was indirect. But the original document provided some provisions expressly aimed at protecting individual rights. The Bill of Rights, added very soon after the new federal government came into being, added more, although they were understood to restrict only the federal government. After the Civil War, however, the Thirteenth, Fourteenth, and Fifteenth Amendments added important rights applicable to state conduct.

While this Chapter comprehends a number of the Constitution's individual rights provisions, the focus rests on the multi-faceted concept of due process. The Due Process Clauses of the Fifth and Fourteenth Amendments[1] have been invoked in a number of distinct contexts to protect various classes or categories of rights. Although it has limits, one classification occasionally used describes some due process rights as property rights and others as personal rights. Another classifying principle for rights guaranteed by the Due Process Clause involves the distinction between substantive and procedural rights. Using the Due Process Clause to guarantee substantive rights, despite its seeming focus on process, has caused considerable scholarly debate and controversy. Still another distinction is between enumerated rights and unenumerated rights. This latter distinction refers to the Court's use of the Fourteenth Amendment's Due Process Clause to make applicable to, or "incorporate" against, the states the rights explicitly protected against federal infringement in the Bill of Rights. As against such "enumerated" rights stand the "unenumerated" rights the Court has found in the Clause, such as the right to abortion, to certain intimate

---

1. For ease of reading, the rest of this book refers to the Due Process Clause in the singular. Many such references will be to the clause that appears in the Fourteenth Amendment, given the historical importance of the Fourteenth Amendment's Due Process Clause in protecting rights against state government infringement. Nevertheless, unless the context suggests otherwise, any such reference should be understood as pertaining to both the Fourteenth Amendment's Due Process Clause, applicable to the states, and the Fifth Amendment's Due Process Clause, applicable to the federal government.

family and interpersonal relationships, and, for a time in our history, the right to participate in the marketplace free of government regulation.

The Chapter begins in Section 9.01 by sketching out the concept of substantive Fourteenth Amendment rights. Section 9.02 considers what, chronologically, was the first general category of Fourteenth Amendment rights to which the Court accorded serious protection: economic rights generally and, particularly in the late nineteenth and early twentieth centuries, the so-called right to contract—that is, the right to buy and sell in the marketplace as one wished. While the right to contract has largely faded from the scene, other economic rights considered in Section 9.02 have continued to enjoy protection, sometimes quite robustly so.

Continuing with this very approximate chronological examination, Section 9.03 then considers the "incorporation" doctrine—that is, the process by which most of the individual rights guarantees of the Bill of Rights have been "incorporated" via the Fourteenth Amendment Due Process Clause, with the result that those rights now apply against states as well as the federal government. Section 9.04 then examines unenumerated rights that are non-economic in nature—for example, the right to contraception, abortion, and sexual intimacy. Section 9.05 considers the Second Amendment, which was only recently recognized to bestow an individual right to possess firearms.

Again, this treatment is very roughly chronological: the right to contract developed in the late nineteenth century, the Court began incorporating Bill of Rights provisions into the Fourteenth Amendment around the turn of the twentieth century, unenumerated non-economic liberties began to appear in the 1920s and have taken on even greater prominence since the 1960s, and the Second Amendment has become prominent only recently. Nevertheless, the story is substantially more complicated than a simple chronology would suggest.

The Chapter ends in Section 9.06 by considering the procedural dimension of the Due Process Clause—that is, the question whether, and to what degree, the government must provide a hearing before depriving any person of "life, liberty, or property."

§ 9.01 Introduction to Substantive Individual Rights

[1] The Sources of Constitutional Individual Rights

The Constitution, as originally ratified, contained relatively few individual rights provisions. This is not to suggest that the Framers were unconcerned with individual rights; to the contrary, they were deeply concerned about protecting liberty. However, they believed that, for the most part, individual rights were best protected by creating a structure of limited government that would be incapable of infringing on individual liberties. Nevertheless, the original document did specify some rights, including the right to seek a writ of *habeas corpus* except in cases of "Rebellion or Invasion"[2] and the right to be free of state government actions that impair "the Obligations of Contracts."[3]

During the ratification debate, opponents of the Constitution charged that the proposed new national government would be too strong and too capable of oppressing the people's liberties. As a concession to those forces, proponents agreed to add a set of individual rights guarantees to the new Constitution, should it be ratified. When it was, work immediately began on what became first 10 Amendments, which eventually became known as the Bill of Rights. But, as the Court, speaking through Chief Justice Marshall, held in the 1833,[4] the Bill of Rights only applied to the federal government, not to the states. It would not be until the addition of the Fourteenth Amendment, in 1868, and, indeed, until several decades later, that the Court seriously began to consider whether all or particular Bill of Rights provisions also applied to the states, through a process by which those rights were said to have been "incorporated" so as to apply against the states via the Fourteenth Amendment's Due Process Clause.[5]

But the Fourteenth Amendment's Due Process Clause protects more than the Bill of Rights provisions it has been deemed to have incorporated. Beyond those rights, the clause's protection for "liberty"[6] has been understood to provide Americans with an additional set of rights, originally focusing on economic liberties but eventually emphasizing personal autonomy. Judicial protection of such "unenumerated" rights

---

2. U.S. Const. art. I § 9, cl. 2.

3. U.S. Const. art. I § 10, cl. 1.

4. Barron v. City of Baltimore, 32 U.S. (7 Pet.) 243 (1833).

5. Obviously, the Bill of Rights is a critical component of the constitutional rights Americans enjoy. However, space limitations, as well as the conventions of how American law is categorized and subdivided, restrict this book's consideration of the Bill of Rights generally to those that do not speak to criminal procedure. Thus, this book will consider the First Amendment rights of speech, press, assembly, and of religion (both free exercise and non-establishment) (Chapters 11 and 12, respectively), the Second Amendment right to keep and bear arms (Section 9.05) and the Takings Clause of the Fifth Amendment (Section 9.02[3]). All of these rights have been incorporated and thus apply to both the states and the federal government. Most of the other rights in the Bill of Rights (most of which have also been incorporated) deal with the rights of criminal defendants. (A notable exception is the Seventh Amendment right to a jury trial in most *civil* cases, which is also not treated in this book.) Readers interested in such rights should consult sources focusing on criminal procedure or, in the case of the Seventh Amendment, sources focusing on civil procedure.

The Constitution provides other important rights as well. Most notably, the Thirteenth Amendment abolished slavery, the Fifteenth Amendment prohibited racial discrimination in voting, the Nineteenth Amendment gave women the right to vote, and later amendments abolished the poll tax and gave eighteen-year-olds the right to vote. Space limitations preclude discussions of these rights, except that Congress' power to enforce the Thirteenth and Fifteenth Amendments is discussed, along with its cognate power to enforce the Fourteenth, in Chapter 13. The Court's sex discrimination jurisprudence more generally is discussed in Section 10.02.

6. U.S. Const. amend. XIV, § 1 ("nor shall any state deprive any person of life, liberty, or property, without due process of law").

has always been controversial. But there is a long tradition of such protection; while the modern Court may not significantly expand the unenumerated rights it protects, and indeed may be poised to limit some of them, it appears unlikely that such "substantive due process" review will disappear from the scene.

[2] *Slaughter-House*: The Court's First Examination of the Fourteenth Amendment

In the *Slaughter-House Cases*[7] of 1873, the Court first confronted the Fourteenth Amendment. The case involved the three main rights clauses in Section 1 of the Amendment: the guarantee against state action that "abridge[s] the privileges and immunities of citizens of the United States," "deprive[s] any person of life, liberty, and property, without due process of law," or "den[ies] to any person … the equal protection of the laws."[8] The Court rejected the plaintiffs' claims based on all three of these provisions, as well as their claim based on the Thirteenth Amendment's abolition of slavery. However, *Slaughter-House* is mainly known for the very narrow construction it gave to the first of these provisions, the Fourteenth Amendment's Privileges or Immunities Clause.[9]

Slaughter-House arose out of a Louisiana law granting one corporation exclusive monopoly rights to operate a slaughter-house in New Orleans. The law was justified as a health measure, given the serious public health concerns raised by slaughter-house operations and the resulting desire to centralize those operations in one location.[10] The plaintiffs were local butchers who alleged that the monopoly law prevented them from practicing their trade. The butchers alleged that the law violated the Constitution in several ways, by creating involuntary servitude prohibited by the Thirteenth Amendment and violating Section 1 of the Fourteenth Amendment by (1) abridging the privileges and immunities of citizens of the United States, (2) denying the butchers

---

7. 83 U.S. 36 (1873).

8. The Amendment also specifies that persons "born or naturalized in the United States, and subject to the jurisdiction thereof," are citizens of the United States and the state in which they reside. The Fourteenth Amendment was motivated in part by a desire to provide a firmer constitutional foundation for Reconstruction legislation that was originally based on the Thirteenth Amendment's prohibition on slavery. The Amendment also addressed a number of other issues that remained outstanding after the Civil War, for example, by repudiating confederate government debts. U.S. CONST. amend. XIV, § 4. One Fourteenth Amendment provision — penalizing states for disenfranchising persons with partial loss of congressional representation, *id.* § 2 — remains relevant for questions of what that provision implies about the Fourteenth Amendment's protection of voting rights. *See* Reynolds v. Sims, 377 U.S. 533 (1964) (discussing this issue). *Reynolds* is discussed in Chapter 10.07[3][a].

9. There is another clause that speaks of persons' privileges and immunities, in Article IV of the original Constitution. That clause is examined in Section 7.08.

10. *See generally* RONALD LABBE & JONATHAN LURIE, THE SLAUGHTERHOUSE CASES: REGULATION, RECONSTRUCTION, AND THE FOURTEENTH AMENDMENT (2005).

the equal protection of the laws, and (3) depriving the butchers of their property without due process of law. The Court rejected all four constitutional challenges, relying heavily on its interpretation of the history and purpose of the post-Civil War Amendments.

Justice Miller, writing for a 5–4 majority, began his discussion by indicating that the Civil War Amendments share a strong "unity of purpose," which must be construed in the context of the "history of the times." The Court believed that their "prevailing"[11] purpose was to end slavery, a fact that had to be considered in their interpretation. In identifying slavery as essentially the only trigger for the Amendments, Justice Miller's analysis arguably ignored the Fourteenth Amendment's more general goal of providing a baseline of federal constitutional rights against states. For example, Congress had expressed concern with the antebellum South's restrictions on freedom of speech related to slavery and with the post-war South's treatment of whites who had remained loyal to the Union.

The Court majority quickly disposed of three of the four constitutional challenges made by the butchers. It concluded that the prohibition of the Thirteenth Amendment was limited to slavery and similar forms of involuntary servitude — conditions the Court said did not characterize the position of the butcher-plaintiffs. The Court also rejected their equal protection challenge, suggesting that racial discrimination was the main, although not necessarily the exclusive, focus of the Equal Protection Clause. In dismissing the due process challenge, the Court reasoned that no previous interpretation of the Due Process Clause of the Fifth Amendment had ever held that a restraint on the exercise of a person's trade was a deprivation of property. Thus, it concluded that the Due Process Clause of the Fourteenth Amendment should not, either.

The most important part of the opinion was its rejection of the butchers' challenge under the Fourteenth Amendment's Privileges or Immunities Clause. The butchers argued that gainful employment was a privilege that the law abridged. They had a plausible claim: an early circuit court opinion authored by a Supreme Court Justice had given a broad construction to Article IV's similarly-worded Privileges and Immunities Clause to include, among other things, protection for persons following common trades and occupations.[12] While the Article IV clause prevented a state from discriminating against out-of-staters with regard to the privileges a state chose to give its own citizens, the butchers argued that the Fourteenth Amendment's Privileges or Immunities Clause gave persons substantive rights to those privileges, rather than stating a mere non-discrimination rule. Thus, the plaintiffs argued, the Fourteenth Amendment protected their right to engage in the butchering trade.

In rejecting the butchers' argument, the Court relied on the distinction between state citizenship and American citizenship. The Court cited the first sentence of

---

11. 83 U.S. at 67, 82.
12. The Article IV clause is discussed in Section 7.08.

Section 1 of the Amendment[13] to support this distinction. Justice Miller noted that the first sentence granted persons born in the United States or naturalized, and subject to U.S. jurisdiction, the status of both American citizenship and citizenship of the state in which they reside. Given that the Privileges or Immunities Clause speaks of "the privileges or immunities of citizens of the United States," the Court concluded that the clause protects only the particular privileges and immunities granted by federal, rather than state, citizenship. According to the Court, protection of "fundamental" property and civil rights was within the jurisdiction of the several states, and not the federal government.

By contrast, the Court explained that the federal privileges and immunities protected by the clause were those rights "which owe their existence to the Federal government, its National character, its Constitution, or its laws." Such "national rights" included rights such the right to "come to the seat of government to assert any claim he may have upon that government, to transact any business he may have with it, to seek its protection, to share its offices, to engage in administering its functions," the right of "free access to its seaports, through which all operations of foreign commerce are conducted, to the subtreasuries, land offices, and courts of justice in the several States," the right to peaceably assemble and petition for redress of grievances, and the privilege of the writ of habeas corpus.[14]

This construction of the Privileges or Immunities Clause arguably rendered it meaningless. As Justice Field's dissent protested, the privileges and immunities of national citizenship that the majority addressed were already protected against state infringement by the Supremacy Clause. Thus, it is generally thought that the majority's construction of the Privileges or Immunities Clause essentially wrote that clause out of the Constitution.[15]

The Court's construction of the Privileges or Immunities Clause was likely motivated by a fear of the transfer of power from state governments to the federal courts or to Congress that could have occurred under a broader construction of the Fourteenth Amendment. The Court exhibited its concern throughout the opinion. Stressing its faith in the federal system of checks and balances and a national government of limited powers, the Court stated that a broad construction of the Fourteenth Amendment and a ruling for the butchers would have constituted the Court as a permanent "censor upon all legislation of the states, on the civil rights of their own citizens, with authority to nullify such as it did not approve as consistent with those rights."[16]

---

13. "All persons born or naturalized in the United States, and subject to the jurisdiction thereof, are citizens of the United States and of the State wherein they reside." U.S. CONST. amend. XIV. This Citizenship Clause fundamentally altered the legal source of citizenship, making citizenship primarily federal, not derivative of state citizenship. It also overruled *Dred Scott v. Sanford*, 60 U.S. 393 (1857), which had refused to recognize a slave as an American citizen on the ground that African-Americans could never be citizens.

14. *Id.* at 79.

15. *See, e.g.*, AKHIL REED AMAR, THE BILL OF RIGHTS: CREATION AND RECONSTRUCTION 305 (1998) (in *Slaughter-House*, the Court "strangled the privileges-or-immunities clause in its crib").

16. 83 U.S. at 78.

Obviously, the Court was motivated, at least to some degree, by a desire to prevent such a radical change in the structure of the government as it had existed during the eighty years prior to the adoption of the Fourteenth Amendment.

Justice Field's dissent challenged the majority's interpretation of the Fourteenth Amendment's Privileges or Immunities Clause. He argued that the Fourteenth Amendment made everyone a citizen of the United States first, and that state citizenship reflected only a person's residence. As a result, the national government, rather than the states, protected a person's fundamental rights, privileges, and immunities. Also dissenting, Justice Bradley would have struck down the law because it deprived the butchers of their liberty to choose lawful employment without due process of law. Justice Bradley's view was significant because it marked acceptance of so-called substantive due process, which later became prominent for a time in economic rights cases.[17]

The majority's decision in *Slaughter-House* is still good law. The Privileges or Immunities Clause of the Fourteenth Amendment remains essentially written out of the Constitution. The clause has rarely made an impact since *Slaughter-House*.[18]

Although *Slaughter-House* severely limited the role of the Privileges or Immunities Clause as a source of individual rights, the Court has used the Due Process and Equal Protection Clauses to fill in much of the resulting gap. The Court has used the Due Process Clause as the vehicle for incorporating most of the Bill of Rights so as to apply against the states. It has used that same clause to find unenumerated liberty rights—first, the right to act in the marketplace free of undue state interference (the so-called "due process liberty to contract"), and later, similarly unenumerated but non-economic liberties, such as the right to procreation and other analogous personal liberties. Eventually, the Court also employed the Equal Protection Clause to develop an elaborate jurisprudence protecting against many types of government discrimination. Indeed, at times it has used a combination of due process and equal protection reasoning, an approach that has been labelled "the fundamental rights strand of equal

---

17. *See* Lochner v. New York, 198 U.S. 45 (1905). The substantive due process right to contract, which Justice Bradley presaged and the *Lochner* Court embraced, is discussed in the next section.

18. In recent decades, the only significant use of the clause was in *Saenz v. Roe*, 526 U.S. 489 (1999), where the Court struck down a California law that temporarily restricted new arrivals to the welfare benefits they would have received had they stayed in the state they left. In 2010, a plurality of the Court concluded that the Due Process Clause incorporated the Second Amendment right to keep and bear arms. Justice Thomas concurred, but based his incorporation conclusion on the Privileges or Immunities Clause. *See* McDonald v. City of Chicago, 561 U.S. 742, 805 (2010) (Thomas, J., concurring in the judgment). Nine years later, both Justices Thomas and Gorsuch called for use of the Privileges or Immunities Clause to incorporate a Bill of Rights provision (the Eighth Amendment's Excessive Fines Clause). *See* Timbs v. Louisiana, 139 S.Ct. 682, 691 (2019) (Gorsuch, J., concurring); *ibid.* (Thomas, J., concurring in the judgment). *See also* Ramos v. Louisiana, 140 S.Ct. 1390, 1420 (2020) (Thomas, J., concurring in the judgment) (agreeing with the Court's full incorporation of the Sixth Amendment, but calling for that to be accomplished via the Privileges or Immunities Clause). The standards by which the Court determines whether the Fourteenth Amendment includes and makes applicable to the states, or "incorporates" a particular Bill of Rights provision, and the question of the proper Fourteenth Amendment clause to accomplish that incorporation, are discussed in Section 9.03, *infra*.

protection." Finally, it has used the Due Process Clause as a guarantee of fair procedure when government seeks to infringe on a person's life, liberty, or property interests. This Chapter considers all of these rights, as well as more explicitly enumerated economic rights under the Takings and Contracts Clauses, and the right to possess weapons under the Second Amendment.

§ 9.02 Regulation of Business and Other Property Interests

[1] Liberty of Contract under the Due Process Clauses

This sub-section highlights the Court's use of the Due Process Clause to strike down state and federal economic regulations during the first four decades of the twentieth century. Although *Slaughter-House* rejected the use of the Privileges or Immunities Clause to scrutinize state economic regulations, toward the end of the nineteenth century, the Court's Due Process Clause jurisprudence evolved toward providing protection to business relationships.

An important early case in this evolution was *Munn v. Illinois*.[19] *Munn* considered, among other constitutional claims, a due process challenge to an Illinois law regulating the price grain elevator operators could charge farmers for storing their grain before shipping it to processing facilities. Writing for the Court, Chief Justice Waite analogized those elevators to ferry boat operators and other common carriers that, at common law, had been subjected to limits on the fees they could charge. He explained that the justification for such limits was that those businesses were "affected with a public interest" — that is, the owners of those businesses had "devote[d] [their] property to a use in which the public had an interest," and had thereby "grant[ed] to the public an interest in that use" which justified public control "for the common good."[20] Applying this principle to the grain elevator operators, Chief Justice Waite concluded that those elevator operators constituted a monopoly in what he described as the largest grain market in the world. Thus, just as operators of ferry boats, common carriers, and other operators of important public conveyances were subject to price regulation, so too were the grain elevator owners.

But who would decide whether a business was affected with a public interest, and thus appropriately subject to regulation? *Munn* was unclear on this question. On the one hand, the Court stated that it would give great deference to the legislature's judgments on such questions. But on the other, the *Munn* Court itself engaged in its own analysis of the position of the grain elevators in the wheat market, suggesting that such determinations were for courts to make. This "who decides?" question would remain an important one throughout the Court's encounter with the due process liberty to contract.

---

19. 94 U.S. 113 (1877).
20. *Id.* at 126.

Justices Field and Strong dissented, with Justice Field providing the most detailed analysis. He conceded that legislatures had great power to regulate businesses in pursuit of the public interest, for example, by regulating how a public building such as a theater should be built for safety or by requiring the sanitary disposal of waste that would otherwise threaten human health. But he insisted that the government had no legitimate reason to regulate the prices a business charges. He also challenged the majority's "affected with a public interest" theory as having no logical stopping point, arguing that society had legitimate interests in the operation of essentially any industry.

As the Court continued to examine due process challenges to business and other types of regulation, it developed a jurisprudence that sought to distinguish regulations imposed for the public good from regulations that it called "class legislation"—the Court's term for laws that regulated businesses, not in pursuit of any public goal, but rather for the interests of a private group. This concern with private-regarding legislation permeated American legal thinking even before the Civil War. Most famously, in *Federalist 10* James Madison explained that a limited government with separated powers was the best structure to avoid a self-interested "faction" gaining complete control of government and using it for its own private goals. Eventually, the Court's insistence on policing business regulation to ensure that it truly promoted a public interest—or, in the language of the day, constituted a legitimate "police power" regulation—ripened into recognition of a due process-based liberty to participate in market transactions. This liberty eventually became known as the "substantive due process" "right to contract."

Substantive due process is the concept that there are certain rights so fundamental to our traditions of justice that, no matter what procedural guarantees government affords, government cannot abridge those rights without making a particularly compelling showing of need. The foundation for substantive due process has generally been the "liberty" prong of the Due Process Clause—that is, the inclusion of "liberty," along with "life" and "property," in the interests that government[21] cannot deprive without "due process of law." This is the same substantive due process analysis that the Court uses today in such areas as privacy, birth control, and child-rearing.

The Court embraced the substantive due process concept in *Allgeyer v. Louisiana*.[22] In *Allgeyer*, the Court invalidated, as a violation of the liberty of contract, a statute requiring property owners in Louisiana to obtain property insurance only from insurance companies licensed in the state. Importantly, the Court included within the liberty protected by the Due Process Clause the right to engage in "any of the ordinary callings of life" and to buy and sell property on equal terms with others similarly situated.[23]

---

21. To repeat a point made earlier, the Fifth Amendment protects these interests against deprivation by the *federal* government without due process, while the Fourteenth similarly protects them against *state* government deprivation without due process.

22. 165 U.S. 578 (1897).

23. *Id.* at 590.

Eight years after *Allgeyer*, the Court decided what was destined to become the most famous (or infamous) liberty of contract case in its history, *Lochner v. New York*.[24] In *Lochner*, the owner of a bakery challenged a New York statute that prohibited the employment of bakers for more than 10 hours per day or 60 hours per week. The bakery owner claimed that the statute violated employers' and employees' liberty of contract to bargain for, purchase, and sell labor. In evaluating the substantive due process challenge to the law, the Court considered whether New York's asserted public welfare interests justified the incursion into employers' and employees' contractual liberty.

The Court identified two possible legitimate public goals for the statute: protecting the interests of a group (bakery employees) who were otherwise unable to bargain effectively for their labor, and protecting the public health. The Court quickly dismissed the first justification. It concluded that bakery employees were not unusually hampered in their ability to make their own bargains, distinguishing an earlier case that had interfered in the contractual relations between coal miners and mine owners on the ground that miners were in fact at a bargaining disadvantage relative to their employers.[25]

Thus, the only legitimate police power end was the protection of the safety, morals, or general welfare of the public. Since the healthfulness of bread was not affected by the number of hours worked by the bakers who baked it, the health of the bakers themselves was the only end that the Court was willing to explore. The Court rejected that latter interest. It reasoned that baking was not an unusually dangerous occupation. Thus, upholding this interest as sufficient to regulate bakers' working hours would open the door to regulation of the working hours of many other classes of employees. To the Court, that prospect meant the destruction of a worker's general right to offer his labor on whatever terms he wished, including the number of hours of labor he was willing to offer.

Justice Harlan dissented. Driven by concerns about separation of powers and federalism, he argued that federal courts should not second-guess the wisdom of legislation. He viewed such decisions as policy judgments best left to the legislature. Instead, he urged that the Court limit its scrutiny to whether there is a "real or substantial relation between the means employed by the state and the end sought to be accomplished by its legislation."[26] Applying that analysis to the facts of *Lochner*, and examining labor studies from the U.S. and abroad, he concluded that sufficient evidence existed to justify a conclusion that baking was in fact an unusually unhealthy occupation which justified limiting bakers' working hours. The deference Justice Harlan showed and the majority's skeptical scrutiny of the law can be understood as reflecting different answers to the question left open in *Munn v. Illinois*: to what extent should courts defer to or, conversely, second-guess legislative judgments about the public benefits underlying a law attacked on due process grounds?

---

24. 198 U.S. 45 (1905).
25. *See id.* at 54–55 (distinguishing *Holden v. Hardy*, 169 U.S. 366 (1898)).
26. *Id.* at 69 (Harlan, J., dissenting).

Justice Holmes also dissented, but his opinion was more far-reaching than Justice Harlan's. He accused the Court of constitutionalizing a particular economic theory *(laissez-faire* capitalism). To avoid infusing the Constitution with the justices' personal predilections, Justice Holmes would have applied a reasonableness test to the statute, imposing a stricter review standard only when "a rational and fair man necessarily would admit that the statute proposed would infringe fundamental principles as they have been understood by the traditions of our people and our law."[27] This approach would have largely eliminated any scrutiny of business regulation. Hence it was more radical than Justice Harlan's analysis, which would have deferred to legislative judgments but which nevertheless accepted the conceptual legitimacy of the right to contract.

Between *Lochner* in 1905 and the late 1930s, the Court used substantive due process (along with other theories, including the Commerce Clause[28]) to invalidate various types of economic regulations. To be sure, the Court did not strike down every economic regulation it encountered. For example, in *Muller v. Oregon*[29] and *Bunting v. Oregon*,[30] the Court upheld statutes establishing maximum ten-hour days for female and male factory workers, respectively. In these decisions, the Court emphasized that liberty of contract was not an absolute, and that states could enact laws limiting that liberty in order to protect the public interest.[31] However, in other cases, the Court struck down regulation of wages, working hours, prices, and other business practices.[32] The Court's careful protection of the right to contract eventually led scholars and courts to label this period "the *Lochner* era."

During the 1930s, the programs of President Franklin Roosevelt's New Deal, and analogous regulatory programs in the states, increased the controversy regarding the use of substantive due process to invalidate economic regulation. In its 1934 decision in *Nebbia v. New York*,[33] the Court signaled a possible retreat from its substantive due process jurisprudence. *Nebbia* considered a due process right to contract challenge to a New York law establishing a minimum price at which milk could be sold, a law that was designed to assist dairy farmers by propping up the price they could obtain for their products.

The Court, speaking through Justice Owen Roberts, upheld the law as a valid exercise of the state's police power to protect the public welfare. The opinion's language seemed to signal increased judicial deference to the legislature's judgments: Justice

---

27. *Id.* at 76 (Holmes, J., dissenting).

28. *See* Chapter 6.

29. 208 U.S. 412 (1908).

30. 243 U.S. 426 (1917).

31. Indeed, Chief Justice Taft, writing several years later, suggested that *Bunting* all but overruled the specific holding in *Lochner* itself. *See* Adkins v. Children's Hospital, 261 U.S. 525, 564 (1923) (Taft, C.J., dissenting).

32. *See, e.g., Adkins, supra* (striking down a minimum wage law for female workers); Jay Burns Baking Co. v. Bryan, 264 U.S. 504 (1924) (striking down a law regulating the weights of bread sold by the loaf).

33. 291 U.S. 502 (1934).

Roberts wrote that when a state enacts laws which were "seen to have a reasonable relation to a proper legislative purpose, and are neither arbitrary nor discriminatory, the requirements of due process are satisfied."[34] To be sure, earlier cases had used similar language while applying more stringent review.[35] But in *Nebbia*, Justice Roberts, using the terminology from *Munn v. Illinois*, concluded that a business affected with a public interest was any business the legislature reasonably believed needed to be regulated in order to promote the public good. This recognition of legislative discretion to determine which businesses were properly susceptible to price or wage regulation was a real difference from earlier cases, such as *Lochner* itself, where the Court investigated the facts itself.[36]

Comparing *Nebbia*'s reasonableness review with the stricter scrutiny applied in cases such as *Lochner*, it is easy to see why many observers believed that *Nebbia* marked a shift to more deferential review of economic legislation. During the next two years, however, the Supreme Court continued using Commerce Clause and substantive due process rationales to strike down many key provisions of the New Deal. As explained earlier in the discussion of the Commerce Clause,[37] the Court's continued rejection of much New Deal legislation prompted President Roosevelt to propose his so-called "Court packing" plan in early 1937. However, in the spring of 1937 the Court began upholding federal legislation against Commerce Clause challenges and federal and state legislation against substantive due process challenges. That shift blunted the momentum behind the Court-packing plan, which was already facing heavy criticism. Eventually, the plan was abandoned.

With this crucial shift, the Court relinquished its authority over economic regulation by abandoning its stringent substantive due process scrutiny in favor of tremendous judicial deference to economic legislation. An example of its new deference is *United States v. Carolene Products Co.*[38] *Carolene Products* involved a federal statute prohibiting the shipment into interstate commerce of skimmed milk that had been combined with any fat or oil (other than milk fat) to resemble real milk. The defendant, indicted for violating the Act, claimed that the law both exceeded Congress's Commerce Clause power and violated the due process right to contract.

Writing for the majority, Justice Harlan Fiske Stone quickly dismissed the Commerce Clause challenge. Also rejecting the due process challenge, Justice Stone set forth the Court's deferential review of economic regulations:

---

34. *Id.* at 537.

35. *See, e.g., Jay Burns Baking*, 264 U.S. at 518 (condemning a law as "so arbitrary or whimsical that no body of legislators, acting reasonably, could have imposed it").

36. *See also id.* at 519–20 ("With the wisdom of the legislation we have, of course, no concern. But, under the due process clause as construed, we must determine whether the prohibition of excess weights can reasonably be deemed necessary ... and whether compliance with the limitation prescribed can reasonably be deemed practicable. The determination of these questions involves an enquiry into facts.").

37. *See* Section 6.05[1].

38. 304 U.S. 144 (1938).

regulatory legislation affecting ordinary commercial transactions is not to
be pronounced unconstitutional unless in the light of the facts made known
or generally assumed it is of such character as to preclude the assumption
that it rests upon some rational basis within the knowledge and experience
of the legislators.[39]

Justice Stone further emphasized that the Court would no longer scrutinize the ends
sought to be achieved by legislation, because that was "a matter for the legislative judgment and not that of courts."[40] Applying this analysis to the facts in *Carolene Products*,
Justice Stone concluded that Congress had a rational basis for believing that the statute
would protect the public from skimmed milk thought to be injurious to health. Importantly, and as discussed at length in a later chapter,[41] Justice Stone suggested possible
exceptions to this deference in a footnote, Footnote 4 to the opinion, which eventually
flowered into a great deal of the modern Court's approach to individual rights.

In *Williamson v. Lee Optical*,[42] the Supreme Court established the current standard
of judicial review for due process challenges to economic regulation. In upholding
a state law regulating the fitting of eyeglasses, the Court stated that

> The day is gone when this Court uses the Due Process Clause of the Four-
> teenth Amendment to strike down state laws, regulatory of business and in-
> dustrial conditions, because they may be unwise, improvident, or out of
> harmony with a particular school of thought. We emphasize again what Chief
> Justice Waite said in *Munn v. State of Illinois*, "For protection against abuses
> by legislatures the people must resort to the polls, not to the courts."[43]

Earlier in the opinion, the Court stated that "the law need not be in every respect
logically consistent with its aims to be constitutional. It is enough that there is an
evil at hand for correction, and that it *might be thought* that the particular legislative
measure was a rational way to correct it."[44] Today, this deferential review is expressed
as a rational basis test for such challenges: as long as the legislature could have had
a rational basis for believing that the liberty infringement furthered a legitimate government interest, the law survives. This test meant that a court need not consider
the actual legislative purpose when evaluating economic legislation — rather, as long
as it can hypothesize a legitimate government interest that could conceivably be furthered by the liberty infringement, the infringement is constitutional.[45]

This is, of course, an exceptionally deferential standard, leading commentators
today to conclude that the due process liberty of contract is, if not completely dead,

---

39. *Id.* at 152.
40. *Id.* at 151.
41. *See* Section 10.01[2].
42. 348 U.S. 483 (1955).
43. *Id.* at 488–489 (quoting *Munn*, 94 U.S. at 134).
44. *Id.* at 487–88 (emphasis added).
45. *Lee Optical* also rejected an equal protection challenge to the same law, and employed a very
deferential level of scrutiny, given the law's status as social and economic regulation. That type of
scrutiny is discussed in Chapter 10.01[1].

then nearly so. Indeed, in 1963, the Court was able to say that "[t]he doctrine that prevailed in *Lochner* ... and like cases—that due process authorizes courts to hold laws unconstitutional when they believe the legislature has acted unwisely—has long since been discarded."[46] As strongly suggested in *Lee Optical*, the question left unanswered in *Munn*—who decides (courts or legislatures) that regulation of persons' conduct in the marketplace is in pursuance of a public interest?—has been definitively answered, in favor of judicial deference to legislative decisions.

Modern scholarly opinion generally criticizes *Lochner*-era jurisprudence as reflecting illegitimate judicial interference with legislation that, if not always perfect, at least attempted to mitigate the worst effects of industrialization. However, a strand of modern scholarship questions that critique, and argues, to varying degrees, that that jurisprudence tolerated more regulation than is generally thought and rested, not on illegitimate political disagreement with reform legislation but on good-faith attempts to apply constitutional principles that stretched back at least to *Munn*.[47]

Regardless of one's views on that debate, it is possible to criticize the most extreme versions of that jurisprudence (perhaps reflected in *Lochner* itself) while wondering if the Court's post-1937 reaction has swung too far in the other direction. Today, economic regulation is often criticized as solidifying advantages for incumbent firms and industries at the expense of new entrants into the market. For example, occupational licensing requirements, not just for professionals such as lawyers but also for would-be small entrepreneurs such as hair stylists, are often criticized as motivated by a desire to limit the number of new entrants into a market and hence keep prices high. On the other hand, careful judicial scrutiny of such legislation would inevitably require judges to second-guess policy judgments made by elected legislators. The extent to which such second-guessing is inappropriate and beyond judges' competence or, alternatively, legitimate judicial protection of basic economic freedom remains a live issue today, even if the Court shows no interest in returning explicitly to the days of *Lochner*.

It is critical to understand, however, that the Court's retreat from the due process liberty to contract did not mean a more general judicial retreat from enforcing constitutional limitations on government action. In Footnote 4 to the 1938 *Carolene Products* opinion described above, the Court sketched out a new foundation for constitutional review of state and federal legislation. Chapter 10 discusses Footnote 4 and its underlying theory in detail.[48] For now, suffice it to say that it is not a coincidence that the Court sketched out this new theory justifying judicial review at the very moment it was abandoning its old, police power/class legislation/liberty of contract-grounded approach.

---

46. Ferguson v. Skrupa, 372 U.S. 726, 730 (1963).
47. *See, e.g.,* DAVID BERNSTEIN, REHABILITATING *LOCHNER*: DEFENDING INDIVIDUAL RIGHTS AGAINST PROGRESSIVE REFORM (2012).
48. *See* Section 10.01[2].

Importantly, the Court eventually reaffirmed one jurisprudential thread that had developed during the *Lochner* era. As explained later,[49] starting in the 1920s, the Court relied on *Lochner*-type economic precedents (including *Lochner* itself) to find *non-economic* interests to be included in the "liberty" the Fourteenth Amendment protected. When the Court repudiated *Lochner* and cases like it in 1937, a question arose whether it had implicitly rejected these non-economic rights cases as well. As Section 9.04 explains, those non-economic rights cases survived. In fact, by the 1970s, they had had become the foundation for the Court's further expansion of non-economic liberty interests.

The demise of the due process liberty of contract does not mean that modern Court has completely abandoned safeguarding property rights. The modern Court affords some limited protection to property under the Contracts Clause of Article I (which is different from the due process-based liberty of contract). It provides much more robust protection to property rights via the Takings Clause of the Fifth Amendment, which has been incorporated to apply against the states. The next two subsections discuss those provisions in that order.

[2] The Contracts Clause

The Contracts Clause of Article I, § 10 prohibits a state, but not the Federal government, from enacting any "law impairing the Obligation of Contracts."[50] Although the modern Court exerts some scrutiny over economic regulation under the Contracts Clause, it currently does so only in limited circumstances.

The Contracts Clause was motivated by states' tendencies during the Articles period to enact legislation benefitting debtors, thus essentially destroying the contractual rights enjoyed by creditors. During the decade between 1776 and 1787, the nation witnessed many instances of such legislation, as pro-debtor groups would gain political power in a state and enact laws that, for example, required legislative approval of contract judgments reached in court and authorized the use of paper money or other debased currency for loan repayment.

During the nineteenth century, the Court used the Contracts Clause actively. In *Trustees of Dartmouth College v. Woodward*,[51] the Court struck down a New Hampshire law that purported to change the state charter granted to Dartmouth College, to convert the school from a private to a state institution. In *Sturges v. Crowninshield*,[52] it struck down a New York bankruptcy law's applicability to discharge a debt that had

---

49. *See* Section 9.04[1].

50. Thus, this is one of the few instances in the Constitution where a right applies against one level of government but not the other. However, the Fifth Amendment's Due Process Clause imposes some minimal restrictions on federal government impairment of contractual obligations, via its requirement that all legislation be at least rational.

51. 17 U.S. (4 Wheat.) 518 (1819).

52. 17 U.S. (4 Wheat.) 122 (1819).

been incurred before the law was enacted. However, in *Ogden v. Saunders*,[53] the Court held that the Clause applied only to laws that interfered with existing contracts, rather than laws that regulated the terms of future contracts.

As the due process liberty of contract gained ascendancy in the late nineteenth century,[54] the Contracts Clause receded in importance. Importantly, when the Court began withdrawing from strict enforcement of the liberty of contract, it did not resurrect the Contracts Clause as a substitute. Most notably, in *Home Building and Loan Association v. Blaisdell*,[55] the Court upheld a Minnesota law that established a temporary moratorium on mortgage foreclosures, in order to prevent a large number of persons from losing their homes due to non-payment of mortgages during the Great Depression. Even though this sort of debt relief legislation was exactly the sort of law the Contracts Clause was probably meant to prohibit, the Court explained that the emergency created by the Great Depression established the public purpose behind the moratorium, and thus rendered it constitutional.

The Court continued this deferential approach until the 1970s. Beginning in 1977, however, the Court began considering whether it was appropriate to give greater scrutiny to laws alleged to violate the Clause. After a period of experimentation with such greater scrutiny, the Court appears to have returned to a more deferential approach, at least in cases involving governmental interference with purely private contracts.

The Court's modern Contracts Clause jurisprudence began with *United States Trust Co. v. New Jersey*.[56] In *United States Trust*, the Court on a 4–3 vote invalidated legislation rearranging states' financial obligations to bondholders. The case involved New York and New Jersey repealing a covenant promising private investors in a joint-state entity (the Port Authority of New York and New Jersey) that their money would not be invested in mass transit. Writing for the plurality, Justice Blackmun held that the states' legislative authorization to the Port Authority to invest in the unprofitable field of mass transit violated the Contracts Clause.

Unlike state interference with private contracts, which deserved legislative deference, Justice Blackmun concluded that a state's interference with a contract in which the government was itself a party required more careful scrutiny because "the state's self-interest is at stake."[57] Without such scrutiny, the state could reduce, at will, its own financial obligations under the contract. Consequently, the Court would uphold a law impairing public contracts involving the Port Authority only if it was "both reasonable and necessary to serve the admittedly important purposes"[58] of reducing automobile use and promoting mass transit. The means used—totally repealing the bond covenant—were neither necessary to achieve those goals nor reasonable under

53. 25 U.S. (12 Wheat.) 213 (1827).
54. *See* Section 9.02[1].
55. 290 U.S. 398 (1934).
56. 431 U.S. 1 (1977).
57. *Id.* at 26.
58. *Id.* at 29.

the circumstances. Indeed, the states could have pursued such goals with means that left untouched the states' covenant with the Port Authority's bondholders. For example, they could have taxed parking or tunnel use and utilized the revenues to subsidize mass transit.

In a dissent joined by Justices White and Marshall, Justice Brennan objected to the Court's use of the Contracts Clause to reverse legislative policy decisions. He criticized the "reasonable and necessary" standard, as the word "reasonable" generally indicated *de minimis* scrutiny, while the word "necessary" normally suggested strict scrutiny.

The next year, the Court increased Contracts Clause scrutiny of governmental interference in *private* contracts. In *Allied Structural Steel Co. v. Spannaus*,[59] the Court invalidated a Minnesota law modifying existing company pension plans by imposing a surcharge on inadequate plans. Writing for the majority, Justice Stewart declared that the Contracts Clause "must be understood to impose some limits upon the power of a state to abridge existing contractual relationships, even in the exercise of its otherwise legitimate police power."[60]

The Court identified several justifications for not applying its normal post-1937 deference to economic and social legislation. The law did not even purportedly deal with a broad, generalized economic or social problem. Nor did it operate in an area already subject to state regulation at the time the parties agreed to the contract; rather, it invaded an area never before subject to state regulation. The legislation did not temporarily alter contractual relationships, but instead worked a severe, permanent, and immediate change — irrevocably and retroactively. Its narrow aim was leveled, not at every Minnesota employer, and not even at every Minnesota employer who left the state, but only at those who had in the past agreed voluntarily to establish pension plans for their employees. Many of these justifications for increased Contracts Clause scrutiny were vague and amorphous, and left open the possibility for greatly expanded judicial scrutiny.

Again speaking for himself and Justices White and Marshall, Justice Brennan dissented, arguing that the Contracts Clause applied only when existing contractual obligations were diminished or nullified. He argued that the Court improperly expanded the Clause's scope to prohibit the creation of new legislatively-imposed duties, such as those he understood Minnesota to have created in the challenged law.

Although *United States Trust* and *Allied Structural Steel* suggested more stringent scrutiny under the Contracts Clause, subsequent cases have demonstrated a renewal of deference to state legislative decisions impacting private contracts.[61] The Court announced the now-prevailing standard for Contracts Clause challenges in *Energy Reserves Group, Inc. v. Kansas Power & Light Co.*[62]

---

59. 438 U.S. 234 (1978).

60. *Id.* at 242.

61. Since *U.S. Trust*, the Court has not decided a Contracts Clause case involving state interference with a contract to which it was a party.

62. 459 U.S. 400 (1983).

Energy Reserves involved a state law that interfered with a price escalation clause in a private natural gas contract. The Court applied a three-part test for reviewing Contracts Clause challenges to laws that regulated purely private contracts. Under that test, the threshold inquiry asked whether the challenged law "substantially impaired" the contractual relationship. This requirement has proven fairly difficult to satisfy. In making this determination, courts have emphasized whether the affected industry has been subject to prior regulation. If a court determines that the challenged law substantially impaired the contractual relationship, the second element requires the state to justify its action with "a significant and legitimate public purpose." If that requirement is satisfied, the court inquires into "whether the adjustment of the rights and responsibilities of contracting parties" was "reasonable" and "appropriate," an inquiry on which courts "properly defer to legislative judgment."[63]

Applying the test, the *Energy Reserves* Court questioned whether the price controls substantially impaired the contract's price escalator provisions, given the reasonable expectations of the contracting parties. In so concluding, the Court noted that natural gas was a heavily regulated industry in which the imposition of price controls could have been reasonably expected. Even if the law constituted a substantial impairment, the Court concluded that the price controls advanced the legitimate interest of protecting consumers against higher prices in the context of ongoing natural gas deregulation. Finally, the means chosen satisfied the Court's deferential requirement of reasonableness and appropriateness, given the limited nature of the contractual interference and the connection between that impairment and larger regulatory developments in the industry.

In *Exxon Corp. v. Eagerton*,[64] the Court rejected a Contracts Clause challenge to an act prohibiting oil companies from passing on several taxes to consumers, even though pre-existing "pass-through" contracts required consumer absorption of such tax increases. The Court held that a substantial impairment did not exist when a "generally applicable rule of conduct"[65] had an incidental effect on contracts. The Court viewed the restriction at issue in *Eagerton* was just such a generally applicable rule, since it applied regardless of whether a particular contract contained a pass-through provision. *Eagerton*'s unwillingness to find a substantial impairment in this context accentuated the renewed deference of Contracts Clause jurisprudence.

The Contracts Clause does not apply to the federal government. However, the Due Process Clause of the Fifth Amendment restricts it from impairing its own contractual obligations or those of others. But that clause affords little protection. In *National Railroad Passenger Corp. v. Atchison, Topeka & Santa Fe Railway Co.*,[66] the Court unanimously upheld a federal statute altering the reimbursement scheme compelling railroads to indemnify Amtrak for the cost of providing pass privileges to the railroads' employees. The railroads argued that Congress violated the agreements by

---

63. *Id.* at 411–413.
64. 462 U.S. 176 (1983).
65. *Id.* at 191.
66. 470 U.S. 451 (1985).

which the railroads had turned their passenger service over to Amtrak. The Court rejected the claim that Congress had violated the Due Process Clause by impairing a private contractual right. The Fifth Amendment notwithstanding, the Court stated that Congress remained free to "adjus[t] the burdens and benefits of economic life."[67] To meet the due process standard, Congress need only show that it acted rationally in spreading the costs of employee passenger travel among the various parties.

[3] The Takings Clause

The Fifth Amendment's Takings Clause guarantees that "nor shall private property be taken for public use, without just compensation."[68] It was perhaps the first Bill of Rights provision incorporated into the Fourteenth Amendment.[69] The power of "eminent domain" allows federal, state, or local governments to take private property for public use, as long as government pays the owner just compensation, which is understood as the fair market value of the property. Takings Clause claims raise several different issues: whether a taking has occurred; if so, whether it was for a public purpose; and, if so, whether compensation was "just." This discussion focuses on the first and second of these issues. It begins with the public purpose requirement before delving into the often-sticky question of whether a taking has occurred.[70]

[a] The Public Use Requirement

The Takings Clause permits appropriately-compensated takings only when the taking is for a "public use."[71] In *Hawaii Housing Authority v. Midkiff*,[72] the Court interpreted the "public use" requirement broadly. A Hawaii statute sought to redistribute the state's heavily concentrated land ownership by transferring fee simple title to tenants occupying privately-owned property. The law allowed the state to condemn the property, compensate the landowner, and sell title to the tenant. Writing for a unanimous Court, Justice O'Connor upheld the statute. Although it transferred title from one private owner to another, Justice O'Connor found the attempt to distribute ownership more evenly among the community to be a valid public purpose.[73] Deferring to the legislature's judgment, the Court stated that the exercise of eminent domain need only be rationally related to its objective.

---

67. *Id.* at 476.

68. U.S. Const. amend. V.

69. *See* Chicago, Burlington & Quincy R. Co. v. Chicago, 166 U.S. 226 (1897).

70. For a discussion of the "just compensation" question, see Christopher Serkin, *The Meaning of Value: Assessing Just Compensation for Regulatory Takings*, 99 Nw. L. Rev. 677 (2005).

71. A taking of property for private use would been understood as a violation of the Due Process Clause, the provision that immediately precedes the Takings Clause in the Fifth Amendment. *See, e.g.*, Mo. Pac. Ry. Co. v. Nebraska, 164 U.S. 403 (1896) (holding that an order authorizing a private grain elevator on railroad right-of-way violated due process as a "taking" of private property for a private use).

72. 467 U.S. 229 (1984).

73. *Id.* at 244.

The Court reaffirmed *Midkiff* in *Kelo v. City of New London*.[74] *Kelo* held that a city's taking of property for an economic development program involving private corporations did not violate the public use requirement. In *Kelo*, the City of New London, Connecticut took property in order to construct a project near a privately-owned research facility. The targeted area would contain research and development office space and support the nearby state park and marina with visitor parking and retail facilities. Thus, it was a classic mixed-use project involving both public and private facilities, which the city hoped would revitalize the area.

Writing for a five-justice majority, Justice Stevens stated that "it has long been accepted that the sovereign may not take the property of A for the sole purpose of transferring it to another private party B, even though A is paid just compensation." However, government "may transfer property from one private party to another" for future public use.[75] The Court held that the city's takings fell into the second category, given the goal of revitalizing the local economy. The Court recognized the implications of its analysis: public purposes, it wrote, "will often benefit individual private parties."[76] The Court deferred to the legislature regarding the existence of those public purposes and the plan's likely effectiveness in achieving them.

Justice Kennedy concurred, cautioning that the Takings Clause might prohibit transfers of this sort that provided "only incidental or pretextual public benefits," a situation he found did not exist with New London's plan.[77] Justice O'Connor, the author of *Midkiff*, dissented for four justices. She complained that the majority opinion allowed forced property transfers between private parties simply to allow upgrading of the property to increase tax revenue. In a separate dissent, Justice Thomas called for reconsidering *Midkiff*, and insisted that the "public use" requirement required, literally, that the public be able to use the taken property.

[b] Determining Whether a Taking Occurred: Physical and Regulatory Takings

One basic rule of the Takings Clause is that government's permanent physical occupation of property constitutes a taking.[78] But government regulation, short of occupation, may also constitute a taking. The foundational regulatory takings case is *Pennsylvania Coal Co. v. Mahon*.[79] In *Pennsylvania Coal*, a state law prohibited mining in areas where it might cause a building to sink. Writing for the majority, Justice Holmes delineated the approach that would dominate the Court's regulatory takings

---

74. 545 U.S. 469 (2005).

75. *Id.* at 477.

76. *Id.* at 485.

77. *Id.* at 490 (Kennedy, J., concurring).

78. *See, e.g.*, Loretto v. Teleprompter Manhattan CATV Corp., 458 U.S. 419 (1982) (finding a taking when a city law required a property owner to place a cable television receiver box on the top of the owner's apartment building). Of course, the compensation due such a trivial taking would be similarly trivial.

79. 260 U.S. 393 (1922).

jurisprudence for decades. He balanced the extent of the property right's diminution with the public interest the regulation served. Some regulation was permissible, but regulation that "goes too far"[80] was considered a taking. Finding a taking in *Pennsylvania Coal*, Justice Holmes found that less burdensome measures, such as giving homeowners notice of the mining, would have addressed the state's health and safety concerns. He also observed that the law made coal mining in the affected areas economically unfeasible.

Pennsylvania Coal's rationale—that when regulation "goes too far" it will be considered a taking—is, of course, exceptionally vague and malleable.[81] In 1978, the Court built on Justice Holmes's intuitions and crafted a more detailed test to judge regulatory takings claims. In *Penn Central Transportation Co. v. New York*,[82] the Court rejected a takings challenge to a New York City landmarks preservation statute that was applied to restrict a developer's right to build a skyscraper over Grand Central Station, one of many historic buildings the city had designated as a landmark.

Writing for the majority, Justice Brennan identified several factors to determine whether a taking had occurred: "[t]he economic impact of the regulation on the claimant and, particularly, the extent to which the regulation has interfered with distinct investment-backed expectations"; "the character of the governmental action"; whether "the interference with the property can be characterized as a physical invasion" as opposed to "interference [that] arises from some public program adjusting the benefits and burdens of economic life to promote the common good."[83]

Applying these factors, he noted that the owner retained air rights that it could use either to build an approved structure or to sell to the owners of adjacent parcels. It also noted that the owner could continue to use the station for its historical purpose as a train station. The Court also rejected the argument that the parcel-by-parcel nature of landmark designation amounted to discriminatory or arbitrary decision-making, noting the availability of judicial review of any landmark designation.

Despite its increased specificity as compared with *Pennsylvania Coal*, the *Penn Central* test is still a vague, multi-factor test. In one limited area, the Court has adopted more of a *per se* rule. The Court in *Lucas v. South Carolina Coastal Council* held that regulations which "prohibit all economically beneficial use of land" constitute a taking.[84] *Lucas* involved a South Carolina law prohibiting construction in certain coastal zones, which barred a property owner from building homes on beachfront land he had recently purchased. Justice Scalia, writing for the Court, explained that compensation must accompany a regulation which "declares 'off-limits' all economically productive or beneficial uses of land," unless the limitation "inhere[s] in the

---

80. *Id.* at 415.

81. Indeed, the test, even as made more concrete by subsequent cases, is vague enough that it allowed the Court to uphold a very similar statute decades later. *See* Keystone Bituminous Coal Ass'n v. DeBenedictis, 480 U.S. 470 (1987).

82. 438 U.S. 104 (1978).

83. *Id.* at 124.

84. 505 U.S. 1003, 1029 (1992).

title itself, in the restrictions that background principles of the state's law of property and nuisance already place upon land ownership."[85] The Court explained that such pre-existing property rules constituted limits on an owner's ability to use the property as the owner wished; because they pre-existed acquisition of the property, those limits essentially came with the land and thus could not serve as a foundation for a takings claim.

One might think that this limitation on the *Lucas* rule meant that any acquiror of property on a given day could not complain about *any* legal limitation on the use of his property that existed on the day of acquisition. The Court repudiated that understanding of *Lucas* in a case decided nine years later. In *Palazzolo v. Rhode Island*,[86] a developer sought to develop coastal property, but failed to obtain the necessary permits. Eventually, the development company's corporate charter was revoked, and title to the land passed to the company's sole shareholder. But before that happened, the state had enacted significant new restrictions on development of coastal property. When the new owner sought to develop the land, his permit was denied on the strength of those intervening regulations. The Court rejected the state's attempt to bring these facts within *Lucas*' exception, reasoning that doing so would allow a state to impose whatever unreasonable limitations on land use it wished and apply them to subsequent acquirors of land.

Regardless of whether one finds this latter proposition attractive, it is difficult to square with the Court's suggestions to the contrary in *Lucas*. It may be that *Lucas* intended, or should be read as intending, to refer to common law rules when it spoke of "the restrictions that background principles of the State's law of property and nuisance already place upon land ownership."[87] But if that reflects *Lucas*' intentions, then the Court has created an unstable regime, given legislatures' power to amend, repeal, or simply codify common law rules of property and nuisance.

As suggested by *Lucas* and *Palazzolo*, timing issues play important roles in takings litigation. In *First English Evangelical Lutheran Church of Glendale v. County of Los Angeles*,[88] the Court stated that the Takings Clause could require government compensation for government actions that effected a temporary taking. An interim ordinance, enacted after fire and flooding destroyed a church retreat, temporarily prohibited the church from rebuilding on the site. Writing for the majority, Chief Justice Rehnquist found that temporary takings, depriving a landowner of all use of his land, were conceptually indistinguishable from permanent takings. The Court held that a constitutionally sufficient remedy required just compensation for the use of property during the time the invalidated ordinance was in effect.[89]

---

85. *Id.* at 1030, 1029.
86. 533 U.S. 606 (2001).
87. *Lucas*, 505 U.S. at 1029.
88. 482 U.S. 304 (1987).
89. In *Tahoe-Sierra Preservation Council, Inc. v. Tahoe Regional Planning Agency*, 535 U.S. 302 (2002), the Court held that a government order stopping all development pending creation of an area-wide land-use plan did not constitute a *per se* taking. However, the Court, speaking through

[c] Taking as a Government Condition for
Granting a Permit

A distinct takings issue arises when the government insists that a landowner act in a way that would normally constitute a taking, but justifies the requirement as a condition for granting a development permit it was not obligated to approve. In *Nollan v. California Coastal Commission*,[90] the Court held that conditioning a building permit on a beachfront landowner's grant of a public easement across his property constituted a taking. When the plaintiff wanted to rebuild on his property, the state conditioned the building permit on the landowner giving the state a 10-foot easement running parallel to the beach. The state contended that since it was not required to permit development at all, it could require such an easement to further legitimate public purposes of beach and ocean access.

The Court held that the access condition violated the Takings Clause. Writing for the Court, Justice Scalia found that the government had not established a nexus between a legitimate governmental objective of nondevelopment and the exaction of the easement. In the majority's opinion, the permit condition did nothing to aid the public already using the community beaches to view or enjoy the waterfront. It did not reduce obstacles to viewing the beach caused by the construction of the new home, or alleviate either the psychological barriers to using the beach or remedy beach congestion, both of which were allegedly also caused by the construction of the new home. Dissenting, Justice Brennan, joined by Justice Marshall, criticized the majority's introduction of the nexus requirement, which he found inappropriately stringent and inconsistent with the deference legislative judgments normally enjoyed.

The Court more precisely defined this nexus requirement in *Dolan v. City of Tigard*.[91] In *Dolan*, a 5–4 majority of the Court invalidated a zoning commission's conditioning of a building permit on the landowner dedicating some property for public use, because "rough proportionality"[92] did not exist between the property development's impact and the required conditions. *Dolan* featured a business owner who wished to pave the parking lot of her downtown store. As a condition of approving that request, the city required her to dedicate part of her property for a greenway that would serve flood control purposes and allow a path for a municipal bikeway. That dedication would entail Dolan having to transfer title of that part of her property to the city.

Justice Stevens, was willing to accept the possibility that the *Penn Central* factors might, in a particular case, justify a finding of a taking. In *Knick v. Township of Scott*, 139 S. Ct. 2162 (2019), the Court decided that a property owner did not have to go to state court to seek compensation before claiming in federal court that she had suffered a taking. The Court reasoned that takings claims mature immediately upon the occurrence of an uncompensated taking. Moreover, the Court, speaking through Chief Justice Roberts, noted the procedural oddity that, if a state court ruled that no taking had occurred and thus no compensation requirement had arisen, that finding would be preclusive in any subsequent litigation in federal court.

90. 483 U.S. 825 (1987).
91. 512 U.S. 374 (1994).
92. *Id.* at 391.

Writing for the Court, Chief Justice Rehnquist invalidated both conditions. He explained that what set this case apart from zoning and other land use regulations was (1) the specific, adjudicative nature of the conditions rather than their status as generalized requirements as part of a zoning master plan, and (2) the fact that the conditions did not simply regulate Dolan's use of her property, but required her to surrender part of her property to public access.

To evaluate the constitutionality of such permit conditions, the Court asked two questions: (1) does the "essential nexus," required by *Nollan*, exist between the conditions and the legitimate state interests that the city seeks to advance by them; and (2) does a sufficient connection exist between the conditions and the impact of the new development? The dedication of land for a public drainage system theoretically could advance the city's interest in flood control, given the paving project's exacerbation of flooding problems, and the bicycle path requirement could reduce traffic congestion, given the extra auto traffic that might result from paving the parking lot. Thus, the Court concluded, both conditions satisfied the "essential nexus" prong.

Turning to the second prong, the Court outlined a "rough proportionality" test requiring the city to make "some sort of individualized determination that the required dedication is related both in nature and extent to the impact of the proposed development." In applying this requirement to the greenway condition, the Court emphasized that the "city has never said why a public greenway, as opposed to a private one, was required in the interest of flood control."[93] A public greenway deprived Dolan of her right to exclude others, a foundational property right. Depriving Dolan of her right to decide when and where the public would enter her property was not proportional to her development's potential impact on flooding. The bicycle path dedication condition likewise encroached on Dolan's right to exclude. While the Court did not require a "precise mathematical calculation," the city had to "make some effort to quantify its findings in support of the dedication for the pedestrian/bicycle pathway beyond the conclusory statement that it could offset some of the traffic demand generated."[94]

Justice Stevens dissented, joined by Justices Blackmun and Ginsburg. Justice Stevens first asserted the absence of any doubt that the impact of Dolan's development would justify the city in denying her permit outright. He conceded that this fact did not give the city unlimited discretion to impose arbitrary conditions in lieu of a permit denial. Nevertheless, he criticized the Court's new "rough proportionality" test, emphasizing the inherent uncertainty in predicting the effects of urban development. In a separate dissent, Justice Souter argued that the city had satisfied the *Nollan* nexus through its calculations of increased traffic flow and its studies correlating decreased traffic congestion with alternative means of transportation. He also objected that the majority's expansion of regulatory takings doctrine was resurrecting the kind of substantive due process approach exemplified by the discredited *Lochner* case.[95]

---

93. *Id.* at 391, 393.

94. *Id.* at 395–96.

95. Lochner v. New York, 198 U.S. 45 (1905). *Lochner*, and economic substantive due process more generally, is discussed in Chapter 9.02[1].

[d] Takings Analysis in Other Contexts

Beyond the regulatory cases discussed earlier, takings claims can also arise in other, less obvious contexts. For example, in *Goldblatt v. Hempstead*,[96] the Court denied a takings challenge to a zoning ordinance that forced the plaintiff out of the sand and gravel business by prohibiting, for safety reasons, excavations below the water table. The Takings Clause can also apply to property interests beyond real estate. For example, *Ruckelshaus v. Monsanto Co.*[97] addressed trade secrets. A federal pesticide safety statute required pesticide companies to submit information about certain products monitored by the Environmental Protection Agency (EPA). When a company claimed that EPA disclosure of that information constituted a taking, the Court agreed in part. First, it agreed that disclosure of information submitted to EPA under a legal regime protecting the confidentiality of that information constituted a taking when the law subsequently changed allowing disclosure. However, disclosure of information the company submitted during a later period, when the law allowed EPA to disclose, did not constitute a taking. Nor was there a taking when the agency disclosed information the company provided at a much earlier time, before any confidentiality provision was promulgated, since in such a heavily regulated industry as pesticides, the company could have had no reasonable, investment-backed expectation of confidentiality.

In *Andrus v. Allard*,[98] the Court upheld a law prohibiting the sale of property because the law only deprived the owner of one strand of his whole property interest. The statute at issue prohibited commercial dealing in parts of birds that had been legally killed before the law became effective. The challenge arose when the government prosecuted a person for selling Indian artifacts containing such bird parts. The statutes did not however, prohibit possession, transportation, donation, or exhibition of the property for a profit. The Court considered the entire scope of the plaintiff's property interest to determine whether the regulation deprived owners of their reasonable investment-backed expectations. For example, it noted that the law did not physically occupy (that is, confiscate) the items, and it suggested that the owner might still be able to profit from them, for example, by exhibiting or donating them, even if those were not the items' most profitable uses. This analysis may sound familiar, given its relationship to the familiar idea of "property" as a "bundle of rights."[99]

The Court has also considered whether courts can violate the Takings Clause. In *Stop the Beach Renourishment, Inc. v. Florida Department of Environmental Protection*,[100] the Florida Supreme Court had concluded that the legal doctrine of avulsion allowed the state to reclaim restored beach as public land when the state rebuilt beachfront

---

96. 369 U.S. 590 (1962).

97. 467 U.S. 986 (1984).

98. 444 U.S. 51 (1979).

99. *See id.* at 65–66 ("At least where an owner possesses a full 'bundle' of property rights, the destruction of one 'strand' of the bundle is not a taking, because the aggregate must be viewed in its entirety.").

100. 560 U.S. 702 (2010).

that had eroded. The property owners alleged that that decision constituted a taking of their property.

Justice Scalia wrote for a unanimous Court in holding that no taking occurred. However, Justice Scalia was joined only by three other justices in maintaining that "the particular state *actor* is irrelevant" in a takings claim.[101] In his partial concurrence, Justice Kennedy, joined by Justice Sotomayor, agreed with Justice Breyer's partial concurrence that the case did not require the Court to decide the judicial takings question. But he suggested that, instead of the Takings Clause, the Due Process Clause offers a "strong footing" for overruling as "arbitrary or irrational" a judicial taking.[102] Justice Breyer also concurred in part and in the judgment, joined by Justice Ginsburg. He worried that, since state courts decide so many property rights cases each year, the plurality's approach may result in constitutional review of large numbers of state law cases dealing with state property law matters unfamiliar to federal judges.

The Takings Clause is the most active area of economic constitutional rights jurisprudence today. This may be because of its textual grounding or perhaps in part because of the special status of real estate (which constitutes the most common subject-matter of takings litigation). For whatever reason, the Court has shown a continuing interest in exploring the Takings Clause. Nevertheless, the same difficult trade-offs between public interests and private economic interests that led the Court to retreat from the due process liberty of contract exist as well in the takings area. This difficulty will likely continue to result in a Takings Clause jurisprudence that avoids *per se* rules and attempts to find room for reasonable legislative regulation even when it invades property interests.

[4] Economic Penalties

A final area of the Court's economic rights jurisprudence involves excessive fines and other economic penalties. The Court has been willing to review such penalties, when imposed by the government, under the Eighth Amendment's Excessive Fines Clause.[103] While the Excessive Fines Clause does not apply to punitive damages assessed in litigation between private parties,[104] the Court has sometimes found such damages to violate the Due Process Clause. Before 1996, such decisions focused on the clause's procedural dimensions. Thus, for example, it has upheld such awards against due process challenges because the state court procedures provided for thorough inquiries

---

101. *Id.* at 715.

102. *Id.* at 737.

103. United States v. Bajakajian, 524 U.S. 321 (1998) (striking down a forfeiture penalty of $357,144 for the crime of failing to report the transportation of more than $10,000 in currency). To be sure, the underlying offense involved the unreported transportation of exactly that amount—that is, $357,144. Nevertheless, the Court concluded that a forfeiture penalty of that entire amount was "grossly disproportionate" to the crime, which referenced the lower amount. The Excessive Fines Clause has recently been incorporated so as to apply against the states. Timbs v. Indiana, 139 S. Ct. 682 (2019).

104. Browning-Ferris Industries, Inc. v. Kelco Disposal, Inc., 492 U.S. 257 (1989).

into potential jurors' impartiality, careful jury instructions, and appellate review of any verdicts.[105]

In 1996, in *BMW of North America v. Gore*,[106] the Court struck down a large punitive damages award as substantively unconstitutional. *Gore* involved a lawsuit by a car purchaser who proved that a dealer had repainted a car to repair paint damage before selling it as new. The actual damages amounted to approximately $4,000; however, based in part on the number of cars the defendant sold across the country, the jury assessed punitive damages of four million dollars, which the state court later reduced to two million dollars.

Writing for a 5–4 majority, Justice Stevens conceded that Alabama's legitimate interests in punishing and deterring unlawful conduct afforded it considerable flexibility in determining punitive awards. However, Alabama could not punish the company for behavior that was legal in other states and did not impact Alabama or its residents. BMW was entitled to fair notice of the potential magnitude of the penalty that Alabama might impose. "Three guideposts" indicated that BMW did not receive such notice, and consequently, that the $2 million punitive damages award was "grossly excessive."[107]

First, and perhaps most importantly, BMW's conduct was not particularly reprehensible. The harm was purely economic, as repainting did not diminish the car's safety, performance, or appearance. Moreover, the record did not establish "indifference to or reckless disregard for the health and safety of others."[108] Second, the ratio of the punitive award the plaintiff's actual harm suggested excessiveness. While the Court had previously allowed ratios of 4 to 1 and 10 to 1,[109] the $2 million punitive award at issue was 500 times the amount of compensatory damages. However, the Court did not base reversal simply on a "mathematical bright line,"[110] since in some instances, small compensatory awards might justify a higher ratio than large ones. Third, the punitive damages award far exceeded civil or criminal sanctions for similar misconduct. The maximum penalty under Alabama's Deceptive Trade Practices Act was $2,000, and no state's penalty exceeded $10,000. Neither these statutes nor any judicial decisions anywhere afforded BMW fair notice that its policy of not disclosing repainting work might subject it to a multi-million dollar penalty.

---

105. *See, e.g.*, TXO Production Corp. v. Alliance Resources, 509 U.S. 443 (1993) (juror questioning and appellate review); Pacific Mutual Life Ins. Co. v. Haslip, 499 U.S. 1 (1991) (juror instructions). The procedural aspects of the Due Process Clause are discussed in Section 9.06.

106. 517 U.S. 559 (1996).

107. *Id.* at 574, 562.

108. *Id.* at 576.

109. *See* TXO Production Corp. v. Alliance Resources, 509 U.S. 443 (1993); Pacific Mutual Life Ins. Co. v. Haslip, 499 U.S. 1 (1991). To be sure, in *TXO*, the disparity between the actual damages suffered and the punitive damages awarded was far more than 10 to 1. However, the Court stressed that the plaintiff *could have* suffered much more harm, which would have brought the disparity closer to 10 to 1. *See BMW*, 517 U.S. at 581 (explaining *TXO*).

110. 517 U.S. at 583.

Justice Breyer, joined by Justices O'Connor and Souter, concurred in the judgment, emphasizing both Alabama's vague standards that failed to sufficiently constrain the jury's discretion and his conclusion that the punitive damages award grossly exceeded Alabama's "legitimate punitive damages objectives."[111]

Justice Ginsburg dissented, joined by Chief Justice Rehnquist, to emphasize that the Court was unnecessarily addressing an issue traditionally left to states and had failed to provide states with adequate standards. Justice Scalia also dissented, joined by Justice Thomas. He argued that the Due Process Clause did not provide substantive protection against unreasonable punitive awards, but only protected the opportunity to challenge the award in state court.

In *Philip Morris USA v. Williams*,[112] the Court held that the Due Process Clause prohibited juries from considering harm to third parties when awarding punitive damages. As a result of a jury trial and subsequent appeals, the plaintiff was awarded $821,000 in compensatory damages and $79.5 million in punitive damages. While the Court prohibited juries from taking into account harms to "strangers to the litigation,"[113] it still allowed them to consider those harms when considering the reprehensibility of the conduct. This distinction, while conceptually plausible, raises serious questions about how appellate courts will be able to review large punitive damages awards in the future.

As with other areas of due process jurisprudence, due process-based limits on punitive damages may seem intuitive, especially when juries impose exceptionally large punitive damages awards.[114] But difficult questions immediately arise. For example, the Court has concluded that such awards cannot be intended to induce the defendant to change its conduct performed outside the state, since that would represent the punishing state foisting its regulatory choices onto the rest of the nation.[115] Similarly, it has concluded that such awards cannot take into account the harm suffered by third parties.[116] On the other hand, juries can take into account the reprehensibility of the defendant's conduct.[117] But how can a jury do that, consistent with the scope of these limits on its awards?

Another difficult problem is presented by the problem of ratios between compensatory and allowable punitive damages awards. While the Court has abjured any "mathematical" rule,[118] it makes intuitive sense that a small amount of actual damage may justify limits on a punitive damages award. But conduct triggering a small dam-

---

111. *Id.* at 595.

112. 549 U.S. 346 (2007).

113. *Id.* at 353.

114. *See, e.g.*, State Farm Mutual Automobile Ins. Co. v. Campbell, 538 U.S. 408 (2003) (striking down, as "grossly excessive," a punitive damages award of $145 million assessed along with an actual damages award of $1 million).

115. *See Gore*, 517 U.S. at 572.

116. *See Phillip Morris*, 549 U.S. at 353.

117. *See ibid.*

118. *See TXO*, 509 U.S. at 458.

ages award may still be quite reprehensible in a moral sense. If the Court is willing to accept that moral intuition,[119] then how is an appellate court to weight a seemingly massive disparity between awards of actual and punitive damages, when the latter award is challenged? In a 2003 case, the Court stated that "in practice, few awards exceeding a single-digit ratio between punitive and compensatory damages, to a significant degree, will satisfy due process."[120] That statement does not provide much guidance. But perhaps the Court can offer little more than such vague statements in this area.

§ 9.03 Due Process Liberty, the Bill of Rights, and Incorporation

"Incorporation" refers to the phenomenon by which the Due Process Clause of the Fourteenth Amendment makes applicable to the states, or "incorporates," the protections of the Bill of Rights. In *Barron v. City of Baltimore*,[121] decided in 1833, the Court held that the protections of the Bill of Rights did not apply against the states. The holding in *Barron* settled the question until the ratification of the Fourteenth Amendment reopened it. Between the turn of the twentieth century and the 1960s, the Court gradually incorporated almost all of the Bill of Rights. In recent years, it has incorporated many of the few remaining provisions that remained unincorporated by approximately 1970.

Despite the largely-settled nature of the subjects of incorporation cases, the incorporation controversy itself reflects fundamentally different views, not just about incorporation itself but by extension about the nature of constitutional rights and the judicial role in discovering and enforcing them. As such, the Court's incorporation jurisprudence remains important for current constitutional law issues. On the one side of the incorporation debate was Justice Hugo Black, who insisted on a theory of "total incorporation" that found the substantive meaning of due process liberty comprehensively, but exclusively, in the Bill of Rights. In other words, Justice Black insisted that the Fourteenth Amendment's Due Process Clause protected all the liberties provided for in the Bill of Rights, but only those liberties. On the other side were justices such as Felix Frankfurter, who took a more nuanced and selective approach — but also a potentially more expansive one. Justice Frankfurter argued that due process liberty included some, but not all, of the Bill of Rights, while also implying that unenumerated rights might also count as due process liberty.

As one can imagine, Justice Black's approach made for a simple, even mechanical, judicial task. For him, this was a positive feature of his approach, since it avoided the need (and, indeed, the temptation) for judges to import their own personal

---

119. *See, e.g., Gore*, 517 U.S. at 582.
120. *Campbell*, 538 U.S. at 425.
121. 32 U.S. 243 (1833).

predilections into incorporation decisions. But he also argued that his approach was the one more historically grounded in the intentions of the Fourteenth Amendment's drafters.[122]

Justice Frankfurter, often joined by other justices, maintained that the Fourteenth Amendment imposed on the states "certain minimal standards which are 'of the very essence of a scheme of ordered liberty,'"[123] and "those personal immunities which ... are 'so rooted in the traditions and conscience of our people as to be ranked as fundamental' or are 'implicit in the concept of ordered liberty.'"[124] The internal quotations in the last sentence came from earlier opinions by Justice Benjamin Cardozo. Justice Cardozo, often speaking for a majority of the Court, used such language when determining which Bill of Rights provisions were incorporated so as to apply against the states. But Justice Frankfurter explicitly recognized that the same test could lead to a conclusion that other rights, beyond those in the Bill of Rights, could also count as due process "liberty."

This point reflects an important insight about Justice Frankfurter's approach — an insight that will matter beyond the incorporation issue itself. Justice Frankfurter readily agreed that some protections found in the Bill of Rights also applied against the states. However, for Justice Frankfurter, the fact that the liberty in question was specifically enumerated in the Bill of Rights did not determine whether it therefore applied against the states via the Due Process Clause. In other words, he believed that the "liberty" that clause protected had meaning separate and independent of the content of the Bill of Rights. While there might be overlap between the Bill of Rights and due process liberty, for Justice Frankfurter, any such overlap did not depend on the fact that the right in question appeared in the Bill of Rights. Eventually, this approach opened the door to the Court's recognition of due process liberties that were not enumerated in the Bill of Rights — the rights to contraception, abortion, and other unenumerated personal autonomy rights recognized today.[125]

The Black-Frankfurter debate ended in an odd sort of draw. On the one hand, the Court has incorporated nearly every liberty in the Bill of Rights.[126] However, the Court reached those results through a process of selective incorporation that asked, in the words of a recent incorporation decision, whether the liberty in question was "fundamental to our scheme of ordered liberty" or "deeply rooted in this Nation's

---

122. Indeed, in one incorporation case, Justice Black submitted with his dissent a thirty-page appendix presenting his research into the history of the Fourteenth Amendment as it related to the incorporation issue. *See* Adamson v. California, 332 U.S. 46, 92 (1947) (Appendix to opinion of Black, J., dissenting).

123. *Adamson*, 332 U.S. at 65 (Frankfurter, J., concurring).

124. Rochin v. California, 342 U.S. 165, 169 (1952).

125. These rights are discussed in Section 9.04.

126. As of the date of this book's publication, only the Third Amendment's prohibition on quartering soldiers, the Fifth Amendment's requirement of criminal indictment by grand jury, and the Seventh Amendment's civil jury trial right remain unincorporated.

history and tradition."[127] That approach—to consider each liberty claim on its own merits rather than simply ask whether it can be shoehorned into a Bill of Rights provision[128]—eventually allowed the Court to expand the scope of due process liberty beyond the Bill of Rights.

But the matter is not quite that simple. One indication that Justice Black's theory of total incorporation enjoyed at least a partial triumph lay in the result of the battle over so-called jot-for-jot incorporation. That battle concerned whether incorporated Bill of Rights provisions carried with them the exact same meanings they had when interpreted in their original versions, applicable to the federal government—in other words, whether they were incorporated in their precise original forms, "jot for jot."

As one might expect, Justice Black's total incorporation theory would suggest that the incorporated versions of those provisions apply exactly as their federally-applicable counterparts did—that is, jot for jot. By contrast, it is at least plausible that a selective incorporation approach, one focusing on the underlying importance of the right rather than its appearance in the Bill of Rights *per se*, would allow room for different versions of the right to apply against the states and the federal government, respectively. But as the Court has recently made clear, an incorporated Bill of Rights provision applies to the states exactly as its original provision applies to the federal government.[129] A recent incorporation opinion revealed (perhaps unwittingly) the draw between Black and Frankfurter when it stated that "While Justice Black's theory was never adopted, the Court eventually moved in that direction by initiating [the] process of selective incorporation."[130] Thus, the Court suggested that Black's approach had triumphed ("the Court eventually moved in [Black's] direction") even when it identified that approach as a process of "selective incorporation" (which Black would have opposed).

---

127. McDonald v. City of Chicago, 561 U.S. 742, 767 (2010) (majority opinion) (incorporating the Second Amendment right to keep and bear arms).

128. For an interesting example such shoehorning, see Justice Black's opinion in Rochin v. California, 342 U.S. 165 (1947). *Rochin* considered a due process attack on a drug possession conviction premised on evidence gained when the police entered Rochin's home and, seeing him ingest drugs laying on his nightstand, took him to a hospital and had his stomach pumped. Justice Frankfurter's majority opinion found a due process violation, on the ground that the police conduct "shock[ed] the conscience" and "offend[ed] a sense of justice." *Id.* at 172 & 173. Justice Black agreed with the result, but only because he considered the stomach pumping compelled self-incrimination in violation of the Fifth Amendment. *See id.* at 174–175 (Black, J., concurring).

129. Until recently, the one exception had been the requirement of unanimity in jury verdicts, derived from the Sixth Amendment. While the Court applied a unanimity requirement in federal criminal prosecutions as part of the Sixth Amendment right to a jury trial in criminal cases, until 2020, it did not apply the unanimity requirement to the incorporated version of the Sixth Amendment jury trial right. However, this exception to the general rule may have resulted from an anomalous voting pattern in the relevant Sixth Amendment incorporation case. *See McDonald*, 561 U.S. at 766 n.14 (explaining this anomaly). In 2020, the Court overruled the precedent allowing non-unanimous state criminal verdicts. Ramos v. Louisiana, 140 S. Ct. 1390 (2020).

130. *McDonald*, 561 U.S. at 763.

§ 9.04 Non-Economic Liberties

[1] Parental Control over Child-Rearing

During the *Lochner* era, the Court occasionally extended substantive due process rights to cases not involving economic interests. For example, in *Meyer v. Nebraska*,[131] the Court reversed the conviction of a teacher who had violated a state law restricting foreign language instruction. The *Meyer* Court gave content to due process liberty beyond the then-dominant liberty to contract understanding, explaining:

> Without doubt, [the Due Process Clause] denotes not merely freedom from bodily restraint but also the right of the individual to contract, to engage in any of the common occupations of life, to acquire useful knowledge, to marry, establish a home and bring up children, to worship God according to the dictates of his own conscience, and generally to enjoy those privileges long recognized at common law as essential to the orderly pursuit of happiness by free men.[132]

Immediately after this quotation, the Court cited as support for the Court's statement a variety of liberty of contract cases, including *Lochner* itself.

Another early example of substantive due process analysis in the personal rights area was *Pierce v. Society of Sisters*. In this 1925 case, the Court invalidated a law requiring most parents to send their children to public schools, relying on parents' due process right to direct their children's upbringing and education.[133] In other cases, the Court rejected related rights claims. Most infamously, in *Buck v. Bell*,[134] the Court rejected a due process challenge to a Virginia law authorizing the forced sterilization of intellectually disabled persons committed to state institutions. Eight justices voted to uphold the law. Writing for that majority, Justice Holmes, referring to the fact that the plaintiff's mother and grandmother were similarly disabled, remarked "three generations of imbeciles are enough."[135]

In the modern era, the Court has continued to accord protection to family and other intimate relationships. Those protected relationships include the one between a parent and her child, which in turn implicates the parent's right to direct the child's upbringing. Those modern family relationship cases are discussed later in this chapter.[136]

[2] Sterilization and Contraception

The demise of *Lochner*-style liberty of contract reasoning in 1937 raised questions about the fate of the *Meyer* line of cases, which, as noted above, was grounded in

---

131. 262 U.S. 390 (1923).

132. *Id.* at 399.

133. 268 U.S. 510 (1925). *See also* Farrington v. Tokushige, 273 U.S. 284 (1927) (invalidating a federal territorial law restricting foreign-language instruction in Hawaiian schools).

134. 274 U.S. 200 (1927).

135. *Id.* at 207.

136. *See* Section 9.04[4][a].

the Court's liberty of contract jurisprudence.[137] One notable case in which the Court struggled with the continued viability of non-economic unenumerated liberties was *Skinner v. Oklahoma*.[138] Decided in 1942, *Skinner* invalidated an Oklahoma statute that allowed the state to sterilize habitual criminals guilty of crimes reflecting "moral turpitude." In doing so, the majority relied on a mixture of due process and equal protection concepts, holding that the law treated similarly-situated criminals unequally, for example, by mandating sterilization for those thrice-convicted of robbery but not for those thrice-convicted of embezzlement. While the distinctions the Oklahoma law drew could potentially suggest discrimination based on the types of crimes committed by persons of different economic classes, the Court did not explicitly embrace such a theory. Instead, it rested on the state's failure to prove that the disfavored class of criminals was particularly liable to have genetically inherited their criminal tendencies.

But a notion of fundamental rights also played a role in *Skinner*. Even though those who were sterilized were not a protected class for equal protection purposes, Justice Douglas held that the statute discriminated with respect to a fundamental right. He wrote: "We are dealing here with legislation which involves one of the basic civil rights of man. Marriage and procreation are fundamental to the very existence and survival of the race."[139] Chief Justice Stone and Justice Jackson both wrote separate concurrences. Chief Justice Stone's opinion relied heavily on the state's failure to provide individual prisoners with an adequate hearing at which they could attempt to demonstrate the non-heritability of their criminal tendencies. Justice Jackson's opinion agreed with both Justice Douglas's majority and Chief Justice Stone's concurrence, but also sought to make clear that Justice Jackson reserved the question whether, leaving aside equal protection and questions of fair procedure, individuals had a substantive right to be free of "biological experiments"[140] of the sort Oklahoma was conducting.

Justice Jackson's reservation of that question, and indeed, the majority's invocation of the importance of procreation to individual liberty, may have reflected both *Skinner*'s historical context and larger jurisprudential concerns. *Skinner* was decided in 1942, soon after America's entry into the war against Nazi Germany, a regime explicitly devoted to eugenics theories that by the late 1930s had started falling out of favor in the United States. The Court may have worried that a decision upholding the Oklahoma law would be seen as an implicit endorsement of some version of those theories. More generally, with the *Lochner* era behind it, the Court may have wanted to signal that it had not definitively lumped the *Meyer* line of cases with the *Lochner* line that it had just discarded. On this theory, the majority's combination of due process and

---

137. Today, cases such as *Meyer* could conceivably be based on First Amendment theories of free speech and free religious exercise, but those doctrines were still insufficiently developed in the late 1930s to justify such a doctrinal move.

138. 316 U.S. 535 (1942).

139. 316 U.S. at 541.

140. *Id.* at 546 (Jackson, J., concurring).

equal protection reasoning might have been seen as a way of avoiding, for the time being, the question about the fate of the *Meyer* line, which, to repeat, had originally sprung forth as a branch of *Lochner*-era jurisprudence.[141] The Court would not definitively resolve that question for several more decades.

The process of deciding that question began in earnest in 1965, in *Griswold v. Connecticut*.[142] In *Griswold*, administrators of the Planned Parenthood League of Connecticut were arrested and charged under a Connecticut law prohibiting the use or provision of contraceptives, because of their conduct in counseling married couples about contraceptives. They sued on behalf of the couples they counseled. Writing for the majority striking down the Connecticut law, Justice Douglas explicitly refused to rely on substantive due process analysis, asserting, as the Court had since 1937, that the Court does not sit as a "super-legislature" to review legislation on social and economic matters.[143] Instead, Justice Douglas argued that "specific guarantees in the Bill of Rights have penumbras, formed by emanations from those guarantees that help give them life and substance."[144] Specifically, he argued that the First Amendment right of association, the Fourth Amendment protection against unreasonable searches, the Fifth Amendment protection against self-incrimination, and the Ninth Amendment[145] combined to create a "zone of privacy" impenetrable by government.

Douglas's basic idea was that these explicit constitutional guarantees all spoke, in one way or another, to the idea of privacy, which he thus embraced as a "penumbral" constitutional right. Based on this "penumbras" analysis, the Court held that the statute in *Griswold* was overbroad in infringing on the privacy of the marital relationship. (The defendants counseled married couples about contraception and were allowed to assert those couples' rights.) In prohibiting the use of contraceptives (as opposed to their manufacture or sale), the law appeared to allow police to pry into the marital relationship in their search for evidence of contraceptive use.

In their separate concurrences, Justices Goldberg, Harlan, and White agreed with Justice Douglas' conclusion that the Connecticut statute was unconstitutional, but their analyses differed. Justice Goldberg, joined by Chief Justice Warren and Justice Brennan, used the Ninth Amendment to support his position that the Fourteenth Amendment Due Process Clause protected a fundamental right to "marital privacy." He did not argue for "incorporating" the Ninth Amendment via the Fourteenth Amendment, acknowledging that the Framers had intended the Ninth Amendment to limit the power of the federal government, not the states. Nevertheless, he construed the Ninth Amendment as expressing the Framers' belief that the first eight amendments were not to be considered an exhaustive list of fundamental rights. In finding

---

141. For more information about *Skinner*, see Victoria Nourse, In Reckless Hands: *Skinner v. Oklahoma and the Near-Triumph of American Eugenics* (2008).

142. 381 U.S. 479 (1965).

143. *Id.* at 482.

144. *Id.* at 484.

145. "The enumeration in the Constitution, of certain rights, shall not be construed to deny or disparage others retained by the people." U.S. Const. amend. IX.

a right of marital privacy, Justice Goldberg looked to "'the traditions and [collective] conscience of our people'" to determine whether the principle was "'so rooted [there] ... as to be ranked as fundamental.'"[146] Concluding that the right was indeed fundamental, he applied strict scrutiny to the statute, which he concluded it failed.

Justice Harlan concurred in the judgment. He found that the statute violated the Due Process Clause by infringing on "basic values 'implicit in the concept of ordered liberty.'"[147] He denied that his theory hinged constitutional interpretation on the personal predilections of individual judges. He listed as restraints on judicial power a reliance on history in identifying fundamental rights and the continued vitality of federalism and separation of powers. In identifying historical American tradition as relevant, however, he cautioned that that tradition continued to evolve, and urged that courts performing due process analysis recognize that ongoing evolution. In discussing his approach to substantive due process, Justice Harlan drew heavily on a dissenting opinion he had written in a case four years earlier, *Poe v. Ullman*,[148] in which the Court considered a due process challenge to the same Connecticut law, but ultimately refrained from reaching the merits. Justice Harlan reached the merits in *Poe*, and wrote an opinion setting forth his views that would become highly influential in later justices' thinking about substantive due process.

Justice White also concurred in the judgment. He imposed a less exacting standard than Justices Goldberg and Harlan, requiring the statute to be "reasonably necessary for the effectuation of a legitimate and substantial state interest."[149] Justice White read Connecticut's argument in *Griswold* as resting purely on a state purpose of discouraging extra-marital sex. He found the law—which applied to unmarried and married couples' use of contraceptives—to be lacking any reasonable connection to that goal, and struck it down given its significant encroachment into the liberty interests of the married couple in the case.

Justices Black and Stewart each wrote separate dissents. Neither could find support for a "right of privacy" in any specific constitutional provision. Although they both personally disagreed with the Connecticut statute (with Justice Stewart dismissing it as "an uncommonly silly law"[150]), they both worried about courts enforcing rights that were not expressly provided in the constitutional text. In particular, Justice Black accused the Court of returning to *Lochner*-era jurisprudence despite the majority's explicit disavowal of the Due Process Clause as the source of the privacy right.

Although the marital relationship was the central tenet in *Griswold*, a series of subsequent cases expanded the decision's scope. In *Eisenstadt v. Baird*,[151] the Court invalidated a Massachusetts statute banning distribution of contraceptives to unmar-

---

146. *Griswold*, 381 U.S. at 487 (quoting Snyder v. Commonwealth of Massachusetts, 291 U.S. 97, 105 (1934) (Cardozo, J.)).

147. *Id.* at 500 (Harlan, J., concurring).

148. 367 U.S. 497, 522 (1961) (Harlan, J., dissenting).

149. *Griswold*, 381 U.S. 504 (White, J., concurring in the judgment).

150. *Id.* at 527 (Stewart, J., dissenting).

151. 405 U.S. 438 (1972).

ried individuals. Somewhat like *Skinner v. Oklahoma*,[152] *Eisenstadt* employed a combination of equal protection and substantive due process analyses. Most importantly for current purposes, Justice Brennan, writing for the Court, stated that "[i]f the right of privacy means anything, it is the right of the individual, married or single, to be free from unwarranted governmental intrusion into matters so fundamentally affecting a person as the decision whether to bear or beget a child."[153]

The Court further broadened access to contraceptives in *Carey v. Population Services International*.[154] The statute at issue required a licensed pharmacist to distribute contraceptives, prohibited distribution of contraceptives to persons under 16 (except by licensed physician to married females between 14 and 16), and prohibited their advertisement. Again writing for the Court, Justice Brennan invalidated the requirement that a licensed pharmacist distribute contraceptives, because it significantly burdened an individual's right to make childbearing decisions without serving a compelling state interest. The Court also struck down the advertising ban.[155]

Denying access to minors presented a much closer question. The statute was draconian: it even prohibited parents from distributing contraceptives to their own children, and limited minors' access to situations where a physician prescribed it. A plurality opinion by Justice Brennan held that the restriction could be upheld only if it served "'any significant state interest ... that is not present in the case of an adult.'"[156] Reflecting the diminished decision-making capacity of minors, this test imposed less scrutiny than the analogous test used to evaluate laws prohibiting contraceptive use by adults. Nevertheless, the plurality found that the near-blanket prohibition on contraceptives for minors was foreclosed by decisions like *Planned Parenthood v. Danforth*,[157] which had invalidated a parental veto provision over a minor's decision to seek an abortion. The plurality also doubted that limiting access to contraceptives would discourage sexual activity among the young, given the lack of evidence the state presented to support that proposition.

Justices White, Powell, and Stevens each wrote separate opinions concurring only in the judgment striking down the distribution ban. All three Justices appeared ready to apply a more relaxed standard of scrutiny than the plurality for regulating the distribution of contraceptives to minors if parents remained free to distribute them to their children. Chief Justice Burger and Justice Rehnquist each dissented. With their votes, it would appear that a majority of five justices would have allowed substantial regulation of the distribution of contraceptives to minors so long as parents were exempted.

---

152. 316 U.S. 535 (1942).
153. 405 U.S. at 453.
154. 431 U.S. 678 (1977).
155. First Amendment protection for such commercial speech is discussed in Section 11.01[2][e].
156. *Id.* at 693 (quoting *Planned Parenthood v. Danforth*, 428 U.S. 52, 75 (1976)).
157. 428 U.S. 52 (1976).

[3] Abortion

[a] Roe v. Wade

Critical to the Court's modern substantive due process jurisprudence are the cases involving a woman's right to choose an abortion. The first case to guarantee that right was *Roe v. Wade*.[158] The Texas statute invalidated in *Roe* made it a crime to procure or attempt an abortion except to save the life of the mother.

The *Roe* Court,[159] speaking through Justice Blackmun, premised the right to have an abortion on the constitutional right of privacy which derived from the concept of personal liberty in the Due Process Clause. Against this due process privacy or liberty right, the state asserted an interest in protecting fetal life. Justice Blackmun first rejected the argument that the fetus was a person for purposes of Fourteenth Amendment protection. Relying on various constitutional provisions referring to "persons," Justice Blackmun concluded that the Constitution only protected those who were already born. By focusing on legal personhood, the Court avoided the question of when life begins, a question on which the Court acknowledged deep medical, philosophical, and theological disagreement.

The Court's refusal to recognize a fetus as a person for constitutional purposes did not mean, however, that it accorded no weight to the state's interest in fetal life. Rather, the Court recognized what it called the state's interest in the "potential life"[160] present in the fetus. Importantly, the Court concluded that that interest grew over the course a pregnancy, becoming compelling enough to justify most restrictions and even prohibitions on abortion once the fetus reached the point of viability—that is, the point at which it became capable of life outside the womb. To be sure, though, even after viability, the Court recognized the woman's right to an abortion in order to protect her life or health.

The Court also recognized that the state itself had an interest in the woman's own health that might justify regulating the abortion decision. Nevertheless, he noted that, at the then-current state of medicine, abortion in the first trimester of pregnancy was safer than taking a pregnancy to term. Based on that observation, the Court concluded that, prior to the first trimester, the state lacked a woman's health justification for restricting abortions.

Thus, Justice Blackmun's opinion created a "trimester" approach to state regulation of abortion. During approximately the first trimester, the abortion decision must be left strictly to the mother and her physician, without state interference. Starting with the second trimester, as the relative health risks shifted between abortion and childbirth, the state could regulate to protect the health of the mother. At the point of viability, which occurs at approximately the start of the third trimester, the state could

---

158. 410 U.S. 113 (1973).
159. *Roe* was a 7–2 opinion, with Justices White and Rehnquist dissenting.
160. *Id.* at 150.

assert its interest in fetal protection to regulate or even forbid abortion except to protect the mother's life or health. In essence, the scheme *Roe* adopted reflected a sliding scale of state interests in abortion regulation, with those interests (the woman's health and the potentiality of life in the fetus) becoming more compelling as the pregnancy moved forward.

Justice Douglas concurred, but he found it more difficult to justify the result in *Roe* with the "penumbras" analysis he employed in *Griswold*. Instead, Justice Douglas relied more heavily on the Ninth Amendment and the Due Process Clause. Although he had dissented in *Griswold*, Justice Stewart concurred largely based on *Griswold's* *stare decisis* effect. Chief Justice Burger also concurred, to emphasize that the Court was not announcing a constitutional right to what he called "abortions on demand."[161]

In separate dissents, Justices White and Rehnquist criticized the Court for engaging in a brand of social policy analysis they argued was reminiscent of *Lochner*. Justice Rehnquist characterized the majority's weighing of the individual and state interests as reflecting more of a legislative judgment than a judicial analysis. His dissent also noted that most states had restricted abortions for over a century, including during the period when the Fourteenth Amendment was ratified. Consequently, quoting Justice Cardozo's description of fundamental rights, he concluded that "the asserted right to an abortion was not so rooted in the traditions and conscience of our people as to be ranked as fundamental."[162] Justice White similarly accused the majority of "fashion[ing] and announcer[ing] a new constitutional right for pregnant women."[163] Both dissenters would have imposed a rationality standard of review for abortion restrictions.

Roe's reasoning applied to a much broader range of abortion restrictions than those in the restrictive Texas statute. In *Doe v. Bolton*,[164] a companion case to *Roe* decided the same day, the Court invalidated a much less restrictive Georgia law based on the new Model Penal Code's abortion provisions. The Georgia law allowed abortion only to protect the life or health of the mother, to prevent the birth of a fetus with a serious birth defect, or to end a pregnancy resulting from rape. The Court also invalidated various procedural requirements, but it upheld a requirement that a physician exercise medical judgment "in light of all factors—physical, emotional, psychological, familial, and the woman's age—relevant to the well-being of the patient."[165]

Following *Roe*, state legislatures attempted to restrict abortion in many ways. Supreme Court decisions reviewing such legislation fall into four principal categories.

---

161. 410 U.S. at 208.

162. *Roe*, 410 U.S. at 174 (Rehnquist, J., dissenting) (quoting Snyder v. Massachusetts, 291 U.S. 97, 105 (1934) (Cardozo, J.)). By contrast, Justice Blackmun's reading of the history led him to conclude that "throughout the major portion of the 19th century, prevailing legal abortion practices were far freer than they are today." *Id.* at 158 (majority opinion).

163. *Id.* at 221 (White, J., dissenting).

164. 410 U.S. 179 (1973).

165. *Id.* at 192.

Withdrawal of public funding for abortion has been upheld. Spousal notification and consent requirements have generally been struck down. Parental notification and consent requirements have been upheld as long as those requirements included a judicial bypass option. Finally, in more recent years, the Court has often upheld restrictions on types of abortions as well as waiting periods, but has invalidated laws imposing onerous requirements on abortion providers. Many of these results, however, flow from closely-divided Court decisions that may well be subject to reconsideration.

[b] Public Funding

The Court has allowed government extensive discretion in deciding whether to fund abortions. Three cases decided in 1977 concluded that neither the Constitution nor any federal legislation required states to fund non-therapeutic abortions for indigent women.[166] According to these cases, constitutional protection was limited to noninterference by the government with the abortion decision.

Three years later, *Harris v. McRae*[167] made clear that government could refuse to provide public funding for even medically necessary abortions, despite funding all other medically necessary procedures, including childbirth services, through its Medicaid program. The Court upheld several versions of a federal law that prohibited federal funding for abortions, including several categories of medically necessary abortions. The Court relied heavily on the philosophical distinction between positive rights — that is, rights to government assistance in exercising liberties — and negative rights — that is, rights simply to government non-interference when doing so. The underlying rationale in *Harris* was that the right to choose an abortion did not amount to a government entitlement. The dissent argued that the *Harris* line of cases made the right established in *Roe* unavailable to poor persons.

[c] Notification and Consent Requirements

In an early post-*Roe* case, *Planned Parenthood v. Danforth*,[168] the Court struck down a law requiring a married woman to obtain her husband's written consent in order to receive an abortion. The Court reasoned that the woman's interest outweighed her husband's interest in the pregnancy, as she was more directly and immediately affected by the pregnancy. Sixteen years later, *Planned Parenthood v. Casey*[169] struck down a spousal notification requirement. The Court held that such a notification requirement generally would only be necessary in dysfunctional, including violent, marriages and could be a substantial obstacle to a woman in such a relationship obtaining an abortion.

The Court has been somewhat more accepting of laws requiring minors to obtain parental consent before obtaining an abortion, although it has attempted to account

---

166. Beal v. Doe, 432 U.S. 438 (1977); Maher v. Roe, 432 U.S 464 (1977); Poelker v. Doe, 432 U.S. 519 (1977).
167. 448 U.S. 297 (1980).
168. 428 U.S. 52 (1976).
169. 505 U.S. 833 (1992).

for the minor's interest in deciding for herself whether to terminate a pregnancy. In *Danforth*, the Court struck down a law requiring parental consent for a minor to have an abortion unless a doctor certified that the abortion was necessary to save the minor's life. The plurality opinion held that a state seeking to impose a parental consent requirement must add an alternative process to give her access to an abortion, such as an opportunity to appear before a judge. The so-called "judicial bypass" option has since become an important part of the Court's jurisprudence on minors' access to abortion.

The Court re-examined the issue of parental consent for minors three years later in *Bellotti v. Baird*.[170] Eight members of the Court held unconstitutional a Massachusetts provision requiring an unmarried minor to obtain the consent of both parents or the authorization of a state judge if parental consent was denied. They expressed concern with the law's provision that a judge could withhold approval even if he concluded that the minor was capable of making an informed and reasonable decision and in fact had made such a decision. Four justices also expressed concern with the fact that the law required parental notification before the minor could even seek judicial approval for obtaining an abortion.

The Court again confronted parental notice in *Hodgson v. Minnesota*.[171] The *Hodgson* Court struck down a Minnesota statute requiring that both parents of an unemancipated minor be notified 48 hours before the minor had an abortion. However, a different majority of justices upheld the same notification requirement with the addition of a judicial bypass option. This judicial bypass allowed a judge to order an abortion without parental consent if the judge determined that the minor was mature and capable of making the decision herself or if the judge determined that the abortion would be in the best interest of the child.

[d] Direct Restrictions on Abortion

Before the late 1980s, few direct restrictions on abortion procedures survived judicial scrutiny. For example, in *Planned Parenthood v. Danforth*,[172] the Court invalidated a prohibition on saline amniocentesis abortions, the most frequent method used for abortions performed after the first trimester. The Court concluded that the prohibition was unreasonably designed to inhibit, and actually did inhibit, second trimester abortions. In *City of Akron v. Akron Center for Reproductive Health, Inc.*,[173] the Court invalidated informed-consent requirements on the ground that they were designed to deter abortions. Among other things, the law required that the woman be informed that the unborn child constituted a life at conception, that she have the physiology of the fetus described to her, and that she be informed of the particular risks of the abortion procedure to be employed. The *Akron* Court also invalidated a requirement that all second and third trimester abortions be performed in full-care

---

170. 443 U.S. 622 (1979).
171. 497 U.S. 417 (1990).
172. 428 U.S. 52 (1976).
173. 462 U.S. 416 (1983).

hospitals. However, in *Simopoulos v. Virginia*,[174] a companion case to *Akron*, the Court upheld a requirement that second trimester abortions be performed in a full-care hospital or a licensed outpatient clinic.

Justice O'Connor's dissent in *Akron* was particularly important, as it articulated the "undue burden" standard as an alternative approach to the trimester framework. This approach, which a three-justice plurality opinion ultimately adopted in 1992 and which has since become established as the law, was less rigid than *Roe*'s trimester scheme, and provided state legislatures with greater latitude in regulating abortion. It applied strict scrutiny to abortion regulations only if they created an "undue burden" on the woman's right to choose an abortion. If a court did not find such a burden, it would review the regulation under a rationality standard. Additionally, the standard treated the state's interests in maternal health and the fetus's potential life as substantial throughout the pregnancy.

By 1989, changes on the Court had made the abortion right less secure. In *Webster v. Reproductive Health Services*,[175] the Court rejected the Solicitor General's request that the Court overrule *Roe*. Nevertheless, the Court upheld various provisions of a Missouri statute restricting abortion, including a requirement that a doctor performing an abortion on a woman he believed to be at least 20 weeks pregnant perform tests on the fetus to determine its viability. In upholding this testing requirement, three justices would have overruled *Roe*'s trimester framework while not disturbing its holding striking down the Texas law completely banning non-therapeutic abortions. Another justice, Justice Scalia, would have overruled *Roe* entirely. Justice O'Connor provided the fifth vote for the result upholding the testing requirement at issue in *Webster*, but she would have done so by finding the law consistent with *Roe*. Four justices dissented from most of the Court's holding and criticized the justices in the majority for seeking either implicitly or explicitly to overrule *Roe*.

[e] Planned Parenthood v. Casey

In *Planned Parenthood of S.E. Pennsylvania v. Casey*,[176] the controlling opinion formally adopted the "undue burden" analysis Justice O'Connor had previously developed. Justices O'Connor, Kennedy, and Souter, writing a joint opinion, rejected *Roe*'s trimester framework while explicitly reaffirming what it called *Roe*'s "essential holding," which it described as follows:

> First is a recognition of the right of the woman to choose to have an abortion before viability and to obtain it without undue interference from the State. Before viability, the State's interests are not strong enough to support a prohibition of abortion or the imposition of a substantial obstacle to the woman's effective right to elect the procedure. Second is a confirmation of the States' power to restrict abortions after fetal viability, if the law contains exceptions

---

174. 462 U.S. 506 (1983).
175. 492 U.S. 490 (1989).
176. 505 U.S. 833 (1992).

for pregnancies which endanger the woman's life or health. And third is the principle that the State has legitimate interests from the outset of the pregnancy in protecting the health of the woman and the life of the fetus that may become a child.[177]

The statute at issue in *Casey* imposed a number of restrictions on a woman's ability to obtain an abortion. Four of the statute's provisions were challenged: the requirement of informed consent, combined with a 24-hour waiting period; a spousal notification requirement; a parental consent requirement for minors; and the requirement of record-keeping for abortion providers.

In reaffirming parts of *Roe*, the joint opinion relied heavily on the doctrine of *stare decisis*. It began that discussion with what it described as the standard factors to consider when deciding whether to overrule a precedent. First, although the rule in *Roe* had encountered opposition, it had not proven unworkable. Second, reliance on *Roe* had shaped the reproductive attitudes of the populace for nearly 20 years; moreover, women had reasonably relied on *Roe*'s continued force. Third, no evolution in constitutional law supported alteration of the rule. Fourth, although certain medical advances had called into question the trimester approach, viability remained a valid point for government intervention.

The joint opinion then went further, acknowledging the heated disagreement about *Roe* and abortion more generally, and comparing calls to overrule *Roe* with analogous calls during the 1930s to overrule the Court's liberty of contract jurisprudence and in the 1950s to overrule its acceptance of racial segregation. Rejecting the comparison to those (ultimately successful) calls to overrule controversial lines of cases, the joint opinion stated that overruling *Roe* in response to political pressure would undermine the Court's legitimacy and Americans' faith in the Court as a body that sought to announce constitutional principles free from political pressure. It described those earlier overrulings as based on the Court's new understanding of facts (respectively, the inability of an unregulated economic marketplace to ensure basic human needs and the stigmatizing effects of racial segregation). By contrast, it concluded that no such new understanding of facts accompanied the calls to overrule *Roe*. Consequently, even though the authors of the joint opinion stated that they might not decide *Roe* the same way had the case come before them as an initial matter, they concluded that to "to overrule under [political] fire in the absence of the most compelling reason to reexamine a watershed decision would subvert the Court's legitimacy beyond any serious question."[178]

Nevertheless, as noted earlier, the joint opinion reaffirmed only what it called *Roe*'s "essential holding." By contrast, it rejected *Roe*'s trimester framework due to its unnecessarily rigid character and its diminishment of the importance of the substantial state interest in potential life and women's health that existed throughout the preg-

---

177. *Id.* at 846.
178. *Id.* at 867.

nancy. Instead, the Court adopted the "undue burden" standard Justice O'Connor offered in previous opinions. Under that approach, a regulation was unconstitutional if it unduly burdened a woman's right to choose an abortion. A regulation imposed an undue burden if "it has the purpose or effect of placing a substantial obstacle in the path of a woman seeking an abortion of a nonviable fetus."[179] But it retained *Roe*'s focus on viability, making that point the dividing line before which a state could not promote its interest in fetal life by prohibiting abortion, but after which it could.

The undue burden standard contrasted with the Court's previous strict scrutiny approach to abortion restrictions. It allowed "structural mechanisms" through which the state, or a parent or guardian of a minor, could demonstrate its respect for the potential life in the fetus by attempting to persuade a woman to choose childbirth over abortion.[180] It also allowed the state to advance its legitimate interest of furthering women's health; unlike *Roe*, it did not limit regulations furthering maternal health to the second and third trimesters of the pregnancy. The Court would uphold measures that did not amount to undue burdens and were reasonably related to expressing respect for life and protecting women's health. After viability, the *Casey* Court would allow regulation and even proscription of abortion unless the abortion was necessary to preserve the life or health of the mother.

Toward the end of its analysis, the joint opinion provided the following summary of the state's ability to regulation abortion:

(a) To protect the central right recognized by *Roe v. Wade* while at the same time accommodating the State's profound interest in potential life, we will employ the undue burden analysis as explained in this opinion. An undue burden exists, and therefore a provision of law is invalid, if its purpose or effect is to place a substantial obstacle in the path of a woman seeking an abortion before the fetus attains viability.

(b) We reject the rigid trimester framework of *Roe v. Wade*. To promote the State's profound interest in potential life, throughout pregnancy the State may take measures to ensure that the woman's choice is informed, and measures designed to advance this interest will not be invalidated as long as their purpose is to persuade the woman to choose childbirth over abortion. These measures must not be an undue burden on the right.

(c) As with any medical procedure, the State may enact regulations to further the health or safety of a woman seeking an abortion. Unnecessary health regulations that have the purpose or effect of presenting a substantial obstacle to a woman seeking an abortion impose an undue burden on the right.

(d) Our adoption of the undue burden analysis does not disturb the central holding of *Roe v. Wade*, and we reaffirm that holding. Regardless of whether exceptions are made for particular circumstances, a State may not prohibit

---

179. *Id.* at 877.
180. *Ibid.*

any woman from making the ultimate decision to terminate her pregnancy before viability.

(e) We also reaffirm *Roe*'s holding that subsequent to viability, the State in promoting its interest in the potentiality of human life may, if it chooses, regulate, and even proscribe, abortion except where it is necessary, in appropriate medical judgment, for the preservation of the life or health of the mother.[181]

In applying these rules to the Pennsylvania statute, the three justices in the joint opinion voted to uphold three of the four challenged provisions (with the four dissenters who would have overruled *Roe* in its entirety providing the remaining votes needed to form a majority on those issues). That coalition upheld the 24-hour waiting period and the requirement that a woman must certify in writing that her physician had informed her of the availability of state-published materials describing the fetus, the medical assistance available for childbirth, the availability of paternal child support and adoption agencies, and other abortion alternatives. (This provision could be waived to avert severe adverse effects on the woman's mental or physical health.)

Analogizing the provision of information to normal medical informed-consent requirements, the joint opinion endorsed the mandated provision of such information as long as it was not misleading. While the waiting period could impose a burden on poor women, three authors of the joint opinion concluded that it did not impose a substantial obstacle based on the facts before the Court. The Court overruled the 1983 *Akron* case[182] to the extent that it was inconsistent with its opinion.

A majority of the justices (the three authors of the joint opinion and Justices Blackmun and Stevens) struck down the requirement that a woman certify in writing that she had notified her spouse of her abortion. Under the statute, a woman could certify that another man impregnated her, that her husband could not be found, that the pregnancy resulted from spousal sexual assault, or that such notification would subject her to the danger of physical assault. In light of the district court's findings of spousal abuse surrounding pregnancy, the Court held the notification requirement unconstitutional, with the joint opinion reasoning that it posed a substantial obstacle due to its probable effect of deterring a significant number of women from exercising their right to choose abortion.

The *Casey* Court upheld the provision requiring a minor to receive one parent's consent before having an abortion. That provision included an exception for medical emergencies and allowed a judicial bypass if a determination could be made that the minor seeking an abortion had given informed consent and that the abortion was in her best interests. The Court upheld the record-keeping provisions except the one related to the invalidated spousal notification requirement.

Justices Blackmun and Stevens each wrote partial concurrences and partial dissents that would have reaffirmed *Roe* in its entirety, although Justice Stevens voted to uphold

---

181. *Id.* at 878–79.
182. *See supra.* note 173.

several of the Pennsylvania law's provisions. Chief Justice Rehnquist wrote an opinion, joined by Justices White, Scalia, and Thomas, that would have applied a rational basis test to uphold every challenged provision of the Pennsylvania statute. His opinion largely reprised the arguments in his dissent to *Roe* itself. He also criticized the joint opinion's *stare decisis* rationale as unprincipled, noting that the joint opinion itself did not follow *Roe* in many significant respects. The Chief Justice also criticized its reliance on *Roe*'s political divisiveness as a reason to refuse to overrule it.

Justice Scalia, joined by Chief Justice Rehnquist and Justices White and Thomas, authored a separate dissent. Among many other arguments, he insisted that the abortion right was the product of judges' personal predilections rather than constitutional principle, and that decisions about abortion should be left to the judgment of the legislative branches.

[f] Abortion Restrictions after Casey

Casey's partial reaffirmation of *Roe* did not stop states' attempts to regulate abortion. After *Casey*, much abortion regulation focused on state restrictions on particular types of abortion procedures and, separately, on abortion regulations defended as measures designed to protect the health of women seeking abortions.

[i] Regulation of Abortion Procedures

In *Stenberg v. Carhart*,[183] the Court invalidated Nebraska's "partial birth abortion" statute, holding that it violated *Casey* by placing an undue burden on a woman's right to choose an abortion. The challenged statute made it a felony for a doctor to perform a "partial birth abortion," which the law defined as " 'an abortion procedure in which the person performing the abortion partially delivers vaginally a living unborn child before killing the unborn child and completing the delivery.' " The statute "further defines 'partially delivers vaginally a living unborn child before killing the unborn child' to mean 'deliberately and intentionally delivering into the vagina a living unborn child, or substantial portion thereof, for the purpose of performing a procedure that the person performing such procedure knows will kill the unborn child and does kill the unborn child.' "[184]

Writing for the five-justice majority, Justice Breyer concluded that the statute raised serious constitutional issues because it regulated both pre- and post-viability abortions, even though the state's regulatory interest was weaker pre-viability. He also explained that, although the statute "regulates only a *method* of performing abortion," the state could not place women's health at risk either due to complications arising from the pregnancy itself or by forcing them to choose riskier abortion procedures.

Applying this latter principle, the Court found two problems with the statute. First, it was worded in a vague way that appeared to cover not just "dilation and extraction" ("D&X") procedures, but also "dilation and evacuation" ("D&E") procedures

---

183. 530 U.S. 914 (2000).
184. *Id.* at 922 (quoting the statute).

that were far more common in second-trimester abortions; as such, it imposed a substantial obstacle on the woman's right. With regard to the D&X procedure, the Court found that the statute's blanket prohibition was unconstitutional, because it lacked an exception for situations when the D&X procedure was safer for the woman's health. Thus, the Court applied in a more particularized context *Casey*'s general insistence that abortion regulations always provide for women's health exceptions. Importantly, when considering these questions, the Court did not simply defer to the Nebraska legislature's judgment, but instead relied heavily on the conclusions the lower court reached after carefully considering medical opinion about the safety of and need for particular types of abortion procedures.

Justice Stevens concurred, joined by Justice Ginsburg. Justice Stevens argued that the choice of abortion procedure should remain with the doctor, rather than dictated by the state. Justice O'Connor concurred, emphasizing that since even a post-viability prohibition of abortion required a health exception, it followed that pre-viability proscriptions also required it. She would have voted to uphold a ban on D&X procedures that exempted situations where the procedure was selected to protect the mother's health or life. Justice Ginsburg, joined by Justice Stevens, concurred to point out that the challenged law "does not save any fetus from destruction, for it targets only a *method* of performing abortion."[185]

Justice Kennedy wrote a dissenting opinion joined by Chief Justice Rehnquist. Justice Kennedy disagreed with the majority's conclusion about the law's ambiguity, arguing that Nebraska's intent was simply to ban D&X procedures. He further argued that the majority's approach effectively deferred to an individual physician's judgment about the safest procedure to use in a given case. As medical opinion was divided on both the safety and ethics of the technique in question, he argued that the legislature had the authority to decide that issue as a general matter.

Justice Thomas dissented, joined by the Chief Justice and Justice Scalia. He disagreed with the majority's analysis of *Casey*'s women's health exception, arguing that, while *Roe* and *Casey* protected abortion procedures "necessary" to protect the mother's health, the majority gave constitutional protection to any procedure that "has any comparative health benefits."[186] Echoing Justice Kennedy's argument, Justice Thomas argued that the majority's actual standard was "whether *any* doctor could reasonably believe"[187] that a particular abortion method would protect the woman. Justice Scalia also dissented, critiquing *Casey*'s undue burden standard as impossible to apply in a principled way.

The Court returned to the "partial birth" abortion question in *Gonzales v. Carhart*.[188] In *Gonzalez*, the Court upheld against a facial challenge the federal Partial Birth Abortion Act of 2003, a statute Congress enacted in reaction to the Court's opinion in

---

185. *Id.* at 951 (Ginsburg, J., concurring) (emphasis in original).
186. *Id.* at 1012 (Thomas, J., dissenting).
187. *Id.* at 1017.
188. 550 U.S. 124 (2007).

Stenberg, discussed immediately above. Justice Kennedy wrote the opinion for the Court and was joined by Chief Justice Roberts, and Justices Scalia, Thomas and Alito. The line up in *Gonzalez* was exactly the same as in *Stenberg* (with Chief Justice Roberts voting as his predecessor Chief Justice Rehnquist had), except that Justice O'Connor, who voted to strike down the Nebraska law in *Stenberg*, was replaced by Justice Alito, who voted to uphold the federal law in *Gonzalez*.

Writing for the Court, Justice Kennedy stated that, in enacting the statute, Congress responded to the Court's holding in *Stenberg* in two ways. First, it made a series of factual findings asserting that the *Stenberg* Court was required to accept the "'very questionable [fact] findings issued by the district court judge.'" Congress further found that a "'moral, medical and ethical consensus exists and that the practice of performing a partial-birth abortion ... [was] a gruesome and inhumane procedure that [was] never medically necessary and should be prohibited.'"[189] Second, the federal statute used more precise language to describe the prohibited procedure than did the Nebraska law in *Stenberg*, and thus cured the ambiguity the *Stenberg* majority had identified in the analogous Nebraska law.

In rejecting the plaintiff's facial challenge, the Court concluded that the federal law was not unconstitutionally vague and did not impose an undue burden from any overbroad impact on the abortion right. Justice Kennedy concluded that the law explicitly defined the conduct that comprised the banned procedure and also contained intent or knowledge requirements that pertained to each of the specified acts the statute identified as part of the prohibited abortion method. In the next major part of the opinion, the Court held that the Act did not impose an undue burden on second trimester abortions because it did not prohibit the standard D&E procedure; indeed, it specifically excluded most D&E procedures. More generally, the Court also rejected the argument that the Act imposed a substantial obstacle to a woman's choice to have an abortion. In so concluding, the Court relied heavily on Congress's findings and conclusions about the procedure's coarsening impact on society and the medical community. He concluded that the law furthered "legitimate [governmental objectives] in regulating the medical profession ... to promote respect for life, including life of the unborn."[190]

Still, even though it advanced legitimate state interests, the law could nevertheless impose an unconstitutional burden on the right to an abortion if it barred a procedure "'necessary, in appropriate medical judgment for [the] preservation of the ... health of the mother.'"[191] While the law would be unconstitutional had it subjected women to unnecessary health risks, the Court concluded that there existed "documented medical disagreement whether the Act's prohibition would ever impose significant health risks on women.... The law need not give abortion doctors unfettered choice in the course of their medical practice, nor should it elevate their status above other

---

189. *Id.* at 141 (quoting the statute's findings).
190. *Id.* at 158.
191. *Id.* at 161 (quoting *Casey*, 505 U.S. at 879).

physicians in the medical community."[192] Given that disagreement, the Court deferred to Congress's judgment on the women's health question. It further observed that if the prohibited procedure was truly necessary, the law permits alternatives such as an injection that kills the fetus prior to the delivery. Finally, the Court acknowledged that a woman for whom the banned procedure was indeed necessary for her health could challenge the law as applied to her particular circumstances.

Justice Ginsburg dissented, joined by Justices Stevens, Souter and Breyer. She accused the Court of blurring the line between pre- and post-viability abortions, and further accused it of upholding, for the first time since *Roe*, an abortion regulation lacking a woman's health exception. She objected that the absence of that statutory safeguard forced women into riskier abortion methods—a result that she said was inconsistent with *Casey*'s requirement of a health exception, even for post-viability abortion prohibitions. Turning to the congressional findings to which the majority deferred, Justice Ginsburg disputed Congress's finding that the banned procedure was never necessary, arguing that as "the evidence very clearly demonstrates the opposite."[193] She observed that every district court that considered Congress's findings about the banned procedure's lack of necessity viewed those findings as unreasonable and unsupported by the evidence.

More generally, Justice Ginsburg noted that the law did not even protect fetal life, as it only targeted a method of abortion. She characterized the Court's use of the term "abortion doctor" and "baby" and "unborn child" for fetus as evidencing its "hostility to the right *Roe* and *Casey* secured."[194] Finally, she argued that a facial challenge to the Act was appropriate. She stated that a health exception does not apply in the large fraction of cases, as it is intended "to protect women in *exceptional* cases."[195]

[ii] Restrictions Justified as Protecting Women's Health

In recent years, states seeking to restrict abortions have often justified their laws as health measures designed to protect women seeking abortions. While these measures vary from state to state, they often include requirements that abortion clinics possess certain equipment or that physicians performing abortions have admitting privileges at nearby hospitals. In *Whole Women's Health v. Hellerstedt*,[196] the Court considered a Texas law that required facilities performing abortions to meet "minimum standards ... for ambulatory surgical centers" and that required doctors performing abortions to have admitting privileges at a hospital within 30 miles of the facility at which the doctor performs abortions. The district court, after extensive fact-finding, concluded that those requirements were extremely costly and would cause a significant number of abortion clinics to close, but that abortion was already an extremely safe procedure, safer, in fact, than many medical procedures that were not subject to such

---

192. *Id.* at 163.
193. *Id.* at 176 (Ginsburg, J., dissenting).
194. *Id.* at 186.
195. *Id.* at 189 (emphasis in original).
196. 136 S. Ct. 2292 (2016).

requirements. The district court found that the law imposed an undue burden, and thus struck it down. The appellate court reversed.

A five-justice majority reversed the appellate court and struck the Texas law down. Writing for that majority, Justice Breyer wrote that the appellate court had erred in stating and applying the legal standard from *Casey*. First, he concluded that the appellate court had failed to consider whether the challenged law provided medical benefits. Second, he concluded that the lower court's statement that such laws are constitutional if " 'reasonably related to (or designed to further) a legitimate government interest' "[197] was too deferential, and ignored *Casey*'s requirement that such laws not constitute an undue burden.

Applying what it explained as the correct standard, the majority endorsed the findings made by the district court (and rejected by the appellate court). Those findings indicated that the law's requirements would not further women's health, given the safety with which abortions were already being conducted in Texas (as indicated by factors such as the rate at which such procedures produced medical complications). In particular, he noted that several of these requirements were simply unrelated to abortion procedures: for example, the law's requirements for facilities and practices more suited to surgical operations were unnecessary in the context of abortion facilities, since abortions are generally not performed via methods that pierce the skin or involve general anesthesia or deep sedation.

Moreover, the Court found that the law's provisions would cause a number of abortion facilities in the state to close, thus reducing access for women. In addition, it was anticipated that the facilities remaining open would be clustered in the four largest cities, far away (given the state's geographical size) from many women who might otherwise wish to obtain an abortion.

Justice Thomas dissented, both to repeat his opposition to *Casey* but also to argue that the majority itself had misapplied *Casey* by requiring consideration of the medical benefits provided by a health-justified abortion regulation, failing to defer to the legislature's judgments with regard to those benefits, and ratcheting up the general level of review under the undue burden standard. Justice Alito, joined by Chief Justice Roberts and Justice Thomas, also dissented. His dissent questioned whether it was the statute that was responsible for the closure of clinics in Texas (as opposed to other factors). He also took issue with the majority's doubt that the remaining clinics would have had the capacity to serve the Texas women who desired an abortion.

[g] Concluding Thoughts on Abortion

The authors of the joint opinion in *Casey* probably hoped that their opinion would settle the abortion issue. It clearly did not. Abortion remains a controversial issue, and both the inherent subjectivity of the undue burden standard and the continued political inflammation of the abortion issue probably mean that that the Court will

---

197. *Id.* at 2309 (quoting 790 F.3d 563, 572 (5th Cir. 2015)).

continue to be pressed to decide abortion rights cases, either by applying the undue burden standard, chipping away at it without overruling *Casey*, or taking the step the *Casey* Court would not — overruling *Roe* in its entirety.

As a topic of constitutional law, abortion also has a broader salience. For many critics of substantive due process, abortion is a prime example of the problems inherent in that doctrine. It is a highly-contentious political and moral issue and yet, these critics maintain, the Court, without any textual basis, has constitutionalized it and thus removed its resolution from the political process. Recall that in *Roe v. Wade*, Justice Rehnquist's dissent accused the majority of employing *Lochner*-style analysis to find an unenumerated right to an abortion, just as *Lochner* itself had found a similarly-unenumerated right to contract.

On the other hand, defenders of *Roe* argue that the decision flowed naturally from the child-rearing, procreation, and contraceptive cases stretching from *Meyer v. Nebraska* in 1923 up to *Eisenstadt v. Baird*, decided in 1972, one year before *Roe*. More conceptually, defenders of *Roe* argue that if "liberty" has any meaning, it must include the personal autonomy inherent in a woman's decision whether to bear a child. The joint opinion in *Casey* spoke to both precedent and this larger conceptual idea about the content of due process liberty:

> Our law affords constitutional protection to personal decisions relating to marriage, procreation, contraception, family relationships, child rearing, and education. Our cases recognize "the right of the *individual*, married or single, to be free from unwarranted governmental intrusion into matters so fundamentally affecting a person as the decision whether to bear or beget a child." *Eisenstadt v. Baird* (emphasis in original). Our precedents have respected the private realm of family life which the state cannot enter. These matters, involving the most intimate and personal choices a person may make in a lifetime, choices central to personal dignity and autonomy, are central to the liberty protected by the Fourteenth Amendment. At the heart of liberty is the right to define one's own concept of existence, of meaning, of the universe, and of the mystery of human life. Beliefs about these matters could not define the attributes of personhood were they formed under compulsion of the State.[198]

Critics of this argument counter that abortion is unique, in that it involves not just the woman but the potentiality of life (and, many people believe, the actual presence of life) in the fetus.[199] They also argue that such profound issues should be resolved through the democratic process, at least when there is no constitutional text explicitly speaking to the right in question.

Added onto this difficult debate are the equality dynamics abortion raises. *Roe* was argued and decided as a due process liberty case. Ironically, it was decided just

---

198. *Casey*, 505 U.S. at 851.

199. For a presentation of these various legal-moral arguments, see LAURENCE TRIBE, ABORTION: THE CLASH OF ABSOLUTES (1992).

as the Court was embarking on its still-ongoing campaign to ensure sex equality via the Equal Protection Clause.[200] Many thoughtful defenders of the abortion right have suggested that the right would be more firmly protected today if it had been articulated as an equality rather than a liberty right. Regardless of whether that is true, the fact remains that issues of sex equality mix with deep-seated moral and philosophical questions to make even more complex the doctrinal question about the existence of a due process right to abortion.

[4] Intimate Relationships

The Court has also extended substantive due process protection to familial and marriage relationships. The Court's recognition of this due process liberty interest extends back to *Meyer v. Nebraska*,[201] where the Court struck down a Nebraska law that prevented teaching schoolchildren a foreign language until after the child had graduated the eighth grade. Speaking through Justice McReynolds, the Court held that a parent had a constitutional right to direct the upbringing of his child, which included the right to make choices about the child's education. The Court reiterated and applied this principle in two other cases from the 1920s that sought to restrict parents' options regarding their children's education.[202]

[a] Family Relationships

In the modern era, the Court has often critically scrutinized state laws that interfere with the maintenance of the family unit or with individual rights exercised within the family context. In resolving conflicts among the interests of spouses, parents, children, and the state, the Court has relied on a number of constitutional sources. In *Wisconsin v. Yoder*,[203] the Court invoked the First Amendment's Free Exercise of Religion Clause to invalidate a state's application of its compulsory education law to Amish children whose parents wished to withdraw them from school earlier than state law allowed. In *Caban v. Mohammed*,[204] the Court found a violation of the Equal Protection Clause in a law that denied a father the right to bar adoption of his illegitimate children, while permitting a mother to do so. State laws that draw distinctions between legitimate and illegitimate children have also been invalidated on equal protection grounds.[205]

The Court has also often found a Due Process Clause right to particular family structures. In *Moore v. City of East Cleveland*,[206] the Court struck down a law that essentially prohibited extended family living arrangements. *Moore* dealt with a city or-

200. The Court's sex equality jurisprudence is discussed in Section 10.02.
201. 262 U.S. 390 (1923).
202. Pierce v. Society of Sisters, 268 U.S. 510 (1925) (invalidating a law requiring most children to attend public schools); Farrington v. Tokushige, 273 U.S. 284 (1927) (invalidating a federal territorial law restricting foreign-language instruction in Hawaiian schools). These cases are also discussed in Section 9.04[1].
203. 406 U.S. 205 (1972). *Yoder* is discussed in Section 12.03[2][b].
204. 441 U.S. 380 (1979).
205. These cases are discussed in Section 10.03[1].
206. 431 U.S. 494 (1977).

dinance that prohibited a woman from living with her adult son, that son's child, and the woman's grandson from another child—that is, it prevented the two grandchildren, first cousins, from living together. Writing for the plurality, Justice Powell distinguished *Moore* from *Village of Belle Terre v. Boraas*,[207] which upheld an ordinance prohibiting unrelated individuals from sharing a single dwelling unit, on the ground that the law in *Moore* infringed on family relationships. As the tradition of extended families living together was one deeply embedded in American society and values, the plurality concluded that the state could not impair it without very good reason. Scrutinizing those reasons carefully, the plurality concluded that the ordinance had "but a tenuous relation"[208] to the interests the city asserted, such as overcrowding and traffic congestion.

Justice Brennan, joined by Justice Marshall, joined Justice Powell's opinion, but also wrote separately to suggest that the tradition of the extended family was one that in the modern era was particularly favored by racial minorities. Conceding that the evidence did not support the conclusion that the city was engaging in racial discrimination, he nevertheless cautioned that due process liberties such as family relationships had to be protected so that even versions of the liberty embraced by minority groups were protected. Justice Stevens concurred in the judgment, concluding that the ordinance was an arbitrary restriction on Ms. Moore's right to use her property as she saw fit. Three of the four dissenters (Justices Stewart, White, Rehnquist) refused to find the right Ms. Moore asserted to be fundamental.[209]

In other cases, the Court was less protective of family relationships that extended beyond the nuclear family. In *Lyng v. Castillo*,[210] the Court rejected a challenge to a federal statute providing lower food stamp allotments to close relatives living together than to more distant relatives, or unrelated persons, living together. The law treated the former grouping as a single household for purposes of food stamp allotments, while treating the latter as separate households unless they customarily purchased food and prepared their meals together. Writing for the Court, Justice Stevens rejected the argument that the statute burdened the "fundamental right" of a person to determine her family living relationships: "The 'household' definition does not order or prevent any group of persons from dining together.... It is exceedingly unlikely that close relatives would choose to live apart simply to increase their allotment of food stamps."[211]

In *Michael H. v. Gerald D.*,[212] the justices engaged in a heated debate about the proper methodology for identifying due process liberties, in the context of a family structure case. The Court in *Michael H.* upheld against a due process challenge a California statute conclusively presuming that the father of a child was the man married to the child's mother. California had applied this statute to deny visitation rights to

---

207. 416 U.S. 1 (1974).
208. 431 U.S. at 500.
209. Chief Justice Burger dissented on an unrelated ground.
210. 477 U.S. 635 (1986).
211. *Id.* at 638.
212. 491 U.S. 110 (1989).

a man who, based on modern genetic testing, was almost certainly the child's biological father and who had held out the child as his own during periods where the mother and the mother's husband were separated.

Justice Scalia wrote for a plurality of four in finding that the interest asserted by the likely father was not one deeply rooted in American history or tradition. In an important footnote to his opinion, Justice Scalia insisted that the methodology he employed to reach that decision—a methodology that insisted on identifying the right in its narrowest formulation—was the only way to prevent due process analysis from devolving into judges' importing their own subjective preferences into the liberty the Due Process Clause protects.[213] Two members of the four-justice plurality, Justices Kennedy and O'Connor, declined to join that footnote. In an opinion by Justice O'Connor, joined by Justice Kennedy, they cautioned that the approach Justice Scalia offered was not the only way the Court had identified due process liberties in the past.[214] Justice Stevens concurred on a different ground, but expressed his disagreement with Justice Scalia's due process analysis.

Justice Brennan, joined by Justices Marshall and Blackmun, dissented. Justice Brennan focused on the methodological footnote discussed above, arguing that it reflected an overly-restrictive approach to identifying due process rights. He also argued that Justice Scalia's approach failed to cabin judicial discretion as much as Justice Scalia claimed, was inconsistent with how the Court had analyzed due process cases in the past, and failed to take account of historical reasons for rules that may no longer be persuasive.[215] Rather than identifying the right as narrowly as Justice Scalia would have, Justice Brennan identified the right as the right of a parent and child to have a relationship with each other. Analogizing to other cases involving non-custodial parents, he concluded that the likely father in this case had a due process right to seek to be named the child's legal father. Justice White, joined by Justice Brennan, also dissented, relying on the Court's earlier cases dealing with non-custodial parents to reach a conclusion similar to Justice Brennan's.

In *Troxel v. Granville*,[216] the Court invalidated a court order granting visitation rights to grandparents, when the parent objected, not to their visits entirely but to the amount of visitation time the grandparents desired. Writing for a plurality of four, Justice O'Connor noted that the "breathtakingly broad" statute under which the lower court acted allowed a court to "grant such visitation rights whenever visitation may serve the best interest of the child,"[217] without any deference to the parent's determination of which visitors would be in the child's best interest.

---

213. *See* 491 U.S. at 127, n. 6.

214. *See id.* at 132 (O'Connor, J., concurring in part). Only Chief Justice Rehnquist joined Justice Scalia in the footnote at issue.

215. For example, Justice Brennan observed that the plurality's conclusion that persons in the plaintiff's position did not have a due process right to prove paternity, to the extent that conclusion flowed from the historical inability to conclusively determine paternity and thus the disruption such claims would cause, was outdated in a world in which DNA testing was quite accurate.

216. 530 U.S. 57 (2000).

217. *Id.* at 67.

Concurring in the judgment, Justice Souter would have affirmed the decision of the Supreme Court of Washington that invalidated the non-parental visitation statute on its face, because it allowed courts to grant visitation rights to anyone at any time. Also concurring in the judgment, Justice Thomas would have invalidated the law under strict scrutiny, because it violated the fundamental right of parents to rear their children articulated in *Pierce v. Society of Sisters*.[218]

Justice Stevens dissented, maintaining that the statute was neither invalid on its face nor as applied. He feared that the Court's decision threatened the "best interests of the child standard," on which visitation laws around the nation heavily relied. Justice Scalia also dissented. He criticized the Court's reliance on the pre-1937 due process family cases such as *Meyer* and *Pierce*, and would not have accorded them heavy precedential weight. Given the difficult choices posed by policy decisions about child visitation, Justice Scalia would have allowed states to craft the relevant standards regarding such issues.

The Court has also confronted challenges to the *procedures* by which family relationships can be altered, or the status of children changed. Such claims are usually decided by recourse to general principles of so-called procedural due process, which inquires into the importance of the interest at stake and the likely accuracy of the challenged procedures.[219] Procedural due process is discussed in later in the chapter.[220]

[b] Marriage

The Court has found a substantive due process right to marriage. Often, it has considered marriage claims in the context of cases that also raised significant equality concerns. For example, in *Loving v. Virginia*,[221] the Court struck down one of the few remaining state-law prohibitions on interracial marriage. In addition to finding the law to be unconstitutional discrimination violating the Equal Protection Clause,[222] the Court also concluded that it deprived the interracial couple-plaintiffs of liberty without due process of law. In so doing, the Court described marriage as one of "the basic civil rights of man," and a "fundamental freedom." Combining the equality and due process theories, the Court wrote: "To deny this fundamental freedom on so unsupportable a basis as the racial classifications embodied in these statutes, classifications so directly subversive of the principle of equality at the heart of the Fourteenth Amendment, is surely to deprive all the State's citizens of liberty without due process of law."[223]

---

218. 268 U.S. 510 (1925). *Pierce* is discussed in Section 9.04[1].

219. *See, e.g.*, Parham v. J.R., 442 U.S. 584 (1979) (upholding the procedures for a parent's civil commitment of a child, based on the likely accuracy of the state's procedures for approving such a commitment, and the presumption that parents act in the best interests of their children); Santosky v. Kramer, 455 U.S. 745 (1982) (striking down a state's use of the "preponderance of the evidence" standard for depriving allegedly-neglectful parents of custody of their children, and, given the importance of the interest, insisting on application of a "clear and convincing evidence" standard).

220. *See* Section 9.06.

221. 388 U.S. 1 (1967).

222. The equal protection aspect of *Loving* is discussed in Section 10.04[2][b][ii].

223. 388 U.S. at 12.

The Court again combined liberty and equality reasoning in *Zablocki v. Redhail*.[224] In *Zablocki*, the Court struck down a Wisconsin law that required state approval before a person could obtain a marriage license if that person was the subject of a child support court order. Writing for the Court, Justice Marshall cited *Loving* for the proposition that marriage is a fundamental right. Turning to equal protection, he then concluded that "[w]hen a statutory classification significantly interferes with the exercise of a fundamental right, it cannot be upheld unless it is supported by sufficiently important state interests and is closely tailored to effectuate only those interests."[225] He rejected as "grossly underinclusive"[226] any goal of preventing the individual from incurring future debts, since the law targeted only one type of pre-existing debt—that related to child support obligations. He also noted that the law did nothing to ensure that the individual actually kept up on those obligations.

Justice Stewart concurred only in the judgment. He rejected the majority's use of equal protection, and instead would have grounded the result solely in the Due Process Clause. Justice Rehnquist dissented to express his disagreement with both the equal protection and due process theories for striking the statute down. He would have applied rational basis review to uphold the Wisconsin law. *Zablocki* and cases like it have come to be understood as occupying a doctrinal position encompassing elements of both due process and equal protection—the so-called fundamental rights strand of equal protection. That doctrinal hybrid is discussed in Chapter 10.[227]

In *Turner v. Safley*,[228] the Court invalidated a state prison regulation that allowed an inmate to marry only with the permission of the prison superintendent, and even then only for "compelling reasons." Applying a "reasonable relationship" test in light of the special deference accorded prison officials, the Court nevertheless struck down the regulation. Justice O'Connor's majority opinion rejected the government's claim that the regulation was reasonably related to prison security. She concluded that interpersonal jealousies threatening prison security could arise in prisons apart from marriage and that ready alternatives existed to address security concerns short of the regulation's broad prohibition. While Justice Stevens, joined by Justices Brennan, Marshall, and Blackmun, concurred separately to object to what he called the majority's vague standard, the Court's willingness to second-guess prison operations—something the Court rarely does—illustrates the importance the Court accords the marriage right.

In 2015, in *Obergefell v. Hodges*,[229] the Court struck down state law bans on same-sex marriage. While relying on the fundamental right to marry, *Obergefell* also focused heavily on the protection of the rights of same-sex couples in particular to enter into

224. 434 U.S. 374 (1978).
225. *Id.* at 388.
226. *Id.* at 390.
227. *See* Section 10.07.
228. 482 U.S. 78 (1987).
229. 135 S. Ct. 2584 (2015).

marriage. *Obergefell* is discussed in the section dealing with the rights to same-sex intimacy and intimate relationships, below.[230]

[c] Same-Sex Intimacy

Bowers v. Hardwick[231] arose when police arrested a man in his bedroom for having sex with another man in violation of Georgia's sodomy statute, which prohibited a variety of sex acts regardless of whether the participants were of the same or the opposite sex. Although the prosecutor dropped the charges, Hardwick sued for declaratory judgment to have the statute declared unconstitutional. He was joined in the suit by an opposite-sex couple that claimed that the law chilled their own exercise of their right to sexual intimacy. The lower court dismissed the opposite-sex couple as plaintiffs, concluding that there was no realistic chance that the law would be applied to them. Thus, although the statute's ban extended to conduct engaged in by opposite-sex couples, as the case reached the Court, it involved a claim focused on same-sex sexual conduct.

Justice White's majority opinion, stating the question as "whether the Federal Constitution confers a fundamental right upon homosexuals to engage in sodomy and hence invalidates the laws of the many States that still make such conduct illegal and have done so for a very long time," rejected the plaintiff's due process argument. Writing for a five-justice majority, he rejected the plaintiff's reliance on the Court's substantive due process procreation and family cases, concluding that "[n]o connection between family, marriage, or procreation on the one hand and homosexual activity on the other has been demonstrated."[232]

Moving beyond precedent, Justice White rejected the argument that tradition revealed a fundamental liberty interest in Hardwick's conduct, noting that 32 of 37 states outlawed sodomy when the Fourteenth Amendment was ratified. He also noted that, until 1961, all 50 states had come to outlaw sodomy, and 24 still banned it when the case reached the Court. To support this analysis, he cautioned against an expansive application of substantive due process, noting its non-textual foundation and the resulting risk that upholding such claims would simply import justices' own subjective value preferences into constitutional analysis, as he suggested the Court had done during the *Lochner* era. He concluded by finding a rational basis for the Georgia law in the state's desire to promote its chosen morality.

Chief Justice Burger joined the majority but also wrote a separate concurrence to emphasize what he saw as the lack of a tradition protecting sodomy. Justice Powell also joined the majority and wrote a separate concurrence, in which he suggested that any prison sentence for homosexual sodomy, particularly one of long duration, could violate the Eighth Amendment.

---

230. *See* Section 9.04[4][c].
231. 478 U.S. 186 (1986).
232. *Id.* at 190, 191.

Somewhat previewing the analogous dispute three years later in *Michael H. v. Gerald D.*,[233] the majority and dissent differed in characterizing the traditions at stake in *Bowers*. Justice White characterized the constitutional right as the right to engage in sodomy. In contrast, Justice Blackmun's dissent understood the relevant issue as whether the Constitution protected a "right to be left alone" or a right to privacy. He also criticized the Court's refusal to consider the statute's regulation of heterosexual behavior, given the sex-neutral character of the Georgia sodomy statute. He noted that the majority left open challenges under the Eighth and Ninth Amendments and the Equal Protection Clause of the Fourteenth Amendment. In a separate dissent joined by Justices Brennan and Marshall, Justice Stevens said that *Griswold v. Connecticut*, *Eisenstadt v. Baird*, and *Carey v. Population Services International*[234] stand for a right to engage in non-reproductive sexual conduct. He argued that selectively restricting sexual conduct by lesbian, gay, or bisexual (LGB) people must be justified by something more than a dislike for them.

Seventeen years later, the Court reconsidered *Bowers* in *Lawrence v. Texas*.[235] As in *Bowers*, the police in *Lawrence* entered a residence where they observed two men engaging in sex and arrested them. They were convicted under a Texas statute that, unlike the statute in *Bowers*, applied only to sexual conduct between persons of the same sex.

The Court, speaking through an opinion by Justice Kennedy for five justices,[236] began its analysis by recounting the Court's right to privacy cases beginning with *Griswold v. Connecticut*,[237] which the Court identified as "the most pertinent beginning point"[238] of the Court's analysis. Turning to *Bowers*, it critiqued Justice White's framing of the issue as concerning "the right of homosexuals to engage in sodomy" as "fail[ing] to appreciate the extent of the liberty at stake." Rather, he said, the statutes in both *Bowers* and *Lawrence* "touch[ed] upon the most private human conduct, sexual behavior, and in the most private of places, the home."[239] The Court then disagreed with the *Bowers* Court about the history of anti-sodomy laws, noting that those laws targeted sodomy of any sort, rather than same-sex practices in particular. He also noted the modern trend of repealing those laws — a trend that he said mirrored similar trends in European legal systems.

Justice Kennedy then suggested that *Planned Parenthood v. Casey*[240] and a gay rights case decided on an equal protection ground, *Romer v. Evans*,[241] undercut *Bowers*, re-

---

233. 491 U.S. 110 (1989). *Michael H.*, dealing with parenthood rights, is discussed in Section 9.04[4][a].

234. These cases, dealing with access to contraceptives, are discussed in Section 9.04[2].

235. 539 U.S. 558 (2003).

236. Justice O'Connor concurred in the judgment only, relying instead on the Equal Protection Clause. Her opinion is discussed in Section 10.06[3].

237. 381 U.S. 479 (1965). *Griswold*, which established a right to use contraceptives, is discussed in Section 9.04[2].

238. 539 U.S. at 564.

239. *Id.* at 567.

240. 505 U.S. 833 (1992). *Casey*, an abortion rights case, is discussed in Section 9.04[3][e].

241. 517 U.S. 620 (1996).

spectively by reinforcing the due process protection for interests such as procreation and family relationships and by rejecting laws that stigmatize LGB persons. Quoting and embracing Justice Stevens' dissent in *Bowers*, the Court rejected the proposition that a political majority's opinion about the immorality of particular conduct, without more, justified a prohibition on that conduct.

Toward the end of this opinion, Justice Kennedy reasoned as follows:

> Th[is] case ... involve[s] two adults who, with full and mutual consent from each other, engaged in sexual practices common to a homosexual lifestyle. The petitioners are entitled to respect for their private lives. The State cannot demean their existence or control their destiny by making their private sexual conduct a crime. Their right to liberty under the Due Process Clause gives them the full right to engage in their conduct without intervention of the government.[242]

Justice Scalia dissented, joined by Chief Justice Rehnquist and Justice Thomas. He observed that the Court did not declare same-sex sodomy a "fundamental right" under the Due Process Clause and, in turn, did not subject the statute to strict scrutiny. He criticized the Court's decision nevertheless to strike the Texas law down, concluding that its rejection of morality as a legitimate basis for the law "decrees the end of all morals legislation."[243] Justice Thomas wrote a short concurrence to note his disagreement with the policy behind the Texas law, but to explain that that policy disagreement did not authorize him to strike it down as unconstitutional.

In 2015, the Court considered state law bans on same-sex marriage. In *Obergefell v. Hodges*,[244] a five-justice majority, again speaking through Justice Kennedy, struck down those laws. The Court noted its earlier decisions recognizing marriage as a fundamental right,[245] and concluded that same-sex couples sought to marry for the same reasons opposite-sex marriage has been considered so important throughout American history. As he had in *Lawrence*, Justice Kennedy also explained how laws singling them out for exclusion from marriage "demeans" same-sex couples and "teach[es] that gays and lesbians are unequal in important respects."[246]

Toward the end of the opinion, Justice Kennedy acknowledged the argument that allowing same-sex couples to marry would discourage opposite sex couples from marrying by "sever[ing] the connection between accidental procreation and marriage." He rejected this justification for reserving marriage to opposite-sex couples as "counterintuitive" and "unrealistic."[247]

Chief Justice Roberts and Justices Scalia, Thomas, and Alito all dissented; all four wrote separate opinions, some of which gained the assent of one or more of the other

---

242. 539 U.S. at 578.
243. *Id.* at 599 (Scalia, J., dissenting).
244. 135 S. Ct. 2584 (2015).
245. These cases are discussed in Section 9.04[4][b].
246. 135 S. Ct. at 2602.
247. *Id.* at 2606–2607.

dissenters. A unifying theme of these dissents was that there was no fundamental right to same-sex marriage, and that the fundamental right to marriage itself was analytically distinct from same-sex marriage since, until recent years, marriage had always been defined as a union of a man and a woman. For this reason, the dissenters maintained, the Court's right to marry cases did not support the majority's result.

In *Pavan v. Smith*,[248] the Court summarily reversed a state court decision upholding an Arkansas law that treated same-sex married couples differently from their opposite-sex married counterparts. Under that law, when a woman married to a man gives birth, the husband is automatically named as the father on the child's birth certificate, even if the mother conceived via artificial insemination. The law did not extend that automatic treatment to a woman married to another woman who gives birth — that is, the non-birthing spouse was not automatically named as one of the child's parents. In a *per curiam* opinion, the Court held that this differential treatment violated *Obergefell*. Justice Gorsuch, joined by Justices Thomas and Alito, dissented on the ground that the case should have been subjected to full briefing and argument.

The sexuality cases are important and fascinating. The gay rights movement has been perhaps the most successful civil rights movement of the last quarter-century, accomplishing a remarkable shift in Supreme Court doctrine from a regime that tolerated criminalization of same-sex sex to one that required legal recognition of same-sex marriage. Yet gay rights litigators have won these battles without winning on the conventional legal questions the relevant doctrines consider. In the substantive due process area, for example, same-sex intimacy was never identified as a fundamental right, while in the equal protection context, LGB status was never deemed sufficiently "suspect" to justify explicitly heightened judicial scrutiny.[249] Indeed, after *Lawrence*, commentators wondered whether the Court had abandoned its conventional methodology to substantive due process in favor of a more amorphous approach.[250] Similarly, *Obergefell*'s mixing of equality and liberty ideas raises fascinating questions about how those guarantees might intermix and provide mutual support to individual rights claims.[251] These issues have yet to be worked out, and await further development in either sexuality or other cases.

[5] The "Right to Die"

The right to die is one of the most complex liberty issues to face the Court. Advances in medical technology and changing attitudes toward suicide have triggered sharp disputes about personal autonomy and the legitimacy of a state's interest in forbidding a person from taking actions to end her own life. Thus, advocates of the right to die, who argue that technological advances threaten to reduce life to an undig-

---

248. 137 S. Ct. 2075 (2017).

249. The equal protection aspect of the gay rights cases is discussed in Section 10.06[3].

250. *See, e.g.*, RANDY BARNETT, RESTORING THE LOST CONSTITUTION: THE PRESUMPTION OF LIBERTY (2004).

251. *See, e.g.*, Laurence Tribe, *Equal Dignity: Speaking Its Name*, 129 HARV. L. REV. F. 16 (2015).

nified machine-like state, compete against a strong interest in preserving life and ensuring that it is not terminated lightly.

The United States Supreme Court first addressed the so-called "right to die" in 1990 in *Cruzan v. Director, Missouri Department of Health.*[252] Nancy Cruzan sustained severe injuries in an automobile accident that left her in a persistent vegetative state. When it became apparent that Nancy's condition was irreversible, her parents sought a court order allowing them to remove their daughter's artificial nutrition and hydration apparatus, an action that would cause Nancy's death. The Missouri Supreme Court denied the parents' request, finding that the life support systems could not be removed absent clear and convincing evidence that Nancy herself would have chosen death under these circumstances. The narrow issue before the Supreme Court was whether the Constitution prohibited Missouri's requirement of the "clear and convincing" evidence standard in the withdrawal of life-sustaining treatment.

Chief Justice Rehnquist's opinion began with an analysis of informed consent. Tort law provided that a patient had the right to refuse medical treatment; indeed, at common law, the administration of medical treatment without consent constituted battery. Chief Justice Rehnquist also observed that state courts applying both common law and constitutional principles had recognized a right of competent people to refuse medical treatment, but differed as to what happened when the patient was incompetent to make that decision. The Chief Justice indicated that Supreme Court precedent also suggested a constitutional right for a competent patient to terminate her own treatment, perhaps even to refuse food and water, and assumed *arguendo* that the Fourteenth Amendment afforded such a right. Because in Nancy's case, that right had to be asserted by a surrogate, the Chief Justice construed Missouri's evidentiary rule as helping to ensure that the surrogate's decision conformed to what the patient would have selected.

Missouri asserted interests in protecting and preserving human life and in protecting the personal wishes of the patient. With regard to the latter, the Court noted that the state may choose not to second-guess decisions about quality of life, and may also recognize that family surrogates may not always place the patient's interests first. The Court found Missouri's interests sufficient to justify its heightened clear and convincing evidence standard. According to the Court, this standard was a permissible means for the state to place an increased burden on those seeking to terminate an incompetent patient's life-sustaining equipment, especially since the consequence of mistaking the patient's desire for death was irreversible.

In a concurrence necessary to form a majority, Justice O'Connor indicated that the right to terminate medical treatment, including food and water, implicated substantive due process rights. As few persons leave written or oral instructions about what to do in these situations, Justice O'Connor suggested that there may be a constitutional duty for states to honor the decisions of certain surrogate decision-makers to terminate the treatment of an incompetent patient. In a separate concurrence with a very different thrust, Justice Scalia flatly rejected any substantive due process right

---

252. 497 U.S. 261 (1990).

in situations such as Nancy Cruzan's. He analogized the right to die controversy to the similarly controversial abortion issue, and urged the Court not to involve itself in such deep philosophical and values disputes. He insisted that the Equal Protection Clause sufficiently protected against irrational laws requiring the preservation of life, since such laws, in order to be valid under equal protection, had to apply to all persons and thus were subject to political checks.

In a dissent joined by Justices Marshall and Blackmun, Justice Brennan challenged Missouri's asserted interest in preserving Nancy's life. Justice Brennan argued that the only legitimate state interest Missouri possessed was an interest in protecting the *accuracy* of a determination of the patient's wishes. He said that misreading the patient's wishes by continuing medical treatment was a decision just as irrevocable as permitting the patient to die. He objected to the rejection of informative evidence indicating a patient's wishes, particularly as few Americans formalize their preferences with written wills or health care directives. According to Justice Brennan, conversations with Nancy, her mother, her sister, and a close friend, in addition to a court-appointed guardian *ad litem*, all concluded that she would have wanted her life support systems terminated under the circumstances at issue. Justice Brennan also argued that in cases where it is impossible to determine the incompetent patient's wishes, the decision to terminate treatment should rest with the patient's family. In a separate dissent, Justice Stevens objected to a state policy asserting an interest in preserving life that might conflict with the patient's best interests.

In *Washington v. Glucksberg*,[253] the Court considered and rejected a facial attack on a Washington law prohibiting any person from assisting in another's suicide. Washington afforded criminal and civil immunity to a physician honoring a patient's request to withhold or withdraw medical treatment. However, the plaintiffs, mentally competent terminally ill persons, asserted a due process right to assistance in the project of affirmatively terminating their lives.

The Court, speaking through Chief Justice Rehnquist, recognized that the Due Process Clause protected the right to refuse medical treatment. However, echoing earlier justices' warning about due process analysis threatening to devolve into the justices' own policy preferences, he urged judicial restraint before constitutionalizing policy issues by finding due process rights. That restraint, he insisted, required that substantive due process rights be limited to "those fundamental rights and liberties which are, objectively, 'deeply rooted in this Nation's history and tradition.'" It also required that fundamental liberty interests be carefully described, using the country's "history, legal traditions, and practices" as guideposts.[254]

Turning to the that history, the Court observed that assisted suicide is a crime in almost every state and that, for more than 700 years, the Anglo-American common

---

253. 521 U.S. 702 (1997).

254. *Id.* at 721 (quoting Moore v. City of E. Cleveland, 431 U.S. 494, 503 (1977)). Chief Justice Rehnquist also cited two opinions by Justice Cardozo using similar language to decide whether a particular Bill of Rights provision was incorporated into the Due Process Clause.

law has discouraged or punished suicide and assisted suicide. All states except Oregon have rejected legislative proposals to legalize assisted suicide. Moreover, virtually every western democracy criminalized assisted suicide. The Court thus rejected the argument that suicide, or assisting another in suicide, was a practice deeply rooted in American tradition and law. The Court distinguished *Cruzan* on the ground that that case dealt with an asserted right to refuse hydration and nutrition interventions — a right the *Cruzan* plurality had found to have been historically protected by the common law.

The Court then concluded that the state had a legitimate interest in protecting human life, particularly as those who contemplate suicide often suffer from depression or other mental disorders. It also had an interest in medical ethics. The state had an additional interest in protecting vulnerable groups, such as elderly, poor, disabled, and socially-marginalized persons against coercion, negligence, or indifference that may result in suicide decisions that do not truly reflect that person's wishes. Finally, it concluded that Washington's ban prevented a slide into voluntary or involuntary euthanasia. As the ban on assisted suicide was "at least reasonably related" to "important and legitimate"[255] state interests, the Court did not weigh the relative strengths and weaknesses of each, but concluded that the ban did not violate the Due Process Clause.

Justice O'Connor concurred, joined by Justices Ginsburg and Breyer. She stated that the Court need not decide whether patients have a constitutional right to receive palliative care even if it would hasten death, as the law at issue permitted such care. In her view, the difficulties in defining terminal illness and the danger that assisted suicide may not be voluntary justified the ban at issue. Justice Breyer concurred, largely to express his general agreement with Justice O'Connor's analysis. Justice Stevens concurred in the judgment, asserting that a person's life was too valuable for society to grant complete autonomy in deciding whether to end it. However, just as the Court held some applications of capital punishment statutes unconstitutional, some specific situations could warrant invalidating prohibitions on assisted suicide.

Concurring in the judgment, Justice Souter applied the approach drawn from Justice Harlan's dissenting opinion in *Poe v. Ullman*.[256] That test led him to believe that the plaintiffs had stated a plausible argument for a narrowly-cabined right for mentally competent, terminally ill patients to obtain assistance in ending their lives. Nevertheless, Justice Souter did not decide whether that interest was fundamental (and thus triggered heightened scrutiny), because he found sufficiently weighty the state's interests in protecting against patients mistakenly or involuntarily deciding to commit suicide and protecting against voluntary and involuntary euthanasia. However, he accepted those justifications only after considering the plaintiffs' responses to them and the state's reply to those responses, thus suggesting that his review encompassed more than the deferential scrutiny the majority accorded the state's rationales.

---

255. *Id.* at 735.
256. 367 U.S. 497, 543 (1961) (Harlan, J., dissenting). *See* Section 9.04[2] (discussing his opinion).

[6] Informational Privacy

Substantive due process issues have also arisen in areas other than marriage, family, procreation, and child rearing. In particular, in several cases, the Court has considered substantive due process claims surrounding informational privacy. In *Whalen v. Roe*,[257] the Court rejected a challenge to New York's maintenance of computer records of the names and addresses of persons who had received a doctor's prescription for certain drugs for which lawful and unlawful markets existed. The state kept the information private, having used it only sparingly for investigations. The *Whalen* Court recognized the potential harm to individual privacy that such storehouses of information present, but it found the risk of inappropriate disclosures and therefore of privacy violations to be small. However, the Court did not foreclose future substantive due process challenges to unwarranted disclosures of sensitive information.

In *NASA v. Nelson*,[258] the Court upheld, as applied to NASA contract employees, a Homeland Security Presidential Directive requiring background checks as applied to employees at the Jet Propulsion Laboratory (JPL), a space research facility owned by NASA and operated by a private university under a government contract. The background check process involved the completion of several forms, one of which asked about illegal drug use, and reference checks sent to persons the employee identified on the form.

Writing for six justices, Justice Alito assumed that the "the Government's challenged inquiries implicate a privacy interest of constitutional significance."[259] Nevertheless, the Court rejected the challenge. It observed that the government was not acting as a regulator but instead as a manager of its own operations, and that the government's inquiries reflected background check inquiries made by private employers and the government since the nation's earliest days.

Justice Scalia, joined by Justice Thomas, concurred only in the judgment. Justice Scalia commented that informational privacy was one of many "desirable things not included in the Constitution."[260] Thus, he would have rejected the plaintiffs' claim on the ground that their asserted privacy interest was not protected by substantive due process.

[7] Concluding Thoughts on Substantive Due Process

Due process is an exceptionally contentious area of constitutional law. The unenumerated nature of the rights at issue and the existence of deep moral, philosophical, and policy conflicts about them lead many judges and scholars to criticize this entire area of jurisprudence, and to urge the Court to withdraw from the

---

257. 429 U.S. 589 (1977).
258. 562 U.S. 134 (2011).
259. *Id.* at 148.
260. *Id.* at 159 (Scalia, J., concurring in the judgment).

field and let the political process resolve these questions. Others argue that the Fifth and Fourteenth Amendments' guarantee of "liberty" would be hollow if government were free to impose severe burdens on decisions as fundamental as those relating to marriage, reproduction, sexual intimacy, family life, and, indeed, when life itself should be ended. Defenders of substantive due process also note the long history of due process review at the Supreme Court, and argue that such review is itself a tradition that merits respect.[261]

It is difficult to predict the course of the Court's due process jurisprudence. While the Court currently appears inclined to cut back on the abortion right it originally found in *Roe*, its last major substantive due process case—*Obergefell v. Hodges*[262]— resulted in the Court finding a due process right for same-sex couples to marry. Probably the only thing that can be predicted with confidence is that due process cases will continue to divide the justices.

As suggested by some of the cases discussed above, equal protection sometimes presents an alternative approach for protecting important rights. The theory—a powerful one—is that as long as laws must be equally applied, oppressive laws will be rare, since the majority will have to live under the same rules it prescribes for the minority. But that theory assumes that we know what "equal applicability" really means and, as with due process analysis, how much deference legislatures should enjoy when they decide that question in a given context. The difficulties surrounding the intuitively straightforward requirement that laws provide "equal protection" are explored in Chapter 10 of this book.

§ 9.05 The Second Amendment

The Supreme Court has interpreted the Second Amendment "right to bear arms" as securing an individual right to possess firearms, unrelated to service in a militia.[263] Two years later, the Court incorporated the Second Amendment, understood as including an individual right to possess firearms, to apply against the states.[264]

In *District of Columbia v. Heller*,[265] the Court held that the District of Columbia's law severely restricting the possession of handguns and requiring that firearms be kept inoperable when stored violated the Second Amendment. Writing for the five-justice majority, Justice Scalia began by reciting the Second Amendment: "A well regulated Militia, being necessary to the security of a free State, the right of the people to keep and bear Arms, shall not be infringed." The Court interpreted the Constitution

---

261. *See, e.g., Glucksberg*, 521 U.S. at 756 (Souter, J., concurring in the judgment) ("The persistence of substantive due process in our cases points to the legitimacy of the modern justification for such judicial review").

262. 135 S. Ct. 2584 (2015).

263. District of Columbia v. Heller, 554 U.S. 570 (2008).

264. McDonald v. City of Chicago, 561 U.S. 742 (2010).

265. 554 U.S. 570 (2008).

using the ordinary everyday meaning of its words and phrases that voters at the time of the Framing could understand.

The Second Amendment consists of a prefatory clause and the operative clause. The Court concluded that the prefatory clause described the purpose of the operative clause but did not limit it — that is, the prefatory clause did not limit the right to bear arms to militia service. Moreover, the term "keep Arms," protected individuals regardless of service in a militia. The term "bear" implied carrying a weapon for "offensive or defensive action," but did not connote "participation in a structured military organization." In addressing the relationship between the prefatory and operative Clauses, the Court argued that it was understood that the right to bear arms allowed for a citizen militia that could be used to oppose an oppressive military force. Justice Scalia noted the Second Amendment could not have played that purpose if it simply had guaranteed a right to keep and use weapons as part of an organized militia that Congress could control.

Justice Scalia also conducted a detailed historical analysis. Examining English authorities, he concluded that an English precursor to the Bill of Rights contained a provision stating that Protestants could never be disarmed. This predecessor to the Second Amendment was an individual right that had nothing to do with military service. He also found support for the individual rights provision in pre-Civil War caselaw, state constitutions' Second Amendment analogues, and early treatises on constitutional law.

The Court was careful to note that the Second Amendment right to bear arms was not unlimited. In an important passage, he wrote that nothing in the opinion should be "taken to cast doubt on longstanding prohibitions on the possession of firearms by felons and the mentally ill, or laws forbidding the carrying of firearms in sensitive places such as schools and government buildings, or laws imposing conditions and qualifications on the commercial sale of arms." Moreover, the Court recognized that the Second Amendment protected weapons "in common use at the time," thus exempting from its coverage "dangerous or unusual weapons."[266]

Pivotal to the Second Amendment right has been the inherent right of self-defense. As the handgun is the most popular weapon to protect the home and family, banning possession of such guns was unconstitutional under any standard of scrutiny. The District of Columbia's requirement that all firearms in the home be kept inoperable at all times was also unconstitutional, because it impeded the core lawful purpose of self-defense.

Justice Stevens dissented, joined by Justices Souter, Ginsburg, and Breyer. Justice Stevens thought that the Second Amendment and its drafters evidenced no intention to impede government regulation of personal firearms outside of military use by state militias. He noted that *United States v. Miller*[267] held that the Second Amendment protected the right to possess arms as part of state militia service but not for non-

---

266. *Id.* at 626–27.
267. 307 U.S. 174 (1939).

military use, a holding the Court reaffirmed 40 years later[268] and that hundreds of lower courts have followed.

Justice Stevens' textual analysis noted that the term "bear arms" is commonly meant to refer to military service, and that the Second Amendment did not include any additional language protecting the use of weapons for hunting or self-defense, as did the Pennsylvania and Vermont constitutions of that era. Such drafting choices illustrated the purpose of prohibiting Congress from disarming state militias. More generally, Justice Stevens understood the Second Amendment as a federalism provision that allowed Congress to call up and organize the militia and govern that part of it employed by the national government, while states commissioned and trained it. Justice Stevens found the majority's historical sources only vaguely instructive, if at all.

Justice Breyer filed a separate dissenting opinion, joined by Justices Stevens, Souter, and Ginsburg. Justice Breyer reiterated Justice Stevens' arguments in favor of the militia-only interpretation of the Second Amendment. But he added that historical evidence revealed significant regulation of firearms possession and worried that the Court's holding would impair similar public safety gun regulation today.

McDonald v. City of Chicago held that the Second Amendment right established in *District of Columbia v. Heller* was "fully applicable to the States" through incorporation by the Fourteenth Amendment.[269] A four-justice plurality, speaking through Justice Alito, incorporated the Second Amendment through the Due Process Clause, while Justice Thomas' decisive fifth vote accomplished incorporation through the Privileges or Immunities Clause. By applying the Second Amendment to the states, the Court invalidated Chicago laws that banned possession of handguns.

In considering the incorporation question, the plurality declined to adopt Justice Black's theory of "total incorporation," but noted that very few provisions of the Bill of Rights remained unincorporated.[270] It also noted that incorporated protections applied in the same way against the states as they did against federal encroachment.[271] The plurality used the familiar legal formulas asking whether a particular Bill of Rights provision was "fundamental to *our* scheme of ordered liberty," or whether the right was "deeply rooted in this Nation's history and tradition."[272] It found that the debates of the 39th Congress about the Fourteenth Amendment referred to this right as fundamental, as did legal commentators at the time. The plurality rejected arguments that it should consider other nations' practices when answering the fundamentality question.

Justice Thomas concurred in part and in the judgment. He disagreed that the Second Amendment "is enforceable against the States through a clause that speaks only

---

268. *See* Lewis v. United States, 445 U.S. 55 (1980).

269. 561 U.S. 742, 767 (2010).

270. The justices' different theories of incorporation more generally are discussed in Section 9.03.

271. *But see* 561 U.S. at 766 n. 14 (noting and explaining one exception to this rule, since resolved).

272. *Id.* at 767.

to 'process,' " and instead would incorporate it through the Privileges or Immunities Clause of the Fourteenth Amendment.[273] Instead, he concluded that "the right to keep and bear arms was understood to be a privilege of American citizenship guaranteed by the Privileges or Immunities Clause."[274]

Justice Stevens dissented for the same four *Heller* dissenters. He argued that an early post-Civil War case, *United States v. Cruikshank*,[275] resolved the Second Amendment incorporation issue, a claim both the plurality and Justice Thomas rejected. More generally, he argued that the Court's holding mistakenly applied a national standard when local variation was more appropriate, given the different circumstances present in different parts of the nation as relevant to firearms issues. Indeed, returning to his *Heller* dissent, he characterized the Second Amendment as a federalism provision intended to protect state militias, and thus not appropriately susceptible to incorporation against states. Justice Breyer, joined by Justices Ginsburg and Sotomayor, also dissented, largely to argue that historians had reached a consensus rejecting *Heller's* historical analysis, and to note the very difficult regulatory and constitutional issues that will arise with the Second Amendment's incorporation against states. On that point, he repeated Justice Stevens' argument that state latitude to experiment on gun issues would help reach innovative and politically legitimate resolutions of those difficult questions.

§ 9.06 Procedural Due Process

In addition to providing substantive protections for the individual liberties discussed above, the Due Process Clause also has a procedural aspect, guaranteeing a fair process before government can deprive a person of "life, liberty, or property." This procedural aspect of the Due Process Clause is related to, but distinct from, the substantive aspect discussed immediately above. This section considers procedural due process by considering three questions, in turn: (1) Is there a "life, liberty, or property" interest at stake in the case? (2) If so, has there been a deprivation of that interest? (3) If so, has the government provided "due process" before accomplishing that deprivation?

[1] The Existence of a Life, Liberty, or Property Interest

This sub-section considers how the Court has gone about defining "liberty" and "property" for purposes of the procedural due process guarantee. But it begins with a very quick statement about life. Of course, in the domestic context, government can deprive persons of life, most notably through the death penalty and fatal police action. The latter situation presents a difficult problem of determining what it means

---

273. *Id.* at 806 (Thomas, J., concurring in part and in the judgment).
274. *Id.* at 838.
275. 92 U.S. 542 (1875).

to "deprive" someone of life, given the split-second, unplanned nature of such conduct, and is treated in the next sub-section. But executions, of course, are carefully planned, and constitute "deprivations" in any sense of the word. Procedural due process doctrine *per se* does not consider such deprivations of "life," however, because the criminal procedure provisions of the Bill of Rights, many of which (for example, the right to counsel) apply with special force to death penalty cases,[276] are generally thought to satisfy any requirements that would otherwise apply as a matter specifically of procedural due process. Government killings in wartime are governed by the law of war, which, for example, allows killing enemy soldiers actively in the fight. In recent years, interesting questions have been raised by so-called targeted killings of terrorists, for example, with drones. When scholars have studied the procedures different presidential administrations have instituted for ensuring that such strikes in fact target guilty people, they have often done so through the lens of procedural due process doctrine, as set forth below.[277]

The Court's method for identifying due process-protected liberty and property interests has changed markedly over the last half-century. Before approximately 1970, the Court enforced a distinction between so-called rights and privileges. Rights — usually described as interests protected by the common law — were considered to be protected by the guarantee of procedural due process. Privileges — usually described as interests granted by statute — were not. Instead, their statutory grounding led courts to describe them as mere "gratuities" that, because bestowed by legislatures, could be withdrawn by government with no due process protections.

Beginning in the 1930s, this rights-privileges distinction began to break down. With the onset of the New Deal, legislatures (both state and federal) began allocating interests that took on great importance in people's lives. Commentators and eventually judges began wondering why such important interests were not protected from arbitrary deprivation. In particular, there came to be less and less justification for considering the common law nature of "rights" to be meaningfully relevant to the question of whether they merited due process procedural protection. Finally, the ultimate mixing of statutory and common law rights in society led to seemingly arbitrary results, in which the common law foundation of one interest justified robust procedural protections while the statutory foundation of another, very similar, interest received nothing.

In 1972, the Court decided two cases that formalized the new understanding that even statutorily-granted rights could be protected by due process. In *Board of Regents v. Roth*,[278] the Court considered whether a university professor had a property interest in his continued employment with the university. Roth had been hired on a one-year contract; after that year, the university declined to renew his contract. He sued, demanding a hearing to challenge the reasons for that refusal.

---

276. *See, e.g.*, Michael Mello, *Is There a Federal Constitutional Right to Counsel in Capital Post-Conviction Proceedings?*, 79 J. CRIM. L. & CRIMM. 1065 (1989).

277. *See, e.g.*, William Funk, *Deadly Drones, Due Process, and the Fourth Amendment*, 22 WM. & MARY BILL OF RTS. J. 311 (2013).

278. 408 U.S. 564 (1972).

The Court held that Roth did not have a property interest. But this was not because the interest was based merely on statute (that is, the legislation establishing the university and the regulations promulgated by the university). Rather, Justice Stewart, speaking for the Court, explained that "property" was comprised of an individual's objectively reasonable expectations in the continuation of whatever benefits the property interest conveyed—*e.g.*, "property" in a real estate leasehold conveyed an expectation of occupancy, but not an expectation of being able to mortgage the real estate. Thus, for someone to have "property" in a statutorily-granted interest (such as Roth's teaching job), he had to have "more than an abstract need or desire for it" and "more than a unilateral expectation of it." Rather, he must have "a legitimate claim of entitlement to it," one "created and [its] dimensions ... defined by existing rules or understandings that stem from an independent source such as state law—rules or understandings that secure certain benefits and that support claims of entitlement to those benefits."[279] In other words, for Roth to have a property interest in his job, he needed to have an objectively reasonable expectation, based on law (whether common law, statutory, or regulatory, state or federal) that he would continue to be entitled to the interest if he satisfied the qualifications. Because Roth's one-year contract did not give Roth any such reasonable expectation that he would be rehired, the Court held that he did not have a due process interest in the job that entitled him to a hearing when his contract was not renewed.

The Court reached a slightly different result in a companion case decided that same day. *Perry v. Sindermann*[280] raised a facially-similar issue as *Roth*: a professor whose one-year contract was not renewed and who sued, demanding a hearing at which he could challenge the failure to renew. But *Perry* was different: the professor in that case had had a long series of one-year contracts, and the Court also noted that, while his college did not have a tenure system, it included in its "Faculty Guide" an "unusual provision" that hinted that well-performing instructors should feel as though they have tenure.[281] That provision suggested to the Court the possibility that the college had provided the professor with the sort of reasonable claim of entitlement to the continuation of his job that would qualify that job as a due process-protected property interest. Moreover, the Court concluded that the fact that, unlike the teacher in *Roth*, the teacher in *Perry* had had a long series of one-year contracts could also justify a conclusion that the teacher in *Perry* had a property interest in his job, because the long series of one-year contracts had given him a reasonable expectation that his employment would continue on those terms. The Court remanded the case for more fact-finding on those issues.

Together, *Roth* and *Perry* state the modern rule that generally governs due process cases. To have a liberty or property interest, the claimant must show that some source

---

279. *Id.* at 577.

280. 408 U.S. 593 (1972).

281. *See id.* at 600 (" 'Teacher Tenure: Odessa College has no tenure system. The Administration of the College wishes the faculty member to feel that he has permanent tenure as long as his teaching services are satisfactory and as long as he displays a cooperative attitude toward his co-workers and his superiors, and as long as he is happy in his work.' ") (quoting the *Faculty Guide*).

of law provides him with a legitimate claim to the benefit if he satisfies the legal requirements (*e.g.*, if in *Perry*, the professor's teaching was "satisfactory").[282] Note the caveat — "if he satisfies the legal requirements." All procedural due process does is give the claimant a right to a hearing at which he can contest the deprivation of the interest. For example, if the professor in *Perry* prevailed in showing that he had a due process interest in his job, all that would mean is that he would have a right to a hearing to challenge his firing — not that he would have to be rehired. In order to have that right to a hearing, he has to show that, *if he satisfies the legal criteria for the benefit*, then he would have a legitimate claim to it. The point of the hearing would be to establish whether or not he actually satisfied those requirements.

Roth and *Perry* apply to both due process liberty and property claims. But an important distinction needs be drawn between these types of claims. Recall *Roth*'s statement that some source of law must provide the claim of entitlement that then renders the interest one protected by due process. When it comes to liberty interests, any source of law will do — from a local government regulation to the Constitution, which itself denominates some interests as liberty interests — for example, the "substantive due process" liberty interests to personal autonomy.[283] The same is true for property, but with one exception. Unlike liberty, the Constitution itself does not create property interests. Thus, while, for example, the professor in *Perry* might be able to cite the *Faculty Guide* as a source of his property interest in his job, he could not cite the Fifth or Fourteenth Amendments.

The Court has created exceptions to this general approach to identifying liberty and property. In *Paul v. Davis*,[284] the Court held that one's reputation did not count as a due process-protected liberty interest. *Paul* involved a police department program distributing to town merchants flyers containing the names and photos of "active shoplifters." The plaintiff's name was on the list, even though his shoplifting case had been filed away without adjudication. The Court rejected the plaintiff's due process claim, concluding that only material interests, rather than merely reputation, constituted interests protected by due process. For example, *Paul* cited an earlier case where a government posting of "habitual drunkards" not only impaired the good name of a person listed on the flyer but also prevented him from purchasing liquor at a bar.[285]

Paul is a difficult case to understand. If one carries *Roth* and *Perry* to their logical conclusions, then the fact that state common law protects people's reputations (by providing for defamation causes of action) should mean that the interest in one's reputation is one to which a person has a legitimate, law-backed, claim of entitlement — that is, it constitutes a due-process protected interest. The Court in *Paul* expressed a federalism-based concern about turning every common law cause of action

---

282. *See id.* (quoting the *Faculty Guide*).

283. Substantive due process is discussed early in this Chapter.

284. 424 U.S. 693 (1976).

285. *See* 424 U.S. at 707–09 (distinguishing Wisconsin v. Constantineau, 400 U.S. 433 (1971), on this basis).

a person may have against her state—for example, a defamation action on the facts of *Paul* itself—into a federal due process claim. But that seems to be the logical end-point of the *Roth* and *Perry* approach to due process.

The Court has carved out another exception to the *Roth* and *Perry* approach. Recall that even government statements such as the *Faculty Guide* in *Perry* could suffice to create a legitimate, law-backed entitlement that thereby counts as a due process-protected interest. In 1995, the Court cut back on that approach in the prison context. In *Sandin v. Conner*,[286] the Court held that only "atypical, significant" deprivations of liberty would create due process-protected liberty interests in the prison context. The Court noted that prison terms already involved significant deprivations of liberty. But even more, the Court observed that the *Roth* and *Perry* approach would incentivize prisoners to find in prison regulations and other official legal statements government commitments to provide prisoners with certain goods or opportunities, which would trigger due process claims when the prison failed to provide them. The Court observed that this dynamic incentivized prison officials to not make such commitments, thus introducing an unwelcome tone of arbitrariness into prison administration.

Sandin may have been motivated by the special circumstances of prisons, in which prisoners may be incentivized to tie up prison administrators in the minutiae of regulatory details that took the form of legal commitments and thus, under *Roth*, legal entitlements triggering due process protection. But its identification of that problem points to a larger issue with the *Roth* and *Perry* approach to identifying due process liberty and property. Under that approach, the language of a statute, a regulation, or even a faculty or student handbook take on outsized importance. If that language uses mandatory language—for example, if a student handbook says that "every student shall be assigned a locker"—then a deprivation of that interest—say, a school's confiscation of a student's locker for using it to hide drugs—triggers the protections of due process. But if that language is permissive, rather than mandatory—if the handbook says, for example, that "every student may, in the discretion of the principal, be assigned a locker"—then no due process right is created. It is fair to ask whether such small differences should define a constitutional line. On the other hand, *Roth* and *Perry* respond to a real impulse to define liberty and property in terms of people's legitimate, law-backed expectations. The Court's response so far has been to honor that impulse except in special situations, such as prisons and with regard to inchoate interests such as reputation.

[2] Has There Been a Deprivation?

After the complexity of defining due process-protected interests, one might think that it is a simple thing to determine whether a deprivation of such an interest has occurred. Indeed, in most cases, the issue is straightforward. But some twists lurk in the caselaw.

---

286. 515 U.S. 472 (1995).

First, the Court has held that negligent government action does not constitute a deprivation of a due process interest. In *Daniels v. Williams*,[287] a prisoner brought a due process claim when he was injured by tripping over a pillow a guard negligently left on a staircase. The Court held that the guard's negligence did not constitute the sort of "abuse of power"[288] the Due Process Clause sought to guard against. Whatever one might think of that rationale, one can understand the holding in *Daniels* as a matter of procedural due process if one considers the possible remedy. If procedural due process fundamentally sounds in notions of fair procedure, one might wonder what sort of procedure the prison could have provided to protect against this sort of negligence. In other words, government might be legitimately required to provide a hearing before intentionally depriving someone of an interest, but how can it provide a hearing before an accident happens? To be sure, this is not a complete response. The Court has upheld post-deprivation procedures in situations where a pre-deprivation hearing is not practical. Perhaps more conceptually, one could argue that the proper "process" before a "deprivation" like this is better training and supervision of guards.

The Court has also held, perhaps counter-intuitively, that a prison guard's private vendetta, involving a search of a prisoner's cell and destruction of his possessions, did not constitute a government deprivation of the prisoner's property. In *Hudson v. Palmer*, the Court reasoned that "when deprivations of property are effected through random and unauthorized conduct of a state employee, predeprivation procedures are simply impracticable since the state cannot know when such deprivations will occur."[289] In essence, if the guard's conduct reflected his own private actions rather than government-authorized action, the government could not provide a meaningful pre-deprivation hearing. Indeed, the Court connected this concern with the impracticability of a remedy with its decisions about the similar lack of due process "deprivation" when the government actor "merely" acts negligently, as in *Daniels*, rather than maliciously and without government authorization, as in *Hudson*.[290] In such cases where a predeprivation remedy is impracticable, a court might say, as it said in these cases, that there has been no deprivation. Or it might say that a postdeprivation remedy—for example, a tort suit—provides all the process that is constitutionally required.[291]

[3] Constitutionally-Required Procedures

During the era in which the Court enforced the rights/privileges distinction when determining which interests due process protected, it generally insisted on the right

---

287. 474 U.S. 327 (1986).

288. *Id.* at 332.

289. 468 U.S. 517, 533 (1984).

290. *See id.* at 532–33 (discussing negligence claims).

291. *See, e.g.*, Parratt v. Taylor, 451 U.S. 527 (1981) (finding a postdeprivation tort remedy adequate for due process purposes when the deprivation of the property occurred as a result of state negligence).

to at least some informal oral hearing before such interests could be deprived. However, once the Court started expanding the universe of due process-protected property and liberty interests, it also started contracting its understanding of what procedures constituted "due process."

During the first years of its more expansive understanding of due process-protected interests, the Court held to relatively stringent requirements for what the required hearing had to include. In *Goldberg v. Kelly*,[292] the Court considered the amount of process due when the government concluded that a recipient of welfare no longer qualified for that benefit. The state provided a generous set of procedures, including an oral hearing, but most of those procedures applied only after the government had terminated the benefits. The plaintiffs demanded more robust procedures *before* the government stopped supplying them.

The Court agreed with the plaintiffs, and held that due process required the government to provide a pre-termination evidentiary hearing before cutting off welfare benefits. While that hearing did not have to conform to the procedural requirements of a formal adjudication, it had to provide the recipient with fair notice and the opportunity to be heard before the government could terminate an individual's benefits. The recipient also had to have the right to confront adverse witnesses, present evidence orally, employ counsel (although the state need not provide counsel), and have an impartial hearing officer who had not participated in the initial termination decision. The decision-maker had to articulate the reasons for the decision and indicate the evidence it relied on.

In the years after *Goldberg*, pressure grew on governments to provide robust procedures before terminating welfare and similar benefits. The vast expansion in the types of benefits that qualified for due process protection, and the sheer scale of many such benefits programs, eventually led the Court to begin scaling back the procedures it was willing to hold were required by due process. That same dynamic may also have been encouraged by the gradual realization that the different factual contexts of the interests that were newly-recognized as due process-protected called for different types of procedural protections.[293]

In 1976, the Court decided an important case, *Mathews v. Eldridge*, in which the Court established the general elements to consider when determining the procedures required before the government could deprive a person of a due process-protected interest:

> First, the private interest that will be affected by the official action; second, the risk of erroneous deprivation of such interest through the procedure used, and the probable value, if any, of additional or substitute procedural safeguards; and finally, the Government's interest, including ... the fiscal

---

292. 397 U.S. 254 (1970).

293. *See, e.g.*, Goss v. Lopez, 419 U.S. 565 (1975) (recognizing a student's due process interest in not being suspended from school, but accepting more informal adjudicative procedures given the nature of the school environment).

and administrative burdens that the additional or substitute procedural requirements would entail.[294]

The Court's application of this test in *Mathews* is instructive. *Mathews* dealt with a government decision to terminate a person's disability benefits, based on an official's conclusion that the recipient was no longer disabled. The Court upheld the government's procedures, which included the ability to submit written information and arguments before the benefits were terminated, but which reserved oral appeals until after termination.

The Court first had to consider the importance of the benefits to the class of recipients. (This issue was decided as it related to the entire class of disability recipients, since case-by-case estimations of the benefits' importance to the particular recipient would require a pre-hearing process to make that determination, before determining how much process would have to be required and then, finally, actually holding the eligibility hearing.) The Court recognized that it could not precisely quantify this figure, but it argued that, if nothing else, the benefits were less important to their recipients than were the welfare benefits in *Goldberg*, since welfare benefits were, by design, intended for persons who had no other means of support.

The Court then considered the accuracy of the written procedures the government provided before terminating the benefits, and whether the plaintiff's demand for a pre-termination *oral* hearing would increase that accuracy. Noting that the question to be decided in each of these hearings was a medical one (*i.e.*, was the person still disabled), the Court concluded that written information, including, if the recipient wished, a doctor's report, would usually lead to an accurate eligibility decision. One might compare this analysis with the situation in *Goldberg*, in which eligibility determinations might turn on questions (*e.g.*, was the recipient living with someone who had a job) for which oral testimony (including the testimony of the recipient himself) would be particularly useful. Indeed, if termination decisions were based on reports about the recipient (*e.g.*, that she was living with someone employed, or was herself working), it might assist in reaching accurate decisions to give the recipient a chance to cross-examine the sources of that information.

Finally, the Court considered the government's interest. The Court identified two such interests. First, it recognized that the prospect of continued benefits during the pendency of the oral appeals process would make that process attractive to claimants even if they knew they were likely to lose. Thus, the government would face more demands for such hearings and in turn would have to hire more adjudicators. Second, that same dynamic would increase pay-outs, especially since the government would likely be unable to recapture payouts found to have been erroneous (*i.e.*, made to people who were ultimately deemed ineligible). Based on a consideration of these factors, the *Mathews* Court found that a pre-termination oral hearing was not constitutionally required.

---

294. 424 U.S. 319, 335 (1976).

Mathews has since become the presumptive test used to judge questions of the constitutional adequacy of processes used to determine eligibility for due process-protected benefits. At times, the Court has applied *Mathews* broadly. For example, in *Cleveland Board of Education v. Loudermill*,[295] the Court required a pre-termination oral hearing even though the matter to be decided was easily discernable from a paper record, since that oral hearing would give the government decision-maker an opportunity to use her discretion not to withdraw the benefits, based on the equities of the case. In that same case, the Court also concluded that the government's interest (the third *Mathews* factor) actually cut in favor of *more* process, not less, given the government's own interest in making an accurate eligibility determination. On some occasions, the Court has used other approaches to the question of how much process is due.[296]

One should not assume that the *Mathews* factors constitute a mathematical formula, in which the importance of the recipients' interest, discounted by the accuracy of the current procedures, must be compared with the magnitude of the government's interest, with the larger figure dictating the result. Justice Powell warned against that use of the test in *Mathews* itself, and later cases have made it clear that *Mathews* set forth factors for a holistic review of the adequacy of the challenged procedures. But even understood as a more holistic inquiry, one might still ask if it is appropriate to balance away procedural rights to assert one's eligibility to constitutionally-protected interests.[297]

---

295. 470 U.S. 532 (1985).

296. *See, e.g.*, Dusenbery v. United States, 534 U.S. 161, 168 (2002) (finding that the claimant had not received constitutionally-adequate notice of the impending forfeiture of his property, concluding that such notice must be "reasonably calculated, under all the circumstances, to apprise" the individual of the impending forfeiture).

297. *See, e.g.*, Lassiter v. Dept. of Social Services, 452 U.S. 18 (1981) (upholding the government's refusal to provide court-appointed counsel to a mother in a proceeding to terminate her parental rights, after applying the *Mathews* factors); *id.* at 60 (Stevens, J., dissenting) ("the value of protecting our liberty from deprivation by the State without due process of law is priceless").

Chapter 10

Equal Protection

§ 10.01 Introductory Concepts

The Equal Protection Clause is deceptively straightforward, requiring simply that "nor shall any State ... deny to any person within its jurisdiction the equal protection of the laws." But this seemingly straightforward requirement of equality raises a host of difficult questions, once one realizes that it cannot be a mandate for completely equal treatment. Government laws classify, or treat people or groups unequally, all the time: a tax law taxes different types of income differently, jaywalkers are treated differently than people who cross streets in crosswalks, and the requirements for a commercial driver's license are different than those for a simple operator's license. When do these and other inequalities violate the constitutional guarantee of "equal protection"?

Since its ratification in 1868 as part of the Fourteenth Amendment, the Equal Protection Clause has been the subject of different judicial approaches that have attempted to answer these basic questions. This section lays out that history. Subsequent sections consider particular applications of the Equal Protection Clause. Section 10.02 considers sex equality. Section 10.03 considers equality claims based on discrimination grounded in traits other than sex or race. Section 10.04 considers race. Race is considered last in this discussion of the different types of constitutionally-problematic discrimination because race alone has been the equality topic that has concerned the Court throughout its encounter with the Equal Protection Clause—and indeed, even before. Thus, it is important to understand how the Court has grappled with other equality concepts and topics before considering race.

Section 10.05 considers the discriminatory intent requirement, a proof requirement that applies to all equal protection claims. Section 10.06 examines a more modern approach to equal protection, one that focuses on the thus-far undertheorized concept of "animus." Section 10.07 concludes this Chapter by considering a hybrid doctrine combining elements of traditional equal protection concepts and substantive rights: the so-called fundamental rights strand of equal protection.

[1] The Class Legislation Era, and Equal Protection for Social and Economic Regulation

During the nineteenth century, courts and lawyers did not think in the terms we use today when we think about individual rights. Today, we think about rights as trumps—that is, as particularly special legal claims that justify a higher burden of justification before the government can impair them. This approach thus focuses on whether a plaintiff successfully states a claim to a legal right. But in the nineteenth century, the focus was different. During that era, the dominant concept was the legitimate scope of government action. If a government action fell within that legitimate scope—if it was, in the terminology of the time, a valid use of the state's "police power"—then it had the right to act, regardless of the individual's claim. Conversely, if the action was not a legitimate use of the state's police power, then the individual's claim prevailed. (Just to be clear, the idea of the "police power" went far beyond what today we would think about as law enforcement activities. Instead, it included anything a state might to do to further the public good.) A prime example of a state action that was *not* a legitimate use of its police power, and thus would be unconstitutional, would be an action taken for the benefit, not of the public good, but of a particular class of persons—what nineteenth century jurisprudence called "class legislation."

An example of this police powers/class legislation approach is *Barbier v. Connolly*.[1] In *Barbier*, the Court upheld a local ordinance regulating laundries—for example, requiring them to close between 10PM and 6AM and requiring a permit for their operation, to allow city officials to confirm that the operation was sanitary and safe. Despite the fact that the ordinance singled out laundries, the Court upheld the ordinance. It explained:

> [N]either the [Fourteenth] amendment—broad and comprehensive as it is—nor any other amendment, was designed to interfere with the power of the state, sometimes termed its police power, to prescribe regulations to promote the health, peace, morals, education, and good order of the people, and to legislate so as to increase the industries of the state, develop its resources, and add to its wealth and prosperity. From the very necessities of society, legislation of a special character, having these objects in view, must often be had in certain districts, such as for draining marshes and irrigating arid plains. Special burdens are often necessary for general benefits,—for supplying water, preventing fires, lighting districts, cleaning streets, opening parks, and many other objects. Regulations for these purposes may press with more or less weight upon one than upon another, but they are designed, not to impose unequal or unnecessary restrictions upon any one, but to promote, with as little individual inconvenience as possible, the general good. Though, in many respects, necessarily special in their character, they do not furnish just ground of complaint if they operate alike upon all persons and property under the same circumstances and conditions. Class legislation,

---

1. 113 U.S. 27 (1884).

discriminating against some and favoring others, is prohibited; but legislation which, in carrying out a public purpose, is limited in its application, if within the sphere of its operation it affects alike all persons similarly situated, is not [prohibited by] the amendment.[2]

The police power/class legislation approach to equal protection was attractive to nineteenth century courts for many reasons. Perhaps most notably, it reflected the underlying concerns about the proper structure of government expressed by James Madison. In *Federalist 10*, one of the most celebrated of the *Federalist Papers* authored by Madison, Alexander Hamilton and John Jay to promote the ratification of the Constitution by New York State, Madison expressed concerns about "factions" — that is, self-interested groups of persons who sought to capture government power to promote their own private goals rather than the public interest.

The class legislation idea expressed in *Barbier* reflected Madison's insistence that government power existed only to promote the public good. By scrutinizing legislation to ensure that it did indeed seek to promote the public good, the class legislation concept sought to vindicate this core commitment of American republicanism. At the same time, by refusing to demarcate certain rights as fundamental (or certain types of discrimination as particularly problematic, or in modern terms, "suspect"), the police power/class legislation approach also sought to promote the idea that individual liberty extended broadly, and allowed any conduct that wasn't the subject of reasonable police power regulation.

Despite its attractiveness, this approach required courts to distinguish between statutes that promoted a legitimate public interest, and those that instead sought to promote the private interest of a class of persons. Given that most statutes classify in some ways (as illustrated, for example, in *Barbier*, which singled out laundries for regulation), the imperative to distinguish between valid police power regulations and invalid class legislation required courts to second-guess an enormous amount of legislation. When, as explained in Chapter 9, the Court stepped back from such second-guessing in due process cases featuring liberty of contract claims,[3] the Court similarly stepped back from second-guessing the validity of most legislative classifications challenged on equal protection grounds. An important exception to this new deference was suggested in a footnote in a 1938 case, *United States v. Carolene Products Co.*[4] This footnote, and theory that underlay it, is presented in the next sub-section.

While that footnote ultimately provided the foundation for more stringent scrutiny of certain types of statutory classifications starting in the late 1930s, around that same time most types of classifications — that is, those dealing with general economic and social matters — started receiving very deferential judicial scrutiny. *Railway Express v. New York*[5] exemplifies this deference. *Railway Express* evaluated due process and

---

2. *Id.* at 31–32.
3. The Court's liberty of contract jurisprudence is discussed in Section 9.02[1].
4. 304 U.S. 144, 152 n. 4 (1938).
5. 336 U.S. 106 (1949).

314 · EQUAL PROTECTION

equal protection challenges to a city ordinance that banned advertising on the sides of trucks, unless the ads were for the products of the truck's owner. (Thus, the ordinance prohibited truck owners from renting out the sides of their trucks for other firms' advertising.)

In addition to rejecting the substantive due process claim, the Court, speaking through Justice Douglas, concluded that it was not competent to second-guess the city's argument that the law was a measure designed to promote traffic safety. In response to the argument that rented-out advertising was no more distracting to drivers than the advertising showcasing a truck owner's own products, the Court stated that rejecting the reasonableness of the law's classification "would take a degree of omniscience which we lack." It also observed that governments could attack problems (such as traffic safety) one step at a time: "the fact that New York City sees fit to eliminate from traffic this kind of distraction but does not touch what may be even greater ones in a different category, such as the vivid displays on Times Square, is immaterial. It is no requirement of equal protection that all evils of the same genus be eradicated or none at all."[6] Of course, that statement, if taken to its logical conclusion, would render the Equal Protection Clause a nullity, since it would allow government to single out particular "evils of the same genus" for regulation while leaving equally-problematic exemplars untouched.

Justice Jackson wrote an influential concurring opinion, in which he set forth his preference for dealing with challenges such as the one in *Railway Express* on equal protection, rather than due process grounds.[7] He explained that this preference flowed from the consequences of relying on one as opposed to the other of these theories. He observed that a due process-based strike-down of a law disables any government action regulating that particular conduct. As he put it, such a strike-down leaves "leaves ungoverned and ungovernable conduct which many people find objectionable."[8] By contrast, an equal protection strike-down allows government to regulate the conduct in question, as long as it applies the challenged regulation equally to all similarly-situated parties. This requirement of equal application had the benefit of preventing regulation that truly was arbitrary, by requiring that such regulations apply to all similarly-situated persons, rather than simply a small targeted group. He wrote:

> The framers of the Constitution knew, and we should not forget today, that there is no more effective practical guaranty against arbitrary and unreasonable government than to require that the principles of law which officials would impose upon a minority must be imposed generally. Conversely, nothing opens the door to arbitrary action so effectively as to allow those officials to pick and choose only a few to whom they will apply legislation and thus to escape the political retribution that might be visited upon them if larger

---

6. *Id.* at 110.
7. *Id.* at 111 (Jackson, J., concurring).
8. *Id.* at 112.

numbers were affected. Courts can take no better measure to assure that laws will be just than to require that laws be equal in operation.[9]

Thus, Justice Jackson's approach had the benefit of both allowing government to regulate rather than leaving some conduct "ungoverned and ungovernable" while also ensuring that such regulation was not oppressive or unreasonable. But the key to this dynamic, of course, is ensuring that courts impose a meaningful requirement of equal application — that is, insisting that legislation apply to all similarly-situated persons. With regard to the case before him, Justice Jackson reasoned as follows:

> The question in my mind comes to this. Where individuals contribute to an evil or danger in the same way and to the same degree, may those who do so for hire be prohibited, while those who do so for their own commercial ends but not for hire be allowed to continue? I think the answer has to be that the hireling may be put in a class by himself and may be dealt with differently than those who act on their own. But this is not merely because such a discrimination will enable the lawmaker to diminish the evil. That might be done by many classifications, which I should think wholly unsustainable. It is rather because there is a real difference between doing in self-interest and doing for hire, so that it is one thing to tolerate action from those who act on their own and it is another thing to permit the same action to be promoted for a price.[10]

Speaking very generally, when dealing with social and economic legislation, the modern Court's equal protection review has been exceptionally deferential.[11] For example, in *U.S. Railroad Retirement Board v. Fritz*,[12] the Court upheld a federal law that reorganized the retirement benefits structure for railroad workers.[13] The Court found the justification for that reorganization statute in the classifications the statute drew.[14] This is remarkable, in that it seemingly opens the door to a circular analysis in which the statute's classifications — that is, what the statute did — furnishes the justification for those classifications — why the legislature drew the classifications it did. A moment's thought will make it clear that this approach necessarily means that

---

9. *Id.* at 112–13.

10. *Id.* at 115–16.

11. One classic statement of this deferential standard, dating from the *Railway Express* era, is found in *Williamson v. Lee Optical*, where the Court stated: "The problem of legislative classification is a perennial one, admitting of no doctrinaire definition. Evils in the same field may be of different dimensions and proportions, requiring different remedies. Or so the legislature may think. Or the reform may take one step at a time, addressing itself to the phase of the problem which seems most acute to the legislative mind. The legislature may select one phase of one field and apply a remedy there, neglecting the others." 348 U.S. 483, 489 (1955).

12. 449 U.S. 166 (1980).

13. The Equal Protection Clause appears only in the Fourteenth Amendment and thus does not apply to the federal government. However, the Court has found in the Due Process Clause of the Fifth Amendment an equality mandate that has come to be understood as imposing requirements identical to those imposed by the Equal Protection Clause. *See* Bolling v. Sharpe, 347 U.S. 497 (1954).

14. *Id.* at 176 ("the plain language of [the statute] marks the beginning and end of our inquiry").

any challenged statute will be upheld because the classifications it draws are a perfect fit with the justifications for those classifications (which, again, the *Fritz* Court finds in the classifications themselves).[15]

To be sure, individual justices and sometimes even the full Court agree that a government action, including some regulating social and economic matters, is so irrational as to violate equal protection.[16] Nevertheless, as a general matter, equal protection review of social and economic legislation remains quite deferential. There may be good reasons for this extreme deference. Recall from the discussion of the Court's earlier police powers/class legislation analysis that that sort of scrutiny required courts to second-guess legislative judgments about the public benefits a law provides. With the Court having abandoned such second-guessing in its due process liberty of contract jurisprudence, one can understand why it would not want to reintroduce that same skepticism through equal protection doctrine. But the price for this deference is that the political process dynamic Justice Jackson described in his *Railway Express* concurrence fails to operate.

[2] Suspect Class Analysis

In 1938, as the Court was turning away from careful scrutiny of classifications involving social and economic matters, a plurality of the Court added a footnote to an opinion that suggested a new approach to equal protection issues. That opinion, in *United States v. Carolene Products Company*,[17] rejected Commerce Clause and due process right to contract challenges to a federal law prohibiting the shipment in interstate commerce of a particular food product thought to be injurious to the public

---

15. *See, e.g., id.* at 186–87 (Brennan, J., dissenting) ("The Court states that 'the plain language of [45 U.S.C.] § 231b(h) marks the beginning and end of our inquiry.' This statement is strange indeed, for the 'plain language' of the statute can tell us only what the classification is; it can tell us nothing about the purpose of the classification, let alone the relationship between the classification and that purpose. Since [the statute] deprives the members of appellee class of their vested earned dual benefits, the Court apparently assumes that Congress must have intended that result. But by presuming purpose from result, the Court reduces analysis to tautology. It may always be said that Congress intended to do what it in fact did. If that were the extent of our analysis, we would find every statute, no matter how arbitrary or irrational, perfectly tailored to achieve its purpose."); *id.* at 180 (Stevens, J., concurring in the judgment) ("Justice Brennan correctly points out that if the analysis of legislative purpose requires only a reading of the statutory language in a disputed provision, and if any 'conceivable basis' for a discriminatory classification will repel a constitutional attack on the statute, judicial review will constitute a mere tautological recognition of the fact that Congress did what it intended to do.").

16. *See, e.g.,* Armour v. City of Indianapolis, 566 U.S. 673, 688 (2012) (Roberts, C.J., joined by Scalia and Alito, JJ., dissenting) (dissenting from an opinion rejecting an equal protection challenge to a local law that excused homeowners from further contributing to a construction fund while not refunding other homeowners who had already paid their contributions in full); Allegheny Pittsburgh Coal Co. v. County Comm'r of Webster County, 488 U.S. 336 (1989) (unanimous opinion, by the author of the majority opinion in *Fritz*, striking down, on equal protection grounds, a county's property valuation decision when that decision violated state law principles and created massive disparities in tax liabilities for owners of similar property).

17. 304 U.S. 144 (1938).

health. By 1938, the Court's doctrine on both of those issues had evolved to the point where a majority of the Court had little difficulty rejecting those claims.[18]

In a part of the opinion that spoke for a plurality of four justices, Justice Stone wrote that "the existence of facts supporting the legislative judgment is to be presumed, for regulatory legislation affecting ordinary commercial transactions is not to be pronounced unconstitutional unless in the light of the facts made known or generally assumed it is of such a character as to preclude the assumption that it rests upon some rational basis within the knowledge and experience of the legislators."[19] That statement reflects the newfound deference with which social and economic legislation of this sort would be reviewed. However, he appended to that statement a footnote— Footnote 4 to his opinion—that alluded to a new theory of when the Court would *not* be so deferential. That footnote is reprinted here, in its entirety:

> There may be narrower scope for operation of the presumption of constitutionality when legislation appears on its face to be within a specific prohibition of the Constitution, such as those of the first ten Amendments, which are deemed equally specific when held to be embraced within the Fourteenth. See *Stromberg v. California*, 283 U.S. 359 (1931); *Lovell v. Griffin*, 303 U.S. 444 (1938).
>
> It is unnecessary to consider now whether legislation which restricts those political processes which can ordinarily be expected to bring about repeal of undesirable legislation, is to be subjected to more exacting judicial scrutiny under the general prohibitions of the Fourteenth Amendment than are most other types of legislation. On restrictions upon the right to vote, see *Nixon v. Herndon*, 273 U.S. 536 (1928); *Nixon v. Condon*, 286 U.S. 73 (1932); on restraints upon the dissemination of information, see *Near v. Minnesota*, 283 U.S. 697 (1931); *Grosjean v. American Press Co.*, 297 U.S. 233 (1936); *Lovell v. Griffin, supra.*; on interferences with political organizations, see *Stromberg v. California, supra.*; *Fiske v. Kansas*, 274 U.S. 380 (1927); *Whitney v. California*, 274 U.S. 357 (1927); *Herndon v. Lowry*, 301 U.S. 242 (1937); and see Holmes, J., in *Gitlow v. New York*, 268 U.S. 652, 673 (1925); as to prohibition of peaceable assembly, see *De Jonge v. Oregon*, 299 U.S. 353 (1937).
>
> Nor need we enquire whether similar considerations enter into the review of statutes directed at particular religious, *Pierce v. Society of Sisters*, 268 U.S. 510 (1925), or national, *Meyer v. Nebraska*, 262 U.S. 390 (1923); *Bartels v. Iowa*, 262 U.S. 404 (1923); *Farrington v. Tokushige*, 273 U.S. 284 (1927), or racial minorities. *Nixon v. Herndon, supra.*; *Nixon v. Condon, supra.*; whether prejudice against discrete and insular minorities may be a special condition, which tends seriously to curtail the operation of those political processes ordinarily to be relied upon to protect minorities, and which may call for a

---

18. The evolution of the Court's Commerce Clause doctrine is discussed in Chapter 6. The evolution of its right to contract doctrine is discussed in Section 9.02[1].

19. 304 U.S. at 152.

correspondingly more searching judicial inquiry. Compare *McCulloch v. Maryland*, 4 Wheat. 316 (1819); *South Carolina State Highway Department v. Barnwell Bros.*, 303 U.S. 177 (1938), note 2, and cases cited.

Footnote 4 thus identified three situations in which the deference the Court would normally accord legislation would be replaced by more careful scrutiny: first, when laws seemed to violate rights that were textually provided for in the Bill of Rights (and when those rights were incorporated so as to apply against states via the Four-teenth Amendment); second, when laws impaired participation in the political process (as with laws restricting speech and voting rights); and, third and most relevantly for equal protection purposes, when laws burdened groups ("discrete and insular minorities") that suffered from "prejudice" in a way that causes the political process to malfunction and fail to protect minority interests. Note that none of these situations applied to the law at issue in *Carolene Products*; thus, Justice Stone's footnote was *dicta*—and, indeed, *dicta* speaking for only four justices.[20]

Nevertheless, Footnote 4 (as it has come to be known) became enormously influ-ential in American constitutional law, for offering a theory justifying careful judicial review of democratically-enacted legislation. The first paragraph suggested that tex-tually-explicit rights provided in the Bill of Rights merited careful judicial protec-tion—unlike, perhaps, the unenumerated due process right to contract that the Court had then-recently abandoned. The second and third paragraphs suggested that careful judicial review was also legitimate when it focused on laws that somehow did not have a valid democratic pedigree—either because the law itself sought to restrict democratic participation (for example, by restricting speech or voting rights) or be-cause the law targeted a group (a "discrete and insular" minority that suffered from social "prejudice") that, because of that status, was not able to participate fully in the political process. Correspondence from Justice Stone suggested that he was thinking about African-Americans in particular when he made this suggestion.[21]

The first paragraph of Footnote 4 implicates the meaning of various Bill of Rights provisions (for example, the First Amendment's Speech Clause), topics that this book takes up in part, but also topics that are partially left to sourcebooks on criminal and civil procedure. It also implicates the question of when those provisions have been "incorporated" so as to apply against the states via the Fourteenth Amendment.[22] The second paragraph speaks both to the First Amendment rights of speech and assembly[23] and to voting and other political rights, some of which are constitutional in nature.

Footnote 4's third paragraph provided the foundation for much of the Court's equal protection jurisprudence in the decades after 1938. In particular, it provided

---

20. Justices Cardozo and Reed did not participate in the case. Justice McReynolds dissented, Justice Butler concurred separately, and Justice Black joined Justice Stone's opinion except for the section that included Footnote 4.

21. *See* Letter from Harlan Fiske Stone to Irving Lehman, *quoted in* ALPHEUS THOMAS MASON, HARLAN FISKE STONE: PILLAR OF THE LAW 515 (1956).

22. The Court's incorporation jurisprudence is discussed in Section 9.03.

23. The Court's freedom of speech and assembly jurisprudence is discussed in Chapter 11.

the foundation of the Court's doctrine governing when a legislative classification would receive the deferential "rational basis" scrutiny normally accorded government action challenged on equal protection grounds,[24] and when, by contrast, it would receive heightened scrutiny. That heightened scrutiny would itself eventually be subdivided into two very general levels, one denominated "intermediate" scrutiny and the other, more stringent version denominated "strict scrutiny."

The next three sections trace how Footnote 4 influenced this evolution and set forth its ultimate results in the present day. Section 10.02 considers the evolution of the Court's thinking about sex discrimination. Section 10.03 considers other types of discrimination that the Court began to consider carefully in the last third of the twentieth century. Section 10.04 then rewinds the tape and considers how the Court has considered race throughout American history, from the founding, through the Civil War and subsequent police powers/class legislation era, and up to today. Race is unique, in that racial equality issues have gotten the Court's serious attention throughout its history; thus, this chapter's brief introduction to class legislation/police power analysis and its illustration of how suspect class analysis has developed will help illuminate the Court's treatment of race over the course of its history. After discussing the intent requirement in Section 10.05, Section 10.06 considers the ultimate fate of the suspect class analysis grounded in Footnote 4. Finally, Section 10.07 considers the so-called fundamental rights strand of equal protection, a concept, as its name implies, combining aspects of substantive rights and equality reasoning.

§ 10.02 Sex Equality

After World War II, the social movement for sex equality compelled a re-evaluation of the role of women in American society and of long-standing social attitudes toward women. The law had long embodied these roles and attitudes. Many such laws, seemingly designed to protect women, reflected and had the effect of perpetuating long-held stereotypical views about the characteristics of both men and women, usually to women's detriment.[25] Other statutes and common law rules, often quite longstanding, reflected assumptions about women's fundamentally subordinate status. For example, under the common law doctrine of coverture, a woman's legal standing — for example, her legal obligations — became subsumed into her husband's upon marriage, on the theory that the husband was the legal representative of the married couple. While some *Lochner*-era liberty of contract cases nodded toward evolving notions of women's equality when striking down women's protective legislation, the Court did not seriously engage the question of sex equality until the 1970s.

---

24. That baseline deferential standard is discussed in Section 10.01[1].

25. Many laws were derived in part from reform-minded legislation intended to protect women and children from sweatshop working conditions. For example, *Muller v. Oregon*, 208 U.S. 412 (1908), upheld an Oregon law setting maximum hours for women factory workers, with the Court referring to women's supposed inherent weaknesses and fragilities that, in the Court's view, justified such protective legislation.

Over time, the Court changed its approach to sex classifications. Using the Equal Protection Clause, it fashioned a middle-tier standard of scrutiny in the gender area. The first sub-section below traces the evolution of this middle-tier standard and the scope of its application in gender cases. The next two sub-sections consider the particular problems of sex classifications justified as compensating women for past discrimination and those justified as reflecting physical or "real" differences between men and women.

[1] Changing Attitudes toward Sex Classifications

[a] Development of the Intermediate Scrutiny Standard

For much of our constitutional history, the Supreme Court did not construe the Equal Protection Clause to speak to sex discrimination. For example, in *Bradwell v. Illinois*,[26] the Court upheld a state law barring women from practicing law. In a concurring opinion, Justice Bradley justified the law by asserting that "[t]he paramount destiny and mission of woman are to fulfil the noble and benign offices of wife and mother" and that "the natural and proper timidity and delicacy which belongs to the female sex evidently unfits it for many of the occupations of civil life."[27] Sometimes during the *Lochner* era of judicial protection for the substantive due process right to contract, courts would use sex equality reasoning to strike down labor laws aimed at protecting women on the ground that those laws deprived women of their contractual rights.[28]

However, after the repudiation of the Court's liberty of contract jurisprudence, the Court adopted an extremely deferential stance toward laws that classified based on sex. For example, in *Goesaert v. Cleary*,[29] the Court upheld a Michigan statute prohibiting a woman from tending bar unless she was the wife or daughter of the male owner. Using a rationality standard, the Court stated that the Michigan legislature could have completely prohibited women from being bartenders. Thus, it could also make exceptions when circumstances, such as the presence of the woman's husband or father, supposedly shielded women from the moral and social hazards the law was designed to address. Similarly, in *Hoyt v. Florida*,[30] the Court upheld a Florida law allowing women to excuse themselves from jury duty. The Court acknowledged "the enlightened emancipation of women from the restrictions and protections of bygone years, and their entry into many parts of community life formerly considered to be

---

26. 83 U.S. (16 Wall.) 130 (1873).
27. *Id.* at 141 (Bradley, J., concurring).
28. *See, e.g.*, Adkins v. Children's Hospital, 261 U.S. 525, 553 (1923) (citing "the great—not to say revolutionary—changes which have taken place ... in the contractual, political, and civil status of women" as a reason to reject a women's protection justification for a minimum wage law aimed at women).
29. 335 U.S. 464 (1948).
30. 368 U.S. 57 (1961).

reserved to men." Nevertheless, it held that, because "woman is still regarded as the center of home and family life,"[31] the state could allow women to excuse themselves from jury duty in order to attend to those domestic responsibilities.

The Court first struck down an instance of sex discrimination in *Reed v. Reed.*[32] *Reed* struck down a statute that preferred males to serve as estate administrators over females who were equally closely-related to the decedent. The state based its preference on an assumption that men generally possessed more business experience than women, thus better qualifying them to administer estates. The Court rejected the state's argument, characterizing the statutory preference as arbitrary. The Court did not explicitly apply heightened scrutiny to the sex discriminatory statute. Still, its scrutiny of the law suggested that it was doing more than applying the conventional deferential rational basis review that governed such claims at that time.[33]

Two years after *Reed*, the Court made its most serious attempt to extend strict scrutiny to sex discrimination. In *Frontiero v. Richardson*,[34] the Court struck down federal statutes that allowed a uniformed serviceman to claim his wife as a dependent regardless of whether she was actually dependent upon him, while requiring a servicewoman claiming her husband as a dependent to demonstrate that he was in fact dependent upon her for over half of his support.[35] Justice Brennan's plurality opinion for four justices concluded that classifications based on gender "are inherently suspect and must therefore be subjected to close judicial scrutiny."[36] In support of that conclusion, the plurality noted first the extensive history of discrimination against women, which Justice Brennan analogized to the history of discrimination faced by African-Americans. Second, he observed that sex, like race, was an immutable characteristic determined at birth that was irrelevant to the actual capabilities of the individual. Third, he noted women's lack of political power, as evidenced by their under-representation in important government positions. Finally, the plurality cited federal statutes prohibiting sex discrimination as evidence that Congress had concluded that gender classifications were "inherently invidious."[37]

The government argued that administrative convenience justified the statutes' sex classifications, because women often were actually dependent upon their husbands, but the converse was rarely true, thus making it rational to require only female members to establish their spouses' dependency. Applying the heightened scrutiny he had called for, Justice Brennan rejected this argument, because the government offered

---

31. *Id.* at 61–62.

32. 404 U.S. 71 (1971).

33. For a discussion of rational basis review of social and economic legislation, see Section 10.01[1].

34. 411 U.S. 677 (1973).

35. As noted earlier, *see* note 13, *supra*, the Equal Protection Clause does not apply to the federal government. However, the Fifth Amendment's Due Process Clause, which does apply to federal action, has been construed to include an equality component whose requirements are identical to the requirements of the Fourteenth Amendment's Equal Protection Clause.

36. *Frontiero*, 411 U.S. at 682.

37. *Id.* at 687.

no evidence that the sex classification made the statute cheaper or easier to administer, and, regardless, because administrative convenience was an insufficient justification for a law subject to strict scrutiny. Justice Stewart concurred in the judgment, on the ground that the law's sex discrimination was arbitrary. Justice Powell, joined by Chief Justice Burger and Justice Blackmun, concurred in the judgment but objected to characterizing gender as a suspect classification. He observed that the Equal Rights Amendment, then currently in the ratification stage,[38] should be allowed to work its way through the political process before the Court branded all sex classifications as inherently suspect.

Frontiero is important, because it reflected the plurality's attempt to apply the political process-based reasoning Justice Stone had suggested in Footnote 4 of *Carolene Products*. Justice Brennan's identification of a history of discrimination, the immutability of the classifying characteristic, and the burdened group's current political powerlessness can be understood as an attempt to create a doctrinal test reflecting Footnote 4's insight that "prejudice against discrete and insular minorities was a special condition" that rendered the political process dysfunctional. Justice Brennan's first and third inquiries (the group's history of discrimination and its current lack of political power) both relate to a group's exclusion from full political participation. Somewhat more distantly, Justice Brennan's focus on the immutability of the classifying characteristic suggests that discrimination would be particularly problematic if it focused on characteristics that others simply could not share. On a political process theory, discrimination based on such a characteristic is particularly problematic, because there is no risk that the dominant group will ever find itself sharing that characteristic, and thus might feel itself free to use it as the basis for discrimination.[39] While Justice Brennan failed to find a majority for his analysis in *Frontiero*, and while, as noted immediately below, sex discrimination analysis took a different turn, his attempt to implement Footnote 4's insights remained an attractive tool for the Court when it considered other types of discrimination in the decade after *Frontiero*.

After *Frontiero*'s failure to assemble a majority for applying strict scrutiny to sex classifications, the Court's focus shifted. In the years immediately after *Frontiero*, Court majorities sometimes focused on whether the challenged sex classification reflected archaic or overbroad stereotypes, or instead reflected real differences between men and women. For example, in *Weinberger v. Wiesenfeld*,[40] the Court struck down a federal Social Security benefit payable to a parent-wife whose working husband had died, but not to a parent-husband whose working wife had died. Such benefits were designed to assist the surviving parent, who was presumed to be not working in order to attend to parental responsibilities; the law's sex classification, however, revealed an assumption that a surviving father would likely be working rather than engaged

---

38. That process eventually stalled just short of the 38 states required to ratify the amendment. In recent years, a campaign has begun to complete the ratification process.

39. *Compare Carolene Products*, 304 U.S. at 152 n. 4 (identifying "prejudice against *discrete and insular* minorities" as the problematic phenomenon) (emphasis added).

40. 420 U.S. 636 (1975).

in full-time parenting. Justice Brennan, writing for the majority, rejected what he called the law's "gender-based generalization"[41] that men, not women, were the primary breadwinners for their families. By contrast, in *Schlesinger v. Ballard*,[42] the Court upheld a statute that allowed female Navy officers more time than men to advance or face discharge, on the theory that women's then-existing exclusion from combat and most sea duty made it harder for them to advance, thus justifying the extra advancement time.

In *Craig v. Boren*, the Court settled on what became known as an intermediate standard of scrutiny for sex discrimination. Under this standard, a sex classification "must serve important governmental objectives and must be substantially related to achievement of those objectives."[43] Applying that standard, the Court struck down an Oklahoma statute that prohibited the sale of low-strength beer to males under the age of 21, but allowed females to purchase it starting at age 18.

In defense of the law, the state introduced statistical evidence designed to show that arrest and accident rates involving alcohol were far greater for males in the 18–21 age category than for their female counterparts. Although the Court acknowledged the importance of highway safety, it found the state's evidence unpersuasive. The Court noted the relatively small percentages of young men and women who drank and drove, but also the apparent fact that young women who were apprehended for the offense were sometimes simply escorted home rather than arrested and thus included in the statistics. It worried that such sex-stereotyped behavior could create the sex-differentiated statistics that in turn could be used to justify sex discriminatory legislation based on stereotypes about male "reckless[ness]."[44] It also questioned the relevance of the statute to combatting this problem, observing that the state had not connected the drunk driving problem to consumption of low-strength beer. Even more strikingly, the Court questioned the entire enterprise of justifying classifications on the basis of statistical correlations—a practice the Court described as "one that inevitably is in tension with the normative philosophy that underlies the Equal Protection Clause."[45]

Justices Blackmun, Powell, and Stevens all joined the Court's majority but wrote separate concurrences. Most notably, Justices Powell and Stevens both indicated discomfort with a middle, intermediate tier of equal protection scrutiny. Chief Justice Burger and Justice Rehnquist each dissented. Justice Rehnquist criticized the Court for striking down a law that, in his view, favored women by allowing them to buy alcohol at an earlier age. He acknowledged the view that such laws effectively disadvantaged women by reinforcing old notions of female passivity and delicacy, but he dismissed that concern as "insubstantial."[46] He also critiqued the Court's embrace of

---

41. *Id.* at 645.
42. 419 U.S. 498 (1975).
43. 429 U.S. 190, 197 (1976).
44. *Id.* at 202 n.14.
45. *Id.* at 204.
46. *Id.* at 220 n.2 (Rehnquist, J., dissenting).

intermediate scrutiny, remarking that such a middle-ground standard would be too vague for courts to apply consistently and would thus become a vehicle for judges to import their own value preferences into constitutional law.

[b] Application of the Standard

In cases after *Craig*, the Court struggled to implement the intermediate scrutiny standard. In *Rostker v. Goldberg*,[47] the Court upheld Congress's exclusion of women from registration for the draft. Justice Rehnquist's majority opinion reflected some of the criticisms he had raised in his *Craig* dissent, such as his reluctance to extend heightened scrutiny to discrimination against men. Nevertheless, the majority appeared at times to rely on the *Craig* middle tier standard in upholding the statute. For example, the majority stated that the government's interest in raising an army was important and concluded that that exempting women from draft registration was closely related to Congress's purpose of preparing a draft for combat troops.

In deciding that the exemption of women was closely related to the stated purpose of a draft, the Court seemed to suggest that women were not similarly situated to men in the draft context, given the then-existing exclusion of women from combat (which the *Rostker* plaintiff did not challenge). The Court afforded great deference to what it concluded was Congress' determination that women could not serve in combat roles or be drafted for specific non-combat roles. In particular, it emphasized the care with which Congress reached this conclusion, and the corresponding absence of any unthinking stereotypes that might otherwise have infected its determination. The Court also noted the deference that the Court has often extended to congressional decisions regarding the military.

Justice White, joined by Justice Brennan, dissented, largely to challenge the Court's conclusion that Congress actually found that the exclusion of women from draft registration, and hence from any future draft, was appropriate because any need for women in a future conflict could be supplied by volunteers. He emphasized that persons of either sex could perform non-combat missions, and that a draft of women could thus free up men for combat roles. In a separate dissent, Justice Marshall, again joined by Justice Brennan, argued that the government had not demonstrated that a gender-based draft satisfied the demands of intermediate scrutiny. Instead, even leaving aside the possibility of a peacetime draft for which women would serve in needed positions, he noted the government's own statement that, in a future wartime draft, approximately two-thirds of the need would be for combat positions. Thus, Justice Marshall concluded that substantial needs would exist for inductees to perform non-combat positions for which women were eligible.

The same year as *Rostker*, in *Michael M. v. Superior Court*,[48] the Court upheld a California statutory rape law that imposed criminal liability on a male who had sexual

---

47. 453 U.S. 57 (1981).
48. 450 U.S. 464 (1981).

intercourse with a female under 18 but not on a female who had sex with an underaged male.[49] Addressing the proper standard to apply to the male defendant's equal protection challenge, Justice Rehnquist, writing for a four-justice plurality, stated that gender-based classifications were not inherently suspect and were subject only to a rationality test applied with a " 'sharper focus' when gender-based classifications are challenged."[50] His opinion concluded that the classification was "sufficiently related"[51] to the goals sought by the state, because men and women were not similarly situated as to the problems and risks of sex, given the possibility women uniquely faced of becoming pregnant. By imposing criminal sanctions on men, Justice Rehnquist reasoned that the statute provided a deterrent for men, while the risk of pregnancy already provided a substantial deterrent for women.

Justice Stewart joined the plurality opinion and wrote a separate concurrence to emphasize his view that young men and young women were differently situated with regard to underage sex, thus justifying the California law. Justice Blackmun concurred only in the result, finding the California law to satisfy, among other standards, the one announced in *Craig v. Boren*. Justice Brennan, joined by Justices White and Marshall, dissented, arguing that the California law failed *Craig*'s intermediate scrutiny standard. He argued that the pregnancy-prevention rationale for the law was not the actual justification for the law. Rather, Justice Brennan, tracing the law back to its nineteenth century origins, argued that it reflected a stereotyped view of young women as fragile and in need of protection. Justice Stevens also dissented, to argue that a desire to protect women from the risk of pregnancy should logically require that they, as well as men, be subject to whatever criminal punishment the state chose to impose.

In both *Rostker* and *Michael M.*, the Court's view that men and women were differently-situated for purposes of the challenged classification resulted in what appears to be substantially reduced scrutiny. In 1982, however, the Court appeared to heighten its scrutiny of sex classifications in *Mississippi University for Women v. Hogan*.[52] In *Hogan*, the Court struck down a state statute excluding males from a state-run nursing school. Writing for the Court, Justice O'Connor, the first woman to serve on the Court, stated that to justify sex classifications, the government had the burden of establishing an "exceedingly persuasive justification."[53] That standard required the government to demonstrate a direct and substantial relationship between the classification and the legitimate and important government objective it purported to serve. It also required that the state's decision be free of preconceived or stereotyped ideas concerning the roles and abilities of males and females. Consequently, if the stated

---

49. The statute spoke in terms of the victim, criminalizing sex with a female minor who was not married to the perpetrator. Conceivably, the law could have applied to a woman who had sex with a female minor, but that Court appears to have ignored that possibility.
50. *Id.* at 468.
51. *Id.* at 473.
52. 458 U.S. 718 (1982).
53. *Id.* at 724.

purpose of the classification was to protect one gender because of supposed inherent handicaps or inferiorities, then the objective itself was illegitimate.

Often, when the Court strikes down a program using heightened scrutiny, it summarily accepts the government's proffered objectives, but disapproves of the means used to reach those objectives. By contrast, in *Hogan*, the Court rejected both the government's objectives and the means used to advance them. Mississippi argued that the purpose of its admission policy was to compensate for past discrimination against women. Justice O'Connor stated that a compensatory purpose would not be accepted here, because there was no evidence of past discrimination against women in nursing or that women lacked opportunities to obtain nursing training. Thus, the policy only perpetuated the stereotype that nursing was exclusively a women's profession. Mississippi also failed to prove that its policy was substantially and directly related to its stated objectives. For example, the fact that the school allowed men to audit classes undermined the state's argument that the presence of men in classrooms adversely affected female students.

Justices Powell and Blackmun dissented, making First Amendment-related arguments about universities' discretion to make pedagogical and academic judgments. They both argued that the goal of educational diversity authorized the state to give students choices between single-sex and co-educational schools. In his dissent, Justice Blackmun worried that the decision jeopardized virtually all government-run single-sex educational institutions. His dissent also emphasized that publicly-supported nursing programs were available to men at other campuses in Mississippi. Chief Justice Burger's brief dissent argued that the holding was limited to professional nursing schools.

One could read *Hogan* and *Craig* on the one hand and *Michael M.* and *Rostker* on the other as reflecting inconsistent approaches to gender discrimination. Alternatively, one could attempt to reconcile these two lines of cases by arguing that *Michael M.* and *Rostker* relaxed their scrutiny because the laws in those cases reflected real sex differences, while the discrimination in *Craig* and *Hogan* was based on stereotypes. To be sure, others — for example, the dissenters in *Michael M. and Rostker* — would argue that the classification in all these cases rested on stereotypes. Regardless of one's view, these representative cases[54] illustrate that, as the Court's sex equality jurisprudence developed, it became clear that the Court was increasingly focused on ferreting out what it believed to be invidious stereotypes, as opposed to applying a purely political process-based standard of review of the sort sketched out by Justice Brennan in his plurality opinion in *Frontiero*.

[c] *Sex Equality Jurisprudence Today*

In *United States v. Virginia*,[55] the Court firmly signaled that it would apply a significantly high degree of scrutiny to sex classifications. *Virginia* considered both

---

54. The Court decided a number of other sex equality cases during this period.
55. 518 U.S. 515 (1996).

whether Virginia Military Institute (VMI), a state university, could exclude women as students and, assuming such discrimination was unconstitutional, whether the remedy VMI proposed when the lower court found against it—the creation of the Virginia Women's Institute for Leadership (VWIL) at a neighboring women's college—was adequate.

Writing for six justices of a 7–1 majority (with Justice Thomas not participating), Justice Ginsburg[56] held that VMI's all-male policy violated equal protection because it denied access to a prestigious educational institution to women who were "capable of all the individual activities required of VMI cadets."[57] Beginning her analysis by stating the applicable level of scrutiny, she cited *Hogan*'s "exceedingly persuasive justification" requirement. She described that burden of justification as "demanding" and stated that "it rests entirely on the State." In addition to repeating the formula from *Craig v. Boren* that the challenged law must serve an important government objective through means substantially related to that goal, she also wrote that "[t]he justification must be genuine, not hypothesized or invented *post hoc* in response to litigation. And it must not rely on generalizations about the different talents, capacities, or preferences of males and females."[58]

Importantly, however, Justice Ginsburg cautioned that not all sex classifications are proscribed. Contrasting the impermissibility of racial or national origin classifications based on purported "inherent differences," she wrote: "[p]hysical differences between men and women, however, are enduring." But she warned that government could not cite such differences as a justification for "denigration of the members of either sex or for artificial constraints on an individual's opportunity." However, she stated that government could distinguish between men and women in order to compensate women "for particular economic disabilities [they have] suffered," [and] to "promot[e] equal employment opportunity."[59]

Applying this standard, Justice Ginsburg found that VMI's exclusion of women violated the Constitution. She did not question the legitimacy of the state's proffered interest in providing Virginia students with a diverse menu of educational opportunities. However, citing the history of higher education in that state (in particular, its longstanding opposition to providing high-level educational opportunities for women), she doubted that was really the reason for VMI's exclusionary policy.

Justice Ginsburg also rejected Virginia's second argument, that admitting women would alter VMI's adversative pedagogical method, which features a rigorous, military-style system of education, including grueling physical demands and a strict rank system of hierarchy. She acknowledged the finding below that coeducation would

---

56. Ruth Bader Ginsburg, the second woman to serve on the Supreme Court, led the ACLU's women's rights litigation effort in the 1970s, the decade during which the Court created much of its sex discrimination jurisprudence. She was a leader in developing constitutional sex equality arguments presented to the Court during that time.

57. 518 U.S. at 530.

58. *Id.* at 533.

59. *Id.* at 533.

undoubtedly affect certain aspects of VMI's program. However, she noted that both sides acknowledged that VMI's methods could be applied to women. She also noted that women had successfully completed studies at the federal military academies and served in the armed forces.

Turning to the remedy, the Court concluded that the VWIL program for women failed to compensate for their exclusion from VMI. The Court observed that, judged under objective metrics such as faculty quality and endowment, VWIL was markedly inferior to VMI. Just as importantly, VWIL did not feature the kind of adversative pedagogical approach for which VMI was renowned. While the state argued that most women did not prefer that approach, Justice Ginsburg insisted that if any women did in fact prefer it, "generalizations about 'the way women are,' estimates of what is appropriate for *most women*, no longer justify denying opportunity to women whose talent and capacity place them outside the average description."[60]

Chief Justice Rehnquist concurred in the judgment, to express concern about the vagueness of the "exceedingly persuasive justification" standard, and to suggest that a more modest remedy than admitting women into VMI might have been adequate under different circumstances. Justice Scalia dissented. He asserted that the Court lacked authority to invalidate a practice that the Bill of Rights did not expressly prohibit and that has enjoyed "a long tradition of open, widespread, and unchallenged use"[61] since the beginning of the Republic. He also complained about the Court's substitution of the "exceedingly persuasive justification" test for the *Craig* standard. He closed his dissent by suggesting that an honest application of suspect class analysis as performed in cases such as *Frontiero* would justify ratcheting down judicial scrutiny of sex classifications to mere rational basis review, given that women are a numerical majority and have won many legislative victories in the form of anti-discrimination laws.

After *Virginia*, one might have thought that sex classifications were presumptively unconstitutional. However, in *Nguyen v. Immigration and Naturalization Service*,[62] the Court upheld a federal statute requiring U.S. citizen-fathers to satisfy more onerous requirements than U.S. citizen-mothers to establish the U.S. citizenship of a nonmarital child born outside of the United States. In conferring citizenship on a nonmarital child, the law required a U.S. citizen-father, before his child turned 18, either to legitimize the child, declare paternity under oath, or receive a court order of paternity. In contrast, the child automatically received its U.S. citizen-mother's nationality as long as the mother had resided in the U.S. for one year. Since Nguyen's father failed to take one of these three affirmative steps required by the statute, his son remained a citizen of Vietnam and could be deported as a result of his criminal conduct.

A five-justice majority, speaking through Justice Kennedy, found that the statute did not violate equal protection, even though it required more of fathers than mothers.

---

60. *Id.* at 550 (emphasis in original).
61. *Id.* at 568 (Scalia, J., dissenting).
62. 533 U.S. 53 (2001).

First, he argued that the statute served Congress's interest in ensuring that a biological relationship existed between the father and child. Even though Nguyen's father had taken a DNA test, this was not one of the specified ways to establish paternity under the statute. Rather than require DNA tests, which may be costly, unreliable, and unavailable in some areas, the Court held that Congress was "reasonable" in imposing other methods to establish paternity. Justice Kennedy also wrote that it would be a "hollow neutrality"[63] to impose sex-neutral requirements ensuring a biological relationship, since the mother gives birth to the child. Second, Justice Kennedy concluded that Congress sought to ensure that a meaningful relationship existed between the parent and child. While a mother knew her child from the moment she gave birth, there was no guarantee that an unwed father even knew his child existed. This, the Court said, was fact, "not a stereotype." Based on these considerations, the Court concluded that the statute acknowledged "basic biological differences"[64] between men and women in the birth process.

Justice O'Connor dissented, joined by Justices Souter, Ginsburg, and Breyer. Justice O'Connor argued that Congress could have achieved the same objectives by imposing sex-neutral requirements, such as DNA testing of both mothers and fathers. She also suggested that the majority had applied nothing more than rational basis review to the statute. She also argued that the majority's decision validated the notion that sole parental responsibility rested on the unmarried mother, while freeing the father from such responsibility.

In *Sessions v. Morales-Santana*,[65] the Court resumed more critical scrutiny of sex classifications to determine if they reflected unconstitutional sex stereotypes. *Morales-Santana* dealt with a federal immigration statute requiring unmarried U.S. citizen-fathers of children born outside of the country to spend more consecutive time in the United States than unmarried U.S. citizen-mothers in order for the U.S. citizen-parent to be able to pass along U.S. citizenship to the child. The plaintiff in *Morales-Santana* was the child of an unmarried U.S. citizen-father who had failed to live in the U.S. for the required number of consecutive years, and thus, under the statute, had failed to pass along his U.S. citizenship to his child. However, if the plaintiff's citizen-parent had been his mother, who was subject to the shorter residency requirement, he would have qualified for U.S. citizenship.

The Court struck the provision down. Writing for six justices, Justice Ginsburg condemned the statute's sex classification as resulting from a stereotyped view of fathers and mothers. The theory of the residency requirement was that the U.S. citizen-parent needed to have spent time in the United States in order to counteract any foreign influences the other (non-citizen) parent might have on the child, before the child would be considered a U.S. citizen. But, as Justice Ginsburg understood the statute, the amount of time the U.S. citizen-parent needed to spend in the United

---

63. *Id.* at 63, 64.
64. *Id.* at 68, 73.
65. 137 S. Ct. 1678 (2017).

States in order to counteract those influences was less when the U.S. citizen-parent was the mother, since an unmarried father was presumed to be absent from the child's life, given the stereotype that child rearing fell to the mother in cases of unmarried parenthood. Justice Thomas, joined by Justice Alito, did not reach the merits of the sex equality claim. Justice Gorsuch did not participate in the case.

The Court's sex equality jurisprudence has evolved considerably since *Reed* and *Frontiero*. Today, the Court appears particularly concerned about ferreting out sex classifications that reflect stereotyping. Interestingly, the Court has never found a majority for a comprehensive theory justifying such scrutiny. The most explicit attempt at such a theory—Justice Brennan's political process-based approach in *Frontiero*—commanded only four votes, and while he continued to press for it in the years after that case, in no sex equality case did a majority sign on to that approach. To be sure, however, the Court's modern sex equality cases speak in resounding terms about men's and women's equal rights to participate fully in society.[66]

Regardless of any lack of theoretical underpinning, the intermediate scrutiny the Court eventually settled on in *Craig* has evolved into an approach that is intensely skeptical of laws that appear to the Court to reflect stereotyped views of women's interests and capabilities, such as the view that women do not engage in risky behavior such as drinking and driving and do not prefer the rugged, individualism-focused training offered by VMI, and the view that unmarried mothers, and not unwed fathers, are the natural caregivers of the children they bear. Recall, for example, Justice Ginsburg's conclusion in *Virginia* that women's *general* lack of interest in the VMI program does not justify denying admission to VMI to women who are in fact interested in its pedagogical approach.[67]

On the other hand, *Virginia*'s statement of the judicial scrutiny appropriate for sex classifications makes clear that the Court will not strike down laws that either reflect real differences between men and women or compensate women for past discrimination. In this sense, the intermediate scrutiny standard applicable to sex discrimination provides the Court with a more nuanced tool than the strict scrutiny Justice Brennan called for in *Frontiero*, since strict scrutiny in the race context has evolved to the point that even race classifications justified as benign or compensatory receive skeptical judicial review.

---

66. *See, e.g., Virginia*, 518 U.S. at 532 ("Since *Reed*, the Court has repeatedly recognized that neither federal nor state government acts compatibly with the equal protection principle when a law or official policy denies to women, simply because they are women, full citizenship stature—equal opportunity to aspire, achieve, participate in and contribute to society based on their individual talents and capacities.").

67. *Compare* Bradwell v. Illinois, 83 U.S. (16 Wall.) 130, 141–142 (1872) (Bradley, J., concurring in the judgment) ("It is true that many women are unmarried and not affected by any of the duties, complications, and incapacities arising out of the married state, but these are exceptions to the general rule.... [T]he rules of civil society must be adapted to the general constitution of things, and cannot be based upon exceptional cases.").

[2] Sex Classifications Justified as Benefitting Women

As suggested by the conclusion to the previous sub-section, the Court's current approach to sex equality combines skeptical scrutiny of most sex classifications with a willingness to accommodate sex classifications successfully justified as compensating women for past discrimination. These cases have forced the Court to draw difficult lines between laws that truly compensate women and those that reflect unflattering sex stereotypes.[68]

In the 1970s the Court confronted a number of cases that posed this issue. In *Kahn v. Shevin*,[69] the Court upheld a Florida statute that afforded widows an annual $500 property tax exemption but did not extend an analogous benefit to widowers. Writing for six justices, Justice Douglas reasoned that the law was an attempt to alleviate the disproportionately heavy burden that fell on widows, given the employment discrimination that often resulted in the husband being the principal wage earner. Justice Brennan, the author of *Frontiero*, dissented, joined by Justice Marshall. Repeating his call for strict scrutiny, he concluded that the law had an insufficiently-precise fit to that justification, given that it would benefit a wealthy widow or a widow who was the family's principal wage-earner. Justice White dissented separately, to raise similar points.

In two cases decided in 1975, both discussed earlier, the Court reached opposite results on the compensation-or-stereotype question. In *Schlesinger v. Ballard*,[70] the Court upheld a law allowing female Navy officers more time than their male counterparts to advance, and thus avoid being discharged. Writing for six justices, Justice Stewart concluded that the differential reflected "not archaic and overbroad generalizations, but, instead, the demonstrable fact that male and female officers ... [were] *not* similarly situated" with regard to advancement opportunities, given women's then-limited opportunities for sea and combat duty. Justice Brennan again dissented, joined by Justices Douglas and Marshall, to argue that the differential failed strict scrutiny.

However, that same year, in *Weinberger v. Wiesenfeld*,[71] the Court struck down a Social Security provision that paid benefits to a widow when a working husband died, but not the widower when a working wife died. The Court concluded that the law was indistinguishable from the program invalidated in *Frontiero v. Richardson*,[72] as they both embodied archaic notions of the role of women and men in a family structure by assuming that men were never dependent on their wives. It rejected the gov-

---

68. *See* C. Edwin Baker, *Neutrality, Process, and Rationality: Flawed Interpretations of Equal Protection*, 58 Tex. L. Rev. 1029 (1980).
69. 416 U.S. 351 (1974).
70. 419 U.S. 498 (1975).
71. 420 U.S. 636 (1975).
72. 411 U.S. 677 (1973). For additional discussion of *Frontiero*, see Section 10.02[1][a].

ernment's argument that the law, like the one upheld in *Kahn*, helped offset the effect of sex discrimination in employment.

In *Califano v. Webster*,[73] the Court upheld a Social Security Act provision that allowed women to exclude three additional lower-earning years than similarly-situated men when computing average wages for Social Security benefits purposes. The Court concluded that the statutory scheme at issue more closely resembled those upheld in *Kahn* and *Schlesinger* than the law struck down in *Wiesenfeld*. The *Webster* Court found in the legislative history a deliberate intention to compensate women for prior discrimination, rather than to sustain stereotypical views about women's capabilities or proper roles. What appears to distinguish these cases, then, is whether the legislative purpose of Congress was compensatory rather than indicative of a stereotyped view of women. While the opinion in *Webster* was unanimous, four justices concurred only in the judgment to question whether Court was competent to distinguish between invidious sex discrimination and benign sex discrimination intended to compensate for past discrimination.

These cases make clear that distinguishing benign from invidious sex classifications can present the Court with a difficult challenge. Still, some cases present fairly clear-cut situations. In *Mississippi University for Women v. Hogan*,[74] the Court dismissed the state's argument that preserving a nursing school as women-only served to compensate women for past discrimination. The Court noted that the state had not shown that women had historically been denied opportunities to become nurses. Instead, it concluded that the state's purported affirmative action on behalf of women actually served to reinforce the traditional stereotype that nursing was an inherently female profession.

[3] Sex Classifications Based on Inherent Differences between the Sexes

In *United States v. Virginia*, Justice Ginsburg cautioned that "[p]hysical differences between men and women ... are enduring,"[75] thus suggesting that sex classifications may be valid if they reflect those differences. In two 1981 cases discussed earlier, *Rostker v. Goldberg*[76] and *Michael M. v. Superior Court*,[77] the Court appeared to base its decisions upholding the challenged laws on the theory that males and females were differently situated as relevant to the challenged classification: in *Rostker*, only men could serve in combat while in *Michael M.*, only women could get pregnant. The first of these differences is, of course, not a physical one: indeed, Congress has now repealed the combat exclusion. But if a legislative distinction (such as the female combat exclusion) is not challenged or at least questioned by the plaintiff, it exists

---

73. 430 U.S. 313 (1977).
74. 458 U.S. 718 (1982).
75. 518 U.S. 515, 533 (1996).
76. 453 U.S. 57 (1981).
77. 450 U.S. 464 (1981).

as a background assumption in the case against which the validity of any sex classification might be judged.

Identifying a sex difference as "natural" or "physical" is a fraught enterprise.[78] Justice Bradley's concurrence in *Bradwell v. Illinois* referred to the "natural and proper timidity and delicacy which belongs to the female sex [and which] evidently unfits it for many of the occupations of civil life."[79] Today, invocations of physical differences often relate to the fact that only women are capable of giving birth.[80] But that difference might well encourage legislative assumptions about the likely closeness of the relationship between a mother and her child, as compared to the father-child relationship, and in turn, assumptions about caregiving roles and responsibilities.[81] More generally, debate has long raged about whether men and women are, as an overall matter, fundamentally different in their psychological make-ups. Some researchers insist that men and women are, in fact "hard wired" differently, for example, with men more predisposed to competitive, individualistic, and mechanically logical approaches to issues and social interactions, while women are more predisposed to cooperative, communitarian, and holistic approaches. Others insist that such differences, if they exist at all, reflect nothing more than ingrained patterns imposed by society, rather than "inherent" differences.

Beyond these deep questions, other, less fundamental ones also make this area challenging. Consider single-sex education. In *Virginia*, Justice Ginsburg recognized the pedagogical value of single-sex education. Indeed, she explicitly acknowledged that "the two sexes are not fungible; a community made up exclusively of one sex is different from a community composed of both."[82] While the Court struck down single-sex education programs in *Virginia* and in *Mississippi University for Women v. Hogan*,[83] her recognition of the value of same-sex education presumably means that there is a significance about sex that renders it a pedagogically sound (and thus, at least a potentially constitutionally valid) classification tool. While it might be easy, at least in retrospect, to spot stereotyping in *Virginia*'s reservation of military-style training to men and *Mississippi*'s reservation of nursing training to women, harder cases will inevitably arise. Those cases will stretch the Court's capacity to determine when sex is a "real" difference that justifies differential treatment.

---

78. The Court has yet to confront a case posing the question of the constitutional status of transgender identity. For speculation about the issues such a case might pose, see William D. Araiza, *New Groups and Old Doctrine: Rethinking Congressional Power to Enforce the Equal Protection Clause*, 37 Fla. St. L. Rev. 451 (2010).

79. 83 U.S. at 141 (Bradley, J., concurring in the judgment).

80. *See, e.g.*, Nguyen v. INS, 533 U.S. 53 (2001) (relying on this fact to uphold a sex classification making it easier for a mother to pass along her U.S. citizenship to her child than it is for a father); Michael M. v. Superior Court, 450 U.S. 464 (1981) (relying on this fact to uphold a sex-specific statutory rape law).

81. *See, e.g.*, Sessions v. Morales-Santana, 137 S.Ct 1678 (2017); Weinberger v. Wiesenfeld, 420 U.S. 636 (1975) (both critiquing such assumptions).

82. 515 U.S. at 533.

83. 458 U.S. 718 (1982). *Hogan* is discussed earlier in this section.

§ 10.03 Classifications Other Than Race and Sex

During the same period the Court was working out its approach to sex discrimination, it was also considering its approach to other types of discrimination to which it had given little or no serious consideration before. This section considers the Court's responses to those types of discrimination: legitimacy (the status of being born to unmarried parents), alienage (the status of not being a U.S. citizen), age, and poverty. It was in these cases, as well as the sex discrimination cases presented in the previous section, that the Court worked out its jurisprudence of "suspect classes" and "suspect classifications" — that is, the types of discrimination that, as particularly problematic (or "suspect"), merit heightened judicial scrutiny. The Court's treatment of two other classifications — intellectual disability and sexual orientation — are considered in Section 10.06, as those cases were decided at a later period when the Court's approach had further evolved.

[1] Legitimacy

Laws that treat illegitimate children differently from legitimate children are not subject to strict scrutiny.[84] However, such distinctions must be "substantially related to permissible state interests,"[85] which the Court has called "intermediate" scrutiny.[86]

The modern Court's first consideration of legitimacy discrimination occurred in two cases decided in 1968, *Levy v. Louisiana*[87] and *Glona v. American Guaranty & Liability Ins. Co.*[88] These cases involved different Louisiana laws that treated illegitimate children differently from other children with regard to recovery for tort damages in case of death when the illegitimate child was either the claimant or the decedent. The Court struck both laws down, without concluding whether such classifications merited heightened scrutiny. In *Levy*, a case dealing with illegitimate children as tort claimants suing after the wrongful death of their mother, the Court, speaking through Justice Douglas, wrote that:

> Legitimacy or illegitimacy of birth has no relation to the nature of the wrong allegedly inflicted on the mother. These children, though illegitimate, were dependent on her; she cared for them and nurtured them; they were indeed hers in the biological and spiritual sense; in her death they suffered wrong in the sense that any dependent would.[89]

---

84. Lalli v. Lalli, 439 U.S. 259, 265 (1978); Mathews v. Lucas, 427 U.S. 495, 506 (1976).

85. *Lalli*, 439 U.S. at 265.

86. *See* Clark v. Jeter, 486 U.S. 456, 461 (1988) ("Between [the] extremes of rational basis review and strict scrutiny lies a level of intermediate scrutiny, which generally has been applied to discriminatory classifications based on sex or illegitimacy.").

87. 391 U.S. 68 (1968).

88. 391 U.S. 73 (1968).

89. *Levy*, 391 U.S. at 72.

Four years later, in *Weber v. Aetna Casualty and Surety Co.*,[90] the Court struck down yet another Louisiana law, this one placing illegitimate children at a lower priority for recovering under a parent's workman's compensation claim. The Court wrote:

> [T]his Court requires, at a minimum, that a statutory classification bear some rational relationship to a legitimate state purpose. Though the latitude given state economic and social regulation is necessarily broad, when state statutory classifications approach sensitive and fundamental personal rights, this Court exercises a stricter scrutiny. The essential inquiry ... is, however, inevitably a dual one: What legitimate state interest does the classification promote? What fundamental personal rights might the classification endanger?[91]

Thus, while the Court was hinting that legitimacy classifications might trigger heightened scrutiny of some sort, the Court had not yet settled on the appropriate scrutiny level.

The Court began to answer that question in 1976, in *Mathews v. Lucas*.[92] *Lucas* involved a provision of federal Social Security law that required illegitimate children to make showings about their relationships with a deceased parent before they could collect survivors' benefits when the claimed parent died, while not imposing those requirements on children born within a marital unit. The Court described earlier cases striking down legitimacy classifications as resting on those classifications' arbitrariness. According to the Court, the reasoning in those cases "does not itself demonstrate that that other, possibly rational, distinctions made in part on the basis of legitimacy are inherently untenable."[93]

Considering for the first time whether legitimacy should be a suspect classification, the Court conceded that "the law has long placed the illegitimate child in an inferior position relative to the legitimate in certain circumstances." Nevertheless, it continued that, "perhaps in part because the roots of the discrimination rest in the conduct of the parents rather than the child, and perhaps in part because illegitimacy does not carry an obvious badge, as race or sex do, this discrimination against illegitimates has never approached the severity or pervasiveness of the historical legal and political discrimination against women and [African-Americans]." The Court thus concluded that the challenged law's legitimacy-based discrimination "does not command extraordinary protection from the majoritarian political process which our most exacting scrutiny would entail."[94] Twelve years later, in *Clark v. Jeter*, the Court cited *Lucas* for the proposition that legitimacy discrimination triggers intermediate scrutiny, which the Court seemed to equate with the scrutiny accorded sex discrimination.[95]

---

90. 406 U.S. 164 (1972).

91. *Id.* at 172–73.

92. 427 U.S. 495 (1976).

93. *Id.* at 505.

94. *Id.* at 505–06.

95. 486 U.S. 456, 461 (1988) ("Between [the] extremes of rational basis review and strict scrutiny lies a level of intermediate scrutiny, which generally has been applied to discriminatory classifications

Despite this seeming equation of the standards for legitimacy and sex discrimination,[96] the scrutiny applied in *Lucas* appeared, if not deferential, then at least not particularly demanding. The Court upheld the legitimacy classifications challenged in *Lucas* as "permissible ... because they are reasonably related to the likelihood of [the child's] dependency [on the decedent] at death." It concluded that the presumptions about actual dependency reflected in the law's requirements on illegitimate children, "though they may approximate, rather than precisely mirror, the results that case-by-case adjudication would show, are permissible ... so long as that lack of precise equivalence does not exceed the bounds of substantiality tolerated by the applicable level of scrutiny."[97]

Referring to the analysis in the then-recent case of *Frontiero v. Richardson*, where the plurality applied strict scrutiny to the sex classification it struck down, the *Lucas* Court stated that "[i]n cases of strict scrutiny, such approximations must be supported at least by a showing that the Government's dollar 'lost' to overincluded benefit recipients is returned by a dollar 'saved' in administrative expense avoided. Under the standard of review appropriate here, however, the materiality of the relation between the statutory classification and the likelihood of dependency they assertedly reflect need not be 'scientifically substantiated.'"[98] Given the relative looseness of the standard these statements suggest, it should not be surprising that the Court upheld the law challenged in *Lucas*, given its relationship to Congress's ultimate goal of ensuring that only children actually dependent on decedents receive survivor benefits.

Laws discriminating based on legitimacy often deal with inheritance and probate matters. In *Trimble v. Gordon*,[99] the Court addressed an Illinois law that allowed illegitimate children to inherit by intestate succession from their mothers, but not their fathers. To legitimate the child, the law required that the putative father not only acknowledge the child but marry the mother, after which Illinois law pronounced the child legitimate. After a court had decided that Gordon was Trimble's father, Gordon acknowledged paternity and paid child support but did not marry Trimble's mother. Accordingly, when Gordon died intestate, Trimble was barred from inheriting the estate.

The state asserted two interests in support of the statute. First, it claimed that the law promoted legitimate family relationships. While the Supreme Court recognized the importance of this interest, it found virtually no relationship between this purpose and the statute. Second, the state claimed an interest in establishing an accurate and efficient method of property distribution upon death of the intestate. While this in-

---

based on sex or illegitimacy."). At this point, the Court cited both sex and legitimacy discrimination cases starting with *Craig v. Boren*, 429 U.S. 190 (1976), and *Mathews v. Lucas*.

96. Whether the standards for these two types of discrimination are still the same is open to question, after cases such as *United States v. Virginia*, 518 U.S. 515 (1996), appeared to heighten the requirements the state had to satisfy in order to justify at least some types of sex discrimination.

97. 427 U.S. at 509.

98. *Id.* at 509–10.

99. 430 U.S. 762 (1977).

terest was valid, the statute was not "'carefully tuned to alternative considerations,'"[100] such as the state court's determination, for child support purposes, that Gordon was in fact Trimble's father. Therefore, the statute violated equal protection.

By contrast, the next year, in *Lalli v. Lalli*,[101] the Court upheld a New York statute that required an illegitimate child to obtain a court order declaring paternity in order to inherit by intestate succession. The order had to be issued during the father's lifetime, in a proceeding commenced while the child's mother was pregnant or within two years of birth. The child in *Lalli* acknowledged that he could not produce the required order, but presented other evidence that the decedent was his father. The Court upheld the statute, distinguishing *Trimble* because, unlike the Illinois law in *Trimble*, the New York law did not require the parents to marry; rather, it merely stated an evidentiary requirement. While it stated the rule as asking whether the law was "substantially related to permissible state interests,"[102] at another part of its opinion, it hinted at a more deferential standard of review.[103]

However, in *Clark v. Jeter*,[104] the case that announced the intermediate scrutiny standard for legitimacy classifications, the Court unanimously invalidated a Pennsylvania statute imposing a six-year limitation on the time in which a suit can be brought to prove paternity of an illegitimate child, when the state placed no limitation on the period in which a legitimate child could seek support through a paternity determination. Applying intermediate scrutiny, the Court concluded the law was not substantially related to the state's interest in avoiding litigation of fraudulent claims, given the existence of longer limitations periods for similar actions.

The legitimacy cases reveal no clear pattern, except perhaps a hostility to laws that conclusively disfavor illegitimate children with no possibility for their parents to remove the burden by, for example, the father formally acknowledging paternity. Thus, for example, the Court struck down the laws in *Levy* and *Glona* that imposed absolute limits on wrongful death tort recovery when the decedent and claimant were related via the child's status as an illegitimate offspring, and also struck down the law in *Trimble*, which barred illegitimate children's intestate inheritance from their fathers. By contrast, in *Lalli*, the Court upheld the New York law that allowed an illegitimate child to inherit from an intestate father as long as the father's paternity of the child was declared in a judicial proceeding before the father's death.

To be sure, these distinctions may appear to be quite subtle. After all, the illegitimate child in *Trimble* could have inherited had his parents married, just as the illegitimate child in *Lalli* could have inherited had his father had his paternity acknowledged in a court proceeding. Nevertheless, the Court drew a distinction between these situa-

---

100. *Id.* at 772 (quoting *Lucas*, 427 U.S. at 513).

101. 439 U.S. 259 (1978).

102. *Id.* at 265.

103. *See id.* at 273 ("Our inquiry under the Equal Protection Clause does not focus on the abstract 'fairness' of a state law, but on whether the statute's relation to the state interests it is intended to promote is so tenuous that it lacks the rationality contemplated by the Fourteenth Amendment.").

104. 486 U.S. 456 (1988).

tions, finding the one in *Trimble* unconstitutional but upholding the one in *Lalli*. Without more detailed explanations from the Court,[105] perhaps all that one can say is that legitimacy does indeed occupy a middle ground in equal protection law, in which some classifications will be upheld and other more burdensome or absolute ones will be struck down.

[2] Alienage

[a] The General Standard

Scrutiny for classifications based on alienage varies based on the level of government that is discriminating. The Court subjects discrimination against aliens by state or local government bodies to far more rigorous scrutiny than it applies to discrimination against aliens by the federal government.

In *Graham v. Richardson*,[106] a case involving eligibility for state welfare benefits, the Court declared that classifications based on alienage, like those based on nationality or race, are inherently suspect and subject to close judicial scrutiny. Without elaboration, the Court stated that "[a]liens as a class are a prime example of a 'discrete and insular' minority for whom such heightened judicial solicitude is appropriate."[107] Two years later, the Court wrote that the standard for protecting aliens, "though variously formulated, requires the State to meet certain standards of proof. In order to justify the use of a suspect classification, a state must show that its purpose or interest is both constitutionally permissible and substantial, and that its use of the classification is necessary ... to the accomplishment of its purpose or the safeguarding of its interest."[108]

The Court has employed rigorous scrutiny to invalidate state laws that excluded resident aliens from the legal profession,[109] denied them welfare benefits,[110] prevented them from becoming notaries public,[111] barred them from all classes of state competitive civil service jobs,[112] and restricted their access to student financial aid.[113]

---

105. Recall that, in *Trimble*, the mother's and father's decision to marry had the effect of rendering the previously-illegitimate child legitimate. Perhaps the reasoning here is that that provision of the Illinois law would render the child legitimate and thus moot any question of legitimacy discrimination, while continuing to impose an absolute burden on children who remained illegitimate. By contrast, in *Lalli*, a child could remain "illegitimate" and nevertheless be rendered eligible to inherit. If this distinction holds, it suggests that the formal status of legitimacy or illegitimacy is doing much of the work, at least in distinguishing these two cases. For a further discussion of how these two cases fit (or don't fit) together, see LAURENCE TRIBE, AMERICAN CONSTITUTIONAL LAW 1554–57 (2d ed. 1988).

106. 403 U.S. 365 (1971).

107. *Id.* at 372 (citing United States v. Carolene Products Co., 304 U.S. 144, 152 n. 4 (1938)).

108. *In re* Griffiths, 413 U.S. 717, 721–22 (1973). The *Griffiths* Court attributed no significance to the different terms used to describe the required state interest, *i.e.*, "substantial," "important," "overriding," or "compelling." *Id.* at 722 n.9.

109. *Id.*

110. Graham v. Richardson, 403 U.S. 365 (1971).

111. Bernal v. Fainter, 467 U.S. 216 (1984).

112. Sugarman v. Dougall, 413 U.S. 634 (1973).

113. Nyquist v. Mauclet, 432 U.S. 1 (1977).

Even in the context of state and local governments, an important limitation on the application of strict scrutiny to alienage classifications is the "political-function" exception. This exception "applies to laws that exclude aliens from positions intimately related to the process of democratic self-government." The theory behind this exception is that states, as political communities, retain the prerogative to limit self-government rights to full-fledged members of that community.[114] Discrimination that falls within the political function exception is valid if it "bears a rational relationship to this [legitimate state] interest."[115]

A classification based on alienage must satisfy a two-part test in order to fall within the political-function exception. "First, the specificity of the classification will be examined: a classification that is substantially overinclusive or underinclusive tends to undercut the governmental claim that the classification serves legitimate political ends."[116] Second, the classification may be applied "only to 'persons holding state elective or important nonelective executive, legislative, and judicial positions,' those officers who 'participate directly in the formulation, execution, or review of broad public policy' and hence 'perform functions that go to the heart of representative government.'"[117] The Court has upheld, under the political-function exception, laws that exclude aliens from becoming police[118] and probation officers,[119] as well as a law that denied aliens the chance to teach in public schools unless they declared their intent to become citizens.[120]

The Court generally has declined to subject to strict scrutiny federal laws that treat resident aliens differently from citizens. For example, in *Mathews v. Diaz*,[121] the Court upheld a federal law limiting eligibility for Medicare benefits to aliens who were admitted for permanent residency and who had resided in the nation for five years. The Court observed that the federal government's treatment of aliens implicated foreign affairs, a concern of the political branches. In addition, the Court concluded that "Congress may decide that as the alien's tie [to the nation] grows stronger, so does the strength of his claim to an equal share of [its] munificence."[122]

[b] The Special Case of Undocumented Aliens

Plyler v. Doe[123] struck down a Texas law denying free public education to undocumented, school-age children, as violating equal protection. Writing for the Court, Justice Brennan acknowledged that "undocumented status is not irrelevant to any proper legislative goal" and continued that "[n]or is undocumented status an absolutely

---

114. *See, e.g., Bernal*, 467 U.S. at 221.
115. Ambach v. Norwick, 441 U.S. 68, 80 (1979).
116. Cabell v. Chavez-Salido, 454 U.S. 432, 440 (1982).
117. *Ibid.* (quoting Sugarman v. Dougall, 413 U.S. 634, 647 (1973)).
118. Foley v. Connelie, 435 U.S. 291 (1978).
119. Cabell v. Chavez-Salido, 454 U.S. 432 (1982).
120. Ambach v. Norwick, 441 U.S. 68 (1979).
121. 426 U.S. 67 (1976).
122. *Id.* at 80.
123. 457 U.S. 202 (1982).

immutable characteristic since it is the product of conscious, indeed unlawful, action."[124] However, while undocumented aliens were therefore not a suspect class, the law discriminated against children who may not have had a say in the decision to migrate without documentation. Moreover, while education was not a fundamental right, it had higher value than a social welfare benefit in maintaining the fabric of our society, since a complete deprivation of basic education would place those presumptively innocent children at a lifelong disadvantage.

For those reasons, the Court concluded that the state had the burden of showing that the classification was rationally related to a substantial state interest. The *Plyler* Court used this test to reject all three of the interests asserted by the state: (1) that the restriction would deter the flow of undocumented aliens into the state; (2) that the restriction would improve the education of other children in the state; and (3) that the children of undocumented aliens were appropriately singled out because they were less likely to remain in the state. Justices Marshall, Blackmun, and Powell each wrote concurring opinions. In dissent, Chief Justice Burger argued that in allocating its finite resources, "it simply is not 'irrational' for a state to conclude that it does not have the same responsibility to provide benefits for persons whose very presence in the state and this country is illegal as it does to provide for persons lawfully present."[125]

[3] Age

In *Massachusetts Board of Retirement v. Murgia*, the Court held that age classifications are subject only to rational basis review.[126] *Murgia* upheld a Massachusetts law requiring that uniformed state police officers retire at age 50, regardless of an individual officer's continued physical capability to perform the job. In rejecting the argument that age was a suspect classification, the Court, speaking through a *per curiam* opinion, defined a suspect class as one "saddled with such disabilities, or subjected to such a history of purposeful unequal treatment, or relegated to such a position of political powerlessness as to command extraordinary protection from the majoritarian political process." The aged "have not experienced a 'history of purposeful unequal treatment' or been subjected to unique disabilities on the basis of stereotyped characteristics not truly indicative of their abilities."[127] Nor were the aged a discrete and insular group needing protection from the majority, as the Court observed that everyone will be a member of that group if he or she lives a normal lifespan. Applying rational basis scrutiny, the Court in *Murgia* upheld the challenged statute as rationally related to a legitimate state interest.[128]

---

124. *Id.* at 220.

125. *Plyler*, 457 U.S. at 250. (Burger, C.J., dissenting). Chief Justice Burger also identified a number of federal programs from which undocumented aliens were excluded.

126. 427 U.S. 307, 312–13 (1976).

127. *Id.* at 313.

128. The Court has also upheld against equal protection challenges a federal law requiring that foreign service personnel retire at age 60, Vance v. Bradley, 440 U.S. 93 (1979), and a provision of

[4] Poverty

The Court has not regarded poverty as a suspect classification. Accordingly, laws differentiating based on wealth are not subject to heightened scrutiny. However, laws impacting the poor sometimes also implicate the so-called fundamental rights strand of equal protection. This sub-section examines the Court's response to the argument that poverty should be a suspect classification. Arguments on behalf of the poor based on the fundamental rights strand are considered in Section 10.07.

While in earlier cases, the Court had struck down laws that distributed benefits based on wealth,[129] the Court first explicitly confronted the constitutional status of poverty discrimination in 1970. In *Dandridge v. Williams*,[130] it refused to accord heightened scrutiny to a Maryland law setting a maximum amount of welfare benefits, regardless of family size. Writing for a six-justice majority, Justice Stewart recognized that the law dealt, not with business or industry, but what he called "the most basic economic needs of impoverished human beings."[131] Nevertheless, he characterized the law as social and economic legislation that triggered only rational basis review.

Writing for himself and Justice Brennan, Justice Marshall dissented on the constitutional issue.[132] Making an argument he would repeat throughout his tenure on the Court, he argued that equal protection issues should turn on both the nature of the classification and the importance of the interest at stake. Noting the majority's acknowledgement of the human needs at issue in the case, Justice Marshall urged a heightened level of review, which he argued the statute failed.

Three years later, the Court again confronted the suspectness of poverty discrimination. In *San Antonio Independent School District v. Rodriguez*,[133] the Court examined Texas's method of funding its public schools. Texas used a complex system of funding in which school districts paid into a state fund based primarily on assessed property values in the district. The districts then received allotments from the fund that they were free to supplement with additional local property taxes and federal aid. In *Rodriguez*, the Court examined the funding of two districts in San Antonio, the Edgewood School District and the Alamo Heights School District. Edgewood received $222 per pupil from the state fund, $108 per pupil in federal funds, and contributed an additional $26 per pupil from local taxes, for a total of $356 per pupil. The same numbers for the Alamo Heights district were $225, $36, and $333, respectively, for a total of $594 per pupil.

---

the Missouri Constitution requiring that judges retire at age 70, Gregory v. Ashcroft, 501 U.S. 452 (1991).

129. *See, e.g.*, Griffin v. Illinois, 351 U.S. 12 (1956) (striking down a law that charged persons for a copy of the trial transcript that was a necessary part of appealing a criminal conviction).

130. 397 U.S. 471 (1970).

131. *Id.* at 485.

132. Justice Douglas dissented on a statutory ground.

133. 411 U.S. 1 (1973).

The Supreme Court rejected the lower court's conclusions that poverty was a suspect classification and that education was a fundamental right for equal protection purposes. The fundamental rights aspect of this case is discussed in Section 10.07. With regard to the suspectness of poverty, Justice Powell's majority opinion determined that the people discriminated against in the Court's poverty precedents shared two character-istics: "because of their impecunity they were completely unable to pay for some desired benefit, and as a consequence, they sustained an absolute deprivation of a meaningful opportunity to enjoy that benefit."[134] The Court found neither element satisfied in *Ro-driguez*, regardless of how one defined the plaintiff class. First, there was no showing that the funding system discriminated against a definable class of "poor" people.[135] Second, even if such a class could be defined, its members were not completely deprived of educational opportunities. The Court refused "to extend its most exacting scrutiny to review a system that allegedly discriminates against a large, diverse, and amorphous class, unified only by the common factor of residence in districts that happen to have less taxable wealth than other districts." Explicitly referencing the Court's then-evolving criteria for determining suspectness, the Court concluded that "[t]he system of alleged discrimination and the class it defines have none of the traditional indicia of suspect-ness: the class is not saddled with such disabilities, or subjected to such a history of purposeful unequal treatment, or relegated to such a position of political powerlessness as to command extraordinary protection from the majoritarian political process."[136]

Justice White, joined by Justices Douglas and Brennan, dissented, arguing that Texas's funding system was not rationally related to its purpose of increasing local initiative and choice by allowing school districts with low tax bases to fund education using property taxes. Justice Marshall, joined by Justice Douglas, also dissented. Justice Marshall repeated his disapproval of the Court's tiered approach to equal pro-tection scrutiny. Instead, he argued again for a standard in which the more essential an activity was to exercising specific constitutional rights, the more protection it should receive. This approach offered education considerable protection because of its nexus to free speech, since the latter right could not be effectively exercised without an education. Moreover, while he conceded that the Court had not treated the poor as a suspect class, he insisted that the invidiousness of wealth as a classification varied with the good being distributed. Distributing the fundamental right of education based on wealth was invidious and did not survive strict scrutiny.

Although it is unusual, the Court occasionally has invalidated statutes impacting poor persons on the grounds that they lack a rational basis. *Department of Agriculture v. Moreno*[137] struck down a law that denied food stamps to households that included unrelated persons. The Court found that the statute's true purpose was to prevent

---

134. *Id.* at 20.
135. *See id.* at 23 (finding "no basis on the record in this case for assuming that the poorest peo-ple—defined by reference to any level of absolute impecunity—are concentrated in the poorest dis-tricts.").
136. *Id.* at 28.
137. 413 U.S. 528 (1973).

"hippie communes" from receiving food stamps. The Court concluded that was not a legitimate government interest. *Moreno*'s rejection of laws motivated by "a bare congressional desire to harm a politically unpopular group"[138] eventually flowered into a new and thus-far unsettled branch of equal protection law, which is considered in Section 10.06.

It is easy to critique the Court's failure to accord heightened scrutiny to laws discriminating against the poor, given the long history of discrimination against that group and its continued political powerlessness. To be sure, even Justice Marshall, perhaps the Court's leading critic of this failure, acknowledged that poverty is not immutable in the sense that biological and other characteristics are.[139] Still, the prevalence of poverty, and the increasing lack of social mobility across economic classes, suggests that the argument against heightened scrutiny may be weak. On the other hand, the fact that many everyday economic regulations classify based on wealth perhaps explains the Court's unwillingness to embrace the argument for heightened scrutiny, which would entail careful judicial review of a whole panoply of laws. One might, of course, then respond just as Justice Marshall did—by considering a rule that looked at both the characteristics of the burdened class and the importance of the right at stake. This combination—which the Court adopted in some cases under the banner of the fundamental rights strand of equal protection—is considered in Section 10.07.

§ 10.04 Race Equality

[1] Introduction and Historical Background

Following the Civil War, the Thirteenth, Fourteenth, and Fifteenth Amendments were added to the United States Constitution to ensure freedom and equality for previously-enslaved African-Americans and for all Americans more generally. While the Thirteenth Amendment included a provision authorizing Congress to enforce its prohibition on slavery, crucial congresspersons worried that it did not justify the sweeping Reconstruction legislation many in Congress wanted to enact. That worry led to the drafting and ratification of the Fourteenth Amendment and, ultimately, the Fifteenth Amendment.

As background for understanding how the Equal Protection Clause affected the status of racial minorities in the United States, one must understand the status of

---

138. *Id.* at 534.

139. *See Rodriguez*, 411 U.S. at 121 (Marshall, J., dissenting) ("That wealth classifications alone have not necessarily been considered to bear the same high degree of suspectness as have classifications based on, for instance, race or alienage may be explainable on a number of grounds. The 'poor' may not be seen as politically powerless as certain discrete and insular minority groups. Personal poverty may entail much the same social stigma as historically attached to certain racial or ethnic groups. But personal poverty is not a permanent disability; its shackles may be escaped. Perhaps most importantly, though, personal wealth may not necessarily share the general irrelevance as a basis for legislative action that race or nationality is recognized to have.").

race and racial equality before the Civil War. That story begins with African-American slavery. Starting in 1619, slavery gradually took hold across the 13 colonies, although by the eighteenth century, the institution was declining in the northern and middle colonies and becoming concentrated in the South.

At the 1787 Constitutional Convention in Philadelphia, delegates from the southern states, especially Georgia and South Carolina, insisted that the new constitution protect slavery. Northern delegates opposed to slavery ultimately compromised with the pro-slavery forces, inserting several provisions into the document that recognized or protected it, although without using the word "slave" or "slavery." Thus, congressional representatives (and hence, Electoral College votes) were allocated based on a formula counting slaves as three-fifths of a person, states agreed to be required to assist in recapturing escaped slaves, and the international slave trade was protected until 1808. (Indeed, this last provision was one of the two the Constitution proclaimed as not subject to amendment via the normal Article V amendment process.)

Despite these compromises, many hoped that the continued decline of slavery would moot the question of slavery's long-term place in the new American republic. That hope was soon dashed when the cotton gin, invented in 1793, resurrected slavery as an economically viable institution. Soon, large scale plantation agriculture dependent on slave labor came to dominate the South, ending any hope that the institution would disappear on its own force in the South, as it had in the North.

The reemergence of slavery as a dominant institution in the South, and its complete disappearance in the North, soon created a sectional rivalry that eventually dwarfed all other topics of political disagreement. As the nation expanded westward, first through the Louisiana Purchase and then through the annexation of Texas, the acquisition of vast lands from Mexico, and the settlement of the Oregon dispute with Great Britain, competition arose between pro- and anti-slavery forces to settle these lands. Beginning in 1820, Congress crafted a series of compromises that kept a precise balance between slave and free states in the Senate. But the issue of the federal territories — that is, the western lands that would eventually become states — remained a fraught one, as both sides fought to establish the character of those territories as either friendly or unfriendly to slavery, with an eye toward those territories eventually becoming slave or free states.

In 1857, the Supreme Court handed down a case that virtually constitutionalized slavery in the territories. *Dred Scott v. Sandford*[140] involved the status of a slave living with his master in a free jurisdiction. In 1834, the slave, Dred Scott, accompanied his master, Dr. Emerson, from Missouri, a slave state, into Illinois, a free state, and later into a free territory, where Emerson, a member of the military, was stationed. Eventually, Emerson brought him back to Missouri, where Scott sued for his freedom, contending that he was a free man because he had resided in free territories.

After receiving an unfavorable decision in a Missouri federal court, Scott appealed to the United States Supreme Court. The Court addressed the threshold issue of

---

140. 60 U.S. (19 How.) 393 (1857).

whether a person who descended from African slaves could be a United States citizen. In an opinion by Chief Justice Roger Taney, the Court held that the drafters of the Constitution had not intended African-Americans, whether free or not, to be citizens of the United States or of any state. Accordingly, the federal courts did not have diversity jurisdiction over suits they might bring.

Despite this holding on jurisdiction, the Court went on to reach the merits question of whether Scott's sojourn in a free federal territory rendered him free. Chief Justice Taney stated that Scott could not have been freed by virtue of living in a free federal territory, because that would have meant that federal law (the territorial law) had deprived Emerson of his property in his slave. Thus, the Court concluded that the Missouri Compromise, the 1820 law that established the territory in question as free, violated the Fifth Amendment Due Process Clause by depriving slave owners of their property if they moved north of the line that law demarcated as the border between free and slave territories. More generally, this ruling meant that any federal attempt to prohibit slavery in any territory was unconstitutional. The Court then concluded that Scott's sojourn in Illinois, a free state, did not render him free, because he was taken there as a slave and then returned to Missouri, and that Missouri law governed his status.

Dred Scott remains one of the most tragic and heavily-criticized decisions in the history of the United States Supreme Court. Chief Justice Taney has been criticized for reaching out to decide the constitutionality of slavery in the territories, when resolution of that issue might not have been necessary to decide the case. (The matter is somewhat ambiguous, because it is not completely clear which of the other six justices who voted against Scott's claim agreed with Taney's analysis of the jurisdictional issue.) More generally, it is thought that Taney tried to use *Dred Scott* as a vehicle for conclusively settling the slavery issue, in favor of slaveholding interests. The fear that he had accomplished just that enraged many northerners and emboldened many southerners, and helped set the stage for the secession crisis of 1860–1861 and the Civil War. It also prompted Abraham Lincoln, as a politician, presidential candidate, and finally, President to call for understanding *Dred Scott* as not having fully settled the slavery issue. This more limited understanding of the effect of a Supreme Court constitutional decision has surfaced periodically in American constitutional history.[141]

[2] Government-Mandated Segregation

[a] "Separate but Equal"

Following the Civil War, the nation ratified the Thirteenth, Fourteenth, and Fifteenth Amendments. The Thirteenth Amendment prohibited slavery and involuntary servitude. The Fourteenth Amendment included, among other provisions, a citizenship clause that overruled *Dred Scott*[142] and guarantees against any state depriving

---

141. This issue is discussed in Section 2.03[2].

142. U.S. Const. amt. XIV, § 1, cl. 1 ("All persons born or naturalized in the United States, and subject to the jurisdiction thereof, are citizens of the United States and of the state wherein they reside.").

any citizen of the privileges and immunities of citizens of the United States, or denying any person the equal protection of the laws or life, liberty, or property without due process of law. The Fifteenth Amendment prohibited denying the right to vote based on race. All three amendments authorized Congress to enact legislation to "enforce" those provisions. In the first years of these amendments' lives, the Supreme Court sometimes upheld such enforcement legislation aimed at ensuring racial equality.[143] Often, however, the Court gave such laws either limited readings[144] or struck them down altogether as exceeding Congress's enforcement power.[145] With the end of Reconstruction in 1877, white supremacist forces regained control of southern governments and instituted a regime of racial segregation, which the Court upheld for nearly two generations.

The seminal case illustrating this latter development is *Plessy v. Ferguson*.[146] In *Plessy*, the Court upheld a Louisiana law mandating separate railroad cars for African-Americans and whites. The Court quickly rejected the plaintiff's Thirteenth Amendment argument, concluding that segregation could not be equated to the involuntary servitude that amendment prohibited. Turning to the Fourteenth Amendment, the Court concluded that that amendment did not aim at what the Court called "social" equality, and observed that segregation, most notably school segregation, had been practiced throughout the nation — indeed, the Congress that enacted the Fourteenth Amendment also provided for segregated schools in Washington, D.C.

Applying the then-dominant police-power approach to constitutional adjudication,[147] the Court conceded that all state laws had to be reasonable exercises of sovereign power. However, it concluded that laws reflecting local customs and usages were reasonable. Importantly, the Court also concluded that any message of racial inferiority perceived by African-Americans in the Louisiana law derived from their (*i.e.*, African-Americans') own construction of the law's meaning. In other words, the Court concluded that the state itself was not responsible for sending any message of racial inferiority by mandating the separation of African-Americans and whites. This latter conclusion would loom large when the Court struck down school segregation in 1954, in *Brown v. Board of Education*.[148]

In a famous dissent, Justice Harlan took a much broader view of the Fourteenth Amendment, arguing that it guaranteed a wider set of rights. He criticized the majority's formalistic reading of the Louisiana statute, under which the law imposed

---

143. *E.g.*, Strauder v. West Virginia, 100 U.S. 303 (1879) (upholding a law restricting racial discrimination in jury selection).

144. *E.g.*, Blyew v. United States, 80 U.S. 581 (1872) (giving a narrow reading to the category of persons who could remove cases to federal court when they could not enforce their federal rights in state court).

145. *E.g.*, The Civil Rights Cases, 109 U.S. 3 (1883) (striking down, as exceeding Congress's enforcement power, a law prohibiting racial discrimination in public accommodations). Congress's power to enforce the Civil War Amendments is discussed in Chapter 13.

146. 163 U.S. 537 (1896).

147. This approach is discussed in Section 10.01[1].

148. 347 U.S. 483 (1954).

equal burdens on both African-Americans and whites by keeping each group out of the cars reserved for the other. Instead, he argued that it was plain that the law reflected an attempt to keep Blacks out of spaces intended to be set aside for whites. According to Justice Harlan (himself a former slaveholder), "the real meaning" of the law was that African-Americans were "so inferior and degraded that they cannot be allowed to sit in public coaches occupied by white citizens."[149] He summarized his own view of the Fourteenth Amendment: "But in view of the constitution, in the eye of the law, there is in this country no superior, dominant, ruling class of citizens. There is no caste here. Our constitution is color-blind, and neither knows nor tolerates classes among citizens."[150] As will become clear, Justice Harlan's simultaneous focus on both the caste-creating characteristics of racial discrimination and the color-blindness principle has provided support to both sides of the argument about the constitutionality of race classifications, colloquially known as "affirmative action," that are defended as compensatory or otherwise benign.[151]

The majority opinion in *Plessy* introduced an era in which so-called "separate but equal" or "Jim Crow" laws became prevalent in the South (and in other parts of the nation) and were not subject to serious judicial challenge. For example, in 1927, the Supreme Court casually remarked that the constitutionality of racially-segregated education had been "many times decided" in its favor.[152] But starting in the 1930s, the litigation arm of the National Association for the Advancement of Colored People (NAACP) began challenging separate-but-equal. It began by challenging segregation at the graduate school level, on the theory that a segregating state's responsibility to provide equal (if separate) facilities to African-Americans would prove impossible to satisfy in the context of expensive, hard-to-replicate institutions such as graduate school programs. For example, in *Missouri ex rel. Gaines v. Canada*,[153] the Court struck down Missouri's practice of paying tuition for African-Americans to attend law school out of state rather than either allowing them to attend the University of Missouri Law School or establishing a law school for African-Americans. The Court was unmoved by the argument that a law school reserved for African-Americans would have a very small enrollment.[154]

A watershed case in the fight for racial equality was *Korematsu v. United States*.[155] *Korematsu* considered a challenge to the military's policy of removing U.S. citizens of Japanese descent from the west coast during World War II. The military defended

---

149. 163 U.S. at 560 (Harlan, J., dissenting).

150. *Id.* at 559.

151. The Court's affirmative action jurisprudence is discussed in Chapter 10.04[3].

152. Gong Lum v. Rice, 275 U.S. 78, 86 (1927).

153. 305 U.S. 337 (1938).

154. The Court had earlier intimidated that it would not accept a state argument of this sort, when it suggested in *dicta* that a state law mandating racial segregation in railroad cars meant that a railroad would have to offer first-class accommodations for African-Americans if they offered such accommodations to whites, despite the anticipated very low African-American demand for such accommodations. McCabe v. Atchison, Topeka, & Santa Fe R.R., 235 U.S. 151 (1914).

155. 323 U.S. 214 (1944).

the removal policy as a national security measure, and the Court, speaking through Justice Black, deferred to the military's judgment and upheld the policy. However, in doing so, the Court began its analysis by cautioning, for the first time in history, "that all legal restrictions which curtail the civil rights of a single racial group are immediately suspect. That is not to say that all such restrictions are unconstitutional. It is to say that courts must subject them to the most rigid scrutiny."[156] Thus, even though the Court upheld the race-based removal order, it went on record as announcing that it would be suspicious of laws that drew race lines.

Note that the Court referenced "legal restrictions *which curtail the civil rights* of a single racial group." The focus on race-based laws that deprive persons of substantive rights may have been necessary in light of the fact that the Fourteenth Amendment does not apply to the federal government, and that the Fifth Amendment, which *does* so apply, only prohibits the federal government from depriving persons of life, liberty, or property without due process of law. Eventually, the Court found that the Fifth Amendment's Due Process Clause contains an equality guarantee that mirrors that of the Equal Protection Clause.[157] However, the *Korematsu* Court may have felt the need to focus on civil rights, given the fact that the government actor in question was the federal government.

In addition to *Korematsu*'s statement presumptively condemning race classifications, in 1938, Justice Harlan Fiske Stone had suggested in Footnote 4 to his opinion in *United States v. Carolene Products* that "prejudice against discrete and insular minorities" might trigger political dysfunction that would justify heightened judicial scrutiny.[158] Thus, as the NAACP prepared its Supreme Court challenge to primary school segregation in the 1952–1953 term, the Court had a variety of doctrinal tools at its disposal if it wished to strike down school segregation in its entirety. Nevertheless, the Court deadlocked on the question, and ordered re-argument the following year. By then, a new Chief Justice, Earl Warren, had taken his seat, and had set about crafting an opinion by which the Court would unanimously strike down school segregation.

[b] Brown, *Its Implications, and Its Implementation*

[i] *Brown* and *Bolling*

In the landmark case of *Brown v. Board of Education*,[159] the Court rejected the apartheid system that *Plessy* sanctioned by striking down the doctrine of "separate but equal" in education. In *Brown*, Chief Justice Warren began by conceding that it was unclear what the drafters of the Fourteenth Amendment thought about segregated public education. But he dismissed that ambiguity in light of the changed importance

---

156. *Id.* at 216.
157. *See* Bolling v. Sharpe, 347 U.S. 497 (1954).
158. 304 U.S. 144, 152 n. 4 (1938).
159. 347 U.S. 483 (1954).

of education since 1868—in particular, the increased importance of public education to citizenship and full participation in American society.

Crucially, the Court concluded that segregation generated feelings of inferiority in African-American children that were detrimental to their education. Accordingly, the Court found that segregation in public education denied Black children equal educational opportunities. The Court explicitly rejected *Plessy v. Ferguson*'s conclusion about the message sent by segregation, writing as follows: "Whatever may have been the extent of psychological knowledge at the time of *Plessy v. Ferguson*, this finding [that school segregation induces feelings of inferiority in African-American children] is amply supported by modern authority."[160] Appended to that sentence was the famous "Footnote 11" to the Court's opinion, in which the Court supported its findings by citing a number of sociological and psychological studies.[161] Scholars have long debated whether the Court acted properly in basing its decision on those studies,[162] rather than, for example, relying on a simple but broad statement that any use of race to segregate is presumptively unconstitutional.

Brown is a crucial opinion for many reasons. First, it marked a decisive break with the Court's previous jurisprudence tolerating race discrimination. After *Brown* and for years thereafter, the Court would be an aggressive force combatting discrimination. Second, *Brown* committed the Court to a role for the federal courts in overseeing the desegregation the Court demanded in the follow up case, *Brown II*.[163] Lawyers and judges at the time were confident that the desegregation job could be accomplished relatively quickly; however, in reality, the job took decades and was never fully completed. Finally, *Brown* was the first major action of the Court as it was to be led over the next 15 years by Chief Justice Earl Warren. The Warren Court was notable for expanding constitutional rights across an entire array of areas—and triggering criticism for allegedly acting too aggressively.

In *Bolling v. Sharpe*,[164] the companion case to *Brown*, the Court applied *Brown* and the Equal Protection Clause generally to the federal government through the

---

160. *Id.* at 494.

161. Some of these studies involved researchers giving Black and white children dolls of different races and asking them which dolls they liked. The studies' results—both sets of children preferred white dolls—were said to demonstrate the effect of segregation on the self-esteem of Black children.

162. *See, e.g.*, H. Wechsler, *Toward Neutral Principles of Constitution Law*, 73 HARV. L. REV. 1, 32–33 (1959) ("The Court did not declare, as many wish it had, that the fourteenth amendment forbids all racial lines in legislation.... [The decision] must have rested on the view that racial segregation is, in principle, a denial of equality to the minority against whom it is directed.... But this position also presents problems."); L. Pollak, *Racial Discrimination and Judicial Integrity: A Reply to Professor Wechsler*, 108 U. PA. L. REV. 1, 33 (1959) ("judicial neutrality ... does not preclude the disciplined exercise by a Supreme Court Justice of that Justice's individual and strongly held philosophy"); C. Black, *The Lawfulness of the Segregation Decisions*, 69 YALE L.J. 421, 428 (1960) (A rationale for the school segregation cases can be stated more simply, "The fourteenth amendment commands equality, and segregation as we know it is inequality.").

163. Brown v. Board of Education, 349 U.S. 294 (1955).

164. 347 U.S. 497 (1954).

Due Process Clause of the Fifth Amendment. *Bolling* held that the District of Columbia's segregated schools violated the Fifth Amendment Due Process Clause. Since *Bolling*, the Court has never wavered from applying equal protection principles to the federal government, even though, as noted earlier, the Fifth Amendment contains no Equal Protection Clause and the Fourteenth Amendment applies only to the states. At times, the Court's application of equal protection principles against the federal government through the Due Process Clause has been termed "reverse incorporation."[165]

[ii] *Brown* and the Destruction of Jim Crow

For all its importance, *Brown* was nevertheless, at least on its face, an opinion limited to segregation in public education. Its focus on the effects segregation had on schoolchildren, and, indeed, its reliance on sociological evidence to support that point, suggested its limited relevance to the constitutionality of segregation in other aspects of government action. There may have been good reason for the Court's caution in confining *Brown* to education: the justices likely knew that ensuring desegregation of public schools would be challenging enough, without, in one blow, striking down official segregation in all its myriad aspects.

Despite this caution, the very year it decided *Brown*, the Court set about using that case to strike down segregation across most[166] of the rest of official government action. In a series of *per curiam* opinions,[167] the Court struck down segregation in parks, beaches, golf courses, busses, and, a few years later, in restaurants located on public property and courthouses.[168] Most of these opinions are exceptionally short, consisting of simply a statement of reversal or affirmance of the lower court decision, followed by case citations. The first of these cases, decided in 1954, simply cited

---

165. *See* B. Clark, *Judicial Review of Congressional Section Five Action: The Fallacy of Reverse Incorporation*, 84 Colum. L. Rev. 1969 (1984).

166. The caveat is necessary, because the Court did not strike down the last vestige of official segregation—bans on interracial marriages—until 1967. Loving v. Virginia, 388 U.S. 1 (1967). Indeed, when given a chance in 1956, the Court avoided an interracial marriage ban case from Virginia, and in the process, allowed the state courts arguably to flout the Supreme Court's authority. Naim v. Naim, 350 U.S. 985 (1956). For an explanation and criticism of *Naim*, see Gerald Gunther, *The Subtle Vices of the "Passive Virtues*," 64 Colum. L. Rev. 1, 11–12 (1964).

167. At the Supreme Court, the term "*per curiam*," or "by the court," means an opinion whose authorship is attributed to the entire Court, rather than a particular justice. Such opinions are usually, though not always, unanimous, and they usually signal the Court's view that the case is not particularly difficult such that a more detailed opinion by a particular justice is necessary. *But see, e.g.*, Buckley v. Valeo, 424 U.S. 1 (1976) (long, detailed, and controversial Supreme Court opinion, styled as a "*per curiam*").

168. Muir v. Louisville Park Theatrical Association, 347 U.S. 971 (1954) (parks); Mayor and City Council of Baltimore v. Dawson, 350 U.S. 877 (1955) (beaches); Holmes v. City of Atlanta, 350 U.S. 879 (1955) (golf courses); Gayle v. Browder, 352 U.S. 903 (1956) (city busses); New Orleans City Park Improvement Association v. Detiege, 358 U.S. 54 (1958) (parks); Turner v. City of Memphis, 369 U.S. 350 (1962) (restaurant within in an airport); Johnson v. Virginia, 373 U.S. 61 (1963) (courthouses).

Brown;[169] the later cases either cited no cases or the earlier cases in this series and *Brown*. By the last of these cases, decided in 1963, the Court could state confidently, on the bases of these opinions, that "it is no longer open to question that a State may not constitutionally require segregation of public facilities."[170]

The *per curiams* had the effect of dismantling the remainder of the official Jim Crow system, except for interracial marriage bans, which lingered until 1967.[171] But they were controversial, given their tenuous foundation in *Brown*, a case that, as discussed earlier, focused on the special context of education rather than the more general constitutional infirmity of race segregation.[172] Perhaps ultimately more importantly, the Court's use of these brief, unreasoned opinions to strike down segregation deprived it of an opportunity to explain *why* segregation was unconstitutional: was it simply because segregation laws employed race, or was it because they employed race in an oppressive way?

The Court did attempt to explain the problem with race classifications in its 1967 decision striking down interracial marriage bans. In *Loving v. Virginia*,[173] the Court at times seemed to embrace the idea that any use of race was presumptively unconstitutional and had to be subjected to the most rigorous scrutiny.[174] However, the Court also emphasized that Virginia's interracial marriage ban, by allowing non-whites to intermarry among any racial and ethnic group while banning intermarriage with whites, was a measure designed to promote the idea of White Supremacy.[175] Thus, even as confined within equal protection, the Court gave an ambivalent answer to the question of what exactly was unconstitutional about Jim Crow legislation. When one adds to that ambiguity the fact that *Loving* described marriage as a fundamental right,[176] it becomes clear that, as the Jim Crow era came to a close, the Court had failed to provide an unambiguous justification for its long and ultimately successful campaign to stamp out explicit, government-sponsored racial segregation.

In one sense, that failure is only a detail, given the results it achieved in the thirteen years between *Brown* and *Loving*. On the other hand, as the Court faced the future—and, in particular, the prospect of equal protection challenges to race classifications

---

169. *See Muir, supra.*

170. *Johnson*, 373 U.S. at 62.

171. As constitutional law decisions, the *per curiams* did not address themselves to private conduct, such as segregative practices in stores and other privately-owned locations. However, the Civil Rights Act of 1964, which outlawed racial discrimination in employment and public accommodations, accomplished much of that work. The public accommodations provisions of the Act were upheld against a Commerce Clause challenge in 1964. Those cases are discussed in Section 6.05[3].

172. For the classic critique of these opinions, see Herbert Wechsler, *Toward Neutral Principles of Constitutional Law*, 73 HARV. L. REV 1, 22–23 (1959).

173. 388 U.S. 1 (1967).

174. *See id.* at 11 ("At the very least, the Equal Protection Clause demands that racial classifications ... be subjected to the most rigid scrutiny").

175. *See ibid.* ("The fact that Virginia prohibits only interracial marriages involving white persons demonstrates that the racial classifications must stand on their own justification, as measures designed to maintain White Supremacy.").

176. *See ibid. Loving*'s focus on the fundamental right to marry is discussed in Section 9.04[4][b].

defended as compensatory or otherwise benign rather than segregative or oppressive—the Court lacked a full-blown theory that would allow it to address those issues. Its failure to set forth such a theory in the Jim Crow cases would cause future justices difficulty as they grappled with the constitutionality of the new generation of race-conscious legislation, which became colloquially known as "affirmative action." Before the affirmative action material is presented, however, it is important to consider the efforts made by the federal courts, led but also limited by the Supreme Court, to enforce *Brown*.

[iii] Enforcing *Brown*: The Fashioning and Implementation of Judicial Relief

The *Brown* Court was sensitive to the magnitude of the desegregation remedy the Court's opinion implied.[177] Thus, the Court ordered the parties to return to the Court the following year and brief the question of remedy. In *Brown II*,[178] the Court determined that proper implementation of desegregation remedies rested with the good faith efforts of local school authorities. Accordingly, the cases were remanded to the lower courts with instructions to fashion remedies using equitable principles, taking into account speed and the effective functioning of the schools during this massive undertaking. Despite this seeming latitude, the Court also stated that school authorities must make a prompt and reasonable start to desegregating their respective districts. Once such a start was made, the defendant school boards had the burden of establishing the necessity of additional time. Because the lower courts were closer to the problems, the Court gave them supervisory jurisdiction with broad-ranging equitable powers to secure desegregation with what the Court called "all deliberate speed."[179]

Soon, considerable resistance to *Brown* began to appear in the South. *Cooper v. Aaron*[180] involved an attempt by the State of Arkansas to defy *Brown*, including by having forces under the governor's control attempt to prevent the integration of the main high school in Little Rock. Eventually, a federal district court enjoined the Governor from obstructing the integration plan. When the Black students came to the school, however, large demonstrations began outside the building. As a result, President Eisenhower ordered federal troops to the school to protect the African-American students.

The Supreme Court unanimously rejected the school board's petition for a stay of the lower court's desegregation order. The decision, in an extraordinary and unprecedented gesture of solidarity and force, was signed by all nine Justices individually. In reply to claims by the Governor and the Legislature that the state, as a non-party in *Brown*, was not bound by that decision but that instead desegregation would have to await a lawsuit brought against the Little Rock district itself, the Court invoked

---

177. *See Bolling*, 347 U.S. at 490 n.4.
178. Brown v. Bd. of Educ., 349 U.S. 294 (1955).
179. *Id.* at 301.
180. 358 U.S. 1 (1958).

Marbury v. Madison[181] to emphasize that the Court's opinion in *Brown* was itself the Constitution, and thus required obedience by every state official in the nation.[182]

In subsequent cases, the Court started to define the types of remedies that would satisfy *Brown*. In *Goss v. Board of Education*,[183] it rejected a voluntary transfer program, concluding that it perpetuated segregation by only allowing a student to transfer from a school in which she was in the racial minority into one in which her race constituted the majority. A year after *Goss*, the Court stated that "the time for mere deliberate speed has run out."[184] In a major desegregation case decided in 1968, *Green v. County School Board*,[185] the Court rejected a "freedom of choice" plan in which students could choose their high school, which had resulted in every white student and the vast majority of African-American students choosing the school that had formerly been officially assigned to their race. Although such a voluntary choice scheme could be part of an overall desegregation plan, it alone was insufficient to comply with *Brown*. School boards that had operated state-compelled dual systems had "the affirmative duty to take whatever steps might be necessary to convert to a unitary system in which racial discrimination would be eliminated root and branch."[186]

In light of this impatience, it was not surprising that, in 1971, the Court decided a case in which it authorized lower courts to take sweeping actions to ensure desegregation. In *Swann v. Charlotte-Mecklenburg Board of Education*,[187] the Court held that, once a constitutional violation has been established, the district court is empowered to fashion a broad equitable remedy to correct past wrongs. Among other steps, lower courts were authorized to oversee not just decisions about student assignments but also faculty assignments, where to site new schools, allocation of funds for improve facilities, and, to some degree, bussing students from one area to another to achieve a set of racially balanced schools.

For many years, school desegregation focused on the South, where dual systems were often explicitly codified. However, in 1973, the Court focused its desegregation remedies on a non-Southern school district in *Keyes v. School District No. 1, Denver, Colorado*.[188] The school district in *Keyes* had never operated under a constitutional or statutory provision that explicitly mandated or permitted school segregation. Instead, plaintiffs alleged that the school board, by use of various techniques such as manipulation of student attendance zones, school-site selection, and a neighborhood school policy, had created or maintained racially or ethnically segregated schools throughout the district.

---

181. 5 U.S. (1 Cranch) 137 (1803).
182. *Cooper*'s claim of judicial supremacy in interpreting the Constitution is discussed in Section 2.03[2].
183. 373 U.S. 683 (1963).
184. Griffin v. County School Board of Prince Edward County, 377 U.S. 218, 234 (1964).
185. 391 U.S. 430 (1968).
186. *Id.* at 437–38.
187. 402 U.S. 1 (1971).
188. 413 U.S. 189 (1973).

The district court found that there had been intentional segregation in one part of the school district and therefore ordered desegregation of that area. The Supreme Court said that desegregation remedies were generally limited to the part of a district where plaintiffs proved intentional discrimination. However, if the plaintiffs proved that school authorities had carried out a systematic program of segregation affecting a "meaningful portion"[189] of students, schools, teachers, and facilities, a presumption arose of segregation throughout the district. This presumption shifted the burden onto the defendant school board to demonstrate that the district was divided into clearly unrelated segments and that the segregative policies in one unit did not cause *de facto* segregation in other units. If the school board could not make this showing, the district court could find an unconstitutional dual system and impose a duty to integrate schools throughout the district. Writing for the majority, Justice Brennan also stated that even if the school board proved that the district was divided into clearly unrelated segments, demonstrating intentional discrimination in one portion may be probative of intentional segregation in others.

Thus, under *Keyes*, in southern schools where segregation was statutory, the plaintiff effectively only had to prove effect, but in the North, where discrimination was more subtle, the plaintiff also had to prove segregative intent. Justice Powell, concurring in part and dissenting in part, criticized this *de jure/de facto* distinction, and suggested that a discriminatory impact test be used instead. He also criticized the use of large-scale bussing to remedy school segregation. Instead, he suggested drawing attendance zones and planning the construction of new schools in a way that increased integration. Justice Rehnquist's dissent stated that the majority had dramatically extended *Brown*. He criticized the use of presumptions to avoid difficult discriminatory intent findings.

In 1974, the Supreme Court began to limit judicial remedies for intentional segregation. In *Milliken v. Bradley*,[190] the Court refused to allow a district court to involve a suburban school district in a desegregation remedy when the lower court found that only the core urban district (in that case, the Detroit school district) had intentionally discriminated. The Court limited the district court's equitable power despite that lower court's findings that discrimination in the city district caused segregation in suburban districts and that remedies imposed upon the Detroit district would leave many of the district's schools 75–90 percent Black, which would further increase "white flight" into the suburbs. In addition to citing equitable principles limiting the imposition of judicial relief to parties found to have engaged in wrongdoing, Chief Justice Burger's opinion for five justices also stressed the history of local control of school districts, which he said would be threatened by a judicial remedy that combined a large number of independent districts into one for purposes of a desegregation remedy.

Justice White's dissent in *Milliken* cited the unchallenged finding of the district court that an intra-district desegregation plan was both more burdensome for many of Detroit's African-American children and more expensive than an inter-district

---

189. *Id.* at 208.
190. 418 U.S. 717 (1974).

remedy. Moreover, he cited the lower court's conclusion that an intra-district remedy would only aggravate the problems of white flight, thus increasing segregation in Detroit. Justice Marshall's dissent argued that the school board was simply an agent of the state. Because the state was responsible, an inter-district remedy should have been available. Justice Marshall predicted that under the majority opinion, metropolitan areas would be divided into separate entities, divided by race.

While *Milliken* placed geographic limits on school desegregation remedies, *Pasadena City Board of Education v. Spangler*[191] imposed temporal limits. In *Spangler*, the district court had ordered annual readjustments of attendance zones even after the school board had adopted a race-neutral student assignment plan. The Court held that once a school district had implemented such a plan, the district court could not retain its injunction in order to accommodate changes in the school population that were caused by population shifts rather than the segregative actions of school officials. In other words, the district court lacked authority to combat resegregation that was being caused by private choices rather than official action. Thus, while *Milliken* limited desegregative remedies to wrongdoing districts (rather than allowing inclusion of their suburban neighbors), *Spangler* limited the lifespan of judicial remedies by limiting the circumstances under which they could be extended.

Cases such as *Milliken* and *Spangler* made it clear that judicial remedies would not remain in place until they conclusively uprooted all the vestiges of prior segregated systems. Starting with *Board of Education of Oklahoma City v. Dowell*, the Court began speaking of desegregation "to the extent practicable."[192] In *Dowell*, the Court ruled that a district court could dissolve a desegregation order if it found that the school board had complied in good faith with the desegregation decree and that the vestiges of past *de jure* segregation had been eliminated "to the extent practicable."

The next year, in *Freeman v. Pitts*,[193] the Court stated that the judiciary should return the supervision of school districts to local school boards as quickly as possible, including partial returns of control over particular aspects of a district's operations. In determining whether a court should partially withdraw its supervision of some aspects of the district's operations, a court should consider whether the school district had fully complied with the part of the decree to be eliminated, and whether retaining control of those aspects would help compliance with other parts of the decree. In making such determinations, courts should afford particular weight to consistent good faith compliance.

In *Missouri v. Jenkins*,[194] the Court invalidated a lower court order commanding the state to fund salary increases and remedial "quality education" programs for the Kansas City, Missouri, School District (KCMSD). A federal district court found the state and the KCMSD liable for intra-district violations for operating a segregated school system within the KCMSD. In an effort to desegregate the KCMSD, the district

---

191. 427 U.S. 424 (1976).
192. 498 U.S. 237, 250 (1991).
193. 503 U.S. 467 (1992).
194. 515 U.S. 70 (1995).

court ordered a magnet school and capital improvements plan. The state claimed that the district court exceeded its authority in issuing that order.

Relying on *Dowell*, discussed earlier, the Court, speaking through Chief Justice Rehnquist, stated that the appropriate inquiry into the district court's remedies must evaluate whether they helped restore the victims of segregation to the position they would have occupied had such segregation not occurred. The Chief Justice found that magnet schools were a proper remedy when used to achieve desired results within the district found to have segregated. However, the district court's plan used magnet schools in order to attract students from outside the KCMSD. The Court rejected such lower court attempts to use magnet schools to circumvent the constitutional requirement limiting inter-district remedies to inter-district violations.

Concurring, Justice O'Connor maintained that inter-district remedies were appropriate when redressing inter-district violations or when intra-district violations had inter-district effects. In this case, she concluded, the district court's plan redressed neither type of violation. Also concurring, Justice Thomas protested what he believed was the idea implicit in the lower court's decision that schools that have become segregated due to private choices necessarily harm African-American students. Justice Thomas concluded that such an assumption presumed that African-American students were inferior.

Justice Souter dissented, joined by Justices Stevens, Ginsburg, and Breyer. Justice Souter argued that the *de jure* violations in the KCMSD produced the inter-district effects of citizens crossing district borders, which caused increased segregation in both the KCMSD and surrounding suburban districts. He also disputed the majority's assertion that a valid segregation remedy cannot be motivated by a desire to generate effects beyond the borders of the offending district. In a separate dissent, Justice Ginsburg objected to the swift curtailment of the desegregation remedy in a district that remained more than two-thirds Black.

The story of federal courts' attempts to implement *Brown* is, in part, not a story about constitutional law but instead one about the equitable powers of federal courts to refashion large and critical government institutions. But constitutional law looms large in this story. Concerns about state defiance of federal courts prompted many judicial statements about states' obligation to comply with *Brown* and, by extension, Supreme Court decisions more generally. At the same time, the federalism implications of federal court supervision of local school districts also played a role, both in *Brown II*'s embrace of the "all deliberate speed" desegregation formula and, much later, in the Court's insistence that lower courts consider ending their supervision of school districts even before the desegregation job was fully completed.

Of course, most fundamentally, the story of implementing (or not fully implementing) *Brown* concerns the vitality of the racial equality right the Court identified in that case. As Chief Justice Marshall recognized in *Marbury v. Madison*, the existence of a legal right requires the presence of a legal remedy.[195] If federal courts proved

---

195. *See* 5 U.S. (1 Cranch) 137, 163 (1803).

themselves incapable of fully implementing *Brown*, then it is fair to question the vitality of the decision itself. To be sure, other branches can also implement constitutional rights. Most notably, Congress possesses the power to "enforce" the Fourteenth Amendment.[196] President Eisenhower called out federal troops to ensure the integration of Central High School in Little Rock, Arkansas. But still, the incomplete judicial implementation of *Brown* raises questions about the status of constitutional rights when those rights require strong judicial measures to implement them—measures that require remaking large and complex institutions of state and local governments.

[3] Affirmative Action

With the final destruction of official Jim Crow in 1967,[197] the Court's attention soon turned to racial classifications designed to assist racial minorities. The Court took an abortive step toward considering this issue in a 1974 case, *DeFunis v. Odegaard*,[198] which involved a challenge to a state law school's race-based affirmative action plan. However, that case became moot when the law school, in response to a lower court order, admitted the white student-plaintiff and advised the Court that it would allow him to complete his studies regardless of any Supreme Court decision that otherwise would have approved of the affirmative action plan under which he was originally denied admission. It was not until 1978, in *Regents of the University of California v. Bakke*,[199] that the Court first spoke about the constitutionality of race-conscious government action defended as benign.

Perhaps ironically, the same well-known passage from an early race case reflects the two competing paradigms the Court has adopted in this area. In his dissenting opinion in *Plessy v. Ferguson*, the elder Justice Harlan stated:

> But in view of the constitution, in the eye of the law, there is in this country no superior, dominant, ruling class of citizens. There is no caste here. Our constitution is color-blind, and neither knows nor tolerates classes among citizens.[200]

One might read that passage's references to "caste" and a "dominant, ruling class of citizens" to mean that race classifications that did not promote such goals—for example, race-conscious action defended as ensuring truly equal access to a public benefit—would not conflict with the Constitution's aspirations. However, the very next sentence of the passage insists that the Constitution "is color-blind." That approach might treat skeptically *any* governmental use of race, adopted for *any* reason. This

---

196. Congress's enforcement power is discussed in Chapter 13.

197. *See* Loving v. Virginia, 388 U.S. 1 (1967) (invalidating laws prohibiting interracial marriages). *Loving*'s equal protection component is discussed in Section 10.04[2][b][ii] of this Chapter, and its due process component is discussed in Chapter 9.04[4][b].

198. 416 U.S. 312 (1974).

199. 438 U.S. 265 (1978).

200. 163 U.S. 537, 559 (1896) (Harlan, J., dissenting).

tension will reappear throughout the affirmative action cases, especially since Justice Harlan's dissent has come to be understood in a far more positive light than the majority opinion, with modern justices seeking to associate themselves with his opinion.[201]

This sub-section is split in four parts. Due to the importance of educational affirmative action, the first part examines that subject. The second part reviews affirmative action in government employment and contracting, before two final parts briefly consider race-based government action in primary education and then conclude. It is important to keep in mind a rough chronology of all these cases, because the Court's general shifts on affirmative action have impacted its attitudes toward affirmative action in the various contexts in which the issue arises. Thus, while this sub-section treats these topics distinctly—because, in fact, different principles govern them—one can track the Court's overall trends by remaining aware of when a given affirmative action case of any sort was decided. The first inquiry deals with education, however, because that was the subject of the justices' first important statement on affirmative action.

[a] Higher Education

Regents of the University of California v. Bakke[202] struck down the admissions policy operated by the medical school of the University of California at Davis, brought by a white applicant who had been denied admission. The program was designed to ensure the admission of a specified number of minority students who either asserted or were found to have an economic or educational disadvantage. The school maintained essentially two admissions programs, a general admissions process that aimed to fill 84 of the 100 seats in the class, and a special process for disadvantaged/minority students that sought to fill the remaining 16 slots.

Justice Powell wrote an opinion that, except for the facts and an important conclusion toward the end, spoke only for himself. But the last part of his opinion was joined by four other justices and thus spoke for a majority. That part of his opinion, speaking for the Court, concluded that a carefully-tailored program designed to create a diverse medical school class and that considered race as one diversity factor among others, could be constitutional. The four justices who agreed with that conclusion would have also upheld the Davis program on a broader ground. Justice Powell himself found that the Davis program did not satisfy the requirements he set out, and he voted to strike it down, along with the four justices who based their decision on a statutory ground. Thus, while a majority of the Court left open the possibility

---

201. *See, e.g.*, Parents Involved in Community Schools v. Seattle School Dist. No 1, 551 U.S. 701, 772 (2007) (Thomas, J., concurring) ("The dissent attempts to marginalize the notion of a colorblind Constitution by consigning it to me and Members of today's plurality. But I am quite comfortable in the company I keep. My view of the Constitution is Justice Harlan's view in *Plessy*: 'Our Constitution is color-blind, and neither knows nor tolerates classes among citizens.'") (quoting Justice Harlan's dissent).

202. 438 U.S. 265 (1978).

that a university could use race in its admissions, a different majority voted to strike down Davis's program, with four of those justices relying on a statutory ground and only Justice Powell voting to strike it down on constitutional grounds.

Even though race was an acknowledged factor in the school's selection process, the University argued that strict scrutiny was unwarranted, on the theory that the disadvantaged group, white persons, were not a "discrete and insular minority" as the Court had used that term in Footnote 4 of *United States v. Carolene Products*.[203] Writing at this point only for himself, Justice Powell responded that racial and ethnic distinctions were inherently suspect. He noted that the United States was a nation of minorities and concluded that the Court should not single out one racial or ethnic group as meriting special Fourteenth Amendment protection over others. Rather, he concluded, "Racial and ethnic distinctions of any sort are inherently suspect and thus call for the most exacting judicial examination."[204]

Justice Powell continued by questioning the workability of a rule that required courts to determine which groups should receive heightened scrutiny. He suggested that under such a rule, courts would have to evaluate the prejudice and harm a given minority group has suffered, and that as society evolved, courts would be required to reevaluate each group's judicial ranking. He characterized the resulting constitutional principle of equal protection as unstable and based on shifting social and political judgments, thereby undermining consistent construction of the Constitution over time.[205]

He then enumerated several policy reasons for rejecting racial preferences. First, he questioned the notion that racial preferences were always benign, as such preferences could impose burdens on individual members of an ethnic group to advance the interests of the group more generally. Second, he argued that racial preferences could force minorities to labor under the stereotype that they could not succeed without the preference. Third, he observed that racial preferences could burden innocent persons who did not create the harm.

Justice Powell then distinguished the Court's acceptance of preferential classifications in other contexts. For example, bussing and other remedies for school segregation were intended to redress a specific constitutional violation and were not allowed to exceed the scope of that violation. Similarly, employment discrimination remedies also focused on a particular defendant's discrimination against a class of workers, rather than the societal discrimination that underlay the university's argument.[206] He also discounted the Court's then-recent jurisprudence suggesting deferential review

---

203. 304 U.S. 144, 152 n.4 (1938). *Carolene Products* and its famous footnote are discussed in Section 10.01[2].

204. 438 U.S. at 291 (opinion of Powell, J.).

205. Justice Powell also stated that the political and sociological analysis required by such a scheme "simply does not lie within the judicial competence." *Id.* at 297.

206. Justice Powell noted that in the case before the Court, there was no finding of a specific constitutional violation by the university that might require or justify a race-conscious remedy.

of *sex*-based affirmative action programs, concluding that the sex context was different from race for both practical and historical reasons.[207]

Based on these considerations, he argued that for a program like the university's to be upheld it would have " 'show that its purpose or interest is both constitutionally permissible and substantial, and that its use of a classification is necessary ... to the accomplishment of its purpose or the safeguarding of its interest.' "[208] Justice Powell's approach has come to be understood as the application of strict scrutiny.[209]

The University posited four interests to justify its special admissions program. First, it sought to reduce "the historic deficit of traditionally disfavored minorities in medical schools and the medical profession."[210] Still writing for himself only, Justice Powell stated that if the purpose of the special admissions program was to guarantee a certain percentage of a particular minority within the student body, the purpose was the equivalent of preferring one group for the sake of race, which the Constitution prohibited.

Justice Powell also rejected the second asserted interest of curing societal discrimination suffered by particular minorities. He stated that the Court has never approved a classification that aided members of victimized groups at the expense of innocent people absent judicial, legislative, or administrative findings of specific discrimination. He rejected the third asserted purpose of promoting health care services for currently underserved communities on the ground that the record contained no evidence that the special admissions program would effectuate that goal, and that other admissions criteria, such as a stated career goal of serving such communities, could accomplish it at least equally as well.

Justice Powell did accept as compelling the fourth proffered interest, that a diverse student body encouraged a robust exchange of ideas. This argument implicated the university's First Amendment interest in freedom of speech, which encompassed the academic freedom that was implicit in its decisions about which students to admit. This argument allowed the Court to invoke a justification of constitutional magnitude in favor of some university consideration of race, rather than simply accepting that a university could choose the interests of one race over those of another. Moreover, this approach was flexible in not asserting an absolute preference for one group but an assortment of preferences to achieve diversity. Outside of the educational context, however, where the First Amendment interests were not so clearly at stake, this argument would likely not apply. Indeed, in practice, the diversity argument has not provided significant support for affirmative action in contexts other than higher education.[211]

---

207. The Court's review of those sex-based programs is discussed in Section 10.02[2].

208. *Id.* at 305 (quoting *In re* Griffiths, 413 U.S. 717, 721 (1973) (internal quotations omitted)).

209. *See, e.g.,* Grutter v. Bollinger, 539 U.S. 306 (2003). *Grutter* is discussed later in this subsection.

210. *Id.* at 306.

211. *Compare, e.g.,* Wygant v. Jackson Bd. of Educ., 476 U.S. 267 (1986) (rejecting a race-based layoff preference scheme for public school teachers that was justified on the ground that protecting

Although diversity was a compelling state interest, Justice Powell concluded that the university's separate admissions program was not a necessary means of achieving that end. That program focused solely on ethnic diversity. Justice Powell insisted that true diversity encompassed a wide range of characteristics, of which racial background was a single, albeit important, feature. Justice Powell identified the Harvard College admissions program as a likely acceptable method of achieving diversity. The Harvard program considered factors such as economic disadvantage, race, and ethnicity along with geographical location and special talents such as music and athletics in assessing potential contributions to the diversity of the university. The Harvard program emphasized that it did not impose a quota in connection with race, just as it did not impose a quota for football players. In addition, the weight attributed to a particular quality could vary from year to year, depending on the mix of applicants for the incoming class.

Again, though, the UC-Davis program was not like the Harvard program. Thus, despite Justice Powell's suggestion that a Harvard-style program would survive his understanding of what the Equal Protection Clause required, he voted to strike down the Davis plan. His vote, when combined with the votes of the four justices who voted to reject the Davis plan on statutory grounds, constituted a majority for striking the program down.

Justices Brennan, White, Marshall, and Blackmun each wrote separate opinions concurring in the judgment in part and dissenting in part.[212] These four justices disagreed with Justice Powell about the constitutionality of the Davis program and with his color-blind paradigm of the Constitution. Justice Brennan argued that the term "color-blind" could not be used to mask the use of race to disadvantage minority groups for over 200 years, a reality that had contemporary effects.

For the Brennan group, the classification in *Bakke* differed from traditional racial classifications because white persons did not exhibit any of the traditional indicia of suspect classes discussed in Footnote 4 of *Carolene Products*. Nevertheless, racial classifications, like those based on gender, had too often been used to stigmatize politically powerless segments of the society. Both classifications were also immutable. The Brennan group thus fashioned a two-part test to scrutinize affirmative action plans. The first prong applied the middle-tier scrutiny afforded to sex-based classifications: affirmative action programs must serve an important government interest and utilize means substantially related to achieving those interests. This formula would allow affirmative action programs to remove disparate racial impacts that were the product of specific past discrimination or of more general societal discrimination. The second prong of the Brennan group's test would require that affirmative action programs not stigmatize a group or single out those least represented in the political process

minority teachers from layoffs helped ensure that minority students had role models among the faculty).

212. Justice White's opinion focused on the statutory issue, but he joined Justice Brennan's discussion of the constitutional issue.

to bear the burden of the program. The hope was that this requirement would avoid both paternalistic stereotyping and the foisting of the costs of such programs on politically powerless non-minorities.

Applying the two-part test, the four-justice Brennan bloc would have upheld the Davis program. Justice Brennan argued that the program advanced the important government interest of addressing substantial and chronic societal discrimination and did not stigmatize any discrete group or individual—for example, it did not have the effect of demeaning Allan Bakke when it led to his rejection. Further, the plan imposed no ceiling on the number of minority admittees, and it used race in a reasonable manner considering the percentage of the beneficiaries of the Davis program relative to their representation in the population as a whole.[213]

While this group did not constitute a majority, those four justices joined the last, brief, part of Justice Powell's opinion (Part V-C), which stated that "the State has a substantial interest that legitimately may be served by a properly devised admissions program involving the competitive consideration of race and ethnic origin."[214] This statement, which left open the door for "a properly devised admissions program involving the competitive consideration of race and ethnic origin," constituted the opinion of the Court. As discussed immediately below, that sliver of an opening for race-based university affirmative action was endorsed by a majority of the Court a quarter-century later.

Bakke did not resolve what constitutional standard applied to affirmative action in education. Justice Powell applied one standard, the four-justice Brennan group applied another, and Justice Stevens' opinion for the remaining four justices did not reach the constitutional question. However, twenty-five years later, in *Grutter v. Bollinger*,[215] a majority adopted Justice Powell's analysis and his standard of review.

Grutter involved the admissions program followed by the University of Michigan Law School. After explicitly adopting Justice Powell's approach, the five-justice majority held that the law school's program satisfied strict scrutiny, because, like the Harvard plan Justice Powell had mentioned favorably, it entailed "a highly individualized, holistic review of each applicant's file, giving serious consideration to all the ways an applicant might contribute to a diverse educational environment."[216] Despite the Court's conclusion that the law school took various types of diversity into account, the Court emphasized in particular the importance of a racially diverse class to the

---

213. Justices White, Marshall, and Blackmun, the other members of this four-justice bloc, all wrote separate opinions as well. Justice White focused on the statutory issue on which the other four-justice bloc had focused. Justice Marshall's opinion focused on the history of discrimination against African-Americans and the constitutional and legal underpinnings of that discrimination. In his view, the Constitution should not be used as a barrier to undo the discrimination that it originally helped to effectuate. Analogizing affirmative action to desegregation, Justice Blackmun's short opinion characterized this remedy as an interim measure toward an integrated society.

214. 438 U.S. at 320 (opinion of the Court).

215. 539 U.S. 306 (2003).

216. *Id.* at 337.

law school's pedagogical goals, given the importance of legal education in training the next generation of American leaders. Indeed, the Court stated that "The Law School's judgment that [racial] diversity is essential to its educational mission is one to which we defer."[217]

The Court acknowledged that race-conscious government action, even when taken to promote a compelling government interest, must be narrowly tailored. However, the Court insisted that such strict scrutiny was not "strict in theory, but fatal in fact"[218]— in other words, it cautioned that strict scrutiny was not invariably fatal. Even more significantly, the Court rejected arguments that that law school could have attained its goals through less race-conscious measures. Instead, the Court stated: "Narrow tailoring does not require exhaustion of every conceivable race-neutral alternative." It concluded that the law school's program—for example, the "highly individualized, holistic review of each applicant's file"[219] recounted in the previous paragraph—satisfied the Court's narrow tailoring requirement. The Court ended its opinion by reflecting on the fact that 25 years had elapsed since *Bakke*. It suggested that, in another 25 years, the use of such race-conscious admissions policies would no longer be necessary.

Justice Ginsburg, joined by Justice Breyer, joined the majority opinion but wrote separately to note her caution about Justice O'Connor's 25-year forecast. All four dissenters (Chief Justice Rehnquist and Justices Scalia, Kennedy, and Thomas) wrote separate opinions, sometimes joined by other of the dissenters. A common thread was their dispute with the majority over whether in fact the law school's race preference reflected holistic review of individual candidates rather than a proportional system that was designed to admit particular percentages of a given minority group—the sort of quota Justice Powell rejected in *Bakke* and that the majority in *Grutter* purported to reject as well.

In a case decided the same day as *Grutter*, a different majority struck down the University of Michigan's undergraduate admissions policy. The Court's concern in *Gratz v. Bollinger*[220] was that the undergraduate admissions policy, which assigned point preferences for certain types of diversity, rendered that policy less than the individualized, holistic review the Court had held characterized the law school's admissions policy in *Grutter*. The Court also concluded that the size of the point preference for racial minorities (20 points on a scale that had a maximum score of 150) made race a decisive factor "for virtually every minimally qualified underrepresented minority applicant."[221] (By contrast, for example, an applicant would receive, at most, five points for artistic talent.)

The Court's final encounter to-date with educational affirmative action has centered on the University of Texas at Austin's undergraduate admissions program. That pro-

---

217. *Id.* at 328.
218. *Id.* at 326.
219. *Id.* at 339, 337.
220. 539 U.S. 244 (2003).
221. *Id.* at 272.

gram, like the programs in *Grutter* and *Gratz*, was defended as promoting the First Amendment-grounded goal of the university's academic freedom to select a class that promoted its pedagogical goals. That plan included a so-called "Ten Percent" provision, which guaranteed admission to the university's Austin campus to any student who graduated in the top 10 percent of their Texas public high school class. Even though it was facially race-neutral, Texas legislators adopted that plan with the clear intent of ensuring that Black and Latino Texas students, who were concentrated in predominantly Black and Latino high schools, would have a meaningful chance to attend the university. The rejected white applicant (Abigail Fisher) did not challenge the Ten Percent provision. Instead, she challenged the university's use of race beyond the Ten Percent plan, which the university defended as necessary to ensure an appropriate critical mass of minority students.

In the first of two cases challenging the university's program, *Fisher v. University of Texas* ("*Fisher I*"),[222] Justice Kennedy, writing for seven justices of an eight-justice Court,[223] agreed with the lower court that courts should defer to the university's expertise about its educational mission—here, its judgment that racial diversity was essential to that mission. However, he concluded that the court had inappropriately deferred to the university's judgment whether the means it adopted were narrowly tailored to achieve the goal of fulfilling that mission. Justice Ginsburg dissented, relying heavily on the fact that the Top Ten Percent plan, which the plaintiff did not challenge, was also enacted with race in mind.

On remand, the lower court upheld the university's plan. The Court affirmed that decision in *Fisher v. University of Texas* ("*Fisher II*").[224] Writing for a 4–3 majority,[225] Justice Kennedy concluded that the university's admissions plan satisfied strict scrutiny. He rejected Fisher's argument that the university had not specified its educational diversity goal more precisely, observing that to do so might result in the university adopting numerical goals for students of different races, a step that might itself violate the Fourteenth Amendment.

Justice Kennedy also upheld the means by which the university sought to achieve that goal. He rejected arguments that the Top Ten Percent plan already achieved a critical mass of minority students, citing both minority enrollment statistics and studies the university had done. He also rejected the plaintiff's argument that the small admissions effects of the race-based component of the university's admissions procedure rendered its use of race unconstitutional, concluding that that component had led to "meaningful, if still limited,"[226] increases in diversity. Finally, he rejected Fisher's argument that race-neutral means could have achieved the university's goals. In particular, in response to her suggestion that the university simply uncap the num-

---

222. 570 U.S. 297 (2013).

223. Justice Kagan did not participate.

224. 136 S. Ct. 2198 (2016).

225. Justice Kagan again did not participate, and Justice Scalia had died by the time the case was decided.

226. 136 S. Ct. at 2212.

ber of admissions offered through the Top Ten Percent plan, he quoted Justice Ginsburg's concurring opinion in *Fisher I* observing that that plan itself was motivated by race-consciousness.

Justice Alito, writing for the three dissenters, argued that the Court had applied a more deferential level of scrutiny than the strict scrutiny it had required the lower court to apply in *Fisher I*. Justice Thomas, writing for himself, called on the Court to overrule *Grutter*.

At present, it is fair to say that affirmative action in higher education stands on unstable ground. Large blocs of justices, while thus-far in the minority, have called for a stringent level of strict scrutiny to be applied to race-based university admissions programs, in contrast to what appears to be the more deferential variety of strict scrutiny applied in *Grutter* and perhaps in *Fisher II*. At the same time, the end of the 25-year time limit Justice O'Connor set in *Grutter* is starting to come into view. But more important than that, the addition Justice Gorsuch in 2017 and Justice Kavanaugh in 2018 may well herald the creation of a new majority that is more hostile to university affirmative action than were the Courts that featured Justice O'Connor or Justice Kennedy as the center, swing justice.

[b] Government Employment and Contracting

The term "affirmative action" appears to have originated in an executive order issued by President John F. Kennedy, which called for government contractors to take "affirmative action" to ensure equal employment opportunity. However, it was not until two years after the 1978 *Bakke* case discussed in the prior sub-section that the Court considered a constitutional challenge to an employment or contracting affirmative action program.[227] It took an additional decade before the Court settled on a standard of review for such programs.

In the first of these cases, *Fullilove v. Klutznick*,[228] the Court rejected a facial challenge to provisions of a federal public works law requiring state or local recipients of federal public works funds to spend at least ten percent of the funds on minority business enterprises (MBEs). While the Court upheld the plan on a 6–3 vote, the case produced a fractured response from the Court, with two opinions upholding the law, each speaking for three justices.

Writing one of those opinions, Chief Justice Burger upheld that set-aside program using the Commerce Power, the Spending Power, and Congress's power to enforce the Fourteenth Amendment.[229] The Chief Justice appeared to use a rationality standard in upholding the congressional purpose of eliminating barriers to minority access to

---

227. The year after *Bakke*, the Court upheld an affirmative action plan voluntarily agreed to by an employer and a union, against a claim that it violated federal employment non-discrimination law. Steelworkers v. Weber, 443 U.S. 193 (1979).

228. 448 U.S. 448 (1980).

229. Section 5 of the Fourteenth Amendment authorizes Congress to "enforce" the rest of the amendment. The enforcement power is discussed in Chapter 13.02.

public contracting funds. While he stated that the congressional means should be narrowly tailored, he exhibited considerable deference to Congress. Justices White and Powell joined Chief Justice Burger's opinion.

Consistent with his opinion in *Bakke*,[230] Justice Powell's concurrence upheld the challenged affirmative action program using strict scrutiny. Justice Marshall, joined by Justices Brennan and Blackmun, relied heavily on his views from *Bakke* to conclude that such race-based contracting set-asides are subject to intermediate scrutiny—that is, that they had to be substantially related to an important government interest. Three justices dissented. In his dissent, Justice Stewart, joined by Justice Rehnquist, cited Justice Harlan's dissent in *Plessy v. Ferguson*[231] as authority for a color-blind Constitution. Justice Stevens recognized in theory the legitimacy of race-based remedial legislation, but he criticized the imprecision of the racial lines the challenged legislation drew.

The next two affirmative action cases after *Fullilove*, decided in 1986 and 1987, considered contexts other than contracting. However, they reflected the Court's continued inability to coalesce around a standard governing challenges to affirmative action plans.

Wygant v. Jackson Board of Education[232] involved a layoff scheme designed to protect minorities by laying off some non-minority teachers with greater seniority before laying off minority teachers with less seniority. Writing for a four-justice plurality, Justice Powell concluded that the layoff provision was not narrowly tailored to serve a compelling state interest. The plurality refused to uphold the plan on the ground that it aimed at remedying societal discrimination—a justification the Court held was inappropriately broad. Instead, that justification required some discrimination by the governmental unit involved in the affirmative action plan. The plurality also rejected the rationale of providing minority teachers as role models for minority students. According to Justice Powell, such a rationale extended far beyond any legitimate remedial purpose and had no logical stopping point before it reached the race-based educational systems rejected in *Brown v. Board of Education*.

In her concurrence, Justice O'Connor argued that school districts need not be required to make specific findings that they had engaged in racial discrimination as a predicate to taking race-conscious action. She agreed, however, that the district had not articulated a constitutionally-sufficient justification for the race-conscious layoff plan. Justice White's concurrence focused heavily on what he perceived as the similarity between the challenged layoff plan and a plan that simply laid off white employees in order to make room for Black employees until a particular racial balance was achieved. In his view, the latter plan would be a clear violation of equal protection, and thus, by extension, the former one would be as well.

Justice Marshall's dissent, joined by Justices Brennan and Blackmun, emphasized that the affirmative action plan at issue had been the product of collective bargaining.

---

230. The *Bakke* case, dealing with university admissions affirmative action, is discussed in the previous sub-section.
231. 163 U.S. 537, 552 (1896) (Harlan J., dissenting).
232. 476 U.S. 267 (1986).

He also maintained that nothing was sacrosanct about a seniority system, noting that *United Steelworkers v. Weber*[233] had approved a collective bargaining agreement altering a seniority system for promotion. Resembling Justice Powell's analysis in *Bakke*, Justice Stevens' dissent emphasized the important public purpose of maintaining an ethnically diverse faculty that can better reflect the diversity of the nation as a whole.

The next year, in *United States v. Paradise*,[234] the Court upheld a court-ordered hiring scheme requiring that Alabama hire one qualified Black state trooper for every white state trooper hired until 25 percent of the force was Black. This remedy followed a finding that the Alabama Department of Public Safety had systematically excluded Blacks from employment as state troopers, and after the Department's implementation of previous consent orders had not remedied the past discrimination.

Writing for a four-justice plurality, Justice Brennan acknowledged the lack of consensus on the Court about the appropriate standard of review to be applied to such an order, but found that the program would meet even the most stringent test. He emphasized that the remedy was imposed only after the Department's consistent history of failure to comply with the district court's prior remedial orders, and that it applied only if there were qualified African-Americans in the applicant pool. Moreover, the remedy was temporary, focused, and did not involve layoffs. Justice Brennan stated that appellate courts should afford deference to district courts in fashioning relief of this sort.

Justice Powell concurred, characterizing the relief as narrow, fair, and flexible. Justice Stevens concurred in the judgment, analogizing the court order in the case to those issued by courts in school desegregation cases. Writing for three dissenters, Justice O'Connor concluded that the order was not sufficiently narrowly tailored to remedy the discrimination the court had found. The fourth dissenter, Justice White, largely agreed with Justice O'Connor's analysis, concluding that the district court had exceeded its equitable powers when it issued the challenged order.

Two years after *Paradise*, and nine years after *Fullilove*, in *City of Richmond v. J.A. Croson Co.*,[235] the Court was able to assemble a (narrow) majority position on the question of affirmative action in government contracting. In *Croson*, the Court invalidated a Richmond, Virginia requirement that prime contractors working for the city award 30 percent of their subcontracts to minority contractors.

Writing at this point for only four justices, Justice O'Connor concluded that the state had to demonstrate that the program served remedial purposes rather than "illegitimate notions of racial inferiority or simple racial politics."[236] The means had to be closely tailored to advancing this goal as to eliminate any inference of such an illegitimate purpose. That same plurality also noted that African-Americans occupied five of the nine seats on the Richmond City Council. Under a *Carolene Products* Foot-

---

233. 443 U.S. 193 (1979).
234. 480 U.S. 149 (1987).
235. 488 U.S. 469 (1989).
236. *Id.* at 493 (plurality opinion).

note 4-type analysis, this fact reinforced the necessity for strict scrutiny, because, on the plurality's view, the City Council's racial make-up indicated that white persons disadvantaged by the program constituted a political minority in city government.

Speaking now for a five-justice majority, Justice O'Connor applied strict scrutiny to the affirmative action plan. Applying that scrutiny, the Court found that the factual findings of the Richmond City Council did not establish a compelling purpose of remedying past discrimination in the Richmond contracting industry. According to the Court, neither conclusory recitations of past discrimination nor of a remedial purpose justified the 30 percent quota. While the city did find that minorities comprised 50 percent of its population yet received only 0.67 percent of its prime contracts, the Court was unwilling to infer from that statistic the existence of race discrimination that justified a race-based remedy.

The majority also concluded that any remedial purpose was further undercut by the gross over-inclusiveness of the program. First, it noted that that the program extended beyond African-Americans to include Aleuts, Asians, Indians, and Spanish-speaking people for whom Richmond had not even attempted to make findings of past discrimination. Indeed, there was no evidence that members of some of these groups had ever resided in Richmond. Second, the majority noted that the city did not consider race-neutral means to accomplish this goal. Third, it noted that 30 percent comprised a rigid numerical quota based on assumptions that minorities would choose certain jobs in proportion to their representation in the population.

Speaking again only for four justices, Justice O'Connor afforded guidance regarding what steps state and local governments had to take in formulating appropriate plans. Findings necessary to underpin an affirmative action plan included (1) direct evidence that nonminority contractors had systematically excluded minority contractors; (2) significant statistical differences between the number of qualified minority contractors available and interested in performing a particular service and the number actually doing work; or (3) individual instances of discrimination supported by statistical proof. It added that individual instances standing alone support individual remedies rather than a broader affirmative action plan.

Even when appropriate findings existed, the plurality cautioned that an affirmative action plan should be proposed only "in the extreme case."[237] The state or local government should first attempt to remedy the problem through anti-discrimination legislation or race-neutral measures, such as helping to finance small businesses, a step that could assist many minority businesses. Finally, any plan should be a temporary measure tailored in duration and scope to the injury described by the government's findings.

Still writing only for a plurality, Justice O'Connor distinguished *Fullilove* on the ground that the plan upheld in that case emanated from the federal government, which has a special power to enact race-conscious remedies for discrimination under

---

237. *Id.* at 509 (plurality opinion).

Congress's Fourteenth Amendment enforcement power. Later in the opinion, writing at that point for a majority, she also noted that the plan upheld in *Fullilove* featured some flexibility that the Richmond plan did not.

Justice Stevens filed a separate opinion concurring in part and concurring in the judgment, in which he disagreed that findings of past discrimination were always necessary to institute an affirmative action plan. Instead, he focused on the imperfections and overbroad generalizations he discerned in the Richmond plan. Concurring in the judgment, Justices Scalia and Kennedy, each writing separately, broadly condemned all affirmative action plans, embracing instead a color-blind interpretation of the Equal Protection Clause.

Dissenting, Justice Marshall, joined by Justices Brennan and Blackmun, criticized the majority for disaggregating the City's factual findings supporting its set-aside plan, rather than considering them together. He also noted that the City had modeled its 30 percent figure on the federal program upheld in *Fullilove*, observing that that figure fell roughly halfway between the percentage of minority contractors and the percentage of minorities in Richmond's population. Justice Marshall was also troubled by Justice O'Connor's emphasis on the fact that minority groups controlled Richmond city government. He found it "insulting" to apply strict scrutiny on the basis that minorities controlled the government.[238]

The next year, in *Metro Broadcasting, Inc. v. FCC*,[239] a majority of the Court afforded Congress considerable authority to enact affirmative action programs. *Metro Broadcasting* upheld two affirmative action rules of the FCC. The first enhanced the positions of groups with some active minority ownership in the competition for broadcast licenses. This policy deemed minority ownership a plus among six other race-neutral factors in allocating broadcast licenses. The second policy allowed "distress sale" stations to be assigned only to FCC-approved enterprises with over 50 percent minority ownership before any competitive process took place.

Writing for a 5–4 majority (the three *Croson* dissenters plus Justices White and Stevens), Justice Brennan relied on the plurality's test in *Fullilove* to apply middle-tier scrutiny to race-conscious rules fashioned by Congress. In *Metro Broadcasting*, the important government objective was promoting diversity in programming. Somewhat akin to Justice Powell's reliance in *Bakke* on the university's academic freedom-based interest in how it selected its students, this interest also had at least some foundation in the First Amendment.

The majority concluded that the FCC's race-based policies were substantially related to achieving this important objective. Congress found severe under-representation of minorities in the broadcast media. Both Congress and the FCC found a relationship between minority ownership and programming diversity. While the Court did not simply defer to this judgment, it gave "great weight" to Congress and the FCC in re-

---

238. *Id.* at 555 (Marshall, J., dissenting).
239. 497 U.S. 547 (1990).

solving such empirical questions.[240] In addition, the policies at issue did not stereotype, for example, in assuming that a discrete category of programming appealed to minority audiences. Congress also limited the plans' duration by appropriating money for limited periods and holding annual hearings to reevaluate it. Finally, the burdens on non-minorities were slight: one policy merely allocated a plus in the multi-factor selection process while the other gave an absolute preference only in the area of distress sales that had accounted for 0.4 percent of all broadcast sales since 1979. Concurring, Justice Stevens emphasized the plan's relationship to the legitimate objective of broadcast diversity. He concluded that pursuing this objective did not stigmatize favored or disfavored ethnic groups.

In a dissent joined by three other Justices, Justice O'Connor relied on *Croson* to apply strict scrutiny. She distinguished *Fullilove* on the ground that the statute in *Metro Broadcasting*, while a federal law, did not involve an exercise of Congress's power to enforce the Fourteenth Amendment. Nor did Congress fashion these measures to remedy specific discrimination. She also questioned the validity of the broadcast diversity rationale, observing that its status as a First Amendment value was, at best, unsettled. At any rate, she insisted that the law was not narrowly tailored to advance this objective, because the policies stereotypically assumed a strong nexus between race and particular programming viewpoints. Finally, the measures imposed considerable burdens on non-minority groups. The burden was particularly strong in distress sales, as the plan created an exclusive market available only to minorities, but even the licensing enhancement was a strong factor that could be pivotal in a competitive market. Justice Kennedy filed a separate dissent, broadly criticizing benign classifications as stigmatizing their beneficiaries and fostering intolerance among disfavored classes.

Five years later, the Supreme Court overruled *Metro Broadcasting* in *Adarand Constructors, Inc. v. Pena*.[241] Writing for a 5–4 majority, Justice O'Connor extended strict scrutiny to a race-based affirmative action program established by the federal government. The federal program sought to award at least five percent of federal prime and sub-contracts to businesses that were at least 51 percent owned by "socially and economically disadvantaged"[242] individuals. Under the Act, Black, Hispanic, Asian Pacific, Asian Subcontinent, Native American, and other groups designated by the Small Business Administration enjoyed a presumption of disadvantage which others had to establish by clear and convincing evidence.

According to the majority, the Court's adoption of an intermediate scrutiny standard for federal racial classifications in *Metro Broadcasting* conflicted with prior precedent such as *Croson*. Given her insistence that federal and state race-based set-asides be judged by the same standard, Justice O'Connor applied strict scrutiny notwithstanding Congress's special power to enforce the Equal Protection Clause. The Court

---

240. *Id.* at 569.
241. 515 U.S. 200 (1995).
242. *Id.* at 205.

also overruled *Fullilove v. Klutznick* insofar as *Fullilove* subjected federal racial classifications to less rigorous standards than strict scrutiny. The Court did not decide, however, whether the *Fullilove* program would have survived strict scrutiny. Indeed, the Court was confident that the strict scrutiny standard would not invalidate all governmental affirmative action, with Justice O'Connor writing, "we wish to dispel the notion that strict scrutiny is 'strict in theory, but fatal in fact.'"[243] The Court remanded the case for review of whether the program at issue satisfied that test.

Justice Stevens dissented, joined by Justice Ginsburg. He believed that a lesser level of scrutiny should apply to programs that benefit historically oppressed groups than to programs that perpetuate such oppression. Justice Stevens would also afford greater deference to federal programs designed to promote equality than he would afford to state programs. Justice Souter also dissented, joined by Justices Ginsburg and Breyer. Justice Souter argued that the Court should have upheld the program based on the *Fullilove* precedent; he also argued that the Court had left unresolved the scope of Congress' authority to enact race-based measures as part of its Fourteenth Amendment enforcement power. Justice Ginsburg wrote a separate dissent, joined by Justice Breyer. She would have left improving the program at issue to the political branches.

[c] *Primary and Secondary Education*

The final context for considering race-based government action is primary and secondary education. This context is distinct from both higher education and employment and contracting, given its particular factual circumstances, which in turn have triggered the government's assertion of different interests in justifying its use of race.

In *Parents Involved v. Seattle School Dist. No. 1*,[244] the Court struck down student-assignment plans at the kindergarten and primary school levels. In order to promote classroom settings where students could experience students of different races, the Seattle and Louisville, Kentucky school districts instituted plans that used the race of a student as a tie-breaker when assigning young students to particular schools. The Court struck down the districts' uses of race. Writing for a five-justice majority, Chief Justice Roberts observed that the Seattle district had never been adjudged guilty of racial segregation (although it had been accused of doing so, and had settled a lawsuit making such an allegation), and that Louisville, while having been so adjudged, had been released from the court's desegregation decree with the court having found that the district had desegregated "to the greatest extent practicable."[245] Thus, he wrote, the districts could not rely on the argument that the districts' use of race was necessary to remedy unconstitutional discrimination.

Nor could the districts' use of race survive on any other basis. Perhaps unsurprisingly, given the young ages of the students involved, the Court noted the absence of

---

243. *Id.* at 237.
244. 551 U.S. 701 (2007).
245. *Id.* at 716.

any claim that such use of race was necessary in order to create the free speech/ academic freedom-grounded educational diversity Justice Powell had endorsed in *Bakke* and the Court had endorsed in *Grutter*. Without considering whether other possible justifications were legitimate, the majority noted that the Seattle and Louisville plans failed because, perhaps ironically, they used race so sparingly that the districts' use of race would be expected to have very little beneficial effect on any goal the districts might assert. One might be tempted to characterize this reasoning as a suggestion that the districts might have prevailed had they used race more aggressively. But perhaps the best reading of the majority is as cautioning that uses of race that had very little beneficial effect would be understood almost as gratuitous uses of race, and on that ground constitutionally impermissible.

Justice Kennedy provided the fifth vote, and while he joined the analysis discussed in the paragraph above, he did not join other parts of the Court's opinion. Most notably, he suggested, *contra* the part of the Chief Justice's position that lacked Kennedy's vote and was thus was only a plurality, that districts could legitimately work to ensure racial balance in schools, in order to encourage a diverse student body. But Justice Kennedy insisted that such efforts not themselves allocate educational opportunity by race. Thus, for example, a school district could make decisions such as drawing school attendance zones with attention to racial demographics, as long as it did not actually assign individual students to particular schools based on the student's race.

Dissenting for four justices, Justice Breyer cited the inclusive local decision-making that had gone into the districts' attendance policies and urged that such good-faith local efforts to integrate schools not be subject to such skeptical judicial review. He questioned the majority's insistence that voluntary integration efforts of the sort the majority struck down were meaningfully different from the judicially-compelled desegregation efforts the Court had upheld in the wake of *Brown*.[246]

A remarkable aspect of *Parents Involved* is the debate among the justices about which side was more faithful to *Brown v. Board of Education*. Both Justice Breyer's and Justice Stevens' dissents sharply attacked the idea that the districts' conduct in these cases was analogous to the exclusionary segregation practiced by the districts in *Brown*. By contrast, both Chief Justice Roberts' majority and Justice Thomas's concurrence insisted that their side was more faithful to the civil rights litigators' argument in *Brown* that the Fourteenth Amendment prohibited any use of race in assigning students to schools. Yet again, *Brown*, and what it means, cast a long shadow over the Court's race jurisprudence.

[d] Concluding Thoughts about Affirmative Action

The cases discussed above reflect the justices' sharp disagreements on the constitutionality of affirmative action. The arguments reflect foundational concerns. On the one hand, opponents of the constitutionality of such programs rely on the fun-

---

246. The Court's jurisprudence dealing with desegregation remedies is discussed in Section 10.04[2][b][iii].

damentally problematic nature of race-based government decision-making, the potential for its overbroad use, and the Fourteenth Amendment's commitment to equal government treatment based on race. On the other hand, those who believe in the constitutionality of race-based affirmative action point to the lengthy history of racial discrimination in the United States, which in their view justifies carefully-drawn remedial measures that are themselves conscious of race. This view is reflected in Justice Blackmun's candid statement in *Bakke* that "In order to get beyond racism, we must first take account of race. There is no other way. And in order to treat some persons equally, we must treat them differently."[247] Those proponents also observe that the Reconstruction Congresses enacted a variety of race-based legislation designed to assist newly-freed slaves and African-Americans more generally.

Bakke preserved a sliver of a justification for affirmative action in the higher education context, via the student body diversity rationale Justice Powell endorsed and the *Grutter* majority later adopted. That justification remains confined to higher education admissions, however, and has provided no support for affirmative action in other contexts. In those other contexts, cases such as *Croson* and *Parents Involved* make it clear that, at least under current law, discrimination remediation and other rationales will be subject to careful judicial scrutiny. For example, plans defended as remedying past discrimination will be reviewed carefully to ensure that that rationale does not flower into a justification for a broad use of race to combat general societal discrimination.

The debate over the constitutionality of race-based affirmative action is not likely to end soon, even if a particular point of view happens to gain a temporary ascendancy at the Court. The persistence of current discrimination and the effects of past discrimination will continue to trigger calls for race-conscious government action in response. In turn, those responses will generate legal challenges. Those challengers will force the Court to continue to confront the foundational question whether the spirit of Justice Harlan's dissent in *Plessy* is one of a color-blind Constitution or, rather, a Constitution that tolerates race-consciousness undertaken in the pursuit of eradicating any vestige of previous racial caste systems and ensuring equal opportunity.

§ 10.05 The Intent Requirement

Courts apply the level of scrutiny appropriate for a particular classification (for example, strict scrutiny for a race classification) only if there is indeed a race classification in issue. In many cases, that threshold requirement does not pose difficult questions: for example, a law that explicitly requires Black schoolchildren to attend one school and white schoolchildren to attend another constitutes a facial race classification and would be subject to strict scrutiny. But sometimes the government's

---

247. 438 U.S. 265, 407 (1978) (opinion of Blackmun, J.).

use of race—or any other classification tool—is not obvious from the face of the law or the government action. In such cases, courts require the plaintiff to show that the government's action reflected an intent to discriminate. This requirement applies throughout equal protection—that is, the plaintiff must establish discriminatory intent anytime a plaintiff alleges that government has discriminated on grounds not explicit on the face of the government action.

The first sub-section below examines the basic doctrine of discriminatory intent. Subsequent sub-sections consider the precursors of the modern rule (Section 10.05[2]), special contexts that might require special applications of the rule (Section 10.05[3]), and, finally, the policy arguments about an intent requirement (Section 10.05[4]).

[1] The Basic Doctrine

The Court formally announced the intent requirement in 1976, in *Washington v. Davis*.[248] In *Davis*, African-American police academy applicants who scored low on a communications test and thus were rejected for entrance into the academy sued, alleging that the test constituted unconstitutional race discrimination. The foundation of their claim was that African-American applicants failed the test at a higher rate than white applicants.

The Court rejected their argument, concluding that they had not made out a claim of unconstitutional race discrimination, because they had not shown intentional race discrimination. The Court based its conclusion on its caselaw, which it conceded was ambivalent but which it read as ultimately rejecting the proposition that mere disparate impact based on a certain characteristic sufficed to state a claim of unconstitutional discrimination based on that characteristic. The Court cautioned that this did not mean that any discrimination claim had to feature government use of the alleged unconstitutional characteristic on its face. Rather, a law would still, for example, be considered "racially discriminatory" even if it was neutrally-worded, as long as a court could discern a racially discriminatory intention underlying it. Disparate impact was relevant to that intent inquiry: as the Court said, "an invidious discriminatory purpose may often be inferred from the totality of the relevant facts, including the fact, if it is true, that the law bears more heavily on one race than another." Thus, disparate impact remained relevant to the discriminatory intent inquiry, even if it did not by itself make out a claim of discrimination.

Confronting the intent/impact question directly, the Court then stated that it was hard to see how the *Davis* plaintiffs could claim race discrimination simply because other African-Americans had failed the facially-neutral test in a greater proportion than white applicants. Echoing the Court's description in other cases of equal protection rights as personal rights, the Court stated that the fact that other African-Americans had failed the test did not establish that the *Davis* plaintiffs "individually"

---

248. 426 U.S. 229 (1976).

had suffered racial discrimination.[249] Viewing the situation more broadly, the Court suggested that the government was acting appropriately—that is, in a non-intentionally discriminatory way—in seeking to ensure that police officers possessed reasonable verbal communication skills of the sort evaluated by the test. It concluded by warning that adoption of an impact test for identifying discrimination would subject to strict scrutiny a whole range of government laws that discriminated based on wealth and income, which the Court noted were correlated with race. It suggested instead that adoption of an effects test in any given context was a decision best left to Congress.

Davis' analysis implied that contextual factors—such as the extent of the disparate impact of the government action and the extent to which it appeared to be promoting an interest the government could legitimately pursue—might be relevant to the intent inquiry. In *Village of Arlington Heights v. Metropolitan Housing Development Corporation*,[250] the Court set forth a set of factors that it identified as relevant to the discriminatory intent inquiry. First, it acknowledged that the extent of the disparate impact was relevant, observing that "[s]ometimes a clear pattern, unexplainable on grounds other than race, emerges from the effect of the state action even when the governing legislation appears neutral on its face."[251] Other factors included the historical background of the decision, the specific sequence of events leading up to the challenged decision, a sudden substantive deviation or deviation from normal decisional processes, and the legislative or administrative history of the action (that is, the existence of statements by decision-makers revealing the alleged intent).

The Court suggested that it was the plaintiff's burden, using these factors, to show that the alleged intent (*e.g.*, to classify on the basis of race) was *a* factor motivating the decision. If the plaintiff succeeds in making that showing, the burden then shifts to the defendant to show that, despite the existence of the alleged ground as a factor motivating its decision, it would have made the same decision even had that alleged ground not been present as a motivating factor.[252]

The Court added an additional component to its discriminatory intent jurisprudence two years later, in *Personnel Administrator v. Feeney*.[253] *Feeney* considered whether the State of Massachusetts discriminated against women when it provided a point bonus to applicants for certain state civil service positions if the applicant was a veteran. The plaintiff claimed that the veterans bonus constituted sex discrimination, because the vast discrepancy between the number of male and female veterans meant that, in practice, the bonus benefitted far more men than women.

The Court rejected the argument. Writing for seven justices, Justice Stewart concluded that the veteran/non-veteran distinction could not be reasonably understood

---

249. *Id.* at 246.
250. 429 U.S. 252 (1977).
251. *Id.* at 266.
252. *See id.* at 270 n.21.
253. 442 U.S. 256 (1979).

as a covert sex classification, despite its sex-based disparate impact. He noted that the state's veterans preference had always been sex-neutral, and he rejected the plaintiff's argument that the lifetime duration of the preference and its impact on women's job opportunities in the state civil service necessarily required a conclusion that the sex-based impact was intentional. Importantly, he explained that discriminatory intent implies not just intent as volition or awareness of the likely consequences of the action, but instead "implies that the decisionmaker, in this case a state legislature, selected or reaffirmed a particular course of action at least in part 'because of,' not merely 'in spite of,' its adverse effects upon an identifiable group."[254] Thus, the foreseeability of any disparate impact does not suffice to make out a claim of intentional discrimination. However, he appended to that quoted phrase a footnote that reads as follows:

> This is not to say that the inevitability or foreseeability of consequences of a neutral rule has no bearing upon the existence of discriminatory intent. Certainly, when the adverse consequences of a law upon an identifiable group are as inevitable as the gender-based consequences of [the challenged state law], a strong inference that the adverse effects were desired can reasonably be drawn. But in this inquiry—made as it is under the Constitution—an inference is a working tool, not a synonym for proof. When, as here, the impact is essentially an unavoidable consequence of a legislative policy that has in itself always been deemed to be legitimate, and when, as here, the statutory history and all of the available evidence affirmatively demonstrate the opposite, the inference simply fails to ripen into proof.[255]

Justice Stevens, joined by Justice White, concurred, to suggest that the impact/intent distinction was not as sharp as the Court's language might suggest. He agreed with the majority's result, though, because he noted that the veterans preference disadvantaged large numbers of males as well as females (indeed, in numbers that were relatively close to each other). Justice Marshall, joined by Justice Brennan, dissented, arguing that the structure of the veterans preference—in particular, its inapplicability to civil service jobs traditionally held by women—was enough to justify a finding of intentional sex discrimination.

[2] Precursors to the Modern Rule

As Justice White noted in *Washington v. Davis*, the Court had previously decided cases that bore on the intent question, even if those cases did not definitively resolve it. One of the earliest and most famous examples is *Yick Wo v. Hopkins*.[256] *Yick Wo* involved a San Francisco ordinance that required laundries to be located in brick or stone buildings (to reduce the chance of fire) unless the proprietor obtained a waiver from the local government. However, local officials were alleged to have denied such

---

254. *Id.* at 279.
255. *Id.* at 279, n.25.
256. 118 U.S. 356 (1886).

waivers to 200 ethnic Chinese proprietors, while granting all but one waiver request made by proprietors of other races. The Court described the law as "applied by the public authorities ... with a mind so unequal and oppressive as to amount to a practical denial by the state of that equal protection of the laws."[257]

In 1960, the Court encountered another law whose effects were so skewed as to suggest intentional unequal treatment. *Gomillion v. Lightfoot*[258] considered a challenge to the Alabama Legislature's decision to alter the boundaries of the City of Tuskegee. The change allegedly resulted in the city's borders changing from a square to what the Court called an "uncouth twenty-eight-sided figure"[259] that, importantly, excluded all but four or five African-American voters from the city while excluding no white voters. The Court stated that if these allegations were proven, the conclusion would be "irresistible" "that the legislation is solely concerned with segregating white and colored voters by fencing [African-American] citizens out of town so as to deprive them of their pre-existing municipal vote."[260] These cases thus suggest that the Court had long considered disparate impact to be relevant—perhaps strongly so—even if such impact was not formally the trigger for finding discrimination the Constitution might forbid.

[3] Special Applications of the Intent Requirement

As suggested by *Arlington Heights*, the intent inquiry is a nuanced, contextual one, and at least ideally is attuned to the circumstances of the case before the court.[261] The Supreme Court has recognized that certain contexts as a general matter present occasions for applying special rules when performing the intent inquiry.

[a] Criminal Sentencing

In *McCleskey v. Kemp*,[262] the Court rejected an equal protection claim that Georgia administered its capital punishment law in a racially discriminatory manner. The death row inmate, McCleskey, supported his claim with an extensive statistical analysis. That analysis showed that defendants who murdered whites were much more likely to receive a death sentence than those who murdered Blacks. It also alleged that Black defendants were generally more likely to receive the death penalty than whites. Finally, the study claimed that people in McCleskey's position—that is, Black defendants who killed whites—were most likely of all to be sentenced to death.[263]

---

257. *Id.* at 373.

258. 364 U.S. 339 (1960).

259. *Id.* at 340.

260. *Id.* at 341.

261. *See, e.g.,* Rogers v. Lodge, 458 U.S. 613 (1982) (holding that a finding of discriminatory intent was one of fact rather than law, which thus merited significant deference from an appellate court).

262. 481 U.S. 279 (1987).

263. The study examined over 2,000 murders that occurred in Georgia in the 1970s and accounted for 230 variables that could have provided a non-racial explanation for the disparities. The raw numbers indicated that those charged with killing whites were sentenced to death in 11 percent of the cases while those charged with killing Blacks were sentenced to death in one percent of the cases.

A five-justice majority, speaking through Justice Powell, stated that McCleskey's equal protection challenge[264] would succeed only if he proved that the decision-makers in his particular case acted with discriminatory purpose in sentencing. McCleskey presented no evidence directly indicating such a particularized discriminatory purpose. Instead, he contended that the study supported an inference from its general statistics to a specific conclusion that his sentence was racially biased. Of course, the sort of individualized evidence Justice Powell insisted on would be hard to produce given, for example, the immunity to review enjoyed by jury verdicts and courts' traditional reluctance to review prosecutors' discretionary decisions, such as the decision to charge a particular crime or seek a particular punishment.

Justice Brennan, joined by Justice Marshall and for the most part by Justices Blackmun and Stevens, focused on the Eight Amendment implications of McCleskey's claim. Justice Blackmun's dissent, joined by those same justices,[265] focused on the equal protection argument. Justice Blackmun argued that it would be appropriate for a court to focus on the actions of prosecutors in seeking the death penalty in some cases but not others. He further suggested that, in McCleskey's case, there was evidence that the prosecutors in the office that charged him enjoyed largely-unconstrained discretion to seek death or a lesser penalty, thus raising the risk of abuse— a risk the state was never required to disprove by way of a court requiring prosecutors to justify their charging decision in McCleskey's case. Applying *Arlington Heights*, Justice Blackmun also cited the history of Georgia's race-based criminal system, although he recognized the limited probative value of long-ago racist practices.

McCleskey is a controversial decision. At one level, the majority's conclusion follows from the Court's discriminatory intent requirement, which, by requiring intent, discounts evidence based solely on statistical impacts. On the other hand, even *Arlington Heights* conceded that some discriminatory impact would be "unexplainable" except as reflecting an intent to classify on the alleged ground.[266] To be sure, were it forced to do, so the state would have a difficult time rebutting a claim based on discriminatory impact alone, if prosecutors and juries were not required to explain their decisions. Justice Blackmun's dissent suggested that the rule against prosecutors being forced to explain their actions was less absolute than the Court insisted.

Perhaps most fundamentally, an implicit theme of the majority opinion is that a ruling for McCleskey based on his statistical evidence alone would open the door to statistics-grounded attacks on other aspects of the criminal justice system that reveal disparate racial impacts. Of course, one can object that this concern essentially trans-

---

In cases involving white victims, 22 percent of the Black defendants and eight percent of the white defendants received a death sentence. The study also found that prosecutors sought the death penalty in 70 percent of the Black defendant/white victim cases, 32 percent of the white defendant/white victim cases, 15 percent of the Black defendant/Black victim cases, and 19 percent of the white defendant/Black victim cases.

264. The Court also rejected McCleskey's Eighth Amendment challenge.
265. Justice Brennan did not join one part of Justice Blackmun's opinion.
266. *See* 429 U.S. at 266.

lates into a fear of "too much justice."[267] Regardless of what one thinks about this latter argument, or more generally about the merits of McCleskey's claim as one that can be effectively resolved by courts, racial disparities in the criminal justice system would seem to be an appropriate target for legislative action, either by Congress via its power to enforce the Equal Protection Clause, or by the states themselves.

[b] Voting

Early voting rights cases attempted to eliminate racially gerrymandered districts that were drawn to dilute or eliminate African-Americas' voting strength. For example, recall *Gomillion v. Lightfoot*,[268] discussed earlier in this section. In *Gomillion*, the Court invalidated a state legislature's alteration of a city's borders, which changed the city's shape from a neat square to a highly irregular, twenty-eight-sided figure, which the Court observed had the effect of excluding nearly all African-American voters from the city without excluding a single white voter. Even after *Washington v. Davis* announced a generally-applicable discriminatory intent requirement, the Court has continued to express serious concerns about racial impacts flowing from the processes by which voters are sorted into governmental units and districts.

In *Shaw v. Reno*,[269] the Court applied *Gomillion* to invalidate a racially-based gerrymander designed to foster the election of Black candidates. The Court held that "bizarrely"-shaped legislative districts that are unexplainable on any other grounds but race are subject to strict scrutiny.[270] Although it remanded the case for further consideration, the Court did suggest certain race-based districting that might satisfy strict scrutiny. For example, it suggested that states could use race to create a narrowly-tailored districting plan that was reasonably necessary to avoid the retrogression of a racial minority's voting strength that would itself violate the Voting Rights Act (VRA).

In *Miller v. Johnson*,[271] the Court invalidated an electoral district designed predominantly with racial motivations. The congressional district in question split 26 counties, connected some neighborhoods 260 miles apart and covered 6,784.2 miles sometimes being connected only by narrow land bridges. Justice Kennedy, writing for the 5–4 majority, stated that *Shaw v. Reno* did not require the demonstration of a bizarrely drawn district to establish an equal protection violation. However, a bizarrely-drawn district might provide powerful circumstantial evidence that race was the predominant legislative purpose.

---

267. *See, e.g.*, *McCleskey*, 481 U.S. at 339 (Brennan, J., dissenting) (using this term to characterize the majority's concern); *id.* at 365 (Blackmun, J., dissenting) (suggesting that this concern "may be the most disturbing aspect of [the majority's] opinion").

268. 364 U.S. 339 (1960).

269. 509 U.S. 630 (1993).

270. *Id.* at 644 (agreeing with the proposition that "redistricting legislation that is so bizarre on its face that it is 'unexplainable on grounds other than race' demands the same close scrutiny that we give other state laws that classify citizens by race") (quoting *Arlington Heights*, 429 U.S. at 266).

271. 515 U.S. 900 (1995).

To establish an equal protection violation, the Court concluded that the plaintiff had to show, "either through circumstantial evidence of a district's shape and demographics or more direct evidence going to legislative purpose, that race was the predominant factor motivating the legislature's decision to place a significant number of voters within or without a particular district."[272] If the plaintiff made this showing, then the district would be considered a racial gerrymander that was subject to strict scrutiny as an intentional race classification.

While the Court has broadly proscribed race-based gerrymandering except in narrowly-tailored remedial cases, it has encountered greater difficulty ferreting out race-based discrimination in decisions to fill elected positions via at-large elections.[273] In *Mobile v. Bolden*,[274] the Court upheld a city's at-large procedure for electing city commissioners. The Supreme Court reversed the lower court's finding of a constitutional violation. Writing for a four-justice plurality, Justice Stewart found no Fourteenth Amendment violation, as there was no evidence of discriminatory intent behind the decision to adopt that voting system.[275] While at-large voting naturally disadvantaged minority parties, the plurality concluded that that effect did not establish purposeful discrimination. Concurring in the judgment, Justice Stevens voted to uphold the at-large system since, in his view, valid reasons, not invidious discrimination, had prompted it. Justice Blackmun concurred only in the result. He agreed with the district court's finding of discriminatory intent, but thought that the district court should have considered remedies other than forcing the city to change its governance structure. Justices Brennan, White, and Marshall filed dissenting opinions.

Rogers v. Lodge[276] involved the use of at-large elections to fill positions on a county board of commissioners. Despite the fact that African-Americans constituted nearly 40% of the population, the county had never elected an African-American to the board. In contrast to *Bolden*, the Court struck down the at-large voting system because of the district court's specific finding of discriminatory intent, which the Court described as not clearly erroneous. *Rogers* indicated that the Supreme Court would grant substantial deference to district courts in determining discriminatory intent.

---

272. *See id.* at 916.

273. At-large elections are those that are conducted by the entire political unit—for example, a city—rather than by geographical sub-divisions of the unit. For example, a decision that all of a city's council members would be elected by all citizens, rather than each council slot being filled by voters of a particular district, represents an at-large method of voting. At-large voting raises the risk that, in a racially or politically-polarized city, a small majority can outvote a sizable minority and obtain complete control of government.

274. 446 U.S. 55 (1980).

275. The district court had found discriminatory intent. However, the plurality stated that the finding was based on disparate impact and purposeful discrimination that was irrelevant to the voting system or too long-ago to be probative. The Court also found no Fifteenth Amendment violation, as there were no claims of race-based interference with registration or actual voting.

276. 458 U.S. 613 (1982).

The key distinction between *Bolden* and *Rogers* appears to be the district court's explicit (and apparently more supportable) finding of discrimination in *Rogers*.

[4] The Policy Debate Underlying the Intent Requirement

Should there be an intent requirement? On the one hand, one might think that the primary concern of the Equal Protection Clause is, or should be, equal treatment by the government. Such a view might suggest that an intent requirement is appropriate, as a way of determining whether in fact government is indeed "treating" people differently based on the alleged ground (*e.g.*, race). Further, one might agree with Justice White in *Davis* that a pure disparate impact rule would call into doubt many laws that, by classifying based on wealth or income, have disparate racial impact, given the unfortunate reality that many racial minorities in the United States are less wealthy and earn less than whites.

But arguments can be marshaled on the other side, too. One can argue that a fundamental purpose of the Equal Protection Clause is ensure that government act with equal consideration to all people and members of all groups. On this theory, a law's disparate impact might suggest the presence of the government's failure to consider the interests of all groups when legislating, and might thus justify a closer judicial look if the impact is based on a characteristic (such as race) that is particularly problematic or "suspect." One might make this argument in particular in the context of race, given the nation's long history of oppressing racial and ethnic minorities, which might create a situation where inertia "naturally" leads the government to act in ways that impose disparate harm on minorities.

One additional concern is that many scholars have argued that the intent requirement, at least as applied by courts, is very hard to satisfy. By definition, laws where the intent requirement applies are facially neutral (and hence require the plaintiff to satisfy the intent requirement). Given the ease with which a government can cite a neutral (*e.g.*, a race-neutral) justification for such a facially-neutral law, an intent requirement, if applied stringently, might render most such laws largely immune from constitutional scrutiny. Indeed, one irony of the current state of American race relations is that, for the most part, the only facially race-based laws remaining are those that are defended as benign for minorities, such as race-based affirmative action plans implemented by state universities. Thus, the strict scrutiny that is currently applied to race-based laws ends up applying only to such benignly-justified laws, while invidious laws that oppress minorities through covert mechanisms escape scrutiny when plaintiffs fail to satisfy the intent requirement.

§ 10.06 Equal Protection Today

Equal protection review today has evolved away from a focus on new suspect classes. To be sure, the Court continues to apply the scrutiny levels that have been determined by previous suspect class analyses. For example, sex continues to get intermediate (or sometimes heightened intermediate) level review,[277] while age continues to get only rational basis review.[278] Lower federal courts and state courts interpreting their state constitutional equality provisions have also continued to experiment with finding new suspect classes.[279]

Nevertheless, the Supreme Court has not found a new suspect or quasi-suspect class since the 1970s, and has not performed a serious suspect class analysis since 1985. Instead, when it has ruled for plaintiffs who are not making an already-established claim for heightened review, the Court has concluded that the challenged discrimination was irrational and based in what the Court has called "animus."

[1] The Roots of Animus Doctrine

The foundational case for this approach to equal protection was *Department of Agriculture v. Moreno*,[280] decided in 1973. *Moreno* involved a challenge to an amendment to the federal food stamp law that reduced food stamp eligibility for unrelated persons living together. While the plaintiffs in *Moreno* were people living conventional lives (including, for example, an elderly woman who had moved in with an unrelated family so they could pool expenses), the (sparse) legislative history of the amendment reflected a congressional desire to deny benefits to "hippies" and "hippie communes."

The Court, citing the lack of any rational justification for the law, struck the amendment down. It did not find that hippies were a suspect class. But at the same time, its rational basis review was more stringent than normal, a fact remarked upon by Justice Rehnquist's dissenting opinion.[281] Perhaps a clue to that more stringent review lay in the Court's commentary on the anti-hippie justification: "The challenged classification clearly cannot be sustained by reference to this congressional purpose. For if the constitutional conception of 'equal protection of the laws' means anything, it must at the very least mean that a bare congressional desire to harm a politically unpopular group cannot constitute a legitimate governmental interest."[282] One reading of *Moreno* is that the direct evidence of such a clearly illegitimate goal gave the Court reason to suspect that the law was in fact based on that goal, and prompted stricter review of the more legitimate justifications the government offered. Later Court opinions applying this approach relied heavily on *Moreno*'s warning that "a bare ... desire to harm a politically unpopular group cannot constitute a legitimate governmental interest."

---

277. *See, e.g.*, Sessions v. Morales-Santana, 137 S. Ct. 1678 (2017).

278. *See, e.g.*, Kimel v. Board of Regents, 528 U.S. 62 (2000).

279. *See, e.g.*, SmithKline Beecham Corp.v. Abbott Labs, 740 F.3d 471, 481 (9th Cir. 2014) (finding sexual orientation to merit "heightened scrutiny"); Varnum v. Brien 763 N.W.2d 862 (Iowa 2009) (finding sexual orientation to be a quasi-suspect classification under the Iowa Constitution).

280. 413 U.S. 528 (1973).

281. *See id.* at 545–47 (Rehnquist, J., dissenting).

282. *Id.* at 534 (majority opinion).

[2] *City of Cleburne v. Cleburne Living Center*

The anti-animus language from *Moreno* did not immediately bear fruit.[283] However, in 1985, the Court resurrected the idea as support for its conclusion that a city violated the Equal Protection Clause when it denied a permit allowing the establishment of a group home for intellectually disabled persons. In *City of Cleburne, Texas v. Cleburne Living Center*,[284] the appellate court had held that the intellectually disabled were a "quasi-suspect" class entitled to more than a rationality standard of review, which the court concluded it failed. The Supreme Court agreed that the decision violated equal protection, but on a different ground.

The Court first rejected the lower court's conclusion that intellectual disability triggered intermediate scrutiny review. It gave four reasons for its conclusion. First, the disabilities of the intellectually disabled were both real and diverse, requiring carefully tailored legislative assistance informed by professional advice. Second, the Court noted that the legislative response to their needs (such as special employment and educational opportunities) "belies a continuing antipathy or prejudice and a corresponding need for more intrusive oversight by the judiciary."[285] The Court also worried that according heightened scrutiny to these laws—which, after all, treated the intellectually disabled differently and thus could be understood as discriminating against them—might deter or obstruct such helpful legislation. Third, and relatedly, this legislative response demonstrated that the intellectually disabled were not politically powerless. Finally, and perhaps most tellingly, the Court worried that accepting the intellectually disabled's claim for heightened scrutiny would open the floodgates to similar claims:

> [I]f the large and amorphous class of the [intellectually disabled] were deemed quasi-suspect ... it would be difficult to find a principled way to distinguish a variety of other groups who have perhaps immutable disabilities setting them off from others, who cannot themselves mandate the desired legislative responses, and who can claim some degree of prejudice from at least part of the public at large.[286]

Despite holding that intellectual disability was not a suspect or quasi-suspect classification, the Court struck down the challenged law because it was based on "irrational prejudice"[287] against the intellectually disabled. The Court led off this part of the

---

283. One of the very few early post-*Moreno* references to that idea was in *New York City Transit Authority v. Beazer*, 440 U.S. 568 (1979), where the Court, in a footnote, concluded that a city transit authority's rule refusing to employ drug users, including those using methadone to end their drug addictions, did not reflect "any special animus against a specific group of persons." *Id.* at 593 n.40. *See also id.* at 609 n.15 (White, J., dissenting) (suggesting that the law might have been motivated by animus against former drug users).

284. 473 U.S. 432 (1985).

285. *Id.* at 443.

286. *Id.* at 445–46. The Court listed the aging, disabled, infirm, and mentally ill as examples of other groups which might also deserve quasi-suspect class protection if the intellectually disabled received it.

287. *Id.* at 450.

analysis by observing that the City Council "was concerned with the negative attitude of the majority of property owners located within 200 feet of the Featherston facility, as well as with the fears of elderly residents of the neighborhood." The Court rejected this justification—which it characterized as "mere negative attitudes, or fear"—as an illegitimate ground for government action.[288] The city then offered a variety of other, more legitimate, rationales for its actions, such as the problem of evacuating the residents in the event of a flood and the density of the living arrangements in the proposed home. While the Court recognized these as legitimate interests, it questioned why the city was citing them for the permit denial, when it allowed other institutions posing similar concerns to locate in that area. In questioning the rational connection between these justifications and the city's decision, and, indeed, in seeming to require record evidence demonstrating that such concerns existed in this case, the Court appeared to engage in rational basis review that was substantially more intrusive than what that review normally entails—a point made by the partial concurrence in the case.[289]

As noted earlier, the Court ended its opinion by concluding that the city's decision rested on "irrational prejudice"[290] against the intellectually disabled. This phrasing suggested simple application of the rational basis test, as a subsequent opinion suggested.[291] But the "prejudice" part of the Court's phrase, and its earlier invocation of *Moreno*'s "bare ... desire to harm" language,[292] allowed *Cleburne* to come to be seen as an application of the animus idea.

Concurring in the judgment, Justice Stevens criticized the Court's suspect class/ tiered scrutiny analytical framework for equal protection cases. He maintained that the various cases applying that framework "reflect a continuum of judgmental responses to differing classifications,"[293] but characterized all those responses as focusing on whether the classification was rational. But Justice Stevens' understanding of "rationality" was more robust than the classic deferential rational basis review associated with cases such as *Fritz v. Railroad Retirement Board*.[294] Instead, he argued for a rational basis test that featured "a requirement that an impartial lawmaker could logically believe that the classification would serve a legitimate public purpose that transcends the harm to the members of the disadvantaged class." He argued that this test would result in the "virtually automatic invalidation of racial classifications,"[295] while

---

288. *Id.* at 448. The Court also dismissed a somewhat analogous concern, that the students at the junior high school across the street might harass the residents. *See id.* at 449.

289. *See id.* at 458–59 (Marshall, J., concurring in the judgment in part and dissenting in part). Justice Marshall, joined by Justices Brennan and Blackmun, would have applied explicitly heightened scrutiny to the city's decision.

290. *Id.* at 450 (majority opinion).

291. *See* Board of Trustees v. Garrett, 531 U.S. 356, 367 (2001).

292. *See Cleburne*, 473 U.S. at 446–47.

293. *Cleburne*, 473 U.S. at 451 (Stevens, J., joined by Burger, C.J., concurring in the judgment).

294. 449 U.S. 166 (1980). *Fritz*, and this deferential style of rational basis scrutiny, is discussed in Section 10.01[1].

295. *Cleburne*, 473 U.S. at 453 (Stevens, J., concurring in the judgment).

leaving most economic legislation intact. Cases involving classifications based on sex and alienage would have varying results. These differing results would not be the product of different tiers of review, but rather of the fact that the characteristics of these groups were relevant to legitimate legislative choices to different degrees, from frequently to almost never, and thus required different results under the application of the same test.

Justice Marshall, joined by Justices Brennan and Blackmun, also criticized the majority's approach. He argued, as he had argued for his entire career on the Court, for a suspect class analysis that considered, along a sliding scale, both the characteristics of the class in question and the importance of the interest at stake in that case.[296]

Despite these separate opinions, the majority's suggestion of animus soon became the focus of the Court's jurisprudence relating to sexual orientation.

[3] Sexual Orientation

In *Romer v. Evans*, the Court struck down a voter-enacted amendment to the Colorado Constitution (Amendment 2) that forbade all laws prohibiting "discrimination on the basis of 'homosexual, lesbian or bisexual orientation, conduct, practices or relationships.'"[297]

Writing for a six-justice majority, Justice Kennedy first construed the reach of Amendment 2. He concluded that it not only repealed existing local ordinances prohibiting discrimination against LGB persons but also prohibited all future "legislative, executive or judicial action at any level of state or local government designed to protect" those individuals.[298] Rejecting Colorado's argument that Amendment 2 simply placed LGB persons in the same position as all other Coloradans, the Court stated that Amendment 2 placed them in a class by themselves, depriving them and only them of protection against discrimination. Indeed, he suggested that the broad language of Amendment 2 might not be limited to overturning laws passed specifically to protect LGB people, but it could also prohibit broader laws that generally banned arbitrary decisions or discrimination in a large variety of settings, as those broader laws applied to LGB persons.

So construed, the Court concluded that Amendment 2 violated equal protection. Ignoring the question whether sexual orientation discrimination merited heighted

---

296. *See Cleburne*, 473 U.S. at 460 ("I have long believed the level of scrutiny employed in an equal protection case should vary with 'the constitutional and societal importance of the interest adversely affected and the recognized invidiousness of the basis upon which the particular classification is drawn.'"). He appended to that statement citations to his separate opinions in San Antonio Independent School District v. Rodriguez, 411 U.S. 1, 99 (1973) (dissenting); Plyler v. Doe, 457 U.S. 202, 230–231 (1982) (concurring); and Dandridge v. Williams, 397 U.S. 471, 508 (1970) (dissenting). *Rodriguez* is discussed in Sections 10.03[4] & 10.07[5]; *Plyler* in Section 10.03[2][b], and *Dandridge* in Section 10.3[4].

297. 517 U.S. 620, 624 (1996) (quoting Amendment 2 to the Colorado Constitution).

298. *Ibid.*

scrutiny, he relied on the rational basis standard, concluding that "Amendment 2 fails, indeed defies, even th[e] conventional inquiry" that standard required. First, he said, Amendment 2 imposed "a broad and undifferentiated disability on a single group." In other words, the law named a status (LGB orientation) and simply made that status ineligible for any government protection. That oddity, he argued, "defies" conventional equal protection ends-means scrutiny, even when that scrutiny is performed deferentially, as it is under the rational basis standard. He concluded that a law such as Amendment 2 that declared "that in general it shall be more difficult for one group of citizens than for all others to seek aid from the government is itself a denial of equal protection of the laws in the most literal sense."[299]

Second, he concluded that the state's justifications for the amendment (to conserve state anti-discrimination enforcement resources and to protect landlords who did not wish to rent to LGB persons) were so removed from the law's broad reach that they could not be credited. Instead, the only justification that remained plausible was that Amendment 2 was based simply on animus toward LGB persons. At this point he cited *Moreno*'s language condemning "'a bare ... desire to harm a politically unpopular group.'"[300]

Justice Scalia, joined by Chief Justice Rehnquist and Justice Thomas, dissented. He questioned the majority's broad interpretation of Amendment 2's actual effects, and on that basis characterized Amendment 2 as a "rather modest attempt by seemingly tolerant Coloradans to preserve traditional sexual mores against the efforts of a politically powerful minority to revise those mores through use of the laws."[301]

Seven years after *Romer*, the Court decided *Lawrence v. Texas*,[302] which struck down Texas's sodomy statute under the Due Process Clause. The *Lawrence* majority's discussion of due process is discussed elsewhere in this book.[303] However, Justice O'Connor did not join the Court's due process analysis. Instead, she concurred in the result on the ground that the Texas law, which singled out same-sex sodomy rather than sodomy more generally, failed equal protection. In reaching that conclusion, she cited *Moreno*, *Cleburne*, and *Romer*, describing them as cases in which "a law exhibits ... a desire to harm a politically unpopular group," and thus triggers "a more searching form of rational basis review" that the Court has used "to strike down such laws under the Equal Protection Clause."[304] She concluded that the Texas law was similarly based on a simple desire to harm LGB people, and on that basis voted to strike it down as violating equal protection.

In more recent years, the Court has decided two significant cases dealing with same-sex marriage. One of these cases, *Obergefell v. Hodges*,[305] relied on the Due

---

299. *Id.* at 632, 633.
300. *Romer*, 517 U.S. at 634–635 (quoting *Moreno*, 413 U.S. at 534).
301. *Id.* at 636 (Scalia, J., dissenting).
302. 539 U.S. 558 (2003).
303. *See* Section 9.04[4][c].
304. *See* 539 U.S. at 580 (O'Connor, J., concurring in the judgment).
305. 576 U.S. 644 (2015).

Process Clause to strike down bans on same-sex marriage, although the Court's analysis employed components of equality reasoning. That case is also discussed in the due process materials.[306] But two years before *Obergefell*, the Court used equal protection reasoning more explicitly to strike down a federal law[307] (Section 3 of the Defense of Marriage Act ("DOMA"))[308] that defined marriage for federal purposes to consist only of unions between a man and a woman. Section 3 was challenged by a lesbian couple New York State considered as married, when the death of one of the women triggered a federal estate tax bill higher than it would have been had the federal government recognized them as married.

In *United States v. Windsor*,[309] the Court began by remarking on the oddity of the federal government enacting its own across-the-board definition of marriage, rather than adopting the marriage laws of the state where the couple lived. (To be sure, some previous federal statutes had defined marriage, but only for limited regulatory purposes.) That oddity seemed to prime the Court for more careful scrutiny of the law.[310] When it performed that scrutiny, it concluded that Section 3 of DOMA "seeks to injure the very class New York seeks to protect"[311] by the state's decision to grant same-sex couples marriage rights. Examining the law's legislative history, the arguments offered in the law's defense, and the law's effects, the Court further concluded that "[t]he history of DOMA's enactment and its own text demonstrate that interference with the equal dignity of same-sex marriages, a dignity conferred by the States in the exercise of their sovereign power, was more than an incidental effect of the federal statute. It was its essence."[312] After a lengthy analysis of the evidence of Congress's intentions in enacting Section 3 of DOMA, the Court concluded at the end of its opinion that "no legitimate purpose overcomes the purpose and effect to disparage and to injure those whom the State, by its marriage laws, sought to protect in personhood and dignity."[313] To be clear, the Court did not identify a legitimate purpose and conclude that it was "overcome" by the law's more problematic purpose and effects—rather, the Court seemed to conclude that no such legitimate purpose existed.

Dissenting for four justices, Justice Scalia did identify legitimate purposes underlying Section 3 of DOMA. He argued that it could be understood as Congress's attempt

---

306. *See* Section 9.04[4][c].

307. Because the law in question was federal, the Court technically used the Due Process Clause, but employed equal protection reasoning, at it had in earlier cases dealing with federal, rather than state, discrimination. *See, e.g.*, Bolling v. Sharpe, 347 U.S. 497 (1954) (striking down federal racial segregation of the Washington, D.C. schools on due process grounds). *Bolling* is discussed in Section 10.04[2][b][i].

308. 1 U.S.C. §7.

309. 570 U.S. 744 (2013).

310. *See id.* at 768 ("[D]iscriminations of an unusual character especially suggest careful consideration to determine whether they are obnoxious to the constitutional provision.") (quoting *Romer*, 517 U.S. at 633).

311. *Id.* at 769.

312. *Id.* at 770.

313. *Id.* at 775.

avoid the difficult cross-jurisdictional issues, such as federal taxation questions, that might arise if the federal government recognized same-sex marriages when many states did not. He also argued that Section 3 "preserves the intended effects of prior legislation against then-unforeseen changes in circumstance," by retaining the opposite-sex marriage assumption underlying federal law unless and until Congress decided to dispense with that assumption in particular cases.[314]

[4] The Animus Doctrine

Windsor's practical effect today is, at most, quite limited, given the Court's subsequent opinion in *Obergefell* striking down all bans on same-sex marriage. However, its continued use of the animus idea originated in *Moreno* continues to give that idea credence as an approach to equal protection law.[315] To be sure, animus is a controversial theory. It is deeply under-theorized in the Court's opinions. For example, Justice O'Connor's equal protection concurrence in *Lawrence* stated that "[w]hen a law exhibits ... a desire to harm a politically unpopular group, we have applied a more searching form of rational basis review to strike down such laws under the Equal Protection Clause."[316] Does that statement mean that a finding of animus automatically means that a law should be struck down, or is she simply stating that such a finding triggers "a more searching form of rational basis review," thus implying that that review could lead to the law being upheld? In that latter case, wouldn't it be odd for the Court to uphold a law that it had concluded rested on animus?

Animus doctrine also raises other difficult questions. As an inquiry into a legislature's intent, it presupposes a judicial ability to determine that intent. That idea is highly controversial. It is even more problematic when, as in *Romer*, a court must determine the animus-intent, not of a legislature or a city council, but a state's electorate. (Recall that Amendment 2, struck down in *Romer*, was enacted as a voter initiative.) These and other questions mean that the *Moreno* line of cases is likely to remain controversial and may not find wide and consistent acceptance at the Court. On the other hand, the Court's seeming abandonment of suspect class analysis raises a serious question of how the Court will confront new forms of discrimination burdening groups that have not yet had their suspect class status conclusively determined by the Court. Unless the Court either resurrects that approach or develops something entirely new, animus may remain an attractive doctrinal approach.[317]

---

314. *See id.* at 796–97 (Scalia, J., dissenting).

315. The idea has also migrated into other areas of law. In *Masterpiece Cakeshop v. Colorado Civil Rights Commission*, 138 S. Ct. 1719 (2018), the Court held that a member of a state civil rights commission exhibited unconstitutional animus against religion when rejecting a baker's religion-based request for an exemption from a public accommodations law. *Masterpiece Cakeshop* is discussed in Chapter 12.03[2][c].

316. Lawrence v. Texas, 539 U.S. 558, 580 (2003) (O'Connor, J., concurring in the judgment).

317. For more discussion about the animus theory, see WILLIAM D. ARAIZA, ANIMUS: A SHORT INTRODUCTION TO BIAS IN THE LAW (2017).

§ 10.07 Equal Protection Fundamental Rights

[1] Introduction

Most equal protection claims are triggered by, and based on, the simple fact of government classification. However, in a relatively small set of cases, the Court has suggested that equal protection analysis is also triggered when the subject-matter of the unequal government action is particularly important. This "fundamental rights strand of equal protection" maintains that, regardless of the suspectness of the classification tool government uses, if the benefit the government is distributing unequally is particularly important—an "equal protection fundamental right"—then courts will apply strict scrutiny.

This can be a confusing concept, as reflected in one case normally classified as an equal protection fundamental rights case, *Zablocki v. Redhail*.[318] In *Zablocki*, the Court struck down a statute requiring that persons owing court-imposed child support obligations obtain the state's approval before marrying. One can perhaps understand the Court's instinct to treat that case as one implicating both liberty and equality: the right to marry had been recognized as a fundamental right by the time *Zablocki* was decided,[319] yet the statute clearly did not deprive everyone of that right, and thus implicated equal protection interests. On the other hand, a concurring justice argued that the case should have been resolved simply as a matter of due process, arguing that equal protection added little to the analysis.[320]

Part of the confusion may stem from the temptation to make too much of the fact that statutes like the one in *Zablocki* distribute fundamental right unequally. After all, even cases analyzed purely as matters of due process sometimes involve unequal distributions of benefits.[321] One way to distinguish between "pure" due process cases and "hybrid" cases involving the fundamental rights strand of equal protection might be to consider which analytical questions are most suited for deciding the issue. The concurring justice in *Zablocki* suggested this approach.[322]

Another approach, not inconsistent with the first, considers the underlying right and asks whether government was obligated to provide it at all. If the answer is no,

---

318. 434 U.S. 374 (1978). *Zablocki* is also discussed in Section 9.04[4][b].

319. For a discussion of the due process right to marry, see Section 9.04[4][b].

320. *See* 434 U.S. at 391 (Stewart, J., concurring in the judgment).

321. For example, *Michael H. v. Gerald D.*, 491 U.S. 110 (1989), considered a state law that denied legal paternity rights only to some likely biological fathers, but was nevertheless analyzed as a case about fathers' due process rights. *Michael H.* is discussed in Section 9.04[4][a].

322. *See* 434 U.S. at 395–96 (Stewart, J. concurring in the judgment) ("The Court is understandably reluctant to rely on substantive due process. But to embrace the essence of that doctrine under the guise of equal protection serves no purpose but obfuscation. Couched in slogans and ringing phrases, the Court's equal protection doctrine shifts the focus of the judicial inquiry away from its proper concerns, which include the nature of the individual interest affected, the extent to which it is affected, the rationality of the connection between legislative means and purpose, the existence of alternative means for effectuating the purpose, and the degree of confidence we may have that the statute reflects the legislative concern for the purpose that would legitimately support the means chosen.").

but if the interest is nevertheless important, then it might be appropriate for the Court to consider carefully whether unequal distribution of the right was nevertheless unconstitutional. For example, due process does not obligate government to provide a right to a criminal appeal. But that right might nevertheless be sufficiently important that unequal provision of criminal appeal rights might be properly analyzed under the fundamental rights strand of equal protection.[323] Similarly, the Constitution does not provide persons with the right to vote for their states' presidential electors — rather, if a state chooses, it could assign that authority to the state legislature. However, once a state does give people the right to vote for its electors, it must not discriminate, for example, by treating one vote as worth more than another.[324]

While the Court has not been completely clear, rights analyzed exclusively under the fundamental rights strand of equal protection appear to include the right of would-be litigants to access the judicial process, the right to vote, the right of candidates to access the ballot, and possibly the right to interstate travel. It has also rejected education as a fundamental right for equal protection purposes. The rights the Court has protected under this theory are not fundamental in an absolute, due process sense; however, they are important enough that their unequal distribution triggers heightened scrutiny under the fundamental rights strand. Of course, unequal deprivations of rights that *are* fundamental in the due process sense — for example, the right to marry — are also subject to analysis under the fundamental rights strand if they are distributed unequally.[325]

[2] Access to the Justice System

In a line of cases stretching back more than 60 years, the Court has considered claims that a combination of due process and equal protection requires states to waive fees necessary to access the judicial process.[326] In *Griffin v. Illinois*,[327] the Court used

---

323. *See, e.g.*, M.L.B. v. S.L.J., 519 U.S. 102 (1996) (recognizing that "most decisions" in the area of indigent persons' access to judicial processes, such as appeals, "rest on an equal protection framework ... for due process does not independently require that the State provide a right to appeal."). Of course, standard equal protection analysis would also come into play if the government distributed the right unequally based on a ground that is considered inherently suspect or quasi-suspect — for example, if the government granted the right to appeal a conviction only to defendants of one race.

324. *See, e.g.*, Bush v. Gore, 531 U.S. 98, 104 (2000) ("The individual citizen has no federal constitutional right to vote for electors for the President of the United States unless and until the state legislature chooses a statewide election as the means to implement its power to appoint members of the electoral college.... When the state legislature vests the right to vote for President in its people, the right to vote as the legislature has prescribed is fundamental; and one source of its fundamental nature lies in the equal weight accorded to each vote and the equal dignity owed to each voter.").

325. *See, e.g.* Zablocki v. Redhail, 434 U.S. 378 (1978) (discussed earlier in this sub-section).

326. Beyond these cases, the Court has found, as a matter of the Sixth Amendment's right to counsel, a right to a government-provided attorney in criminal cases. Gideon v. Wainwright, 372 U.S. 335 (1963). For more information about *Gideon* and the line of Sixth Amendment cases it spawned, the reader is referred to books on constitutional criminal procedure. However, the same day the Court decided *Gideon*, it also decided that equal protection required that indigent criminal defendants be provided a lawyer for their first appeal. Douglas v. California, 372 U.S. 353 (1963).

327. 351 U.S. 12 (1956).

a combination of due process and equal protection reasoning to strike down a state law requiring a criminal defendant to provide the appellate court with a trial transcript in order to perfect an appeal but failing to provide one for free for indigent persons. Notably, the four-justice plurality relied on equal protection and due process, even though it conceded that due process did not require the right to appeal a criminal conviction. Justice Frankfurter concurred, emphasizing the equal protection aspects of the case.

In subsequent years, the Court built on *Griffin.* It struck down financial impositions on the right to appeal petty misdemeanor convictions,[328] the right to seek a divorce,[329] and the right to appeal a court order terminating parental rights.[330] However, it has maintained that a right to fee waivers in civil actions remains "the exception, not the general rule."[331] In *M.L.B. v. S.L.J.*, the case addressing a court order terminating parental rights, the Court noted the line the Court's cases had drawn between ordinary civil actions and those, such as the one in *M.L.B.*, that impacted the family relationships otherwise protected as fundamental by the Due Process Clause. In considering whether the Constitution required a fee waiver in a given context, that same opinion explained that such claims require the Court to "inspect the character and intensity of the individual interest at stake, on the one hand, and the State's justification for its exaction, on the other."[332]

In *Douglas v. California*, the Court found a constitutional right—seemingly based in concerns about both equal protection and due process—to have a lawyer appointed at no charge for an indigent criminal defendant's first appeal.[333] In later cases, the Court has considered the boundaries of that right. It concluded that the right bestowed in *Douglas* would be "a futile gesture" if it did not encompass a right to effective representation; thus, in *Evitts v. Lucey*, it reversed a state court decision to refuse to hear an appeal as of right when the defendant's court-appointed attorney failed to file the required statement of appeal when filing his appellate brief.[334] On the other hand, it refused to expand that right to discretionary appeals to a state's highest court or the United States Supreme Court, relying on the discretionary nature of the appeal and the fact that a lawyer may be less necessary at that stage given the existence of materials developed at the first appellate stage of the process.[335] Based on that decision, it also

---

328. Mayer v. City of Chicago, 404 U.S. 189 (1971).

329. Boddie v. Connecticut, 401 U.S. 371 (1971).

330. M.L.B. v. S.L.J., 519 U.S. 102 (1996).

331. *Id.* at 114 (citing United States v. Kras, 409 U.S. 434 (1973) (upholding a fee requirement for filing for bankruptcy)). *See also* Ortwein v. Schwab, 410 U.S. 656 (1973) (upholding a fee requirement for filing an appeal to an agency decision reducing a person's welfare benefits).

332. *Id.* at 120–21. *See also* Bearden v. Georgia, 461 U.S. 660 (1983) (using this same inquiry to invalidate a state law that revoked a person's probation and imprisoned him for the rest of his sentence when he was unable to pay a restitution penalty for a theft offense).

333. 372 U.S. 353 (1963); *see also id.* at 360–61 (Harlan, J., dissenting) (explaining the Court's decision as based on a combination of equal protection and due process reasoning).

334. 469 U.S. 387 (1985).

335. Ross v Moffitt, 417 U.S. 600 (1974).

refused to find a right to a government-appointed lawyer in a post-conviction proceeding.[336]

[3] An Equal Right to Vote

[a] The Basic Principle

Citing the centrality of voting rights in a democracy, the Court has accorded strict scrutiny to laws that make it difficult to exercise voting rights or dilute the value of a vote. The seminal modern case establishing the equal right to vote is *Reynolds v. Sims*.[337] In *Reynolds*, the Court imposed a requirement that legislative districts be as nearly equal in population as possible. The Court described the right to vote as fundamental, and concluded that, since unequally-sized legislative districts essentially mean that some votes have more weight than others in determining the make-up of the legislature, any districting scheme featuring such unequally-sized districts requires careful scrutiny under the Equal Protection Clause.[338] *Reynolds* dealt with the make-up of the Alabama legislature. Because of decades-long failures to reapportion state legislative districts in response to population changes, approximately 25% of Alabama voters were in districts that collectively elected a majority of both houses of the Alabama legislature.[339]

Tracing a long history of cases in the voting rights area, *Reynolds* stated that "the Constitution of the United States protects the right of all qualified citizens to vote, in state as well as federal elections."[340] The Court had previously held that a state could not establish districts that diluted a person's vote for members of the United States House of Representatives[341] or in state-wide primary elections.[342] In *Reynolds*, the Court extended the "one-person-one-vote" standard to state legislatures. Because the right to vote was fundamental, restrictions on it had to be "meticulously scrutinized."[343] The Court rejected the state's proffered justifications for the unequal weight it accorded different voters' preferences. Most notably, it rejected the state's attempt to point to the United States Senate as a model of such unequal weight, concluding that the Senate's structure flowed from unique compromises that were made at the Constitutional Convention and the resulting unique structure of American federalism.

The Court recognized the "practical impossibility"[344] of attaining exact equality in population across districts. However, as the Court's jurisprudence developed, the

---

336. Pennsylvania v. Finley, 481 U.S. 551 (1987).

337. 377 U.S. 533 (1964).

338. The Court recognized that states may, for example, wish to draw district lines based on political subdivisions, for example, cities and towns. But the Court insisted that any such decisions not deviate from the general equality principle the Court announced.

339. There was no claim of racial discrimination in this mal-apportionment.

340. *Id.* at 554.

341. Wesberry v. Sanders, 376 U.S. 1 (1964).

342. Gray v. Sanders, 372 U.S. 368 (1963).

343. *Reynolds*, 377 U.S. at 562.

344. *Id.* at 577.

Court began to insist on exceptionally small deviations from equally-sized legislative districts[345] and has also expanded the one-person-one-vote rule to nearly all state government units.[346]

Dissenting, Justice Harlan insisted that the Court's analysis lacked any foundation in the Fourteenth Amendment. Indeed, he argued that the Court completely ignored Section 2 of the Amendment, which in his view authorized states to restrict voting rights as they wished, subject to the that state having its House delegation reduced if it disenfranchised persons from voting in elections for federal or state office. Justice Harlan examined the history of the amendment and concluded that it was not intended to limit states' power to apportion their own legislatures as they deemed fit.

In *Harper v. Virginia State Board of Elections*,[347] the Court struck down, as violating equal protection, a law requiring voters to pay a $1.50 poll tax as a prerequisite for voting in state elections. Citing *Reynolds*, Justice Douglas' majority opinion found that voting was a fundamental right because it preserved other basic civil and political rights. Justice Douglas stated that "once the franchise is granted to the electorate, lines may not be drawn which are inconsistent with the Equal Protection Clause of the Fourteenth Amendment."[348] The Court further found that the poll tax did not further the state's asserted interest in encouraging citizens to vote intelligently, given the irrelevance of wealth to a person's ability to make intelligent electoral choices. Justice Black dissented, arguing that the poll tax should be abolished via the political process and criticizing what he saw as the Court's use of the Equal Protection Clause to impose its own views of good government policy. Also dissenting, Justice Harlan claimed that the Court should have upheld the law after employing a rational basis test, because the classification in question did not involve race.

In 2000, the Court decided a case about the right to cast an equal ballot that had the effect of deciding the 2000 presidential election. In *Bush v. Gore*,[349] the Court reversed the Florida Supreme Court's decision which had allowed several Florida counties to recount ballots for the 2000 presidential election, holding that a lack of uniform standards for determining voter intent violated equal protection. In light of an exceptionally close race in Florida, the result of which would determine the victor of the entire election, the Supreme Court of Florida ordered a lower court to recount a number of ballots in particular localities where officials had been unable to determine whether the voter had intended to vote for one or the other, or neither, presidential candidate. The ambiguity arose from the type of marking process the ballot required

---

345. *See, e.g.*, Karcher v. Doggett, 462 U.S. 725 (1983) (invaliding 0.7% deviation in sizes of congressional districts); *but see* Mahan v. Howell, 410 U.S. 315, 322 (1973) (recognizing more latitude for deviations in cases of state legislative district sizes).

346. For one of the few exceptions to the one-person-one-vote rule, see Salyer Land Co. v. Tulare Lake Basin Water Storage District, 410 U.S. 719 (1973) (allowing a water district to apportion voting rights based on the value of the land affected by the district's decisions).

347. 383 U.S. 663 (1966).

348. *Id*. at 665.

349. 531 U.S. 98 (2000).

for the voter to register a vote. Many counties used procedures requiring voters to punch through the ballot next to the name of the candidate for whom they wished to vote; sometimes, punch-throughs either only indented that part of the ballot or left the punched-out part hanging by a corner, thus creating either a "dimpled" or "hanging" chad. The state court required partial, geographically-limited recounts of ballots that did not register a presidential vote, but different counties and different personnel within each county used different standards to determine which partially-stamped out ballots would count as a vote for a given candidate.

In *Bush*, seven justices concluded that this process violated equal protection by tolerating different standards by which the same state sought to determine the intent of its voters, and thereby counting votes unequally. The five-justice majority opinion insisted that its decision was exceptionally narrow. Indeed, it wrote that its "consideration is limited to the present circumstances"[350] and thus did not suggest that a state violated equal protection if, for example, it allowed different counties to use different types of ballots or different mechanisms for tallying votes. Two additional justices agreed that the recount raised constitutional problems. But they proposed remanding the case for the state court to correct the problem and giving the state more time to certify its election results. By contrast, the five justices comprising the majority for the result concluded that the state had expressed a policy of adhering to the then-upcoming federal safe-harbor date for certifying results, such that the lack of time to complete the recount by then meant that the recount had to stop.

In more recent years, voter identification laws have been a major area of political and constitutional controversy. In *Crawford v. Marion County Election Board*,[351] the Court rejected a facial challenge to an Indiana law requiring its citizens to present government-issued photo identification to vote in person. A three-justice plurality rejected a facial attack on the statute but suggested that a court could still hear any subsequent challenge to the law as it applied to particular voters' circumstances. Relying on both *Harper* and some of the ballot access cases discussed in the next subsection, Justice Stevens, writing for the plurality, explained that even-handed burdens on the right to vote, if intended to enhance the integrity of the electoral process, were not necessarily unconstitutional, depending on the weight of the government interests justifying the burden. It found Indiana's interests in protecting against the reality and the appearance of electoral fraud and in modernizing its election procedures adequate to defeat the plaintiffs' facial challenge, given the plurality's conclusion that the law imposed only modest burdens on voters.

Three other justices concurred, to state their disagreement with even the possibility that particular voters might be able to bring challenges focused on their particular circumstances. In these justices' view, the law's minimal burdens and reasonable jus-

---

350. *Id.* at 109.
351. 553 U.S. 181 (2008).

tifications rendered the law generally valid, without regard to its impact on particular would-be voters.[352] Justices Souter, Ginsburg, and Breyer dissented.

[b] Other Barriers to Political Participation: Ballot Access and Gerrymandering

The Court has scrutinized various state restrictions on parties seeking to be placed on an election ballot. The Court has explained that those restrictions interfere with the related rights of political association and voting. In some cases, it has applied strict scrutiny to such restrictions, while in others, it has shrunk back from doing so.[353] It is hard to discern a consistent pattern to these cases. To be sure, the rights the Court identifies as implicated by ballot access claims are quite important—indeed, fundamental to democracy. On the other hand, the government has legitimate interests in preventing the ballot confusion and even deception that might arise from unfettered access to an election ballot.[354] To the extent such restrictions impose serious burdens on parties' and candidates' attempts to get on a ballot, the Court is likely to accord them at least some meaningful scrutiny. On the other hand, less burdensome restrictions will likely receive more generous scrutiny, given the undeniable interests government has in controlling access to the ballot—interests that might not be easily susceptible to review under a strict scrutiny standard.[355]

The right to vote could also effectively be impaired by political gerrymandering. Gerrymandering involves the drawing of political district lines to create a particular type of advantage for a group. For example, racial gerrymandering might involve drawing district lines so as to "pack" as many members as possible of the disfavored racial group into just a few districts; that group would see its preferred candidates win by overwhelming margins in those districts, but would have little impact on other districts, with the result that the group's overall political power would be lower than what might be suggested by its raw percentage of the state's total voting population. Alternatively, drafters of district lines might "crack" such groups, by splitting them up and dispersing them into many districts, with the result that they fail to dominate any district and thus again enjoy less political power than they otherwise would. Such practices can apply beyond racial groups, to members of political parties. Thus, for example, a state whose districting apparatus is controlled by Republicans might "pack" and "crack" likely Democratic voters so as to minimize Democratic in-

---

352. *See id.* at 204 (Scalia, J., joined by Thomas and Alito, JJ., concurring in the judgment).

353. *Compare, e.g.,* Williams v. Rhodes, 393 U.S. 23 (1968) (applying strict scrutiny) *with, e.g.,* Clements v. Fashing, 457 U.S. 957 (1982) (plurality opinion) (finding ballot access rights to not be fundamental).

354. *See, e.g.,* Jenness v. Fortson, 403 U.S. 431 (1971) (upholding a law requiring a new third party to make a threshold showing of support before being allowed onto a ballot).

355. For example, in *Jenness*, the Court distinguished analogous ballot access requirements struck down in *Williams v. Rhodes, supra.*, by noting the comparative strictness of the requirements struck down in *Rhodes. See* 403 U.S. at 438.

fluence in state government (and, of course, states where Democrats control the apparatus might attempt to do the same thing to likely Republican voters).

Such partisan gerrymandering triggers claims that the members of the disfavored party are suffering violations of their constitutional rights, whether to cast a meaningful, equal vote or to associate politically. As intuitive as such injuries might seem, in a long series of cases the Court struggled to find a justiciable standard governing such claims. In *Davis v. Bandemer*,[356] six justices concluded that political gerrymandering claims were justiciable — that is, the majority concluded that such claims did not constitute political questions.[357] However, only four of those justices could agree on a standard governing such claims, which they argued included inquiries into possible intentional discrimination against the disfavored party coupled with effects that transcended one election, along with factors drawn from racial gerrymandering cases such as a "strong indicia of lack of political power and the denial of fair representation."[358] The plurality concluded that those factors were not satisfied in the case before them. Three justices concurred in the decision to dismiss the lawsuit on the ground that such claims constituted political questions. Two justices, based on a somewhat more detailed standard than the one offered by the plurality, concluded that the plaintiffs had in fact made out a claim of political gerrymandering.

Almost twenty years later, in *Vieth v. Jubelirer*,[359] a four-justice plurality stated that political gerrymandering was non-justiciable due to a lack of any judicially-discoverable or manageable standards. After reviewing previous attempts after *Davis v. Bandemer* to develop such standards, the plurality determined that *Davis* had been incorrectly decided. It also rejected what it saw in *Davis* as an attempt, via its focus on the effects of a political gerrymander, to constitutionalize a requirement that elections result in proportional representation. In other words, the *Vieth* plurality saw any focus on the effects of a political gerrymander as an implicit requirement that, say, an election in which Republicans won 45% of the total vote result in a state legislature comprised of approximately 45% Republicans. The *Vieth* plurality found no such requirement in the Constitution,

Justice Kennedy concurred in the judgment, agreeing with the plurality that there were at that time no judicially manageable standards by which courts could judge political gerrymandering claims. However, he left open the possibility of future challenges, due to technological developments that may "make more evident the precise nature of the burdens gerrymanders impose on the representational rights of voters and parties." He wrote that when a gerrymander has the "purpose and effect of imposing burdens on a disfavored party," the First Amendment may supply a better basis than the Equal Protection Clause for intervention.[360]

---

356. 478 U.S. 109 (1986).
357. The political question doctrine is discussed in Section 2.08[5].
358. *Davis*, 478 U.S. at 139 (plurality opinion).
359. 541 U.S. 267 (2004).
360. *Id.* at 313, 315 (Kennedy, J., concurring).

Four justices dissented. Justice Stevens, relying on the racial gerrymandering cases, stated that he would "ask whether the legislature allowed partisan considerations to dominate and control the lines drawn, forsaking all neutral principles."[361] Justice Souter, joined by Justice Ginsburg, argued for a five-factor approach, which spoke to (1) the cohesiveness of the burdened political group; (2) the disregard the challenged district lines showed for traditional districting principles; (3) correlations between that disregard and the distribution of the burdened group's population; (4) the presentation of a hypothetical comparison district that exhibited less gerrymandering; and (5) intentional "packing" or "cracking" of the burdened group.[362] In his dissent, Justice Breyer urged the Court to focus on "extreme cases." Specifically, he would remedy "the unjustified entrenching in power of a political party that voters have rejected."[363]

In 2019, the Court for the first time assembled a majority for the proposition that political gerrymandering claims present non-justiciable political questions. In his opinion for a five-justice majority in *Rucho v. Common Cause*,[364] Chief Justice Roberts reprised the arguments justices had made previously in support of that position. He recognized that in cases of racial gerrymanders and denials of the one-person-one-vote principle of *Reynolds v. Sims*,[365] the Court had acknowledged that it had the authority to review state districting decisions. But outside of those two areas, he concluded that the Framers' decision to allocate such decisions to the states, and the lack of any judicially manageable standard short of a constitutionally-unrequired principle of proportional representation, mandated the conclusion that such claims were non-justiciable political questions.

Justice Kagan, speaking for four justices, wrote a heated dissent. She argued that over the years, lower courts had coalesced around a three-part test that examined the state's intent when drawing its district lines, the effects of those lines in diluting plaintiffs' votes by creating results that under-represented their preferences, and whether the state had offered a neutral justification for the lines it had drawn — a three-part test she described as one familiar to the law. She also criticized the majority for suggesting that plaintiffs could bring such claims under state constitutional provisions, asking why state courts could be expected to develop manageable standards when the Supreme Court had expressed its own inability to do so.

[4] The Right to Travel

In *Shapiro v. Thompson*,[366] the Court held unconstitutional laws of three states that limited welfare assistance to persons who had lived in the state for at least one year.

---

361. *Id.* at 339 (Stevens, J., dissenting).
362. *See id.* at 347–50 (Souter, J., dissenting).
363. *Id.* at 365 (Breyer, J., dissenting).
364. 139 S. Ct. 2484 (2019).
365. 377 U.S. 533 (1964). *Reynolds* is discussed in the prior sub-section.
366. 394 U.S. 618 (1969).

The states involved gave several justifications for the laws. The Court first rejected as illegitimate any state interest in preventing indigent people from traveling into the state, concluding that such a justification collided with the constitutional right to travel from state to state. It then rejected a state justification in preventing indigents from entering a state simply to take advantage of its welfare benefits, concluding that such a justification was overbroad since it penalized both indigents who migrated for this reason and those who came to improve their circumstances but found themselves having to rely on welfare. The Court did accept that a state might possibly wish to compensate long-term residents who had previously contributed to the state, but it nevertheless rejected this justification on the ground that, if taken to its logical conclusion, it would allow a state to withhold from new arrivals any otherwise-available public benefit.[367] Finally, the Court rejected administrative convenience and fraud deterrence rationales for the laws, concluding that they failed the requirement that infringements on the right to travel had to be "shown to be necessary to promote a compelling governmental interest."[368]

Chief Justice Warren, joined by Justice Black, dissented, arguing that Congress could overrule these statutes by enacting Commerce Clause legislation. They worried that the Court's opinion could lead to the invalidation of in-state preferences for such matters as state university tuition. Justice Harlan filed a lengthy dissent. In light of the purposes of the Fourteenth Amendment, he argued that strict scrutiny should apply only to racial classifications. He also more specifically attacked the "fundamental rights" prong of equal protection jurisprudence, observing that virtually all statutes affected some important interest. Justice Harlan felt that this branch of equal protection jurisprudence was unnecessary, because restrictions on rights secured by the Constitution should be subject to scrutiny under substantive due process analysis.[369] Applying these principles, he found various state interests adequate to outweigh the liberty to travel he found protected by the Due Process Clause.

Since *Shapiro*, the Court has reviewed durational residency requirements in several other contexts. In so doing, it has not formalistically applied the compelling state interest test to invalidate all restrictions on the right to travel. Instead, it appears to examine the importance of the state interest, the need for the disparate treatment in accomplishing the state's goals, and the actual burden or deterrent effect the disparate treatment has on interstate travel. While the Court has rejected a one-year residency requirement for eligibility to vote,[370] it has upheld 50-day residency requirements.[371] The Court invalidated a one-year residency requirement on indigents seeking non-

---

367. The Court later read this analysis as prohibiting this rationale for a state law according fewer benefits to new arrivals than to long-time residents. *See* Zobel v. Williams, 457 U.S. 55, 63 (1982).

368. *Shapiro*, 394 U.S. at 634.

369. *Compare* Zablocki v. Redhail, 434 U.S. 378, 391 (1978) (Stewart, J., concurring in the judgment) (criticizing the Court's use of the fundamental rights strand of equal protection and arguing that the case in question should be decided simply under the Due Process Clause). *Zablocki* is discussed earlier in Section 10.07[1].

370. Dunn v. Blumstein, 405 U.S. 330 (1972).

371. Marston v. Lewis, 410 U.S. 679 (1973); Burns v. Fortson, 410 U.S. 686 (1973).

emergency medical care in a public hospital.[372] It has upheld a one-year residency requirement as a condition of instituting a divorce action.[373] Finally, the Court has recognized states' authority to impose durational requirements as a condition of qualifying for lower, in-state tuition for colleges.[374]

In *Saenz v. Roe*,[375] the Supreme Court struck down, as violating the right to travel, a California statute according new residents, for their first year of California residency, only the level of welfare benefits they would have received in their previous home state. Writing for a seven-justice majority, Justice Stevens explained that the right to travel contains at least three components: "[The] right of a citizen of one State to enter and leave another State, the right to be treated as a welcome visitor rather than an unfriendly alien temporarily present in the second State, and, for those travelers who elect to become permanent residents, the right to be treated like other citizens of that State."[376] The California statute was held to violate the third aspect of the right to travel, which he located in the Fourteenth Amendment's Privileges and Immunities Clause.[377]

Chief Justice Rehnquist and Justice Thomas joined each other in separate dissents. The Chief Justice criticized the Court's use of the Privileges and Immunities Clause, which he noted had been used only very sparingly since the Fourteenth Amendment's ratification. He found no difference between California's one-year limitation on the amount of welfare benefits and one-year residency requirements previously upheld by the Court for in-state tuition benefits, access to divorce proceedings, and voting in primary elections. Justice Thomas said that the Privileges and Immunities Clause did not establish "the right of the newly arrived citizen to the same privileges and immunities enjoyed by other citizens of the same state."[378]

[5] Education

In 1973, the Court concluded that education was not a fundamental right. *San Antonio Independent Sch. Dist. v. Rodriguez*[379] involved a challenge to Texas's system of public school funding, which featured a complex formula emphasizing revenues from property taxes assessed on real property located within the district. The formula

---

372. Memorial Hosp. v. Maricopa County, 415 U.S. 250 (1974).

373. Sosna v. Iowa, 419 U.S. 393 (1975).

374. Starns v. Malkerson, 326 F. Supp. 234 (D. Minn. 1970), *aff'd*, 401 U.S. 985 (1971). *But cf.* Vlandis v. Kline, 412 U.S. 441 (1973) (striking down Connecticut's in-state tuition preference on the ground that it created an "irrebuttable presumption" preventing individuals in certain categories from ever establishing *bona fide* residency).

375. 526 U.S. 489 (1999).

376. *Id.* at 500.

377. That clause is discussed in Section 9.01[2]. The Court did not speculate about the constitutional foundation for the first version of this right, except to cite cases where the Court relied on the Commerce Clause to protect it. The Court located the second version of this right in the Article IV Privileges and Immunities Clause. That Clause is discussed in Section 7.08.

378. 526 U.S. at 521 (Thomas, J., dissenting).

379. 411 U.S. 1 (1973).

effectively meant that some districts were much more easily able to provide higher expenditures per student than other districts.

The Court in *Rodriguez* rejected both of the plaintiffs' main arguments—that poverty was a suspect class and that education was a fundamental right that had to be distributed equally. The suspect class component of the Court's analysis is discussed in Section 10.03[4]. After rejecting that argument, the Court turned to the fundamental rights issue. Justice Powell, writing for the five-justice majority, denied that fundamental rights were determined by deciding whether the right in question was in some ways important. Such an approach, he warned, turned courts into super-legislatures vested with the power to make policy determinations about which interests were important enough to protect.

Instead, he argued that in order to determine which rights were fundamental, the Court asked whether the interest in question was "explicitly or implicitly guaranteed by the Constitution."[380] He noted that the Constitution did not explicitly protect education. He also refused to hold education implicitly protected as essential to exercising other constitutional rights, such as speaking and voting. Justice Powell conceded that a fully informed citizenry would be better equipped to exercise speech and voting rights, but he concluded that it was not the Court's job to implement such values by "intrusion into otherwise legitimate state activities."[381] Moreover, he observed that even if the Constitution guaranteed some minimum level of education as necessary to meaningfully exercise other constitutional rights, the plaintiffs had failed to show that the Texas system failed to provide that minimum level. Because the Texas funding system did not affect a suspect class or deprive the plaintiffs of a fundamental right, the Court did not apply strict scrutiny; instead, it held that the system satisfied the required rational basis test. In upholding the system, the Court also noted the complex policy decisions implicit in the operation of a school funding system, and worried that courts would be incapable of developing judicially-manageable standards for overseeing a constitutional mandate of equal funding.

Justice Marshall, dissenting for himself and Justice Douglas,[382] engaged the majority's analysis on both the suspect class and the fundamental rights issue. With regard to the latter, he argued that the close nexus between education and the full exercise of constitutionally-protected speech and voting rights established education as a fundamental right. He noted that the Court had identified other unenumerated rights—such as voting in state elections, protected by *Reynolds v. Sims*, and the right to appeal one's criminal conviction, protected by *Griffin v. Illinois*—as fundamental.[383] He argued that the right to education should also be considered fundamental, given precedents emphasizing the importance of education, such as *Brown v. Board of Ed-*

---

380. *Id.* at 33–34.

381. *Id.* at 36.

382. Justice Brennan dissented separately but expressed his agreement with Justice Marshall's approach. Justice White dissented on a ground distinct from the fundamental rights issue.

383. Reynolds v. Sims, 377 U.S. 533 (1964); Griffin v. Illinois, 351 U.S. 12 (1956). Both of these cases are discussed earlier in this Section.

ucation,[384] the general importance society accords to education, and "the close relationship between education and some of our most basic constitutional values."[385]

As previously noted, some language in *Rodriguez* and *Plyler v. Doe*[386] suggests that a complete deprivation of education for lack of wealth or other reasons violates the Constitution. In *Kadrmas v. Dickinson Public Schools*,[387] the Court upheld a poor family's challenge to a North Dakota program charging a fee for school bus services. The Court reiterated *Rodriguez*'s conclusion that education is not a fundamental right, and, distinguishing cases such as *Griffin v. Illinois*,[388] noted that the state had not completely deprived any child of the ability to be transported to school.

---

384. 347 U.S. 483 (1954). *Brown* is discussed in Section 10.04[2][b][i].

385. 411 U.S. at 111 (Marshall, J., dissenting).

386. 457 U.S. 202 (1982). *Plyler*, which struck down a Texas law prohibiting children of undocumented immigrants from attending state public schools, is discussed in Section 10.03[2][b].

387. 487 U.S. 450 (1988).

388. 351 U.S. 12 (1956).

Chapter 11

Freedom of Speech, Press, and Assembly

At one level, American free speech law is quite complex. Rules lead to sub-rules, which in turn feature poorly-defined exceptions or limitations. This should not be surprising. Speech is prominent in nearly every human interaction. Calls for political change in a street protest, recitations of the facts of cases in law school classrooms, testimony in a court, novels, and offers to sell products in a grocery store are all speech. In addition, a wide variety of conduct—depending on the context, burning an American flag, dancing nude, or sleeping in a park—can all count as expression that also merits First Amendment protection. One should not be surprised, therefore, when First Amendment doctrine features a wide variety of rules and sub-rules.

This Chapter begins in Section 11.01 by considering the building blocks of free speech law. After a brief introduction (Section 11.01[1]), it explains that those fundamental elements include the identification of so-called unprotected categories of speech (Section 11.01[2]), the content-neutrality rule that governs most (although not all) government attempts to restrict speech and in turn the rules that govern content-neutral speech restrictions (Sections 11.01[3] and [4]), and the relevance of the location in which speech occurs for the amount and type of constitutional protection it enjoys (Section 11.01[5]). Section 11.02 considers a variety of special contexts in which speech and speech regulation occur. Section 11.03 considers the particular problems of speech in the mass media and the press, which are governed by a combination of rules derived from the Free Speech Clause and the Free Press Clause.

§ 11.01 The Fundamentals of Free Speech Law

[1] Introduction

One can identify some foundational principles of American free speech law. First, some speech is deemed "unprotected" by the First Amendment. Second, protected speech enjoys the protection of a rule—the "content-neutrality" rule—that looks askance at laws that restrict speech based on its subject-matter, its viewpoint, or the identity of the speaker. These two rules constitute the building blocks of Free Speech Clause doctrine. To be sure, these rules are not absolute: even ostensibly "unprotected" speech enjoys *some* First Amendment protection, and the content-neutrality rule does not always apply in full force, even to otherwise fully-protected speech. But understanding those exceptions requires, first, understanding the rules themselves.

This section begins by considering the categories of speech that are either unprotected or that enjoy reduced First Amendment protection. It then considers the content-neutrality rule. Section 11.02 then discusses specialized speech situations and doctrines.

Before that discussion begins, it is worthwhile realizing some free speech fundamentals. The 45 words contained in the First Amendment underwrite several important guarantees. The Amendment states, in its entirety, as follows:

> Congress shall make no law respecting an establishment of religion, or prohibiting the free exercise thereof; or abridging the freedom of speech, or of the press; or the right of the people peaceably to assemble, and to petition the Government for a redress of grievances.

While the Amendment only explicitly restricts Congress, there has never been any serious modern challenge to its applicability to all branches of the federal government.[1] Moreover, in 1925, the Court presumed that the guarantees of the Free Speech Clause applied to the states via the Fourteenth Amendment's Due Process Clause, and has never since questioned that idea.[2] Since then, the Court has "incorporated" the remainder of the First Amendment.[3]

Some commentators have suggested that the First Amendment has primacy over other constitutional provisions. In the middle years of the twentieth century, some justices argued that the First Amendment enjoyed a "preferred position" among constitutional rights.[4] Justices William O. Douglas and Hugo Black even maintained that the First Amendment was an *absolute*. A majority has never adopted the absolutist approach of Justices Douglas and Black. But, while the "preferred position" language has not survived into more modern cases, it is clear that the Court values free speech to an unusually high degree, even as compared to other Bill of Rights guarantees.

Scholars have identified a variety of theories justifying free speech. Some, such as Seana Shiffrin, have focused on the self-development role speech plays.[5] Another prominent speech theorist, Alexander Meiklejohn, argued that the essential reason for protecting speech was that the free exchange of different ideas was necessary for a democratic society.[6] On his view, if the people were truly to be the ultimate deci-

---

1. This oddity has been remarked on. *See* Nicholas Quinn Rosenkranz, *The Subjects of the Constitution*, 62 STAN. L. REV. 1209, 1253 (2010).

2. Gitlow v. New York, 268 U.S. 652 (1925).

3. For a discussion of the incorporation process, see Section 9.03.

4. *See, e.g.*, Murdock v. Pennsylvania, 319 U.S. 105, 115 (1943). For a discussion of this idea, see G. Edward White, *The First Amendment Comes of Age: The Emergence of Free Speech in Twentieth Century America*, 95 MICH. L. REV. 299, 327 (1996).

5. *See, e.g.*, Seana Shiffrin, *A Thinker-Based Approach to Freedom of Speech*, 27 CONST. COMM. 283, 287 (2011) (advocating an approach based on an "individual agent's interest in the protection of the free development and operation of her mind.").

6. *See* A. MEIKLEJOHN, FREEDOM OF SPEECH AND ITS RELATION TO SELF-GOVERNMENT (1948); Meiklejohn, *The First Amendment is an Absolute*, 1961 SUP. CT. REV. 245. *See also* W. Brennan, *The Supreme Court and the Meiklejohn Interpretation of the First Amendment*, 79 HARV. L. REV. 1 (1965).

sion-makers in government, they had to be informed enough, not just about political issues, but also literary, scientific, and cultural matters, to exercise effective choice in voting and influencing government. In contrast to Meiklejohn, Thomas Emerson offered four rationales for protecting free speech: (1) individual self-fulfillment; (2) the pursuit of knowledge and truth; (3) participation in democracy and in other aspects of our culture; and (4) political dissent to effect social change.[7]

The Court has never conclusively adopted one of these approaches, instead moving between them as needed in order to decide cases. One of the implications of that refusal to choose is that all speech is presumptively protected by the First Amendment. Nevertheless, the Court has recognized a limited number of cases in which government may regulate content more freely. The next sub-section considers those categories of "unprotected" speech.

[2] Categories of Unprotected and Partially Protected Speech

[a] Incitement

[i] The Early Cases

The Court's first serious engagement with the First Amendment occurred in the context of speech calling for radical revolutionary change. On the one hand, as speech addressing social and political affairs, such speech lies at the core of many understandings of the First Amendment's importance. Certainly, such speech is, almost by definition, critical to self-government. Moreover, to the extent one adopts the marketplace of ideas/search for truth rationale for free speech, political and social ideas (*i.e.*, ideas about how society should be organized and what it should value) surely rank among the most important. On the other hand, calls for radical change imply violence, or at least extra-legal political activity. Government surely has a compelling interest in preventing violence and activity that ignores and even undermines the normal processes of governmental change.

The Court's first encounter with the free speech implications of such speech occurred in the context of the nation's entry into World War I. The decision to enter the war sparked criticism and resistance both from socialists, who saw the war as simply a way for capitalists to retain power, and from pro-German forces in the nation, based particularly in German immigrant communities.

The speech cases involving these speakers, and those who continued to speak into the 1920s, are no longer good law. However, they contributed to the development of the principles that have provided strong protection for the freedom of speech today. Many of these principles were developed in the classic concurring and dissenting opinions written during this era by Justices Oliver Wendell Holmes and Louis Brandeis.

---

7. T. Emerson, The System of Freedom of Expression 6–7 (1970).

As noted above, World War I provided the impetus for the Court's first serious encounters with the Free Speech Clause. During World War I, Congress enacted two statutes to suppress opposition to the war. The Espionage Act of 1917 proscribed the publication or utterance of statements intended to obstruct the armed forces, including its recruiting efforts. The Sedition Act of 1918 made it a felony to publish or utter mere criticism of the government. These laws generated almost two thousand prosecutions and approximately one thousand convictions. In 1919 and 1920, the Supreme Court reviewed five major cases that challenged these laws as violations of the First Amendment.[8]

In *Schenck v. United States*,[9] Justice Holmes first articulated his famous "clear and present danger" test. In a unanimous opinion, the Court affirmed the convictions of Socialist Party officials under the Espionage Act. Schenck, the party's general secretary, distributed 15,000 pamphlets criticizing the war. One side of the pamphlet attacked the war and conscription, quoting, among other things, the Thirteenth Amendment's prohibition on slavery. The other side of the pamphlet was a more focused attack on conscription, which quoted, among other things, the First and Ninth Amendments.[10] Neither side directly urged disobedience to the draft, although it did urge legal action to have conscription repealed. There was no evidence that Schenck or his pamphlets actually obstructed the draft.

Nevertheless, the Court upheld Schenck's conviction, because he only had to intend to obstruct the draft. Writing for the Court, Justice Holmes reasoned that the defendant "intended to have some effect, and we do not see what effect [the pamphlet] could be expected to have upon persons subject to the draft except to influence them to obstruct the carrying of it out."[11] Consequently, the publication and distribution of the pamphlet alone established the intent required for a conviction under the statute.

Answering Schenck's First Amendment defense, Justice Holmes insisted that First Amendment protection is contingent. He wrote: "We admit that in many places and in ordinary times the defendants in saying all that was said in the circular would have been within their constitutional rights. But the character of every act depends upon the circumstances in which it is done." He continued: "The most stringent protection of free speech would not protect a man in falsely shouting fire in a theater and causing a panic." He therefore concluded: "The question in every case is whether the words used are used in such circumstances and are of such a nature as to create a clear and present danger that they will bring about the substantive evils that Congress has a right to prevent."[12]

---

8. *See* Gilbert v. Minnesota, 254 U.S. 325 (1920); Abrams v. United States, 250 U.S. 616 (1919); Schenck v. United States, 249 U.S. 47 (1919); Frohwerk v. United States, 249 U.S. 204 (1919); Debs v. United States, 249 U.S. 211 (1919).

9. 249 U.S. 47 (1919).

10. The Ninth Amendment recognizes the existence of rights not otherwise specified in the Constitution.

11. 249 U.S. at 51.

12. *Id.* at 52.

One week after *Schenck* was decided, Justice Holmes again wrote for a unanimous Court in *Debs v. United States*.[13] *Debs*, even more than *Schenck*, illustrated the lack of protection that the clear and present danger test afforded speech. Eugene Debs, a Socialist Party leader and five-time presidential candidate,[14] was convicted under the Espionage Act for remarks he made in a speech delivered to his supporters. The trial court sentenced Debs to ten years in prison for obstructing the recruitment of servicemen and for inciting a mutiny.

Before the speech, Debs signed an "Anti-war Proclamation and Program," which served as the Socialist Party's platform. The platform recommended "continuous, active, and public opposition to the War through demonstrations, mass petitions, and any other means within [the people's] power." Although Debs was not prosecuted for signing the proclamation, the Court relied in part on Debs' signature to "infer" his intent to obstruct the war effort. In reviewing Debs' First Amendment challenge to his conviction, Justice Holmes focused on the part of Debs' speech in which he told his audience that he had just returned from visiting fellow socialists who were incarcerated for aiding and abetting one another in failing to register for the draft. After praising several of them for their efforts, Debs said that he had to be "prudent" and might not be able to say all that he thought, intimating to the listeners that they could infer that he meant more. Justice Holmes considered this innuendo incriminating. This part of the decision may have exerted the greatest chilling effect on speech. Since language often is ambiguous, most people would be reluctant to discuss controversial political issues if they feared that their words might be construed in a way that violates a statute. Rather than finding specific intent to obstruct the war, Justice Holmes allowed the jury to find that such obstruction was the "natural and intended effect"[15] of Debs' speech.

Eight months after *Schenck* and *Debs*, the Court adopted a standard even less protective of speech than the clear and present danger test. In *Abrams v. United States*,[16] the Court upheld the convictions of five Bolshevik sympathizers under the Espionage Act as amended in 1918. The defendants, who opposed American intervention in the Russian Revolution, published two anti-war pamphlets that called on munitions factory workers to stop producing bullets that would be used in that intervention. The pamphlets also called for a general strike to halt the production and shipment of arms. Although the Court relied on *Schenck* to summarily dispose of the defendants' First Amendment challenges, the majority paid little attention to the "clear and present danger" test. Focusing on the "probable effect" that a general strike would have on the war effort against Germany, the Court noted that the general strike they advocated necessarily impeded that effort, even if their intent was merely to obstruct the Russian intervention.

---

13. 249 U.S. 211 (1919).

14. Debs won nearly a million votes in 1920, running his campaign from his jail cell. David Yassky, *Eras of the First Amendment*, 91 COLUM. L. REV. 1699, 1718 (1991).

15. 249 U.S. at 215.

16. 250 U.S. 616 (1919).

Justice Holmes, joined by Justice Brandeis, dissented. He construed the Espionage Act to require a specific intent to interfere with the American war effort against Germany and her allies. He found such an intent lacking in the flyers, given their focus on the intervention in Russia. Turning to the First Amendment, he wrote that "It is only the present danger of immediate evil or an intent to bring it about that warrants Congress in setting a limit to the expression of opinion where private rights are not concerned."[17] He insisted that what he called "the competition of the market" had to be relied on in order to reach ultimate truth. He thus called upon the government to tolerate even detested ideas "unless they so imminently threaten immediate interference with the lawful and pressing purposes of the law that an immediate check is required to save the country."[18] By bolstering it with concepts such as specific intent and immediacy, Justice Holmes began to tighten up the clear and present danger test that he had originally fashioned in *Schenck*.

Many have speculated whether *Abrams* reflected a change of heart on Justice Holmes's part, and, if it did, what caused it. Professor Gerald Gunther maintained that Holmes' chance encounter and subsequent correspondence with a young Judge Learned Hand deeply influenced his ideas about protection for speech.[19] Regardless of what his intentions were and how they evolved, it is notable that between *Schenck* and *Abrams*, Holmes changed the language of his formula from "clear and present"[20] to "clear and imminent."[21]

In *Gitlow v. New York*,[22] the Court for the first time applied the First Amendment against the states by incorporating it under the Fourteenth Amendment. Nevertheless, the Court still upheld Benjamin Gitlow's conviction against the constitutional challenge. Gitlow, a member of an extremist faction of the Socialist Party, was convicted for publishing "The Left Wing Manifesto," a document that called for a socialist revolution. He was arrested, tried, and convicted under New York's Criminal Anarchy statute, which made a felony of advocating or teaching the duty to overthrow government by force.

Writing for the majority, Justice Sanford held the statute to be valid as an exercise of New York's police power that advanced the state's fundamental interest in self-preservation. Justice Sanford found the clear and present danger test inapplicable in this case, because the New York statute only punished speech. Thus, unlike the World War I cases that involved prohibitions of conduct that the government claimed was intended and made more likely by the defendants' speech, *Gitlow* did not require the Court to look into the nexus between the speech and the harm. In the Court's view, the New York legislature had made the decision that all such speech carried with it

---

17. *Id.* at 628 (Holmes, J., dissenting).
18. *Id.* at 630.
19. *See* G. Gunther, *Learned Hand and the Origins of Modern First Amendment Doctrine: Some Fragments of History*, 27 STAN. L. REV. 719 (1975).
20. *Schenck*, 249 U.S. at 52.
21. *Abrams*, 250 U.S. at 627.
22. 268 U.S. 652 (1925).

the requisite danger, and courts had to respect that decision, with the result that it was unnecessary for the Court to examine Gitlow's particular speech to determine whether it specifically raised that danger.

Justice Holmes dissented, again joined by Justice Brandeis. Addressing the majority's position that the manifesto was not merely a theory but an incitement, Justice Holmes responded: "Every idea is an incitement. It offers itself for belief and if believed it is acted on unless some other belief outweighs it or some failure of energy stifles the movement at its birth." Building on that point, he added that "[e]loquence may set fire to reason"[23] — that is, the eloquent expression of an idea always carries the risk that a listener or reader would act upon it. This analysis suggests that Justice Holmes was continuing to probe the proper meaning of the clear and present danger test. But that very project highlighted the test's subjectivity and malleability, since the words "clear," "present," and "danger" inherently involved questions of degree.

Two years later, in *Whitney v. California*,[24] the Court upheld an individual's conviction for conspiring to overthrow the government under California's Criminal Syndicalism Act. The California statute prohibited the "advocacy" of crimes or unlawful violent acts as a means to bring about political change. It also forbade the assembly or formation of groups teaching criminal syndicalism. The Court inferred Whitney's "specific intent" to overthrow the government from her membership in and association with the Communist Labor Party. At the Party's convention, Whitney had supported a resolution seeking to move the Party away from its militant stance and toward participation in the electoral process. Nevertheless, the Court upheld her conviction because she remained a member after the resolution was defeated.

Joined by Justice Holmes, Justice Brandeis concurred in the result in *Whitney* because there was evidence that Whitney's conduct did in fact associate her with a conspiracy to commit serious crimes. Nevertheless, he criticized the Court's application of the clear and present danger test. Brandeis defined "present" danger as "imminent" danger, reasoning that, in order to be properly subject to punishment, the evil to society must be so immediate that it may transpire before the opportunity for full discussion. He then added that "even imminent danger cannot justify resort to prohibition of these functions essential to effective democracy, unless the evil apprehended is relatively serious."[25] Thus, according to Justice Brandeis' definition of the clear and present danger standard, government could only suppress speech in times of emergency when the danger of harm was *both* imminent and serious.

Justice Brandeis' opinion contained most of the rationales for the modern Court's strong protection for freedom of political speech. Toward the start of his discussion of the First Amendment issue, he wrote:

> Those who won our independence believed that the final end of the state
> was to make men free to develop their faculties, and that in its government

---

23. *Id.* at 673.
24. 274 U.S. 357 (1927).
25. 274 U.S. at 377 (Brandeis, J., concurring).

the deliberative forces should prevail over the arbitrary. They valued liberty both as an end and as a means. They believed liberty to be the secret of happiness and courage to be the secret of liberty. They believed that freedom to think as you will and to speak as you think are means indispensable to the discovery and spread of political truth; that without free speech and assembly discussion would be futile; that with them, discussion affords ordinarily adequate protection against the dissemination of noxious doctrine; that the greatest menace to freedom is an inert people; that public discussion is a political duty; and that this should be a fundamental principle of the American government.[26]

[ii] Increased Toleration and Renewed Repression

Justice Brandeis's rationales for protecting free speech, particularly the promotion of democracy and self-fulfillment, presaged the theories adopted by later First Amendment theorists. That broad understanding of the First Amendment's goals helped provide the foundation for the Court's turn toward more speech protection starting in the 1930s and 1940s. Among other examples of this more protective attitude, the Court in 1931 struck down a law prohibiting flying a red flag as a symbol of revolutionary socialism,[27] and in 1937, it struck down a conviction of a person who had presided over a meeting of an organization dedicated to revolutionary change, but a meeting in which such violent action was not discussed.[28] This new attitude reflected complex dynamics, including not only changing attitudes toward individual rights but the Court's response to external developments such as the rise of totalitarian regimes abroad.[29] But just as external developments led toward a more tolerant attitude toward freedom of speech during that era, the fear caused by the onset of the Cold War led it to turn in a more repressive direction in an important 1951 case, *Dennis v. United States*.[30]

In *Dennis*, the Court reviewed the convictions of 11 national leaders of the American Communist Party for violations of the Smith Act, a 1940 law that was America's first peacetime sedition act since 1798. The Smith Act outlawed organized advocacy that called for changing the government by force or violence. With the onset of the Cold War after 1945, the Smith Act became a prime tool for government prosecutors who sought to suppress domestic Communist activity, most spectacularly in *Dennis*.

The Court upheld the Act's constitutionality, although it did not review the actual evidence developed against the defendants.[31] In a plurality opinion, Chief Justice Vin-

---

26. *Id.* at 375.
27. Stromberg v. California, 283 U.S. 359 (1931).
28. De Jonge v. Oregon, 299 U.S. 353 (1937).
29. *See, e.g.*, Mark Tushnet, *The Hughes Court and Radical Political Dissent: The Case of Dirk DeJonge and Angelo Herndon*, 28 Ga. St. L. Rev. 333 (2012).
30. 341 U.S. 494 (1951).
31. Ironically, the Court declined to perform that evidentiary review even though Chief Justice Vinson's plurality repudiated the idea from *Gitlow* and *Whitney* that the Court had to defer to the legislature's determination that all speech of the banned type necessarily posed the requisite danger. *See id.* at 507–08.

son found that the clear and present danger test, as developed by Justices Holmes and Brandeis, had little relevance to the Communist threat, because it would prevent the government from meeting the slow and secretive danger of Communist infiltration. Instead, the four-justice plurality applied a watered-down version of that test by adopting the lower court's test,[32] which turned on the severity of the harm the government sought to prevent by suppressing the speech, as discounted by the probability that such harm would come to pass if the speech were allowed. Chief Justice Vinson dismissed the argument that any Communist uprising would likely be put down easily, concluding instead that the relevant harm was the *attempted uprising*—something he concluded a court could not discount as necessarily highly improbable. This tactic of substituting one harm for another as the one government had a right to try to prevent illustrates the malleability of any test based on vague "clear and present danger" language.

Justice Frankfurter's concurrence recognized that Chief Justice Vinson's open-ended balancing approach needed to be confined. He offered three rules, based on historical analysis, to accomplish this. His first and most important principle required that the judiciary give substantial deference to the legislature when balancing competing interests. Because the legislature had access to more information concerning national security, it was better able to assess the risks domestic Communism posed. Justice Frankfurter's second rule allowed this balancing of interests to adapt to the demands of the current situation. This made speech protection situation-specific. His third principle asserted that the Court could determine that certain types of speech were protected and other types were not. In *Dennis*, he distinguished between speech as an interchange of ideas, which was protected, and "advocacy," which was not. Applying that distinction in *Dennis*, he cautioned that the advocacy speech made by the defendants, while "not a conspiracy to overthrow the Government," was also not merely "a seminar in political theory."[33]

In his concurrence, Justice Jackson criticized the entire idea of applying a clear and present danger test in the circumstances raised by *Dennis*. In his view, that test, as developed by Justices Holmes and Brandeis, was suitable for speech made by individuals and small-scale groups, but not speech by individuals associated with a group like the Communist Party, which was a large, disciplined and foreign-directed organization, the threat from which could not be discerned by judges who lacked access to top-secret intelligence.

Justices Douglas and Black wrote separate dissenting opinions. Justice Douglas described the case as involving a criminal prosecution for "conspiracy to advocate and teach."[34] Rather than suppressing the teachings of Stalin, Marx, and Engels, he

---

32. In another irony, the lower court judge who wrote the appellate opinion affirming the convictions of the *Dennis* defendants was Learned Hand, whose conversations with Justice Holmes in 1919 might have led the latter to move toward a more tolerant attitude toward free speech. *See* text accompanying note 19, *supra.*

33. 341 U.S. at 546 (Frankfurter, J., concurring).

34. *Id.* at 582 (Douglas, J., dissenting).

argued that the government should allow them to be exposed to the light of criticism, to allow the public to repudiate Communism. Justice Black insisted that the First Amendment's phrasing, "Congress shall pass no law," should be interpreted literally. His absolutist approach to free speech, also embraced by Justice Douglas, was criticized by Justice Frankfurter as being simplistic and naive. Justice Frankfurter warned: "Absolute rules would inevitably lead to absolute exceptions, and such exceptions would eventually corrode the rules."[35] While the Court never adopted the absolutist approach to freedom of speech, Justices Black's and Douglas' position powerfully influenced the modern Court's stringent protection for free speech.

Six years after *Dennis*, the Court overturned the Smith Act convictions of 14 lower-level Communist Party leaders in *Yates v. United States*.[36] In contrast to *Dennis*, the *Yates* Court construed the Smith Act to require incitement of action forcibly to overthrow the government. While the case was decided on statutory interpretation grounds, constitutional concerns very likely influenced that more speech-friendly interpretation of the statute. Moving away from a balancing approach toward a bright lines approach, the *Yates* test maintained that certain speech was presumptively protected unless that speech essentially constituted a call to actual violence.

[iii] *Brandenburg* and the Modern Rule

Cold War tensions had eased somewhat by *Yates*. By 1969, they had eased even more. This development made it easier for the Court, in *Brandenburg v. Ohio*,[37] to announce the modern, much more speech-protective rule for incitement. In *Brandenburg*, the Court reviewed the conviction of a Ku Klux Klan leader under Ohio's Criminal Syndicalism statute, a law similar to the one the Court sustained in *Whitney v. California*, discussed earlier. The defendant in *Brandenburg* had invited a television reporter and camera operator to film a Klan rally, where Brandenburg made a speech to fellow Klansmen. Although most of the content of the speech was inaudible, Brandenburg clearly made several derogatory remarks about African-Americans and Jews. Boasting that the Klan had the largest membership of any organization in the state, Brandenburg proclaimed that 400,000 of its members were planning a march in Washington, D.C., and then in Florida and Mississippi, approximately a week after the Ohio rally. He continued: "We're not a revengent [sic] organization, but if our President, our Congress, our Supreme Court continues to suppress the white, Caucasian race, it's possible that there might have to be some revengance [sic] taken."[38] Although Brandenburg himself was not armed, several people in one film carried weapons.

In overturning the conviction, the Court declared that the First Amendment did "not permit a State to forbid or proscribe advocacy ... except where such advocacy is directed to inciting or producing imminent lawless action and is likely to incite or

---

35. *Id.* at 524 (Frankfurter, J., concurring).
36. 354 U.S. 298 (1957).
37. 395 U.S. 444 (1969).
38. *Id.* at 446.

produce such action."[39] Thus, to meet the *Brandenburg* test and be subject to prohibition, the speech must fit within certain categories. First, the speech must be an incitement—that is, it could not take the form of mere abstract advocacy of violence, no matter how likely such advocacy would be in producing the violent effect. *Brandenburg* also required that the speech be objectively likely to produce imminent lawless action, and that the speaker intended to produce such imminent lawless action. The speech must meet all three of these criteria before government can proscribe it. To illustrate the test, the Court contrasted teaching the moral necessity of using force (which would be protected under this test), with preparing or steeling a group for violent action (which would not).

Hess v. Indiana[40] illustrated the speech-protectiveness with which the *Brandenburg* test could be applied. In *Hess*, the Court summarily overturned the conviction of a protester for disorderly conduct.[41] After police forced Hess and his fellow demonstrators off a street and onto the curb, a sheriff arrested Hess when he overheard him say something that was later stipulated to be, "We'll take the fucking street later" or "We'll take the fucking street again."[42] In a *per curiam* opinion, the Court characterized Hess' speech as "[at] best ... counsel for present moderation; at worst, it amounted to nothing more than advocacy of illegal action at some indefinite future time."[43] The Court's summary reversal of his conviction, in a factual context that featured a greater danger of "imminent lawless action" than the small group of Klansmen talking about future conduct in *Brandenburg* itself, demonstrated the stringency with which the Court applied the *Brandenburg* test.[44]

In *NAACP v. Claiborne Hardware Co.*,[45] the Court held that *Brandenburg* did not permit a civil action for a speech made by the leader of an economic boycott that called for violence against boycott violators.[46] The Court conceded that if acts of vi-

---

39. *Id.* at 447.

40. 414 U.S. 105 (1973).

41. A summary decision is one that is rendered without briefing or oral argument.

42. 414 U.S. at 107.

43. *Id.* at 108.

44. A related doctrine, known as "true threats," holds that speech that communicates a threat is unprotected. In *Watts v. United States*, the Court reversed the conviction of a person who, at demonstration, stated that if he was inducted into the armed forces and given a rifle, "the first man I want to get in my sights is L.B.J" (the well-known initials of the President at the time). 394 U.S. 705, 706 (1969). The Court recognized that threats against the President were uniquely dangerous to the nation, but concluded, given the First Amendment's commitment to protecting even caustic speech, that the statutory language criminalizing such threats had to be construed as not covering what the Court called "the kind of political hyperbole indulged in" by the speaker. *Id.* at 708. "True threats" are not limited to those made against the President. In 2015, the Court, interpreting a more general federal statute criminalizing threats, held that the statute required that the speaker have a mental state either intending to communicate a threat or knowing that the message will be construed as a threat. However, it did not explicitly ground that conclusion on First Amendment considerations. *See* Elonis v. United States, 575 U.S. 723 (2015).

45. 458 U.S. 886 (1982).

46. The civil action was for a business tort arising out of the boycott leaders' alleged interference with contractual relationships.

olence had followed the speech, a "substantial question"[47] would have arisen about whether the speakers could be liable. This *dicta,* suggesting that actionability hinges on what happened after the speech, contrasts with the apparent thrust of *Brandenburg, i.e.,* that the objective assessment of imminent lawless action should focus on the time that the speech was uttered. On the other hand, the factual context of the *Claiborne Hardware* suit—an after-the-fact tort suit, rather than an on-the-spot decision by police that speech is raising the risk of violence—helps explain the Court's focus on what actually happened as opposed to, as in *Hess,* what was likely to happen or what the speaker intended.

In sum, the Court's incitement jurisprudence has followed a long path from upholding restrictions on core political speech based on common law notions of constructive intent toward a much more speech-protective insistence on a speaker's actual specific intent to incite immediate lawless activity and the likelihood that such incitement would be successful. But this path has not been a straight line: at times of national anxiety, such as in the early years of the Cold War, the Court has been much more willing to tolerate restrictions on political speech. Some feared that the shock the nation felt after the September 11, 2001, terrorist attacks would similarly trigger such a retrenchment; for the most part, that seems not to have occurred in the United States.[48] Whether some future international crisis could cause such a reaction remains an open question.

[b] Fighting Words and Other Offensive Speech

The Court has long allowed government to restrict certain types of offensive speech. One notable category of unprotected offensive speech is "fighting words." This category was recognized in *Chaplinsky v. New Hampshire,* where the Court upheld a criminal conviction for calling a police officer "a God damned racketeer" and "a damned Fascist."[49] The Court defined "fighting words" as "those which by their very utterance inflict injury or tend to incite an immediate breach of the peace."[50] The idea, according to *Chaplinsky,* is there are some words that, if said without what it called "a disarming smile,"[51] would normally provoke a person to respond not with more speech, but with violence. Several cases since *Chaplinsky* appear to have narrowed the fighting

---

47. 458 U.S. at 928.

48. Some European nations, however, have imposed more draconian restrictions in the wake of the September 11 attacks and similar attacks in Europe itself. *See, e.g.,* Shawn Marie Boyne, *Free Speech, Terrorism, and European Security: Defining and Defending the Political Community,* 30 PACE L. REV. 417 (2010) (discussing various European nations' laws regarding incitement in the early twenty-first century).

49. 315 U.S. 568, 568 (1942). The law under which Chaplinsky was convicted prohibited addressing "any offensive, derisive, or annoying word" to any other person lawfully in public. *See ibid.* (quoting the statute).

50. *Id.* at 572. The Court provided this definition in the context of explaining why several types of speech, including but not limited to fighting words, are unprotected by the First Amendment. That explanation is discussed in Section 11.01[2][f][i], below.

51. *Id.* at 573.

words doctrine.[52] The concept is still the law, however. Indeed, a number of lower court decisions in the modern era have upheld convictions for disturbing the peace and similar charges, on the basis of uttering fighting words.[53]

Venturing beyond fighting words *per se*, the modern Court has declined to restrict speech because it is merely offensive. Most famously, in *Cohen v. California*,[54] the Court reversed an individual's conviction for wearing in a courthouse a jacket on which the words "Fuck the Draft" were written. After recognizing that the First Amendment protected expressive conduct as well as pure speech,[55] the Court declined to find the jacket constituted fighting words, since the message was not directed at a particular individual. The Court also rejected the state's argument that it sought to protect the sensibilities of other persons in the courthouse who might have seen the jacket. Writing for the Court, Justice Harlan observed that, while the state might have an interest in protecting other persons from having to hear unwelcome speech in their homes, that interest was much weaker in public. The Court also rejected the state's interest in excising offensive language from public discourse. It explained that the First Amendment protected both reasoned and immoderate expressions, and noted that strong, immoderate words often convey a unique intensity of feeling.

Offensive speech touches upon at least two additional First Amendment concepts. Because of the inherent vagueness of many statutes on which offensive speech convictions are based, cases involving offensive speech are often decided based on the First Amendment concepts of overbreadth and vagueness. These closely-related ideas are discussed in Section 11.02. Second, the Court has held that police must take significant steps to prevent opponents of a speaker from effectively shutting down speech by threatening violence if the speaker continues. This phenomenon—known as the "heckler's veto"—is discussed later in this sub-section.[56]

[c] Libel, Defamation and Other Speech Torts

Libel, defamation, infliction of emotional distress, and invasion of privacy are classic tort claims that implicate First Amendment interests. The Court's treatment of these issues has attempted to strike a balance between those First Amendment in-

---

52. Several cases may indicate a narrowing of the fighting words doctrine by overturning convictions on overbreadth grounds. *See, e.g.,* Lewis v. City of New Orleans, 415 U.S. 130 (1974); Gooding v. Wilson, 405 U.S. 518 (1972). Overbreadth doctrine is discussed later in this Chapter. *See* Section 11.02[2]. Both *Lewis* and *Gooding*, as well as *Chaplinsky* itself, involve police officers, as do many other cases. *See, e.g.,* ARTHUR HELLMAN, WILLIAM ARAIZA, THOMAS BAKER & ASHUTOSH BHAGWAT, FIRST AMENDMENT LAW: FREEDOM OF SPEECH AND RELIGION 71–75 (4th ed. 2018) (discussing other cases). It is likely not a coincidence that many fighting words cases involve police officers as the recipients of the verbal abuse, given the stressful nature of many encounters with the police and the simple fact that arrests are easier to make when the police officer happens to be on site when the verbal abuse occurs.

53. *See* HELLMAN ET AL. FIRST AMENDMENT LAW, *supra*, at 71–75.

54. 403 U.S. 15 (1971).

55. The First Amendment rules governing the regulation of such expressive conduct are discussed later in this Chapter. *See* Section 11.01[4][b].

56. *See* Section 11.01[5][c].

terests and, on the other hand, plaintiffs' longstanding and well-recognized common law rights to, among other interests, their reputations and their privacy.

[i] Libel and Defamation

In *New York Times v. Sullivan*,[57] the Court held that the First Amendment constrained common law defamation actions.[58] The defamation plaintiff in *New York Times* was the Police Commissioner of the City of Montgomery, Alabama, who brought a libel action against four Alabama clergymen and the New York Times Company for, respectively, placing and publishing an allegedly defamatory advertisement about him. The ad called for solidarity with civil rights protesters in the South and was signed by a large number of prominent persons. It also contained several factual inaccuracies. Some errors were trivial (*e.g.*, it misidentified a patriotic song the protesters sang), while others were more serious (*e.g.*, it misstated details about police activity near a college that was one of the centers of the protest). A jury awarded the Commissioner damages of $500,000.

Under Alabama defamation law, the statements at issue were libelous *per se* because they damaged the Commissioner's reputation in his trade or business. Consequently, the law imposed strict liability for publishing the material, unless the defendant could prove truth in all its particulars. Moreover, actual damages were presumed — that is, they did not have to be proven in order to be assessed.

The Court began its analysis by refusing to accept the claim that the status of the speech as "libel" removed it from First Amendment protection. The Court described "libel" as simply a label attached by state law, which did not by its own force immunize the speech from First Amendment scrutiny. Explaining that falsity and reputational harm did not strip speech of constitutional protection, Justice Brennan cited the Sedition Act of 1798, which had imposed criminal fines and imprisonment for publishing defamatory material about the President, Congress, or the national government. Congress and the President subsequently rejected the Act, repealing it and making amends to those punished. In *New York Times*, the Court for the first time stated that criminal penalties for defamatory speech were unconstitutional.

Justice Brennan then added that large civil damage awards could chill government criticism even more dramatically than the Sedition Act. However, the Court did not immunize from tort liability any and all false statements of fact. Rather, the Court held that a public official plaintiff in a defamation action relating to his official conduct must prove that the defendant published the defamatory falsehood with actual knowledge of its falsity or with reckless disregard as to its truth or falsity — a standard the Court called "actual malice." Moreover, the Court required plaintiff to prove this

---

57. 376 U.S. 254 (1964).

58. In order to reach the First Amendment issue, the Court held that, first, the actions of the Alabama courts in assessing the tort liability constituted "state action" subject to the First Amendment, and second, the fact that the alleged defamation occurred in an advertisement did not remove the speech from First Amendment protection. "State action" is discussed in Chapter 14, while the First Amendment's treatment of "commercial speech" is discussed in Section 11.01[2][e].

standard with "convincing clarity,"[59] or as later decisions have indicated, with clear and convincing evidence.[60] The standard applied to media and non-media defendants, which were both involved in this case. Applying that standard to the newspaper's conduct, the Court concluded that its failure to check the facts of the proposed ad against its own files and its reliance on the good names of those who signed the ad constituted at most negligence rather than the actual malice required to impose liability.

To meet the reckless disregard standard, a plaintiff must establish that the defendant in fact entertained serious doubts about the truth of the statement. This is generally thought to be a subjective standard.[61] To determine lack of good faith, the plaintiff could prove, for example, that the story was the product of the reporter's imagination or of an unverified telephone call, or that "there are obvious reasons to doubt the veracity of the informant or the accuracy of his reports."[62] Building on its application of the standard in *New York Times*, the Court in *Curtis Publishing Co. v. Butts*[63] found reckless disregard based on deficiencies in investigatory procedures that resulted in serious charges being published in a context that did not involve "hot news" and thus allowed for deeper investigation. The defendant had almost exclusively relied on the affidavit of one source who was on probation for a crime of dishonesty, and the publisher-defendant had not attempted to corroborate this story.

In *New York Times*, the Court did not give careful consideration to the definition of "public official," since it was clear that Commissioner Sullivan satisfied any definition. Two years later, in *Rosenblatt v. Baer*,[64] the Court held that a county recreation area supervisor was a public official for *New York Times* purposes. It explained that the test for determining whether a particular plaintiff was a public official was whether "the position in government has such apparent importance that the public has an independent interest in the qualifications and performance of the person who holds it, beyond the general public interest in the qualifications and performance of all governmental employees."[65] The Court also ruled that such an official should "appear to [have] substantial responsibility for or control over the conduct of governmental affairs."[66]

The Court has articulated a similarly broad definition of official conduct. In *Monitor Patriot Co. v. Roy*, the Court applied the *New York Times* standard to a charge that a candidate for the United States Senate had been a "small-time bootlegger."[67] At least for candidates running for public office, the Court found it difficult to determine

---

59. *Id.* at 285–86.
60. *See* Gertz v. Robert Welch, Inc., 418 U.S. 323 (1974).
61. St. Amant v. Thompson, 390 U.S. 727 (1968).
62. *Id.* at 732.
63. 388 U.S. 130 (1967).
64. 383 U.S. 75 (1966).
65. *Id.* at 86.
66. *Id.* at 85.
67. 401 U.S. 265, 266 (1971).

what statements about private or public life would be irrelevant. The Court did imply that the definition might be narrower, and thus the liability standard less stringent, for public officials who were not candidates in an election when the libel occurred.

After *New York Times*, the Court handed down several decisions extending that case's "actual malice" liability standard rule beyond "public officials," to also include "public figures." In *Curtis Publishing Co. v. Butts*[68] and *Associated Press v. Walker*,[69] the Court applied it to, respectively, the University of Georgia football coach and a retired army general. Although neither was a public official, both were held to be public figures. The Court reached a different conclusion about the plaintiff in *Gertz v. Robert Welch, Inc.*[70] *Gertz* involved a lawyer who was defamed by a publication after he took on a high-profile civil rights case. Writing for the Court, Justice Powell provided a rationale for affording less tort law protection for public official or public figure defamation plaintiffs, as opposed to plaintiffs who were merely private individuals. He explained that because public officials and public figures have greater access to the media to respond to charges made against them, they have less need to use the judicial system to clear their names. In addition, because such persons have thrust themselves into the limelight, they assume the risk of public scrutiny. Neither of these considerations applies when the defamation concerns a private figure. For these reasons, in cases involving defamation of a private figure (but still on a matter of public concern), *Gertz* permitted states to define the standard for compensatory damages, as long as that standard was not strict liability. Thus, for example, a state could apply a negligence standard. However, punitive and presumed damages still required a showing of actual malice.

Because *Gertz* drew a constitutional distinction between public figures and private figures, it had to consider the definition of those terms. The Court identified a class of persons as "voluntary general public figures" who have "such pervasive fame or notoriety"[71] or who "occupy positions of such pervasive power and influence" that they always have public figure status in all defamation actions. Other persons were "limited public figures" who, having voluntarily thrust themselves into a particular controversy, are public figures only for defamation claims related to that controversy. Justice Powell acknowledged that in "exceedingly rare"[72] cases, there could be involuntary public figures, who are drawn into controversies without any action on their part. In *Gertz* itself, the Court concluded that the attorney-defamation plaintiff fell into none of these categories. He took a high-profile case but did not seek out press attention relating to it—for example, he never called a press conference to discuss the case. None of the jurors in the case recognized his name, and the defendant-pub-

---

68. 388 U.S. 130 (1967).

69. 389 U.S. 28 (1967). In *Walker*, the Court, without discussing the facts, simply reversed the lower court decision and remanded the case to allow the lower court to apply the principles announced in *Butts*.

70. 418 U.S. 323 (1974).

71. *Id.* at 351.

72. *Id.* at 345.

lisher offered no evidence that that lack of recognition failed to reflect the wide recognition he actually enjoyed in the local community.

Since *Gertz*, the Court has further narrowed the public figure concept by focusing on whether a defamation plaintiff had thrust herself into a public controversy. In *Time, Inc. v. Firestone*,[73] the Court refused to hold the wife of a wealthy industrialist to be a public figure, even after a well-publicized divorce proceeding. According to the Court, she "did not assume any role of especial prominence in the affairs of society ... and she did not thrust herself to the forefront of any particular public controversy in order to influence the resolution of the issues involved in it."[74] In *Hutchinson v. Proxmire*,[75] the plaintiff was a scientist who had been awarded a satirical award by a senator, for alleged government waste. Neither the award nor the small number of writings that plaintiff had published in professional journals transformed him into a public figure. Finally, in *Wolston v. Reader's Digest, Inc.*,[76] the Court refused to extend public figure status to a plaintiff who had been convicted in 1958 for failing to appear before a grand jury investigating Soviet espionage. The 1958 conviction did not transform him into a public figure when he sued in 1974 after a publication called him a "Soviet agent." The Court again concluded that the plaintiff had not thrust himself into any controversy, and the fact that he had previously been convicted of a crime was not enough to render him a public figure.

The other component of the *New York Times* rule involves the public's interest in the subject-matter of the defamation. In *Dun & Bradstreet v. Greenmoss Builders, Inc.*,[77] the Court held that the Constitution imposed only mild restrictions on the ability of a state to allow a private figure to recover presumed or punitive damages for statements that did not involve matters of public concern. *Dun & Bradstreet* involved a credit reporting agency's allegedly false statement about the plaintiff's business conduct, which was communicated privately to the agency's client. In that factual context, a three-justice plurality allowed state law to control the award of presumed and punitive damages, as long as the state did not allow such damages on a showing of strict liability. Chief Justice Burger and Justice White each wrote separate concurrences to establish a majority for the proposition that the private matters the speech addressed justified imposition of a more plaintiff-friendly liability standard.[78]

In determining whether allegedly defamatory speech involved a matter of public concern, the plurality listed a number of relatively amorphous factors. Writing for those three justices, Justice Powell noted the report in this case did not involve public issues; rather, the speech interested only the credit reporting agency and its five business clients who could not circulate it. It was both false and damaging, but unlike

73. 424 U.S. 448 (1976).

74. *Id.* at 453.

75. 443 U.S. 111 (1979).

76. 443 U.S. 157 (1979).

77. 472 U.S. 749 (1985).

78. *Id.* at 763 (Burger, C.J., concurring in the judgment); *id.* at 765 (White, J., concurring in the judgment).

advertising, did not involve the free flow or exchange of information. Justice Powell also noted that the speech was more objectively verifiable than certain other forms of speech deserving greater protection and was solely motivated by a desire for profit, a fact suggesting that it was resilient enough to withstand more plaintiff-friendly liability rules.[79]

With regard to private defamation plaintiffs, the law remains somewhat uncertain. The narrow holding of *Dun & Bradstreet* is that with a non-media defendant, state law largely (although not completely) controls the imposition of presumed and punitive damages if the speech does not involve a matter of public concern. That holding arguably implies that a state could impose liability without fault for actual damages under such circumstances, but no decisions since *Dun & Bradstreet* have altered *Gertz*'s requirement that a private-figure plaintiff at least show negligence.

[ii] Other Speech Torts

In *Hustler Magazine v. Falwell*,[80] the Court extended the *New York Times* reckless disregard standard to a tort action for intentional infliction of emotional distress (IIED) brought by well-known minister. *Hustler* involved a parody magazine ad that made outrageous statements about the minister. At the bottom of the page, the ad contained a small print disclaimer "ad-parody — not to be taken seriously." The Court unanimously reversed the trial court's allowance of a claim for IIED. The Court required a public figure or public official to meet the reckless disregard standard to recover for this tort, and further required that liability could only rest on a false statement of fact. Since no reasonable person could believe that the ad's outrageous statements were true instead of constituting a parody, there could be no liability.

In 2011, the Court reversed an IIED verdict against religious protesters at a military funeral. In *Snyder v. Phelps*,[81] members of a church picketed a funeral of a soldier killed in action, claiming that his death was welcome retribution for the nation's sin of tolerating homosexuality. The soldiers' parents obtained an IIED verdict, which the Court reversed on First Amendment grounds. The Court noted that the church members were speaking on matters of public concern, did not trespass but rather stayed on public property, did not disrupt the funeral, and otherwise complied with the law. The Court stressed the narrowness of its holding, implying that protests characterized other than in these terms might still be vulnerable to IIED liability.

Defamation actions apply to false statements of fact that damage reputation. *Milkovich v. Lorain Journal Co.*[82] held that a statement of opinion was subject to a defamation action if it implied underlying facts which were defamatory. Prefacing a factual statement with words like "I think" or "[i]n my opinion" did not insulate it from a defamation action. Thus, in *Milkovich*, the Court held actionable a statement

---

79. 472 U.S. at 762.
80. 485 U.S. 46 (1988).
81. 562 U.S. 443 (2011).
82. 497 U.S. 1 (1990).

implying that the plaintiff had perjured himself. The Court said that the language was not "loose, figurative, or hyperbolic,"[83] but instead was capable of being proven true or false. In dissent, Justice Brennan feared that the Court's decision would chill conjecture that was "a means of fueling a national discourse on such questions and stimulating public pressure for answers from those who know more."[84]

Separate from protection against damage to reputation is protection against public revelation of private facts. These private facts need not even be damaging to reputation.[85] As with defamation, the Constitution has imposed certain limitations on these privacy actions. In *Zacchini v. Scripps-Howard Broadcasting Co.*,[86] a television station broadcast an entire "human cannonball" performance. The case upheld against a First Amendment defense a state-law right of publicity, which implicated a commercial, proprietary interest in the performance. The majority reasoned that allowing uncompensated display of such events would deprive performers of any economic incentive to create and perform them. Important to the plaintiff's case was the fact that the broadcaster aired the entire act, and that the plaintiff had specifically asked the reporter not to film it. With regard to damages, the majority stated that if the publicity caused more people to attend so that he made more money, the performer could recover nothing.

Time, Inc. v. Hill[87] involved another sort of privacy action. False light privacy involves discussing private facts about an individual and casting them into a false and objectionable (although not necessarily defamatory) light. An example of this could be using someone's picture in an offensive advertisement. *Time* required that the *New York Times* standard be met in all false light privacy actions. However, *Time* was decided before *Gertz*. *Gertz*'s distinction between public and private figures in the defamation context may mean that the First Amendment does not require a private plaintiff in a false light privacy action to meet the actual malice standard.[88]

In *Florida Star v. B.J.F.*,[89] a reporter trainee published the name of a rape victim, violating both police policy and the newspaper's own policy, when the police had inadvertently released the victim's name. While the Court ruled in favor of the newspaper, it did not rule out the possibility that publication of such information could trigger an invasion of privacy action under some circumstances. Instead, it decided the case on what it described as narrow grounds. Quoting an earlier case, the Court,

---

83. *Id.* at 21.

84. *Id.* at 35 (Brennan, J., dissenting).

85. A famous article co-authored by future Supreme Court justice Louis Brandeis catalogued the then-developing jurisprudence of privacy rights, in the context of the growth of the popular press during that era. Samuel Warren & Louis Brandeis, *The Right to Privacy*, 4 HARV. L. REV. 193 (1890).

86. 433 U.S. 562 (1977).

87. 385 U.S. 374 (1967).

88. However, noted torts theorists William Prosser and Page Keeton have suggested that the reckless disregard test was inherent to a false light privacy cause of action, as the culpable conduct must have involved deliberately falsifying or sensationalizing information. PROSSER & KEETON ON THE LAW OF TORTS, § 113, at 804–5 (W. Page Keeton ed., 5th ed.).

89. 491 U.S. 524 (1989).

speaking through Justice Marshall, stated: "'[I]f a newspaper lawfully obtains truthful information about a matter of public significance then state officials may not constitutionally punish publication of the information, absent a need to further a state interest of the highest order.'"[90]

Thus, there might be more room for an invasion of privacy lawsuit when the publisher acquires information unlawfully. Indeed, as the above quotation indicates, there remained room, under limited circumstances, for such a tort suit even when the publisher acquired the information lawfully. The Court found this possibility not to apply in *Florida Star*, given the fact that it was the government itself that (inadvertently) provided the information, the "broad sweep of the negligence *per se* standard"[91] under which the rape victim sued in *Florida Star*, and the fact that the prohibition on disclosing rape victims' names applied only to dissemination in an "instrument of mass communication,"[92] thus allowing disclosure through other methods.

In *Bartnicki v. Vopper*,[93] the Court struck down an application of a federal wiretapping statute that imposed liability on persons who knowingly disclosed unlawfully obtained electronic communications. In *Bartnicki*, an unidentified person illegally intercepted and taped a cell phone conversation between plaintiffs Bartnicki and Kane, who were involved in heated negotiations between a teacher's union and a school board. Eventually, the tape fell into the hands of Vopper, who broadcast the conversation on his radio talk show. Under the statute, Vopper could be punished for disclosing the conversation even though he was not the one who illegally taped it.

In striking down the prosecution, the Court rejected the government's argument that penalizing the disclosure of innocently-obtained information that the provider had procured illegally was an appropriate way of deterring illegal procurement of such information. Though the Court found the government interest in protecting privacy interests more persuasive, it concluded that the privacy concerns at stake in this case were outweighed by the interest in disclosing matters of public importance. Thus, the First Amendment continues to protect speech about public matters despite unlawful conduct in the chain by which the ultimate disseminator acquired it.

[d] Sexual Speech

[i] Obscenity

In *Chaplinsky v. New Hampshire*,[94] the Court, in *dicta*, stated that obscenity did not receive constitutional protection. In 1957, the Court first established that the First Amendment did not protect obscenity. Balancing the state's interest in preserving

---

90. *Id.* at 533 (quoting Smith v. Daily Mail Pub. Co., 443 U.S. 97, 103 (1979)).
91. *Id.* at 539.
92. *Id.* at 540.
93. 532 U.S. 514 (2001).
94. 315 U.S. 568 (1942). *Chaplinsky* is discussed in Section 11.01[2][b].

morality and order with an individual's right to freedom of expression, the Court in *Roth v. United States* posited that "material which deals with sex in a manner appealing to prurient interest" was unprotected obscenity.[95]

In its 1966 decision in *Memoirs v. Massachusetts*, a plurality of the Court formulated a new three-part test for obscenity, writing that: "It must be established that (a) the dominant theme of the material taken as a whole appeals to a prurient interest in sex; (b) the material is patently offensive because it affronts contemporary community standards relating to the description or representation of sexual matters; and (c) the material is utterly without redeeming social value."[96] The *Roth* Court had used the language "utterly without redeeming social value" to explain why the Constitution did not protect obscenity. The *Memoirs* Court transformed that reasoning into a required part of the test for defining obscenity that would receive no constitutional protection. Tremendous protection for sexually explicit speech ensued.

Nevertheless, because *Memoirs* was only a plurality opinion, and because the *Memoirs* test itself was susceptible to many different interpretations, the Court found itself having to review material that had been adjudged obscene by lower courts, to determine whether it satisfied a majority of justices' views about what constituted obscenity. This practice, which began with *Redrup v. New York*,[97] put unacceptable strain on the Court, and did nothing to provide certainty and predictability to lower courts, prosecutors, and businesses that trafficked in sexual material.

Seeking to establish a more durable standard, in 1973, the Court announced a majority test for obscenity in *Miller v. California*.[98] Writing for the Court, Chief Justice Burger set out the following test for the type of material that would be unprotected as obscenity:

(a) whether the average person, applying contemporary community standards would find that the work, taken as a whole, appeals to the prurient interest;

(b) whether the work depicts or describes, in a patently offensive way, sexual conduct specifically defined by the applicable state law; and

(c) whether the work, taken as a whole, lacks serious literary, artistic, political or scientific value.[99]

Amplifying on the second element, Chief Justice Burger offered some examples of what a state could define as patently offensive sexual depictions:

(a) Patently offensive representations or descriptions of ultimate sexual acts, normal or perverted, actual or simulated.

---

95. 354 U.S. 476, 489 (1957).
96. 383 U.S. 413, 418 (1966). While a plurality of four supported the *Memoirs* test, two other Justices, Black and Douglas, would have afforded absolute protection to obscene material.
97. 386 U.S. 767 (1967).
98. 413 U.S. 15 (1973).
99. *Id.* at 24.

(b) Patently offensive representation or descriptions of masturbation, excretory functions, and lewd exhibitions of the genitals.[100]

The critical difference between the *Memoirs* and *Miller* tests was that *Miller* did not require that the work be "utterly without redeeming social value," a criterion that was virtually impossible to meet. Instead, the third element simply required that the work lack "serious literary, artistic, political, or scientific value." As the Court said in *Miller*, "A quotation from Voltaire in the flyleaf of a book will not constitutionally redeem an otherwise obscene publication."[101]

While the *Miller* test specified that both the prurient interest and patent offensiveness tests were based on community standards, just one year later, in *Jenkins v. Georgia*,[102] the Court rejected a jury finding that the film "Carnal Knowledge" was patently offensive. (That film was a major Hollywood film, starring Jack Nicholson, rather than a film designed and intended as pornography.) The Court stated that the film was "simply not the public portrayal of hard core sexual conduct for its own sake" and thus "could not, as a matter of constitutional law, be found to depict sexual conduct in a patently offensive way."[103]

While *Jenkins* established that the patent offensiveness prong of *Miller* was subject to a constitutional law minimum, or floor, the third element of the *Miller* test, whether the work "lacks serious literary, artistic, political or scientific value," has become understood as reflecting a national standard, which asked whether a reasonable person would find that value.[104]

Several pre-*Miller* cases shed further light on other factors involved in determining whether material is obscene. *Smith v. California*[105] established that obscenity convictions carry a scienter requirement. The Court found that imposing strict liability on the bookseller would cause him "to restrict the books he sells to those he has inspected."[106] In 1974, the Court explained that this does not mean that the seller must have known that the materials are legally obscene; it does, however, require that the seller knew of the material's "nature and character."[107] The manner in which dealers sell sexually explicit material could also determine whether it would be afforded constitutional protection. In *Ginzburg v. United States*,[108] the Court held that juries could consider the way in which particular materials were marketed in determining whether they were obscene. The Court stated that "pandering" tactics demonstrated the seller's intent to appeal "solely" to prurient interests.

---

100. *Id.* at 25.
101. *Id.* at 25 n.7.
102. 418 U.S. 153 (1974).
103. *Id.* at 161.
104. *See* Pope v. Illinois, 481 U.S. 497 (1987).
105. 361 U.S. 147 (1959).
106. *Id.* at 153.
107. Hamling v. United States, 418 U.S. 87 (1974).
108. 383 U.S. 463 (1966).

While *Miller* sets the current standard for obscenity protection, *Paris Adult Theatre I v. Slaton*,[109] decided the same day, renders it broadly applicable by extending the standard to willing recipients of sexually explicit material in public venues. Thus, *Paris Adult Theater* upheld the conviction of exhibitors of obscene movies who warned would-be patrons of the content of the material. In upholding that conviction, the Court distinguished *Stanley v. Georgia*,[110] which held that one cannot be convicted for having obscene materials in one's home.[111] The Court in *Paris Adult Theater* refused to extend the protection afforded the private exhibition of obscene materials in one's home to public displays of obscenity.

Justice Brennan's dissent in *Paris Adult Theater* rejected the Court's attempt to define obscenity. Despite having authored the opinion in *Roth* denying obscenity constitutional protection, Justice Brennan argued in *Paris Adult Theater* that that attempt had simply failed.[112] Nevertheless, he did suggest that government might have a stronger interest in protecting children or unwilling viewers from sexual speech, despite the fact that he could not offer a standard for defining the speech that could be regulated for that reason.[113] By contrast, Justice Douglas, dissenting separately, argued that obscenity should be fully protected. He expressed concern that suppression limited the exchange of ideas within society and that the Court was thus engaging in censorship when it allowed obscenity to be prosecuted.[114]

Since the 1980s, the Court's only significant foray into the sexual speech question, beyond the unique category of child pornography, has focused on the special problems posed by distribution of obscenity on the Internet. In *Ashcroft v. ACLU*,[115] the justices debated the implications of the Internet's world-wide reach in the context of a federal law that banned the online communication of material that, applying "contemporary community standards," was harmful to minors. Writing for three justices, Justice Thomas rejected the argument that the community standards-based components of the Court's obscenity test had to be modified since, as a practical matter, it meant that the most pornography-hostile jurisdiction in the nation could set the standard

---

109. 413 U.S. 49 (1973).

110. 394 U.S. 557 (1969).

111. The right to possess obscenity in the home does not extend to child pornography. *See* Osborne v. Ohio, 495 U.S. 103 (1990). Child pornography, which adds in the factor of the exploitation of children, is discussed in Section 11.01[2][d][iii].

112. *See* 413 U.S. at 103 (Brennan, J., dissenting) ("I am forced to conclude that the concept of 'obscenity' cannot be defined with sufficient specificity and clarity to provide fair notice to persons who create and distribute sexually oriented materials, to prevent substantial erosion of protected speech as a byproduct of the attempt to suppress unprotected speech, and to avoid very costly institutional harms.").

113. *See id.* at 114 ("Difficult questions must still be faced, notably in the areas of distribution to juveniles and offensive exposure to unconsenting adults."). Justice Brennan argued that that question should be deferred until the Court had before it a case squarely presenting that issue. *See id.* at 114 n.29.

114. *See id.* at 70 (Douglas, J., dissenting).

115. 535 U.S. 564 (2002).

for what would be allowed online. Concurring in the decision to remand the case, Justices O'Connor and Breyer, each writing separately, suggested that online distribution of sexual material required a nationwide standard. In another concurrence speaking for three justices, Justice Kennedy edged close to this position as well. Despite this seeming five-justice position, it remains uncertain how the national character of the Internet interacts with *Miller*'s community standards components.

[ii] Non-Obscene Pornography

Beyond the question of what constitutes unprotected obscene sexual speech, the regulation of sexual speech has raised a variety of related, but distinct issues.

In *American Booksellers v. Hudnut*,[116] the Court summarily affirmed a lower court decision invalidating a city ordinance that imposed civil penalties for "pornography," which the ordinance had defined in a way that focused not on prurience or offensiveness but rather the material's portrayal of men's dominance over women. The lower court had held the definition defective, because it was not viewpoint neutral — that is, it banned sexual speech that expressed particular viewpoints (*e.g.,* that women enjoyed being sexually subordinate to men) but not sexual speech expressing other viewpoints. As discussed later in this section,[117] a fundamental rule of free speech strongly disfavors speech restrictions that are based on the viewpoint of the regulated speech.

A different issue also involving non-obscene pornography deals with attempts by cities to zone businesses offering such speech, such as adult bookstores and theaters. Despite the seeming obvious content basis of such zoning regulations, the Court has traditionally considered such laws to be content-neutral, and has accorded them relatively deferential review. The doctrine governing such zoning laws is discussed later, in this section's discussion of content-neutral regulations of speech.[118]

A recurring issue in the regulation of sexual speech has been the question of limiting the access of minors to sexual material. In 1989, in *Sable Communications v. FCC*,[119] the Court upheld against a facial challenge a federal statute's ban on obscene commercial telephone messages. At the same time, the Court unanimously struck down that part of the statute banning messages that were merely indecent. As First Amendment protection does not extend to obscene speech, the Court found no constitutional impediments to a ban on obscene "dial-a-porn." In contrast, the outright ban on indecent messages was not narrowly tailored to serve the "compelling interest of protecting the physical and psychological well-being of minors"[120] who might attempt to access the dial-a-porn service. The Court concluded that access to such indecent messages could be restricted using technological means or simply by requiring use of a credit card number.

---

116. 475 U.S. 1001 (1986).
117. *See* Section 11.01[3][c].
118. *See* Section 11.01[4][c].
119. 492 U.S. 115 (1989).
120. *Id.* at 126.

The issue of minors' access to pornography long pre-dates *Sable Communications*. In *Ginsberg v. New York*,[121] the Court applied a different obscenity standard for materials sold to minors. Decided before *Miller*, the *Ginsberg* Court refashioned the old *Memoirs v. Massachusetts*[122] test specifically to apply to minors, by withholding protection for material which "(i) predominantly appeals to the prurient, shameful or morbid interest of minors, and (ii) is patently offensive to prevailing standards in the adult community as a whole with respect to what is suitable material for minors, and (iii) is utterly without redeeming social importance for minors."[123] In subsequent years, Congress has attempted to regulate Internet display of indecent speech deemed harmful to minors, but those attempts have foundered because of the impact those restrictions had on adults' access to that material. Thus, in *Reno v. ACLU*,[124] the Court struck down the first federal attempt to regulate online sexual speech in the interest of protecting minors, finding the law to be so vaguely-worded as to provoke uncertainty among would-be online speakers, and to ban too much adult access to speech that is constitutionally protected for adults. The Court, speaking through Justice Stevens, also suggested that then-developing technologies might allow parents to control their children's access to online sexual speech, thus obviating the need for the law's broader prohibitions. A decade later, the Court ultimately let stand an appellate ruling striking down a follow-up federal statute regulating online sexual speech, enacted after *Reno*.[125] The appellate court had concluded that the statute, the Child Online Protection Act, was unconstitutionally vague and overbroad, and failed the strict scrutiny applicable to laws imposing content-based restrictions on speech. Whether Congress or the states can find a formula that would allow regulation of online pornography allowable for adults but potentially not suitable for children, and, indeed, whether they will ever again try, remains a doubtful question.

[iii] The Special Case of Child Pornography

A different child protection issue is posed by child pornography—that is, sexual speech, whether obscene or not, that depicts children. In 1982, the Court unanimously held that child pornography was not protected by the First Amendment. Writing in *New York v. Ferber*[126] for six of those justices,[127] Justice White emphasized, among other reasons, the need to safeguard the physical and psychological well-being of children who were used as models in child pornography. Moreover, the Court explained that there was little value in sexual representations of actual children, because

---

121. 390 U.S. 629 (1968).

122. 383 U.S. 413 (1966).

123. *Ginsberg*, 390 U.S. at 633.

124. 521 U.S. 844 (1997).

125. ACLU v. Mukasey, 534 F.3d 181 (3d Cir. 2008) (affirming trial court holding striking down the Child Online Protection Act), *cert. denied*, 555 U.S. 1137 (2009).

126. 458 U.S. 747 (1982).

127. Justice Brennan (joined by Justice Marshall) and Justice Stevens each wrote a separate concurrence in the judgment. Justice O'Connor joined the majority opinion but also wrote a separate concurrence.

youthful-looking adult actors could simulate children. The Court relied heavily on *Ferber* in *Osborne v. Ohio*,[128] where it upheld a conviction for possessing child pornography in one's home. The Court distinguished *Stanley v. Georgia*,[129] which protected a right to view obscene materials in the privacy of one's home. The Court reasoned that the statute in *Osborne* destroyed "a market for the exploitative use of children," while the one in *Stanley* served a "paternalistic interest in regulating [the defendant's] mind."[130]

However, in *Ashcroft v. The Free Speech Coalition*, the Court invalidated as substantially overbroad parts of the Child Pornography Prevention Act of 1996 (CPPA) that prohibited "sexually explicit images that appeared to depict minors but were produced without using any real children."[131] Writing for the Court, Justice Kennedy concluded that the law banned an overly large category of speech, and its age cut-off (eighteen) was "higher than the legal age for marriage in many States, as well as the age at which persons may consent to sexual relations."[132] Perhaps most importantly, the law criminalized both real and virtual child pornography—that is, sexual depictions using adult actors or computer-generated images, and thus, according to the Court, depictions that did not directly implicate the child protection rationale the Court relied on in *Ferber*. The Court rejected the government's argument that protecting simulated child pornography would make it difficult to prosecute actual child pornography, as the images would be too hard to distinguish. Justice Kennedy wrote: "Government may not suppress lawful speech as the means to suppress unlawful speech."[133]

[e] Commercial Speech

[i] The General Doctrine

In 1976, in *Virginia State Board of Pharmacy v. Virginia Citizens Consumers Council, Inc.*,[134] the Court extended constitutional protection to commercial speech. Before *Virginia Pharmacy*, the Court specifically declined, in several decisions, to afford commercial speech constitutional protection.[135] In the period immediately prior to *Virginia Pharmacy*, the Court began moving toward constitutional protection of commercial speech.[136]

Virginia Pharmacy involved a challenge to a Virginia law preventing licensed pharmacists from advertising drug prices. Writing for the majority, Justice Blackmun de-

---

128. 495 U.S. 103 (1990).
129. 394 U.S. 557 (1969).
130. 495 U.S. at 109.
131. 535 U.S. 234, 239 (2002).
132. *Id.* at 247.
133. *Id.* at 255.
134. 425 U.S. 748 (1976).
135. *See* Valentine v. Chrestensen, 316 U.S. 52, 54 (1942) ("We are ... clear that the Constitution imposes no ... restraint on government as respects purely commercial advertising.").
136. *See, e.g.*, Bigelow v. Virginia, 421 U.S. 809 (1975) (reversing a conviction under a Virginia statute prohibiting advertising the availability of abortion).

scribed the speech in straightforward terms. According to the Court, the pharmacist wishing to engage in such speech simply wished to communicate the idea that, " 'I will sell you the X prescription drug at the Y price.' "[137] Justice Blackmun elaborated on this definition, stating that commercial speech was speech that did no more than propose a commercial transaction and was removed from any exposition of ideas and from discussion of truth, science, morality, the arts, or even commercial matters in general. As discussed below, the Court later refined its definition of commercial speech.

Justice Blackmun stated that such straightforward offers to buy and sell should not lie wholly outside the First Amendment's protection. First, he found that the public could well be more interested in price information about products than debate about any particular public issue. Second, he stated that our free market economy requires that individuals' economic decisions be intelligent and well-informed. In addition, commercial speech was indispensable to the free flow of information, and thus to the formation of intelligent opinions about how the free market system should be regulated.

Defending the regulation, the state argued that allowing pharmacists to advertise competitive prices would encourage them to cut corners, ultimately damaging the health of their customers, undermining the professional relationship between pharmacists and patients, and affecting the status of pharmacists as professionals. The Court responded that pharmacists were constrained by the disciplinary rules of their profession. Justice Blackmun also argued that the state's asserted interests were predicated on enforcing ignorance, and a particular view of the pharmaceutical profession, rather than letting individuals make informed decisions in their own self-interest. He insisted that whatever problems might be caused by advertising could be averted by regulating the underlying market, rather than its advertising.

Justice Blackmun nevertheless recognized that legitimate reasons existed to regulate at least some commercial speech. Most notably, the market-efficiency and consumer information justifications for protecting such speech would, at the same time, justify restrictions on false or misleading speech or speech that proposed an unlawful transaction. (Note that these justifications for regulation do not apply to political speech: the Court has insisted that there is no such thing as "a false idea" that, on that ground, could be regulated, and, of course, much protected incitement speech proposes illegal conduct.[138]) Justice Blackmun also suggested that prohibiting false commercial speech might be acceptable, because the speaker would be particularly well-placed to know whether that speech (which, after all, concerned the speaker's own products) was false. He also suggested that, since it was economically motivated, commercial speech may be more "durable" than other types and thus more likely not to be chilled by appropriate government regulation.[139]

---

137. 425 U.S. at 761.
138. Incitement speech is discussed in Section 11.01[2][a].
139. 425 U.S. at 771 n. 24.

Justice Rehnquist dissented. He found the state's concerns sufficient to justify the regulation. He also worried that protecting commercial speech would reintroduce *Lochner*-era style judicial review, in which courts accorded careful scrutiny of business regulation.[140]

Virginia Pharmacy attempted to define commercial speech. The Court gave further guidance on the definitional question in *Bolger v. Youngs Drug Products Corp.*[141] *Bolger* invalidated a federal law that prohibited the mailing of unsolicited advertisements for contraceptives. At issue were pamphlets mailed to private homes. The pamphlets were entitled "Condoms in Human Sexuality," and "Plain Talk About Venereal Disease." One pamphlet repeatedly described the drug company's product by name, while the other pamphlet referred to condoms generally. Thus, unlike the advertisements at issue in *Virginia Pharmacy*, the pamphlets were more than mere proposals to engage in commercial transactions.

Writing for the majority, Justice Marshall held that this material was nevertheless commercial speech. In reaching that conclusion, however, the Court did not rely exclusively on any particular characteristic of the speech. Thus, the fact that the pamphlets were advertisements or referred to particular products, or the fact that the sender of the material had an economic motivation for mailing them, did not in isolation establish the character of the speech as commercial. Nonetheless, the combination of all these characteristics supported the lower court's determination that these mailings amounted to commercial speech. In a later case, *City of Cincinnati v. Discovery Network, Inc.*, the Court, attempting to bring clarity to this area, stated that "the proposal of a commercial transaction is *the test* for identifying commercial speech."[142] This test arguably allows a broader swath of speech to be identified as core political speech that receives full First Amendment protection.

Four years after *Virginia Pharmacy* formally identified commercial speech as deserving of at least some protection, it provided the standard for judging restrictions on such speech. In *Central Hudson Gas & Electric Corp. v. Public Service Commission*,[143] the Court invalidated a state public service commission's regulation prohibiting public utility advertising that promoted the use of electricity. The Court established a four-part, middle-tier test to judge restrictions on commercial speech. First, in order to come within First Amendment protection, the speech must concern lawful activity and not be misleading. Second, if the speech falls within that protection, the regulation must serve a substantial government interest. Third, the regulation must directly advance the state's asserted interest. Fourth, the regulation must not be more extensive than necessary to serve that interest.

In *Central Hudson* itself, the Court recognized as substantial the state's interest in conserving energy, and it concluded that the regulation directly advanced that interest.

---

140. *Lochner v. New York*, 198 U.S. 45 (1905), and the type of substantive due process review of business regulations that case characterized, are both discussed in Section 9.02[1].

141. 463 U.S. 60 (1983).

142. 507 U.S. 410, 423 (1993) (emphasis in original).

143. 447 U.S. 557 (1980).

However, the complete suppression of the utility's commercial speech was broader than necessary to protect that interest. For example, the Court suggested that the regulation would prohibit speech promoting the purchase of new, energy-efficient electric appliances—thus, the regulation was broader than necessary to promote the commission's energy conservation goal.[144]

In *Posadas de Puerto Rico Associates v. Tourism Co.*,[145] the Court took what it ultimately concluded was a wrong turn. In *Posadas*, the Court upheld a Puerto Rican statute restricting gambling advertisements directed at residents of Puerto Rico while allowing gambling ads directed at tourists. Writing for the majority, Justice Rehnquist found that the state's interest in reducing gambling by residents was substantial. The Court also characterized as "reasonable"[146] the legislature's belief that the regulation directly advanced that interest. Importantly, the Court concluded that since the government could prohibit gambling altogether if it so chose, it could take the lesser course and only ban certain speech advertising gambling. While a majority of the Court has not explicitly overruled this case, *Posadas*'s deferential scrutiny is probably no longer good law.[147]

A notable example of the Court's more careful scrutiny of commercial speech regulations is *44 Liquormart, Inc. v. Rhode Island*.[148] In *44 Liquormart*, a unanimous Court invalidated two Rhode Island statutes prohibiting the advertisement of retail prices of alcoholic beverages. Although the justices spoke through a fractured set of opinions, the Court was clearly moving toward more careful scrutiny of such laws. The crucial parts of Justice Stevens' lead opinion spoke only for a plurality of justices. In one of those parts, Justice Stevens construed key commercial speech precedents as invalidating blanket bans on truthful commercial speech relating to lawful activity. He maintained that neither commercial speech's "greater objectivity" nor "greater hardiness" justify deferential review of complete bans on truthful, non-misleading commercial speech. While the typical reason for allowing relatively greater regulation of commercial speech is protecting consumers from "commercial harms," bans on truthful, non-misleading commercial speech rarely serve that purpose. Therefore, the plurality used "special care"[149] to review the Rhode Island ban, which was a ban on truthful and non-misleading price information.

Perhaps unsurprisingly, the plurality then found that Rhode Island's price advertising prohibition failed its application of the *Central Hudson* test. Justice Stevens concluded that that test required the state to show "not merely that its regulation

---

144. The commission had also offered a second justification for the restriction—easing the implementation of a fairer rate structure. While the Court accepted that justification as substantial, it found an insufficient connection between it and the advertising ban.

145. 478 U.S. 328 (1986).

146. *Id.* at 342.

147. *See, e.g.*, Ass'n of Charitable Games of Missouri v. Missouri, 1998 WL 602050, *6 (W.D. Mo. 1998) (suggesting that subsequent caselaw effectively overruled *Posadas*).

148. 517 U.S. 484 (1996).

149. *Id.* at 502, 504.

will advance its interest, but also that it will do so to a material degree."[150] He understood that requirement as demanding evidence that the speech prohibition would significantly advance the state's interest in reducing alcohol consumption. Moreover, he concluded that less restrictive alternatives, such as mandating higher prices for alcohol, increasing regulation, or instituting public education programs, were "more likely to achieve the State's goal of promoting temperance."[151] Finally, still speaking for four justices, Justice Stevens explicitly rejected much of the reasoning of *Posadas*, discussed immediately above, in particular, its conclusion that government can treat speech regulations simply as another means to achieve its regulatory objectives. This analysis strongly suggested that the possibility of regulating the underlying conduct itself would usually constitute a preferable alternative to regulating speech about the conduct.

In separate concurrences, Justices Thomas and O'Connor (the latter joined by three other justices) would have applied careful scrutiny of whether other alternatives open to the state would have served the state's objectives as well as the challenged speech regulations. While these opinions and Justice Stevens' plurality approached the issue slightly differently,[152] they all signaled heightened protection for commercial speech.

In *Lorillard Tobacco Co. v. Reilly*,[153] the Court continued its trend toward stringent application of *Central Hudson*. *Lorillard* invalidated several Massachusetts restrictions focused on signs advertising tobacco products, enacted in order to prevent minors from using tobacco. The first set of regulations banned outdoor advertising of tobacco products "within a 1,000 foot radius of any public playground, playground area in a public park, elementary school or secondary school."[154]

These outdoor restrictions satisfied the third prong of *Central Hudson* (that the law "directly advance" the state's interests), as the restriction would in fact decrease youth smoking. Nevertheless, the restrictions failed the fourth part of *Central Hudson*, which examines the fit between the government's means and the ends it sought to accomplish. The Court explained that the outdoor regulations were too broad and did not carefully consider the "costs and benefits associated with the burden on speech."[155] For example, the impact of the regulations on speech would vary depending on whether the area was rural, suburban, or urban. This analysis suggests that the fourth prong of *Central Hudson* requires, as part of the fit analysis, a consideration of the impact the speech restrictions have on the speaker.

---

150. *44 Liquormart*, 517 U.S. at 505.

151. *Id.* at 507.

152. Most notably, Justice Thomas expressed doubt about the correctness of *Central Hudson*'s decision to accord lesser protection to commercial speech. *See id.* at 518 (Thomas, J., concurring in part and concurring in the judgment).

153. 533 U.S. 525 (2001).

154. *Id.* at 534–35.

155. *Id.* at 561.

The Court also struck down indoor point-of-sale regulations requiring retailers located within 1,000 feet of a school or playground to place smokeless tobacco products and cigar advertisements at least five feet above the floor. This restriction failed both the third and fourth prongs of *Central Hudson*. The Court concluded that the regulation would likely prove ineffective, since some children are taller than five feet, and even those who are not can still simply look up to see the advertisements.[156]

The Court's increasingly stringent application of *Central Hudson* has led to it strike down, on First Amendment grounds, state regulations defended as regulations not of speech but of business practices. In *Sorrell v. IMS Health, Inc.*,[157] the Court invalidated a Vermont statute limiting pharmacists' sales of the doctor-specific prescribing information they possessed to firms that wished to use that information to market their drugs to doctors. Pharmacists could, however, sell that information to other persons, such as medical researchers. The state's goal in restricting those sales was to lower health care costs by discouraging doctors from prescribing the name-brand drugs the marketers promoted, in favor of lower-cost generic drugs.

Writing for the Court, Justice Kennedy described the law as enacting content, viewpoint, and speaker-based restrictions on speech, characteristics that he noted would trigger strict judicial scrutiny in a normal First Amendment case.[158] Nevertheless, because the law involved commercial speech, he applied the *Central Hudson* test. But he described that test in terms that echoed the justifications for the content-neutrality rule, stating that *Central Hudson*'s "standards ensure ... that the law does not seek to suppress a disfavored message."[159] He found the law to fail that test. First, the fact that pharmacists could sell the information to individuals other than pharmaceutical marketers defeated any claim that the law advanced any interest in physician privacy. Second, the Court concluded that state's goal of reducing health costs, while legitimate, was being advanced in an unacceptable way — that is, by trying to prevent physicians from receiving information from marketers that would be more tailored to the particular physician (and thus more persuasive) if the marketers could obtain that doctor's prescribing history. Justice Kennedy characterized this as an attempt to keep information away from persons out of fear it would be too persuasive.

Despite applying *Central Hudson*, Justice Kennedy stated that the law required "heightened judicial scrutiny."[160] That conclusion may again reflect the Court's increasing tendency to review commercial speech restrictions carefully, at least when

---

156. The Court upheld another provision of the law, requiring that tobacco products be kept within reach only of store personnel and thus requiring customers to access those products only through an interaction with salespersons who could verify the customer's age.

157. 564 U.S. 564 (2011).

158. These aspects of First Amendment doctrine are discussed later in this chapter. *See* Section 11.01[3].

159. *Id.* at 572.

160. *See id.* at 565 ("Act 80 is designed to impose a specific, content-based burden on protected expression. It follows that heightened judicial scrutiny is warranted.").

the speech in question is truthful and pertains to legal transactions, and when the Court suspects, as it did in *Sorrell*, that the law was designed to keep listeners from hearing truthful messages the state did not want them to hear.

On the other hand, the Vermont law appeared closely related to the state's attempt to regulate the healthcare industry. Dissenting for four justices, Justice Breyer worried that according heightened scrutiny to such laws would hobble states' ability to impose such economic regulation. He reasoned that business, like most human activity, is performed largely by speech—for example, by disclosing terms of a business offer or explaining a product or simply directing customers how to place an order. Under the majority's approach, those business practices would gain significant immunity from government regulation if speech of the sort in *Sorrell* were subjected to stringent judicial protection. Echoing Justice Rehnquist's dissent in *Virginia Pharmacy*, the case that first accorded commercial speech First Amendment protection, Justice Breyer thus worried that the majority's approach heralded a return to *Lochner*-era jurisprudence, where the Court gave constitutional protection to business practices.[161]

[ii] Professional Speech

Professional advertising—for example, advertising by lawyers—has traditionally been regulated on the theory that it raises the risk of professionals acting unethically. In recent decades, the Court has scrutinized such regulations on First Amendment grounds. One year after *Virginia Pharmacy*, the Court extended First Amendment protection under the commercial speech doctrine to advertising by lawyers in *Bates v. State Bar*.[162] *Bates* struck down a state disciplinary rule prohibiting lawyer advertising. The advertisement in question appeared in a newspaper and offered routine legal services such as adoption proceedings and uncontested divorces and personal bankruptcies at "very reasonable rates."

The state bar offered several justifications for its ban on price advertising, such as adversely affecting lawyer professionalism, diminishing the quality of legal services, and inherently misleading the public because legal services were by nature individualized. Writing for the Court, Justice Blackmun rejected those justifications. He did, however, express a willingness to allow regulation of false or misleading advertising based on the public's lack of sophistication in legal services. For example, statements concerning the quality of legal services could be deceptive or misleading and thus warrant restrictions. These reasons might also justify restriction of in-person solicitation or require warnings or disclaimers in advertisements. None of these considerations, however, permitted suppression of generic price advertising.

---

161. The *Lochner* era of due process jurisprudence is discussed in Section 9.02[1].

162. 433 U.S. 350 (1977). In a footnote in *Virginia Pharmacy*, Justice Blackmun had suggested that the Court's holding applied specifically to pharmacists, and that other factors might be involved in considering the commercial speech of lawyers and doctors. Chief Justice Burger, in his concurrence, also stressed that the decision was strictly limited to pharmacists. Despite this language limiting the holding, Justice Rehnquist, the only dissenter to the opinion, correctly predicted that the decision would pave the way for lawyer and doctor advertising.

The Court has protected a wide variety of lawyer solicitations. In *Zauderer v. Office of Disciplinary Counsel*,[163] the Court extended constitutional protection to newspaper advertisements in which, among other offers, an attorney offered to represent women who had suffered injuries from using a particular consumer product. The Court held that the lawyer's offers to represent women were, with one exception, truthful and not misleading commercial speech that thus enjoyed First Amendment protection. It also protected the advertisement's use of an accurate drawing of the product, rejecting the state's argument that use of such diagrams impaired the dignity of the profession and raised the risk of misleading would-be clients through sub-conscious means. However, the ad's promise of a fully contingent fee arrangement was unprotected, because, by failing to mention the client's responsibility for costs regardless of outcome, the statement was misleading.

Despite the protection *Zauderer* provided for lawyer (and presumably other professional) advertising, the Court has been more accepting of regulation of in-person solicitations, which it considers to raise special risks of overreaching. In *Ohralik v. Ohio State Bar Ass'n*,[164] the Court held that a state can discipline lawyers for soliciting clients in person, because the potential for overreaching is great when a lawyer personally solicits an unsophisticated, injured, or distressed layperson. The Court expressed a slightly different concern in *Florida Bar v. Went For It, Inc.*,[165] where, on a 5–4 vote, it upheld a Florida Bar regulation prohibiting lawyers from soliciting accident or disaster victims until 30 days after the date of the event. Speaking through Justice O'Connor, the Court concluded that the regulation satisfied the *Central Hudson* test, because it "directly and materially" advanced a "compelling" state interest in protecting citizens' privacy and upholding the integrity of the legal profession.[166]

Dissenting for four justices, Justice Kennedy questioned the regulation's compliance with every prong of the *Central Hudson* test. In particular, he distinguished the in-person solicitation *Ohralik* allowed to be regulated from the mail solicitations at issue in *Florida Bar*, concluding that privacy interests were implicated less in the latter situation. In contrast to the result in *Florida Bar*, the Court in *In re Primus*[167] accorded constitutional protection to the solicitation of prospective litigants by a civil liberties organization. The Court relied heavily on the fact that the representation was solicited as part of a non-profit organization's political and associational activity, rather than as a for-profit venture.

In *National Institute of Family and Life Advocates* ("*NIFLA*") *v. Becerra*,[168] the Court elaborated on its understanding of the constitutional status of professional speech. *NIFLA* dealt with a California law requiring any "pregnancy crisis center" to post certain information about the center's licensing status and the availability of state-paid

---

163. 471 U.S. 626 (1985).
164. 436 U.S. 447 (1978).
165. 515 U.S. 618 (1995).
166. *Id.* at 624, 625.
167. 436 U.S. 412 (1978).
168. 138 S. Ct. 2361 (2018).

abortion services. The Court rejected the lower court's theory that the law survived First Amendment scrutiny because it regulated " 'professional speech.' "[169] The Court denied that it had created such a category of speech, subject to special First Amendment rules. However, it did note that the Court:

> has afforded less protection for professional speech in two circumstances — neither of which turned on the fact that professionals were speaking. First, our precedents have applied more deferential review to some laws that require professionals to disclose factual, noncontroversial information in their "commercial speech." See, e.g., *Zauderer v. Office of Disciplinary Counsel of Supreme Court of Ohio*; *Ohralik v. Ohio State Bar Assn*. Second, under our precedents, States may regulate professional conduct, even though that conduct incidentally involves speech.[170]

The Court explained that the latter category encompassed situations where a state punished a professional for malpractice or directed that the professional obtain informed consent from a client or patient.[171]

[iii] The Future of Commercial Speech Doctrine

Commercial speech doctrine is in flux. As suggested by cases such as *Sorrell*, the Court at times appears to be edging toward according commercial speech full First Amendment protection—most notably, the application of strict judicial scrutiny when a law regulates speech on the basis of its content. But as the dissent in *Sorrell* pointed out, the ubiquity of speech in business conduct means that according commercial speech full First Amendment protection would effectively immunize much business conduct from government regulation. Indeed, that dissent also observed that most commercial speech regulation is content-based by definition, since it regulates speech about particular business activities (for example, advertising about a particular product or service). Thus, giving that speech the full protection accorded speech more generally would more or less automatically subject all commercial speech restrictions to strict scrutiny.

According full First Amendment protection to commercial speech raises other issues, as well. Most notably, First Amendment law does not generally allow government to regulate speech simply because it is untruthful,[172] but commercial speech doctrine does. Moreover, political speech is fully protected even if it proposes illegal conduct, as long as that proposition does not satisfy that *Brandenburg v. Ohio* incitement test.[173] Commercial speech doctrine assumes that much of the point of protecting commercial

---

169. *Id.* at 2371 (quoting lower court opinion).

170. *Id.* at 2372.

171. *See id.* at 2373. The Court's resolution of the speech claim in *NIFLA* is discussed in Section 11.02[3][a], which considers claims that the government has unconstitutionally compelled an individual to speak.

172. *See* United States v. Alvarez, 567 U.S. 709 (2012).

173. The *Brandenburg* test, and incitement doctrine more generally, is discussed in Section 11.01[2][a].

speech—giving consumers information and allowing efficient market transactions—
is inconsistent with protecting speech that proposes an illegal transaction.

On the other hand, some commercial speech jurisprudence fits neatly within the
larger stream of First Amendment doctrine. Most notably, the Court's hostility to
commercial speech regulations motivated by a fear that speech will be too persuasive
fits easily within more general First Amendment principles condemning government
attempts to keep valuable information away from would-be listeners. Ultimately, the
Court may find itself compelled to retain special rules for commercial speech while
trying to the extent possible to harmonize those rules with the principles underlying
more generally-applicable First Amendment doctrine.

[f] Identifying and Understanding Unprotected Categories of Speech

This sub-section's enumeration of categories of speech that, according to the Court,
enjoy no First Amendment protection is not necessarily intuitive—that is, it is not
necessarily intuitive to understand why categories such as fighting words and obscenity
fall into the "unprotected" category. Moreover, despite the common statement that
such speech is "unprotected," it is inaccurate to say that speech within these categories
enjoys "no" First Amendment protection—hence the quotation marks around "unprotected." The next sub-section considers the "why" question—why is certain speech
deemed to be unprotected? The one following considers the "consequences" question—that is, what are the consequences of a category of speech falling into the "unprotected" category?

[i] The Methodology for Identifying Unprotected Categories of Speech

The doctrinal origin for the modern Court's placement of certain speech in the
"unprotected" category is the classic statement from *Chaplinsky v. New Hampshire*,[174]
the 1942 case dealing with fighting words. Going beyond fighting words, the Court
said the following about the types of speech that lack First Amendment protection:

> There are certain well-defined and narrowly limited classes of speech, the
> prevention and punishment of which have never been thought to raise any
> Constitutional problem. These include the lewd and obscene, the profane,
> the libelous, and the insulting or 'fighting' words—those which by their very
> utterance inflict injury or tend to incite an immediate breach of the peace.
> It has been well observed that such utterances are no essential part of any
> exposition of ideas, and are of such slight social value as a step to truth that
> any benefit that may be derived from them is clearly outweighed by the social
> interest in order and morality.[175]

---

174. 315 U.S. 568 (1942).
175. *Id.* at 571–72.

Chaplinsky thus provides the foundation for the Court's subsequent statements about the unprotected status of these classes of words—obscenity, libel, and fighting words.[176]

But what about categories of speech not mentioned in *Chaplinsky* that the government argues should also lack First Amendment protection? Consider *Chaplinsky*'s explanation for the unprotected status it accorded to the categories of speech it mentioned—"that such utterances are no essential part of any exposition of ideas, and are of such slight social value as a step to truth that any benefit that may be derived from them is clearly outweighed by the social interest in order and morality." That explanation suggests that the Court excluded from First Amendment protection the categories it listed because it weighed the benefits of such speech and its costs in terms of "the social interest in order and morality," and reached a result excluding those categories. On this reading of *Chaplinsky*, one might expect the Court to be open to identifying additional categories of speech as unprotected, based on that same balancing approach.

Not so. In a series of cases starting in 2010, the Court rejected that approach. In the first of these cases, *United States v. Stevens*, the Court described as "startling and dangerous" the government's argument that the Court should balance the value of the speech category in question (in *Stevens*, depictions of animal cruelty) against the harm it caused.[177] In later cases involving violent video games and false statements relating to the speaker's receipt of military honors, the Court repeated this rejection.[178] Instead, the Court in *Stevens* explained that *Chaplinsky*'s catalogue of unprotected speech categories should be understood simply as a description of categories that had historically been unprotected, rather than a statement that past Courts had engaged in such balancing (and thus an implication that the current Court should do the same when faced with a claim for a new category of unprotected speech).

Thus, after the set of cases starting with *Stevens*, a Court faced with a claim that a new category of speech should be deemed unprotected will not perform an explicitly policy-based balancing of the costs and benefits of that speech category. Instead, it will inquire whether historically that category of speech had lacked First Amendment protection. The Court has recognized at least the possibility that categories of unprotected speech remain to be discovered. But if they exist, those categories will be "discovered," not "created"—that is, the Court will have to conclude that such categories were always unprotected, and there simply had been no occasion for the Court to uncover them.

The Court's understanding of *Chaplinsky* is controversial. Scholars have questioned whether it is accurate to describe the *Chaplinsky* categories as reflecting long-

---

176. *See, e.g.,* Roth v. United States, 354 U.S. 476, 481 (1957) (citing *Chaplinsky*, among other cases, for the proposition that obscenity is not protected). Profanity, to the extent it can be subsumed within a more general category of offensive speech, has been held to be protected in at least some circumstances. *See* Cohen v. California, 403 U.S. 15 (1971). *Cohen* is discussed in Section 11.01[2][b].
177. 559 U.S. 460, 470 (2010).
178. Brown v. Entertainment Merchants Ass'n, 564 U.S. 786, 792 (2011) (violent video games); United States v. Alvarez, 567 U.S. 709, 717 (2012) (false statements about receipt of military honors).

standing jurisprudential history.[179] Justices, too, have questioned this approach. In *Stevens* itself, the justices debated whether this historical understanding accounts for the Court's post-*Chaplinsky* precedents dealing with new categories of unprotected speech. Most notably, they debated how the Court had handled the question of child pornography.

Recall from an earlier subsection[180] that, in *New York v. Ferber*,[181] the Court held that child pornography is unprotected. The majority in *Stevens* argued that *Ferber* reached that decision by reasoning that such depictions were inextricably linked to criminal conduct — the sexual exploitation of children — and thus fell within a category (speech that is an integral part of a crime) that had historically lacked First Amendment protection. By contrast, Justice Alito, dissenting in *Stevens*, argued that in *Ferber* the Court relied heavily on the lack of that speech's social value and the serious harm that speech caused (by necessarily involving the sexual exploitation of children). Thus, he argued, in *Ferber*, the Court had indeed performed the kind of balancing that the *Stevens* majority insisted was "startling and dangerous" and thus inappropriate as a methodology for identifying unprotected speech.

Commercial speech appears to be another area in which the Court has found speech to enjoy less than full First Amendment protection based on a judicial weighing of the costs and benefits of speech. While individual justices have suggested that commercial speech should be accorded First Amendment protection based on the historical pedigree for such protection,[182] the Court's foundational explanation for why commercial speech is protected — the majority opinion in *Virginia Board of Pharmacy v. Virginia Citizens Consumer Council*[183] — reflected the interest balancing the Court in *Stevens* rejected.

Nevertheless, since *Stevens*, the Court has been clear: when dealing with a category of speech whose unprotected status has not yet been determined, the Court will not employ an explicit policy-balancing approach. To repeat, this does not mean that that the Court will never add to the list of categories of unprotected speech. But, unless and until the Court changes its mind about its methodology, such a result must flow from a conclusion that, as a historical matter, the speech in question had never been protected, with that lack of protection simply not becoming a question for the Court until the present moment.[184]

---

179. *E.g.*, Genevieve Lakier, *The Invention of Low-Value Speech*, 128 Harv. L. Rev. 2166 (2015).

180. *See* Section 11.01[2][d][iii].

181. 458 U.S. 747 (1982).

182. *See, e.g.*, 44 Liquormart v. Rhode Island, 517 U.S. 484, 522 (2996) (Thomas, J., concurring in part and concurring in the judgment) ("I do not see a philosophical or historical basis for asserting that 'commercial' speech is of 'lower value' than 'noncommercial' speech. Indeed, some historical materials suggest to the contrary.").

183. 425 U.S. 748 (1976).

184. *See Stevens*, 599 U.S. at 472 ("Maybe there are some categories of speech that have been historically unprotected, but have not yet been specifically identified or discussed as such in our case law.... We need not foreclose the future recognition of such additional categories to reject the Government's highly manipulable balancing test as a means of identifying them.").

[ii] The Consequences of Speech Being Unprotected

Courts and commentators usually refer to speech *Chaplinsky* identified as "unprotected" speech. In 1992, the Court cautioned that this description was not "literally true."[185] In *R.A.V. v. City of St. Paul*, the Court struck down a city ordinance that read as follows:

> Whoever places on public or private property a symbol, object, appellation, characterization or graffiti, including, but not limited to, a burning cross or Nazi swastika, which one knows or has reasonable grounds to know arouses anger, alarm or resentment in others on the basis of race, color, creed, religion or gender commits disorderly conduct and shall be guilty of a misdemeanor.[186]

The Court unanimously agreed that the law was unconstitutional. However, it split badly in its reasoning. Writing for five justices, Justice Scalia argued that, even though the state supreme court had construed the statute as applying only to unprotected "fighting words," the statute nevertheless drew unconstitutional content- and even viewpoint-based distinctions. As already alluded to and as explained in more detail later in this section, a fundamental free speech requirement accords content-based laws strict scrutiny and considers viewpoint-based laws nearly *per se* unconstitutional. In *R.A.V.*, the Court extended the protection of the content-neutrality rule to ostensibly unprotected speech, such as fighting words.

Justice Scalia explained that the identification of a category of speech — for example, obscenity — as "unprotected" by the First Amendment implied a conclusion that the very reasons for finding obscenity unprotected justified content-based restrictions taking the form of a ban on obscenity. This sort of content-based regulation — *e.g.*, between obscene and non-obscene speech — was allowable by the very fact that obscenity as a category is unprotected. Moreover, he continued that government could even subdivide obscenity — banning some obscene speech but not other such speech — if the government's justifications tracked the very reason obscenity as a category lacked constitutional protection. Thus, for example, since obscenity can be banned in part because of its prurience, government could, if it wished, ban only the most prurient of all obscenity. More generally, government can ban only some but not all obscenity (or any other type of "unprotected" speech) "so long as the nature of the content discrimination is such that there is no realistic possibility that official suppression of ideas is afoot."[187]

But Justice Scalia cautioned that other content-based discriminations between subcategories of unprotected speech might trigger more serious First Amendment problems. For example, he posited a government entity that punished libel (an unprotected category) but only if the libel was critical of the government. That sort of content (or, indeed, viewpoint) discrimination, he concluded, was still banned by the First Amendment, even though the overall category (here, libel) was itself unprotected.

---

185. R.A.V. v. City of St. Paul, 505 U.S. 377, 383 (1992).
186. 505 U.S. at 380 (quoting the ordinance).
187. 505 U.S. at 390.

Applying this approach, the majority condemned the city ordinance for singling out certain types of fighting words (those "which one knows or has reasonable grounds to know arouses anger, alarm or resentment in others on the basis of race, color, creed, religion or gender" while not, for example, also prohibiting fighting words that cause such reactions on the basis of sexual orientation), and thus crossing the line into forbidden content discrimination.[188]

Four concurring justices, speaking through opinions by Justices White and Stevens, strongly disagreed with this analysis. They agreed that the ordinance was unconstitutional, but they grounded their analysis on their conclusion that it was overbroad.[189] Had it not been — in other words, had the ordinance truly been limited to targeting only unprotected "fighting words" — the concurring justices would have upheld it.

R.A.V. complicates analysis of otherwise-unprotected speech. Now, a law that targets unprotected speech must be further examined to determine whether there is a risk that the law is seeking to suppress particular ideas. This may be an intricate inquiry. Recall that Justice Scalia explained that government can draw content-based sub-divisions of unprotected speech if the prohibited sub-category is defined by the characteristic that renders the entire category unprotected — thus, for example, since government can ban obscenity because of its prurience, it can therefore limit its ban to the most prurient obscenity. Apply that reasoning to *R.A.V.* itself. Could the city have argued that fighting words based, say, on race are those fighting words most likely to cause a violent reaction? Not according to the Court. First, without any analysis, it simply doubted the empirical basis for such an argument. Second, it objected that such a theory would still be inadequate because any such unusually violent reaction to racial fighting words would be based on the listener's reaction to those words — that is, the listener's reactions to the ideas those words conveyed.[190]

At the very least, this explanation complicates free speech analysis, since it distinguishes between two seemingly analogous applications of the same principle. Whether such complications are appropriate — for example, whether they are necessary to prevent government from hiding behind the unprotected status of some speech categories to repress particular ideas, or whether other doctrines might solve that problem — is a question that will likely remain prominent in debates about the First Amendment, especially during eras that feature debates about government's ability to suppress so-called "hate speech."

---

188. Indeed, the Court argued that the law was not just content-based, but also favored certain viewpoints, by, for example, banning fighting words that caused alarm on the basis of religion (and thus banning fighting words that attacked a religion) while allowing fighting words to be used by proponents of religious toleration. *See id.* at 391–92. As the next sub-section will explain, viewpoint discrimination is thought to be even more problematic than content discrimination.

189. "Overbreadth" doctrine is a distinct category of free speech analysis. It is discussed later in this chapter. *See* Section 11.02[2].

190. *See* 505 U.S. at 394 n.7.

[3] The Content-Neutrality Rule

[a] The Basic Rule

Beyond the categories of unprotected and partially-protected speech lay vast areas of speech that enjoy full First Amendment protection. While there are important exceptions, as a general matter, speech is protected by what is called the "content-neutrality rule." That rule requires that any government regulation of protected speech that is based on the content of the speech must satisfy strict scrutiny—that is, it must be narrowly tailored to achieve a compelling government interest.

The content-neutrality rule derives from a 1972 case, *Police Dept. of City of Chicago v. Mosley*.[191] *Mosley* considered a Chicago ordinance that prohibited picketing near schools, but exempted labor picketing from the prohibition. The opinion striking down the ordinance, written by Justice Marshall, is best known for its sweeping statement that "above all else, the First Amendment means that government has no power to restrict expression because of its message, its ideas, its subject matter, or its content."[192] Nevertheless, the Court considered the justifications Chicago offered for its labor speech exemption, finding them inadequate to justify the content discrimination.

Fascinatingly, Justice Marshall described *Mosley* mainly as an equal protection case, even though he mentioned the First Amendment several times. Nevertheless, *Mosely* has come to be understood as stating a rule strongly disfavoring content-based laws. To be sure, while one could read *Mosley* as insisting on flat-out invalidations of such laws, the rule that has developed allows the possibility of such laws surviving, but only, as noted above, if the law satisfies strict scrutiny.[193] Over time, such strict scrutiny has also come to be applied to laws that discriminate based on the identity of the speaker.

Why the content-neutrality rule? Scholars and judges have offered several related reasons. Allowing government to restrict speech based on the topic the speech addresses allows government to skew public debate by marking some subjects as off-limits to discussion. Relatedly, content discrimination raises the prospect of something even worse: viewpoint discrimination, *i.e.*, discrimination based on a particular point of view. In *Mosley*, for example, while the carve-out for labor picketing might be seen as "merely" content discrimination in favor of speech about labor issues, one might also be able to understand it as a viewpoint-based carve-out, since most labor

---

191. 408 U.S. 92 (1972).

192. *Id.* at 95. *See also id.* at 99 ("In this case, the ordinance itself describes impermissible picketing not in terms of time, place, and manner, but in terms of subject matter. The regulation 'thus slip(s) from the neutrality of time, place, and circumstance into a concern about content.' This is never permitted."). Of course, this statement raises questions about whether government is similarly disabled from restricting, via a content-based rule, speech that falls into one of the unprotected categories. Chief Justice Burger, concurring in *Mosley*, implied this caveat in his brief concurring opinion. *See id.* at 102 (Burger, C.J., concurring).

193. *See, e.g.*, Williams-Yulee v. Florida Bar, 575 U.S. 433 (2015) (upholding a content-based law after concluding it survived strict scrutiny).

picketing tends to be on the pro-worker side of any labor-management dispute. More generally, it is easy to intuit that content-based laws fail to rationally further any legitimate government interests. (Of course, they further quite well an illegitimate government interest in skewing public debate.) For example, in *Mosley* itself, the Court discounted the city's interest in keeping order around schools, remarking that "peaceful" labor picketing (which the ordinance allowed) was no more disruptive than other types of peaceful picketing which the ordinance prohibited.

A straightforward example of strict scrutiny is *Brown v. Entertainment Merchants Association*.[194] *Entertainment Merchants* involved a California law that restricted minors from purchasing violent video games unless they had the approval of a parent or guardian. Thus, the law was clearly content-based: minors could freely access some speech (the speech in non-violent games) but not other speech, based on its content. Applying strict scrutiny, the Court, implicitly conceding that the state had a strong interest in protecting minors and ensuring their proper development, concluded that the law was not narrowly tailored to achieve those goals. Among other things, it argued that the evidence linking exposure to such content with the development of anti-social attitudes was at best mixed. Indeed, it noted that some studies had even found such a connection even to content such as certain Saturday morning cartoons, which California had not attempted to restrict. Moreover, the Court noted that the law allowed minors to access such games as long as a parent or guardian approved. Lest that parental override be thought to find support in a state interest in ensuring parental control over what their children are exposed to, the Court pointed out that the video game industry had already instituted a ratings system that allowed parents to inspect and forbid any video game the parent thought might be inappropriately violent.

Much of this analysis can be critiqued. It might well be hard to draw solid connections between video games and anti-social development, given the complexity of the issue. California likely had no power to regulate broadcast television content. And finally, the sales ban might assist parents who are too harried or otherwise unaware of what their children purchase and view. Nevertheless, the Court's narrow tailoring analysis reveals how stringent strict scrutiny often is in First Amendment cases.[195]

[b] Identifying Content Discrimination

What constitutes a content-based law? One might think this is a relatively straightforward question. And sometimes it is. In *Reed v. Town of Gilbert*,[196] the Court applied strict scrutiny to a city's sign ordinance that prescribed different size and duration

---

194. 564 U.S. 786 (2011).

195. On the other hand, sometimes the Court's strict scrutiny is not as strict as it appeared to be in *Entertainment Merchants*. *See, e.g., Williams Yulee*, 575 U.S. at 462 (Scalia, J., dissenting) (criticizing the majority's application of strict scrutiny to uphold a content-based law, arguing that the majority had applied a watered-down version of strict scrutiny).

196. 576 U.S. 155 (2015).

limits for private signs placed on public property, depending on the content of the sign. The lower court had upheld the ordinance as content neutral, citing earlier Supreme Court caselaw stating that the content-neutrality question was answered by asking whether the law in question "was justified without reference to the content of the regulated speech."[197]

The Supreme Court agreed that that formula stated one criterion for determining content discrimination, but it concluded that the lower court had ignored another, preliminary one: whether the law *on its face* drew content-based distinctions. In response to arguments that not all facially content-based laws reflect illegitimate government attempts to skew debate or otherwise impair First Amendment values, the Court cautioned that even a well-meaning content-based law could be used for inappropriate ends by a future government official. Thus, because the town's sign ordinance drew facial content-based distinctions, the Court subjected it to strict scrutiny without analyzing whether such inappropriate goals actually underlay the law. Given the city's lack of any strong argument in defense of the law, the Court struck it down.[198] But the more important point is that, after *Reed*, a law will be considered content-based if it either draws a facial content-based distinction (as the statute in *Reed* itself did) or if it is facially neutral, but is justified based on concern about the content of particular speech.

Justices Breyer and Kagan wrote separate opinions that concurred in the result only. Writing only for himself, Justice Breyer conceded that sometimes content discrimination suggested bad government motivations, such as the skewing of debate and even viewpoint discrimination. But he also observed that the ubiquity of speech regulations meant that many content-based laws reflected straightforward government regulation of social and business affairs, for example, content-based laws requiring that energy consumption information be placed on consumer electronics. Justice Breyer repeated his call, which he has made in other First Amendment cases, to ask "whether the regulation at issue works harm to First Amendment interests that is disproportionate in light of the relevant regulatory objectives," an inquiry that would require "examining the seriousness of the harm to speech, the importance of the countervailing objectives, the extent to which the law will achieve those objectives, and whether there are other, less restrictive ways of doing so."[199]

Justice Kagan, writing for herself and Justices Breyer and Ginsburg, also questioned the utility of a rigid requirement of strict scrutiny anytime a law was facially content-based. Using an example of a city ordinance that prohibited illuminated lawn lights except for those that illuminated the home's street number and the name of the family that lived there, she worried that the Court's approach would lead either to such everyday laws being upheld after application of a watered-down version of

---

197. Reed v. Town of Gilbert, 707 F.3d 1057, 1068 (9th Cir. 2013), *rev'd*, 576 U.S. 155 (2015).

198. *See* 576 U.S. at 184 (Kagan, J., concurring in the judgment) ("The Town of Gilbert's defense of its sign ordinance ... does not pass strict scrutiny, or intermediate scrutiny, or even the laugh test.").

199. *Id.* at 179 (Breyer, J., concurring in the judgment).

strict scrutiny, or struck down, resulting in gratuitous invalidations of laws that pose no threat to First Amendment values. Instead of imposing a rigid content-neutrality requirement, Justice Kagan urged the Court to "apply strict scrutiny to facially content-based regulations of speech ... when there is any realistic possibility that official suppression of ideas is afoot,"[200] but not otherwise.

These differing views notwithstanding, in *Reed*, a six-justice majority announced a stringent requirement that any content-based law be subjected to strict scrutiny. Whether such a rule is wise presents a controversial question. On the one hand, facially content-discriminatory laws do seem to present the most obvious instances of the favoritism and skewing of public debate that, at its core, the First Amendment prohibits. Moreover, even an innocently motivated content-discriminatory law might, in the hands of an unscrupulous administrator, be used for such illegitimate goals.

On the other hand, it is difficult to see how First Amendment values are threatened by, for example, a requirement that landlords posting signs directing tenants to the trash cans also note the location of the recycling bins, in order to encourage recycling. While one can always make the argument that such a law, as innocuous as it sounds, skews debate toward favoring recycling, one could say the same thing about nearly any law that regulates social relationships by regulating certain speech. As Justice Breyer pointed out, such economic and social regulation is present everywhere we look in our society. Nevertheless, it is a fair objection that his and Justice Kagan's suggested approaches are so vague and subjective that they might invite judges to play favorites with regard to certain speech.

[c] Content versus Viewpoint Discrimination

The Court often speaks of speech regulations that discriminate on the basis of *viewpoint*, rather than content. Conceptually, it is at least somewhat easy to understand the difference between content-based and viewpoint-based laws. Content-based laws are those that are based on the topics that are either allowed or prohibited as subjects for speech. Thus, for example, a law that prohibited any speech about abortion, pro or con, would be content-based. A sub-set of content-based laws, however, discriminate on the viewpoint the speaker wishes to espouse. Thus, a law that prohibited pro-choice but not anti-choice speech would be viewpoint-based.

Given this explanation, one can perhaps intuit why viewpoint-based laws are considered even more problematic than content-based ones. Viewpoint-based laws prohibit one side of a controversy from speaking. As such, they skew debate even more than laws that prohibit *any* speech on a given topic — that is, content-based laws. And indeed, while the Court has sometimes upheld speech restrictions that are content-based (but viewpoint-neutral),[201] it would be extraordinarily rare for a view-

---

200. *Id.* at 182 (Kagan, J., joined by Breyer and Ginsburg, JJ, concurring in the judgment).

201. *See, e.g.*, Burson v. Freeman, 504 U.S. 191 (1992) (upholding a state law prohibiting speech about candidate elections within a certain distance of a polling place, in order to prevent voter intimidation and election fraud).

point-based law to survive judicial review. This is because of both the problematic nature of viewpoint discrimination and the likelihood that, while government may be able to give a good explanation of why certain topics of speech are off-limits, it would be very hard-pressed to give a legitimate reason for banishing one side of a political debate while allowing the other to speak. As will be explained later in this section, government is allowed to impose content-based regulations on speech made in certain locations but remains prohibited from imposing viewpoint-based regulations in those same places.[202]

Nevertheless, some ambiguity clouds the distinction between content discrimination and viewpoint discrimination. For example, in *Rosenberger v. Rectors of the University of Virginia*,[203] the Court confronted a university's decision to deny student activity funding to a group that wished to publish a religiously-oriented newspaper. The majority concluded that the university's action constituted viewpoint-based discrimination that was not allowed in the forum created by the student activity fund. It argued that the university had discriminated against a particular outlook on public affairs and social issues more generally — the religiously-based outlook. By contrast, the dissenters argued that the university had "merely" discriminated on the basis of content, something they concluded was justifiable given the nature of the forum created by the student activity fund.[204]

This example should make it clear that, as conceptually straightforward as the distinction might be, it is not always easy to tell the difference between a law that discriminates on the basis of content and one that discriminates on the basis of viewpoint. To be sure, a viewpoint-discriminatory law quite likely also discriminates based on content. But the reverse is not necessarily true, as the dissenters in *Rosenberger* argued. This distinction matters, given the particularly strong rule against viewpoint discrimination.

[4] Analysis of Content-Neutral Laws

Content-neutral speech restrictions are much more likely to survive judicial review than restrictions that are content- or viewpoint-based. Nevertheless, such laws are still subject to First Amendment scrutiny. This sub-section considers three varieties of laws that are considered to be content-neutral: regulations of the "time, place, or manner" of speech, regulations of conduct that has an expressive element, and regulations of speech that are defended as combatting harmful, non-speech "secondary effects."

---

202. *See* Section 11.01[5].

203. 515 U.S. 819 (1995).

204. The dissenters also argued that university funding of the religious group would unconstitutionally fund religion in violation of the First Amendment's Establishment Clause. The Establishment Clause is discussed in Chapter 12.

[a] Time, Place, and Manner Restrictions

The classic type of content-neutral law is called a "time, place, or manner" law since, as a content-neutral law, such a regulation typically regulates when, where, or how speech is allowed. Such restrictions can still severely impact speech: think, for example, of a law that bans speech on weekends or in the town square. On the other hand, government often has quite legitimate reasons for imposing such regulations.

The Court has scrutinized such laws at least since the late 1930s, when it decided a series of cases over the course of a decade that established the basic First Amendment principles governing such laws. In *Schneider v. State*,[205] the Court struck down a group of city ordinances that severely restricted handbilling on public streets. The Court recognized the cities' interest in preventing the litter that followed when the recipients of handbills tossed them into the street. However, it concluded that less speech-restrictive means, such as punishing actual littering, would promote that interest at less cost to speech.

Similarly, in *Martin v. Struthers*,[206] the Court struck down a city ordinance that prohibited door-to-door distribution of handbills of any kind, including those addressing political topics. The city—an industrial city whose factories were then engaged in around-the-clock war production—justified the ordinance on the ground that the around-the-clock nature of residents' work meant that there was no time when a handbiller could be sure that the resident summoned to the door was not trying to sleep. The Court, speaking through Justice Black,[207] observed that the law did not just balance speech rights with residents' rights to be undisturbed in their homes, but also denied residents the right, if they wished, to receive information. It noted that residents who did not wish to receive information at their doorstep or who wished to not be disturbed could simply put up a placard to that effect, and that the city could enforce violations of those instructions. Finally, the Court extolled the importance of door-to-door solicitation of support for ideas, describing that practice as "essential to the poorly financed causes of little people."[208]

On the other hand, in *Kovacs v. Cooper*,[209] the Court upheld a city's ban on sound trucks. Emphasizing the volume of the speech emanating from sound trucks, the Court distinguished both *Schneider* and *Martin* on the ground that people on the streets, in businesses, and in residences could not help but hear the unwanted information, conveyed in a raucous manner. Dissenting for three justices, Justice Black

---

205. 308 U.S. 147 (1939).

206. 319 U.S. 141 (1943).

207. Interestingly, Justice Black originally voted the other way in this 5–4 case and was assigned to write the opinion. He tried, but he apparently concluded that the opinion didn't even convince him, and he switched his vote. *See* ARTHUR HELLMAN, WILLIAM ARAIZA, THOMAS BAKER & ASHUTOSH BHAGWAT, FIRST AMENDMENT LAW: FREEDOM OF SPEECH AND RELIGION 344–348 (4th ed. 2018) (reprinting excerpts from both the original draft opinion and the final opinion).

208. 319 U.S. at 146.

209. 336 U.S. 77 (1949).

repeated his concern in *Martin* that the speech being restricted was made in a manner favored by poorly-financed causes.

These and other early cases laid out the ideas that ultimately coalesced into modern time, place, and manner doctrine. That doctrine requires that (1) a content-neutral law be (2) narrowly tailored (3) to further a significant government interest and (4) leave open ample alternative means of communication. One can find the foundations for these rules in the earlier cases. *Schneider*, for example, insisted on a tighter fit between the government interest in street cleanliness and the speech regulation than would be the case if the law simply regulated non-expressive conduct. Indeed, *Schneider* even questioned whether the city's cleanliness interest was sufficiently important to justify such a broad speech regulation at all. In *Martin*, the Court worried that "the poorly financed causes of little people" would not receive a hearing if the inexpensive manner of door-to-door solicitation was completely closed off to them.

These earlier cases thus laid the foundation for the modern rule requiring that the government seek to further an interest of some magnitude, that there be more than a trivial connection between the law and that government interest, and that the law allow speakers ample opportunity to express themselves. More generally, this test responds to the intuition that even a content-neutral law risks suppressing speech to an unacceptable degree, and thus requires more than cursory judicial review.[210]

The Court has sent mixed signals on the stringency of the time, place, and manner test. In *Ward v. Rock Against Racism*,[211] the Court made clear that that test's narrow tailoring prong did not require the government to use the least speech-restrictive means of furthering the government's regulatory interest. Instead, the Court suggested what amounts to a mid-range level of ends-means review:

> Lest any confusion on the point remain, we reaffirm today that a regulation of the time, place, or manner of protected speech must be narrowly tailored to serve the government's legitimate, content-neutral interests but that it need not be the least restrictive or least intrusive means of doing so. Rather, the requirement of narrow tailoring is satisfied so long as the ... regulation promotes a substantial government interest that would be achieved less effectively absent the regulation. To be sure, this standard does not mean that a time, place, or manner regulation may burden substantially more speech than is necessary to further the government's legitimate interests. Government may not regulate expression in such a manner that a substantial portion of the burden on speech does not serve to advance its goals. So long as the means chosen are not substantially broader than necessary to achieve the government's interest, however, the regulation will not be invalid simply be-

---

210. Of course, the requirement of content-neutrality is a prerequisite for any law potentially being upheld as a valid time, place, or manner regulation. If instead the law is deemed content-based, then it receives the strict scrutiny required by the content-neutrality rule.

211. 491 U.S. 781 (1989).

cause a court concludes that the government's interest could be adequately served by some less-speech-restrictive alternative.[212]

Applying that standard, the Court in *Rock Against Racism* upheld a New York City ordinance requiring that bands playing at a bandshell in Central Park use a city-employed sound mixer rather than their own personnel, in pursuit of the city's interest in controlling volume and quality for the benefit of both concert-goers and nearby residents. The Court reasoned that the ordinance advanced the city's interest in expert and appropriate sound management, while still allowing bands ample opportunity to speak by performing at the bandshell. More generally, *Rock Against Racism* makes it clear that the narrow tailoring requirement in time, place, and manner analysis imposes nowhere near the same stringent least-restrictive-means condition that it does in other areas of constitutional law, most notably in equal protection.[213]

In other contexts, however, the Court has been more demanding in its time, place, and manner scrutiny. In *City of Ladue v. Gilleo*,[214] the Court struck down a law that prohibited the placement of many, but not all signs on private property in the town, as applied to a homeowner who wished to place an antiwar sign on her lawn. While the exemptions would have justified a holding that the ordinance was content-based and thus deserving of strict scrutiny, the Court instead assumed the law was content neutral. Applying time, place, and manner scrutiny, the Court relied heavily on the communicative value of speech made by residents from their property. Such speech communicated not just a message but also the identity of the person speaking—*i.e.*, the resident. Moreover, echoing *Martin v. Struthers'* recognition of "the poorly financed causes of little people," Justice Stevens insisted that "residential signs are an unusually cheap and convenient form of communication. Especially for persons of modest means or limited mobility, a yard or window sign may have no practical substitute."[215] Given their communicative value and the Court's conclusion about a lack of ample alternative means of communication, the Court struck down the law on time, place, and manner grounds.

Another example of relatively careful time, place, and manner analysis, in a very different context, was the Court's 2014 decision in *McCullen v. Coakley*.[216] *McCullen* struck down, on time, place, and manner grounds, a Massachusetts law that created a 35-foot buffer around abortion clinic entrances, to ease access to clinics for women seeking abortions who would otherwise have to make their way through a scrum of protesters. Despite vociferous dissents from Justices Scalia and Alito, the Court concluded that the law was content-neutral. Speaking through Chief Justice Roberts, the

---

212. *Id.* at 798–800.
213. *Compare, e.g.*, City of Richmond v. J.A. Croson Co., 488 U.S. 469 (1989) (imposing a stringent narrow tailoring requirement on a city's race-based affirmative action plan). *Croson*, and the stringency of the scrutiny the Court imposes on race-based affirmative action plans generally, is discussed in Section 10.04[3][b].
214. 512 U.S. 43 (1994).
215. *Id.* at 57.
216. 573 U.S. 464 (2014).

majority found irrelevant the fact that the law might have a content-based *effect*— that is, that the law, with its exceptions for passers-by, women seeking access to the clinic, clinic employees, and construction and fire and police personnel, had the effect of excluding only anti-abortion protesters.

Nevertheless, the Court concluded that the law failed time, place, and manner scrutiny. The Court explained that the type of speech the plaintiff in *McCullen* wanted to make was quiet, intimate anti-abortion counseling rather than raucous shouting of the sort that could be accomplished outside the 35-foot buffer. Such intimate counseling, the Court concluded, could not easily occur outside of the buffer zone, since the would-be counselor could not determine who was seeking to enter the clinic until the woman got closer to the entrance, within the buffer zone. Thus, the law imposed serious burdens on the counselors' speech.

In addition, the Court held that the law failed the narrow tailoring requirement. It suggested that "the Commonwealth has too readily forgone options that could serve its interests just as well, without substantially burdening the kind of speech in which petitioners wish to engage."[217] The Court pointed to anti-harassment laws and laws against obstructing traffic on sidewalks as measures the state could have tried before enacting the buffer zone's more draconian remedy. In response to the state's arguments that it had indeed tried such laws, the Court simply disbelieved them, noting the lack of prosecutions under existing laws of that sort. Finally, it observed that perhaps only one clinic in the state, on one day a week, had experienced problems of the sort the state had cited as justification for the law.

Any doctrinal formula as vague as the time, place, and manner test will be applied in ways that will sometimes seem inconsistent. Comparing the Court's deferential language and application of the test in *Rock Against Racism* with its more stringent applications in *Ladue* and *McCullen* suggests that, like other such formulas, time, place, and manner doctrine will be applied with an eye toward the particular context of the speech regulation in question and, quite likely, the particular judge's or justice's intuition about the severity of the speech infringement and the reasonableness of the law's attempt to promote the government's goals.

[b] Regulation of Expressive Conduct

Sometimes, government regulation of expression takes the form of regulation of conduct, rather than what is sometimes called "pure speech." For example, burning a flag (or saluting it) constitutes conduct that is highly expressive. Such conduct enjoys at least some First Amendment protection, limited by government's obvious authority to regulate conduct for reasons having nothing to do with its expressive elements (for example, prosecuting a person who has burned a flag for violating a general prohibition on open fires).

---

217. *Id.* at 490.

In *United States v. O'Brien*,[218] the Court announced the rule applicable to such government regulation of expressive conduct. *O'Brien* involved a federal prosecution of an anti-war activist who burned his draft card on the steps of a courthouse. O'Brien later explained that he burned his card as a protest against the government's military policies. The Court held that such expressive conduct was entitled to at least some First Amendment protection. The Court held that the government could penalize such conduct:

> if [the law] is within the constitutional power of the Government; if it furthers an important or substantial governmental interest; if the governmental interest is unrelated to the suppression of free expression; and if the incidental restriction on alleged First Amendment freedoms is no greater than is essential to the furtherance of that interest.[219]

Applying that test, the Court observed that it was within Congress's constitutional power to regulate the treatment of draft cards, that the government had an important interest in persons retaining their draft cards, that that interest was unrelated to the suppression of any expression that might accompany the destruction of such a card, and that the statutory prohibition on destroying such cards was narrowly drawn in order to further that interest. Note that the relevant interest was not the interest in maintaining armies, or even an effective draft system: presumably, if the Court had identified one of those as the relevant interest, it would have faced a much harder question about whether the prohibition on draft card destruction was "greater than ... essential to the furtherance of that interest." In subsequent years, the Court has explicitly acknowledged that the *O'Brien* test and the test for time, place, and manner restrictions are largely identical.[220]

O'Brien raises a number of questions. First, when does conduct in fact become sufficiently expressive that the First Amendment is triggered? The *O'Brien* Court acknowledged this issue when it began its analysis by stating that "[w]e cannot accept the view that an apparently limitless variety of conduct can be labeled 'speech' whenever the person engaging in the conduct intends thereby to express an idea."[221] However, the Court did not resolve that question, instead assuming that O'Brien's conduct in burning his draft card was expressive and thus did implicate the First Amendment.

Six years later, in *Spence v. Washington*,[222] the Court confronted this question. *Spence* dealt with a prosecution of a person for using tape to create a peace sign on an American flag, which he then displayed, causing his prosecution under a statute prohibiting the placing of any marks on a U.S. or state flag. The Court noted both the individual's statement that he intended to communicate a point of view about

---

218. 391 U.S. 367 (1968).

219. *Id.* at 377.

220. *See, e.g.*, Clark v. Community for Creative Non-Violence, 468 U.S. 288, 298 (1984).

221. 391 U.S. at 376.

222. 418 U.S. 405 (1974).

government policy and the background context of his conduct, which took place after a major escalation of the Vietnam War and an incident in which National Guard troops killed several anti-war protesters at a college. After considering those facts against *O'Brien*'s recognition that not every act can be thought of as triggering First Amendment scrutiny, the Court concluded that Spence's conduct did implicate the First Amendment. Speaking through a *per curiam* opinion, the Court wrote: "An intent to convey a particularized message was present, and in the surrounding circumstances the likelihood was great that the message would be understood by those who viewed it."[223] Since then, the "*Spence* test" has largely governed when expressive conduct is deemed to trigger First Amendment scrutiny.

A further question, answered two decades after *O'Brien* itself, concerned when the *O'Brien* test applied. There are two diametrically different situations in which it might not. Consider first *Arcara v. Cloud Books*.[224] *Arcara* involved a local prosecutor's application for an order closing a bookstore when the store was alleged to be knowingly allowing illegal sexual activities on the premises. The sexual activities themselves were not protected by the First Amendment — however, the sale of books clearly was. Did the order closing the bookstore thus reflect regulation of expressive conduct that in turn triggered *O'Brien*? The Court said no. It explained that the conduct being regulated was itself not expressive — unlike in *O'Brien*, where the conduct being regulated (the draft card burning) was in fact the exact conduct that was expressive. Based on this distinction, the Court concluded that the closure order did not implicate the First Amendment at all: even though the order ended up impacting expression, the order did not itself aim at the expressive conduct.

At the other end of the spectrum is regulation of conduct that is itself expressive when, unlike *O'Brien*, that regulation *was* related to the suppression of expression. This situation occurred in *Texas v. Johnson*.[225] In *Johnson*, the Court reversed the conviction of a person who had burned a flag as part of a political protest. After dispensing with other arguments, the Court confronted the state's claim that it had a legitimate interest in criminalizing flag burning in order to protect the flag as a symbol of national unity. The Court reasoned that this interest necessarily was related to expression, since it allowed the state to criminalize conduct (the flag burning) when it communicated a particular message (a negative message about national unity). Thus, the state's action fell outside of *O'Brien*'s test, just like it had in *Arcara*. In *Johnson*, however, the state's action triggered, not the complete lack of any First Amendment analysis as in *Arcara*, but instead what the Court in *Johnson* called "the most exacting scrutiny."[226] Given that the state could only claim an interest in suppressing a particular viewpoint about the nation (*i.e.*, that the nation was not united), the Court easily found the prosecution to have failed that scrutiny.

---

223. *Id.* at 410–11.
224. 478 U.S. 697 (1986).
225. 491 U.S. 397 (1989).
226. *Id.* at 412.

Combining *Arcara* and *O'Brien* leads, then, to a conclusion that *O'Brien*'s test applies in only a relatively narrow set of circumstances. First, the challenged government action must target the actual conduct that is alleged to be expressive. Thus, the expressive conduct cannot be mere "collateral damage" in the government's regulation of other, non-expressive conduct. (If it is mere "collateral damage," as it was in *Arcara*, then the First Amendment simply does not apply.) At the other extreme, though, if the government action does in fact target the actual expressive conduct itself, then *O'Brien* applies only if that regulation is unrelated to the expression that is communicated by that conduct. If it fails that test—that is, if, as in *Johnson*, the regulation *is* targeted at suppressing the expression that comes with that conduct—then *O'Brien* does not apply, but instead a higher level of scrutiny: what *Johnson* called "the most exacting" scrutiny. In sum, then, *O'Brien* only applies when the government regulates the actual conduct that is alleged to be expressive, but does so, as in *O'Brien* itself, in support of an interest that is unrelated to the suppression of expression.

[c] Secondary Effects Regulation

"Secondary effects" regulations refer to restrictions on speech, usually non-obscene sexual speech,[227] that generally take the form of limits on where businesses making such speech may locate. The commonest examples of such regulations are those that either cluster sex-oriented businesses, essentially creating "red light districts," or separating them out, for example, by requiring them to locate a certain distance away from any other such business, or from places where children may congregate.

In *City of Renton v. Playtime Theaters*,[228] the Court held that such regulations merited relatively deferential First Amendment scrutiny. *Renton* involved a city ordinance that required "adult motion picture theaters" to locate 1,000 feet away from a variety of places, including residential zones, churches, parks, and schools. Thus, in a basic way, it was content-oriented (since, for example, motion picture theaters showing family films were not restricted). Nevertheless, the Court concluded that the law should be analyzed as a content-neutral regulation because it was *justified* without reference to the content of the speech restricted.[229] The City denied that it had anything against adult sexual speech *per se*, but instead expressed concern that businesses catering to the demand for such speech were correlated with pernicious "secondary effects" such as public drunkenness and prostitution.

The Court concluded that such regulation of secondary effects was constitutional if the challenged law "is designed to serve a substantial governmental interest and allows for reasonable alternative avenues of communication."[230] As applied in *Renton*, this is a deferential standard. The Court did not insist that the city develop its own evidence connecting adult businesses to the secondary effects the city desired to elim-

---

227. *But see* Boos v. Barry, 485 U.S. 312 (1988) (considering a claim that regulation of political speech was justified under the secondary effects doctrine).

228. 475 U.S. 41 (1986).

229. *See id.* at 48.

230. *Id.* at 50.

inate — rather, the city could rely on data derived from other cities' experiences. Moreover, the city was given broad leeway either to concentrate such businesses or disperse them. The Court rejected the argument that, by singling out theaters for the location requirement (rather than including, say, adult bookstores) the city had acted in an unconstitutionally underinclusive way, reasoning that there was no evidence that, when enacted, any other types of adult businesses were in Renton.

Finally, the Court rejected the argument that the ordinance's location requirements made it impossible to find suitable venues for the speech. Even though the ordinance's various requirements apparently removed almost 95% of the city's acreage as legal locations for such theaters, the Court concluded that the remaining acreage gave them adequate places to locate. In response to the theater's argument that the remaining land was unsuitable for adult theaters, the Court shrugged its shoulders and essentially disclaimed any responsibility for the real estate market in Renton.[231]

Sixteen years later, in *City of Los Angeles v. Alameda Books*,[232] the Court expressed a more ambivalent attitude toward *Renton*'s deferential approach. In *Alameda Books*, a five-justice majority reversed a grant of summary judgment to an adult bookstore challenging a Los Angeles ordinance that sought to disperse adult businesses, including by prohibiting two such businesses from existing under the same roof (*e.g.*, in a mini-mall or other such structure). A four-justice plurality applied *Renton* to demand relatively little of the city. Most notably, the city was allowed to rely on a study that showed a correlation between high concentrations of adult businesses and crime, even though the businesses that were the subject of that study had separate locations, in contrast to the shared-location status of the plaintiff in *Alameda Books*.

Concurring, Justice Kennedy provided the fifth vote but expressed concern with calling such regulations content-neutral. Nevertheless, because the city was seeking to diminish the "externalities"[233] of the speech — that is, the secondary effects — he concluded that *Renton* provided the appropriate analysis. However, Justice Kennedy did caution that dispersal regulations such as the Los Angeles ordinance must not result in the affected entities shutting down and thus reducing the amount of speech created and available to consumers of that speech. In other words, the city could not attempt to limit the unwanted secondary effects simply by suppressing the speech it believed to be correlated with those effects. Four dissenters would have subjected the Los Angeles ordinance to more careful scrutiny. They faulted the city for failing to demonstrate that multiple sexual speech businesses operating under one roof caused the same secondary effects as multiple operations located separately from each other—

---

231. *See id.* at 54 ("That respondents must fend for themselves in the real estate market, on an equal footing with other prospective purchasers and lessees, does not give rise to a First Amendment violation. And although we have cautioned against the enactment of zoning regulations that have the effect of suppressing, or greatly restricting access to, lawful speech, we have never suggested that the First Amendment compels the Government to ensure that adult theaters, or any other kinds of speech-related businesses for that matter, will be able to obtain sites at bargain prices.").

232. 535 U.S. 425 (2002).

233. *Id.* at 446 (Kennedy, J., concurring in the judgment).

the situation that was the subject of the city's study on which it based its dispersal ordinance.

The Court's 2015 decision in *Reed v. Town of Gilbert*[234] calls into question the continued viability of secondary effects doctrine. Regulations such as those in *Renton* and *Alameda Books* are facially content-based; thus, *Reed* suggests that such laws automatically trigger strict scrutiny, regardless of any content-neutral justification the city offers (such as combatting the secondary effects of that speech). At some point, a litigant will likely force the Court to confront *Reed*'s implications for this particular sub-part of free speech law.

[5] Forum Doctrine

Speech has to occur somewhere. Even electronic speech, such as speech on the Internet, can be understood as occurring "in" the wires and servers and other physical facilities that comprise the World Wide Web or, more conceptually, in a virtual forum. And of course, much speech still takes place on unambiguously physical property, such as a street, an auditorium, or a bookstore.

One might intuit that the First Amendment has great force on private property, since one would naturally think that, for example, a bookstore should be able to sell whatever types of books it wants and host whatever types of readings it wants. But speech also naturally occurs on government-owned property. Streets, the classrooms of state universities, and Social Security offices are but three of the nearly-limitless types of government-owned property where speech occurs as a matter of course. First Amendment doctrine pays attention to the location at which a speech restriction operates, and provides different rules depending on that location. The resulting rules are just as foundational as the rules governing content-based and content-neutral speech restrictions.

[a] The Foundations of Forum Doctrine

The strength of the First Amendment's free speech guarantee varies according to the place in which an individual wishes to speak. At a very basic level, one can begin with the simple insight that any owner of property, whether governmental or private, enjoys the latitude to allow or prohibit whatever speech it wishes on its property. As far as private property owners are concerned, this basic rule is largely accurate as a statement of the law today. At the very least, restrictions on speech a private property owner wishes to host are subject to strict scrutiny if the restriction is content-based, and to time, place, and manner or similar scrutiny if content-neutral.[235]

With regard to government-owned property the situation is more complicated. Before the twentieth century, government ownership of property was, for purposes of the First Amendment, thought to be analogous to private ownership, with the

---

234. 576 U.S. 155 (2015). *Reed* is discussed in Section 11.01[3][b].
235. These standards are discussed in Sections 11.01[3]–[4].

result that government, like any other landowner, exercised complete dominion over speech activities on its property. In 1895, Oliver Wendell Holmes, then a justice on Massachusetts' highest court, said the following: "For the legislature absolutely or conditionally to forbid public speaking in a highway or public park is no more an infringement of the rights of a member of the public than for the owner of a private house to forbid it in his house."[236]

However, over the course of the middle decades of the twentieth century, the Supreme Court's gradually increasing protection for free speech led it to embrace the idea that individuals enjoyed particularly strong speech rights on certain types of government property. In 1939, in *Hague v. CIO*, the Court described public parks and streets as places that "have immemorially been held in trust for the use of the public and [places that], time out of mind, have been used for purposes of assembly, communicating thoughts between citizens, and discussing public questions."[237] In conjunction with a series of other cases dating from that same era,[238] *Hague* established the idea that certain types of government-owned property were places where speech rights were guarded particularly carefully. *Hague*'s focus on the historical purpose of such venues, while perhaps a legal fiction,[239] has come to play an important role in determining which categories of government-owned property possess this speech-friendly status.

However, with regard to other types of government-owned property, the private landlord/private control analogy applies with stronger force. In *Adderly v. Florida*, a 1966 case involving protesters who wished to make their speech at a jail facility, the Court observed that "[t]he State, no less than a private owner of property, has power to preserve the property under its control for the use to which it is lawfully dedicated."[240] The Court's acceptance of this idea[241] has led, at the very least,[242] to a bifurcated approach to speech on government property, in which speech in parks and on streets and sidewalks enjoys more constitutional protection than speech on other types of government-owned property.

[b] The Modern Rule

The foundational ideas discussed in the previous sub-section have led the Court to announce a set of rules varying the protection speech enjoys based on where it oc-

---

236. Commonwealth v. Davis, 39 N.E. 113, 113 (Mass. 1895).

237. 307 U.S. 496, 515 (1939).

238. *See, e.g.*, Schneider v. State, 308 U.S. 147 (1939); Cantwell v. Connecticut, 310 U.S. 296 (1940).

239. *See, e.g.*, Int'l Soc'y for Krishna Consciousness v. Lee, 505 U.S. 672, 696 (1992) (Kennedy, J., concurring in the judgment) (calling "a most doubtful fiction" the idea that historically the primary purpose of streets, parks, and sidewalks was to facilitate speech).

240. 385 U.S. 39, 47 (1966).

241. The quote from *Adderly* has reappeared a number of times in Supreme Court opinions, for example, in *Greer v. Spock*, 424 U.S. 828, 836 (1976), and *Cornelius v. NAACP Legal Def. Fund*, 473 U.S. 788, 800 (1985).

242. As the text will make clear, there may well be more than two categories of government property for purposes of the First Amendment.

curs. The basic rule—which this discussion later expands on and makes more complex—is that government-owned property can either be a public forum or a non-public forum. Speech in public forums enjoys heightened protection: regulations of speech in such places are subject to strict scrutiny if content-based, and, if content-neutral, are subject to the various intermediate scrutiny tests identified earlier (most notably, the time, place, and manner and expressive conduct tests). By contrast, speech in non-public forums can be regulated based on its content. The only limits on such restrictions is that they be viewpoint-neutral and reasonable.

Thus, a lot turns on what government-owned property counts as a public forum.[243] At the most basic, certain places—streets, sidewalks, and parks—are considered "traditional public forums." Such places, as locations that, to use the reasoning in *Hague*, have "have immemorially been held in trust for the use of the public and, time out of mind, have been used for purposes of assembly, communicating thoughts between citizens, and discussing public questions,"[244] are where speech rights are protected most carefully. In the 1992 case *Lee v. International Society for Krishna Consciousness*, the Court relied heavily on a historical analysis—most notably, the relative recentness of air travel and thus of the development of airports—to conclude that John F. Kennedy Airport in New York City was not a traditional public forum.[245] The Court also observed that, while traditional public forums are also characterized as having, "as a principal purpose ... the free exchange of ideas," airports are "commercial establishments funded by user fees and designed to make a regulated profit."[246] Thus, airports again failed the test for status as a traditional public forum.

But other places may also be public forums. In addition to "traditional" public forums, the Court has identified "designated" public forums as places where speech enjoys the same level of protection as speech in traditional public forums. Essentially, a designated public forum is a place that is not a traditional public forum, but which government opens up for speech.[247] The act of creating such a forum and opening it up for speech subjects government to the same rigorous rules for restricting speech as those that apply in traditional public forums.

The most straightforward understanding of the Court's forum structure lumps all other government-owned property into the category of non-public forums. Places such as military bases,[248] government-run charity campaigns conducted within a gov-

---

243. Again, speech restrictions on private property are fully subject to the content-neutrality rule—that is, such restrictions are analyzed the same as restrictions on speech in a public (government-owned) forum.

244. 307 U.S. at 515.

245. 505 U.S. 672, 680–81 (1992).

246. *Id.* at 682.

247. One scholar has identified, among other spaces, art displays in a city hall building and municipal theaters as forums courts have identified as designated public forums. *See* Michael Friedman, *Dazed and Confused: Explaining Judicial Determinations of Traditional Pubic Forum Status*, 82 TUL. L. REV. 929, 934 (2008).

248. *See* Greer v. Spock, 424 U.S. 828 (1976).

ernment workplace,[249] and an inter-school mail system operated by a school district[250] have all been held to constitute non-public forums, where viewpoint neutrality (*not* content neutrality) and reasonableness are the only requirements for government speech restrictions. One way to understand such places is that government operates them, not as a trustee for the public's use (as with traditional public forums), and not as a venue explicitly dedicated to speech (as with designated public forums), but instead for the conduct of the government's own business. As a proprietor, the government, like any property owner, can decide which speech to welcome and which speech to exclude (with the caveat, again, that when the government is the owner, even non-public forums are subject to the viewpoint-neutrality and reasonableness requirements).[251]

However, the Court has introduced additional complexity into this structure. In *Perry Educators' Association v. Perry Local Educators' Association*,[252] the Court, in the course of setting forth this traditional public forum/designated public forum/non-public forum division, suggested that the second of these categories (designated public forums) could be sub-divided into forums "designated" for discussion of any topic and forums designated for discussion of particular topics. As the *Perry* Court stated in a footnote: "A public forum may be created for a limited purpose such as use by certain groups, or for the discussion of certain subjects."[253]

While perhaps confusing conceptually, this idea of a "limited public forum" (or a "limited designated public forum") makes sense when one considers the myriad ways in which government facilitates speech. The two cases the *Perry* footnote cited dealt with a university that opened up a forum for speech for student groups (but nobody else)[254] and a school board that opened up a forum for discussion of school board business (but no other topics).[255] One can easily imagine similar cases occurring across the entire sphere of government action.

The difficult question is the standard to be applied to such "limited" public forums. At times, the Court has suggested that the same standard applies to all public forums, whether limited or not.[256] But this seems to conflict with the entire idea of a limited

---

249. *See* Cornelius v. NAACP Legal Def. Fund, 473 U.S. 788 (1985).

250. *See* Perry Educators' Ass'n v. Perry Local Educators' Ass'n, 460 U.S. 37 (1983).

251. The "reasonableness" caveat may be understandable in terms of the baseline requirement that all government regulation be at least rational. Indeed, one could further speculate that the viewpoint-neutrality caveat might be tied to the reasonableness requirement, since government would likely be hard-pressed to defend the reasonableness of a decision to allow speech on a topic but only if the speech takes one side or another on that issue.

252. 460 U.S. 37 (1983).

253. *Id.* at 46 n. 7.

254. *See* Widmar v. Vincent, 454 U.S. 263 (1981).

255. *See* City of Madison Joint Sch. Dist. No. 8 v. Wisconsin Employment Relations Comm'n, 429 U.S. 167 (1976).

256. *See, e.g., Lee*, 505 U.S. at 678 ("The second category of public property is the designated public forum, *whether of a limited or unlimited character*—property that the State has opened for expressive activity by part or all of the public. Regulation of such property is subject to the same limitations as that governing a traditional public forum.") (emphasis added).

public forum as a venue the government has established for the discussion of particular topics or by particular groups.[257] On the other hand, the other obvious standard for speech restrictions in such venues — a requirement that such restrictions be merely *viewpoint* neutral — effectively subjects these forums to the same standard as that imposed on non-public forums. Such a conclusion would render the concept of a designated public forum superfluous. Given this confusion, it is not surprising that lower courts have disagreed on the proper standard to be applied to speech restrictions in such venues.[258]

[c] Government Power to Restrict Speech in Public Forums

Even speech in public forums can be legitimately subjected to government restrictions. Recall that even a content-based restriction on speech in a public forum will be upheld if the Court finds that the restriction satisfies strict scrutiny. More commonly, content-neutral restrictions, such as time, place, or manner restrictions, will often be upheld.

Other, more specialized rules also apply to particular types of speech restrictions in public forums. In one of the foundational public forum cases, *Schneider v. State*, discussed earlier, the Court, in the course of striking down restrictions on hand-billing on streets, acknowledged that the city had the right to prevent persons from forming a human chain across a street, forcing passers-by to take a handbill in order to cross.[259]

Two years later, the Court upheld a restriction on speech in a public forum when that speech threatened the type of blockage the Court warned about in *Schneider*. *Cox v. New Hampshire*[260] involved a group of Jehovah's Witnesses who massed in a large number and proceeded to march on sidewalks in the downtown area of a city, without first obtaining a permit from the authorities. The Court held that the city could constitutionally require such a permit, in order to allow the police to plan for the safety of the marchers and other users of the streets, and to ensure that no conflicting marches were planned for that time and place. The Court noted that the statute did not give the authorities arbitrary discretion to deny a permit for any reason that suited the whim of the official, thus obviating the concern that disagreement with the march's message would allow the official to deny a permit.

Cox also upheld the imposition of a fee designed to defray the cost of providing police protection to any requested march. However, in a 1992 case, *Forsyth County v. Nationalist Movement*,[261] the Court struck down a county ordinance requiring a

---

257. *See Perry*, 460 U.S. at 46 n. 7.
258. *See, e.g.*, Child Evangelism Fellowship of Md., Inc. v. Montgomery County Public Schools, 457 F.3d 376 (4th Cir. 2006) (recognizing the disagreement among the lower courts).
259. *See* 308 U.S. 147, 160 (1939). *Schneider* is discussed in Section 11.01[4][a].
260. 312 U.S. 569 (1941).
261. 505 U.S. 123 (1992).

permit for marches. According to the Court, the county's interpretation of the ordinance failed to provide adequate standards guiding the official's use of discretion when determining how much of a fee to charge. Moreover, the Court worried that the county's interpretation also suggested that, in setting the fee, the county would take into account the likely response to the march (and thus the response to the ideas it conveyed) when determining the policing costs the fee was intended to defray. On these grounds, the Court distinguished *Cox*'s upholding of the similarly-worded New Hampshire law. *Forsyth County* thus reflects not only the content-neutrality rule that plays such a large role in First Amendment law, but also the Court's concern with giving officials unbridled discretion to burden speech with which they may disagree.

The Court has also imposed another requirement on government when a speaker is lawfully engaged in speech in a public forum. In a series of fact-intensive cases, the Court has essentially required police to take strong measures to protect a permitted speaker's right to speak, even in the face of a hostile crowd that is threatening to get violent if the speech continues. This idea is known as a "heckler's veto," because it supposes an opponent of the speaker (a "heckler") who, if not for the police's obligation to protect the speech and the speaker, possesses the power to shut down (or "veto") the speech simply by threatening to start a riot if it continues.

The Court first considered this idea in *Terminiello v. Chicago*.[262] *Terminiello* involved a speaker who gave a fiery speech inside a packed auditorium, with a large crowd of his political opponents protesting outside and inside the building. When the speaker continued with his speech, even taunting his opponents, and when the crowd responded by becoming more and more agitated, the police responded by arresting the speaker for breach of the peace. The Court overturned the conviction, extolling the importance of free speech, even when it "induces a condition of unrest ... or even stirs people to anger."[263] Justice Jackson dissented. He provided a long account of the factual situation inside and outside the auditorium, and warned that the Court's decision threatened to hamstring local authorities who sought to prevent rioting.

The Court reached the opposite conclusion in a case decided two years later. In *Feiner v. New York*,[264] a speaker—this time speaking outdoors—attracted a hostile crowd, which arguably blocked free passage along the sidewalk. According to the Court, the crowd was "restless" and "at least one person threatened violence if the police did not act."[265] At some point, the police arrested the speaker for disorderly conduct, of which he was convicted.

On a 6–3 vote, the Court upheld the conviction. Chief Justice Vinson denied that the speaker was arrested for the content of his speech, but instead insisted that he was arrested because he "passe[d] the bounds of argument or persuasion and

---

262. 337 U.S. 1 (1949).
263. *Id.* at 5.
264. 340 U.S. 315 (1951).
265. *Id.* at 317.

undert[ook] incitement to riot."[266] Justice Black, joined by Justices Douglas and Minton, dissented, concluding that the policemen took inadequate measures to protect the speaker, took no measures to ensure clear passage on the sidewalk, and did nothing to discourage one listener who threatened to assault the speaker.

A similar fact-intensive disagreement marked *Edwards v. South Carolina*,[267] decided in 1963. *Edwards* dealt with civil rights protesters parading on the statehouse grounds in South Carolina. As the majority described the situation, upon being told to disperse, the crowd "sang patriotic and religious songs after one of their leaders had delivered a 'religious harangue.' There was no violence or threat of violence on their part, or on the part of any member of the crowd watching them. Police protection was 'ample.'"[268] Eight members of the Court, speaking through Justice Stewart, distinguished *Feiner* and overturned the protesters' arrest and conviction. Dissenting, Justice Clark noted the situation then prevailing in some southern communities and described the situation as creating "a much greater danger of riot and disorder"[269] than in *Feiner*.

These cases turn largely on their facts—in particular, on the Court's estimation of the combustible nature of the situation, the police's ability to protect the speaker, and the actual actions of the police before arresting the speaker and ending his speech. Still, they suggest that police have some First Amendment-based duty to attempt to protect a speaker's rights, especially if the speaker has secured a legal right to be in that place at that time for speech purposes.

§ 11.02 Special Doctrines in the System of Freedom of Expression

This chapter considers First Amendment doctrines that have application to particular types of speech situations. It begins in Section 11.02[1] by considering the doctrine against so-called prior restraints. A prior restraint is essentially a government command that a speaker or publisher not speak or publish, with the effect that the very act of nevertheless speaking or publishing constitutes a legal violation, even if the speech uttered is itself protected. As one might imagine, such prior (or "previous") restraints are heavily disfavored.

Section 11.02[2] considers two constitutional doctrines that have either unique or special relevance in free speech jurisprudence: overbreadth and vagueness. In the First Amendment context, both of these ideas respond to the same concern for ensuring that constitutionally-protected speech is not chilled by either overbroad or vague laws. Section 11.02[3] considers the protection against being compelled to speak. One might think that being compelled to speak is just as problematic as being

---

266. *Id.* at 321.
267. 372 U.S. 229 (1963).
268. *Id.* at 236.
269. *Id.* at 244 (Clark, J., dissenting).

forbidden from speaking. In a foundational 1943 case, *West Virginia State Board of Education v. Barnette,*[270] the Court implied that, indeed, government compulsion of speech was even more problematic. Until very recently, however, the Court has not suggested a particular doctrinal test to govern government speech compulsions.

Section 11.02[4] considers a First Amendment concept that is sometimes closely related to the freedom from compelled speech: the freedom of association. The Court has recognized that the First Amendment protects persons' rights to associate for political and other speech purposes. This section considers the constitutional analysis applied to laws that restrict such association, either by impairing persons' ability to combine into such associations or, in a manner roughly analogous to compelled speech, by compelling persons to accept unwanted persons into their associative institutions, for example through the application of anti-discrimination laws.

Section 11.02[5] examines constitutional protection for political campaign activity, especially monetary contributions to and expenditures on such campaigns. Such protection constitutes one of the most heated topics of First Amendment law today. Section 11.02[6] examines the restrictions imposed on government when it either funds private speech or acts as the speaker itself. As one might intuit, government has more leeway to govern the content of private speech when the government is paying for it. Similarly, one might suppose that government has even more leeway when it is the entity actually doing the speaking. While these intuitions are essentially accurate, these areas still raise difficult questions. Finally, Section 11.02[7] considers the First Amendment rights of persons in their capacity as public school students or government employees. In these cases, the Court has attempted to strike a difficult balance between recognizing individuals' continued First Amendment rights even when they walk into a government classroom or workplace, while acknowledging the government's interests as educator or employer—interests that often clash with students' and employees' free speech interests.

[1] The Doctrine against Prior Restraints

Understanding the power of information, particularly when widely distributed, governments have long sought to impose restrictions on the press. Before the United States became an independent nation, William Blackstone suggested that the common law looked with considerable disdain on governments imposing prior restraints on publication: "The Liberty of the press is indeed essential to the nature of a free state; but this consists in laying no previous restraint upon publication, and not in freedom from censure for criminal matter when published."[271] While at times it may be difficult to define a prior restraint with precision, the classic, straightforward definition of a prior restraint is a government edict prohibiting the publication of information. A prior restraint thus differs from other restrictions on speaking and publishing in that

---

270. 319 U.S. 624 (1943).

271. W. BLACKSTONE, COMMENTARIES 151–152 (*quoted in* Near v. Minnesota, 283 U.S. 697, 713 (1931)).

it renders illegal the very act of speaking or publishing without any finding that the material itself may be prohibited (for example, because it constitutes incitement or obscenity). In 1993, Justice Kennedy explained the concept of prior restraints and the reason they are particularly disfavored:

> In its simple, most blatant form, a prior restraint is a law which requires submission of speech to an official who may grant or deny permission to utter or publish it based upon its contents. In contrast are laws which punish speech or expression only after it has occurred and been found unlawful. While each mechanism, once imposed, may abridge speech in a direct way by suppressing it, or in an indirect way by chilling its dissemination, we have interpreted the First Amendment as providing greater protection from prior restraints than from subsequent punishments. In [a prior case], we explained that "behind the distinction is a theory deeply etched in our law: a free society prefers to punish the few who abuse rights of speech after they break the law than to throttle them and all others beforehand."[272]

Despite this explanation, Justice Kennedy then conceded the ambiguity of the concept: "It has been suggested that the distinction between prior restraints and subsequent punishments may have slight utility, for in a certain sense every criminal obscenity statute is a prior restraint because of the caution a speaker or bookseller must exercise to avoid its imposition."[273] Justice Kennedy was speaking in the context of an obscenity prosecution that involved significant monetary penalties and forfeitures; hence, his concern that the Court's vague test for obscenity, when coupled with large *ex post* penalties, might serve to chill speech every bit as much as a prior restraint. But regardless of any such ambiguities, the Court has historically treated prior restraints as a particularly disfavored form of speech restriction.

The Supreme Court afforded strong protection against prior restraints in the classic 1931 case *Near v. Minnesota*.[274] The Minnesota statute at issue in *Near* permitted state authorities to seek an injunction against the owner or publisher of any " 'malicious, scandalous and defamatory newspaper, magazine or other periodical.' "[275] If the publisher failed to prove both the truth of the matter published and his good motives in publishing it, a judge suppressed that publication and would punish any further publication by contempt sanctions. To escape this injunction against future publication, the publisher had to satisfy the court that any subsequent publication of his was truly new and different. Thus, the statute authorized prior restraints, in the form of court injunctions against continued publication.

Minnesota sought to use this statute to close a publication called *The Saturday Press* for publishing a series of articles accusing high officials of corruption. The Supreme Court struck down the statute. Writing for a 5–4 majority, Chief Justice

272. Alexander v. United States, 509 U.S 544, 566–67 (1993) (Kennedy, J., dissenting).
273. *Id.* at 567.
274. 283 U.S. 697 (1931).
275. *Id.* at 702 (quoting the statute).

Hughes characterized the Minnesota law as "the essence of censorship."[276] He treated the ban on future publication as a prior restraint even though it had been imposed by a court as a penalty for past behavior. The majority distinguished prior restraints from statutes imposing criminal or civil penalties on speech after it had occurred.

One might wonder why the Court drew this distinction. After all, if the Constitution permits government to exact penalties on speech after it occurs, deterrence theory would predict that those penalties would discourage future speech. This is especially true when, as in the *Alexander* case from which Justice Kennedy's earlier quotation is drawn,[277] the liability standard is vague, and the *ex post* penalties are severe. Thus, whether it compelled silence directly by injunction or indirectly by subsequent penalty, the government has in both cases suppressed ideas. Nevertheless, as reflected in the Blackstone quotation reprinted earlier, a prohibition on prior restraints was the core of the historic British conception of freedom of expression. Moreover, a prohibition on prior restraints at least increases the possibility that an intrepid speaker will speak or publish, hoping that the material will not be found punishable. By contrast, a prior restraint guarantees that the speaker or publisher is violating the law by the very act of speaking or publishing. Whatever the reasons, the tradition strongly disfavoring prior restraints has persisted into the current day, and indeed has evolved into a near-absolute prohibition.

While the Court struck down the statute at issue in *Near*, Chief Justice Hughes did list several possible instances in which it might permit a prior restraint. Among others, the Court suggested that prior restraints might be valid against obscene publications and those revealing the sailing dates of troop carriers.[278] Obscene materials remain among the most likely instances in which a court will issue a prior restraint, although even for these materials, prior restraints are quite difficult to obtain. The example involving troop military maneuvers was quoted approvingly in Justice Brennan's opinion in *New York Times Co. v. United States*, discussed immediately below.

New York Times Co. v. United States[279] — often referred to as *The Pentagon Papers Case* — illustrates the stringency of the modern Court's protection against prior restraints. Shortly after the *New York Times* and *Washington Post* published the first in a series of classified government documents on the Vietnam War (which became known as "the Pentagon Papers"), the United States sued to enjoin further publication. As the culmination of an expedited judicial process, the Supreme Court, in a *per curiam* opinion, stated that any prior restraint bore "a heavy presumption against its

---

276. *Id.* at 713.

277. Alexander v. United States, 509 U.S. 544, 566–67 (1993).

278. *See Near*, 283 U.S. at 716 (also discussing incitement and actual obstruction of the armed forces recruiting services as possible justifications for a prior restraint). Interestingly, Chief Justice Hughes, citing a law review article by the influential legal scholar Roscoe Pound, also suggested that private rights such as defamation and invasion of privacy could also be enforced via prior restraints. *See ibid.* and *ibid.* n.7 (citing Roscoe Pound, "Equitable Relief Against Defamation and Injuries to Personality," 29 Harv. L. Rev. 640 (1916)).

279. 403 U.S. 713 (1971).

constitutional validity," and the Government carried a "heavy burden" of justifying such a restraint.[280] As the government failed to meet its burden, the Court refused to impose any prior restraint. Beyond the short and vague *per curiam* opinion, each of the six justices in the majority wrote separate, and analytically different, concurring opinions.

Justices Black and Douglas each wrote an opinion and joined the other's. Taking an absolutist position, Justice Black stated "that the press must be left free to publish news, whatever the source, without censorship, injunctions, or prior restraints."[281] He summarily rejected the Solicitor General's attempt to justify a prior restraint on national security grounds. Justice Douglas appeared to indicate that under the proper circumstances, Congress may use its "war power" to authorize the Executive to apply for a prior restraint. As Congress had not declared war on North Vietnam, and the Executive had no power to make war, Justice Douglas did not decide the extent to which Congress could have invoked its war power to authorize a prior restraint.[282]

In his concurrence, Justice Brennan criticized even the interim restraints issued by the lower courts in these cases as based on the government's "surmise or conjecture" that publication might impair national security.[283] He stated that precedent limited prior restraints to wartime. Quoting *Near*, he would have permitted a prior restraint to " 'prevent actual obstruction to its recruiting service or the publication of the sailing dates of transports or the number of troops.' "[284] He also suggested that a prior restraint might be issued in peacetime to prevent setting a nuclear holocaust in motion.[285] For even a temporary restraint to issue, Justice Brennan would require government proof "that publication must inevitably, directly, and immediately cause the occurrence of an event kindred to imperiling the safety of a transport already at sea."[286]

Justice Marshall's concurrence emphasized the fact that Congress had specifically declined to enact legislation giving the President the power to request a prior restraint. A court issuing a judicial prior restraint against this legislative backdrop would thus violate the separation of powers. Justice White, joined by Justice Stewart, also emphasized that lack of congressional authorization. He also noted that the Executive had failed to comply with congressional legislation authorizing criminal sanctions for publishing specified intelligence or military information. Justice White did not rule out the possibility that the government could enjoin these materials pursuant to a congressional statute.

---

280. *Id.* at 714.

281. *Id.* at 717 (Black, J., concurring).

282. *Id.* at 722 (Douglas, J., concurring).

283. *Id.* at 726 (Brennan, J., concurring).

284. *Id.* at 727 (quoting *Near*, 283 U.S. at 716).

285. In *United States v. Progressive, Inc.*, 467 F. Supp. 990 (W.D. Wis. 1979), a district court enjoined a magazine from publishing details about the construction of a hydrogen bomb. The appellate court dissolved the injunction when the material was published elsewhere. *See* L.A. Powe, Jr., *The H-Bomb Injunction*, 61 U. COLO. L. REV. 55 (1990).

286. 403 U.S. at 726–27.

Justice Stewart, joined by Justice White, cautioned that an informed citizenry was needed to restrain the tremendous powers of the Executive over national defense and international relations. Nevertheless, to exercise these awesome powers effectively, the Executive requires "confidentiality and secrecy." Unlike the opinions previously discussed, Justice Stewart afforded the President inherent authority to seek prior restraints to protect sensitive information relating to defense and international relations. While Justice Stewart was convinced that some of the documents at issue should remain secret, the government had not established that disclosing "any of them will surely result in direct, immediate, and irreparable damage to our Nation or its people."[287]

Justice Stewart allowed greater possible latitude for a prior restraint than did Justices Black, Douglas, or Brennan. Moreover, because Justice White joined Justice Stewart's position, and three Justices dissented, Justice Stewart's opinion represented the most protection that a majority of the Court afforded against prior restraints.[288]

Chief Justice Burger wrote a dissenting opinion, and Justice Harlan wrote a separate dissent joined by Chief Justice Burger and Justice Blackmun. Both opinions criticized the speed with which the Court acted, a pace that, in their view, did not allow adequate time to decide the many complex questions in this case. Turning to the merits, Justice Harlan limited judicial scrutiny to two inquiries. First, he said, the judiciary must determine that the dispute properly lay in the President's foreign relations authority. Second, the judiciary should require that the head of the relevant department—for example, the Secretary of State or of Defense—make the determination that disclosure would irreparably harm national security. Because Justice Harlan construed the Court's decision as an improper redetermination of the probable national security impact of the *Times* and *Post* disclosures, he dissented.

The Court has also addressed the doctrine against prior restraints in other, less fraught contexts. Specific instances include laws requiring obtaining a permit before mounting a demonstration,[289] laws requiring a license before opening an adult speech business,[290] and contractual limitations on former CIA agents publishing information about the agency.[291] One notable area in which prior restraints operate is when a trial

---

287. *Id.* at 728, 730 (Stewart, J., concurring).

288. *See* Marks v. United States, 430 U.S. 188, 193 (1977) ("When a fragmented Court decides a case and no single rationale explaining the result enjoys the assent of five Justices, the holding of the Court may be viewed as that position taken by those Members who concurred in the judgments on the narrowest grounds.").

289. *E.g.*, Cox v. New Hampshire, 312 U.S. 569 (1941). *Cox* and the constitutional issues surrounding laws requiring permits before staging a march are discussed in Section 11.01[5][c].

290. *E.g.*, Littleton v. Z.J. Gifts, 541 U.S. 774 (2004) (requiring prompt judicial review of any license denial); *see also* Freedman v. Maryland, 380 U.S. 51 (1965) (imposing procedural requirements before the display of allegedly obscene materials could be enjoined).

291. Snepp v. United States, 444 U.S. 507 (1980) (rejecting the imposition of damages for violating an agreement requiring former agents to submit proposed writings about the agency's work to prepublication review by the agency, but imposing a "constructive trust" on proceeds from the book sales).

judge issues a gag order on the press, forbidding coverage of an otherwise highly-publicized trial in order to ensure a fair trial for the defendant.[292] Because this type of prior restraint is closely tied to the press, it is discussed in the section on press freedom.[293]

In *Madsen v. Women's Health Center*,[294] the justices again confronted the difficult question of defining prior restraints. In *Madsen*, the Court declined to apply prior restraint analysis to a broad-ranging injunction issued by a state court against protesters in front of abortion clinics, and instead inquired whether the injunction burdened no more speech than necessary to serve a significant government interest. Using this test, the Court upheld the part of the injunction, including a part that created a protester-free buffer zone around the entrance, and invalidated other parts. Explaining the majority's decision not to apply prior restraint analysis, Chief Justice Rehnquist conceded that "[p]rior restraints do often take the form of injunctions." However, he immediately continued: "Not all injunctions which may incidentally affect expression, however, are 'prior restraints' in the sense that the term was used in *New York Times Co.*" Continuing, he observed that the protestors were not "prevented from expressing their message in any one of several different ways; they are simply prohibited from expressing it within the 36-foot buffer zone." Moreover, the injunction at issue in *Madsen* "was not issued because of the content of petitioners' expression, as was the case in *New York Times Co.*, but because of their prior unlawful conduct."[295]

Dissenting on this point, Justice Scalia, joined by Justices Kennedy and Thomas, insisted that the injunction was a "classic prior restraint":

> an injunction against speech is the very prototype of the greatest threat to First Amendment values, the prior restraint. As the Chief Justice wrote for the Court last Term: "The term prior restraint is used to 'describe administrative and judicial orders *forbidding* certain communications when issued in advance of the time that such communications are to occur.'... [P]ermanent injunctions, *i.e.* — court orders that actually forbid speech activities — are classic examples of prior restraints."[296]

He appended to this text a footnote that read as follows: "This statement should be compared with today's opinion, which says [in the text quoted above], that injunctions are not prior restraints (or at least not the nasty kind) if they only restrain speech in a certain area, or if the basis for their issuance is not content but prior unlawful conduct. This distinction has no antecedent in our cases."[297]

---

292. *E.g.*, Nebraska Press Ass'n v. Stuart, 427 U.S. 539 (1976).

293. *See* Section 11.03[3].

294. 512 U.S. 753 (1994).

295. *Id.* at 763 n.3.

296. *Id.* at 797 (Scalia, J., concurring in the judgment in part and dissenting in part) (emphasis in original) (quoting *Alexander v. United States*, 509 U.S. 544, 550 (1993)).

297. *Ibid.*

In *Tory v. Cochran*,[298] the Court invalidated a permanent injunction as a remedy in a defamation action a well-known litigator brought against a disgruntled client who widely publicized his discontent with the litigator. Based on a finding of a continuous pattern of defamatory activity, the injunction prohibited the defendant "from 'picketing,' from 'displaying signs, placards, or other written or printed material,' and from 'orally uttering statements'" about plaintiff or his law firm "'in any public forum.'"[299] On a 7–2 vote, Justice Breyer held that the plaintiff/litigator's death did not moot the injunction, but that the underlying reason for it was considerably reduced or destroyed. The Court thus held that the injunction was "an overly broad prior restraint upon speech," without "plausible justification."[300] Justice Thomas dissented, joined by Justice Scalia, to argue that the Court should have dismissed the writ of *certiorari*, given the death of the individual who sought the injunction.

[2] Vagueness and Overbreadth

Vagueness and overbreadth are doctrines that play special roles in First Amendment law. Vagueness is a general legal principle that requires laws to be clear enough to allow the average person to understand what is allowed and what is prohibited. Overbreadth is a doctrine that allows a speaker to challenge a law as being overbroad— that is, as punishing speech that cannot constitutionally be subjected to punishment—even if the speaker/plaintiff herself is engaging in speech that government *does* have the authority to punish. In other words, overbreadth doctrine allows a plaintiff lacking a good First Amendment claim herself to sue on behalf of others who might have stronger speech claims, and to reap the benefit of a decision striking down the law as punishing too much speech. Thus, overbreadth doctrine is generally understood as an exception to the general rule limiting standing to sue to plaintiffs asserting their own, rather than a third party's, legal claims.[301]

These doctrines play an important role in First Amendment jurisprudence because one of the Court's great concerns about free speech is that speech not be "chilled"— that is, the concern that would-be speakers will avoid speaking out of fear of punishment. Both vagueness and overbreadth doctrines address this concern. A vague law might leave a would-be speaker guessing about whether her speech is legal; to avoid the risk of punishment, the speaker might decide not to speak and thus not run the risk.[302] Similarly, an overbroad law might chill a would-be speaker who would

---

298. 544 U.S. 734 (2005).

299. *Id.* at 736 (quoting trial court order).

300. *Id.* at 738.

301. Standing doctrine is discussed in Section 2.08[3].

302. *See, e.g.*, Grayned v. City of Rockford, 408 U.S. 104, 109 (1972) ("Uncertain meanings inevitably lead citizens to steer far wider of the unlawful zone than if the boundaries of the forbidden areas were clearly marked.").

have a good First Amendment claim if she was willing to risk speaking, being penalized, and then challenging the penalty as violating the First Amendment. Overbreadth doctrine allows another plaintiff—one whose speech *could be* constitutionally punished—to assert the claims of the chilled speaker and have the overbroad law struck down.

Vagueness is a doctrine that applies generally in constitutional law, as a matter of due process. By contrast, overbreadth is arguably confined to the special circumstances of the First Amendment.[303] Both doctrines are illustrated by *Broadrick v. Oklahoma*.[304] In *Broadrick*, the Court upheld against vagueness and overbreadth challenges a state law prohibiting state government employees from engaging in certain partisan campaign activities. The Oklahoma statute specifically forbade a set of such activities, such as soliciting contributions and "taking part in" a political party's affairs.

Because the Court had already upheld government's ability to enact statutes seeking to depoliticize government workplaces and remove any managerial pressure to engage in partisan work,[305] the government employees limited their challenges to vagueness and overbreadth claims. In rejecting the vagueness challenge, the Court conceded that certain phrases like "take part in" or "partisan" were not entirely clear. The Court recognized, however, that all language lacks perfect clarity. Moreover, it concluded, even if the outermost boundaries of the Act were imprecise, the activities in which appellants engaged fell well within its prohibitions.

As noted earlier, overbreadth doctrine requires that an entire statute be invalidated because of its chilling effect on protected speech. Thus, unlike vagueness, overbreadth will invalidate an entire statute even though the statute could have been validly applied to the plaintiff's conduct. For example, in *Broadrick*, the plaintiffs admitted that their particular conduct could be proscribed by a properly drafted law, but argued that the statute at issue should be struck down because it also restricted protected speech such as wearing campaign buttons or displaying bumper stickers.

Given the broad impact of an overbreadth ruling, the Court in *Broadrick v. Oklahoma* cautioned that overbreadth doctrine was "strong medicine" that had to be "used sparingly."[306] As a threshold requirement, the Court held that it would not hold a statute overbroad if the statute has been or could have been subjected to a limiting construction.[307] Moreover, when conduct rather than pure speech was at issue, the

---

303. Whether overbreadth applies beyond the confines of the First Amendment presents a complex question. *See, e.g.*, Richard Fallon, *Making Sense of Overbreadth*, 100 YALE L.J. 853, 859 n. 29 (1991) (considering this question).

304. 413 U.S. 601 (1973).

305. *See* United Pub. Workers of Am. v. Mitchell, 330 U.S. 75 (1947).

306. 413 U.S. at 613.

307. For example, in *Osborne v. Ohio*, 495 U.S. 103 (1990), the Court rejected an overbreadth challenge to a child pornography conviction. The defendant argued that the statute, which criminalized possession of nude photos of children, was overbroad, given that persons—for example, parents— might have many nude photos of their infants. The Court rejected the challenge, noting that the state

Court also imposed a requirement of "substantial overbreadth"[308] for the statute to be invalidated. While the term "substantial overbreadth" is itself vague, *Broadrick*'s facts indicated that this standard is difficult to meet. The *Broadrick* Court noted that certain activities restricted by the statute may be constitutionally protected (like wearing campaign buttons), but nevertheless refused to hold the statute substantially overbroad.

Two further examples provide a flavor of what overbreadth analysis can look like. In *City of Houston v. Hill*,[309] the Court invalidated a Houston ordinance providing that it "shall be unlawful for any person to assault, strike or in any manner oppose, molest, abuse or interrupt any policeman in the execution of his duty, or any person summoned to aid in making an arrest." The Court struck down the law as substantially overbroad because it "criminalizes a substantial amount of constitutionally protected speech, and accords the police unconstitutional discretion in enforcement."[310]

By contrast, in *Virginia v. Hicks*,[311] a unanimous Court rejected an overbreadth challenge to the trespass policy of the Richmond Redevelopment and Housing Authority (RRHA). RRHA's trespass policy prohibited anyone other than a resident or employee from entering RRHA's property without "a legitimate business or social purpose for being on the premises."[312] To be overbroad, *Hicks* stated that a law must apply to a substantial amount of protected speech "not only in an absolute sense, but also relative to the scope of the law's plainly legitimate applications."[313] The policy at issue extended to all non-residents and non-employees seeking to enter that property for any purpose, expressive or otherwise; thus, its application to would-be First Amendment-protected entrants was not substantial in relation to its application to persons as to whom the policy was unquestionably constitutional.

Vagueness and overbreadth doctrines perform important roles in First Amendment analysis. However, as this sampling of cases illustrates, these doctrines are both imprecise and difficult to apply in a principled manner.[314]

---

supreme court had construed the statute to limit it to "lewd" and "graphic" displays focusing on genitalia, and to possession of photos by persons who were not the parents or guardians of the child.

308. *See Broadrick*, 413 U.S. at 651 n.14.

309. 482 U.S. 451 (1987).

310. *Id.* at 466.

311. 539 U.S. 113 (2003).

312. *Id.* at 115–116.

313. *Id.* at 120.

314. *See, e.g.*, Lewis v. New Orleans, 415 U.S. 130, 136 (1974) (Blackmun, J., dissenting, joined by Chief Justice Burger and Justice Rehnquist) ("Overbreadth and vagueness in the field of speech ... have become result-oriented rubberstamps attuned to the easy and imagined self-assurance that 'one man's vulgarity is another's lyric.' *Cohen v. California*, 403 U.S. 15, 25 (1971). The danger is apparent. Inherent in the use of these doctrines and this standard is a judicial-legislative confrontation. The more frequent our intervention, which of late has been unrestrained, the more we usurp the prerogative of democratic government. Instead of applying constitutional limitations, we do become a 'council of revision.' If the Court adheres to its present course, no state statute or city ordinance will be acceptable unless it parrots the wording of our opinions.").

[3] Compelled Expression

[a] Compelled Speech

Section 11.01 considered the general rules governing when and under what circumstances government can constitutionally restrict speech. Before turning to more context-specific situations, this sub-section considers the opposite of speech restrictions—speech compulsions. One might intuitively understand that, in order to be meaningful, the freedom of speech must include a freedom not to speak. The Court had adopted this idea, although not without confronting some difficult issues along the way.

In 1940, an eight-justice majority upheld a school board's requirement that schoolchildren stand and salute the American flag at the start of every school day, against a challenge that sounded largely in religious freedom. Writing for the Court in *Minersville School District v. Gobitis*,[315] Justice Frankfurter concluded that courts should defer to legislative judgments about the means by which schools should inculcate patriotism in school. He acknowledged that some parents and children might oppose the flag salute, including for religious reasons. (The plaintiffs in *Gobitis* were Jehovah's Witnesses who objected on religious grounds to pledging allegiance to an image, such as a flag.) But he suggested that the political process was open to objectors to argue for an exemption from any such requirement.

Three years later, the Court reversed itself in *West Virginia State Board of Education v. Barnette*.[316] *Barnette* featured very similar facts as those in *Gobitis*, down to the fact that the objectors were again Jehovah's Witnesses. Writing for a six-justice majority that repudiated *Gobitis*, Justice Jackson focused his attention on freedom of speech rather than religion.[317] After recognizing that flags convey ideas and thus are the proper subject of First Amendment claims when conduct toward them is either restricted or compelled, he then suggested that speech compulsions are more problematic than speech restrictions.[318]

One can understand this suggestion as reflecting at least two distinct theories about free speech. First, one might argue that the marketplace of ideas is especially skewed when a person is forced to add content to the marketplace with which she disagrees, rather than simply being required to remain silent. Second, one might understand speech compulsions as especially damaging to a person's ability to self-actualize via speech, since government is essentially commandeering the person's mind by requiring

---

315. 310 U.S. 586 (1940).

316. 319 U.S. 624 (1943).

317. Justice Black, joined by Justice Douglas, wrote a concurrence that placed greater emphasis than the majority on religious freedom. *See id.* at 643 (Black, J., concurring).

318. *See id.* at 633 (majority opinion) ("It is now a commonplace that censorship or suppression of expression of opinion is tolerated by our Constitution only when the expression presents a clear and present danger of action of a kind the State is empowered to prevent and punish. It would seem that involuntary affirmation could be commanded only on even more immediate and urgent grounds than silence.").

her to utter something she doesn't wish to say. While Justice Jackson did not explicitly rely on either of these theories, his opinion is suffused with an anti-totalitarianism that reflects the time when it was written (the middle of the nation's struggle against fascism).

After concluding that speech compulsions were particularly problematic, Justice Jackson then discounted the state's argument that the compelled flag salute was an appropriate means of fostering patriotism. Using the language of the "clear and present danger" test that Justice Holmes had developed two decades before, he found no "clear and present danger" of any significant harm if the state were prevented from compelling schoolchildren to recite the pledge. Indeed, he suggested that encouraging voluntary pledges of allegiance was more likely to inculcate patriotic feelings. Finally, in language that later opinions have often quoted, he suggested what might be an absolute rule against government prescribing what shall be orthodox opinion on public matters.[319] If one looks hard enough, one can find within that statement the origins of the modern stringent rule against viewpoint-based speech restrictions.

The next major compelled speech case did not arise for over thirty years. In *Wooley v. Maynard*,[320] the Court ruled in favor of New Hampshire residents who challenged a state requirement that, as a condition of operating an automobile in the state, they display license plates that featured the state motto, "Live Free or Die." The Court, speaking through Chief Justice Burger, relied heavily on *Barnette*, concluding that the facts in *Wooley* differed from those in *Barnette* only by a matter of "degree." The Court characterized the state's requirement as one that made the Wooleys "a mobile billboard for the State's ideological message."[321]

Despite the Court's analogizing to *Barnette*, *Wooley* raised difficult issues. For example, the Court had to consider the argument, made by Justice Rehnquist's dissent, that the majority analysis seemingly implied that U.S. coinage and currency, with all of its ideological messages (such as "In God We Trust") was unconstitutional. The Court rejected the analogy, concluding that currency was different from license plates, because, for the most part, currency was hidden in pockets and wallets and not displayed publicly. Justice Rehnquist also disputed whether the Wooleys were in fact being compelled to say anything, since, unlike in *Barnette*, the state had not "place[d] the citizen in the position of either apparently or actually 'asserting as true' the message."[322] He queried whether *Wooley* was instead closer to a case where the state had taxed all of its citizens and used the money to erect billboards proclaiming the "Live Free or Die" message—a situation Justice Rehnquist thought plainly did not implicate coerced speech concerns. Finally, he noted that the Wooleys remained free to signal

---

319. *See* 319 U.S. at 642 ("If there is any fixed star in our constitutional constellation, it is that no official, high or petty, can prescribe what shall be orthodox in politics, nationalism, religion, or other matters of opinion or force citizens to confess by word or act their faith therein. If there are any circumstances which permit an exception, they do not now occur to us.").

320. 430 U.S. 705 (1977).

321. *Id.* at 715.

322. *Id.* at 721 (Rehnquist, J., dissenting).

their disagreement with the state's message, for example, by displaying next to the license plate a bumper sticker repudiating the state's message.

Wooley may seem a strange or even idiosyncratic case. But it raises profound conceptual issues. What constitutes a state compulsion to speak? Is it relevant to the First Amendment analysis if a compelled speaker retains ample opportunity to repudiate the message she is being required to communicate? What role is played by listener reactions—if nobody would seriously think that the speaker is communicating a message, can the plaintiff in a compelled speech case really be said to be the victim of a "speech" compulsion?

The Court soon had a chance to consider these matters, from a different angle. The issue in *PruneYard Shopping Center v. Robins*[323] was whether California violated the free speech rights of a shopping center owner when it enacted a law giving the public certain rights to engage in speech activities on the premises of shopping centers. One can immediately see the analogy to *Barnette* and *Wooley*, this time with the shopping center owner claiming that it is being compelled to speak by being forced to host speech it would prefer not to host.

The Court rejected the compelled speech claim. The Court distinguished *Wooley* as follows:

> Most important, the shopping center by choice of its owner is not limited to the personal use of [the owner]. It is instead a business establishment that is open to the public to come and go as they please. The views expressed by members of the public in passing out pamphlets or seeking signatures for a petition thus will not likely be identified with those of the owner. Second, no specific message is dictated by the State to be displayed on appellants' property. There consequently is no danger of governmental discrimination for or against a particular message. Finally, as far as appears here [the owner] can expressly disavow any connection with the message by simply posting signs in the area where the speakers or handbillers stand. Such signs, for example, could disclaim any sponsorship of the message and could explain that the persons are communicating their own messages by virtue of state law.[324]

In the next paragraph, the Court distinguished *Barnette* on the following grounds:

> *Barnette* is inapposite because it involved the compelled recitation of a message containing an affirmation of belief. This Court held such compulsion unconstitutional because it required the individual to communicate by word and sign his acceptance of government-dictated political ideas, whether or not he subscribed to them. Appellants are not similarly being compelled to affirm their belief in any governmentally prescribed position or view, and they are free to publicly dissociate themselves from the views of the speakers or handbillers.[325]

---

323. 447 U.S. 74 (1980).
324. *Id.* at 87.
325. *Id.* at 88.

Consider the arguments in the first excerpt. The first one essentially states that, given the context, nobody would associate the visitors' speech with the shopping center owner. Could one say the same thing about the "Live Free or Die" motto on New Hampshire license plates? The third one relies on the ability of the shopping center owner to disavow any of the visitors' statements by placing his own placard near their table. This option of course was open to the Wooleys as well. Thus, the Court's distinguishing of *Wooley* boils down to the fact that the compelled message in *Wooley* was the state's own preferred message. It is an interesting question whether that fact serves to really make *Wooley* different, since in both cases, from the compelled speaker's point of view, he is being compelled to say something he would rather not say. The arguments in the second excerpted paragraph largely track those in the first.

Given this treatment of *Barnette* and *Wooley*, after these foundational cases, the scope of the prohibition on compelled speech remained unclear. The lack of clarity has continued into the modern day. Thus, in *Rumsfeld v. Forum for Academic and Institutional Rights*,[326] the Court rejected a compelled speech attack on a federal law that withdrew federal funding from universities that did not provide equal access for military recruiters as for non-military recruiters. The plaintiff universities argued that the law compelled them to speak because, for example, if they posted announcements that a private employer was coming to interview on campus, they would have to post a similar announcement about a military recruiter.

The Court rejected the First Amendment claim.[327] Writing for a unanimous eight-justice Court, Chief Justice Roberts downplayed the significance of the speech the law compelled (for example, speech providing the time and room information for the military recruiter's interviews). He also noted that any such speech was compelled only if the university chose to make such speech on behalf of other employers. Thus, the case did not pose a situation where the government required schools to communicate a government-selected pledge or motto. Finally, the Chief Justice cited the Court's cases holding that incidental burdens on speech that arise from a valid regulation of conduct do not violate the First Amendment. On these grounds, he concluded that "compelling a law school that sends scheduling e-mails for other recruiters to send one for a military recruiter is simply not the same as forcing a student to pledge allegiance, or forcing a Jehovah's Witness to display the motto 'Live Free or Die,' and it trivializes the freedom protected in *Barnette* and *Wooley* to suggest that it is."[328]

More recently, the Court has at least suggested that speech compulsions, like speech restrictions, should be evaluated according to the content-neutrality rule — that is, the rule that content-based speech restrictions usually trigger strict scrutiny.[329] In *Na-*

---

326. 547 U.S. 47 (2006).
327. While the law was cast as a funding condition rather than a legal requirement, the Court concluded that, since the law would be constitutional as a legal requirement, it would necessarily be constitutional as a mere funding condition.
328. *Id.* at 62.
329. For a fuller discussion of this rule, see Section 11.01[3].

tional Institute for Family and Life Advocates ("NIFLA") v. Becerra,[330] the Court struck down a California law that required so-called crisis pregnancy centers to post certain notices for their customers. These centers, which were operated by persons who opposed abortion and offered non-abortion pregnancy services, were required to post signs indicating that the State of California offered free and low-cost family-planning services, including abortions, and providing a telephone number. In addition, these centers, to the extent they were unlicensed by the state, were required to post a notice disclosing their unlicensed status.

The Court struck down both provisions. Most importantly for our purpose, it identified the speech compulsions as content-based, and seemed to include speech compulsions within the class of laws that are subject to the content-neutrality rule. However, it found it unnecessary to the case to apply the strict scrutiny that would normally follow from application of that rule.[331] But even the Court's suggestion that the content-neutrality rule might apply to speech compulsions drew criticism in Justice Breyer's dissent for four justices. Justice Breyer argued that full importation of the content-neutrality rule into the realm of speech compulsions threw into doubt many government regulations of the marketplace, which often take the form of requirements that persons in the marketplace—and in society more generally—disclose certain facts as a part of their operations.[332]

It is unclear whether the Court will make good on its suggestion in *NIFLA* that, as a general matter, speech compulsions that require disclosure of certain information will be subject to the content-neutrality rule. Recall that in *NIFLA* itself, the Court did not apply such scrutiny, finding it to be unnecessary to decide the case. If the Court does take that path, however, then it will encounter difficult questions when plaintiffs challenge seemingly everyday speech compulsions that do not require the kind of affirmation of personal belief at issue in *Barnette* or *Wooley*.

---

330. 138 S. Ct. 2361 (2018).

331. The Court in *NIFLA* ended up applying intermediate scrutiny to the California provisions, on the assumption, which the Court did not endorse but merely assumed for purposes of deciding the case, that a particular category of speech restrictions applicable to the speech of professionals (such as lawyers and doctors) might justify such a lower level of scrutiny. But the Court concluded that the California law failed such lower tier scrutiny. *See id.* at 2375, 2377 (addressing the scrutiny standard applicable to each provision of the California law). The scope of government authority to regulate professional speech is discussed in Section 11.01[2][e][ii].

332. *See id.* at 2380 (Breyer, J., dissenting) ("Because much, perhaps most, human behavior takes place through speech and because much, perhaps most, law regulates that speech in terms of its content, the majority's approach at least threatens considerable litigation over the constitutional validity of much, perhaps most, government regulation. Virtually every disclosure law could be considered 'content based,' for virtually every disclosure law requires individuals 'to speak a particular message.' See *Reed v. Town of Gilbert*, 135 S. Ct. 2218, 2234–2235 (2015) (Breyer, J., concurring in judgment) (listing regulations that inevitably involve content discrimination, ranging from securities disclosures to signs at petting zoos). Thus, the majority's view, if taken literally, could radically change prior law, perhaps placing much securities law or consumer protection law at constitutional risk, depending on how broadly its exceptions are interpreted.").

[b] Compelled Subsidization of Speech

Similar issues arise when the government compels, not speech itself, but subsidization by one person of another person's speech. A prominent example of such compelled subsidization has been the requirement under many state laws that public sector workplaces be "closed union shops." That term refers to the requirement that a worker in a unionized workplace pay "agency fees" to defray the union's expenses, even if the particular worker chooses not to join the union.

In 1977, in *Abood v. Detroit Board of Education*,[333] the Court upheld a limited variant on the closed shop idea against a worker's claim that the forced payment of such fees to the union compelled him to subsidize speech with which he disagreed. The Court, speaking through Justice Stewart, conceded that such forced subsidization impacted dissenting employees' speech rights. However, it also concluded that the government had important interests in ensuring labor peace (by requiring that only one union represent all the workers in a given workplace) and preventing "free rider" problems in which employees obtained the benefits of union representation (such as pay negotiations and grievance resolution) without having to pay the expenses of such representation.

However, the Court expressed greater concern about dissenters' forced subsidization of union activities that went beyond the union's collective bargaining functions — for example, unions' practices of engaging in electoral politics by endorsing particular candidates and working for their election. The Court concluded that the First Amendment prohibited the forced collection of fees from union non-members for the purpose of subsidizing the union's speech in "the support of an ideological cause"[334] the non-member might oppose.

Thus, *Abood* drew a constitutional line between forcing a union non-member to subsidize the union's collective bargaining activities (which the Court allowed) and forcing the non-member to subsidize the union's ideological or political speech (which the Court prohibited). The Court conceded that this distinction might create difficult line-drawing problems in the context of the public-sector unions that were the subject of *Abood*. These problems arise because when public-sector unions make demands on their employers (*e.g.*, wage demands), those demands impact state treasuries and the provision of state government services, and thus implicate state government policies. Nevertheless, under *Abood*, such union speech could be supported by compelled subsidization from non-members. In later cases, the Court attempted to delineate the line between collective bargaining expenses and political expenses.[335]

In 2018, the Court abandoned the attempt to distinguish between these types of expenses and ruled instead that *any* forced subsidization of a union by a non-member violated the non-member's First Amendment rights. In thus overruling *Abood*, the

---

333. 431 U.S. 209 (1977).

334. *Id.* at 235.

335. *See, e.g.*, Locke v. Karass, 555 U.S. 207 (2009); Lehnert v. Ferris Faculty Ass'n, 500 U.S. 507 (1991).

Court in *Janus v. American Federation of State, County, and Municipal Employees, Council 31*[336] found insufficient the government's interests in labor peace and in avoiding employee free-riding that the Court had found sufficient in *Abood*. With regard to the first, the Court found that experience since *Abood* in jurisdictions that did not impose agency fees had shown that labor peace did not require the imposition of such fees. With regard to the free-rider argument, the Court concluded that there was nothing unfair or unworkable about unions being required to represent the interests of all workers in the bargaining unit, including those that chose not to join the union. Four justices dissented, arguing that *Abood* had crafted a workable compromise that served important purposes underlying federal labor policy.

Before *Abood* was overruled, the Court had extended its compelled subsidization jurisprudence to other contexts. In *Keller v. State Bar of California*, the Court held that mandatory state bar fees were constitutional only to the extent they defrayed costs the state bar association "reasonably incurred for the purpose of regulating the legal profession or improving the quality of the legal services available to the people of the State."[337] However, the Constitution prohibited the imposition of mandatory fees designed to defray the cost of the bar association's ideological expression.

Another area where the Court has actively reviewed compelled subsidization requirements is federal agricultural marketing programs. Today, agriculture is a heavily-regulated business. As one aspect of that regulation, government often collects money from growers of a given crop and uses the proceeds to fund generic advertising for that food, in order to stimulate demand. Thus, for example, the government may collect fees from apple growers and use the proceeds to fund advertising urging Americans to eat more applies.

Such programs amount to the type of compelled subsidization the Court examined in *Abood*. In 1997, in *Glickman v. Wileman Brothers and Elliott*,[338] the Court rejected a First Amendment compelled subsidization claim growing out of one such program, aimed at California tree fruits (plums, peaches, and nectarines). Writing for a five-justice majority, Justice Stevens explained that the forced subsidization of that advertising was only one part of a broad regulation of that industry. Because that broader regulation is presumed constitutional,[339] the Court declined to review the compelled subsidization program under a heightened standard. Turning to that program, the Court distinguished earlier compelled speech cases:

> Our compelled speech case law ... is clearly inapplicable to the regulatory scheme at issue here. The use of assessments to pay for advertising does not require respondents to repeat an objectionable message out of their own mouths, *cf. West Virginia Bd. of Ed. v. Barnette*, 319 U.S. 624 (1943), require

---

336. 138 S. Ct. 2448 (2018).
337. 496 U.S. 1, 14 (1990).
338. 521 U.S. 457 (1997).
339. The presumption of constitutionality accorded government regulation of business activity is discussed in Section 9.02[1].

them to use their own property to convey an antagonistic ideological message, *cf. Wooley v. Maynard*, 430 U.S. 705 (1977), force them to respond to a hostile message when they would prefer to remain silent, or require them to be publicly identified or associated with another's message, *cf. PruneYard Shopping Center v. Robins*, 447 U.S. 74 (1980). Respondents are not required themselves to speak, but are merely required to make contributions for advertising. With trivial exceptions on which the [lower] court did not rely, none of the generic advertising conveys any message with which [the grower-plaintiffs] disagree. Furthermore, the advertising is attributed not to them, but to the California Tree Fruit Agreement or "California Summer Fruits."[340]

Four years later, in *United States v. United Foods*,[341] the Court distinguished *Glickman* and struck down a forced subsidization program targeting mushroom growers. Like the program in *Glickman*, the forced subsidization in *United Foods* was designed to obtain funds for an advertising program, this time urging consumption of mushrooms. But a six-justice majority, speaking through Justice Kennedy, distinguished *Glickman* on the ground that that earlier case involved forced subsidization of advertising speech as merely one component of a broader regulatory program. By contrast, the compelled subsidization in *United Foods* was a stand-alone advertising program.

A final compelled agricultural subsidy case, *Johanns v. Livestock Marketing Association*,[342] introduced a new twist into the compelled subsidy/compelled speech issue. The program in *Johanns*, dealing with compelled cattle rancher subsidization of beef advertising, was held to be a case of government itself speaking, rather than forcing private parties to speak. The Court based this decision largely on its conclusion that, even though it received the funds for the advertising from the ranchers, the government itself controlled the message of the advertising. The Court recognized the possibility that the advertising, which was credited to "America's Beef Producers," might be mistakenly attributed to the ranchers themselves. However, the Court did not reach that argument, given the lack of evidence on that point in the record. The First Amendment rules applicable to government speech are discussed later in this section.[343]

Whether *Glickman* and *Keller* remain good law in light of *Janus* is an interesting question. The Court in *Janus* overruled *Abood* largely because of its disagreement with *Abood*'s crediting of the government interests in closed union shops — disagreement that seemed specific to the particular context of unionized workplaces. But *Janus* also seemed, at least implicitly, to reflect a general skepticism about such compelled subsidization of speech, regardless of the context. Whether that skepticism seeps into the Court's treatment of compelled subsidization of agricultural marketing, state professional association, or other situations remains to be seen.[344]

---

340. 521 U.S. at 470–71.
341. 533 U.S. 405 (2001).
342. 544 U.S. 550 (2005).
343. *See* Section 11.02[6][b].
344. The Court confronted a slightly different variant of the compelled subsidization question in *Board of Regents v. Southworth*, 529 U.S. 217 (2000). *Southworth* involved a university's imposition

[4] Freedom of Association

In addition to protecting the freedom to speak, the Court also protects the freedom to associate — that is, the freedom to gather for expressive purposes.[345] In a foundational case, *NAACP v. Alabama*,[346] the Court recognized that infringements on the right of persons to associate for speech purposes triggered First Amendment scrutiny. In *NAACP*, the State of Alabama required the NAACP, a major civil rights organization, to disclose to the state the names and addresses of its Alabama members and agents. Coming as it did during a tense period in the civil rights movement, the Alabama law would have likely exposed members to the risk of harassment and violence, with the result that many members might well have rethought their decision to remain part of the organization. Recognizing that risk, and recognizing as well the importance of the right to associate to the exercise of both the First Amendment rights to speech and assembly,[347] the Court subjected the Alabama law to careful scrutiny, requiring that the state's interests be "compelling."[348] While it ultimately did not decide the importance of the interests Alabama asserted, the Court concluded that the compelled disclosure of its membership lists lacked "a substantial bearing" on either of them.[349]

The Court's suggestion in *NAACP* that infringements on associational rights triggered heightened scrutiny was made explicit in 1984, in *Roberts v. United States Jaycees*.[350] *Roberts* considered a Minnesota anti-discrimination law that was applied to the Jaycees, an organization that limited full membership to men. (Women were allowed partial membership.) The Jaycees argued that compelled admission of women as full members would impair the rights of its members to associate for speech purposes by forcing them to include as members persons they wished to exclude.

---

on students of a mandatory student activity fee, which was used to fund the speech of student groups. The Court recognized that the forced subsidization scheme implicated the free speech rights of dissenting students, but it concluded that the point of the fee system — to fund a wide diversity of student speech — made it impossible simply to impose the *Abood/Keller* distinction between subsidizing speech germane to the organization's purposes and, on the other hand, subsidizing the organization's ideological speech. Instead, the Court concluded that the key question was whether the speech the student activity fee subsidized was selected on a viewpoint-neutral basis. Because it was, the Court concluded that the dissenting students' First Amendment rights were not violated.

345. The Court also protects the freedom of intimate association, such as familial associations. This aspect of the freedom to associate is discussed in Section 9.04[4].

346. 357 U.S. 449 (1958).

347. *See id.* at 460 ("Effective advocacy of both public and private points of view, particularly controversial ones, is undeniably enhanced by group association, as this Court has more than once recognized by remarking upon the close nexus between the freedoms of speech and assembly. It is beyond debate that freedom to engage in association for the advancement of beliefs and ideas is an inseparable aspect of the 'liberty' assured by the Due Process Clause of the Fourteenth Amendment, which embraces freedom of speech.").

348. *Id.* at 463.

349. The state asserted that it sought the membership lists "to determine whether petitioner was conducting intrastate business in violation of the Alabama foreign corporation registration statute," *id.* at 464, and whether any such activity justified the ouster of the organization from the state.

350. 468 U.S. 609 (1984).

The Court recognized the seriousness of impositions on the right to associate. Justice Brennan, writing the Court, wrote: "Infringements on that right may be justified by regulations adopted to serve compelling state interests, unrelated to the suppression of ideas, that cannot be achieved through means significantly less restrictive of associational freedoms."[351] However, the Court concluded that the alleged impairment of the Jaycees members' associational rights was more apparent than real. The Jaycees had claimed that its ability to take positions on public issues was impaired by the forced inclusion of women, but the Court found no evidence in the record that such forced inclusion would create that risk. The Court's conclusion is not surprising when one realizes that, by the 1980s, the Court's equal protection jurisprudence was well on the way to presumptively rejecting sex classifications based on supposed differences in how men and women act or feel with regard to public issues.[352] Thus, while recognizing the importance of the right to free association for speech purposes, the Court concluded that that right was not impaired in this case.

Justice O'Connor agreed with the result but disagreed with the majority's approach. She expressed concern that the majority's approach to the question required courts to inquire into and make assumptions about the speech the impacted organization wished to make, an inquiry she found inappropriate. Instead, she would have inquired simply into whether the association in question was formed primarily for expressive purposes or for other purposes. Applying that analysis to the Jaycees, an organization founded to promote knowledge of business practices, she concluded that it was primarily a commercial organization rather than one devoted to speech. As such, she concluded that it could not assert a First Amendment associational right to exclude unwanted members.

Both Justice Brennan's and Justice O'Connor's approaches can be critiqued. As Justice O'Connor objected, Justice Brennan's approach required courts to inquire into the kind of speech the association wanted to make and to speculate about how that speech might be altered if a state or federal anti-discrimination law required it to include unwanted members. Indeed, as exemplified in *Jaycees* itself, that approach required courts to second-guess the extent to which forced inclusion of an unwanted person as a member would impair the association's speech.[353] On the other hand, Justice O'Connor conceded that her own approach might be difficult to apply in certain situations, as it might be difficult to characterize some organizations as primarily

---

351. *Id.* at 623.

352. *See id.* at 628 (citing equal protection cases reflecting the rejection of this idea). The Court's sex equality jurisprudence is discussed in Section 10.02.

353. As an example of this second-guessing, see *Board of Directors of Rotary Int'l v. Rotary Club of Duarte*, 481 U.S. 537 (1987). In that case, the Court rejected the Rotary Club's expressive association-based argument for its right to exclude women, concluding that the organization's own purposes would likely be furthered if it were forced to include women. *See id.* at 548–49 ("by opening membership to leading business and professional women in the community, Rotary Clubs are likely to obtain a more representative cross section of community leaders with a broadened capacity for service").

expressive or commercial. Moreover, her analysis implied that a commercial organization lacked any First Amendment associational right to exclude, even when forced inclusion of a member impacted its speech.

The Court limited the permissible reach of state anti-discrimination laws in *Hurley v. Irish-American Gay, Lesbian and Bisexual Group of Boston*.[354] *Hurley* considered a challenge made by an LGB group in Boston to their exclusion from the annual St. Patrick's Day parade in Boston. The group claimed that the parade was a public accommodation and thus was subject to the Massachusetts law banning sexual orientation discrimination in public accommodations. The Court, in a unanimous opinion, held that the parade organizers had a First Amendment right to exclude the group. Writing for the Court, Justice Souter explained that the case presented an unusual situation in which the claimed public accommodation (the parade) was itself an expressive event. Since every inclusion or exclusion decision made by the parade organizers affected the parade's expression, forced inclusion of the unwanted group would necessarily impair the parade organizers' expression in violation of the First Amendment. This was true even if the parade organizers' inclusion and exclusion choices did not necessarily express a coherent message.[355]

Hurley thus deferred to the exclusion choices made by the association, in the context of a lawsuit that sought forced inclusion into an event (a parade) that the Court deemed inherently expressive. Several years later, a sharply-divided Court expanded on this deference in *Boy Scouts of America v. Dale*.[356] *Dale* considered a Scouting organization's exclusion of a gay man from a scoutmaster position, on the basis of the man's sexual orientation. The excluded person sued under New Jersey's public accommodations law, which, like Massachusetts', banned discrimination in public accommodations on the basis of sexual orientation. The Boy Scouts defended by arguing that they had a First Amendment right to discriminate against Dale, because being forced to include him would contradict the Scouts' teaching about sexual morality.

The Court sided with the Boy Scouts. Writing for a five-justice majority, Chief Justice Rehnquist insisted that courts should defer to organizations' own assertions about both what its expression consists of and what type of forced membership inclusions would impair that expression. Thus, the Court rejected the lower court's examination of the Scouts' policies and its conclusion that exclusion of Dale would be inconsistent with the Scouts' stated desire for a "diverse" and "representative" mem-

---

354. 515 U.S. 557 (1995).

355. *See id.* at 574 ("Rather like a composer, the [parade organizing] Council selects the expressive units of the parade from potential participants, and though the score may not produce a particularized message, each contingent's expression in the Council's eyes comports with what merits celebration on that day. Even if this view gives the Council credit for a more considered judgment than it actively made, the Council clearly decided to exclude a message it did not like from the communication it chose to make, and that is enough to invoke its right as a private speaker to shape its expression by speaking on one subject while remaining silent on another.").

356. 530 U.S. 640 (2000).

bership, as well the lower court's conclusion that the Scouts' own statements about sexuality suggested that the organization took no view on that issue.[357]

Dissenting for four justices, Justice Stevens argued that the majority's deference to the Scouts' own description of their expression and what would impair it gave discriminating organizations "a free pass out of antidiscrimination laws."[358] Analyzing the Scouts' own historical statements about sexuality, Justice Stevens agreed with the lower court that the Scouts had not taken a position on sexual morality issues and thus that forced inclusion of an openly gay man as a scoutmaster would not impair the Scouts' expression.

The justices' disagreement in *Dale* about the proper approach to First Amendment challenges to application of anti-discrimination laws reflects the underlying tensions in the doctrine, as expressed in *Roberts v. Jaycees*. As Justice Stevens notes in *Dale*, the majority's deference to the organization's own claims about its expression does seem to at least put a thumb on the scale of organizations' free association claims, to the detriment of the application of anti-discrimination law. On the other hand, his approach seems to require second-guessing the organization's own expression and what might affect it. There is no easy to answer to this conundrum, unless the Court is going to import its own equal protection jurisprudence into this area and prioritize applications of anti-discrimination statutes only when those applications attack the types of discrimination the Court itself has recognized as suspect or quasi-suspect.[359]

[5] Campaign Finance

The First Amendment protection appropriately accorded campaign finance activities has been the subject of sharp disagreement at the Court. This sub-section begins by setting forth the foundational principles governing this area of First Amendment law, as those principles were set forth in the 1976 case *Buckley v. Valeo*.[360] It then considers a number of controversies that have either continued after *Buckley* or arisen in its wake.

[a] Buckley v. Valeo

In *Buckley*, the Supreme Court decided the constitutionality of certain provisions of the Federal Election Campaign Act of 1971, as amended in 1974 in the wake of

---

357. *Id.* at 651.

358. *Id.* at 688 (Stevens, J., dissenting).

359. *See, e.g., Roberts*, 468 U.S. at 625 ("By prohibiting gender discrimination in places of public accommodation, the Minnesota [public accommodations] Act protects the State's citizenry from a number of serious social and personal harms. In the context of reviewing state actions under the Equal Protection Clause, this Court has frequently noted that discrimination based on archaic and overbroad assumptions about the relative needs and capacities of the sexes forces individuals to labor under stereotypical notions that often bear no relationship to their actual abilities. It thereby both deprives persons of their individual dignity and denies society the benefits of wide participation in political, economic, and cultural life.").

360. 424 U.S. 1 (1976).

the Watergate scandal. The law imposed a wide-ranging set of limits on campaign finance activities, including limitations on campaign contributions, independent expenditures advocating the election or defeat of a candidate, and self-financing of a candidate's campaign, as well as imposing reporting and disclosure requirements for campaign contributions and expenditures. The Court upheld some of these provisions and struck down others.

The *per curiam* opinion treated speaking and spending money to advance an idea as similar for constitutional purposes. Because the Act limited the quantity and diversity of political speech, it implicated political expression and association. In determining the applicable standard of review, the Court rejected the argument that the Act's contribution and expenditure limitations could be analogized to the limitations on conduct allowed in *United States v. O'Brien.* The Court rejected the analogy in large part because it concluded that the Act's restrictions on expression flowed from the perceived harms of that expression, rather than, as in *O'Brien,* from some non-expressive element of the conduct. On this theory, while *O'Brien* concluded that the government prosecuted draft-card burning because of the harm that flowed from destroying draft cards, rather than because of the anti-war expression such conduct communicated, the law in *Buckley* restricted campaign finance activities *because of* those activities' communicative element. The Court also rejected the characterization of the contribution and expenditure limitations as time, place, and manner restrictions, because they "impose[d] direct quantity restrictions on political communication and association by persons, groups, candidates, and political parties in addition to any reasonable time, place, and manner regulations otherwise imposed."[361]

Nevertheless, the Court drew a sharp distinction, for First Amendment purposes, between limits on campaign contributions and limits on independent expenditures in support of a candidate. The Court concluded that expenditure limitations imposed substantial restraints on the quantity and diversity of political speech. By contrast, it concluded that a campaign contribution constituted only a symbolic expression of support for a candidate and her views. Accordingly, limitations on contributions short of a flat prohibition still allowed the contributor both to express her support for the candidate and associate herself with the campaign. Moreover, as long as they were not set too low, the Court found no indication that contribution limitations would adversely affect candidates' ability to fund their own speech.

This did not mean that *Buckley* gave a free pass to limits on campaign contributions. Rather, the *per curiam* opinion stated it would uphold such limits only where the state demonstrates "a sufficiently important interest and employs means closely drawn to avoid unnecessary abridgment of associational freedoms."[362] The Court found that the law's contribution limitations did advance Congress's primary purpose of elim-

---

361. *Id.* at 18. The approach of *United States v. O'Brien,* 391 U.S. 367 (1968), to the regulation of expressive conduct and time, place, and manner restrictions on speech are both discussed in Section 11.01[4].

362. 424 U.S. at 25.

inating corruption or the appearance of corruption in the political process. Further, the contribution limitations focused narrowly on promoting those goals while allowing persons to speak, volunteer services, and even make limited contributions, all of which satisfied supporters' First Amendment interests. In response to the argument that bribery laws were a more direct method of combatting corruption, the Court concluded that the Constitution did not limit congressional regulation only to instances of actual corruption. As explained later in this sub-section, this understanding of contribution limits as a "prophylactic" measure going beyond punishment of actual corruption has come under strain in recent years.

The Court was much less tolerant of the Act's limitations on independent expenditures advocating the election or defeat of a clearly identified candidate. It concluded that those limits did not avoid political corruption, as they concerned expenditures made independent of the candidate and his campaign.[363] It also rejected the government interest in equalizing citizens' voices in the electoral process as "wholly foreign to the First Amendment."[364] For these reasons, the expenditure limits failed to "satisfy the exacting scrutiny applicable to limitations on core First Amendment rights of political expression."[365]

The Court also invalidated the law's limitations on expenditures from a candidate's personal resources, as they infringed the candidate's right to speak on behalf of her own candidacy. The government could not justify these limits on the ground of preventing actual or apparent corruption, given the lack of potential corruption flowing from a candidate's decision to self-finance. The Court also discounted the government's interest in equalizing the financial resources of candidates, maintaining that candidates could also outspend their rivals by being better fund-raisers. For reasons similar to those used to strike down limits on personal campaign expenditures, the Court also struck down the limitations on overall campaign expenditures.

The Court next examined the disclosure provisions, which required campaigns to keep records for the Federal Election Commission (FEC) of the names and addresses of each person making a contribution above $10. The provisions also mandated disclosure of non-candidate campaign expenditures exceeding $100. Because compelled disclosure infringed on privacy and associational interests, it required "exacting scrutiny."[366] Nevertheless, the Court upheld the compelled disclosure provisions as generally being "the least restrictive means" of curbing "campaign ignorance and corruption."[367] First, the disclosure provisions would inform voters about the sources of campaign funds, which would alert voters to the influences on the candidate. Second,

---

363. Under the Act, independent expenditures that were coordinated with the campaign were considered contributions and thus subject to the contribution limits the Court upheld.

364. *Id.* at 49.

365. *Id.* at 44–45.

366. *Id.* at 64. In requiring this level of scrutiny, the Court cited a compelled membership disclosure case, *NAACP v. Alabama*, 357 U.S. 449 (1958). *NAACP*, and the Court's jurisprudence reviewing laws that implicate the right to associate more generally, are both discussed in Section 11.02[4].

367. 424 U.S. at 68.

the requirements would deter corruption by exposing large contributions and expenditures. Third, the information would help the FEC to enforce the law.

The Court recognized that the law's disclosure provisions could adversely affect minority parties espousing unpopular views. Consequently, the Court stated that minority parties could obtain an exemption from those provisions if they showed a probability that compelled disclosure would subject contributors to "threats, harassment, or reprisals from Government officials or private parties."[368] The Court indicated that proof could include specific examples of past harassment against the party or its members. New parties could prove a similar pattern of threats or specific manifestations of hostility against established minority parties with similar views.[369]

Finally, the Court addressed Subtitle H of the Act, which limited the total expenditures for a presidential campaign to $20 million when the candidate accepted public funding. The provision also stated that a candidate from a new or minor party would only get federal funding if her party received more than five percent of the vote in the preceding election. Major party candidates also received some funding for their primary campaigns. The Court upheld Subtitle H, because it furthered the electoral process by facilitating and enlarging discussion, and because it offered candidates a choice to accept public money and abide by its limitations or forego it and remain free of those limits.

A number of justices wrote partial concurring and dissenting opinions to register their disagreement with different aspects of the *per curiam* opinion. In his opinion, Chief Justice Burger expressed concern that the Court's piecemeal analysis of the Act frustrated Congress's intent and rendered the law unworkable. He also criticized the disclosure provisions for chilling political participation, using the example of lower-level employees in a workplace, for whom the prospect of disclosure might dissuade them from contributing to minority parties disfavored by their supervisors. In addition, he criticized as artificial the Court's distinction between campaign contributions and independent expenditures, arguing that limitations on both such activities were unconstitutional. Justice Blackmun, in his own separate opinion, expressed similar doubt about that distinction.

In his opinion, Justice White argued that spending money was not the same as speaking. He added that nothing in the record before the Court indicated that the expenditure or contribution limitations at issue would cripple campaigns. Justice Marshall argued that the Court's decision would diminish confidence in the political system, because the wealthy would be perceived as having a distinct advantage in the electoral process. Thus, he would have upheld the provision limiting a candidate's ability to self-finance. Finally, Justice Rehnquist argued that the public funding provisions indefinitely enshrined the Democratic and Republican parties in a preferred position. He thus dissented from the part of the opinion upholding those provisions.

---

368. *Id.* at 74.

369. In *Brown v. Socialist Workers '74 Campaign Comm.*, 459 U.S. 87 (1982), the Court applied this analysis to invalidate an Ohio law requiring disclosure of campaign contributions and expenditures, as applied to the Socialist Workers Party.

Buckley established several foundational First Amendment principles related to campaign finance. But by far the most consequential was its distinction, for First Amendment purposes, between campaign contributions and campaign expenditures. That distinction has remained a faultline for disagreements about the constitutionality of subsequent campaign finance laws.

[b] Corporate and Union Campaign Speech

One issue *Buckley* did not address in detail was the special status, if any, of corporate and union campaign speech. An important set of cases after *Buckley* involved political expenditures by corporations and unions. These cases culminated in 2010 with the Court's decision in *Citizens United v. Federal Election Commission*,[370] discussed later in this sub-section, which gave corporations and unions an unfettered right to engage in political expenditures.

This line of cases began in 1978, with *First National Bank v. Bellotti*.[371] In *Bellotti*, the Court held that a state could not prohibit corporations from spending money to express their views on pending citizen referenda. *Bellotti* involved a Massachusetts law restricting corporations' expenditures on referendum campaigns to referenda relating to their particular business interests. The law had the effect of prohibiting several Massachusetts companies from publicizing their views on a pending referendum proposing a personal income tax. Writing for the majority, Justice Powell stated that corporations enjoyed free speech rights, although he did not address whether they enjoyed the same speech rights as natural persons.

Massachusetts claimed that the statute protected citizens' participation and confidence in the integrity of the referendum process. The Court responded that there was no showing that corporate political speech had "been overwhelming or even significant in influencing referenda in Massachusetts, or that there has been any threat to the confidence of the citizenry in the government."[372] The Court conceded that these arguments would merit consideration had there been such a showing. But it was careful to note that it was confining its analysis to referendum campaigns; in a footnote, it cautioned that different considerations of political corruption might apply in cases involving campaigns for elective office.[373]

The Court also rejected the state's argument that the statute protected the interests of corporate shareholders who might disagree with the corporation's expressed views and who might not want their money used for that speech. It pointed out that, as a response to that concern, the statute was underinclusive, because it did not cover other corporate activities, such as lobbying, which might also offend minority shareholders. It was also underinclusive in its failure to mention such groups as labor unions, trusts, and other associations which might also have minorities with differing

---

370. 558 U.S. 310 (2010).
371. 435 U.S. 765 (1978).
372. *Id.* at 789–90.
373. *See id.* at 787 n. 26.

views. The Court also argued that the law was overinclusive, because it prohibited corporate speech even when that speech enjoyed unanimous shareholder support. The Court concluded that shareholders were better protected by standard corporate law procedures such as shareholder control over the actions of the corporation's managers—what Justice Powell referred to as "corporate democracy."[374]

Dissenting, Justice White conceded that corporate speech was protected by the First Amendment. However, he argued that corporate speech was not entitled to full First Amendment protection, because it did not further self-actualization, one of the primary justifications for protecting free speech. For Justice White, the state's interest in preventing the economic skewing of the political process was sufficiently important to restrict a corporation's expression when the speech was unrelated to its business. (Recall that the Massachusetts law allowed corporations to speak on referenda that affected their business interests.) Justice White also emphasized that incorporation in a state was a privilege which gave a corporation power to amass great wealth. This privilege, Justice White argued, should not aid a corporation in dominating the political affairs of the state. He also noted that, just the year before, the Court had recognized dissenting union non-members' constitutional rights to not subsidize the political speech of the union that represented their workplace.[375] While recognizing that that situation involved state action different than that in *Bellotti*, Justice White wondered why Massachusetts could not accommodate that analogous interest by restricting corporations' political speech. Justice Rehnquist also dissented, to question whether corporations, which were creations of state law to begin with, had free speech rights.

In *Federal Election Commission v. Massachusetts Citizens for Life, Inc.* ("*MCFL*"),[376] the Court struck down limitations on expenditures by a nonprofit corporation, as applied to an anti-abortion group (MCFL) that published a newsletter disseminating the voting records of particular candidates. The Court found that, since its goal was not to amass capital, the nonprofit corporation created for ideological purposes did not present the same threat of corruption as a typical for-profit corporation that could amass large amounts of money that did not correspond to the public support for its views. The Court, speaking through Justice Brennan, wrote a narrow decision holding the law unconstitutional as applied to MCFL. It relied first on the fact that MCFL was a nonprofit corporation formed to disseminate ideas rather than earn profits. Second, it noted that MCFL had no shareholders who might disagree with its ideas—that is, the shareholder protection rationale for limiting corporate speech offered in *Bellotti* did not apply, since people joined MCFL exactly in order to associate for speech purposes. Third, MCFL was not a conduit established by a labor union or a for-profit corporation to circumvent restrictions on electioneering.

---

374. *Id.* at 794.
375. Justice White was referring to *Abood v. Detroit Bd of Education*, 431 U.S. 209 (1977). *Abood* is discussed in Section 11.02[3][b].
376. 479 U.S. 238 (1986).

The Court again addressed the issue of corporate political speech in *Austin v. Michigan Chamber of Commerce.*[377] In *Austin*, the Court upheld a Michigan statute that prohibited corporations from using general treasury funds for contributions or independent expenditures to support or oppose candidates for state office. The statute did permit corporations to make political expenditures from segregated political funds to which persons could contribute. The law was challenged by the Michigan Chamber of Commerce, a corporate entity that accepted for-profit corporations as members and that some corporations joined for its business advantages, rather than in order to associate with the Chamber's speech.

Relying on *Buckley v. Valeo*, the Court acknowledged that the statute's limitation on a corporation's campaign spending did burden its political speech. However, the Court found the state's expressed interest in preventing corruption sufficiently compelling to uphold the statute. Writing for a six-justice majority, Justice Marshall found that the statute was aimed at "the corrosive and distorting effects of immense aggregations of wealth that are accumulated with the help of the corporate form and that have little or no correlation to the public's support for the corporation's political ideas."[378] The Court found the statute to be narrowly tailored to prevent this corruption because it did not ban all political expenditures by a corporation but only required that the money be spent through segregated funds that were fed through voluntary contributions. As a result, the corporation's political expenditures could accurately reflect the views of those contributing to the separate fund while allowing those not contributing to remain associated with the corporation for economic and other non-political reasons.

The Chamber of Commerce asserted that the law was unconstitutional as applied to nonprofit corporations. In rejecting this contention, the Court distinguished *Massachusetts Citizens for Life* on several grounds. First, the corporation in *MCFL* only engaged in political speech, while the Chamber engaged in more varied forms of activities that might attract members who, unlike the members of the MCFL organization, did not necessarily agree with the Chamber's speech. In addition, three quarters of the Chamber's members were for-profit corporations whose contributions and expenditures could be regulated by the state, thus justifying regulation of the Chamber as well in order to prevent the circumvention of that regulation. Justice Marshall also rejected the argument that the statute was underinclusive because it did not cover entities like labor unions, observing that whatever capital such unincorporated associations may amass was done without the special state help provided by the corporate structure.

Justice Kennedy dissented, arguing that *Austin* marked the first time that the Court allowed restrictions on political expenditures. He also complained that the decision also permitted some nonprofit corporations to speak but not others. Finally, Justice Kennedy pointed out that the statute's distinctions were based on the content of the

---

377. 494 U.S. 652 (1990).
378. *Id.* at 660.

speech (by restricting corporations' political speech) and the identity of the speaker. Justice Scalia also dissented. He criticized the majority's anti-distortion theory as another name for the speech equalization argument rejected in *Buckley*, describing the majority's rationale in *Austin* as reflecting an "illiberal free speech principle of 'one man, one minute' [that] was proposed and soundly rejected in *Buckley*."[379]

Austin's acceptance of restrictions on corporate electoral advocacy led corporations and unions during the 1990s to spend vast sums of money on so-called "issue ads" — advertisements that did not explicitly call for the election or defeat of a candidate for office, but that referenced candidates' positions on issues and expressed agreement or disagreement with those positions. These ads, usually run just before elections, were clearly designed to influence those elections, but because they did not explicitly call for the candidate's election or defeat, they remained unregulated.

Congress tried to close this loophole in 2002 when it enacted the Bipartisan Campaign Reform Act (BCRA). Among many other things, BCRA prohibited corporations and unions from using general treasury funds to fund what it called "electioneering communications," which it defined essentially as issue ads that ran in the period immediately before an election. As had previous legislation, BCRA allowed corporations and unions to make such speech via a segregated fund. In 2003, a divided Court upheld this and most of the rest of BCRA in *McConnell v. Federal Election Commission*.[380]

The Court overruled that part of *McConnell*, as well as *Austin*, seven years later, in *Citizens United v. Federal Election Commission*.[381] Writing for a five-justice majority, Justice Kennedy characterized BCRA's electioneering communications provision as a flat ban on corporate and union political speech. So characterized, the law ran afoul of the Court's content- and speaker-neutrality rule, in a context (political speech) that lay at the core of the First Amendment. The Court found no adequate justifications for those restrictions on First Amendment rights. The Court dismissed *Austin*'s anti-distortion rationale and repeated *Bellotti*'s reliance on "corporate democracy" to protect shareholders who might disagree with a corporation's decision to engage in political speech. It also dismissed the fear that Americans might feel like large corporate speech expenditures favoring certain candidates would be perceived as creating corruption. Justice Kennedy acknowledged that such expenditures might create an appearance of favoritism, but he concluded that such favoritism simply reflected politicians' responsiveness to their supporters, rather than something nefarious.

Writing for four justices, Justice Stevens dissented from the majority's decision striking down BCRA's electioneering communications provision and overruling *Austin*. He disputed the Court's characterization of that provision as banning corporate and union speech, noting that such entities remained free to fund political speech during non-election periods, and anytime if they used a segregated fund. While conceding

---

379. *Id.* at 684 (Scalia, J., dissenting).
380. 540 U.S. 93 (2003).
381. 558 U.S. 310 (2010).

that it was important to ensure that Congress was not entrenching incumbents by limiting campaign speech, he nevertheless urged that the Court defer to Congress's determinations about the corrupting effect of the activities BCRA regulated. On that point, he noted that *Bellotti*'s otherwise broad protection for corporate political speech was limited to referendum campaigns, with that earlier decision explicitly conceding that different considerations might apply in electoral campaigns. Justice Stevens also defended the shareholder protection rationale, and argued that, as a historical matter, corporations were generally thought not to possess wide speech rights.[382]

In overruling *McConnell* and striking down BCRA's electioneering communications restrictions, the Court also overruled *Austin*, given that the same interests were at stake in both the direct candidate endorsements/attacks that *Austin* allowed states to regulate and the issue ads that BCRA regulated. The result is that, after *Citizens United*, corporations and unions are free to use their general treasury funds for either issue ads or for direct endorsements of or attacks on candidates.

Corporate political speech remains a matter of heated public debate, with frequent calls to overrule *Citizens United* and even to amend the Constitution to allow regulation of corporate political speech. The issue is a complex one. One the one hand lies the centrality of political speech to the First Amendment and *Buckley*'s emphatic rejection of a speech equalization justification for restricting campaign finance activities. On the other lies the continuing suspicion that money dominates American politics and the sense that corporations have been able to use legal advantages to amass immense sums they can now use to influence politicians and political debate. It is quite possible that states will continue to impose restrictions on corporate and union political speech, thus creating opportunities for the Court to reconsider *Citizens United*, should it wish to.

[c] Disclosure Provisions

In stark contrast to corporate and union expenditure limitations, the Court has been far more receptive to the imposition of reporting and disclosure requirements. *Buckley* upheld such requirements both as means of informing voters and developing information that would help uncover actual corruption. In more recent years, the Court has remained tolerant of such mandates. In *Citizens United* itself, eight justices of an otherwise deeply-divided Court voted to uphold BCRA's disclosure requirements, which had been previously upheld in *McConnell* but which the plaintiffs requested be struck down as applied to them in particular. The Court refused, citing both *McConnell*'s and *Buckley*'s analysis embracing disclosure requirements as less speech-restrictive methods of ensuring the public's interest in full information about the sources of political speech, as well as shareholders' interest in obtaining information about what speech their corporations were funding. The Court also concluded that the plaintiffs had not made any showing that the required disclosures subjected them to

---

382. Justice Scalia joined the majority but wrote a separate concurrence to engage Justice Stevens' historical argument. *See id.* at 385 (Scalia, J., concurring).

harassment.[383] Justice Thomas was the sole dissenter from this part of *Citizens United*. He adhered to his often-expressed view[384] that the First Amendment protected the right to anonymous political speech.

[d] Continued Debate over Contribution Limits

In the years after *Buckley*, the Court has continued to consider the contexts in and the degree to which contribution limits could be restricted. These cases have focused on two major issues related to contributions.

One issue concerns the severity of those limitations, and the extent to which very low contribution limitations infringe on the First Amendment interests of both contributors and candidates. In *Nixon v. Shrink Missouri Government PAC*, the Court upheld Missouri's system of contribution limits.[385] Under the Missouri system, contributions to a candidate for the position of Missouri State Auditor were capped at an inflation adjusted amount of $1,075, an amount that was lower than the $1000 federal cap upheld in *Buckley*, when that $1,000 amount was adjusted for inflation since 1976.

The Court upheld the limitations. It held that the $1,000 contribution limit upheld in *Buckley* was not a minimum constitutional threshold for such legislation. More generally, the Court, speaking through Justice Souter, recognized the plausibility of the state's argument that candidates for statewide office were able to run effective campaigns despite these limits. The Court also found plausible the state's arguments that voters in Missouri were concerned about the possible corrupting effect of large campaign contributions, especially in light of *Buckley*'s own conclusions about that issue.

Concurring, Justice Stevens would have decided the case under a substantive due process analysis involving the liberty and property rights of the candidates and contributors, arguing that "money is property; it is not speech."[386] Justice Breyer, joined by Justice Ginsburg, also concurred. He expressed concern that too low a limit on contributions could unfairly favor incumbents by amplifying their existing media and reputational advantages. While the $1,075 limit was questionable, he concluded that the features of the statute, including the record of candidates being able to fund their campaigns adequately and the statute's inflation indexing showed that the statute did not severely disadvantage the plaintiff/state auditor candidate. But he cautioned

---

383. *See also* Doe v. Reed, 561 U.S. 186 (2010) (holding that, as a general matter, signatories to petitions seeking to place a referendum on the ballot do not have a First Amendment right to the confidentiality of their signatures, but allowing the plaintiffs to move forward with a claim that disclosure would be unconstitutional as applied to their signatures on a particular petition).

384. *See, e.g.*, McIntyre v. Ohio Elections Commission, 514 U.S. 334, 358 (1995) (Thomas, J., concurring in the judgment).

385. 528 U.S. 377 (2000). The statute placed limits ranging from $250 for offices involving populations under 100,000 to $1000 for offices involving populations of more than 250,000. The state adjusted these amounts for inflation.

386. *Id.* at 398.

that if problems such as these could not be resolved within *Buckley*'s framework, then it might be appropriate to reconsider *Buckley*.

Dissenting, Justice Kennedy also called on the Court to re-evaluate *Buckley*. He substantially agreed with Justice Thomas's dissent that government was not able to limit campaign contributions or expenditures. However, he would not dismiss the possibility that some limits on both expenditures and contribution limitations might allow public officials to focus on their governmental responsibilities instead of fundraising. Justice Thomas, joined by Justice Scalia, also dissented, arguing that *Buckley* should be overruled. He would have accorded strict scrutiny to campaign contribution limitations and would have held the Missouri statute unconstitutional. He pointed out that after the law's enactment, spending on statewide primaries and elections fell sharply.

Six years after *Shrink Missouri*, the Court reached a different result in *Randall v. Sorrell*,[387] and invalidated both Vermont's expenditure and contribution limits. The Court's analysis, however, was highly fractured. Only a three-justice plurality, speaking through Justice Breyer, applied *Buckley* and found the state's limits to fail its requirements. With regard to the law's contribution limits, the plurality admitted that there was no precise metric by which the Court could judge whether unusually low contribution limits violated the Constitution, but Vermont's extremely low limits, the evidence that those limits made it hard for candidates to run effective campaigns, and the lack of an inflation adjustment, among other factors caused the plurality to conclude that the contribution limits were unconstitutionally low.

Three other justices concurred in the judgment, expressing varying degrees of skepticism about *Buckley*'s tolerance for contribution limits. Three justices dissented, and would have upheld the Vermont law. Dissenting, Justice Stevens would have overruled those parts of *Buckley* that struck down expenditure limits. He maintained that expenditure limits were more analogous to time, place, and manner restrictions than to content-based restrictions. Justice Souter, joined by Justice Ginsburg and in part by Justice Stevens, would have deferred to the Vermont legislature's determinations of both appropriate expenditure and contribution limits. With regard to the expenditure limits, Justice Souter would have remanded the case for a trial on the question whether those limits were narrowly tailored to the state's interest in curbing the amount of time candidates felt obliged to spend raising money—an interest the reliance on which Justice Souter suggested had not been foreclosed by *Buckley*. Applying *Buckley*, he would have upheld the contribution limits.

A second important issue surrounding contribution limits concerns government's authority to impose such limits as a prophylactic device to guard against corruption. Recall that in *Buckley*, the Court accepted Congress's argument that actual bribery laws were insufficient to combat corruption, and upheld contribution limits as an indirect, prophylactic measure to achieve that same end. In recent years, the Court has grown skeptical about how far this prophylactic-based argument could be stretched.

---

387. 548 U.S. 230 (2006).

In *California Medical Association v. Federal Election Commission*,[388] the Court upheld a section of the Federal Election Campaign Act limiting the amount that individuals could contribute to a particular PAC that in turn contributed to candidates. The Court reasoned that a contrary holding would allow wealthy contributors to circumvent federal law's restrictions on large campaign contributions by funneling large contributions through a PAC, which could then forward them to a candidate.

The year after *California Medical*, in *Federal Election Commission v. National Right to Work Committee*,[389] the Court found no constitutional invalidity in a law limiting corporations lacking capital stock to seeking contributions from "members" of the corporation when seeking to amass money for electoral speech (including both expenditures and contributions). In other words, such corporations, if they wished to amass money for electoral speech, could only solicit members rather than any and all persons. While the main issue in the case was the correctness of the lower court's interpretation of the statute, the Court, once it interpreted the statute to impose this limitation, concluded that that interpretation did not render the statute unconstitutional. Writing for a unanimous Court, Justice Rehnquist explained that among the legitimate interests justifying the law was a congressional desire "to ensure that substantial aggregations of wealth amassed by the special advantages which go with the corporate form of organization ... not be converted into political 'war chests' which could be used to incur political debts from legislators who are aided by the contributions."[390]

In 2014, the Court struck down one of the contribution limitations *Buckley* had upheld. At issue in *McCutcheon v. Federal Election Commission*[391] was the aggregate contribution limit that federal law had imposed on contributions to all federal candidates and political committees during a given election cycle, beyond the much smaller limits on contributions to individual candidates. *Buckley* had upheld this aggregate limit, on the theory that it prevented large contributors from circumventing the individual contribution limits by giving large amounts either to parties or political committees who could then redistribute them to candidates, including those to whom the contributor had already directly contributed the statutory maximum. *McCutcheon* involved a large contributor who wished to donate the individual maximum contribution to a large number of candidates, thus exceeding the statutory aggregate limit.

The Court struck down the aggregate limit and overruled the part of *Buckley* that had reached a different result. Writing for four justices, Chief Justice Roberts concluded that the aggregate limit imposed too severe of a restraint on contributors' First Amendment rights in light of his conclusion that the limit did not directly further the government's anti-corruption goal. He observed that Congress had judged that contributions up to the contribution limit to any individual candidate did not run the risk of corruption, and he thus questioned why multiple instances of such con-

---

388. 453 U.S. 182 (1981).
389. 459 U.S. 197 (1982).
390. *Id.* at 207.
391. 572 U.S. 185 (2014).

tributions to different candidates did raise that risk. Addressing one possible answer to that question, he discounted the likelihood that candidates would engage in the kind of redistribution of contributions about which the government expressed concern, and concluded that such concerns could be resolved by restricting such redistributions.

Importantly, Chief Justice Roberts also observed that contribution limits in general were prophylactic devices that were designed to deter corruption above and beyond the effect of bribery laws themselves. He expressed impatience with the government's argument, which he described as a double prophylactic — that is, a restriction on aggregate contributions above a certain amount that was designed to prevent circumvention of the prohibition on individual contributions above a certain amount, which was *itself* designed to ensure deterrence of conduct more directly regulated by bribery laws. Justice Thomas provided the fifth vote. He repeated his consistent calls for overruling *Buckley*; applying strict scrutiny, he would have held the law unconstitutional.

Dissenting for four justices, Justice Breyer argued that the Court should defer to Congress, which had superior knowledge of the risks posed by the kind of redistribution the aggregate limit was designed to prevent. He also sketched out a broader theory of corruption, focusing on the undue influence powerful interests exerted over government, and argued that the aggregate limit furthered that broader anticorruption understanding.

In sum, much of the trend since *Buckley* has been toward loosened restrictions on campaign finance activities, both expenditures and, as illustrated by *Randall* and *McCutcheon*, contributions as well. But these topics remain highly controversial, with the Court closely split on many of these cases.

[6] Government Spending on Speech

In addition to regulating speech, government also facilitates speech by providing private parties funds with which they can speak. Government also speaks on its own — think, for example, of government announcements urging people to vote, abstain from drugs, or join the military. As one might suspect, when government funds private speech, it has a great deal of latitude to decide which speech to fund. Nevertheless, even in those situations, the government is subject to at least some First Amendment limits. Those limits become much less stringent when the government itself speaks. But determining when it is in fact government that is speaking often presents a harder question than one might initially think.

[a] Government Funding of Private Speech

The Court has generally imposed relatively loose restrictions on government when it funds private speech. *Regan v. Taxation With Representation*[392] illustrates the general idea. In *Regan*, the Court upheld Congress's general refusal to afford tax-exempt

---

392. 461 U.S. 540 (1983).

status to organizations that engage in lobbying. The Court held that the government was not constitutionally obligated to subsidize any particular speech activity or indeed the exercise of any right, even a fundamental one. The Court also rejected an equal protection challenge grounded on the fact that the government did allow tax-exempt status to veterans organizations that engaged in lobbying. The Court found no basis for the equal protection challenge as, again, government's failure to subsidize the exercise of a fundamental right does not constitute an infringement on that right.

Rust v. Sullivan[393] is an important case that helps delineate the breadth of Congress's power to choose the speech it wishes to subsidize. In *Rust*, the Court rejected a facial challenge to Title X of the Public Health Service Act, which authorized federal expenditures to advance family planning methods but exempted abortion. Entities receiving Title X federal funds could neither engage in abortion counseling nor refer a woman to abortion services, even upon her specific request. The regulations also prohibited funded projects from engaging in activities that "encourage, promote, or advocate abortion as a method of family planning," including lobbying or sponsoring speakers. Finally, the regulations required physical and financial separation of the Title X project from prohibited abortion-related activities, including separate accounting and personnel records. The Court rejected the argument that Title X allowed unconstitutional viewpoint discrimination by permitting counseling which favored bringing a pregnancy to term, while prohibiting counseling of abortion.

Relying on *Maher v. Roe* and *Harris v. McRae*, which upheld government funding of childbirth but not abortion,[394] the Court noted that government may make a value judgment favoring childbirth over abortion. According to the Court, in making that judgment, the government was not engaging in viewpoint-based speech discrimination. Thus, the Court again drew a distinction between interfering with an activity and subsidizing it. Relying on *Regan v. Taxation With Representation*,[395] discussed above, the Court observed that, for example, in establishing the National Endowment for Democracy, the government was under no obligation to subsidize analogous organizations that espoused competing political philosophies. Nor did the law in question impose an unconstitutional condition on the recipients of federal funds. In this regard, the Court noted that the restrictions applied to a Title X-funded *project*, rather than a *grantee* who received money to operate such a project. The grantee could continue to speak about abortion as she wished, but simply had to do it outside the confines of the federally-funded project.

Nevertheless, the Court conceded that the ability of recipients of government funds to speak outside their government-funded work would not always justify government control of the content of government-funded speech. In this connection,

---

393. 500 U.S. 173 (1991).

394. Maher v. Roe, 432 U.S. 464 (1977); Harris v. McRae, 448 U.S. 297 (1980). The Court's abortion jurisprudence, and in particular its jurisprudence finding no constitutional right to federal funding of abortions, is discussed in Section 9.04[3][b].

395. 461 U.S. 540 (1983).

the Court stated that the social importance of universities as "a traditional sphere of free expression" might justify vagueness or overbreadth-based limits on federal funding conditions.[396] The Court similarly acknowledged the social importance of the doctor-patient relationship. But the Court concluded that the limited nature of the doctor-patient relationship in Title X programs—that is, the limitation of that relationship to matters of family planning—defeated any patient expectation that that relationship might include counseling about abortion.[397]

Justice Blackmun dissented, joined by Justice Marshall and in relevant part by Justice Stevens.[398] He based his First Amendment argument on the proposition that the government may not condition federal funds and employment based on acceptance of a particular viewpoint—a demand that he found in the Title X program's conditions on physician speech. He distinguished *Regan* on the ground that the law in that case was content-neutral.[399]

In *Rosenberger v. University of Virginia*,[400] the Court, on a 5–4 vote, invalidated a university decision denying student activity fund resources to a student-run newspaper because of the newspaper's religious viewpoint. The fund denied the newspaper's request to pay for its printing costs on the ground that providing the funding would have violated the Establishment Clause.[401] Writing for the majority, Justice Kennedy wrote that the funding denial amounted to unconstitutional viewpoint discrimination.

The University asserted that it should enjoy substantial discretion in allocating University funds. The Court insisted, however, that government was forbidden from making such allocations in a viewpoint discriminatory way. It distinguished *Rust v. Sullivan* by reading *Rust* as a case in which the federally-funded family planning program constituted the government's own speech.[402] By contrast, the speech in *Rosenberger* was the speech of the student groups the university funded. In support of this latter conclusion, Justice Kennedy noted that each student group had to sign an agreement with the University specifying that the group was not acting as the University's agent. Consistent with *Regan v. Taxation With Representation*, the Court held that

---

396. *Rust*, 500 U.S. at 200. The vagueness and overbreadth doctrines are discussed in Section 11.02[2].

397. *See id.* at 200 ("The program does not provide post conception medical care, and therefore a doctor's silence with regard to abortion cannot reasonably be thought to mislead a client into thinking that the doctor does not consider abortion an appropriate option for her. The doctor is always free to make clear that advice regarding abortion is simply beyond the scope of the program.").

398. Justice O'Connor dissented on a separate, statutory interpretation ground.

399. The Court in *Rust* also split on whether the Title X funding conditions violated the due process right to abortion. That right is discussed in Section 9.04[3].

400. 515 U.S. 819 (1995).

401. The Establishment Clause is discussed in Chapter 12.

402. The question of when the government is held to be speaking, and thus can decide the content and viewpoint of that speech, is considered in Section 11.02[6][b].

government can single out certain *groups*, such as veterans groups, for more favorable treatment in its funding decisions but may not single out any particular viewpoint.

Legal Services Corp. v. Velazquez[403] raised an issue closely analogous to the one in *Rust*; however, the Court in *Velazquez* reached a different result than in *Rust*. In *Velazquez*, the Court struck down a congressional restriction on using federal Legal Services Corporation (LSC) funds to challenge existing welfare laws. Congress established the LSC to distribute funds to local organizations which provided indigent persons with legal assistance. Since the program's inception, Congress has limited the use of LSC funds in various ways, including, as challenged in *Velazquez*, forbidding the use of LSC grants "in litigation, lobbying, or rulemaking, involving an effort to reform a Federal or State welfare system."[404]

Relying on *Board of Regents v. Southworth*,[405] *Rust v. Sullivan*, *Rosenberger v. University of Virginia*, and *FCC v. League of Women Voters*,[406] Justice Kennedy explained that funding decisions based on viewpoint can be upheld in situations where the government is itself the speaker or where the government uses private speakers to communicate information about a governmental program. In contrast, the Court concluded that the LSC "was designed to facilitate private speech,"[407] since, even though LSC attorneys were federally-funded, they spoke on behalf of their clients, not the government.

Thus, the Court observed, Congress, by dictating the claims attorneys could and could not litigate, sought to control "an existing medium of expression," and thereby "distort [the medium's] usual functioning."[408] The restriction interfered with an attorney's ability to fully represent his client and altered "the traditional role of attorneys in much the same way broadcast systems or student publication networks were changed"[409] in *League of Women Voters* and *Rosenberger*, respectively. Justice Kennedy

---

403. 531 U.S. 533 (2001).

404. *Id.* at 538.

405. 529 U.S. 217 (2000). In *Southworth*, the Court upheld a university student activities fund, fed by mandatory student contributions, that was challenged by students who objected to having their money used for speech with which they disagreed. In rejecting the students' challenge, the Court noted that the fund was an important part of the university's efforts to provide students with a diverse array of ideas, and allocated funds in a viewpoint-neutral manner.

406. 468 U.S. 364 (1984). In *League of Women Voters*, the Court struck down a federal law prohibiting public broadcasting stations from editorializing if they received a federal grant. The Court concluded that the law constituted a content-based restriction on speech that the government failed to justify. The Court also rejected the government's argument, based on *Regan*, that government could choose to fund only non-editorializing speech, observing that, unlike in *Regan*, there was no provision in federal law allowing public broadcasters to establish "affiliate" organizations that could engage in the speech the government chose not to fund.

407. *Velazquez*, 531 U.S. at 542.

408. *Id.* at 543.

409. *Id.* at 544. As this case concerned a subsidy, the Court said that limited forum cases, such as *Perry Education Ass'n v. Perry Local Educators' Ass'n*, 460 U.S. 37 (1983), and *Rosenberger*, may be instructive though not controlling. The Court's doctrine governing speech forums is discussed in Section 11.01[5].

concluded that this restriction interfered with the courts' duty to interpret the law articulated in *Marbury v. Madison*,[410] as it prohibited "expression upon which courts must depend for the proper exercise of judicial power."[411] Thus, the Court suggested that, beyond the First Amendment issues it raised, Congress's limitation on LSC attorneys offended separation-of-powers principles by quelling constitutional challenges and insulating its own laws from judicial scrutiny.

The Court also distinguished *Rust* on the ground that indigent clients denied representation for their welfare-related claims by LSC-funded attorneys would probably not seek other legal counsel. Thus, unlike the program in *Rust* in which a patient could participate in government-funded family planning counseling and also could receive abortion counseling from another organization, the LSC program required an attorney to withdraw if a question implicating the validity of a welfare statute arose, leaving the client without the opportunity for joint representation. Further distinguishing *Rust*, the Court said the LSC restriction conveyed "no programmatic message,"[412] presumably unlike the Title X program *Rust* upheld, which conveyed a government message of support for childbirth over abortion.

Justice Scalia dissented, joined by Chief Justice Rehnquist and Justices O'Connor and Thomas. He considered the case directly analogous to *Rust*. The LSC Act did not create a public forum, had always restricted the use of funds, and had never pretended to endorse all viewpoints. Moreover, it did not "discriminate on the basis of viewpoint, since it funds neither challenges to nor defenses of existing welfare law."[413] Echoing earlier courts' distinctions between subsidizing a right and interfering with it, Justice Scalia argued that a client without an LSC attorney stood in "no *worse* condition than he would have been in had the program never been enacted."[414] In Justice Scalia's view, the only plausible way to distinguish this case from *Rust* was on the inability of attorneys to engage in joint representation with a non-government funded attorney challenging welfare laws. Justice Scalia found nothing problematic about this, given generally-applicable canons of legal ethics.

To date, the most recent important statement from the Court on government funding of private speech is *Agency for International Development v. Alliance for Open Society International*.[415] *Open Society* considered a challenge to a federal government limitation on grants it made to organizations fighting the spread of HIV/AIDS. The law governing those grants prohibited recipient organizations from using those funds to promote or advocate for the legalization of prostitution. The recipients of the grants did not challenge that requirement. Instead, they challenged the second re-

---

410. 5 U.S. (1 Cranch) 137 (1803).
411. *Velazquez*, 531 U.S. at 545.
412. *Id.* at 548.
413. *Id.* at 553 (Scalia, J. dissenting).
414. *Id.* at 557.
415. 570 U.S. 205 (2013).

quirement, which prohibited organizations from receiving such grants unless they had a policy explicitly opposing prostitution.

The Court held, on a 6–2 vote,[416] that the second condition violated the First Amendment rights of the organizations that sought such grants. Writing for the majority, Chief Justice Roberts distinguished *Rust v. Sullivan* on the ground that the health care program challenged in that case regulated physician speech only within the scope of the grant—in other words, that program merely specified how government money was to be used. Thus, *Rust*, as well as *Regan v. Taxation With Representation* and *FCC v. League of Women Voters*, drew a distinction "between conditions that define the federal program and those that reach outside it," with conditions of the first type held to be constitutional and those of the second type held not to be. Conceding that this distinction was not always clear, the Chief Justice concluded that the requirement challenged in *Open Society* "falls on the unconstitutional side of the line,"[417] because it restricted how recipient organizations spoke using their own funds, independently of any federal funding.

Justice Scalia, joined by Justice Thomas, dissented. He argued that government had a right not just to speak, but to choose as its funding grantees entities that were generally supportive of (or simply not opposed to) the government's own policy views. Thus, he concluded, as long as groups were free to espouse their own views about prostitution when engaging in anti-HIV/AIDS work, there was no constitutional violation in the government's decision to favor with funding those groups whose general policy views coincided with those of the federal government.

These cases should make clear that the line between constitutional and unconstitutional conditions on government funding is a very blurry one. Sometimes the distinctions will turn on the details of the government funding program, as in *Rust*, where the majority viewed the Title X program as one sufficiently limited that it was not thought to impinge on any broader relationship a doctor may have with her patient. Similarly, in *Velazquez* the Court, in distinguishing *Rust*, laid heavy emphasis on the importance of lawyers not being precluded from raising relevant issues and claims in a lawsuit, as part of their role in assisting judges adjudicate cases. In *Regan*, the Court relied in part on the ability of a group that wished to lobby to establish an affiliate organization for that purpose, a step that would render the original group eligible for tax-exempt status under the law the plaintiffs unsuccessfully challenged.[418] In other cases, the disagreement is more fundamental. In *Open Society*, for example, Justice Scalia took the position that competitors for government grants could not complain if they were denied funding based on broader policy positions they took unrelated to the funding program itself.

---

416. Justice Kagan did not participate.

417. *Id.* at 217.

418. *See also supra.* note 406 (noting that the Court made a similar observation in *FCC v. League of Women Voters*).

But an even deeper ambiguity lurks in these cases: when is government merely funding private speech, and when is it speaking for itself? As the next sub-section explains, the answer to that question is critical to understanding the limitations the First Amendment places on government-financed speech.

[b] Government Speech

Over the last twenty years, the Court has begun experimenting with the doctrinal category of government speech. As one might expect, this category refers to situations in which government itself is understood to be speaking. When that is the case, government, like any private speaker, is largely, although not completely,[419] free to select the topics it wishes to address and even the viewpoint it wishes to espouse. One can immediately understand how this phenomenon appears in everyday life. Government can put out messages such as "Make sure to vote" or "Join the military" without any First Amendment concern with the topic the government selects and even the viewpoint the government espouses. But in some cases, the question whether government is the entity doing the speaking is not as straightforward as these examples might suggest.

While the Court had mentioned the idea of government speech in earlier cases,[420] the Court's explicit invocation of this new doctrinal category began in earnest in the 2005 case *Johanns v. Livestock Marketing Association*.[421] *Johanns* presented the Court with a free speech challenge to a tax imposed on beef producers that was used to fund an advertising program urging Americans to eat beef. The claim was that the targeted tax effectively forced the producers to subsidize speech with which they disagreed.

Rather than deciding the case as one in which the government compelled the producers themselves to subsidize another's message,[422] the Court in *Johanns* concluded that the beef advertising speech was government speech. Writing for five justices, Justice Scalia explained that, while the advertising was controlled by a non-governmental entity, Congress and the executive branch had set "the overarching message."[423] Moreover, the Secretary of Agriculture determined the final content of the advertising,

---

419. *See, e.g.*, Pleasant Grove City v. Summum, 555 U.S. 460, 468–69 (2009) ("This does not mean that there are no restraints on government speech. For example, government speech must comport with the Establishment Clause. The involvement of public officials in advocacy may be limited by law, regulation, or practice. And of course, a government entity is ultimately accountable to the electorate and the political process for its advocacy. If the citizenry objects, newly elected officials later could espouse some different or contrary position."). For a detailed discussion of the connection between the Establishment Clause and the government speech doctrine, see Mary Jean Dolan, *Government Identity Speech and Religion: Establishment Clause Limits After* Summum, 19 WM. & MARY BILL OF RIGHTS J. 1 (2010).

420. *See Summum*, 555 U.S. at 467–68 (citing cases).

421. 544 U.S. 550 (2005).

422. Cases presenting the compelled speech/compelled subsidization issue, including cases involving somewhat analogous targeted taxes aimed at agriculture producers to fund advertising promoting those producers' products, are discussed in Section 11.02[3][b].

423. *Johanns*, 544 U.S. at 561.

appointed half the members of the board that otherwise developed its details, and had firing authority over every member. Justice Scalia recognized the possibility that the advertising, which stated it was presented by "America's Beef Producers," could possibly be misattributed to producers rather than the government, but he noted that the producers had not provided adequate evidence on that point.

Justice Souter, joined by Justices Stevens and Kennedy, dissented. Justice Souter argued that the facts of the case demonstrated that the speech in that case could not be understood as the government's own. Most notably, he insisted that the public accountability that limits government's power to abuse its ability to speak its own message requires that the government explicitly identify itself as the speaker, which it did not do in *Johanns*.

The Court further explained the government speech concept in a case decided in 2009, *Pleasant Grove City v. Summum*.[424] *Summum* involved a small religious group that wished to donate to a city, for placement in a park, a statue that recited the precepts of that religion. The park in question already contained several statues, including one reciting the Ten Commandments, donated by a different private group. When the city declined the donation, the group sued, claiming that the park was a public forum and that the city's action constituted unconstitutional content- and speaker-based discrimination, especially given the city's acceptance of the Ten Commandments monument.

The Supreme Court rejected the claim. Writing for eight justices on a unanimous Court,[425] Justice Alito wrote that, whatever ambiguity might lay in determining whether particular speech was in fact speech made by the government, the permanent placement of monuments in public parks clearly constituted government speech. Justice Alito relied heavily on the history of such placements, which he described as expressing the government's choice to propound certain viewpoints—for example, the government's decision to accept and display the Statue of Liberty as a gift from France, as expressing the government's pro-liberty viewpoint.

Because the city was deemed to be speaking when it placed permanent monuments in the park, the Court concluded that it was inappropriate to view the case through the lens of forum doctrine, in which a park's status as a traditional public forum required government content- and viewpoint-neutrality.[426] The Court also rejected the religious group's argument that the city's government speech defense required it to adopt a resolution formally endorsing "the message" expressed by any monument it accepted. According to the Court, this requirement would be a pointless formality that might accomplish little, given that the meaning of monuments—that is, the message they express—might well change over time.

Several justices wrote concurring opinions. Justice Scalia, joined by Justice Thomas, wrote to reassure the city that its victory on the government speech issue did not

---

424. 555 U.S. 460 (2009).

425. Justice Souter concurred only in the judgment. Several justices joined Justice Alito's opinion but wrote separate concurrences.

426. Forum doctrine is discussed in Section 11.01[5].

mean that it had thus violated the Establishment Clause when it accepted the Ten Commandments monument.[427] Justice Stevens (joined by Justice Ginsburg) and Justice Breyer each wrote to express concern about over-use of the government speech principle. Justice Souter merely concurred in the judgment, and also expressed caution about the government speech concept. He agreed that on the facts of the case before the Court, the city's acceptance of the Ten Commandments monument constituted government speech, but he declined to embrace the majority's seemingly broader rule categorizing all permanent monuments placed in parks as government speech.

After the near-unanimity of *Summum*, the Court split badly in the next case to consider a claim that the challenged government action constituted government speech. In *Walker v. Sons of Confederate Veterans*,[428] the Court considered a challenge from a confederate veterans group challenging the State of Texas's refusal to accept a design for a customized license plate that took the form of a shaded version of the confederate battle flag. The group argued that the state's customized license plate program constituted a public forum the state had created, in which it was prohibited from engaging in content- or viewpoint-based discrimination.

The Court disagreed, finding the program, and the license plates thereby created, to be government speech. Writing for a five-justice majority, Justice Breyer cited several factors that he argued justified that conclusion. First, license plates were historically issued by states and contained state-created messages. Second, the public generally viewed license plates as expressing the government's speech. Third, Texas maintained government control over that speech by approving of every design before it becomes available as an option for motorists.[429]

Justice Alito dissented for four justices. He disputed the idea that the state controlled the message communicated by specialty license plate designs, and instead concluded that Texas had indeed created a limited public forum, in which it could not exercise viewpoint discrimination. Applying his own opinion in *Summum*, Justice Alito argued that, unlike with park monuments, in recent years Texas, like other states, had begun programs allowing privately-created messages to appear on license plates. He also argued that Texas had not been selective in approving offered designs, and thus could not claim that the messages were the state's own. Finally, he noted that, unlike permanent park monuments in *Summum*, there was no inherent limit on the number of designs that could be used on Texas license plates. Beyond these factors which he said distinguished the license plates from the monument in *Summum*, Justice Alito also noted that the Texas program, like similar ones in other states, required persons seeking custom designs to pay extra money. To Justice Alito, that fact buttressed his

---

427. The Establishment Clause is discussed in Section 12.02.

428. 576 U.S. 200 (2015).

429. The fact that the Court found license plates to be government speech did not obviate any First Amendment claim motorists might have for being forced to display the state's message, as in *Wooley v Maryland*, 430 U.S. 705 (1977). *Wooley*, and analogous compelled speech cases, are discussed in Section 11.02[3][a].

argument that the Texas program gave individuals the opportunity to speak via Texas license plates, rather than representing the state's own speech.

In a more recent case, the Court had an easier time rejecting the argument that the speech in question constituted government speech. In *Matal v. Tam*,[430] the Court struck down a provision of federal trademark law that prohibited the registration of a trademark that "disparages ... or ... brings into contemp[t] or disrepute" any person or group of persons.

In a part of the opinion joined by all the justices, the Court, speaking through Justice Alito, rejected the government's argument that any viewpoint discrimination inherent in that provision was constitutional because trademarks registered with the Patent and Trademark Office were government speech. The Court noted the relative lack of government control over the viewpoints of trademark speech (except for the challenged provision itself), and observed that, if such speech was in fact the government's, then it was engaged in a cacophony of contradictory and often-offensive speech.

Justice Alito contrasted the government speech claim in *Matal* with the analogous claims in *Johanns*, *Summum*, and *Walker*. He concluded that in each of those latter three cases, the government exerted significantly more control over the speech in question and there was substantially more public association of the speech with the government. Even *Walker*, which Justice Alito (who dissented in that case) described as the case "which likely marks the outer bounds of the government-speech doctrine,"[431] differed from trademark registration, given the characteristics of the license plate design scheme, as described by the *Walker* majority. He concluded his government speech analysis by worrying that characterizing trademarks as government speech would open the door to a government claim that copyrighting a book rendered that book government speech, with all the attendant discretion government would then have to accord it treatment based on content- and viewpoint-based criteria.

The cases discussed in this sub-section vary widely in their subject-matter, and in the relationship between the speech in question and the government. This fact suggests that the government speech doctrine is likely to remain a highly fact-intensive one, with decisions resting on the unique aspects of the particular context in which the alleged government speech is taking place. The justices may also be tempted to find certain speech to be government speech as a way to avoid having to require the government to open up forums associated with the government (for example, license plates) to offensive or otherwise undesirable speech, as would be required by public forum analysis.[432]

---

430. 137 S. Ct 1744 (2017).

431. *Id.* at 1760.

432. *Compare, e.g.*, Robb v. Hungerbeeler, 370 F.3d 735 (8th Cir. 2004) (finding a violation of the First Amendment in a state's refusal to allow a unit of the Ku Klux Klan to participate in the state's adopt-a-highway program, which entails recognizing highway "adopters" on signs posted on the selected highway, and rejecting the state's argument that the signs constituted government speech).

[7] Speech in Custodial or Proprietary Government Contexts

In addition to regulating speech in public and on private property, government also regulates speech in particular places where it has special authority. Most notably, public schools and government workplaces are locations where government has special need and authority to control speech, but where, respectively, students and employees retain some degree of free speech rights.[433] This sub-section considers these special speech situations.

[a] Students' Speech Rights

The extent of protection granted to speech in the public school setting varies. The Court has recognized that students retain their First Amendment rights even on school grounds. Greater protection has been extended to student expression unrelated to curricular or extracurricular activities over which school officials might be thought to enjoy more authority and control, and thus responsibility for. Moreover, government's need to ensure order and discipline, as well as students' safety, may justify speech restrictions that threaten those imperatives.

The foundational student speech rights case is *Tinker v. Des Moines Independent Community School District*.[434] *Tinker* involved students who were suspended from school for wearing black armbands to protest the Vietnam War. The Court held that the suspensions were an impermissible restriction on the students' free speech rights. The decision was largely driven by the majority's view of schools as a place to exchange ideas. As a starting point for the analysis, the Court, speaking through Justice Fortas, stated: "It can hardly be argued that either students or teachers shed their constitutional rights to freedom of speech or expression at the schoolhouse gate."[435] The Court recognized the schools' interest in preventing disruption, but discounted the school administrators' fear of disruption as unsubstantiated and thus insufficient to overcome the students' speech rights. The Court noted that, in fact, the protesting students'

---

433. Two other custodial contexts require a brief word. In the prison context, the Court has held that in order to justify a restriction on prisoners' constitutional rights, "there must be a reasonable relationship between the restriction at issue and a legitimate penological objective." Turner v. Safley, 482 U.S. 78, 89 (1987). While this was likely intended to be a relatively deferential standard, designed to give wardens the leeway needed to manage prisons, critics have argued that the standard, as applied in the First Amendment context, has been used to excuse wide-ranging infringements on prisoners' speech rights. *See, e.g.*, David Shapiro, *Lenient in Theory, Dumb in Fact: Prison, Speech, and Scrutiny*, 84 GEO. WASH. L. REV. 972 (2016). Second, the restricted nature of military bases and, more generally, courts' deference to Congress and military commanders on military issues often results in restrictions on soldiers' First Amendment rights that would be intolerable if imposed on civilians. *See, e.g.*, Brown v. Glines, 444 U.S. 348 (1980) (deferring to the military in upholding a requirement of prior approval for circulating petitions on Air Force bases); Greer v. Spock, 424 U.S. 828 (1976) (concluding that a military base was a non-public forum in which content-based speech restrictions were allowed, as long as they were viewpoint-neutral and reasonable).

434. 393 U.S. 503 (1969).

435. *Id.* at 506.

speech caused only slight disruption of the school environment.[436] In dissent, Justice Black emphasized that the purpose of school was to learn and that to advance that purpose, discipline, including controls on student speech, had to be maintained.

Nearly two decades later, the Court decided two cases in quick succession that appeared to cut back on *Tinker*. In *Bethel School District No. 403 v. Fraser*,[437] the Court allowed a school to punish a student who delivered a nominating speech for a student government candidate that took the form of an extended set of juvenile sexual references. The Court found the penalties imposed unrelated to any viewpoint discrimination. Emphasizing the *in loco parentis* role of the schools, the Court determined that the First Amendment did not prevent schools from determining when lewd and vulgar speech undermined the school's basic educational mission of inculcating the values of civil and serious discourse on public matters.

Two years after *Fraser*, the Court again ruled in favor of a school in a student speech case. *Hazelwood School District v. Kuhlmeier*[438] dealt with school administrators' impositions of restrictions on the content of a student newspaper, based on their concerns about the fairness and accuracy of the claims made in the article and the mature nature of some of the newspaper's other content (which described students' experiences with pregnancies). The Court held that the school newspaper was not a public forum and, therefore, school authorities could censor it as long as their actions were reasonable. Although students were given some control over the newspaper's content, the control was part of the normal curriculum, with the newspaper understood to have been published as a component of the school's journalism program. The Court thus distinguished *Tinker*, explaining that the *Tinker* standard applied to students' own expression on school premises but not to expression by students using the school's resources. Given that the decision to remove the objectionable content was reasonably related to the school's legitimate pedagogical concerns about proper journalistic practices and its concerns about a school-sponsored publication dealing with mature content, the Court upheld the administrators' actions.

Hazelwood substantially narrowed *Tinker*. If *Tinker* had applied, the prohibition on expression would likely have been invalidated unless the student speech impacted student discipline or the rights of other students. By contrast, *Hazelwood* required courts to determine simply if the school's action was reasonable. The differing results in the two cases largely reflect the dual role of schools, as locations where students enjoy at least some free speech rights but also where those rights were limited by the school's pedagogical and custodial interests. They also quite possibly reflect the *Hazelwood* Court's lesser interest in protecting student speech.

---

436. *See id.* at 508 ("Only a few of the 18,000 students in the school system wore the black armbands. Only five students were suspended for wearing them. There is no indication that the work of the schools or any class was disrupted. Outside the classrooms, a few students made hostile remarks to the children wearing armbands, but there were no threats or acts of violence on school premises.").

437. 478 U.S. 675 (1986).

438. 484 U.S. 260 (1988).

In *Morse v. Frederick*,[439] the Court held that schools can restrict student speech that encourages illegal drug use. In *Morse*, a student was suspended for displaying a sign that read "BONG HiTS 4 JESUS" at an Olympic torch relay event that took place off-campus, but which was held to be an event where the students were still under the school's control. The Court found the banner could be reasonably interpreted to encourage illegal drug use and was not political speech advocating the legalization of marijuana. Writing a narrow opinion for five justices, Chief Justice Roberts cited *Fraser* for the proposition that *Tinker*'s "substantial disruption" analysis was not the sole approach to student speech questions. The Court emphasized the dangers of illegal drug use by minors, and recognized school authority to prevent speech that seemed to promote it.

Concurring, Justice Thomas argued that *Tinker*'s analysis has no basis in the Constitution because it interferes with traditional *in loco parentis* powers school officials have possessed since the framing period. He thus echoed Justice Black's dissent in *Tinker*, several decades earlier. Also concurring but from the other end of the free speech spectrum, Justice Alito, joined by Justice Kennedy, concluded that restrictions on student speech advocating drug use are "at the far reaches of what the First Amendment permits."[440]

Dissenting, Justice Stevens, joined by Justices Souter and Ginsburg, maintained that the banner did not encourage illegal drug use. Rather, he understood the banner as expressing a nonsense message, motivated simply by a desire to attract television coverage. Moreover, he objected that the majority's broad holding would restrict students' legitimate First Amendment rights to debate political issues regarding the legalization of drugs. Concurring in part and dissenting in part, Justice Breyer argued that the case should have been decided on grounds other than the First Amendment.

In recent years, a number of cases have arisen that raise the question of administrators' authority to restrict online speech when it has effects on campus. *Tinker* itself was decided on the assumption that the speech in question took place on school property. In 1969, when the Court decided *Tinker*, it was possible to meaningfully distinguish such on-campus speech from speech made off-campus, where presumably students enjoyed far more robust free speech rights. This assumption no longer applies, however, given that speech made online can easily be consumed on campus, even if the speaker posted her comments anywhere in the world off school property. Some courts have indeed taken the position that off-campus creation of online speech at least tends to insulate that speech from school punishment.[441] On the other hand, courts have been more willing to punish even off-campus created speech when it

---

439. 551 U.S. 393 (2007).

440. *Id.* at 425 (Alito, J., concurring).

441. *See, e.g.*, Layshock ex rel. Layshock v. Hermitage Sch. Dist., 650 F.3d 205 (3d Cir. 2011) (en banc) (finding a student's satirical profile of a school principal, posted on a social networking site, to be protected speech in part because it was created off-campus even though the student used a photo from the school's website).

either threatens or actually causes serious disruption at school, for example, if the speech constitutes a threat of violence.[442] These cases at least imply that the off/on campus nature of the speech operates in tandem with *Tinker*'s substantial disruption inquiry, with more seriously disruptive speech more likely to justify punishment even if made off-campus.

To date, the Court has not taken a case that poses the question of school administrators' authority to punish off-campus speech. It is hard to see how such off-campus speech could be punishable by school authorities, without giving those authorities the ability to punish speech made by a student while she was anywhere in the world, unless punishment of such speech is limited to particularly disruptive speech. As suggested by speech threatening violence, off-campus speech clearly has the potential for causing the on-campus disruption that *Tinker* acknowledged would justify official punishment.[443]

[b] Government Employees' Speech Rights

[i] Speech-Based Claims

Generally, the Court protects a government employee's criticism of government only when it is a matter of "public concern." If, however, the employee speaks pursuant to his "official duties," then the First Amendment is not implicated.[444] Otherwise, the First Amendment does protect such speech. As the Court said in its most recent important employee speech case, "So long as employees are speaking as citizens about matters of public concern, they must face only those speech restrictions that are necessary for their employers to operate efficiently and effectively."[445]

The foundations for this doctrine were laid in 1968, in *Pickering v. Board of Education*.[446] *Pickering* dealt with a school board dismissal of a teacher after the teacher sent a letter to the editor of a local newspaper criticizing the school board's use of educational funds. In rejecting the lower court's upholding of the firing, the Court, speaking through Justice Marshall, observed that the teacher did not work directly with the members of the school board he had criticized in the letter. Thus, there was no issue about immediate supervisors' need to maintain either workplace discipline or harmonious relationships. Nor was there any claim that the content of the letter was necessarily detrimental to the school district.

---

442. *See id.* at 217–18 (discussing such cases and explaining that the disruption the speech caused justified official punishment).

443. *See, e.g.*, J.S. v. Bethlehem Area Sch. Dist., 807 A.2d 847 (Pa. 2002) (upholding punishment of off-campus created speech that threatened to kill a teacher, causing the teacher to take a medical leave of absence and worrying several parents and students).

444. *See* Garcetti v. Ceballos, 547 U.S. 410, 421 (2006) ("We hold that when public employees make statements pursuant to their official duties, the employees are not speaking as citizens for First Amendment purposes, and the Constitution does not insulate their communications from employer discipline.").

445. *Id.* at 419.

446. 391 U.S. 563 (1968).

Importantly, the Court observed that the public issue that sparked the letter—whether to approve additional school funding—was one that teachers, as a class, would be expected to be informed about and have definite opinions about, thus making it essential that they be allowed to speak out free of worry about dismissal or other adverse action. Distilling these ideas, the Court concluded that "[t]he problem in any case is to arrive at a balance between the interests of the teacher, as a citizen, in commenting upon matters of public concern and the interest of the State, as an employer, in promoting the efficiency of the public services it performs through its employees."[447]

Connick v. Myers[448] illustrates how the Court has sought to perform this balancing. In *Connick*, an Assistant District Attorney (Myers) was fired for insubordination after she circulated an intra-office questionnaire soliciting views from her co-workers on matters of office policy and morale, their level of confidence in their supervisors, and whether they felt pressured to work on political campaigns. The Court upheld the discharge, because it viewed the questionnaire as an attempt to gain support for resisting her transfer to another section of the court where she practiced, rather than as speech on matters of public concern. She did not convey the information to the public, and even if she had, it would only have indicated dissatisfaction by one employee. Essentially, with one exception noted immediately below, the Court viewed the questions Myers asked "as mere extensions of Myers' dispute over her transfer to another section of the criminal court."[449]

However, the Court did concede that one question in the questionnaire—the one that asked her co-workers whether they ever felt pressured to work on political campaigns—raised a matter of public concern. But that fact by itself did not win the case for Myers; rather, speech that met this threshold inquiry of being a matter of public concern still had to be balanced against the state's justification for the adverse employment action. At this point, the Court criticized the lower court for holding that the state bore the burden to "'clearly demonstrate' that the speech 'substantially interfered' with official responsibilities."[450] Rather, the Court held that "the state's burden in justifying a particular discharge varies depending upon the nature of the employee's expression." The Court conceded that "such particularized balancing is difficult," but it insisted that "courts must reach the most appropriate balance of the competing interests."[451]

In performing this balance, *Connick* concluded that a court had to consider the nature of the employee's expression. In *Connick* itself, for example, the Court noted that Myers' questionnaire did not impede her ability to perform her job. On the other hand, the Court concluded that it was important for assistant district attorneys to maintain close working relationships with their supervisors, and noted the supervisor's

447. *Id.* at 568.
448. 461 U.S. 138 (1983).
449. *Id.* at 148.
450. *Id.* at 150 (quoting trial court decision).
451. *Ibid.*

and assistant supervisor's conclusions that the questionnaire had caused "a mini-insurrection"[452] in the office. The Court also noted the fact that Myers distributed the questionnaire at the office, and observed that an employee's manner of speaking— for example, via a personal confrontation with her supervisor—might itself threaten the efficiency of the workplace.[453] Finally, the Court noted the context in which Myers circulated the questionnaire—that is, in the aftermath of her transfer to another section of the court. The Court viewed that fact as increasing the weight of the supervisor's view that the employee had threatened the supervisor's ability to manage the workplace.

Dissenting for himself and three other justices, Justice Brennan would have construed matters of public concern more broadly, as involving all subjects in which the public could be reasonably interested when formulating its opinion of the local district attorney. For example, Justice Brennan insisted that it was a matter of public concern how the supervisor's personnel policies impacted workplace morale. Underlying the majority's determination of what issues do and do not constitute matters of public concern appears to have been the concept of efficiency in the provision of government services. The Court seems to have differentiated between government in its role as formulator of policy and its role as provider of services, concluding that the latter responsibility broadens government's discretion to punish employee speech. By contrast, Justice Brennan seemed to stress the public's interest in all aspects of how government operated.

Cases after *Connick* reflect these same concerns. In *Rankin v. McPherson*,[454] a civilian employee in a sheriff's office, upon hearing that President Reagan had been shot, said to a friend at the office, "If they go for him again, I hope they get him." After finding the speech to touch upon a matter of public concern, the Court emphasized that the employee did not discredit the office or interfere with its efficient functioning. She made the remark privately to a friend that another employee overheard. The Court also observed that her position, as a data-entry clerk, lacked any policy-making or confidential role, the performance of which could have been impaired by her comment. Four justices dissented, criticizing both the Court's conclusion that the comment touched on a matter of public concern and its conclusion that the effective functioning of the office did not require the speaker's dismissal. As Justice Scalia, writing for the dissenters and quoting the supervisor's lawyer, insisted, "no law enforcement agency is required by the First Amendment to permit one of its employees to 'ride with the cops and cheer for the robbers.' "[455]

---

452. *Id.* at 151.

453. This is not to say that private communications of grievances or concerns to a manager always render the speech unprotected by the First Amendment. For example, in *Givhan v. Western Line Consolidated School District*, 439 U.S. 410 (1979), the Court reversed the dismissal of an employee who, in a private meeting with her employer, had criticized discrimination in which her employer was allegedly engaging.

454. 483 U.S. 378 (1987).

455. *Id.* at 394 (Scalia, J., dissenting).

The Court's most recent important employee speech case, *Garcetti v. Ceballos*,[456] considered the dismissal of an assistant district attorney for writing a memorandum to his supervisor recommending that a prosecution be dismissed based on discrepancies in a police officer's affidavit that supported a crucial search warrant in that case. The Court, in a 5–4 decision, held that speech made pursuant to the employee's official duties is unprotected by the First Amendment. Speaking through Justice Kennedy, the Court concluded that restricting such speech did not infringe on any rights the employee enjoyed as a citizen, since he made the speech in question as part of his work responsibilities. The Court also stressed the employer's need to manage the work of its employees, including the speech they produced, and expressed concern that a contrary result would embroil courts in second-guessing the employer's management of the workplace.

Four justices dissented in three different opinions. Writing for himself and Justices Stevens and Ginsburg, Justice Souter argued that the Court should apply *Pickering* balancing even to speech made in the course of government employment, as long as the speech is on a matter of public concern. However, he did concede that such balancing should result in a win for the employee only if that speech addressed particularly weighty matters in responsible ways. Writing only for himself, Justice Stevens rejected a categorical difference between a person speaking as an employee and as a citizen, and stressed that in the past, the Court had protected employee speech even when it was made in private to the employer.[457] Finally, Justice Breyer, also writing only for himself, faulted Justice Souter's approach for giving too little weight to the government interests in effective workplace management. However, he noted that in this case, the district attorney's speech was freighted with professional standard-based obligations (that is, as a lawyer, he had an obligation to seek justice and to speak when necessary to do so, which he sought to do through his memorandum) and constitutional obligations (that is, his obligations as a prosecutor to disclose exculpatory evidence).[458]

Sometimes, of course, government employees speak on matters unrelated to their government employment. In *United States v. National Treasury Employees*, the Court struck down a federal law that prohibited federal employees from receiving honoraria for speaking engagements.[459] The five-justice majority, speaking through Justice Stevens, performed *Pickering* balancing and concluded that no government interest justified the ban, which the Court worried would restrict speech by removing any economic reward for making it.

---

456. 547 U.S. 410 (2006).

457. *See id.* at 427 (Stevens, J., dissenting) (citing Givhan v. Western Line Consolidated Sch. Dist., 439 U.S. 410 (1979)).

458. *See id.* at 447 (Breyer, J., dissenting) (citing Brady v. Maryland, 373 U.S. 83 (1963) (establishing a prosecutor's constitutional obligation to reveal exculpatory evidence)).

459. 513 U.S. 454 (1995). The ban had a series of exceptions, but the facts recounted by the Court focused on honoraria paid to government speakers who spoke on matters unrelated to their official position.

First, because most of such speech was unrelated to the speaker's employment,[460] there was no danger of workplace disruption. Nor did any workplace efficiency concerns justify the ban. The Court distinguished an earlier case that had upheld a ban on partisan political activity by a large class of federal workers,[461] on the ground that that earlier ban aimed to protect employees from being coerced into performing such activity by their supervisors. Nor did the Court find compelling the government's concern with employees leveraging their official positions to obtain lucrative speech opportunities, a concern the Court found validated only by evidence regarding higher-ranking federal executives and Members of Congress.

Justice O'Connor concurred in part and dissented in part, to express her general agreement with the Court's application of *Pickering* but also to disagree with the Court's remedy. Chief Justice Rehnquist, joined by Justices Scalia and Thomas, dissented. Applying *Pickering*, the Chief Justice concluded that Congress's interest in avoiding possible improprieties by its employees was reasonable. Moreover, he noted that the ban did not prohibit anyone's speech but simply prohibited the government employees from receiving honoraria.

The Court rejected a lower court's reliance on *Treasury Employees* in a 2004 case, *City of San Diego v. Roe*.[462] In *Roe*, the Court, in a unanimous *per curiam* opinion, held that a police officer's sexually explicit videos, in which he engaged in sexual activity while wearing his uniform, did not constitute speech on a matter of public concern. Consequently, in reviewing that dismissal, a court did not need to engage in *Pickering* balancing. The Court upheld the dismissal.

To determine whether speech involves a matter of public concern, the Court stated that courts should look at the entire record. It wrote that matters of public concern include subjects "of legitimate news interest." They can also include "certain private remarks, such as negative comments about the President." However, the Court concluded that "this is not a close case," as the police officer's activities neither involved political news nor public information about the police department's functioning. Instead, the officer's speech purposefully exploited the police department, harming its "mission and functions."[463]

The Court rejected the lower court's reliance on *Treasury Employees* for the proposition that the videos were unrelated to the police officer's employment and had no impact on the employer. It noted that in *Treasury Employees*, the government had failed to establish that the speech caused any deleterious impact on the government workplace. By contrast, it concluded that the police department in *Roe* had "legitimate

---

460. The Court conceded that higher-ranking federal officials and Members of Congress might well find that the demand for them as speakers might flow from their official position. For this and other reasons, the Court limited its relief to the class of plaintiffs who sued—lower-ranking federal employees.

461. *See* Public Workers v. Mitchell, 330 U.S. 75 (1947).

462. 543 U.S. 77 (2004).

463. *Id.* at 84.

and substantial interests of its own that were compromised by [the officer's] speech,"[464] due to the officer's deliberate attempts to connect his videos with his police work, in ways that injured the police department.

In 1996, the Court extended the First Amendment protection enjoyed by government employees to independent contractors.[465] The plaintiff in *Board of Commissioners v. Umbehr*,[466] an independent contractor, alleged that a county board of commissioners terminated his contract with the county as retaliation for his for open and extensive criticism of the board. Writing for a 7–2 majority, Justice O'Connor noted that government employees and independent contractors were similarly situated in receiving financial benefits. Moreover, fear of losing these benefits might prevent them from speaking, even when they have intimate knowledge about "matters of public concern."[467]

Rather than entirely reject a cause of action for independent contractors, the Court found that *Pickering*'s balancing test could be applied to "accommodate the differences between employees and independent contractors."[468] The Court located independent contractors somewhere between employees and persons having more remote relationships with the government, such as claimants of tax exemptions or small government subsidies. These latter categories of people resemble ordinary citizens whose views cannot be repressed. On remand, the Court held that the plaintiff "must show that the termination of his contract was motivated by his speech on a matter of public concern." If he made that showing, then the Board would have to show that they "would have terminated the contract regardless of his speech," or that "the County's legitimate interests as contractor, deferentially viewed, outweigh the free speech interests at stake."[469] The Court did not address the possibility of suits by bidders or applicants for new government contracts, who lack the existing relationship with government that incumbent contractors have.[470]

[ii] Patronage-Based Claims

"Patronage" is the word used to describe a system of government in which a high-ranking government official installs political loyalists in subordinate government positions. At the federal level, the patronage system dated at least to the Jefferson Administration, became particularly prominent beginning with the administration

---

464. *Id.* at 81.

465. The Court extended this protection both to contractors' claims based on their speech and to claims based on their partisan affiliation. The latter, "patronage"-based type of First Amendment claim is discussed in the next sub-section.

466. 518 U.S. 668, 670 (1996).

467. *Id.* at 676.

468. *Id.* at 678.

469. *Id.* at 685.

470. Justice Scalia dissented, joined by Justice Thomas, and filed the same dissenting opinion in *Umbehr* as in *O'Hare Truck Services v. City of Northlake*, 518 U.S. 712 (1996), a case decided the same day that extended to contractors the First Amendment protection government employees enjoyed against patronage-based dismissals. *O'Hare Truck* is discussed in the next sub-section.

of Andrew Jackson, and began to decay when Congress enacted the civil service system after the Civil War. But state level patronage arrangements have lingered.[471] In the last half-century the Court has begun to find those systems to violate the free speech rights of government officers who find themselves on the opposite side of the political fence from their higher-level supervisors.

In the first of these cases, *Elrod v. Burns*,[472] the Court struck down patronage dismissals of government employees who did not occupy policymaking positions. The plaintiffs in *Elrod* were employees of a sheriff's office who were Republicans, and who were discharged when a Democrat was elected sheriff. Writing for three justices, Justice Brennan noted the impairment on political association rights that flowed from conditioning continued government employment on the employee associating himself with the party that controlled the management of that office. Turning to the government interests furthered by a patronage system, the plurality acknowledged that having lower-ranking employees of the same political persuasion as the elected official helped prevent disgruntled employees from obstructing the policies the newly-elected official sought to implement, thus undermining the democratic majority's decision to embrace the successful candidate's policies. However, the Court concluded that this interest could be served by limiting patronage dismissals to employees who held policymaking positions.

Justice Stewart, joined by Justice Blackmun, concurred in the judgment and thus created a majority for the decision in favor of the plaintiffs. But he spoke narrowly, identifying the sole issue in the case as "whether a nonpolicymaking, nonconfidential government employee can be discharged or threatened with discharge from a job that he is satisfactorily performing upon the sole ground of his political beliefs." He continued: "I agree with the plurality that he cannot,"[473] but he explicitly refrained from suggesting anything broader about the constitutionality of patronage systems.

Justice Powell, joined by Chief Justice Burger and Justice Rehnquist, dissented. He argued that patronage systems stimulated democracy by helping build strong and cohesive political parties and stimulating interest in campaigns for otherwise-obscure elective offices. He argued that these beneficial effects, reflected in American history, outweighed what he considered to be the relatively minimal First Amendment interests asserted by the plaintiffs. Chief Justice Burger also wrote a short separate dissent, to complain about what he considered to be the Court's unwarranted intrusion into state government prerogatives.[474]

Four years later, in *Branti v. Finkel*,[475] the Court applied *Elrod* to strike down a threatened dismissal of Republican assistant public defenders when a Democrat was chosen public defender by the county legislature, which had shifted from Republican

---

471. *See* Elrod v. Burns, 427 U.S. 347, 353–54 (1976) (explaining the patronage system and tracing its history in the United States).

472. 427 U.S. 347 (1976).

473. *Id.* at 375 (Stewart, J., concurring in the judgment).

474. Justice Stevens did not participate in the decision in *Elrod*.

475. 445 U.S. 507 (1980).

to Democratic control. Writing for a six-justice majority, Justice Stevens wrote that the question was not whether the discharged officer held a policymaking or confidential position, but instead whether political affiliation was an appropriate criterion for the effective performance of the office's duties. Justice Stevens provided an example of his standard in application: executive assistants to a governor—those who, for example, write his speeches or explain his views to the public—can be selected based on political affiliation, but football coaches may not. He then concluded that the job of public defenders—to defend indigent defendants—did not require for its effective performance that occupants of the job have the same political orientation as the head of the office.

Justice Powell, joined by Justice Rehnquist, dissented, complaining that the Court had taken yet another step on the path of dismantling the longstanding American system of patronage. In a part of his opinion joined as well by Justice Stewart, he complained that the majority's standard was too vague. In a part joined only by Justice Rehnquist, Justice Powell largely repeated his arguments from his dissenting opinion in *Elrod*. Justice Stewart wrote a dissent only for himself, arguing that a position as a lawyer required a degree of confidential relationship with the supervising attorney (here, the politically-selected public defender) that justified patronage removals of assistant public defenders.[476]

In *O'Hare Truck Service v. City of Northlake*,[477] the Court extended the patronage line of cases beyond government employees, to also protect independent contractors who contract with the government. (The Court decided that case the same day as *Board of Commissioners v. Umbehr*,[478] which similarly extended the *Pickering* line of employee speech cases to contractors.) The plaintiff in *O'Hare Truck*, a towing service, was removed from the defendant's list of available towing companies shortly after its owner had refused to contribute to the Mayor's reelection campaign and instead openly supported the Mayor's opponent. Writing for a seven-justice majority, Justice Kennedy applied *Elrod* and *Branti* to contractors. Because the government simply asserted an interest in having absolute discretion to terminate contracting relationships for any reason, including patronage-based reasons, and because the Court found contractors to have a First Amendment interest in being free of such dismissals, the Court ruled in favor of the contractor's First Amendment rights.

Despite deciding *O'Hare Truck* and *Umbehr* the same day, the Court in *O'Hare Truck* distinguished between cases that turned on the *political affiliation* of the harmed employee or contractor (that is, *patronage* cases), and cases that turned on the *speech* the employee made, and which were governed by the *Pickering* balancing described in the prior sub-section. But it also noted that some cases would combine claims of patronage-based disfavoring and speech-based disfavoring, in which case *Pickering*-

---

476. In *Rutan v. Republican Party*, the Court extended *Branti* to hold that party patronage practices may not affect "promotion, transfer, recall and hiring decisions involving low-level public employees." 497 U.S. 62, 65 (1990).
477. 518 U.S. 712 (1996).
478. 518 U.S. 668 (1996).

type balancing would become inevitable. Indeed, the Court acknowledged that the patronage cases themselves required some balancing, since those cases instructed courts to determine whether it was reasonable for the government to conclude that political affiliation was an appropriate requirement for effective performance of the task.

Despite protecting contractors from patronage-based removals, the Court concluded that the Constitution allows government much discretion in awarding contracts for goods and services. For example, economic factors may lead government to keep certain contractors or to exchange others for new ones without undertaking "the costs and complexities of competitive bidding." So long as the rationale was not pretextual, government might continue with a contractor to "maintain stability, reward good performance, deal with known and reliable persons, or ensure the uninterrupted supply of goods and services." Alternatively, government might switch contractors "to stimulate competition, encourage experimentation with new contractors, or avoid the appearance of favoritism." Governments can terminate a contractor for reasons other than political affiliation — such as unreliability — or when "political 'affiliation is an appropriate requirement for the effective performance' of the task in question."[479]

Justice Scalia dissented, joined by Justice Thomas, and filed the same dissenting opinion in *O'Hare Truck* as in *Umbehr*. Justice Scalia maintained that using patronage to award government contracts should be upheld, as it was a practice not specifically prohibited by the Bill of Rights and an "open, widespread and unchallenged"[480] tradition dating back to the beginning of the Nation. He also criticized the Court's explanation of how lower courts should approach cases where the contractor alleged both patronage- and speech-based reasons for being dropped as a contractor, arguing that it left lower courts with incoherent guidance.

§ 11.03 Government and the Press: Print and Electronic Media

While freedom of speech and of the press are each explicitly specified in the First Amendment, the cases in this Chapter indicate that the Court treats both of these freedoms in much the same way. Still, certain doctrines in First Amendment jurisprudence have particular applicability to the press. Moreover, the special characteristics of various electronic media have at times generated unique rules based on those characteristics. This section considers several situations where the Court has considered the special problems of the press and the media more generally. It begins with a foundational question: should there be special protections for the press?

---

479. *O'Hare Truck,* 518 U.S at 725 (quoting *Branti,* 445 U.S. at 518).
480. *O'Hare,* 518 U.S. at 726 (Scalia, J., dissenting).

[1] Special Protections for the Press?

The First Amendment, in addition to protecting the freedom of speech and assembly, also protects the freedom of the press. An ongoing debate in First Amendment jurisprudence considers whether the Press Clause requires, or perhaps allows, special protections for the press. On one side of the debate are those who argue that the Press Clause would be a nullity if there were no differences between the freedoms all persons enjoy under the Speech Clause and the special protections enjoyed by those invoking the Press Clause. Persons on this side of the debate often cite the special structural role the press plays in providing information about the government and allowing Americans to exercise effectively their power to dictate public policy.[481]

The other side of this debate raises objections that combine history and practicality. Scholars have argued that, historically, the rights of a free press belonged to everyone who had access to a printing press.[482] In light of the broad protections now provided by the Speech Clause, this argument means that the protections of the Speech Clause have largely subsumed any Press Clause-based protections that turn on the identity of the speaker as a member of something called "the press."

Adding practical concerns to those historical ones, persons opposing special protections for the press raise serious questions about how the press is to be defined. These questions arise in a variety of contexts. Within the realm of issues related to the press itself, for example, these questions arise when claims are made that journalists enjoy special privileges to resist having to testify before grand juries, if the testimony would require them to divulge confidential sources.[483] But it also arises in other regulatory areas. For example, in the campaign finance context, justices have sometimes expressed doubts about the constitutionality of limitations on expenditures related to political expression because such limits would seem to severely limit the ability of the press to spend money reporting on politics.[484]

The Court has never conclusively answered this question. However, its doubts about the practicality of defining "the press" for purposes of special Press Clause protection suggest that, as a general matter, the press, however defined, does not enjoy special rights or immunities. Nevertheless, when faced with a plaintiff (or defendant)

---

481. A notable statement of this position was provided by Justice Potter Stewart, in his article, *Or of the Press*, 26 Hastings L.J. 631 (1975).

482. *See, e.g.*, Eugene Volokh, *Freedom of the Press as an Industry, or for the Press as a Technology? From the Framing to Today*, 160 U. Penn. L. Rev. 459 (2012).

483. *See* Branzburg v. Hayes, 408 U.S. 665, 703–04 (1972) ("The administration of a constitutional newsman's privilege would present practical and conceptual difficulties of a high order. Sooner or later, it would be necessary to define those categories of newsmen who qualified for the privilege, a questionable procedure in light of the traditional doctrine that liberty of the press is the right of the lonely pamphleteer who uses carbon paper or a mimeograph just as much as of the large metropolitan publisher who utilizes the latest photocomposition methods."). The issue of whether the Constitution recognizes such a privilege is considered later in this chapter, in Section 11.03[5].

484. *See, e.g.*, Citizens United v. FEC, 558 U.S. 310, 351–52 (2010) (noting that the law under review exempted "the institutional press" but also noting that the rationale offered for the law could also justify restrictions on press coverage of political campaigns).

who is easily understandable as a member of "the press" or a case that appears to implicate the press, however defined, the Court sometimes relies on the Press Clause.

[2] Taxation of the Press

A basic First Amendment limit on government regulation of the press involves taxation. On the one hand, discriminatory taxation of press entities raises the risk of government punishing the press for speaking in ways that displease it. On the other hand, like any business, press entities are appropriately subject to taxation. The cases in this area have attempted to draw a line recognizing these two realities, although at times it has disagreed on the application of these principles.

The foundational case in this line dates from 1936. In *Grosjean v. American Press Co.*,[485] the Court struck down a tax Louisiana had imposed on newspapers with circulations of more than 20,000 copies. The Court explained that such a targeted tax exceeded the state's legitimate power to impose generally-applicable taxes on newspapers and other press outlets, especially given its focus on high-circulation newspapers. Nevertheless, the Court was not clear about the line between permissible and unconstitutional taxation of press entities.

Nearly fifty years later, the Court clarified its understanding of *Grosjean* in *Minneapolis Star and Tribune v. Minnesota Commissioner of Revenue.*[486] In *Minneapolis Star*, the Court held that Minnesota's imposition of a special tax on newspapers violated the First Amendment. While Minnesota exempted newspapers and other periodicals from its general sales and use taxes, it imposed a use tax on the cost of the paper and ink they used. The tax, however, exempted the first $100,000 spent for those supplies. As the *Star and Tribune* newspaper had the largest circulation of all Minnesota papers, it paid nearly two-thirds of the total amount collected under this tax.

Writing for the majority, Justice O'Connor concluded that *Grosjean* appropriately rested on the fact, well-known to the parties and the Court in 1936, that the Louisiana tax was targeted at the enemies of the sitting governor. The Court in *Minneapolis Star* found no such nefarious intent in the case before it. Nevertheless, the Court held that a tax singling out the press for special treatment still had to be "necessary to achieve an overriding government interest."[487] Moreover, despite the lack of any bad legislative intent, the Minnesota tax still singled out those newspapers that used more than $100,000 worth of paper and ink per year—a very small percentage of Minnesota newspapers. The Court viewed such a narrowly focused tax as having great potential for abuse. No interest that Minnesota proposed justified such a risk.

In his dissenting opinion, Justice Rehnquist noted that the newspaper would have paid three times more taxes had it been subject to Minnesota's generally-applicable

---

485. 297 U.S. 233 (1936).
486. 460 U.S. 575 (1983).
487. *Id.* at 582.

taxes. He and Justice White, who concurred only in the judgment, would have upheld special taxes on the press that did not impose a greater burden on them then the generally-applicable ones for which they substituted.[488]

In *Arkansas Writers' Project v. Ragland*,[489] the Court invalidated an Arkansas sales tax that taxed "general interest" magazines but exempted newspapers and religious, professional, trade, and sports journals. Given the law's content-discrimination in the imposition of a tax burden, a majority of seven justices, speaking through Justice Marshall, held that the law failed strict scrutiny.[490] By contrast, in *Leathers v. Medlock*,[491] the Court upheld the application of an Arkansas state sales tax to cable television, even though the tax exempted certain newspaper and magazine sales. The statute as originally written did not mention cable or satellite television. The legislature subsequently amended the sales tax to include cable, but exempted satellite broadcast service in addition to the pre-existing exemptions enjoyed by newspapers and magazine sales. The Supreme Court upheld both versions of the tax. Distinguishing *Grosjean*, *Minneapolis Star*, and *Arkansas Writers'*, the Court, speaking through Justice O'Connor, emphasized that the challenged tax was a broad-based, generally applicable, content-neutral tax not confined to a narrow group and including a large number of diverse cable operators. She concluded that the First Amendment prohibited differential taxation of speakers including press sources only if the tax was "directed at, or presents the danger of suppressing particular ideas."[492]

Justice Marshall dissented in *Leathers*, joined by Justice Blackmun. Justice Marshall concluded that this case was indistinguishable from the ink and paper tax struck down in *Minneapolis Star*. He conceded that *Minneapolis Star* involved discrimination between different sources of the same media, while this case involved differential taxation of different types of press outlets. Nevertheless, echoing the concern in *Minneapolis Star* about the potential for abuse differential tax regimes raise, he wrote: "Because cable competes with members of the print and electronic media in the larger information market, the power to discriminate between these media triggers the central concern underlying the nondiscrimination principle: the risk of covert censor-

---

488. Only Justice Rehnquist would have upheld the $100,000 exclusion that discriminated among Minnesota press sources. Justice White concurred in the judgment, basing his decision on the tax's targeted impact on just a few newspapers. He would not have gone farther than that in striking the law down, and he criticized the Court for casting doubt on the fact that Minnesota chose to tax newspapers via a paper and ink tax rather than a general sales tax.

489. 481 U.S. 221 (1987).

490. Justice Stevens joined all of the Court's opinion except for the proposition that all content-based laws are necessarily unconstitutional. But he nevertheless agreed that strict scrutiny was the appropriate standard to apply in this case, and that the Arkansas law failed it. *Id.* at 234 (Stevens, J., concurring in part and concurring in the judgment). Justice Scalia, joined by Chief Justice Rehnquist, dissented, focusing on the fact that the law in question was a subsidy rather than a direct government regulation. He concluded that the Court had not persuasively distinguished the Arkansas subsidy law from other subsidies that he believed were "unquestionably lawful." *Id.* at 235 (Scalia, J., dissenting).

491. 499 U.S. 439 (1991).

492. *Id.* at 453.

ship."[493] Justice Marshall also noted that the only reason the state offered for discriminating among media was raising revenue, a rationale that usually did not allow discrimination in the free speech area. He argued that discriminating against cable impacted the types of ideas disseminated because cable television often includes ideas that do not appear elsewhere.

[3] The Right to Report on Government Activity

Prior restraints—that is, government orders not to speak—were discussed in a prior sub-section of this Chapter.[494] A particular type of prior restraint that often affects the press in particular takes the form of court orders mandating restrictions on the dissemination of information acquired in criminal or other government investigations. Such orders are issued either to ensure a criminal defendant a fair trial by preventing the potential tainting of the jury pool or to protect the confidentiality or integrity of a government proceeding. Like all prior restraints, these orders come with a heavy presumption against their validity.

A seminal case of this sort is *Nebraska Press Association v. Stuart*.[495] *Nebraska Press* arose out of a sensational mass murder in a small community. Soon after the police apprehended a suspect, the prosecution and defense counsel joined in asking the county court to enter an order restricting news coverage, because widespread coverage would make it very difficult to empanel an impartial jury and ensure a fair trial. The trial judge issued an order aimed at several press outlets and individual reporters. As modified by the Nebraska Supreme Court, the order prohibited reporting "(a) the existence and nature of any confessions or admissions made by the defendant to law enforcement officers, (b) any confessions or admissions made to any third parties, except members of the press, and (c) other facts strongly implicative of the accused."[496]

Writing for the Court, Chief Justice Burger noted that in these rare sensational cases, a tension arises between strong presumption against prior restraints and the Sixth Amendment's guarantee of trial by an impartial jury. The Court refused to resolve it simply by according one right priority over the other; however, the Chief Justice also insisted that these two rights seldom conflict in typical criminal cases that receive little or no publicity. While the trial in *Nebraska Press* was not a typical criminal trial, the Court observed that the prior restraint in the case extended to a prohibition on publishing information that was disclosed in open court. The Court held that prohibition invalid, finding that the press had a right to report on what transpires in open court. As for the order's prohibition on publishing other, still-private, information, the Court concluded that other mechanisms for ensuring a fair trial, such as jury sequestration and carefully questioning of prospective jurors,

---

493. *Id.* at 458 (Marshall, J., dissenting).
494. *See* Section 11.02[1].
495. 427 U.S. 539 (1976).
496. *Id.* at 545.

would serve to protect the defendant's right. Thus, the Court struck down that part of the order as well.

Interestingly, in making that decision, Chief Justice Burger invoked the often-criticized plurality opinion in *Dennis v. United States*,[497] asking whether "'the gravity of the evil discounted by its improbability, justifies such invasion of free speech as is necessary to avoid the danger.'"[498] Rendering this loose balancing test more stringent, the *Nebraska Press* Court took into account the following factors in applying it: "(a) the nature and extent of pretrial news coverage; (b) whether other measures would be likely to mitigate the effects of unrestrained pretrial publicity; and (c) how effectively a restraining order would operate to prevent the threatened danger. The precise terms of the restraining order are also important."[499] The Court's application of this guidance demonstrated the difficulty of crafting a pretrial gag order that would satisfy constitutional requirements. The trial judge only found that pretrial publicity "could impinge" on a fair trial.[500] Moreover, the record contained little evidence that the lower courts considered the availability of alternative measures to secure a fair trial. Questioning the efficacy of the trial court's order, Chief Justice Burger also noted that the trial court lacked the jurisdictional authority to restrain publication in another state. At bottom, the Court concluded that the record did not clearly establish that additional publicity would make it impossible to find twelve jurors who would follow instructions to decide the case based on the evidence presented in court. The speculative findings made by the trial court did not rise to the level of certainty required to issue a prior restraint.

While there were no dissenters to the Chief Justice's opinion, six justices concurred in four separate opinions. Justices White and Powell joined the majority opinion but each wrote a separate concurrence. Justice White expressed considerable doubt that a gag order would ever be constitutional. Justice Powell would allow a pretrial gag order to issue only if it was necessary to prevent the dissemination of prejudicial publicity that otherwise poses a high likelihood of preventing, directly and irreparably, the impaneling of a jury meeting the Sixth Amendment requirement of impartiality. This required a showing that (i) there be a clear threat to the fairness of trial, (ii) such a threat is posed by the actual publicity to be restrained, and (iii) no less restrictive alternatives are available.[501]

Justice Powell's standard is quite important, as the remaining four justices did not join the majority opinion but only concurred in the judgment. Specifically, Justices

---

497. 341 U.S. 494 (1951). *Dennis*, which dealt with First Amendment challenges to laws aimed at speech that sought to incite violent revolution, is discussed in Section 11.01[2][a].

498. *Nebraska Press*, 427 U.S. at 562 (quoting United States v. Dennis, 183 F.2d 201, 212 (2d Cir. 1950), *aff'd*, 341 U.S. 494 (1951)). The Court quoted from the appellate opinion in *Dennis*, but the Supreme Court in *Dennis* adopted the same test.

499. *Nebraska Press*, 427 U.S. at 562.

500. *Id.* at 563. Indeed, the Chief Justice noted that rumors circulating around the town of 850 could have prejudiced the trial more than the press reports. *See id.* at 567.

501. *See id.* at 571 (Powell, J., concurring).

Brennan, Stewart, Marshall, and Stevens all expressed substantial doubt that such a gag order would ever pass constitutional muster. Consequently, Justice Powell's standard—which appears to be more stringent than the standard set forth in the Chief Justice's majority opinion—may represent the minimum test that must be met for a gag order to issue.[502] Indeed, not even this standard may support a gag order, as five justices (when one includes Justice White) expressed varying degrees of doubt that they would ever allow a pretrial gag order.

Other prior restraint on publication cases focus on government attempts to prevent the publication of the names of juveniles or victims of particular types of crimes, especially rape. One year after *Nebraska Press*, the Court invalidated a trial court order prohibiting publication of information identifying a juvenile defendant, issued after a hearing that was open to the public and at which the juvenile's name was disclosed.[503] The Court reasoned that *Nebraska Press*, among other cases, mandated invalidating the order. Two years later, in *Smith v. Daily Mail Publishing Co.*,[504] the Court invalidated a West Virginia statute that prohibited newspaper publication of the name of a person charged as a juvenile offender without the written approval of the juvenile court. The Court in that case stated that it did not matter whether the law was understood as a prior restraint or a subsequent punishment; even under the latter understanding, it explained, government could not prohibit the publication of legally-acquired information "absent a need to further a state interest of the highest order."[505] A year before *Nebraska Press*, in *Cox Communications Corp. v. Cohn*,[506] the Court held unconstitutional a common law privacy action against a television station for broadcasting the name of a rape/murder victim that the station had learned from publicly-available court records. *Florida Star v. B.J.F.*[507] reinforces this point. That case disallowed a privacy cause of action for publishing the name of a rape victim the press obtained legally due to a police error.

When combined with the more general prior restraint cases the Court has decided,[508] this set of cases, most of which were decided within a few years of each other, illustrates the force of the presumption against prior restraints. Conversely, they also reflect the strength of the press's right to disseminate even sensitive information about criminal proceedings, defendants, and victims, at least if that information is acquired legally, without fear of either prior restraint or subsequent punishment.

[4] The Right to Access Government Activity

Affording a right to publish news about governmental and judicial proceedings is different from affording access to those proceedings. To be published, information

---

502. *See supra.* note 288 (setting forth the rule for determining the holding in a case featuring a fractured Court).

503. Oklahoma Pub. Co. v. District Court, 430 U.S. 308 (1977).

504. 443 U.S. 97 (1979).

505. *Id.* at 103.

506. 420 U.S. 469 (1975).

507. 491 U.S. 524 (1989).

508. Those other cases are discussed in Section 11.02[1].

must first be acquired. The issues of access focus on a point in the information stream that is prior to publication. While government can rarely impose a prior restraint to stop the dissemination of information already known,[509] government can block the flow of information at an earlier stage by denying public access to its activities. As a general matter, there is no unlimited First Amendment right to gather information.[510]

In *Houchins v. KQED, Inc.*,[511] a public television station sued when it was denied permission to inspect and take pictures in a prison facility. Although no formal policy regarding public access to the jail existed at the time of the suit, the sheriff reported that a program for access was being implemented at the time the suit was filed. As finalized, that program limited tours to 25 persons and did not allow cameras, tape recorders, or inmate interviews. The station argued that those restrictions were too stringent to permit it to do its journalistic work.

A majority of a seven-justice Court upheld the denial of the station's requested access. Writing for a plurality of three, Chief Justice Burger said that access to the prison was a legislative rather than a judicial question, because the Constitution did not require government to grant access to government information within its control. Moreover, once the government did afford access, it did not have to grant any greater right of access to the press than to the general public. Concurring in the judgment, Justice Stewart agreed that the Constitution did not guarantee a right of access to government institutions. Although he agreed that the press had no greater right of access than that the government chose to grant the general public, Justice Stewart suggested, somewhat obliquely, that a truly equal right for the press required that they be able to bring equipment necessary for effective reporting, including television cameras and sound equipment. Three dissenting Justices would have required a far broader right of general media and public access. While the dissenters recognized the necessity of keeping some governmental affairs secret, they construed the First Amendment to afford a broad right of access to governmental information.

In contrast to *Houchins'* refusal to find a constitutional right to access prisons and jails, *Richmond Newspapers, Inc. v. Virginia*[512] established a right of access to judicial

---

509. *See* Sections 11.02[1] and 11.03[3].

510. *See, e.g.,* Zemel v. Rusk, 381 U.S. 1, 17 (1965) ("The right to speak and publish does not carry with it the unrestrained right to gather information."). To be sure, the plaintiff in *Zemel* did not identify himself as a member of the press. Moreover, the information he sought — about conditions in a foreign country that he was not allowed to visit due to federally-imposed travel restrictions — did not implicate any government duty to open up its own decision-making processes. *But see id.* at 16–17 ("There are few restrictions on action which could not be clothed by ingenious argument in the garb of decreased data flow. For example, the prohibition of unauthorized entry into the White House diminishes the citizen's opportunities to gather information he might find relevant to his opinion of the way the country is being run, but that does not make entry into the White House a First Amendment right.").

511. 438 U.S. 1 (1978).

512. 448 U.S. 555 (1980).

proceedings.[513] In *Richmond Newspapers*, a murder defendant's trial had ended in a mistrial three times, at least one of which was caused by pretrial publicity. The defendant moved to close his fourth trial to the public. The prosecutor had no objection, and the judge ordered the closure. Members of the press sought to vacate the order. As the defendant wanted the trial closed, the case did not implicate a defendant's Sixth Amendment right to a public trial, thus posing the First Amendment issue squarely.

Eight justices concluded that the First Amendment requires a right of access to criminal trials. Chief Justice Burger, writing for three justices, stressed that the access right was supported by the long tradition of open criminal trials. Justice Brennan, writing for himself and Justice Marshall, concurred in the judgment, relying also on that historical tradition as well as the functional importance of press access to the criminal process as providing the public the means of ensuring the fair administration of justice. Citing *Houchins* among other cases, Justice Brennan explained that "our decisions must ... be understood as holding only that any privilege of access to governmental information is subject to a degree of restraint dictated by the nature of the information and countervailing interests in security or confidentiality."[514] Several other justices wrote concurring opinions. Justice Rehnquist dissented.

How can *Richmond Newspapers* be reconciled with *Houchins*? The answer may rest in the history of public trials, which contrasts sharply with the history of closed prisons. On the other hand, Justice Brennan's analysis added into the mix a consideration of both the public interest in accessing the information and the government's interest in restricting access. However the analysis is performed, the language and results of the cases point toward opening court proceedings while allowing legislative and executive proceedings to remain closed.[515]

Since *Richmond Newspapers*, the Court has extended the right of access to many trial and pretrial proceedings. In *Chandler v. Florida*,[516] the Court found that the Sixth Amendment was not violated by a Florida rule allowing the televising of criminal trials over the defendant's objection. In *Globe Newspapers Co. v. Superior Court*,[517] the Court struck down a Massachusetts statute that made closure of a trial mandatory during the testimony of a rape victim under 18 years old. In *Press-Enterprise Co. v. Superior Court (Press Enterprise I)*,[518] the Court unanimously extended the holding

---

513. This access right has been understood to apply equally to the press and the public more generally. *See id.* at 558 ("The narrow question presented in this case is whether the right of the public and press to attend criminal trials is guaranteed under the United States Constitution.").

514. *Id.* at 586 (Brennan, J., concurring in the judgment).

515. Congress has afforded considerable access to information possessed by federal agencies in the Freedom of Information Act, 5 U.S.C. § 552 (1982). States have likewise enacted state-level analogues to the federal statute.

516. 449 U.S. 560 (1981).

517. 457 U.S. 596 (1982).

518. 464 U.S. 501 (1984).

in *Richmond Newspapers* to the *voir dire* process. As in *Richmond Newspapers*, the Court in *Press-Enterprise I* closely examined the history of the *voir dire* process and determined that it had been a public process since at least the sixteenth century. It further found that an order excluding the press from a *voir dire* in a rape-murder case was not narrowly tailored to serve an overriding government interest.

In *Press-Enterprise Co. v. Superior Court* (*Press Enterprise II*), the Court required access to preliminary hearings in California criminal cases unless "closure is essential to preserve higher values and is narrowly tailored to serve that interest."[519] The Court, speaking through Chief Justice Burger, explained that judicial access questions have been answered by examining both the history of public access to the proceeding in question and the degree to which such access assists in the functioning of that proceeding. Applying those principles, the Court noted the traditional openness of California preliminary hearings. It also noted their similarity to trials, which earlier cases had already identified as proceedings where public access assisted in their functioning by making them publicly accountable.[520]

[5] Protection for the Newsgathering Process

While the previous sub-section focuses on access to governmental proceedings and locations, this sub-section focuses on the news-gathering process. Instead of access to information, this sub-section treats the protection of information already gathered. Along an information continuum, then, this section focuses on protecting the sources of information that have already been obtained. Of course, the protection of sources has important implications for obtaining the information in the first place. Without anonymity, many sources simply will not talk to journalists.

This issue was squarely presented in *Branzburg v. Hayes*.[521] *Branzburg* presented the Court with four different cases in which reporters refused to reveal their sources to a grand jury. In each case, a reporter, who had personal knowledge of activities being investigated by the grand jury, was subpoenaed to testify about his knowledge. In each case, the reporter asserted a First Amendment privilege to withhold the information.

The Court framed the issue narrowly, noting that the government was not seeking a prior restraint or commanding the press to publish certain information or to alter its content. Instead, as stated by the Court, the issue was simply whether reporters, unlike other citizens, were exempt from having to comply with grand jury subpoenas and respond to questions relevant to a criminal investigation. Writing for a five-justice majority rejecting a First Amendment-based exemption, Justice White noted that the First Amendment did not exempt the press from every incidental burden

---

519. 478 U.S. 1, 9 (1986).

520. The Court has described as an "open question" whether the public's First Amendment right of access to a criminal trial is "coextensive" with a defendant's analogous right under the Sixth Amendment. Presley v. Georgia, 558 U.S. 209, 213 (2010).

521. 408 U.S. 665 (1972).

imposed by generally applicable civil and criminal statutes. For example, the press could be excluded from grand jury proceedings, Supreme Court conferences, and meetings of officials from the Executive branch and of private organizations. Moreover, the historical evidence demonstrated that the media had never enjoyed a privilege to keep confidential information from a grand jury. The Court found that the important workings of the grand jury outweighed any uncertain burden the obligation to testify imposed on the news-gathering process. While fear of identification in a grand jury investigation could deter some sources, the Court noted that the press had flourished for many years without such a constitutional privilege.

Justice White also listed several difficulties that would impede fashioning any such privilege. Most notably, he mentioned, first, the difficulty of defining who was a newsperson qualifying for the privilege. Second, he observed that a contrary rule would mean that every grand jury subpoena of a privileged newsperson would require courts to make preliminary determinations regarding the justifiability of an exception to the privilege. Justice White also enumerated several protections the press retained even after rejection of its constitutional privilege claim. First, the press could try to persuade Congress, state legislators, or state courts (under state law) to grant a reporter's privilege.[522] Second, the press could write about any unfairness it perceived in the government's subpoena. Third, if the press could prove bad faith or harassment by prosecutors or the grand jury, courts could issue protective orders. Fourth, individual reporters could assert their Fifth Amendment protection against self-incrimination.

Concurring, Justice Powell stressed that although no express privilege was granted, a reporter could not be required to disclose information that was only remotely or tenuously relevant to the grand jury investigation or that revealed confidential sources without a legitimate law enforcement need. Justice Powell's opinion thus appeared to be somewhat more protective than Justice White's, although he joined Justice White's opinion. His ambiguous concurrence is significant, because Justice Powell provided the fifth vote for Justice White's majority.[523]

Justice Stewart, joined by Justices Brennan and Marshall, dissented. He maintained that a right to publish necessitated a right to gather news, which in turn necessitated a right to protect the confidentiality of sources. He argued for a rule under which, before the government could compel a reporter to reveal confidential information before a grand jury, it "must (1) show that there is probable cause to believe that the newsman has information that is clearly relevant to a specific probable violation of law; (2) demonstrate that the information sought cannot be obtained by alternative means less destructive of First Amendment rights; and (3) demonstrate a compelling and overriding interest in the information."[524] Justice Stewart pointed out that law enforcement officials were not the only ones who needed the information at issue in

---

522. Many jurisdictions have enacted such shield laws.

523. Indeed, Justice Stewart later described *Branzburg* as having been decided by a vote of four-and-a-half to four-and-a-half. Potter Stewart, *"Or of the Press,"* 26 HASTINGS L.J. 631, 635 (1975).

524. 408 U.S. at 743 (Stewart, J., dissenting).

Branzburg and cases like it. If sources of such information dried up for fear of exposure, members of society would lack the information to make decisions on these important issues. Dissenting separately, Justice Douglas contended that a newsperson had an absolute right not to respond to a grand jury subpoena or at least to refuse to answer certain questions. He predicted that the Court's opinion would deter potential sources from communicating with reporters.

Since *Branzburg*, the Court has continued to refuse to accord special immunities to newsgathering activities. In *Zurcher v. Stanford Daily*,[525] the Court sustained a warrant to search a college newspaper office, which the police obtained after demonstrating probable cause that it contained photographs taken by the newspaper that could identify demonstrators who had assaulted police. The police searched the newspaper's darkrooms, filing cabinets, and waste baskets, but not locked drawers or rooms. The search afforded the opportunity to read notes and correspondence.

The Court, speaking through Justice White, held that the Fourth Amendment afforded the press no special treatment concerning search warrants. He did, however, require that the Fourth Amendment be applied with "scrupulous exactitude," with the materials in question defined carefully, when the material in question may be protected by the First Amendment. When presumptively protected materials were sought, Justice White wrote, "the warrant requirement should be administered to leave as little as possible to the discretion or whim of the officer in the field."[526]

Similarly, the Court has upheld a state law promissory estoppel action by a confidential source against a newspaper for breaching its promise of confidentiality and identifying the source. Writing again for the Court, Justice Write explained in *Cohen v. Cowles Media Co.* that the press must comply with generally applicable laws that have an incidental effect on newsgathering and reporting.[527] Dissenting, Justice Blackmun said that the burden on free speech was not incidental, because the publication of important political speech was involved. Justice Souter also dissented, stressing the public's interest in the information but suggesting that he might permit a promissory estoppel action by a private individual. (The confidential source in *Cohen* was a person associated with a gubernatorial campaign.)

---

525. 436 U.S. 547 (1978).

526. *Id.* at 564. The Privacy Protection Act of 1980, Pub. L. No. 96-440, 94 Stat. 1879, affords by statute much of the protection the *Zurcher* decision refused to extend under the Constitution. The statute severely limits the use of search warrants to obtain material possessed by the media, requiring law enforcement officials to rely primarily on subpoenas. For more information on the Act, see Elizabeth B. Uzelac, *Reviving the Privacy Protection Act of 1980*, 107 Nw. L. Rev. 1437 (2013).

527. *See* 501 U.S. 663, 669 (1991) ("The press, like others interested in publishing, may not publish copyrighted material without obeying the copyright laws. See Zacchini v. Scripps-Howard Broadcasting Co., 433 U.S. 562 (1977). Similarly, the media must obey the National Labor Relations Act, Associated Press v. NLRB, 301 U.S. 103 (1937), and the Fair Labor Standards Act, Oklahoma Press Publishing Co. v. Walling, 327 U.S. 186 (1946); may not restrain trade in violation of the antitrust laws, Associated Press v. United States, 326 U.S. 1 (1945); Citizen Publishing Co. v. United States, 394 U.S. 131 (1969); and must pay non-discriminatory taxes, Murdock v. Pennsylvania, 319 U.S. 105 (1943); Minneapolis Star & Tribune Co. v. Minnesota Comm'r of Revenue, 460 U.S. 575 (1983).").

[6] Mandated Access to the Media

The cases in this sub-section deal with public access to the means of mass media communication, rather than media and public access to governmental affairs and places. Thus, these materials deal less with direct government restriction of speech and the press and more with government requirements that third parties be allowed to access a person's speech facilities. Of course, that mandated access itself entails regulation of that media outlet and of the speech it is required to make or at least facilitate.

Red Lion Broadcasting Co. v. FCC[528] is an early case of this type. It also stands as one of the few cases in which the Court has promoted a strongly egalitarian view of freedom of speech focusing on the public's right to access the marketplace of ideas. *Red Lion* upheld the Federal Communications Commission's (FCC's) "Fairness Doctrine." The Fairness Doctrine required television and radio broadcasters both to cover important public issues and also "to provide a reasonable opportunity for the presentation of contrasting viewpoints on such issues."[529] While the FCC has since abrogated the Fairness Doctrine as a matter of policy, the constitutional doctrine enunciated in *Red Lion* remains good law.

Red Lion arose when a radio program, discussing a book about a prominent politician, made disparaging statements about the author of the book. The author invoked the Fairness Doctrine and demanded time to reply, which the station refused, relying on the First Amendment. Writing for a unanimous eight-justice Court,[530] Justice White rejected the station's argument. He characterized the broadcast media as a scarce forum in which Congress could stop one voice from drowning out all others. This characterization was underpinned by the fact that the broadcast media use scarce, publicly-owned airwaves which the government allowed the broadcaster to use when it granted the broadcaster its license. The Court observed that this scarcity existed due to the fact that it would be impossible for anyone to communicate via the airwaves if anyone and everyone was allowed to broadcast, because the conflicting signals would interfere with each other. Moreover, even if technological scarcity disappeared, broadcasters that the government had licensed earlier still enjoyed a competitive advantage that others would find difficult to overcome.

For these reasons, the Court found the broadcast spectrum both a technologically and economically scarce resource. Consequently, the Court viewed broadcasting as a privilege rather than a right. It reasoned that, by bestowing a privilege, the government could impose certain duties, such as those in the Fairness Doctrine. Importantly, the Court also grounded that government power in its observation that the First Amendment protected not just the speech rights of the broadcaster forced to

---

528. 395 U.S. 367 (1969).

529. *In re* Rules and Regulations Concerning General Fairness Doctrine Obligations of Broadcast Licensees, 102 F.C.C.2d 143, 146 (1985).

530. Justice Douglas did not participate in *Red Lion*. In the next case discussed in the text, he wrote separately, in part to indicate his disagreement with the Court's decision.

carry a reply it otherwise would have preferred not to carry, but also the rights of the listening public to hear a diverse array of viewpoints. Indeed, the Court in *Red Lion* described listeners' rights as "paramount."[531]

Countering the argument that the Fairness Doctrine fostered diverse views in this scarce marketplace, the broadcaster argued that if airing controversial programming obliged broadcasters to allot no-cost time to speakers whose views they found un-palatable, then self-censorship would severely curtail coverage of controversial public issues. Based on past industry practice, the Court found this argument speculative. It also observed that if such self-censorship occurred, the FCC could simply require broadcasters to cover controversial issues, even though such coverage would trigger a right of reply.

Four years later, the Court displayed a less generous approach to access to the broadcast media. In *Columbia Broadcasting System, Inc. v. Democratic National Com-mittee*,[532] the Court upheld an FCC policy allowing broadcasters to refuse "editorial" advertising—that is, advertising that took a position on public issues. Supporting the Commission's ruling, the Court concluded that the First Amendment did not mandate a private right of access to the broadcast media. Citing *Red Lion*, Chief Justice Burger argued that a private right of paid access to the media would favor those with the wealth to purchase such access. The Chief Justice was also concerned that a broad right of private access would require the FCC to determine which ad-vertisers would enjoy access.

Concurring, Justice Stewart argued that compelling broadcasters to accept adver-tising with which they disagreed violated their First Amendment rights. He laid par-ticular stress on his conclusion that private broadcasters were not government actors, and thus had First Amendments rights to refuse to speak. Also concurring, Justice Douglas said that radio and television have the same First Amendment rights as news-papers. Accordingly, Justice Douglas, who did not participate in *Red Lion*, would have set aside even the Fairness Doctrine.

Justice Brennan dissented, joined by Justice Marshall. Justice Brennan construed *Red Lion* as based on a First Amendment principle valuing the provision to listeners of a wide diversity of views in the broadcast media. He found the Fairness Doctrine inadequate to ensure the debate on diverse views to which the public was constitu-tionally entitled. Justice Brennan complained that the Court permitted broadcasters virtually absolute control over who and what would be covered, how material would be presented, and who would speak.

In an important case from 1974, *Miami Herald Publishing Co. v. Tornillo*,[533] the Court rejected a right of access to the print media. The Court, in a unanimous de-cision, struck down Florida's "right of reply" statute, which required newspapers printing editorials critical of political candidates to publish the candidates' replies at

---

531. 395 U.S. at 390.
532. 412 U.S. 94 (1973).
533. 418 U.S. 241 (1974).

no cost. The candidate defending the statute made arguments similar to the ones that the Court had embraced in *Red Lion*. Citing economic rather than technological scarcity, he focused on the concentration of newspaper ownership, the fact that many cities had only one daily newspaper, and the frequent common ownership of newspapers and television and radio stations in a given market. While the Court was sympathetic to these concerns, Chief Justice Burger's opinion for the Court held the statute unconstitutional, because it forced the newspaper to print material that it would otherwise have refused to print. Consequently, the right exacted economic costs which could deter the publisher from printing what it wished. Just as importantly, the statute also intruded into newspapers' editorial decisions, which included deciding which content to print.

Even though *Tornillo* and *Red Lion* may seem difficult to distinguish, it is noteworthy that *Red Lion* was not mentioned in any of the *Tornillo* opinions.[534] These two cases may reaffirm that the Court sometimes treats the broadcast media and print media differently, without always explaining the reasons for this different treatment. One can speculate that those reasons include the fact that government owns the broadcast spectrum in a way that it does not own a newspaper's printing presses, thus justifying more government regulation of the content of television and radio broadcasts than newspaper content.[535]

Red Lion and *Columbia Broadcasting* dealt with over-the-air broadcasters. Because these cases, and especially *Red Lion*, were largely based on the unique characteristics of broadcasting, government regulation of cable television, not to mention even newer types of media such as Internet-based streaming services, presents different First Amendment issues.

As early as 1986, the Court recognized that cable television operations implicate the First Amendment.[536] But in that same case, three justices explicitly recognized that the unique characteristics of cable television require a First Amendment analysis tailored to those characteristics, on the theory that different media more generally require different First Amendment treatment.[537] Eight years later, in *Turner Broad-*

---

534. Justice Brennan wrote a short concurrence and Justice White wrote a longer one.

535. Justices have at times criticized *Red Lion*'s reasoning. *See* FCC v. Fox Television Stations, 556 U.S. 502, 530 (2009) (Thomas, J., concurring) ("the logical weakness of *Red Lion* ... has been apparent for some time: It is certainly true that broadcast frequencies are scarce but it is unclear why that fact justifies content regulation of broadcasting in a way that would be intolerable if applied to the editorial process of the print media."); Turner Broadcasting v. FCC, 512 U.S. 622, 638 (1994) ("Although courts and commentators have criticized the scarcity rationale since its inception, we have declined to question its continuing validity as support for our broadcast jurisprudence....").

536. *See* City of Los Angeles v. Preferred Communications, 476 U.S. 488, 494 (1986).

537. *See id.* at 496 (Blackmun, J., joined by Marshall and O'Connor, JJ, concurring) ("I join the Court's opinion on the understanding that it leaves open the question of the proper standard for judging First Amendment challenges to a municipality's restriction of access to cable facilities. Different communications media are treated differently for First Amendment purposes. In assessing First Amendment claims concerning cable access, the Court must determine whether the characteristics of cable television make it sufficiently analogous to another medium to warrant application of an already existing standard or whether those characteristics require a new analysis.").

casting System v. FCC ("Turner I"),[538] the Court elaborated on the proper First Amendment analysis applicable to cable television. *Turner I* involved the FCC's "must carry" rules, which require cable operators to carry the signals of local and public television broadcasters, in order to ensure that those broadcasters, which otherwise made their signals available for free via over-the-air transmission, continued to exist by remaining able to draw an audience from cable subscribers.

Writing for the Court, Justice Kennedy concluded that the deferential standard applied in *Red Lion* should not apply to regulations of cable television, because cable television was not marked by the spectrum scarcity and signal interference rationales *Red Lion* relied on. However, because the must-carry rules distinguished based on the manner in which the favored speakers operated (*i.e.*, via over the air broadcasting) rather than the content they provided, the Court concluded that the rules were content-neutral. Thus, the Court held that the rules should be reviewed under the intermediate scrutiny appropriate to government regulation of expressive conduct.

In so holding, the Court distinguished *Tornillo*, on the ground that the characteristics of cable systems were such that the operators of such systems possessed "bottleneck" or "gatekeeper" authority, since the structure of the industry was such that only one cable provider in a given community could reasonably enjoy a franchise given the physical infrastructure needed for cable connectivity. Essentially, the structure of cable television meant that only one cable provider could serve a particular community, while no such institutional impediment prevented a variety of newspapers from simultaneously reaching a given community or household. The Court further distinguished *Tornillo* on the ground that cable operators, unlike newspapers, are generally not assumed to exercise editorial discretion over the content they carry, thus mitigating any First Amendment interest the cable operator might have in resisting the must-carry mandate. A majority of the Court remanded the case to the lower court for factfinding necessary to apply the intermediate scrutiny the Court had called for.[539]

Justice O'Connor dissented, joined by Justices Scalia, Ginsburg, and in substantial part, by Justice Thomas. Justice O'Connor argued that the must-carry provisions expressed content-based preferences for local programming, for educational programming, for news and public affairs programming, and even for diversity of viewpoint. These restraints on the editorial discretion of cable operators had to be justified as means necessary to advance a compelling state interest, which she argued was not satisfied by the government's proffered interest in preserving local broadcast outlets.

---

538. 512 U.S. 622 (1994).

539. The decision to remand was explicitly supported by only four justices. However, Justice Stevens, who would have favored an outright affirmation of the lower court's decision in favor of the rules, concurred in this result in order to create a majority result. *See id.* at 669 (Stevens, J., concurring in part and concurring in the judgment). In *Turner Broadcasting System v. FCC*, 520 U.S. 180 (1997) ("*Turner II*"), the Court held that the must-carry regulations satisfied the *O'Brien* test, as they served substantial government interests such as preventing the disappearance of free over-the-air television broadcasting and did so without burdening substantially more speech than necessary. *United States v. O'Brien*, 391 U.S. 367 (1968), is discussed in 11.01[4][b].

[7] Medium-Specific Standards for Government Regulation

This last sub-section asks whether different judicial standards should apply to government regulation of different media, depending on the unique characteristics of the medium being regulated. It focuses on electronic media—in turn, broadcasting, cable television, and finally, the Internet—but along the way it, contrasts the standards applicable to regulation of those media to those applicable to regulation of print media.

[a] Broadcast Media

The Court's understanding of the uniqueness of broadcasting for First Amendment purposes rests heavily on two cases discussed in the previous sub-section, *Red Lion Broadcasting v. FCC*[540] and *Columbia Broadcasting System v. Democratic National Committee*.[541] In those cases, the Court embraced the argument that the technological and economic scarcity of the broadcast spectrum justifies more intrusive government regulation, at least when the issue centers whether the First Amendment allows the government to require a broadcaster to carry otherwise-unwanted content.[542] To be sure, the spectrum scarcity argument has been subject to heavy critique.[543] Nevertheless, it remains the law today. *Red Lion* and *Columbia Broadcasting* also rest on a related concern that, since the medium (*i.e.*, the broadcast spectrum) is scarce, concern for listeners' rights justifies more intrusive regulation to ensure that listeners receive a broad range of views.

The Court distilled this teaching in 1984, in *FCC v. League of Women Voters*.[544] In *League of Women Voters*, the Court, on a 5–4 vote, struck down a federal statutory provision forbidding any public broadcasting stations that received federal funding from engaging in editorializing. The case announced a general middle tier standard to scrutinize restrictions on the broadcast media. Under that standard, restrictions on the broadcast media would be upheld if they were "narrowly tailored to further a substantial governmental interest, such as ensuring adequate and balanced coverage of public issues."[545] Writing for the majority, Justice Brennan justified the middle tier standard on two grounds. First, it reflected *Red Lion's* and *Columbia Broadcasting's* view that the technological scarcity of the broadcast spectrum allowed the government to regulate the airwaves. Second, the standard allowed leeway for government regulation imposed to ensure that the public received a balanced presentation of views.

Justice Brennan explained these justifications as follows:

---

540. 395 U.S. 367 (1969).
541. 412 U.S. 94 (1973).
542. *Red Lion* and *Columbia Broadcasting* are discussed in Section 11.03[6].
543. *See supra.* note 535.
544. 468 U.S. 364 (1984).
545. *Id.* at 365.

The fundamental distinguishing characteristic of the new medium of broadcasting that, in our view, has required some adjustment in First Amendment analysis is that "broadcast frequencies are a scarce resource that must be portioned out among applicants." *Columbia Broadcasting.* Thus, our cases have taught that, given spectrum scarcity, those who are granted a license to broadcast must serve in a sense as fiduciaries for the public by presenting "those views and voices which are representative of [their] community and which would otherwise, by necessity, be barred from the airwaves." *Red Lion.* As we observed in *Red Lion*, because "it is the purpose of the First Amendment to preserve an uninhibited marketplace of ideas in which truth will ultimately prevail, ... the right of the public to receive suitable access to social, political, esthetic, moral, and other ideas and experiences through the medium of broadcasting is crucial here and it may not constitutionally be abridged either by Congress or by the FCC."[546]

Applying the middle tier test to the editorializing ban at issue, the Court noted that the ban was based on the content of speech and that editorializing was a form of speech central to the First Amendment. The Court rejected the interest in preventing government from propagandizing, saying that Congress had provided other protections against this including a creating bipartisan board for the Public Broadcasting Corporation. The Court also rejected the contention that the ban was a legitimate exercise of Congress's spending power. The Court reasoned that federal funds paid for only a small fraction of the plaintiff-television station's activities, but Congress did not allow the station to confine federal money to non-editorial activities, which would allow it to use other funds for editorializing.[547] The Court emphasized the narrowness of its decision, noting that it did not forbid congressional regulation of the "content, timing, or character"[548] of speech by public broadcasting stations.

Dissenting, Justice Rehnquist, joined by Chief Justice Burger and Justice White, argued that Congress had rationally determined, in the proper exercise of its spending power, that the taxpayers who funded public broadcasting would not like to see their money used to editorialize or endorse political candidates. Justice Stevens also dissented. Recalling the harsh voice of Nazi propaganda, he agreed with Congress's decision to limit the potential impact of government funds on pervasive and powerful organs of mass communication.

[b] Cable Television

Many of the cable television cases the Court has decided have dealt with congressional legislation either authorizing or requiring cable operators to restrict access to

---

546. *Id.* at 377–78.
547. The Court's more general jurisprudence concerning First Amendment limits on government funding of private activity is discussed in Section 11.02[6][a].
548. 468 U.S. at 402.

channels that display offensive content.[549] At times, these opinions have focused on the unique attributes of cable television,[550] while at other times, the Court has applied generally-applicable First Amendment rules.[551] In the mandated access cases discussed earlier,[552] the Court observed that cable television is not subject to the same scarcity as exists in broadcasting.[553] At the same time, it also observed that the mechanics of cable connectivity, especially the requirement of obtaining rights of way to lay physical cable infrastructure, meant that cable operators were more inherently monopolistic as compared with, for example, newspapers.[554] The Court also noted, in the context of the must-carry rules discussed earlier, that unlike, say, newspaper publishers, cable operators were not so identified with the content they carried that requiring them to carry certain broadcast stations would impute in the public's mind the operators' agreement with the speech the government required them to carry.[555]

Technology and the market structure of the information business are quickly outpacing the Court's understanding of at least some facets of cable television. On the

---

549. *See, e.g.* Denver Area Educational Telecommunications Consortium, Inc. v. FCC, 518 U.S. 727 (1996) (invalidating the parts of a law that required cable operators to restrict the availability of patently offensive programming on leased access commercial channels and that empowered cable operators to regulate similar programming on public access channels, but upholding another part of the law that afforded operators discretion to prohibit or restrict patently offensive programming on leased access channels); United States v. Playboy Entertainment Group, 529 U.S. 803 (2000) (invalidating a law that required cable providers to completely scramble all channels which primarily feature sexual programming, in order to prevent the signal from "bleeding" over to nearby channels and thus being viewed, on the ground that the law failed the strict scrutiny that was required given its content discrimination).

550. *See, e.g., Denver Area*, 518 U.S. at 739 & 740 (refusing to adopt "categorical standards" applicable to "a new and changing environment").

551. *See, e.g., Playboy*, 529 U.S. at 813 ("Since [the challenged law] is a content-based speech restriction, it can stand only if it satisfies strict scrutiny.").

552. *See* Section 11.03[6].

553. *See* Turner Broadcasting System v. FCC, 512 U.S. 622, 638–639 (1994) (*Turner I*).

554. *See Turner I*, 512 U.S. at 656 ("[T]he asserted analogy to *Miami Herald v. Tornillo*, 418 U.S. 241 (1974), ignores an important technological difference between newspapers and cable television. Although a daily newspaper and a cable operator both may enjoy monopoly status in a given locale, the cable operator exercises far greater control over access to the relevant medium. A daily newspaper, no matter how secure its local monopoly, does not possess the power to obstruct readers' access to other competing publications—whether they be weekly local newspapers, or daily newspapers published in other cities. Thus, when a newspaper asserts exclusive control over its own news copy, it does not thereby prevent other newspapers from being distributed to willing recipients in the same locale. The same is not true of cable. When an individual subscribes to cable, the physical connection between the television set and the cable network gives the cable operator bottleneck, or gatekeeper, control over most (if not all) of the television programming that is channeled into the subscriber's home. Hence, simply by virtue of its ownership of the essential pathway for cable speech, a cable operator can prevent its subscribers from obtaining access to programming it chooses to exclude."). In *Miami Herald*, the Court struck down a Florida law requiring a newspaper that printed an unfavorable editorial about a political candidate to provide that candidate an opportunity to reply. That case and mandated access to media cases more generally are discussed in Section 11.03[6].

555. *See Turner I*, 512 U.S. at 655 ("Given cable's long history of serving as a conduit for broadcast signals, there appears little risk that cable viewers would assume that the broadcast stations carried on a cable system convey ideas or messages endorsed by the cable operator.").

one hand, the rise of online streaming services threatens to obsolesce the Court's understanding of cable as inherently monopolistic. Those services provide a significant and growing portion of the content available through conventional broadcast and cable operations. On the other hand, to the extent cable companies are becoming more prevalent as providers of Internet service (or, conversely, to the extent those providers acquire cable companies), the Internet provider may find itself in a position where it can slow down such streaming services and exercise, if not complete, then at least some, control over what content enters a home, thereby cementing its monopoly control. How the Court will apply this fast-changing technological and business environment to basic First Amendment principles remains very unclear.

[c] *The Internet*

Much regulation of the Internet, like much regulation of cable television, has sought to prevent young persons from accessing sexual speech. In the Court's first important Internet case, *Reno v. ACLU*,[556] the Court struck down the Communications Decency Act of 1996 (CDA), which was designed to safeguard minors from "indecent" and "patently offensive" transmissions on the Internet.

Much of the Court's analysis consisted of distinguishing earlier cases in which the Court upheld regulation of speech in other media. For example, Justice Stevens, writing for the Court, distinguished the CDA from the statute upheld in a 1968 case, *Ginsberg v. New York*,[557] which upheld a more restrictive standard for selling obscenity to minors than to adults. Unlike the statute in *Ginsberg*, the CDA had no exemption for parental consent or participation. Moreover, the law in *Ginsberg* applied only to commercial dealings, while the CDA applied to all transmissions on the Internet. Also in contrast to *Ginsberg*, the CDA failed to define terms like "indecent" with the precision required by the Court's test for obscenity.[558]

Justice Stevens then distinguished *FCC v. Pacifica Foundation*,[559] which upheld FCC restrictions on the time of day when indecent material could be broadcast over radio. Unlike the regulations upheld in *Pacifica*, the CDA's restrictions were not limited to certain times of the day. Moreover, these restrictions were not overseen by an agency like the FCC that was "familiar with the unique characteristics of the Internet." Additionally, the CDA provided for criminal penalties, unlike the FCC order at issue in *Pacifica*. Addressing the significance of the medium regulated in *Pacifica*, the *Reno* Court added that the broadcast medium has historically "received limited First Amendment protection," in significant part because warnings could not prevent listeners from unintentionally tuning into offensive programming if they happened upon a particular radio program while turning the radio dial.[560] In contrast, the Court con-

---

556. 521 U.S. 844 (1997).
557. 390 U.S. 629 (1968).
558. For a discussion of the constitutional standard for obscenity, see Section 11.01[2][d][i].
559. 438 U.S. 726 (1978).
560. *Reno*, 521 U.S. at 867.

cluded that, at least as of 1997, little risk existed of unintentionally accessing offensive material on the Internet.

In addition to these differences between the Internet and broadcasting, the Court in *Reno* also emphasized the history of government regulation of broadcasting and the scarcity rationale as explained in *Red Lion*, both of which he noted were absent with regard to the Internet. In contrast to broadcasting's limited spectrum capacity, Justice Stevens observed that the Internet allows for broad-based, cost-effective communication of all kinds. Using language that now sounds outdated but that still reflects a larger modern reality, he wrote: "Through the use of chat rooms, any person with a phone line can become a town crier with a voice that resonates farther than it could from any soapbox. Through the use of Web pages, mail exploders, and newsgroups, the same individual can become a pamphleteer."[561]

In addition to these speech-friendly aspects of the Internet, the Court also faulted the CDA's breadth. Far from being narrowly tailored, the Court noted that the CDA would burden communication among adults, since it would criminalize sending an indecent message across the Internet as long as the sender knew or should have known that a minor could view it.[562] The Court expressed concern that the CDA's reach might make it a felony to speak frankly online about topics such as safe sex, rape, or art featuring nude subjects, or for a parent to send her 17-year-old child a message about birth control. The Court observed that less restrictive alternatives existed, included restricting the CDA to commercial sites or allowing parents to select what materials their children may view. While the CDA provided that the use of a credit card requirement or age verification device was an affirmative defense to liability, the Court objected that most non-commercial sites would find such methods economically infeasible.

Seven years after *Reno*, in *Ashcroft v. ACLU*,[563] the Court upheld a preliminary injunction, pending a trial, against enforcement of the Child Online Protection Act (COPA), agreeing with the lower court that COPA was likely unconstitutional. The five-justice majority, speaking through Justice Kennedy, concluded that, as a content-based restriction, the government bore the burden of proof to establish COPA's constitutionality, in particular by showing that no less-restrictive means would have satisfied the government's child-protection interests. COPA imposed more limited restrictions than did the CDA on the online posting of material "harmful to minors," for example, by limiting liability to those who posted "for commercial purposes" and by allowing affirmative defenses for those commercial posters who required adult verification via credit card or " 'any other reasonable measures that are feasible under available technology.' "[564] Nevertheless, the Court found that the government had not carried its burden of proof, given the availability of filtering technology that would

---

561. *Id.* at 870.

562. Relatedly, the Court expressed concern that the statute's definition of the prohibited speech was vague, a characteristic that it feared would chill protected speech. *See id.* at 871–72. First Amendment vagueness doctrine is discussed in Section 11.02[2].

563. 542 U.S. 656 (2004).

564. *Id.* at 662 (quoting the statute).

have better protected minors while restricting less adult access to speech. On remand, the lower court, after a bench trial, entered a permanent injunction against COPA, which the appellate court affirmed. The Supreme Court denied *certiorari*.[565]

Several justices dissented. Most relevantly for understanding the First Amendment status of online speech, Justice Breyer both noted the small expense a commercial online operator would have to incur to store passwords or credit card numbers and questioned the accuracy of the filtering technology. Presumably, both of those estimations of the Internet's capabilities have relatively little value today, given technological change.

In a more recent case, the Court continued to extol the importance of the Internet to communication and free expression, and to insist that any limits on expression online be carefully circumscribed. *Packingham v. North Carolina*[566] dealt with a North Carolina law that made it a felony for a registered sex offender "to access a commercial social networking Web site where the sex offender knows that the site permits minor children to become members or to create or maintain personal Web pages."[567] The Court struck down the law on a unanimous eight-justice vote.[568] Writing for five justices, Justice Kennedy, citing *Reno*, again noted the vast opportunities for expression the Internet made available. Going beyond *Reno*'s celebration of the Internet's free speech implications, he identified social media in particular as "the most important places (in a spatial sense) for the exchange of views."[569]

Justice Kennedy recognized the fast-changing nature of the Internet. Acknowledging that *Packingham* presented "one of the first [cases] this Court has taken to address the relationship between the First Amendment and the modern Internet," he wrote: "As a result, the Court must exercise extreme caution before suggesting that the First Amendment provides scant protection for access to vast networks in that medium."[570] Justice Kennedy then concluded that the North Carolina law restricted too much speech to be constitutional, finding that the law thus failed the intermediate scrutiny that was appropriate for a content-neutral law such as this. He assumed that the law, as written, was broad enough to prevent sex offenders from accessing even sites such as a newspaper's or marketer's website. But he concluded that, even as more narrowly construed to apply only to mainstream social media sites such as Facebook or Twitter, the law "with one broad stroke bars access to what for many are the principal sources for knowing current events, checking ads for employment, speaking and listening in the modern public square, and otherwise exploring the vast realms of human thought and knowledge."[571] Conceding that a more narrowly-tailored law could pass consti-

---

565. ACLU v. Gonzalez, 478 F. Supp. 2d 775 (E.D. Pa. 2007), *aff'd*, ACLU v. Mukasey, 534 F.3d 181 (3d Cir. 2008), *cert. denied*, Mukasey v. ACLU, 555 U.S. 1137 (2009).

566. 137 S. Ct. 1730 (2017).

567. N.C. Gen. Stat. Ann. §§ 14-202.5(a), (e).

568. Justice Gorsuch did not participate.

569. 137 S. Ct. at 1735.

570. *Id.* at 1736.

571. *Id.* at 1737.

tutional scrutiny, the Court concluded that the North Carolina law swept too broadly and thus failed even intermediate scrutiny.

Justice Alito, writing for himself, Chief Justice Roberts, and Justice Thomas, concurred in the judgment, citing (as did the majority) the North Carolina law's broad reach. However, he criticized what he called the majority's "undisciplined dicta" about the importance of online expression, stating concern that "this language is bound to be interpreted by some to mean that the States are largely powerless to restrict even the most dangerous sexual predators from visiting any internet sites, including, for example, teenage dating sites and sites designed to permit minors to discuss personal problems with their peers."[572]

The justices' division in *Packingham* reflects, in a very general way, the central problem the Court has confronted when considering regulation of speech in mass media. On the one hand, those media allow broad dissemination of information. For that reason, they merit special First Amendment protection. On the other hand, with that great potential for communication comes, as in *Packingham*, the great potential for harm. Less nefariously, but still potentially problematic, with that great potential also comes calls for government to open up those media to broader participation.

Of course, more modern media, such as the Internet and social media in particular, do not present the speaker access limitations inherent in, say, broadcast television. Thus, for example, the Court in *Reno* and *Packingham* was able to extol the fact that the Internet allowed persons both broad access to information and broad ability to participate in public dialogue. Nevertheless, in older media and, potentially, in media yet to be developed, access issues may still arise. And at any rate, the broad reach of and access to modern media make such media much more effective tools in the hands of those who wish to do harm.

In all these cases, any government regulation will force the Court to balance, not just the beneficial and dangerous uses of mass media but also the interests of both speakers and listeners/viewers of speech in the regulated medium. And it will have to perform that balancing while recognizing that the medium itself is changing at a rapid rate.[573]

---

572. *Id.* at 1738 (Alito, J., concurring in the judgment).

573. *See, e.g., Packingham,* 137 S. Ct. at 1736 ("The forces and directions of the Internet are so new, so protean, and so far reaching that courts must be conscious that what they say today might be obsolete tomorrow.").

Chapter 12

Government and Religious Freedom

The Bill of Rights begins with the command that "Congress shall make no laws respecting an establishment of religion, or prohibiting the free exercise thereof."[1] At a very broad level, the Establishment Clause prevents state sponsorship of religion in general or a particular religion, and the Free Exercise Clause mandates freedom of religious belief. The textual position of the religion clauses in the First Amendment has come to mirror the central role religious freedom plays in our society and democracy generally. Ideally, the religion clauses work in tandem to preserve a single ideal, religious freedom. The Establishment Clause mandates a kind of mutual noninterference by church and state in each other's affairs. This mutual noninterference helps to foster the freedom of religious belief and practice mandated by the Free Exercise Clause.[2]

The application of this singular ideal has proven to be a complex matter. While the clauses may be mutually sustaining, they also exist in significant tension with each other. In our modern welfare state, stringent separation of government and religion may at times require depriving religion of an otherwise generally-available benefit, thus arguably impairing free religious exercise. Conversely, provisions of such benefits to religious institutions, or liberal exemptions of religious practitioners from otherwise generally-applicable burdens, may amount to favoring religion in a manner inconsistent with that strict separation, even while being defended as promoting free religious exercise. The historical ebbs and flows in the Supreme Court's religion jurisprudence reflect this tension between the clauses.

This chapter explains the Court's highly complex religion jurisprudence. Section 12.01 sets forth the basic divide between the two main approaches to the religion clauses: the separationist and the accommodationist approaches. Section 12.02 then considers the Establishment Clause, examining in turn the variety of contexts in which Establishment Clause challenges arise, including but not limited to government

---

1. U.S. Const. amend. I.

2. Like the rest of the Bill of Rights, the religion clauses originally applied only against the federal government. *See* Section 9.03 (discussing the process by which Bill of Rights provisions eventually became incorporated so as to apply against the states via the Fourteenth Amendment Due Process Clause). State religious establishments, although declining by the late eighteenth century, persisted until the 1830s. The Court incorporated both clauses in 1940. *See infra.* n.6.

aid to religious schools and other religious institutions (respectively, Sections 12.02[1] and [2]), religious displays on government property (Section 12.02[3]), school prayer and actual religious instruction (respectively, Sections 12.02[4] and 12.02[5]), legislative prayers (Section 12.02[6]), exemptions from generally-applicable laws (Section 12.02[7]), and grants of government power to religious groups (Section 12.02[8]), before concluding.

Section 12.03 considers the Free Exercise Clause. After Section 12.03[1] examines the Court's attempt to define "religion" for purposes of the free exercise right, Section 12.03[2] examines the history of the Court's treatment of that right, culminating in the present non-discrimination rule. Section 12.04 concludes the chapter by considering the close, but contested relationship between the Establishment and the Free Exercise Clauses.

§ 12.01 Competing Approaches: A "Wall of Separation" versus Accommodation

The Supreme Court heard relatively few religion cases during the first century and a half after ratification of the First Amendment.[3] These early cases lacked any unifying principle other than a marked deference to the legislature.[4] In the 1940s and 1950s, the Court handed down a series of decisions reflecting two competing approaches to interpreting the religion clauses. These approaches — the "wall of separation" between church and state, and the accommodation of religion — continue to dominate the Court's decisions today.

Everson v. Board of Education[5] construed the Establishment Clause to require a strict separation of church and state. *Everson* involved a New Jersey program reimbursing parents for the cost of their children's bus fare, which included reimbursements for bus fare for children using busses to attend Catholic schools.[6] Writing for the

---

3. It was not until 1899 — over 100 years after ratification of the Bill of Rights — that the Court first reviewed an Establishment Clause claim, in *Bradfield v. Roberts*, 175 U.S. 291 (1899). However, several earlier Supreme Court decisions dealt with constitutional protection of religious liberty. *See* Davis v. Beason, 133 U.S. 333 (1890); Reynolds v. United States, 98 U.S. 145 (1878); Vidal v. Philadelphia, 43 U.S. (2 How.) 127 (1844); Terrett v. Taylor, 13 U.S. (9 Cranch) 43 (1815). *Reynolds* is a particularly important Free Exercise Clause case, and is discussed in Section 12.03[2][a].

4. *Bradfield v. Roberts* exemplifies this deference. The dispute in *Bradfield* involved a congressional appropriation to the Commissioners of the District of Columbia for a hospital to be built and operated by the Roman Catholic Church. The Court upheld the appropriation, reasoning that because the Commissioners acted within the scope of their authority and the Church did not actually hold title to the property, there was "nothing sectarian" in the undertaking. *Bradfield*, 175 U.S. at 299–300.

5. 330 U.S. 1 (1947).

6. *Everson*, 330 U.S. at 29–30. The prohibition of the Establishment Clause applies to state governments as well as the federal government. In 1940, the Court incorporated both religion clauses in *Cantwell v. Connecticut*, 310 U.S. 296 (1940).

Court, Justice Black looked to the historical backdrop against which the religion clauses were promulgated, particularly the colonists' efforts to escape religious persecution but also their willingness to establish their own coercive religious establishments in the colonies they settled. Justice Black concluded that the Establishment Clause "was intended to rid the nation of these policies by erecting 'a wall of separation between Church and State,'"[7] and insisted that "[t]hat wall must be kept high and impregnable."[8]

Despite this strong language, Justice Black concluded that the bus reimbursement program did not breach the wall of separation he extolled. Rather, he reasoned that the transportation subsidy was a generally-applicable one, which he analogized to general police protection provided to all institutions in a city or to all children walking to any school. To be sure, the *Everson* majority did not hold that a failure to reimburse transportation to religious schools would violate the free exercise right to attend them. However, the majority did suggest that providing such reimbursement was consistent with the neutrality mandated by the religion clauses taken together: "State power is no more to be used so as to handicap religions, than it is to favor them."[9] As Justice Black understood them, free exercise and non-establishment in tandem guaranteed state neutrality toward religion.

Everson exhibited a deep tension. In the context of the modern welfare state, one could argue that education itself was a public function. If so, aid to parochial schools in the form of providing textbooks or salaries for teachers who did not teach religion would arguably escape the prohibition of the Establishment Clause because such aid would not benefit religion, but further advance a proper public function, akin to ensuring that children travel to school safely. On the other hand, separation—at least in the absolute terms articulated by Justice Black—would seem to bar the government from aiding even a public function such as transportation if it collaterally benefitted religion. Indeed, in the spirit of that latter idea, Justice Jackson's dissent argued that Catholic education was central to the church's religious function and that subsidizing the transportation of parochial school children supported this essentially religious function in violation of the Establishment Clause.

Establishment Clause decisions subsequent to *Everson* have turned on whether the Court favored protecting freedom of religion by accommodating free exercise or by maintaining a strict wall of separation. In *Illinois ex rel. McCollum v. Board of Education*,[10] the Court invoked the wall metaphor to strike down a program releasing public school students from their secular instruction for a short time to receive optional religious instruction, conducted on public school premises by teachers employed by religious organizations. Again writing for the majority, Justice Black ruled

---

7. 330 U.S. at 16 (quoting *Reynolds v. United States*, 98 U.S. 145, 164 (1878)). The "wall" metaphor was first coined by Thomas Jefferson in a letter to the Danbury Baptist Association in 1802. *See* Lynch v. Donnelly, 465 U.S. 668, 673 (1984).

8. *Everson*, 330 U.S. at 18.

9. *Ibid.*

10. 333 U.S. 203 (1948).

that the program violated the Establishment Clause, because the state's tax-supported public school buildings and compulsory attendance laws were being used to disseminate religious doctrines. In the Court's view, allowing religious school teachers access to public classrooms involved government aid to a religious function rather than provision of a public function such as bus transportation. This program also raised the specter of significant entanglement between church and state, because religious school instructors would have been subjected to the approval and supervision of the school superintendent. In Justice Black's view, such entanglement could not be reconciled with the separation the Establishment Clause required. Recognizing the tension between a strong anti-establishment view and the spirit of the Free Exercise Clause, Justice Black insisted that invalidating the state program in *McCollum* did not evince a hostility to religion inconsistent with the Free Exercise Clause.

By contrast, Justice Reed's dissent took a decidedly accommodationist tone. He observed that Thomas Jefferson and James Madison, leaders in the anti-establishment movement, had approved of the University of Virginia's requirement that students attend worship services. In Justice Reed's view, the Establishment Clause only barred aid to religion that supported some ecclesiastical function, such as aid directly to the church itself. In contrast, education was a public function, with the result that the support of religion in education did not support the church itself. According to Justice Reed, the majority's rigid interpretation of the Establishment Clause was out of step with the nation's long history of permitting incidental benefits to religion.

Just four years later, in *Zorach v. Clauson*,[11] a 5–4 majority upheld a release time program similar to the one struck down in *McCollum*. The pivotal difference was that the religious instruction in *Zorach* was not conducted on public school grounds.[12] A centerpiece for the accommodationist approach, Justice Douglas' majority opinion noted that complete separation would disrupt many religious traditions embedded in the fabric of our society. As examples, he noted legislative chaplains, courtroom oaths, giving religious students days off for holy days, and the prayer, "'God save the United States and this Honorable Court,'"[13] which was recited at the start of Supreme Court sessions.

Justice Douglas reasoned that the First Amendment did not prohibit public schools' efforts to "accommodate [students'] schedules to a program of outside religious instruction." Indeed, again illustrating the tension between anti-establishment and free exercise values, he argued that striking down the program on Establishment Clause

---

11. 343 U.S. 306 (1952).

12. *Id.* at 312–15. The Court also distinguished the case before it from *McCollum* on the grounds that the *Zorach* release time program did not expend public funds. *Id.* at 308–09. In his concurrence in *McCollum*, however, Justice Jackson had pointed out that any expense in the program at issue in that case was "incalculable and negligible." *McCollum*, 333 U.S. at 234 (Jackson, J., concurring). The dispositive factual distinction between the two cases thus appears to have been the location at which the religious instruction took place. *See* William P. Marshall, *"We Know It When We See It"; The Supreme Court and Establishment*, 59 S. CAL. L. REV. 495, 524–25 n.175 (1986).

13. *Zorach*, 343 U.S. at 313.

grounds would undermine government neutrality and constitute "hostility to reli-gion."[14] Justice Douglas distinguished the *McCollum* program, because it was con-ducted inside the school building where the force of the state could be invoked to promote religion. The majority did not consider any coercive effects that the program may have caused by singling out, as non-religious, students who did not attend the religion classes. By contrast, in later cases, the Court recognized that peer pressure could coerce non-religious children to exercise some form of religion.[15]

Dissenting, Justice Jackson focused on the use of state power to compel students to choose between attending secular or religious instruction during school hours. He viewed the off-campus location of the religion classes as too subtle a distinction to be dispositive, particularly in view of the fact that in both *McCollum* and *Zorach*, the state used its compulsory attendance laws to enforce such a choice. Adhering to a strict separationist paradigm, Justice Black's dissent also saw no difference between the programs in *McCollum* and *Zorach*. For Justice Black, the only release time pro-gram that could be constitutionally upheld would be one that involved religious in-struction entirely apart from normal school hours. Jurisprudentially, he characterized the majority's approach as a balancing analysis where the focus was on whether the state has entered too far into the area of religion. Justice Black instead favored a cat-egorical approach denying the state any entry at all.[16]

Regardless of any factual distinctions one might draw between them, the majority opinions in *McCollum* and *Zorach* illustrate, respectively, the separation and accom-modation approaches. Virtually all Establishment Clause decisions of the modern Court represent one or the other of these approaches. The debate between the two remains unresolved, as will become clear by examining the divisions on the Court in more recent aid-to-school cases, discussed in Section 12.02[1], below.

Many of the Court's attempts to reconcile the values embodied in the Free Exercise and Establishment Clauses have arisen in circumstances where the government has provided some form of aid to religious institutions. Often, such cases require the Court to choose, in some measure, between burdening free exercise by striking down the aid program or promoting a religious establishment by upholding it.

Walz v. Tax Commission[17] is a classic example of such a conundrum. At issue in *Walz* was the constitutionality of a New York property tax exemption for charitable

---

14. *Id.* at 315.

15. *Cf.* Lee v. Weisman, 505 U.S. 577, 593 (1992) (expressing concern that a school district's su-pervision and control of a middle school graduation ceremony would place "subtle and indirect public and peer pressure" on students to stand during a prayer opening the ceremony).

16. Thirty years later, the Court explained the *McCollum/Zorach* distinction this way: "The dif-ference in symbolic impact helps to explain the difference between the cases. The symbolic connection of church and state in the *McCollum* program presented the students with a graphic symbol of the 'concert or union of dependency' of church and state. This very symbolic union was conspicuously absent in the *Zorach* program." School Dist. v. Ball, 473 U.S. 373, 391 (1985) (quoting *Zorach*, 343 U.S. at 312).

17. 397 U.S. 664 (1970).

organizations, including religious organizations. If the Court upheld the exemption, religion would have been benefitted; if the Court struck it down, the exercise of religion would have been burdened by taxation. Writing the opinion for the Court upholding the exemption, Chief Justice Burger reflected at length about the competing values in the religion clauses:

> The Court has struggled to find a neutral course between the two Religion Clauses, both of which are cast in absolute terms, and either of which, if expanded to a logical extreme, would tend to clash with the other.... The general principle deducible from the First Amendment and all that has been said by the Court is this: that we will not tolerate either governmentally established religion or governmental interference with religion.

> Short of those expressly proscribed governmental acts there is room for play in the joints productive of a benevolent neutrality which will permit religious exercise to exist without sponsorship and without interference.... Adherence to the policy of neutrality that derives from an accommodation of the Establishment and Free Exercise Clauses has prevented the kind of involvement that would tip the balance toward government control of churches or governmental restraint on religious practice.... No perfect or absolute separation is really possible; the very existence of the Religion Clauses is an involvement of sorts — one that seeks to mark boundaries to avoid excessive entanglement.[18]

Against the background of these general observations, Chief Justice Burger turned to the "purpose" and "effect" test set out by the Court seven years earlier in *Abington School District v. Schempp*.[19] The Chief Justice found that the general purpose of the legislation challenged in *Walz* was to grant a tax exemption to charitable organizations, including religious ones, which the state considered beneficial to the public interest, irrespective of the organizations' religious character. He then explored whether the exemption brought about the impermissible effect of an excessive government entanglement with religion. He concluded that avoiding excessive entanglement required choosing between the lesser of two entanglements:

> [G]ranting tax exemptions to churches necessarily operates to afford an indirect economic benefit and also gives rise to some, but yet a lesser, involvement than taxing them. In analyzing either alternative the questions are whether the involvement is excessive, and whether it is a continuing one calling for official and continuing surveillance leading to an impermissible degree of entanglement.[20]

Applying this test of degree, Chief Justice Burger concluded that exempting religious organizations created less entanglement than taxing them, and tended to "reinforce

---

18. *Id.* at 668–70.

19. 374 U.S. 203 (1963). In *Schempp* the Court struck down a public school prayer policy. *Schempp* and the issue of prayer in public schools is Section 12.02[4].

20. *Walz*, 397 U.S. at 674–75.

the desired separation insulating" church and state from one another. Reflecting an accommodationist position, the Chief Justice said that government must exercise "benevolent neutrality toward churches and religious exercise generally so long as none was favored over others and none suffered interference."[21]

Dissenting, Justice Douglas asserted that the tax exemption amounted to a subsidy which established religion. He argued that the Chief Justice's "benevolent neutrality" could not be squared with the First Amendment's demand that the government be neutral not only as between religious sects but also as between believers and non-believers. Justice Douglas observed that *Everson* prohibited aid to all religions, not just aid to one at the expense of others.

In addition to the accommodationist and separationist positions the two opinions reflected, another important distinction between the opinions of Chief Justice Burger and Justice Douglas appears to have been their differing characterizations of the law's effects. The Chief Justice took the law's benefit at face value, as an exemption. Although he did not expressly rely on free exercise grounds, his opinion contained many references to unburdening religion. By contrast, Justice Douglas viewed the statute as providing a subsidy. From that perspective, free exercise concerns dropped out of the picture, and the benefit derived more clearly violated the mandated separation and neutrality.

The importance of how a benefit is characterized is a recurring theme in religion clause decisions. Its importance would become clear the next year in *Lemon v. Kurtzman*,[22] a case involving an Establishment Clause challenge to government aid to religious schools. More generally, it was in *Lemon* that the Court, again speaking through Chief Justice Burger, formally united the strands of its prior analysis and announced a test that, though often criticized, remains influential today in deciding Establishment Clause cases.

§ 12.02 The Establishment Clause

[1] Aid to Religious Schools

[a] The Lemon Test

Cases involving government aid to religious schools have proved particularly fractious for the Court. The outcome in particular cases has often depended upon whether a majority of the Court leans toward the separation or accommodation paradigm.

Lemon v. Kurtzman[23] is a seminal case in this area, and in Establishment Clause jurisprudence more generally, because it provided the occasion for the Court to attempt to establish a general rule for deciding Establishment Clause cases. *Lemon* in-

---

21. *Id.* at 676–77.
22. 403 U.S. 602 (1971).
23. 403 U.S. 602 (1971).

volved Establishment Clause challenges to Rhode Island and Pennsylvania statutes that subsidized teachers' salaries in non-public schools. Writing for the Court, Chief Justice Burger advanced a textual argument in striking down the subsidies. For the Chief Justice, the word "respecting" in the Establishment Clause evidenced the Framers' intent to prohibit not only laws that actually established a religion, but also laws that tended in that direction.

To determine which laws fell within the proscribed category, Chief Justice Burger articulated the test that would dominate Establishment Clause jurisprudence for the next two decades, and which remains at least somewhat influential today. In *Lemon*, the Chief Justice set forth a test "gleaned" from "the cumulative criteria developed by the Court over many years": "First, the statute must have a secular legislative purpose; second, its principal or primary effect must be one that neither advances nor inhibits religion; finally, the statute must not foster an excessive government entanglement with religion."[24] If a statute failed any one of these requirements, it would be struck down as violating the Establishment Clause.

In applying the test, the Chief Justice indicated that the Pennsylvania and Rhode Island statutes' permissible legislative purposes were to promote quality secular education. Turning to the primary effect prong, the state legislatures had recognized that church-related schools were governed by a religious mission. This recognition was evidenced by legislative efforts designed to ensure that state support furthered only secular purposes without furthering the schools' religious mission. For example, the Rhode Island statute limited aid to teachers of mathematics, languages, physical science, and physical education, since these courses posed less danger of the inculcation of religious values than might arise in courses such as history or literature. Moreover, the Rhode Island statute required that the state subsidy to private school teachers not increase their salaries to the point where they would exceed the salaries of public school teachers and thus incentivize the best teachers to go to private, including religious, schools. However, the Chief Justice did not decide whether these limitations were sufficient to save the statutes under the effect prong, because he concluded that the programs failed the excessive entanglement prong.

Turning to the entanglement issue, the Chief Justice examined the nature of the government aid, the character and purposes of the religious institutions thus assisted, and the resulting relationship between the government and those institutions. First, the Chief Justice summarized the integral role that parochial schools play in the Catholic Church's mission of inculcating religious faith.[25] He observed that teachers, in particular, play an important part in providing a religious atmosphere. Next, he observed that earlier decisions had ruled that state aid in the form of bus transportation, such as that in *Everson*, as well as funding for school lunches, public health services, and even secular textbooks did not constitute excessive entanglements be-

---

24. *Id.* at 612–13.
25. Catholic schools were the largest beneficiaries of the aid in both Rhode Island and Pennsylvania. *See id.* at 608 (discussing the Rhode Island program) & 610 (discussing the Pennsylvania program).

tween church and State. The secular content of textbooks, for example, could be ascertained in advance. By contrast, the content of the teachers' speech could not.

Chief Justice Burger did not predicate his opinion on a finding that teachers would act in bad faith and insidiously inject religion into the classroom. Rather, he assumed that religious content in the classroom would simply be inevitable. He worried that the state would need to conduct a "comprehensive, discriminating, and continuing surveillance" of teachers in order to ensure a wholly secular curriculum. He concluded that such "prophylactic contacts will involve excessive and enduring entanglement between state and church."[26]

Lemon's addition of the entanglement inquiry to the purpose/effect test articulated in the earlier *Abington School District v. Schempp* case[27] placed legislators in a difficult position. If they were insensitive to establishment concerns, they ran the risk of violating the primary effect test. On the other hand, if they were sensitive to those concerns and accorded careful scrutiny to how the government aid programs were implemented, that scrutiny could generate entanglement problems. Ultimately, the Court attempted to resolve this contradiction by collapsing the two inquiries into one.[28]

The Chief Justice also identified a different type of entanglement: the potential for political divisiveness along religious lines. The Rhode Island and Pennsylvania programs required continuing annual appropriations in amounts that would have to keep pace with inflation and population growth. Chief Justice Burger predicted that under such circumstances, candidates and voters might tend to align according to their faiths, creating "political divisions along religious lines [which] was one of the principal evils" the Establishment Clause was meant to prohibit.[29]

Comparing Chief Justice Burger's *Lemon* opinion to his opinion in *Walz*, it becomes apparent that the accommodative tone of the *Walz* opinion was absent in *Lemon*. One might distinguish the cases on the ground that *Walz* involved tax exemptions and *Lemon* involved a subsidy: given the nuanced distinctions the religion clauses together require the Court to draw, such a distinction can easily be understood as a meaningful one. An additional distinction may be that the Court was less inclined to accommodate state involvement in religious affairs in the education context, given the involvement of impressionable children. Whether or not such a concern was at work in *Lemon* is not immediately discernible from the opinion.[30] It would more clearly become a critical factor in later cases.[31]

---

26. *Id.* at 619.

27. 374 U.S. 203 (1963). *Schempp* is discussed in Section 12.02[4]. *See also* note 19, *supra.*

28. *See* Agostini v. Felton, 521 U.S. 203 (1997). *Agostini* is discussed in Section 12.02[1][c].

29. *Lemon*, 403 U.S. at 622.

30. In his analysis of the character and nature of the religious institutions receiving aid, the Chief Justice merely noted that the "process of inculcating religious doctrine is, of course, enhanced by the impressionable age of the pupils." *Id.* at 616.

31. For example, in *Lee v. Weisman*, the Court struck down a school district's practice of offering state-sponsored prayers at middle-school graduation ceremonies, with Justice Kennedy observing

[b] Lemon's Early Applications

In the decade after *Lemon*, the Court charted a mixed course, upholding some state aid programs and invalidating others. As illustrated by the sampling of cases discussed below, the results led to a confusing jurisprudence that some justices critiqued as drawing meaningless distinctions.

In *Committee for Public Education & Religious Liberty v. Nyquist*,[32] the Court applied the *Lemon* test to a program involving three forms of aid: a provision of funds for maintaining and repairing school facilities; a provision reimbursing low-income parents directly for tuition costs; and a provision for tax relief for those parents not qualifying for the tuition reimbursement. Applying the first prong of the *Lemon* test, Justice Powell found legitimate secular purposes in the program, including the provision of safe schools, the promotion of diversity in educational options for parents and children, and the state's interest in preventing further overcrowding of its public schools. However, the Court found the program to fail *Lemon*'s effect prong. Justice Powell modified that prong by stating that in order for a program to be constitutional, any promotion of religion must be only remote and incidental. While later decisions required that "the" primary effect be on that advances religion, in *Nyquist* the Court stated that a law was unconstitutional if it merely had "a" primary effect of advancing religion.

Justice Powell found such an unconstitutional primary effect in the repair funding program, since there was no provision limiting such funds to the repair of structures used for secular education — for example, those funds could be used to repair a chapel. The tuition reimbursement program also failed the effect prong. Even though the aid went to parents rather than the school, the Court concluded that "the effect of the aid [was] unmistakably to provide desired financial support for non-public, sectarian institutions."[33] The Court further found no meaningful distinction between the reimbursement program and the tax benefit given to higher-income parents who were ineligible for the tuition reimbursement; thus, the tax benefit was also held to fail the effect test.

Distinguishing *Walz*, Justice Powell observed that unlike the property tax exemption in that earlier case, the tax relief at issue in *Nyquist* lacked historical precedent.[34] He also distinguished *Walz* as reflecting a more generally applicable set of tax exemptions, in contrast to the "special tax benefits"[35] to religion at issue in *Nyquist*. Finally, Justice

---

that "there are heightened concerns with protecting freedom of conscience from subtle coercive pressure in the elementary and secondary public schools." 505 U.S. 577, 592 (1992).

32. 413 U.S. 756 (1973).

33. *Id.* at 783.

34. *See Nyquist*, 413 U.S. at 792 ("Tax exemptions for church property enjoyed an apparently universal approval in this country both before and after the adoption of the First Amendment.... In sum, the Court [in *Walz*] concluded that 'few concepts are more deeply embedded in the fabric of our national life, beginning with pre-Revolutionary colonial times, than for the government to exercise at the very least this kind of benevolent neutrality toward churches and religious exercise generally.' We know of no historical precedent for New York's recently promulgated tax relief program.").

35. *Id.* at 793.

Powell expressed concern about political pressure that might be applied to enlarge sectarian programs. While such divisiveness alone was not sufficient to invalidate a program, it was "a 'warning signal' not to be ignored."[36]

In dissent, Justice Rehnquist, joined by Chief Justice Burger and Justice White, found that any distinctions between *Walz* and the New York programs actually favored upholding the programs. In *Walz*, the benefit was a complete forgiveness of taxes that had been made directly available to churches themselves; by contrast, in *Nyquist*, the benefit was a reduction in taxes available directly to the parents of school children. Thus, he argued that the benefit only indirectly helped parochial schools. Justice Rehnquist rejected the majority's characterization of the programs as an "incentive to parents to send their children to sectarian schools."[37] Instead, he characterized the programs as neutral assistance to parents of parochial school children to defray the burden of taxes they paid for public services (public education) they did not use.[38]

The Court's division on the question whether *Walz*'s upholding of one type of tax break required it to uphold the tax breaks in *Nyquist* illustrates the line-drawing problems the Court often confronts when deciding Establishment Clause cases. Another example involves government reimbursement of expenses religious schools incur in administering state-mandated tests.

In *Levitt v. Committee for Public Education & Religious Liberty*,[39] an eight-justice majority invalidated a New York law reimbursing private schools for the cost of administering state-mandated tests.[40] Some of the exams were state-prepared; others were traditional teacher-prepared tests. Because the latter tests involved the discretion of teachers supervised by religious institutions, Chief Justice Burger, writing for the Court, explained that they presented "the substantial risk that these examinations ... will be drafted with an eye, unconsciously or otherwise, to inculcate students in the religious precepts of the sponsoring church."[41] The statute failed to provide any means to assure that these internally-prepared tests were free of religious instruction. Moreover, the lump-sum, per-pupil payments did not represent actual costs of performing reimbursable secular services but covered all testing services, some of which were potentially religious. The overall effect of the statute, concluded the Court, would to be advance religious education.

Four years later, a sharply split Court upheld a state's provision of testing services to private schools. In *Wolman v. Walker*,[42] a four-justice plurality concluded that, be-

---

36. *Nyquist*, 413 U.S. at 798.

37. *Id.* at 808 (Rehnquist, J., dissenting).

38. *Compare Everson*, 330 U.S. at 58–60 (Routledge, J., dissenting) (arguing that parents choosing to send their children to religious schools have simply made a choice to forego the generally-available benefit of a public education).

39. 413 U.S. 472 (1973). *Levitt* was decided the same day as *Nyquist*.

40. Justice White dissented, while Justices Douglas, Brennan, and Marshall wrote simply that the result in this case was compelled by the Court's decisions in *Nyquist* and another case the Court decided that day.

41. *Id.* at 480.

42. 433 U.S. 229 (1977).

cause the tests were on secular subjects and were prepared and graded by the state, there was no possibility that a religious school could use the test to advance religious education. This characteristic of the aid also meant that there was no need to monitor how the private school interacted with the test, thus removing any risk of excessive entanglement.

But this analysis only commanded the support of four justices. To reach a majority on this point, it was necessary to add the views of Chief Justice Burger and Justices White and Rehnquist, who in earlier cases had taken more accommodationist views on state aid to private schools. Two justices dissented from this analysis. Thus, the plurality's analysis of the testing issue reflected a minority view on the Court, a fact that reflected the increasing division among the justices on where to draw appropriate lines in this area.

A final pair of cases illustrate yet again the Court's attention during this era to relatively small differences in how a state aid program was structured. In *Meek v. Pittenger*,[43] the Court invalidated all but the textbook loan provisions of two Pennsylvania statutes providing auxiliary services, instructional material, and equipment to private schools. The program supplied extensive educational aid in the form of auxiliary services such as counseling, psychological services, speech and hearing therapy, testing, and related services for exceptional or educationally disadvantaged students, and educational equipment such as maps, charts, films, records, periodicals, projectors, recorders, and laboratory paraphernalia. Of the private schools eligible for the assistance, 75 percent were church-affiliated.

Writing for the Court, Justice Stewart found that it would be unrealistic to attempt to separate the secular educational functions and the religious functions of church-related schools. He concluded that, "Even though earmarked for secular purposes, 'when it flows to an institution in which religion is so pervasive that a substantial portion of its functions are subsumed in the religious mission,' state aid has the impermissible primary effect of advancing religion."[44] He expressed concern that, for example, the therapy services were provided on the premises of the religious school, a fact which might pressure the state-funded therapist to adopt a sectarian approach to her interaction with students. At the same time, the extent of state supervision necessary "to ensure that a strictly nonideological posture is maintained"[45] in the delivery of such services would create an excessive entanglement between church and state. This latter observation again reflects the internal tension between the effect and entanglement prongs of the *Lemon* test. Several justices wrote partial concurrences and partial dissents, reflecting the internal divisions on the Court and the justices' tendencies to draw Establishment Clause-grounded lines in different places.

---

43. 421 U.S. 349 (1975).
44. *Id.* at 365–66.
45. *Id.* at 369.

Two years later, another sharply divided Court upheld a similar program in *Wolman v. Walter*.[46] As discussed earlier, a fractured majority upheld the testing program challenged in *Wolman*, because it was conducted by the state and did not involve religious school personnel in the preparation or grading of the test. *Wolman* also upheld the program's therapeutic and remedial services provisions. Those services would be administered by public employees and, unlike the state provision of similar services in *Meek*, they were provided on neutral sites not identified with sectarian schools, a fact the Court found significant in terms of the temptation the therapist would feel to adopt religious themes in his work with a student. Focusing on the provision of diagnostic, rather than therapeutic services, the Court found that the limited contact of a diagnostician with a child, unlike the teacher-student or therapist-student relationship, provided no opportunity for inculcating sectarian views. Both *Meek* and *Wolman* have been substantially overruled by *Mitchell v. Helms*.[47]

Given the nuanced lines drawn by these cases, one can perhaps understand the difficulty many persons had in understanding what state aid to religious schools the Establishment Clause allowed and what it forbade. Writing in 1985, Justice Rehnquist identified many of the intricate lines the Court had drawn in this area, and he criticized the *Lemon* test for requiring what he clearly thought were unprincipled, *ad hoc* distinctions:

> The results from our school services cases show the difficulty we have encountered in making the *Lemon* test yield principled results. For example, a State may lend to parochial school children geography textbooks that contain maps of the United States, but the State may not lend maps of the United States for use in geography class. A State may lend textbooks on American colonial history, but it may not lend a film on George Washington, or a film projector to show it in history class. A State may lend classroom workbooks, but may not lend workbooks in which the parochial school children write, thus rendering them nonreusable. A State may pay for bus transportation to religious schools but may not pay for bus transportation from the parochial school to the public zoo or natural history museum for a field trip. A State may pay for diagnostic services conducted in the parochial school but therapeutic services must be given in a different building; speech and hearing "services" conducted by the State inside the sectarian school are forbidden, but the State may conduct speech and hearing diagnostic testing inside the sectarian school. Exceptional parochial school students may receive counseling, but it must take place outside of the parochial school, such as in a trailer parked down the street. A State may give cash to a parochial school to pay for the administration of state-written tests and state-ordered reporting services, but it may not provide funds for teacher-prepared tests on secular

46. 433 U.S. 229 (1977). Much of the prevailing opinion commanded only the support of four justices, and four justices wrote separate partial concurrences.
47. 530 U.S. 793 (2000).

subjects. Religious instruction may not be given in public school, but the public school may release students during the day for religion classes elsewhere, and may enforce attendance at those classes with its truancy laws.[48]

[c] The Court's Move toward More Accommodation

Starting in the 1980s, the Court began edging toward a more accommodationist approach to government aid to religion, and away from a strict application of the *Lemon* test as it was then understood. In *Mueller v. Allen*,[49] the Court applied the *Lemon* test to uphold a state statute allowing a tax deduction for educational expenses. Writing for the Court, Justice Rehnquist focused much of its analysis on *Lemon*'s primary effect prong. The Minnesota statute met this part of the test, in part because the deduction was only one among many deductions in the tax code, including for medical expenses and charitable contributions. Notably, the Court in *Mueller* also stated that the benefits of the tax deduction were channeled directly to parents rather than to schools. This distinction would become significant in later cases.

The Court distinguished *Nyquist* on several grounds. However, importantly, it also implicitly criticized that case as being an outlier — the only case, according to the Court, where aid sent to parents rather than to religious schools directly was held to violate the Establishment Clause. By characterizing *Nyquist* as an outlier, Justice Rehnquist was able to set the stage for broader government assistance to religious schools, as long as that assistance was funneled to parents or students directly. Indeed, eventually, the Court began upholding direct assistance to such schools. Writing for four dissenters, Justice Marshall found the challenged tax deduction indistinguishable from the hybrid deduction/credit struck down in *Nyquist*, since both programs afforded parents financial incentives to send their children to sectarian schools.

Two cases decided shortly after *Mueller* demonstrate the importance of the *Mueller* distinction between aid distributed to parents and aid sent directly to sectarian institutions. In *Grand Rapids School District v. Ball*,[50] the Court struck down separate "Shared Time" and "Community Education" programs which respectively took place during and after school hours on religious school premises. The Shared Time program entailed public school teachers offering various remedial and enrichment classes to non-public school students on the premises of non-public schools during the regular school day. Forty of the forty-one schools involved were sectarian, and the record did not indicate that any public school students attended any of these programs. In addition to teachers, the state provided supplies and materials necessary for instruction.

The Community Education program offered pupils at private schools a variety of academic and non-academic courses at the end of the regular school day. Generally, these Community Education courses were taught by private school teachers employed

---

48. Wallace v. Jaffree, 472 U.S. 38, 110–11 (1985) (Rehnquist, J., dissenting).
49. 463 U.S. 388 (1983).
50. 473 U.S. 373 (1985).

part-time by the school district for the purposes of the program. For both programs, the state leased classrooms from the private schools. During Shared Time instruction, a sign was posted denominating the particular room a "public school classroom." The state inspected such classrooms to ensure that they were free of religious symbols; it also adjusted the teaching schedule to accommodate religious holidays.

The Court held that both programs violated the *Lemon* primary effect test in three ways. First, relying on *Meek v. Pittenger*, the majority feared that public school teachers teaching in such pervasively sectarian environments could subtly or overtly convey religious messages. Second, having public school teachers teach at religious schools presented a dangerous symbolic union between church and state which involved concerns similar to those voiced in the early case of *McCollum v. Board of Education*, discussed earlier.[51] Third, the programs subsidized sectarian education by shouldering some of sectarian schools' secular education responsibilities.

In *Aguilar v. Felton*,[52] decided the same day as *Ball*, the Court struck down a similar shared time program. Under the program, New York City used federal funds to pay public school teachers and other personnel to provide remedial educational and guidance services to educationally-deprived children enrolled in both public and private (including religious) schools. Instruction of religious school students occurred on the premises of their schools. City officials told those teachers to avoid religious matters and to minimize contact with private school officials. Moreover, classrooms used for the lessons were cleared of religious symbols. To monitor compliance with these directives, City officials periodically made unannounced visits to the schools during instructional periods. The close state supervision of the program prompted the Court to strike it down as violating *Lemon*'s entanglement prong. Concurring, Justice Powell argued that the program also violated the primary effect prong of *Lemon*, as it relieved religious schools of their duty to provide supplemental and remedial education.

Four justices dissented in four separate opinions that raised objections to the theory and practice of *Lemon*'s entanglement prong—objections that would eventually lead the Court to modify that prong significantly.[53] Justice O'Connor argued that the Court exaggerated the amount of supervision necessary to avert religious indoctrination, as no evidence of such indoctrination by public school teachers existed. Echoing these objections, Chief Justice Burger objected that the majority's worry that state aid like this advances religion "borders on paranoia."[54] In his dissent, Justice Rehnquist said that the Court placed the state in what he called a trap, in which a state's failure to supervise the program violated the primary effect prong of *Lemon* while a state's performance of supervision violated the entanglement prong. Justice White, adhering

---

51. *See* Section 12.01.

52. 473 U.S. 402 (1985).

53. Those four justices also dissented from parts of the *Grand Rapids v. Ball* decision, decided the same day, invalidating an analogous program.

54. 473 U.S. at 419 (Burger, C.J., dissenting).

to the more accommodationist view he held at least from his partial dissent in *Lemon*, would have upheld the program.

As the Court's composition continued to change in the 1980s and early 1990s, it began to embrace these criticisms of *Lemon* and cast serious doubt on its continued vitality. For example, in *Zobrest v. Catalina Foothills School District*,[55] the Court did not even mention the *Lemon* test.[56] *Zobrest* involved a deaf student who invoked the federal Individuals with Disabilities Education Act (IDEA) to request that a public school district provide him with an interpreter at his religious school. The school district refused, arguing that the Establishment Clause barred the student's request. The Court, however, held that the provision of an interpreter did not violate the Establishment Clause. In so doing, it articulated a much more accommodationist approach to Establishment Clause issues.

Writing for the majority, Chief Justice Rehnquist categorized IDEA as a neutral "social welfare program" providing benefits "to a broad class of citizens defined without reference to religion."[57] According to the Chief Justice, the Establishment Clause did not bar such programs merely because religious institutions might receive an incidental benefit. In upholding the program, the Court relied heavily on *Mueller v. Allen*, discussed earlier, and *Witters v. Washington Department of Services for the Blind*.[58] In *Mueller*, incidental aid to sectarian schools occurred "'only as a result of numerous private choices of individual parents of school-age children'" to use the state's tax credit at a religious school.[59] In *Witters*, the Court upheld the extension of a general state program of vocational educational assistance to a blind seminary student. Neither of the cases involved direct assistance to religious institutions, nor did the programs in those cases create financial incentives for parents to seek a sectarian education for their children, as both programs provided benefits regardless of the religious or secular character of the education that was thereby assisted. Chief Justice Rehnquist found the assistance at issue in *Zobrest* to be analogous to the programs upheld in those cases.

The Court rejected the argument that *Zobrest* was distinguishable from *Mueller* and *Witters* because the interpreter was a public employee. In making this argument, the school district relied on two cases, discussed earlier, involving direct governmental aid to sectarian schools. In *Meek v. Pittenger*,[60] the Court invalidated a statute providing "massive aid"[61] to sectarian schools through the direct loan of educational materials

55. 509 U.S. 1 (1993).

56. *See also* Lee v. Weisman, 505 U.S. 577 (1992). In *Lee*, a school graduation prayer case, the majority did not predicate its decision on the *Lemon* test. Justice Kennedy, writing for the Court, struck down the prayer because of its subtle coercive effects and divisive potential. Justice Scalia, joined in his dissent by Chief Justice Rehnquist and Justices White and Thomas, articulated a test of direct or legal coercion grounded in a historical practice.

57. *Zobrest*, 509 U.S. at 8.

58. 474 U.S. 481 (1986).

59. *Zobrest*, 509 U.S. at 9 (quoting *Mueller*, 463 U.S. at 399).

60. 421 U.S. 349 (1975).

61. *Zobrest*, 509 U.S. at 11 (quoting *Meek*, 421 U.S. at 365).

and services, including tape recorders, on-site instruction and counseling by public employees. In *Grand Rapids School District v. Ball*,[62] the Court struck down a statute allowing public school employees and instructional materials to be used in sectarian schools.

Chief Justice Rehnquist concluded that the programs in *Meek* and *Ball* differed from the IDEA program. Those earlier programs involved direct grants of government assistance that relieved sectarian schools of educational expenses they would otherwise have borne. By contrast, IDEA afforded its primary benefits to handicapped students, providing sectarian schools with only incidental benefits to the extent that they benefitted at all. Moreover, the services provided by a sign-language interpreter varied greatly from those supplied by a teacher or counselor. The Court stated that "the Establishment Clause lays down no absolute bar to the placing of a public employee in a sectarian school." The requested interpreter would simply "transmit everything that is said in exactly the same way it was intended."[63]

Justice Blackmun wrote a dissenting opinion, whose constitutional analysis was joined only by Justice Souter.[64] Justice Blackmun noted that public employees would be interpreting religious instruction, Catholic Mass, and communication of secular subjects from a religious perspective. Objecting to the majority's reliance on its characterization of IDEA as a "general welfare program," Justice Blackmun noted that *Meek* and *Ball* struck down general welfare programs providing remedial aid to public and private school students. He relied on *Board of Education v. Allen*,[65] a 1968 case that invalidated the provision of tape recorders and slide projectors to sectarian schools. Like sign-language interpreters, such provisions could impermissibly supply "the medium" for transmission of a religious message. Justice Blackmun distinguished *Mueller* and *Witters*, saying that government involvement with sectarian schools in those cases only entailed tax relief or monetary payments.

In *Agostini v. Felton*,[66] the Court overruled *Aguilar v. Felton* and parts of *Grand Rapids School District v. Ball*, decided the same day in 1985, both of which were discussed earlier. *Aguilar* had construed the Establishment Clause to bar New York City from sending public school teachers into religious school classrooms to offer federally-mandated remedial education. *Agostini* held that *Aguilar* was no longer consistent with the Court's understanding of the Establishment Clause.[67]

Writing for the Court, Justice O'Connor first abandoned the presumption that the mere presence of a public employee in a religious setting has the "impermissible

62. 473 U.S. 373 (1985).

63. *Zobrest*, 509 U.S. at 13.

64. Justices Stevens, O'Connor, and Souter joined a part of his dissent addressing statutory issues.

65. 392 U.S. 236 (1968).

66. 521 U.S. 203 (1997).

67. *Agostini* arose when the school officials bound by the injunction in *Aguilar* petitioned the Court to be released from it, on the ground that the underlying Establishment Clause law had shifted in their favor in the period since the injunction was issued.

effect of state-sponsored indoctrination or constitutes a symbolic union between government and religion."[68] She observed that the Court had moved away from that presumption in *Zobrest v. Catalina Foothills School District*, discussed earlier, which
upheld a publicly-employed sign language interpreter assisting a student in a private
school. Moreover, she argued, no evidence in *Agostini* indicated that any public school
teacher had ever tried to broach the topic of religion. Absent such evidence, it was
unreasonable to assume a "symbolic unions" because of the mere presence of public
school teachers in religious schools.[69]

The Court also rejected the dissent's concern that the funding had the primary
effect of advancing religion by relieving sectarian schools of services that they would
otherwise have had to provide. Instead, it characterized the program as providing
supplementary assistance for children in need. Moreover, the Court refused to consider
the program as a government subsidy to religion based on the number of sectarian
students it helped. Instead, the Court characterized the program as one which allotted
funds on criteria that neither favored nor disfavored religion and were available to
all eligible children. Thus, the Court concluded that the program did not have the
impermissible effect of promoting religion.

Finally, the Court rejected *Aguilar*'s conclusion that the program created excessive
entanglement between church and state. At this point in the analysis, the Court modified *Lemon* by considering entanglement as a part of its inquiry into the law's effect;
thus, the Court effectively combined two of *Lemon*'s three prongs. *Aguilar*'s conclusion
of excessive entanglement had rested on the fear that the program would require significant monitoring of the relationship between the public school teachers and the
religious school in which they were teaching. But the Court concluded that, given
Zobrest's assumption that state employees would not inculcate religion simply because
they found themselves in a sectarian environment, such pervasive monitoring would
not be required, and thus the risk of excessive entanglement was not present. Moreover, Justice O'Connor concluded, *contra Aguilar*, that the state's need to engage in
"administrative cooperation" with religious schools and the danger of "political divisiveness" by themselves did not merit a finding of excessive entanglement.[70]

In summary, the Court found that the program "does not run afoul of any of three
primary criteria we currently use to evaluate whether government aid has the effect
of advancing religion: it does not result in governmental indoctrination; define its
recipients by reference to religion; or create an excessive entanglement."[71] Nor did
the program endorse religion in any way.

Justice Souter dissented, joined by Justices Stevens and Ginsburg. Justice Souter
argued that the program relieved private schools of the responsibilities of teaching
remedial skills, thus subsidizing them by allowing them to focus their resources on

---

68. *Id.* at 223.
69. *Id.* at 227.
70. *Id.* at 233–34.
71. *Id.* at 234–35.

other subjects, including religious instruction. He disputed the Court's reading of *Zobrest*, contending that the sign language interpreter was more of an instrumentality than an instructor. He further distinguished *Zobrest* and *Witters* as cases in which government aid went to individual students who chose to put the aid to use in a religious environment, rather than constituting a broader program of aid featuring extensive participation by students in religious schools.

Together, *Zobrest* and *Agostini* marked retreats from the strict separationism that had marked cases such as *Ball* and *Aguilar* and, even more, *Lemon*. Their more relaxed attitudes toward state instructors working on the site of sectarian institutions and their similarly more relaxed attitude toward both entanglement and the risk of government personnel engaging in religious indoctrination reflected a more accommodationist attitude that was gaining force at the Court during the 1990s.

That trend accelerated with *Mitchell v. Helms*, decided in 2000.[72] In *Mitchell*, the Court upheld a Louisiana school aid program which lent "library services and materials" including "assessments, reference materials, computer software and hardware for instructional use, and other curricular materials."[73] Under the federal statute that funded the Louisiana program, materials had to be "secular, neutral, and nonideological."[74]

Writing for a four-justice plurality, Justice Thomas applied the test in *Agostini v. Felton*,[75] focusing on its effects requirement. The plaintiffs did not challenge the holding below that the program did not involve excessive entanglement. Accordingly, Justice Thomas narrowed his analysis to the other two parts of *Agostini*'s effects test: whether the program results in government religious indoctrination or defines its recipients by religion.

First, the plurality found that no religious indoctrination occurred in religious schools that could be attributed to government action. To avoid government indoctrination, Justice Thomas wrote that the Court had consistently relied on the doctrine of neutrality, which upheld broad-based government aid provided without regard to religion. Justice Thomas explained that one way of ensuring neutrality is to require that government aid reach religious institutions only through the private, independent choices of individuals. The second relevant criterion in the *Agostini* effects test evaluates whether an aid program defines its recipients by reference to religion. Importantly, aid cannot create incentives to choose a religious school. The plurality concluded that this requirement is satisfied if the program's aid is allocated on neutral, secular grounds, as was the Louisiana program.

The plurality also considered two other proposed criteria for judging a program's effect: that the effect prong is violated if either the aid goes directly to schools or if the aid is capable of being diverted to religious instruction. The plurality rejected

---

72. 530 U.S. 793 (2000).
73. *Id.* at 802.
74. *Id.* at 796.
75. 521 U.S. 203 (1997).

both of them. As for the first, it observed that, while passing government aid through private hands makes it more obvious that the aid is neutrally available without regard to religion, it did not regard such a structure as constitutionally required. Indeed, it concluded that such a requirement would be a pointless formalism, as long as the aid reached the school only through the independent choices of parents and students. As for the second argument, the plurality accepted the plaintiffs' contention that aid cannot be religious in nature, but rejected their proposed rule banning any aid that could be diverted to religious use. If a religious school received aid that was non-religious in content and that could be used in a public school, the aid could also be supplied for any use in a private school.

Applying these two factors, the plurality concluded that the challenged law did not have an impermissible effect, as *Agostini* had redefined that term. The program did not determine eligibility for aid based on religion, as it was allocated mainly on a per capita basis by the number of students enrolled in the school. The aid thus followed a private decision to attend a particular school. Nor did the aid result in government indoctrination, as it was made available to public and private schools regardless of religious affiliation and could not have religious content.[76] The plurality, joined on this point by Justice O'Connor and Justice Breyer, overruled *Meek v. Pittenger* and *Wolman v. Walter*, cases striking down such direct aid to religious schools, to the extent that they conflicted with the decision.

Justice O'Connor, joined by Justice Breyer, concurred in the judgment. While agreeing in the result and in overruling *Meek* and *Wolman*, she objected that the plurality had announced an exceptionally broad rule allowing aid to religious institutions so long as it flowed on a neutral basis—a rule she saw as over-emphasizing the concept of neutrality. She also criticized the plurality's permitting direct aid and aid that was actually diverted to promote a sectarian mission. She would have held that actual diversion of government aid for religious purposes violated the Establishment Clause, and thus disagreed with the plurality's conclusion that the only question was whether the material the government provided itself had religious content.

Justice Souter dissented, joined by Justices Stevens and Ginsburg. Like Justice O'Connor, Justice Souter also criticized the majority's emphasis on the law's neutrality. He argued that cases such as *Everson v. Board of Education* forbade government from directly aiding any institution in support of its religious mission. If the Court solely used neutrality as the criterion, he argued, much government aid would flow to religious institutions for religious uses, a result he viewed as inconsistent with the Establishment Clause.

Mitchell, when combined with *Zobrest* and *Agostini*, made it possible for government to provide direct aid to religious schools and to place government instructional personnel within the premises of religious schools. The distance between these results, and the results and analysis in the early cases (*Everson*, *McCollum*, and *Zorach*) are

---

76. The Court noted 191 examples of improper lending of books over the course of three years, but also noted that those problems had been resolved prior to litigation.

striking, and can only be understood as reflecting a different understanding of what the Establishment Clause requires.

In addition to the kind of aid discussed in the cases up to now, in recent years, states have experimented with programs that provide parents with vouchers that can be used to pay the cost of private education, including education in religious schools. In *Zelman v. Simmons-Harris*,[77] the Court upheld against an Establishment Clause challenge an Ohio voucher program, applicable to students in any school district that had come under state control because of sub-standard performance, which allowed the vouchers to be used in religious schools.

Writing for a five-justice majority upholding the program, Chief Justice Rehnquist noted that the Court's decisions consistently have distinguished between government programs that directly funded religious schools and programs in which government funds only reached the schools through "the genuine and independent choices of private individuals." The Court stated, "[w]here a government aid program is neutral with respect to religion, and provides assistance directly to a broad class of citizens who, in turn, direct government aid to religious schools wholly as a result of their own genuine and independent private choice, the program is not readily subject to challenge under the Establishment Clause."[78] The Court held that the Ohio program was neutral toward religion, describing it as "part of a general and multifaceted undertaking" to help the children of a failed school district, conferring its benefits "to a broad class of individuals defined without reference to religion."[79] It also concluded that the program's neutrality and operation through private choices necessitated the conclusion that it did not endorse religious practices or beliefs.

Nor did Chief Justice Rehnquist attach constitutional significance to "the fact that 96% of the scholarship recipients have enrolled in religious schools." He noted that his own 1983 opinion in *Mueller v. Allen* had "found irrelevant that 96% of parents taking deductions for tuition expenses paid tuition at religious schools."[80] Finally, the Court distinguished *Public Committee v. Nyquist*, discussed earlier, as a case where the program's function itself was to assist sectarian institutions.[81] He contrasted that goal with the voucher program's neutrality toward religion and religious schools.

Justice Souter dissented, joined by Justices Stevens, Ginsburg, and Breyer. He objected that the majority had approved of an "unprecedented"[82] scale of government aid to religious schools, which would pay for religious instruction. He also found illogical the majority's application of the neutrality test, in that the majority included public schools among the options that established the program's neutrality. Justice

---

77. 536 U.S. 639 (2002).

78. *Id.* at 649, 652. Recall that it was Justice Rehnquist himself in *Mueller v. Allen*, 463 U.S. 388 (1983), who had focused on whether the program operated through private choices rather than providing support directly to religious schools. *Mueller* is discussed earlier in this sub-section.

79. *Id.* at 653.

80. *Id.* at 658.

81. *Nyquist* is discussed in Section 12.02[1][b].

82. 536 U.S. at 708 (Souter, J., dissenting).

Breyer, joined by Justices Stevens and Souter, also dissented. He insisted that voucher programs differed both in kind and degree from past programs, since, respectively, they help finance teaching religion and entail a significant shift of public resources from public schools to religious schools.

The Court's aid-to-schools cases reflect a complex, intricate jurisprudence that is made even more difficult to understand by the Court's gradual but clear shift toward a more accommodationist approach to government aid to religion. In particular, since *Zobrest*, the Court has been much more willing to accept government aid to religious schools, even if that aid has the effect of advancing religion and involves placing government instructional personnel in schools and sending government resources directly to those institutions, rather than formally funneling them through parents or students. As long as the aid disbursed to the schools is part of a program that is available to all schools, religious and secular, the fact that government aid is flowing directly to schools no longer renders the program a violation of the Establishment Clause. This view clearly reflects a view of the Establishment Clause that is more accommodating to religion.

These more accommodationist decisions, however, have all generated spirited dissents joined by multiple justices. The dissenters' views generally take the form of an insistence that government not directly fund religious schools and not involve the state in directly advancing the teaching of religious doctrine. These views reflect the strict separationist spirit illustrated by the "wall of separation" metaphor Justice Black employed in *Everson*. Given the difficult lines these cases require courts to draw, it is likely that the justices will continue to disagree, not just on the fundamental principles animating the Establishment Clause, but the details of their application.

[2] Government Support for Other Religious Institutions

A number of cases involve government support for religious institutions other than religious schools. This type of support ranges from funding religious institutions' activity as part of a more general secular federal program to exempting religious institutions from generally-applicable burdens. Disputes over these laws raise yet again the tension between the accommodation of religion that the Free Exercise Clause might encourage and the Establishment Clause's mandate to not favor religion.

Sometimes these laws involve tax benefits. For example, in *Texas Monthly, Inc. v. Bullock*,[83] the Court struck down a Texas sales tax exemption applicable only to religious periodicals. Writing for a three-justice plurality, Justice Brennan acknowledged that government policies could have secular benefits that incidentally assist religion. Relying on *Walz* and *Mueller*, tax exemption cases that featured religious expenditures as beneficiaries,[84] Justice Brennan said that the benefits provided to religious organ-

---

83. 489 U.S. 1 (1989).
84. These cases are discussed earlier, in Sections 12.02[1][a], [c].

izations could be characterized as incidental when those benefits were shared by many nonreligious organizations — a situation that did not exist under the Texas law's special exemption for religious publications.

The plurality rejected the argument that the exemption was necessary to avoid either violating the Free Exercise Clause or entangling the state with religion and thus violating the Establishment Clause. It also attempted to distinguish earlier cases that had struck down licensing tax requirements as applied to Jehovah's Witnesses,[85] describing those earlier laws as burdens on preaching, unlike the tax on the religious periodicals in *Texas Monthly*.

In a concurring opinion joined by Justice O'Connor, Justice Blackmun criticized the plurality for sacrificing Free Exercise Clause values in its rejection of the state's argument in defense of the religious-periodical exemption to its sales tax law. But he also criticized Justice Scalia's willingness, in his dissent, to exalt those free exercise values at the expense of the Establishment Clause. Justice Blackmun reasoned that, whatever the constitutionality under the Free Exercise Clause of taxing religious activity as a general matter, it was unconstitutional under the Establishment Clause to limit a tax exemption to religious periodicals. Dissenting, Justice Scalia, joined by Chief Justice Rehnquist and Justice Kennedy, concluded that the exemption of exclusively religious literature was not only permissible, but possibly even "constitutionally compelled in order to avoid interference with the dissemination of religious ideas."[86]

In *Jimmy Swaggart Ministries v. Board of Equalization*,[87] the Court upheld, against both Free Exercise Clause and Establishment Clause challenges, a state's imposition of general use and sales taxes on a religious organization for distributing religious materials. The case involved California sales and use taxes for goods purchased out-of-state, including goods sold by the plaintiff religious organization.

Writing for a unanimous Court, Justice O'Connor rejected the free exercise argument. The California tax was a generally applicable measure that religious organizations must obey along with everyone else. She distinguished license taxes on religious literature or other religious activities of the sort that were struck down in earlier Free Exercise Clause cases, which she described as prior restraints on religious activity, since they had to be paid before the individual could pursue the religious activity. The Court left open the question of whether a more onerous generally applicable tax might violate the Free Exercise Clause. Justice O'Connor also rejected the argument that the tax violated the Establishment Clause by fostering excessive entanglement. On that point, she noted the organization's sophisticated accounting operations, which allowed for easy compliance with the state's tax laws, and also observed that

85. *See* Murdock v. Pennsylvania, 319 U.S. 105 (1943) (striking down occupational tax as applied to seller of religious literature); Follett v. McCormick, 321 U.S. 573 (1944) (same).

86. 489 U.S. at 41 (Scalia, J., dissenting). Justice White concurred on Press Clause grounds. The Press Clause, and the limitations it imposes on taxation of publications and other media, is discussed in Section 11.03[2].

87. 493 U.S. 378 (1990).

government could impose general record-keeping and administrative duties on religious institutions.

As noted throughout this discussion, *Lemon* and other tests have been applied to scrutinize nondiscriminatory government aid to religion. By contrast, when that aid discriminates among religious groups, the Court employs strict scrutiny. In *Larson v. Valente*,[88] a statute imposed registration and reporting requirements on charitable institutions, but exempted those religions that received less than half their support from nonmembers. A church that did not satisfy that criterion successfully argued that the law at issue established an unconstitutional government preference among religions. Employing strict scrutiny, the Court concluded that the state's asserted interest in preventing fraud was not furthered by the law's criterion for the exemption. The Court, speaking through Justice O'Connor, also noted that the law politicized religious affiliation by picking and choosing among favored and disfavored creeds, and thus entangled government in religion in violation of *Lemon*.

[3] Religious Displays on Government Property

Another important series of cases concerns the display of religious symbols on government property. The Court has been deeply split in many of these cases, although the most recent of them, decided in 2019, might portend a consensus on a more accommodating attitude to at least some of these symbols. In most of these cases, the fundamental conflict has been between the Establishment Clause's restriction on government approval of a particular religion, or religion generally, and, on the other hand, the asserted hostility to religion that would be evinced by a requirement that government refrain from displaying any religious iconography, or even to remove some monuments to comply with a court order finding that the display violated the Establishment Clause.

To be sure, even the strictest of separationists would agree that a display of a Renaissance painting of the Madonna and Child in a government art museum would not violate the Establishment Clause. And even the most accommodating of accommodationists would strike down a government erection of a golden calf, accompanied by a placard officially commanding the populace to bow down and worship it. But between these extremes lie many difficult cases.

In the earliest of the modern cases, dating from the 1980s, the Court often attempted to decide these cases based on the *Lemon* test.[89] For example, in *Lynch v. Donnelly*,[90] the Court upheld the display in a private park of a city-owned Christmas nativity scene. In upholding the display, Chief Justice Burger, writing for the Court, applied *Lemon*, but effectively loosened its secular purpose prong by stating that it would be satisfied unless there was no question that the statute or activity was mo-

---

88. 456 U.S. 228 (1982).
89. The *Lemon* test is set forth in Section 12.02[1][a].
90. 465 U.S. 668 (1984).

tivated wholly by religious considerations. He concluded that the crèche at issue was displayed to celebrate the national holiday of Christmas and to depict the origins of that holiday. These amounted to legitimate secular purposes under the highly deferential purpose standard the Court employed.

Turning to *Lemon*'s primary effect prong, the Chief Justice stated that comparisons of the relative benefits to religion of different forms of governmental support were difficult to make. Faced with the task of making such elusive distinctions in the abstract, the Chief Justice devised analogies, finding that the display of the crèche was no more beneficial to religion than was the supplying of books in *Board of Education v. Allen*[91] or transportation for private school students in *Everson v. Board of Education*,[92] both of which were upheld against Establishment Clause challenges.[93] Chief Justice Burger also compared the crèche to practices not ruled upon by the Court, such as the display of religious paintings in public museums. He argued that just as paintings had artistic value apart from their religious symbolism, the crèche had independent worth in that it represented an historical event. For Chief Justice Burger, the benefit to religion in *Lynch* was incidental, indirect, and remote and certainly no greater than any benefit conferred by endorsing a holiday called "Christ's Mass" or displaying religious paintings in government museums.

Finally, the crèche display satisfied *Lemon*'s entanglement prong. The Court focused on administrative entanglement, finding that the city had not specifically designed the crèche, nor had it spent a great deal on its upkeep. Moreover, the Court refused to hold that political divisiveness alone could comprise excessive entanglement. In any event, he observed that, beyond the lawsuit itself, no evidence of divisiveness created by the crèche existed over the entire history of its display.

Several times in *Lynch* the Chief Justice referred to the crèche in the context of the overall holiday display. This has led many to suggest that the outcome was conditioned in part on the crèche's having been part of a general holiday display which included reindeer, a Santa Claus house, and other secular symbols of Christmas. In his dissent, Justice Brennan criticized the majority for focusing only on the general holiday context in which the crèche appeared, rather than the "clear religious import of the crèche" itself.[94] Nevertheless, in a later case, the Court similarly considered the surrounding context of religious displays exhibited during the winter holiday season.[95]

---

91. 392 U.S. 236 (1968).

92. 330 U.S. 1 (1947).

93. Chief Justice Burger also compared the display of the crèche to practices upheld in several other Establishment Clause decisions, including *Marsh v. Chambers*, 463 U.S. 783 (1983) (legislative prayer); *Roemer v. Board of Pub. Works*, 426 U.S. 736 (1976) (federal grants to church-supported colleges); *Tilton v. Richardson*, 403 U.S. 672 (1971) (federal grants for buildings of church-sponsored colleges); *Walz v. Tax Comm'n*, 397 U.S. 664 (1970) (tax exemption for church property); *McGowan v. Maryland*, 366 U.S. 420 (1961) (Sunday closing laws); and *Zorach v. Clauson*, 343 U.S. 306 (1952) (public school release time program for religious education).

94. *Lynch*, 465 U.S. at 705 (Brennan, J., dissenting).

95. *See* County of Allegheny v. ACLU, 492 U.S. 573 (1989), discussed later in the text.

In her concurring opinion, Justice O'Connor first proposed her "endorsement" approach to Establishment Clause cases, which became quite influential on the Court. According to Justice O'Connor, the Establishment Clause was not violated when there was neither excessive entanglement nor government endorsement or disapproval of religion. She de-emphasized the secular purpose test, calling it merely the subjective component of the objective inquiry into the law's effects. Instead, Justice O'Connor reformulated the first two prongs of the *Lemon* test as being concerned with whether a government practice was intended to or had the effect of conveying a message of government endorsement or disapproval of religion. This endorsement test asked whether the governmental practice had the purpose or unintentional effect of making religion relevant, in reality or in public perception, to status in the political community. Applying this inquiry in *Lynch*, she concluded that the government's legitimate secular purposes of "solemnizing public occasions, expressing confidence in the future, and encouraging the recognition of what is worthy of appreciation in society"[96] did not constitute religious endorsement.

In *County of Allegheny v. ACLU*,[97] the Court struck down a crèche display in a government building but upheld a separate display of a Hanukkah menorah next to a Christmas tree. In a part of the opinion supported by a majority of five, Justice Blackmun largely adopted Justice O'Connor's endorsement test by explaining *Lemon*'s effect prong in terms of endorsement. Drawing on the definition of that concept that Justice O'Connor had proposed in her *Lynch* concurrence, Justice Blackmun concluded that endorsement could comprise appearing to take "a position on questions of a religious belief or ... 'making adherence to a religion relevant in any way to a person's standing in the political community.'"[98]

Answering the endorsement question, Justice Blackmun reasoned, required examining the context surrounding the government's employment of religious symbolism. Accordingly, he conducted an extensive analysis of the design elements contributing to the total effect of the crèche display, including the proximity of other decorations to the crèche, the floral frame surrounding it, the performance of Christmas carols in front of it, the general physical setting, and a sign disclosing ownership of the crèche by a religious organization. The Court noted that the crèche in *Lynch* was displayed among a variety of other figures including Santa's house and reindeer. In contrast, the crèche in *County of Allegheny* was displayed alone on the Grand Staircase, an important ceremonial part of the building housing the county seat, with the floral frame accentuating its centrality. A sign noting that the crèche display was owned by the Roman Catholic Holy Name Society, not the City, did not render the display constitutional. Neither did the occasional singing of Christmas carols near the crèche, especially since some of those carols were religious in nature.

---

96. *Id.* at 693 (O'Connor, J., concurring).
97. 492 U.S. 573 (1989).
98. *Id.* at 594 (quoting *Lynch*, 465 U.S. at 687 (O'Connor, J., concurring)).

A different majority of six upheld the combined display of a Christmas tree and a Hanukkah menorah. Justice Blackmun, writing only for himself, wrote that the context of the menorah display with a Christmas tree and a sign saluting liberty during the holiday season sufficiently reduced any danger of endorsement. Justice Blackmun would, however, have remanded the case to determine whether the display had a secular purpose and did not generate excessive entanglement under the *Lemon* test. In her concurring opinion, Justice O'Connor voted to sustain the display of the religious menorah next to the secular Christmas tree. She concluded that, when considered along with the sign saluting liberty, this combination of religious and secular symbols conveyed a message of pluralism rather than endorsement of a particular religion.

In a concurring and dissenting opinion for four justices, Justice Kennedy would have upheld both displays. Justice Kennedy criticized the majority's analysis as resting on the "minutiae"[99] of each display's other features. He also criticized the endorsement test as difficult to apply and one that, if applied in full force, would prohibit many longstanding government practices. In its stead, he proposed the following test: "Noncoercive government action within the realm of flexible accommodation or passive acknowledgment of existing symbols does not violate the Establishment Clause unless it benefits religion in a way more direct and more substantial than practices that are accepted in our national heritage."[100] Justice Kennedy argued that the displays at issue neither coerced nor proselytized; rather, they were representations of holidays that had religious and secular aspects and acknowledgements of those holidays' histories.

In an opinion joined by Justices Marshall and Stevens, Justice Brennan would have struck down both displays. He said that both the menorah and the Christmas tree were religious symbols. Moreover, the Establishment Clause did not permit religious displays for the purpose of conveying pluralism. In an opinion joined by Justices Brennan and Marshall, Justice Stevens worried that governmental displays of any religious symbols could foment differences between citizens on matters of religion.

In *Capitol Square Review Board v. Pinette*,[101] the Court, on a 7–2 vote, held that allowing the Ku Klux Klan to display an unattended cross on government property near the Ohio Statehouse would not violate the Establishment Clause. *Pinette* was factually distinct from most other religious displays cases in that it involved the placement of a religious item on public property by a *private* group, rather than by the government (even if the item was owned by a private group, as the crèche was in *Allegheny County*). Thus, the case implicated the free speech rules appropriate for speech in a public forum. In that context, a four-justice plurality concluded that the endorsement test was inappropriate, since the placement of the cross constituted private speech in a place designated for speech. While three justices agreed with the plurality that the private placement of the cross was protected, they, as

---

99. *Id.* at 674 (Kennedy, J., concurring in the judgment in part and dissenting in part).
100. *Id.* at 662–63.
101. 515 U.S. 753 (1995).

well as two dissenters, argued that it was still appropriate to inquire into whether the government's allowance of that speech constituted endorsement of Christianity. Writing for those three concurring justices, Justice O'Connor argued that the plurality's reading would abandon *Lemon*'s effect prong, since it would allow government sponsorship of private religious speech even when such speech sent a message of government endorsement of religion.

On the same day in 2005 the Court decided two Establishment Clause cases by 5–4 votes, reaching different results on the constitutionality of two challenged displays of the Ten Commandments. *Van Orden v. Perry*[102] held that a monument displaying the Ten Commandments on the grounds of the Texas State Capitol did not violate the Establishment Clause. The monument, a large stone monolith, was donated to the state by a private organization. Located on the grounds surrounding the Capitol, the monument was one of 17 monuments and 21 historical markers said to commemorate Texas history and Texans. The monument in question featured the text of the Ten Commandments, surrounded by religious and patriotic symbols. Forty years passed before anyone brought an Establishment Clause claim against the monument; the plaintiff had passed it frequently for six years before filing his lawsuit.

Writing for a four-justice plurality, Chief Justice Rehnquist observed that the Establishment Clause reflects a constitutional principle that both acknowledges the role played by religion in American life but also the risk that government intervention in religion could impair religious liberty. When considering how to strike that balance, he concluded that *Lemon* did not provide the appropriate approach to fact patterns such as those in *Van Orden*. Instead, he concluded that proper analysis of the case was "driven both by the nature of the monument and by our Nation's history."[103] With regard to the latter, he noted the long history of official government acknowledgement of religion, including by featuring representations of the Ten Commandments in government buildings. With regard to the former, he noted that the monument in question stood among a large number of other stone monuments recognizing other aspects of Texas history and values. He distinguished *Stone v. Graham*,[104] a case where the Court had struck down the posting of the Ten Commandments in public school classrooms, on the ground that that latter practice was far more intrusive on students than the passive monument, sitting on the statehouse grounds, was on passers-by.

Justice Breyer concurred in the judgment, providing the critical fifth vote for the result upholding the monument's constitutionality. He described *Van Orden* as a "borderline case," which requires "the exercise of legal judgment" about the monument's context, rather than a legal test. He wrote that the monolith conveys both religious and secular messages, including "the Commandments' role in shaping civic

---

102. 545 U.S. 677 (2005).
103. *Id.* at 686.
104. 449 U.S. 39 (1980).

morality."[105] (The group donating the monument aimed at helping prevent juvenile delinquency.) While he conceded that a new monument would likely be divisive, he doubted that the current display was, given the 40-year gap between its erection and the legal challenge. Justice Breyer worried that a finding that the monument violated the Establishment Clause would suggest hostility toward religion and foment the religious divisiveness the Clause endeavored to protect against.

Justices Scalia and Thomas joined the plurality opinion, and each wrote a separate concurrence. Justice Scalia insisted that the Clause allowed a state to favor religion generally and honor God through practices such as veneration of the Ten Commandments. Justice Thomas took issue with the very idea of incorporating the Establishment Clause to apply against the states. He also offered a test that centered on legal coercion, such as mandatory religious observances or taxes for a religious purpose.

Four justices dissented in three separate opinions. The opinions all emphasized the role the Ten Commandments played in Judaism and Christianity and argued that the display did not commemorate any aspect of Texas culture or Texas history. Nor, in their view, did it refer to the Commandments in the sense of a tradition of lawgiving, but instead as a religious text, the presentation of which violated the government's Establishment Clause duty of neutrality toward religion.

By contrast, *McCreary County v. American Civil Liberties Union of Kentucky*,[106] decided the same day as *Van Orden*, invalidated a display of the Ten Commandments in certain courthouses. The display at issue was the final version of one that had been the object of previous litigation, with earlier versions having been struck down. The final version of the display consisted of a framed copy of the Ten Commandments alongside nine other framed copies of historical documents, with the Ten Commandments quoted at greater length than the others, and the statement: "The Ten Commandments provide the moral background of the Declaration of Independence and the foundation of our legal tradition."

In striking down the third display, a five-justice majority agreed with the lower courts that the display constituted a rare government failure to satisfy *Lemon*'s purpose prong. The Court, speaking through Justice Souter, insisted that the purpose inquiry had to be "taken seriously,"[107] and concluded that, in light of the previously struck-down religiously-motivated displays and the County's failure to repeal the ordinances authorizing those earlier unconstitutional displays, the third display had to be understood as reflecting a government purpose to promote religion. The Court further concluded that *Lemon*'s secular purpose was to be judged by an "objective observer" who considers the "text, legislative history, and implementation of the statute."[108] The Court concluded that such an observer, aware of the County's previous uncon-

---

105. *Van Orden*, 545 U.S. at 700–01 (Breyer, J., concurring in the judgment).
106. 545 U.S. 844 (2005).
107. *Id.* at 874.
108. *Id.* at 862.

stitutional attempts to promote religion via the earlier displays, would have concluded that the County's third display was indeed an attempt to promote religion.

Justice O'Connor joined the majority opinion and also wrote a separate concurrence to note her conclusion that the third display conveyed an "unmistakable message of endorsement to the reasonable observer."[109] Justice Scalia dissented, joined by Chief Justice Rehnquist and Justices Kennedy and Thomas. He criticized the majority's analysis as reflecting a hostility to religion, and criticized it further for requiring that, under *Lemon*, the asserted secular purpose "predominate."

To date, the Court's most recent statement on the constitutionality of religious displays on public property is *American Legion v. American Humanist Association*.[110] *American Legion* upheld the constitutionality of a large Latin cross that was erected shortly after World War I as a monument to American casualties of that war. Writing for a majority of five justices, Justice Alito critiqued *Lemon*'s appropriateness in the context of Establishment Clause challenges to longstanding monuments such as the cross in that case. He explained that their age made it hard to uncover the true purposes underlying the decisions to erect such monuments, that such purposes may multiply over time (for example, from an original purpose of simply furthering religion to a desire to illustrate the community's history), that the message such monuments actually communicate may similarly evolve, and that, as a monument becomes an accepted part of the community, a court order requiring its removal may be seen as reflecting government hostility to religion.

For those reasons, Justice Alito concluded that the longstanding nature of a monument like the war cross challenged in *American Humanist* gives rise to a presumption of its constitutionality. Applying that presumption and considering the factors he had laid out, he concluded that the war cross, having become a symbol of Americans who died fighting World War I and a recognized feature of the local community, did not violate the Establishment Clause. In a section of the opinion that spoke for only four justices, Justice Alito explicitly called for jettisoning *Lemon* in favor of a more case-by-case approach that relied to a significant degree on the history of the display or the other challenged government action. In particular, the plurality cited previous decisions' reliance on history when deciding the constitutionality of legislative prayers, a topic considered in a later sub-section.[111]

Several justices concurred. Justice Breyer joined Justice Alito's opinion and Justice Kagan joined most of it, but each of them wrote separately to note their caution about over-reliance on history. Justices Thomas and Gorsuch argued for a more thorough repudiation of *Lemon* and a much broader scope for government to acknowledge religion through public displays. Notably, Justice Kavanaugh, in his first Establishment Clause opinion, offered a strong critique of *Lemon*. Justice Ginsburg, joined by Justice Sotomayor, dissented, emphasizing the Christian nature of Latin crosses in general,

---

109. *Id.* at 883 (O'Connor, J., concurring).
110. 139 S. Ct. 2067 (2019).
111. *See* Section 12.02[6].

and suggesting that remedies could be found that did not require the destruction or removal of the particular cross in question.

American Humanist reflects, in the monument and display context, an analogous move toward the accommodationist approach to the Establishment Clause as seen in the school aid cases discussed in 12.02[1]. In both sets of cases, the changing composition of the Court has led it to express increasing sympathy for the argument that a requirement of strict church-state separation would reflect a hostility to religion that is inconsistent with the values underlying the Free Exercise Clause. On the other hand, the decision in *American Humanist* was 7–2, unlike the more closely divided school aid cases. Perhaps the contexts are different enough that some justices willing to accommodate government religious displays will not be as accommodating of aid to religious education.[112]

[4] School Prayer

In contrast to the school funding and display cases, the modern Court has generally not permitted much government support for state-mandated or sanctioned prayer at school events. As in other areas of the Court's religion jurisprudence, however, many school prayer cases exhibit the same tension between separationist and accommodationist positions.

The watershed modern case is *Engel v. Vitale*,[113] in which the Court struck down state-mandated prayer in public school classrooms. The New York Board of Regents required teachers at the beginning of each school day to lead the class in the following recitation: "Almighty God, we acknowledge our dependence upon Thee, and we beg Thy blessings upon us, our parents, our teachers and our Country."

In finding that the prayer violated the Establishment Clause, Justice Black discussed two concerns. First, state involvement in a religious practice poses the danger of religious persecution. Evidence that recitation of the prayer resulted in religious persecution was not readily apparent in *Engel*. Nevertheless, the Court acknowledged that the pressure exerted on students to say the prayer and the exclusion of students if they refused to participate might raise that specter.

Justice Black also worried that state involvement in a religious practice might demean religion. In *Engel*, the state composed the prayer, and civil officials appeared to be assuming the religious duty of leading prayers, thereby impairing the sanctity of religious authorities. Moreover, such state involvement transformed religious practice into a political issue. The state might have allowed ministers, rabbis, and priests to compose the prayers; however, that could have posed entanglement problems. Moreover, free exercise problems might have arisen, as only those individuals who

---

112. *See, e.g.,* note 30, *supra* (noting the possibility that Chief Justice Burger was less willing to accommodate government support of religion in the education context because of the presence of impressionable children).

113. 370 U.S. 421 (1962).

were members of the particular sect composing the prayer might have felt comfortable reciting it. Justice Stewart dissented, stressing the voluntary nature of the prayer in question and the long history of public officials acknowledging God.

The next year, in *Abington School District v. Schempp*,[114] the Court struck down a state law requiring teachers to read, without comment, at least ten verses from the Bible before the school day began. The law also required teachers to lead their classes in a voluntary recitation of the Lord's Prayer. The state claimed that the law furthered such secular purposes as the promotion of moral values, the contradiction of the trend toward materialism, the perpetuation of our institutions, and the teaching of literature.

In an analysis that eventually led to the *Lemon* test,[115] the Court stated that the Bible was clearly a sectarian instrument and that Bible reading had the primary effect of advancing religion. The Court rejected the argument that students' ability to excuse themselves from the Bible reading sessions validated those sessions' constitutionality. Nor did the Court accept the argument that striking down those sessions effectively established secular humanism as a *de facto* state religion. Finally, the Court rejected the argument that the invalidation of those sessions amounted to a violation of the Free Exercise Clause, remarking that that latter Clause did not authorize believers in a given religion to use the mechanism of state power to practice their beliefs. The Court cautioned, however, that it was not disallowing the study of the Bible as a literary or historical text.

Several justices wrote concurring opinions. In his concurrence, Justice Goldberg, joined by Justice Harlan, raised concerns about coercing schoolchildren when the prestige of the state was placed behind the Bible reading sessions. For that reason, he concluded that the state law crossed the line from appropriate accommodation of students' religious beliefs into a violation of the Establishment Clause.

Again dissenting as he had in *Engel*, Justice Stewart elaborated on points that he had raised in his previous opinion. Justice Stewart argued that there was a substantial free exercise claim on the part of those who affirmatively desired to have their children's school day open with Bible readings, and that such a claim could not be overcome without a showing of direct governmental coercion of unwilling students.

Despite *Engel*'s and *Schempp*'s rejection of official school prayer, litigation has continued to arise in contexts in which either the prayers in question were described as non-denominational moments of silence or when the prayer was claimed to be the result of student choice unaffiliated with the decisions of school officials or legislators. For example, in *Wallace v. Jaffree*,[116] the Court used the secular purpose prong of the *Lemon* test to strike down a state law allowing a moment of silence for "voluntary prayer" in public school classrooms. Writing for the Court, Justice Stevens stated that

---

114. 374 U.S. 203 (1963).

115. *See id.* at 222 ("[T]o withstand the strictures of the Establishment Clause there must be a secular legislative purpose and a primary effect that neither advances nor inhibits religion").

116. 472 U.S. 38 (1985).

"one of the questions we must ask is whether the government intends to convey a message of endorsement or disapproval of religion."[117] After reviewing the legislative history of the statute, particularly comments by the bill's sponsor,[118] Justice Stevens concluded that the statute was enacted for the "sole purpose of expressing the State's endorsement of prayer."[119]

This conclusion was buttressed by the fact that the statute was an amendment to an earlier statute which already provided that a one-minute period of silence be "observed for meditation." The amended version was almost identical to the original except the addition of the words "or voluntary prayer" after the word "meditation." Thus, the purpose of the amendment was clearly to promote prayer in the classroom. The Court echoed *Engel* in its concern that the promotion of prayer in the classroom would intrude on the "individual freedom of conscience protected by the First Amendment [which] embraces the right to select any religious faith or none at all."[120] Maintaining a meditative silence could arguably be squared with non-theistic beliefs; prayer could not.

The time at which the Court decided to take up *Wallace* was significant. When the lower court issued its decision, several other cases existed involving simple moments of silence. The Court chose to review *Wallace*, however, and it is not clear what the Court would permit states to do after this decision. Justice Stevens' opinion suggested, and Justices Powell and O'Connor strongly stated, that each would uphold some kind of moment of silence statute. Certainly, the three dissenters would also have upheld a true moment of silence statute as they would have upheld the combined prayer and moment of silence statute at issue in *Wallace*.

Dissenting, Chief Justice Burger maintained that the Court had exhibited hostility toward religion in suggesting that it would uphold a pure moment of silence statute but not one that "includes the word prayer." The Chief Justice also distanced himself from his own *Lemon* test, which in *Wallace* he construed as merely a series of "signposts."[121] In separate dissents, Justices White and Rehnquist called for a broad-ranging reconsideration of the Court's establishment jurisprudence. Justice Rehnquist wrote an extensive critique of the wall of separation metaphor and the *Lemon* test which he viewed as implementing it. He interpreted the primary thrust of the Establishment Clause as preventing discrimination among different religions rather than requiring strict neutrality between religion and irreligion.

The Court again returned to the issue of prayer in public schools in *Lee v. Weisman*.[122] In *Lee*, a five-justice majority ruled that non-sectarian prayers offered under the direction and guidance of school officials at public elementary and middle school

---

117. *Id.* at 61.
118. The bill's sponsor in the state legislature stated that the bill had no other purpose than that of returning voluntary prayer to the classroom. *See id.* at 65.
119. *Id.* at 60.
120. *Id.* at 53.
121. *Id.* at 89 (Burger, C.J., dissenting).
122. 505 U.S. 577 (1992).

graduation ceremonies violated the Establishment Clause. *Lee* arose when a middle-school official in Providence, Rhode Island invited a rabbi to deliver an invocation and benediction at the school's graduation ceremony. Officials choosing to invite clergy to graduation gave the clergy member a copy of a pamphlet providing guidelines for prayers at civic occasions and asked the selected clergy member to recite a non-sectarian prayer.

Writing for the Court, Justice Kennedy declined to reconsider the Court's decision in *Lemon*. Nevertheless, rather than relying on *Lemon*, he focused the Court's attention on the coercive effect of the officially sponsored prayers. Despite the school official's attempt to ensure that the benediction be nonsectarian, the very fact that the official had chosen the clergy member and partially dictated the tone of the prayer involved the state in religious matters. Moreover, the context of a school graduation, in which attendance, even if not formally required, was nevertheless socially expected and highly valued by the graduating students, created a coercive environment of the sort the Court described in *Engel* and *Schempp*. Nor was it constitutionally adequate that the graduating student could simply remain seated during the benediction, given the indirect coercion students might feel to participate in the prayer along with their classmates.

Justices Blackmun and Souter each wrote concurring opinions, both of them joined by Justices Stevens and O'Connor. Justice Blackmun argued that the Court's result flowed from its precedents, in particularly, *Lemon*. Justice Souter stressed that the Establishment Clause was implicated not only by laws that implicate coercion concerns, but also laws that endorse religion. He also wrote a lengthy historical analysis arguing that the Clause was implicated by laws that favored religion generally (rather than only laws that treated particular religions differently). He acknowledged, however, that the Clause's required government neutrality in religious matters still allowed government to accommodate religion by relieving adherents from generally applicable laws that interfere with their religious practices.

Dissenting for four justices, Justice Scalia took issue with what he called Justice Kennedy's "psycho-coercion" test.[123] He noted several examples of public ceremonies where prayer had traditionally been offered, including presidential inaugurations, the opening of congressional sessions, and the opening invocation of the Supreme Court, and he argued that prayers at graduation ceremonies were not sufficiently different to be treated differently. Justice Scalia questioned courts' competence to judge claims of psychological coercion and argued that the only coercion that could invalidate longstanding government practices featuring religion was coercion backed by a threat of official penalty.

Eight years later, the Court explored the meaning of *Lee* in *Santa Fe Independent School District v. Doe*.[124] In *Santa Fe*, the Court invalidated a school district policy

---

123. *Id.* at 641 (Scalia, J., dissenting).
124. 530 U.S. 290 (2000).

allowing prayer at varsity football games. The policy called for a student election to determine whether to present a nonsectarian invocation at home varsity football games and, if so, to select the student-presenter. The six-justice majority, speaking through Justice Stevens, concluded that the decision to recite a prayer and the selection of the presenter were both attributable to the state, given the school's policy of holding an election to decide those issues. The Court then found that the policy had coercive effect akin to the coercion the Court had found in *Lee*, given the mandatory nature of attendance for some students (*e.g.*, players and band members) and the informal social pressure and simple desire to attend football games on the part of other students. The Court also rejected the school's argument that the plaintiff's facial challenge to the policy was premature, observing that the policy on its face failed *Lemon*'s purpose prong.

Chief Justice Rehnquist dissented, joined by Justices Scalia and Thomas. He emphasized that the plaintiffs' challenge came before the district's policy went into effect, a fact that deprived the Court of a record of allegedly unconstitutional action to review. On the merits, he disagreed with the Court's use of what he called the "oft-criticized test of *Lemon*,"[125] and distinguished *Lee* because there, a "graduation prayer given by a rabbi was 'directed and controlled' by a school official."[126]

While the Court has been very circumspect about allowing school-sponsored prayer or instruction in public school classrooms, it has allowed student groups to engage in these activities. These cases often involve claims arising under both the Free Speech Clause and the Free Exercise Clause,[127] which are met by government arguments based on the Establishment Clause. For example, *Widmar v. Vincent*[128] invalidated a regulation that prevented student religious groups from using university facilities. Justice Powell predicated the holding on the Free Speech Clause. The majority rejected the state's argument that its exclusion of religious groups was necessitated by the compelling state interest of avoiding an Establishment Clause violation. Evaluating the regulation under *Lemon*, the Court found that an open forum policy, which included nondiscrimination against religious speech, constituted a secular purpose and would avoid entanglement with religion.

With respect to *Lemon*'s primary effect prong, Justice Powell conceded that religious groups would likely benefit from access to university facilities; however, he stated that the provision of merely "incidental benefits" does not violate *Lemon*'s effect prong, in the context of a forum that was available to a large number of student groups. In a footnote, the Court added that because university students were adults and were less impressionable than younger students, religious influences need not be as strongly guarded against.[129] Justice White dissented.

---

125. *Id.* at 319 (Rehnquist, C.J., dissenting).
126. *Id.* at 319, 324 (Rehnquist, C.J., dissenting).
127. The Free Exercise Clause is discussed in Section 12.03.
128. 454 U.S. 263 (1981).
129. *See id.* at 274 n.14.

Board of Education v. Mergens[130] upheld against an Establishment Clause defense the application of a federal law, the Equal Access Act, to a student religious group. The statute essentially requires that schools receiving federal money provide equal access to non-curricular student groups who wish to use school facilities. When the school in *Mergens* refused to allow the religious group to use its facilities, claiming that to do so would violate the Establishment Clause, the student group sued.

The Court upheld the statutory right to equal access, rejecting the school's argument that the statute on its face and as applied in that case violated the Establishment Clause. A four-justice plurality relied heavily on *Widmar*'s application of *Lemon* to conclude that requiring the school to provide access to the student group would not violate the Establishment Clause. Justice Kennedy, joined by Justice Scalia, concurred in the result on the ground that application of the statute to these facts would neither amount to the establishment of an official church nor coerce any student into participating in religious activity. Justice Marshall, joined by Justice Brennan, concluded that the statute could potentially be applied to a religious group without offending the Establishment Clause, but expressed concern that government neutrality toward religion (and hence compliance with the Establishment Clause) was not assured on the facts of the forum the school created when it allowed student groups. He noted that the school allowed such groups as vehicles for transmitting values, and thus worried that the school could be perceived as endorsing religious values if it was required to give equal access to religious groups.

Five years after *Mergens*, the Court again rejected a government argument that support of a student religious group would violate the Establishment Clause. The issue in *Rosenberger v. Rector and Visitors of the University of Virginia*[131] was whether the University of Virginia could constitutionally refuse to use student activities fund money to fund the publication of a student religious newspaper. Considering this question as a matter of the Speech Clause, a five-justice majority, speaking through Justice Kennedy, concluded that that refusal constituted unconstitutional viewpoint-based discrimination in the forum the university had created via the student activity fund.[132] More relevantly for current purposes, the Court, again relying on *Widmar*, held that a university did not violate the Establishment Clause when it acted neutrally toward religion, and did not have a purpose of promoting religion when it established the forum to which the religious group demanded access. Four justices dissented, characterizing the case as one where "The Court is ordering an instrumentality of the State to support religious evangelism with direct funding."[133]

In addition to considering the rights of student groups to access school facilities for religious purposes, the Court has also considered the rights of outside groups to use school facilities when the school has otherwise opened its facilities for community

---

130. 496 U.S. 226 (1990).

131. 515 U.S. 819 (1995).

132. The Court's Speech Clause jurisprudence dealing with the locations in which speech occurs is discussed in Section 11.01[5].

133. 515 U.S. at 892 (Souter, J., dissenting).

use. As with student groups, the Court has allowed such outside groups to use school facilities as part of a general access program extended to community groups.

In *Lamb's Chapel v. Center Moriches Union Free School District*,[134] the Court held that allowing a religious group to display Christian films on public school property, after school hours, would not constitute an establishment of religion. The Court thus found that compliance with the Establishment Clause did not furnish the school with a compelling justification for engaging in the viewpoint discrimination it performed when it blocked that group's access, despite opening up its facilities to other, non-religious groups. Writing for seven justices on a unanimous Court,[135] Justice White concluded that the government's allowance of the religious activity would neither violate neither *Lemon* nor Justice O'Connor's endorsement test.

In *Good News Club v. Milford Central School*,[136] the Court again ruled in favor of a religious speaker who sought to use school facilities after hours for religious instruction. Writing for the five (and sometimes six[137]) justices, Justice Thomas said the school's exclusion of the religious group constituted "impermissible viewpoint discrimination"[138] that was unnecessary to avoid an Establishment Clause violation. In performing its Establishment Clause analysis, the Court analogized the religious group's activities to those at issue in *Lamb's Chapel*, discussed immediately above: the meetings were held after school, the school did not sponsor the activities, and any student could attend the meetings with a parent's permission.

Rejecting the school's Establishment Clause explanation for its denial of the religious group's access request, the Court explained that "allowing the Club to speak on school grounds would ensure neutrality, not threaten it."[139] Moreover, the parents who must give consent to the children's participation in the meetings would not feel "coercive pressure"[140] to participate in the religious group's activities. The school argued that impressionable elementary school children would automatically believe that it was endorsing religion, since the activities were on school grounds. The Court rejected such a categorical conclusion and further held that the specific facts of the school's access and the religious group's activities did not warrant a finding of unconstitutional endorsement.[141]

Concurring in part, Justice Breyer argued that neutrality was only one factor used to examine an Establishment Clause claim. He suggested that this case turned in particular on whether requiring that the religious group receive access would send a mes-

---

134. 508 U.S. 384 (1993).
135. Justice Scalia, joined by Justice Thomas, merely concurred in the judgment.
136. 533 U.S. 98 (2001).
137. Justice Breyer joined only part of Justice Thomas' analysis.
138. *Id.* at 112.
139. 533 U.S. at 114.
140. *Id.* at 115.
141. First, the Club met after school hours in a special room used by the high school and the middle school, not by elementary school students. Second, the Club's instructors were not schoolteachers. Third, the children who engaged in Good News' activities ranged from ages six to twelve. *See id.* at 117–18.

sage of religious endorsement—an issue that turned on particularized circumstances such as the time and nature of the meetings.

Justice Stevens dissented. He distinguished religiously-focused speech on a particular subject from worship and proselytizing, arguing that in a public forum, government could constitutionally exclude the latter two types of religious activity as long as it was done consistently. Justice Souter also dissented, joined by Justice Ginsburg. He distinguished *Widmar* based on the large number and diversity of student groups using the university's facilities, as compared to the situation in *Good News*, which involved only four groups who sought to use the school's premises, and only one (the religious group itself) that wished to use the facility immediately after school hours.

[5] Religious Instruction

Somewhat related to school prayer is the issue of religious beliefs influencing school instruction in secular subjects. In *Epperson v. Arkansas*,[142] a unanimous Court struck down an Arkansas law mandating the teaching of creationism. Speaking for the Court,[143] Justice Fortas concluded that the law was motivated by sectarian purposes. The law had been enacted in the 1920s, shortly after the famous Scopes "Monkey Trial" challenging a similar Tennessee law; in *Epperson*, the state mounted only a half-hearted defense of the law, and Justice Black, concurring, questioned whether it had even been enforced in recent decades.

Two decades later, in *Edwards v. Aguillard*,[144] the Court faced a more serious defense of a more moderate creationism law. The Louisiana law at issue in *Edwards* required that "creation science" be taught in public schools whenever evolution was taught. Writing for the Court, Justice Brennan struck down the law under the secular purpose prong of the *Lemon* test. Justice Brennan concluded that the Court's usually deferential inquiry into legislative purpose must give way to greater vigilance when the Court dealt with elementary and secondary schools, given those students' impressionability and the fact that their attendance in school was compulsory. In *Edwards*, the Court dismissed the state's argument that the law promoted academic freedom by allowing teachers to teach what they wanted, since the previous regime already allowed teachers that freedom and since the challenged law in fact limited it.

Dissenting, Justice Scalia, joined by Chief Justice Rehnquist, stated that he had understood the secular purpose prong of the *Lemon* test as being satisfied unless there was no secular purpose at all. Given the procedural posture of the case as having reached the Court on a summary judgment motion, Justice Scalia believed that more deference should have been accorded the Louisiana legislature's explicitly-stated secular purpose of protecting academic freedom. More fundamentally, Justice Scalia believed

---

142. 393 U.S. 97 (1968).
143. Two justices voted to strike the law down on vagueness grounds.
144. 482 U.S. 578 (1987).

the purpose prong should be abandoned altogether, because "determining the subjective intent of legislators is a perilous enterprise," not justified by the text of the Establishment Clause.[145]

[6] Legislative Prayers

A basic problem the Court has had to confront in the Establishment Clause context is the one of legislative and other official prayers and statements. Congress invites clergy members to deliver blessings before the start of its sessions, as do most, if not all, state legislatures and many local bodies. Even the Supreme Court begins with the marshal calling out "God save the United States and this Honorable Court." Congress has also provided for military chaplains for nearly all the nation's history. These practices are longstanding, yet they appear, at least on one understanding, a flat-out violation of the Establishment Clause.

In *Marsh v. Chambers*,[146] the Court upheld state-sponsored prayers in state legislatures. Observing that the complaining party was an adult rather than an impressionable child, the Court ruled that Nebraska's payment of chaplains and the opening of each legislative session with a prayer did not violate the Establishment Clause. Chief Justice Burger's majority opinion stressed history and the Framers' intent. He noted that the Congress that drafted the First Amendment also opened its sessions with a prayer. Despite the fact that he had written the opinion in *Lemon* twelve years before, the Chief Justice did not apply it in his opinion for six justices in *Marsh*.

Justice Brennan's dissent, joined by Justice Marshall, traced the Court's Establishment Clause decisions and concluded that the majority opinion could not be squared with the cumulative criteria the Court had developed since *Everson*. Justice Brennan viewed the Constitution as an evolving document. Thus, the diversity of religious thinking—particularly as a result of the entry of large non-Christian populations into the country and the rise of secular humanism, agnosticism, and atheism—might mandate a different set of rules than those existing when the First Amendment was drafted. For Justice Brennan, the issue was whether a particular act of state sponsorship of religious practice would offend the sensibilities of contemporary Americans, in all their diversity. Justice Stevens also dissented. He focused on the fact that the Nebraska Legislature had selected an adherent of one particular religion as its chaplain for the previous sixteen years as evidence that the state's practice violated the Establishment Clause.

More than thirty years after *Marsh*, the Court returned to the question of legislative prayers in *Town of Greece v. Galloway*.[147] In *Town of Greece*, a five-justice majority upheld a town's practice of inviting clergy, chosen from a local directory, to deliver a benediction at the start of town council meetings. The Court, speaking through

145. *Id.* at 638 (Scalia, J., dissenting).
146. 463 U.S. 783 (1983).
147. 572 U.S. 565 (2014).

Justice Kennedy, relied heavily on *Marsh*'s invocation of the historical pedigree of such benedictions in upholding the town's practice. It rejected the plaintiffs' argument that only nonsectarian prayers could be allowed, concluding that such a requirement would involve the government even more deeply in the selection of approved prayers. It also rejected any argument that the town's predominantly Christian character imposed a constitutional requirement on the town to look outside its boundaries for more a more diverse sampling of religions. Relying on the purpose of legislative prayer as one focusing lawmakers on their shared ideals and common ends in the process of governing, the Court cautioned that a practice of invocations that "denigrate nonbelievers or religious minorities, threaten damnation, or preach conversion"[148] might violate the Establishment Clause.

Writing now for only a plurality of three, Justice Kennedy further concluded that the town's practice did not coerce citizens to participate in religious activity, and thus that its practice comported with the Establishment Clause. Justice Thomas, joined by Justice Scalia, concluded, as he had in the past,[149] that the only type of coercion relevant for Establishment Clause purposes was legal coercion, rather than the informal pressure the plaintiffs alleged. Justice Thomas simply concurred in the no-coercion conclusion, but only after applying his own understanding of that concept.

Justice Kagan dissented for herself and Justices Ginsburg, Breyer, and Sotomayor. She did not dispute the correctness of *Marsh*. Nevertheless, she argued that three factors justified a ruling against the town's prayer practices. First, unlike the sessions of the Nebraska Legislature at issue in *Marsh*, ordinary citizens participated in the town council meetings in *Town of Greece*, for example, by requesting zoning variances and other exceptions from generally applicable town rules. Second, the prayers in *Town of Greece* were sectarian. Finally, except when prodded by the prospect of the plaintiffs' lawsuit, the town never sought to broaden the scope of religions represented in the benedictions. Justice Breyer, in addition to joining Justice Kagan's dissent, also wrote a separate dissent to emphasize the case's fact-intensiveness, and, in particular, the fact that the town never reached out to non-Christian clergy about providing the opening benediction.

[7] Religious Exemptions from Generally-Applicable Laws

Cases involving government-granted religion-based exemptions from generally-applicable laws raise yet again the tension between the Free Exercise Clause-based concerns supporting such exemptions and the Establishment Clause-based concerns that cut against them. In *Estate of Thornton v. Caldor*,[150] for example, the Court struck down a Connecticut law that gave an employee an absolute right not to work on the

---

148. *Id.* at 583.
149. *See, e.g.*, Van Orden v. Perry, 545 U.S. 677, 693 (2005) (Thomas, J., concurring).
150. 472 U.S. 703 (1985).

employee's chosen weekly day of worship. A unanimous opinion, authored by Chief Justice Burger, stressed that the Connecticut law made no allowance for the convenience or interests — religious or otherwise — of either the employer or other employees; rather, the employee's religious interests took precedence over all secular interests at the workplace. For that reason, the Court concluded that the law had a primary effect of advancing religion, in violation of *Lemon.* Justice O'Connor's concurrence, joined by Justice Marshall, stressed that the majority opinion did not cast doubt on the validity of Title VII of the 1964 Civil Rights Act's guarantee against discrimination based on religion. She stressed that Title VII required only reasonable, rather than absolute, accommodation of the employee's religion, and applied to religious discrimination generally rather than focusing only on protection of Sabbath observances. For those reasons, she concluded that "an objective observer would perceive [Title VII] as an anti-discrimination law rather than an endorsement of religion or a particular religious practice."[151]

A more generally-applicable federal law, requiring government to satisfy stringent requirements before imposing substantial burdens on religious exercise, is the Religious Freedom Restoration Act (RFRA). Congress made RFRA applicable to the states through its power to enforce the Fourteenth Amendment. In 1997, the Court found RFRA to exceed that enforcement power.[152] However, it remains applicable to the federal government, and the Supreme Court has not yet had opportunity to consider the constitutionality of that aspect of the statute.[153] After RFRA's partial strike-down, Congress enacted a more modest religious freedom law, the Religious Land Use and Institutionalized Persons Act (RLUIPA), which provides for free religious exercise in the contexts of state and local governments' land use decisions and treatment of institutionalized persons. In *Cutter v. Wilkinson,*[154] the Court upheld RLUIPA's institutionalized persons provision against an Establishment Clause challenge. Writing for a unanimous Court, Justice Ginsburg explained that the law relieved burdens imposed on free exercise by the fact of institutionalization (for example, imprisonment). Distinguishing *Estate of Thornton,* the Court also noted that, "[p]roperly applying RLUIPA, courts must take adequate account of the burdens a requested accommodation may impose on nonbeneficiaries." It also noted that courts "must be satisfied that the Act's prescriptions are and will be administered neutrally among different faiths."[155]

A more general type of exemption, one grounded in the religion clauses themselves rather than statute, is the so-called "ministerial exception." The doctrine originated

---

151. *Id.* at 712 (O'Connor, J., concurring).

152. *See* City of Boerne v. Flores, 521 U.S. 507 (1997). *Boerne* is discussed in Section 13.02.

153. *See* Cutter v. Wilkinson, 544 U.S 709, 715 n.2 (2005) (noting that lower courts have continued to apply RFRA to the federal government, and that the Supreme Court has yet to have ruled on that question); *see also, e.g.,* O'Bryan v. Bureau of Prisons, 349 U.S. 399, 401 (7th Cir. 2003) (upholding RFRA's applicability to the federal government under the Necessary and Proper Clause); *ibid.* (noting Justice Stevens's view that statutory accommodations of religion may violate the Establishment Clause but also noting that no other justice has taken this view).

154. 544 U.S. 709 (2005).

155. *Id.* at 720.

in cases beginning in the nineteenth century, in which the Supreme Court held that courts could not adjudicate disputes between competing factions of a church, each claiming church property or some other legal interest, if doing so would require the court to decide questions of proper adherence to religious doctrine.[156] By the late twentieth century, the Court had established that under both the Free Exercise Clause and the Establishment Clause, it was not only inappropriate for courts to adjudicate such intra-church disputes, but also that government more generally lacked the authority to determine who could serve as minister in any given religion.[157]

An important recent illustration of the ministerial exception was in a 2012 case, *Hosanna-Tabor Evangelical Lutheran Church and School v. Equal Employment Opportunity Commission*.[158] *Hosanna-Tabor* raised questions about both the existence and scope of the ministerial exemption. It involved an employment dispute between a religious school and an instructor at the school who had attained a special, "called" position that marked her as more than a secular employee. When the instructor threatened to assert her legal rights under federal employment law, the congregation terminated her. The instructor sued, alleging that the school had violated federal employment law banning retaliation against an employee for asserting her legal rights.

The Court unanimously upheld the firing, concluding that, based on the facts of the instructor's status in her religious community, the school could invoke the ministerial exemption to avoid federal anti-discrimination law. Much of the Court's analysis was taken up by explaining how the details of the instructor's status within her religious community qualified the school for the exception in its dealings with the instructor. But the Court also explained more generally that the exception was grounded both in the church's Free Exercise Clause right to select its own leaders and in the Establishment Clause's prohibition on government involvement in those selections.

Hosanna-Tabor involved a litigant who had significant indicia of official status in the religion, including her status as a "called" instructor, obtained after a formal, religiously-based process. In 2020, the Court arguably expanded the scope of the exception in two cases involving lay teachers in Roman Catholic schools. In *Our Lady*

---

156. For a brief history of the ministerial exception, see Ralph Mawdsley & Allan Osborne, *Shout Hosanna: The Supreme Court Affirms the Free Exercise Clause's Ministerial Exemption*, 278 EDUC. L. REP. 693, 700 (2012).

157. As the Court explained in a recent statement on the exception, this latter variant of it developed after Congress enacted a comprehensive federal employment discrimination law in 1964. *See Hosanna-Tabor Evangelical Lutheran Church and School v. Equal Employment Opportunity Commission*, 565 U.S. 171, 188 (2012) ("Since the passage of Title VII of the Civil Rights Act of 1964, and other employment discrimination laws, the Courts of Appeals have uniformly recognized the existence of a 'ministerial exception,' grounded in the First Amendment, that precludes application of such legislation to claims concerning the employment relationship between a religious institution and its ministers.").

158. 565 U.S. 171 (2012).

of Guadalupe School v. Morrissey-Berru,[159] the Court ruled in favor of the schools and against the teachers who had brought federal employment law claims against them. Writing for seven justices, Chief Justice Roberts explained that the factors relevant to the Court's decision in *Hosanna-Tabor* were not a "checklist" that had to be satisfied. Rather, he wrote that "implicit in our decision in *Hosanna-Tabor* was a recognition that educating young people in their faith, inculcating its teachings, and training them to live their faith are responsibilities that lie at the very core of the mission of a private religious school." Thus, it was not determinative that the teachers in question were not ordained or "called" in any way, or, indeed, that one of the instructors had asserted after the litigation commenced that she was not a practicing Catholic. Instead, the Court said, what mattered was what the individual did. In ruling for the schools, the Court noted that the instructors taught religion (among other subjects), accompanied students to Mass, and generally were expected to model the Catholic faith.

Concurring, Justice Thomas, joined by Justice Gorsuch, would have invoked the ministerial exception simply upon concluding that the religious employer sincerely believed that the individual's position was "ministerial." He argued that courts did not have the competence to engage in a more searching inquiry. Dissenting for herself and Justice Ginsburg, Justice Sotomayor argued that the majority had abandoned its more context-specific approach for a "functional" one that simply focused on the individual's duties. She worried that this approach would greatly expand the reach of the ministerial exception.

Hosanna-Tabor was a unanimous opinion, perhaps because its facts were relatively straightforward. *Morrissey-Berru* attracted two dissenting votes. One can probably expect continued litigation over this issue, and perhaps increased disagreement at the Court, as religious employers attempt to utilize this attractive immunity from employment law restrictions. If so, the Court may find itself drawing difficult distinctions that potentially entangle it in matters of religious doctrine and practice.

[8] Grants of Government Power to Religious Groups

A final Establishment Clause area concerns situations where the government has delegated sovereign power to a religious institution or sect. In *Larkin v. Grendel's Den, Inc.*,[160] the Court struck down a Massachusetts law providing that premises within five hundred feet of a church or school could not receive a liquor license if the governing body of the church or school objected. Writing for an eight-justice majority, Chief Justice Burger noted that deference was normally due to legislative zoning judgments and recognized the legitimacy of keeping the areas around churches and schools free of tumult. Nevertheless, the Court found that that goal could be

---

159. 140 S.Ct. 2049 (2020).
160. 459 U.S. 116 (1982).

served by other means, that the power it granted to religious institutions had the primary effect of promoting religion, and that it deeply entangled the government with religion by giving religious institutions power to make controversial public policy decisions.

In *Board of Education of Kiryas Joel Village School District v. Grumet*,[161] the Court invalidated a New York law that created a separate school district tracking the boundaries of an exclusively religious community, a Jewish sect known as the Satmar Hasidim. A group of Satmar had moved to an unincorporated subdivision of a town and formed their own village. After Supreme Court cases prevented government instruction on religious school premises,[162] handicapped children in the village were left without educational opportunities, as the community would not allow the children to travel to other communities where such programs existed. The state responded by creating a separate school district for the village, which allowed it to establish public school opportunities for handicapped children.

The Court struck down the state's action. Writing at this point for a five-justice majority, Justice Souter noted that the state's action was not one that made a benefit available on a generally-applicable basis. Rather, he cautioned that there was no guarantee that any other community would receive similar beneficial treatment. Writing now only for four justices, he relied on *Larkin* for the proposition that the state in this case had delegated political power to a community that the legislature knew was defined by religion. Concurring in the judgment and supplying the fifth vote to strike the state law down, Justice Kennedy disagreed with the plurality's critique of the state law as singling out the Satmar community for a special religious accommodation. However, he nevertheless concluded that the state had unconstitutionally drawn a political line based on religion.

Justices Blackmun and Stevens both joined the majority opinion but also wrote separate concurrences. Justice Blackmun emphasized that the majority opinion did not depart from *Lemon v. Kurtzman*. Justice Stevens, joined by Justices Blackmun and Ginsburg, noted the other steps public schools could have taken to accommodate the community's distinct culture and values. But he also noted that the state-created district served students from outside the district's lines that also happened to be of the same religious sect, thus suggesting the religiously-motivated character and effect of the state's action.

Justice O'Connor, concurring in part and concurring in the judgment, emphasized equal treatment irrespective of religious or nonreligious beliefs. She noted that New York could have enacted a general law allowing all villages to operate their own school districts. Alternatively, the Court could have allowed the state to revive the kind of publicly-funded programs on religious school grounds, taught by public school teachers, something that would have violated then-existing Supreme Court precedent but

---

161. 512 U.S. 687 (1994).

162. *See* Aguilar v. Felton, 473 U.S. 402 (1985); Sch. Dist. of Grand Rapids v. Ball, 473 U.S. 373 (1985). *Aguilar* and *Ball* are both discussed in Section 12.02[1][c].

precedent she was willing to reconsider.[163] But regardless, the state could not favor the Satmar because of their religion.

Justice Scalia, joined by Chief Justice Rehnquist and Justice Thomas, dissented. Justice Scalia charged that the majority treated tolerance of a religious group's special needs as an impermissible establishment of religion. He distinguished an (unconstitutional) transfer of civic authority to a religious institution from what he characterized in *Kiryas Joel* as a transfer to a group of citizens who happened to share the same religion. Finally, Justice Scalia advocated that the *Lemon* test be abandoned and replaced by reliance on the longstanding traditions of the American people, which he concluded would have allowed the state's accommodation of the Satmar.

[9] Conclusion

As exemplified in much of the material provided above, the Establishment Clause has given rise to perhaps the most intricate and confusing jurisprudence the Court has created on any constitutional law topic. Much of this intricacy results from the inherent vagueness of the idea of prohibiting government from "establishing" a religion, especially given the transformation of American society from a society where government provided very little by way of services to one in which it provides for many major social needs. In that latter context, it arguably makes little sense to conceive of religious establishments in the narrow sense of official government religions or penalties for not belonging to particular religions. Rather, today, government provides services from bus transportation to fire protection to a robust system of public education. The Court has thus confronted the question of when provision of those services to religious institutions furthers their religious efforts in a way that should be thought to violate the anti-establishment principle.

Complicating matters significantly is the coupling of the anti-establishment principle with the free religious exercise principle of the other religion clause, the Free Exercise Clause. As this chapter has noted numerous times, the free exercise principle stands in significant tension with the anti-establishment principle, since any accommodation of religion in support of the former arguably implicates government in supporting religion, in violation of the latter. (Of course, this tension works in the other direction as well: any government attempt to avoid an Establishment Clause violation by steering well clear of religion arguably implicates interests protected by the Free Exercise Clause.)

This realization makes it clear that one cannot fully understand the issues at stake in the Establishment Clause cases without understanding the Free Exercise Clause. The next section of this Chapter examines that clause.

---

163. Three years after *Kiryas Joel*, the Court did in fact overrule its earlier precedent invalidating government teachers from coming into religious schools to provide specialized instruction. Agostini v. Felton, 521 U.S. 203 (1997). *Agostini* is discussed in Section 12.02[1][c].

§ 12.03 Free Religious Exercise

[1] The Meaning and Scope of "Religion"

Any examination of the right to free religious exercise requires consideration of an antecedent issue: the meaning of "religion" for purposes of the Free Exercise Clause. The Court, perhaps mindful of discriminating among religions by defining the term too narrowly, has provided a broad definition. A foundational case is *Torcaso v. Watkins*.[164] In *Torcaso*, the Court struck down a religious test for public office that required the candidate to profess a belief in God. In invalidating the test, Justice Black explained that the state could not "aid those religions based on a belief in the existence of God as against those religions founded on different beliefs." In a footnote appended to the language just quoted, Justice Black expanded on that passage: "Among religions in this country which do not teach what would generally be considered a belief in the existence of God are Buddhism, Taoism, Ethical Culture, Secular Humanism and others."[165] Thus, the Court's concept of what is "religious" is broad enough to include practices motivated by non-theistic ideologies, including secular "religions."

The Court has shed some indirect light on the issue in its conscientious objector cases.[166] While those cases ostensibly involved merely the proper interpretation of the federal conscription statute rather than constitutional issues, many commentators think that the Court's broad interpretation of that federal law has free exercise dimensions. In *United States v. Seeger*, for example, the Court interpreted the federal conscription law's conscientious objector provision to define religion to include a "sincere and meaningful belief which occupies in the life of its possessor a place parallel to that filled by the God of those admittedly qualifying for the exemption."[167]

The breadth of this definition, which again was likely influenced by Free Exercise Clause concerns,[168] has been matched by the Court's willingness to credit an individual's own view about what his religion requires. For example, in *Thomas v. Review Board*,[169] the Court considered a Jehovah's Witness's free exercise claim, even though a fellow Jehovah's Witness who worked with the claimant testified that that the religion did not impose the obligations the claimant stated he felt religiously obligated to satisfy. The Court expressed great hesitancy about second-guessing a claimant's interpretation of his own religion, noting the obvious difficulties that would ensue if courts sought to ensure that the claimant was interpreting his own religion correctly.

---

164. 367 U.S. 488 (1961).

165. *Id.* at 495, 495 n.11.

166. *See* Gillette v. United States, 401 U.S. 437 (1971); Welsh v. United States, 398 U.S. 333 (1970); United States v. Seeger, 380 U.S. 163 (1965).

167. 380 U.S. at 176.

168. *See, e.g.*, Welsh v. United States, 398 U.S. 333, 344 (1970) (Harlan, J., concurring in the judgment) (concluding that the conscription statute's conscientious objector provision could not be read as embracing the broad definition of religion stated in *Seeger*, but nevertheless adopting that broad definition as a matter of interpreting the Free Exercise Clause).

169. 450 U.S. 707 (1981).

Indeed, one need not even belong to an organized religion in order to claim a constitutional right to free religious exercise. In *Frazee v. Illinois Department of Employment Security*,[170] the Court struck down Illinois' denial of unemployment benefits to William Frazee, who refused to work on Sundays because it was "the Lord's day." Frazee claimed to be a Christian, but not a member of a particular sect. Writing for a unanimous Court, Justice White read the Court's precedents to require only that the individual have a sincere belief in the religious precepts he asserts as the basis for his religious exercise claim. There was no need that such precepts reflect the views of any organized religious sect.

Still, "purely secular views"[171] do not count as religion for purposes of the Free Exercise Clause. For example, in *Wisconsin v. Yoder*,[172] the Court considered a variety of factors when concluding that the free exercise claim made by the Amish plaintiffs was in fact based on religion rather than merely Amish culture. Among the factors the Court considered were whether the practice was a shared belief by an organized group rather than a personal experience; whether the belief related to certain theocratic principles and the interpretation of religious literature; whether the belief system pervaded and regulated the daily lives of the Amish; and whether that system and the resultant lifestyle had existed for a substantial period of time. Again, though, *Thomas* and *Frazee*, which both came after *Yoder*, make it clear that, respectively, a person's religious beliefs do not have to track those of the sect to which he claims to belong and that those beliefs may be personal, as long as they are not "purely secular views."[173]

[2] The Scope of Free Exercise Clause Protection

[a] The Development of Heightened Protection for Free Exercise

Establishment and free exercise jurisprudence developed somewhat concurrently. Like the Establishment Clause, the Free Exercise Clause was seldom the subject of litigation prior to the mid-twentieth century.[174] In the Court's few early free exercise cases, the balance between religious liberty and the general welfare was usually struck in favor of the latter. *Reynolds v. United States*[175] is typical of the Court's early hostility toward recognizing free exercise-based exemptions from generally-applicable laws. In *Reynolds*, a Mormon claimed that his conviction under a territorial anti-polygamy law violated the Free Exercise Clause because polygamy was mandated by church

---

170. 489 U.S. 829 (1989).

171. *Id.* at 833.

172. 406 U.S. 205 (1972).

173. *Frazee*, 489 U.S. at 833.

174. For an historical perspective on the history of free exercise exemptions from generally applicable laws, see M. McConnell, *The Origins and Historical Understanding of Free Exercise of Religion*, 103 Harv. L. Rev. 1409 (1990).

175. 98 U.S. 145 (1878).

doctrine. The Court upheld the conviction by constructing a belief/practice dichotomy defining the scope of protection afforded by the Clause. Religious beliefs, according to the *Reynolds* Court, received absolute protection. Religious practices, however, received no protection. The Court expressed concern that mandating exemptions from generally-applicable regulations of conduct would "permit every citizen to become a law unto himself,"[176] able to claim an exemption from otherwise-valid laws.[177]

A half-century later, in *Cantwell v. Connecticut*,[178] the Court appeared more sympathetic to free exercise concerns than it had in *Reynolds*. In *Cantwell* a Jehovah's Witness was convicted under a statute forbidding solicitation without a license. The Court was particularly troubled by the unfettered discretion given public officials under the licensing statute, and concluded that the statute imposed an unconstitutional prior restraint on both free speech and on the free exercise of religion when the licensing requirement was applied to religious solicitations. In its analysis, the *Cantwell* Court maintained the *Reynolds* belief/practice distinction, albeit without the heavy overtones of majoritarian morality suggested in *Reynolds*. According to *Cantwell*, religious belief was afforded "absolute" protection, while religious practice may be regulated "for the protection of society." However, it added that even the power to regulate religious practice must not be exercised so as to "unduly ... infringe" on freedom of religion.[179] This "undue infringement" concept, while more protective than the almost nonexistent level of scrutiny accorded laws burdening religious exercise in *Reynolds*, still favored state power over individual religious liberty.[180]

The Court took another step toward heightening judicial protection for religious freedom in *Braunfeld v. Brown*.[181] In *Braunfeld*, Jewish merchants challenged a state's Sunday closing law as violating their free exercise rights.[182] The merchants claimed that, because their religion already required them to close on Saturdays, the Sunday closing law had the effect of allowing them to conduct business only five days per week, placing them at a competitive disadvantage with respect to merchants who could remain open six days a week. The Court upheld the Sunday closing law against a free exercise challenge, distinguishing between laws that directly prohibited a particular religious practice and laws, like the Sunday closing law, that only indirectly burdened a religious practice as an unintended consequence of pursuing an appropriate public goal. The Court also suggested that states could enact laws exempting

---

176. *Id.* at 167.

177. To be sure, the *Reynolds* Court made clear its distaste for polygamy, thus suggesting another motive for its refusal to allow the polygamist to assert a religiously-based exemption from the anti-polygamy law.

178. 310 U.S. 296 (1940).

179. *Id.* at 303–04.

180. *Cantwell* is also important for having incorporated both the Establishment and Free Exercise Clauses. *See id.* at 303.

181. 366 U.S. 599 (1961).

182. *Braunfeld* was a companion case to *McGowan v. Maryland*, 366 U.S. 420 (1961), in which the Court upheld a Sunday closing law against a claim that it violated the Establishment Clause by establishing Christianity.

from the Sunday closing laws those merchants whose religious beliefs required them to close on another day, thus signaling that such a law accommodating Sabbath keepers would not be struck down as an invalid establishment. Importantly, while upholding the law against a free exercise challenge, the Court added that the law would have been invalid if the state could have accomplished its purpose in a manner that did not burden religious practice.

[b] The Rise and Decay of Heightened Protection

Braunfeld's observation that the Sunday closing law might have been invalid had the state had an alternative way of achieving its goals that did not burden religious exercise would play an important role two years later in the Court's watershed decision in *Sherbert v. Verner.*[183] *Sherbert* marked the beginning of the modern Court's application of heightened scrutiny to laws burdening free exercise. In *Sherbert,* South Carolina denied unemployment compensation to a Seventh-day Adventist because she refused available employment that would require her to work on Saturdays, her faith's day of rest. Writing for the majority, Justice Brennan stated that a challenge to a law burdening a person's free exercise requires the plaintiff to demonstrate that the law substantially infringed on her religious practices. The Court noted, though, that the infringement need only be incidental. Justice Brennan found that the denial of unemployment benefits because of the plaintiff's religious conduct constituted a "substantial infringement" and had a "coercive effect"[184] on her free exercise of religion.

Once the challenger demonstrated a substantial burden on her free exercise of religion, the government must then justify that infringement with a compelling state interest. In *Sherbert,* the state claimed that the law was intended to prevent the filing of spurious claims by claimants falsely citing a religious objection to Saturday work. The Court found no evidence that such a concern was well-founded. Moreover, even if the interest was compelling, the Court concluded that the government program must constitute the least restrictive means to effectuate that interest. In *Sherbert,* the government failed to demonstrate that less restrictive means would not have combatted the alleged fraudulent claims.

Justice Brennan distinguished *Sherbert* from *Braunfeld* on several grounds. First, he argued that the state's interest in *Braunfeld*—to ensure a uniform day of rest— was compelling, in a way that South Carolina's anti-fraud justification in *Sherbert* was not. Second, he observed that *Braunfeld* had concluded that administrative difficulties justified the state's refusal to make exemptions. Finally, Justice Brennan concluded that the unemployment law at issue in *Sherbert* discriminated against Sabbath observers, since another provision of that law accommodated Sunday-observers and yet another provision recognized at least some personal reasons to refuse work. (Of course, that latter provision also undercut any claim that a system of exemptions was unworkable, in contrast to the Court's conclusion in *Braunfeld.*) Justice Brennan's

---

183. 374 U.S. 398 (1963).
184. *Id.* at 406, 404 n.5.

characterization of the South Carolina law as discriminatory would become important when, in 1990, the Court attempted to limit *Sherbert*'s doctrinal significance.

Justice Harlan, joined by Justice White, dissented. He disputed the majority's attempt to distinguish *Braunfeld*, concluding instead that the Court had effectively overruled that previous case. He also expressed concern with a rule that states are constitutionally compelled to provide religious exemptions from generally-applicable rules of conduct. While he acknowledged that states could legislatively choose to provide such accommodations without violating the Establishment Clause, he cautioned against requiring too many such accommodations as a matter of constitutional right under the Free Exercise Clause. Citing their temporary nature, Justice Harlan concluded that the unemployment benefits at issue were too minor to justify heightened scrutiny of a state's failure to provide a religion-grounded exemption.

In *Wisconsin v. Yoder*,[185] the Court continued on *Sherbert*'s path of according significant protection to free religious exercise, even as against undeniably legitimate countervailing government interests. In *Yoder*, parents of Amish children challenged the state's compulsory education laws requiring that students remain in school at least until age 16, claiming that they should be able to withdraw their children from school earlier, after graduating the eighth grade. After concluding that the parents' objection was indeed based on their religious beliefs rather than merely their distinctive cultural values[186] and that the state's compulsory school attendance law threatened to substantially impair their exercise of those beliefs, the Court considered, and rejected, the state's arguments in favor of the law mandating that children remain in school until age 16. Those interests — in ensuring that children were educated to be well-socialized, productive members of society and educated citizens — were significant. Nevertheless, the Court, focusing on the particular practices of the Amish community, concluded that that community's child-raising practices were likely to satisfy those state interests while not impairing the parents' exercise of their religious duties. The Court's conclusion was aided by the fact that the entire dispute in the case centered on the parents' objection, not to any formal education for their children, but simply the approximately two additional years the state law demanded that the parents did not wish to comply with.

The Court returned to the employment context in several cases from the 1980s, in which, applying *Sherbert*, it held that states could not deny unemployment benefits when the reason for the claimant's unemployment was a religiously-based refusal to perform certain work. For example, in *Thomas v. Review Board*,[187] the Court struck down the denial of unemployment benefits to an employee who refused, based on religious reasons, a transfer to a part of his employer's factory producing armaments. As noted in the previous section, the Court in *Thomas* ruled for the plaintiff even though a co-religionist in the factory testified that their religion did not prohibit that

---

185. 406 U.S. 205 (1972).
186. The question of defining religion is discussed in the prior sub-section.
187. 450 U.S. 707 (1981).

type of work. The Court held that neither of the state's asserted interests—in preventing widespread unemployment caused by voluntary departures from the workforce and avoiding the need to probe a claimant's religious beliefs—was supported by the record; thus, they did not justify the burden placed on the plaintiff's religious beliefs. Similarly, in *Hobbie v. Unemployment Appeals Commission*,[188] the Court deemed it irrelevant for purposes of the claimant's free exercise claim that her conversion to the religion imposing the obligation in question occurred while she was working for the employer.

Cases such as *Sherbert, Yoder, Thomas*, and *Hobbie* marked the apex of the Court's protection of free exercise of religion. In a line of cases beginning in the 1980s, the Court began to become less receptive to free exercise-based claims for exceptions to generally-applicable laws. Sometimes, those decisions rested on the special context of the claimed free exercise right. For example, in *Goldman v. Weinberger*,[189] the Court upheld a regulation forbidding a Jewish member of the military from wearing his yarmulke while on duty. Justice Rehnquist, writing for the majority, emphasized the deference courts owed military judgments about the desired uniformity implemented through dress regulations. At other times, the government interest was particularly compelling. For example, in *Bob Jones University v. United States*,[190] the Court upheld an Internal Revenue Service decision denying tax-exempt status to a university that refused to admit persons in interracial relationships. Writing for the Court, Chief Justice Burger acknowledged that the school's policies were grounded in sincerely-held religious beliefs protected by the Free Exercise Clause. Nevertheless, the Court held that the government's compelling interest in preventing racial discrimination in education outweighed any burden the withdrawal of tax-exempt status imposed on the university's free exercise interests.

Even outside of such special situations, the Court in the 1980s often allowed government programs to prevail over free exercise concerns. In *Bowen v. Roy*,[191] the Court rejected a free exercise claim brought by persons challenging a federal law requiring the use of social security numbers to access federal benefits. The plaintiffs argued that the use of numerical identifiers for their children would inflict spiritual harm on them. The Court rejected the claim, concluding that the government could not be required "to conduct its own internal affairs" in ways conducive the plaintiffs' religious beliefs.

The Court relied heavily on *Roy* two years later when, in *Lyng v. Northwest Indian Cemetery*,[192] it permitted the United States Forest Service to construct a road through Native American burial grounds in a national forest that three native tribes considered sacred. Justice O'Connor's majority opinion distinguished the free exercise burden in this case from those in *Sherbert, Yoder*, and *Thomas*, concluding that,

---

188. 480 U.S. 136 (1987).
189. 475 U.S. 503 (1986).
190. 461 U.S. 574 (1983).
191. 476 U.S. 693 (1986).
192. 485 U.S. 439 (1988).

unlike in those cases, the government road-building in *Lyng*, just like its use of social security numbers in *Roy*, imposed only an indirect burden on religious exercise. Although the Court had consistently held that even indirect burdens on free exercise were subject to strict scrutiny, Justice O'Connor, speaking for a five-justice majority, insisted that:

> This does not and cannot imply that incidental effects of government programs, which may make it more difficult to practice certain religions but which have no tendency to coerce individuals into acting contrary to their religious beliefs, require government to bring forward a compelling justification for its otherwise lawful actions. The crucial word in the constitutional text is "prohibit."[193]

Justice Brennan, joined by Justices Marshall and Blackmun, dissented, challenging the idea that the Free Exercise Clause prohibited only government actions that coerced conduct inconsistent with religious belief.

[c] Smith *and the Non-Discrimination Rule*

The Court's increasing resistance to free exercise conduct-based claims culminated with its seminal 1990 decision in *Employment Division v. Smith*.[194] The dispute in *Smith* began when the plaintiffs, who were members of the Native American Church, were fired from their jobs at a private drug rehabilitation center for ingesting peyote as part of a sacramental ritual. The State of Oregon then determined that they were ineligible for unemployment benefits because they had been fired for work-related misconduct.

The Court upheld the denial of unemployment benefits. Writing for the five-justice majority,[195] Justice Scalia first asserted that the only governmental action ever invalidated by the Court under the *Sherbert* test was the denial of unemployment benefits in cases such as *Sherbert* and *Thomas*. He distinguished the unemployment cases as involving exemption systems that entailed "individualized government assessment"[196] of the reasons for the relevant conduct; by contrast, despite *Smith*'s ostensible dispute about unemployment benefits, Justice Scalia described the case as one involving a generally-applicable criminal law (which in turn triggered a disqualification for those benefits). He reasoned that cases such as *Sherbert* stood for the proposition that when government provides for a system of individualized exemptions, as it does in states' unemployment programs, it had to make an exemption equally available for religious-based exemption requests. Only if it does not—that is, only if the law discriminates against religion—does *Sherbert* require the government to show a compelling reason for burdening religious exercise. Continuing, Justice Scalia distinguished cases such as *Yoder* as involving "hybrid"[197] situations involving the conjoining of a free ex-

---

193. *Id.* at 450–451.
194. 494 U.S. 872 (1990).
195. Justice O'Connor concurred in the judgment on a different ground.
196. *Id.* at 884.
197. *Id.* at 882.

ercise claim with another constitutional claim (in *Yoder*, for example, a due process claim based on parents' right to direct their children's upbringing).

In contrast to these cases (as Justice Scalia described them), *Smith* was a non-hybrid case involving a neutral, generally applicable statute. Quoting the foundational case of *Reynolds v. United States*, discussed earlier, Justice Scalia argued that using the *Sherbert* test to require government to show a compelling interest under such circumstances would allow a religious objector, "by virtue of his beliefs, 'to become a law unto himself.'"[198] He continued that applying *Sherbert* to all cases involving a religiously-grounded objection to a neutral, generally-applicable law "would open the prospect of constitutionally required religious exemptions from civic obligations of almost every conceivable kind."[199] Oregon's prohibition of peyote use was a generally applicable law that itself easily satisfied rational basis scrutiny and thus, under *Smith*'s analysis, could be applied even to religiously-motivated conduct.

Justice O'Connor concurred in the judgment. In a part of her opinion joined by Justices Brennan, Marshall, and Blackmun, she disputed Justice Scalia's reading of the caselaw and further argued that *Sherbert* had provided a workable balance between government needs and free exercise interests. Nevertheless, in a part of her opinion speaking only for herself, she concluded that the Oregon law satisfied *Sherbert*, given the importance of combatting drug use. Justice Blackmun dissented, joined by Justices Brennan and Marshall. He argued that the sacramental use of peyote was "integral" to the plaintiffs' worship and that the state's justification for refusing to exempt such use from its criminal laws was based on speculation, given its record of not enforcing criminal prohibitions on peyote use. Thus, he concluded, application of *Sherbert* should have led the Court to uphold the plaintiffs' free exercise claim.

In *Smith*, the Court conceded that *Sherbert*'s compelling interest test applied when the challenged law discriminated against religion. The Court applied that non-discrimination rule in *Church of the Lukumi Babalu Aye, Inc. v. City of Hialeah*.[200] In *Lukumi*, the Court invalidated, under the Free Exercise Clause, a set of ordinances a city had enacted to prevent members of the Santeria faith from performing the animal sacrifices that are a principal tenet of their religion. In response to the imminent founding of a Santeria church in Hialeah, Florida, the city council enacted several ordinances relating to animal slaughter. While some were worded so as to clearly regulate animal sacrifice, others were worded more generally but included carve-outs that left their impact solely focused on Santeria sacrifice.

Justice Kennedy wrote for the majority in all but one section of the opinion. Relying on *Smith*, the Court scrutinized the neutrality and general applicability of the ordinances at issue. Justice Kennedy observed that an ordinance's language or context could indicate a lack of facial neutrality. Although the ordinances at issue mentioned "sacrifice" and "ritual," these terms did not conclusively demonstrate a lack of neu-

---

198. *Id.* at 885 (quoting *Reynolds*, 98 U.S. at 167).
199. *Id.* at 888.
200. 508 U.S. 520 (1993).

trality. He continued, however, that the ordinances' wording and exemptions meant that Santeria rituals were nearly the only conduct affected by the ordinances. For example, the ordinances' restrictions on killing animals contained many exceptions, including for kosher slaughter, veterinary euthanasia, and hunting. Justice Kennedy concluded that providing such exceptions without also providing an exception for Santeria religious practices demonstrated a lack of neutrality that government must justify with compelling reasons. In addition to lacking neutrality, the ordinances were not generally-applicable. The ordinances were substantially underinclusive with regard to achieving the asserted government interests. For example, rather than generally promoting the City's purported interest in preventing cruelty to animals, the ordinances prohibited few slaughters other than those performed during Santeria worship. Similarly undercutting the City's asserted public health concerns, the ordinances failed to address improper carcass disposal after nonreligious animal killings.

Regulations that were not neutral or not generally applicable had to be narrowly tailored to advance a compelling state interest. Perhaps unsurprisingly, the ordinances failed that strict scrutiny given their demonstrated under-inclusiveness. In separate opinions, Justice Souter and Justice Blackmun (the latter joined by Justice O'Connor) concurred in judgment but called for a reexamination of *Smith*. Justice Scalia (the author of *Smith*), joined by Chief Justice Rehnquist, also wrote a separate concurrence.

In *Masterpiece Cakeshop v. Colorado Civil Rights Commission*,[201] the Court reversed a state civil rights agency's decision rejecting a baker's claim for a religious exemption to the state's public accommodations laws. The state law banned discrimination based on sexual orientation, and the charge against the baker arose from his religion-based refusal to sell a wedding cake to a same-sex couple. Applying *Lukumi*, the Supreme Court faulted one member of the agency's tribunal that rejected his claim for making comments that appeared to disparage the baker's religion. The Court also concluded that the tribunal's different treatment of other, non-religiously motivated, exemption claims revealed the tribunal's hostility to the baker's religious beliefs. The Court concluded that the tribunal's hostility to the baker's religious beliefs violated *Lukumi*'s non-discrimination rule. Justice Ginsburg, joined by Justice Sotomayor, dissented, finding the majority's evidence insufficient to show hostility to the baker's religious beliefs.

Smith's imposition of a mere non-discrimination rule, rather than the more religion-protective rule from cases such as *Sherbert*, was controversial. In 1993, Congress enacted a statute, the Religious Freedom Restoration Act (RFRA),[202] which expressly aimed at restoring the *Sherbert* compelling interest test to free exercise jurisprudence. In the statute's findings, Congress explicitly stated its approval of the *Sherbert* test, and expressed its intention to reinstate it. The statute essentially codifies *Sherbert*,

---

201. 138 S. Ct. 1719 (2018).
202. Religious Freedom Restoration Act of 1993, Pub. L. No. 103-141, 107 Stat. 1488 (codified at 42 U.S.C. § 2000bb).

providing that government may substantially burden a person's exercise of religion only if it demonstrates that its interest is compelling and that the means chosen are the least restrictive possible.[203]

Congress made RFRA applicable to the federal government via its general power to regulate federal action.[204] But to make it applicable to the states, it employed its power to enforce the Fourteenth Amendment, through which the Free Exercise Clause was incorporated to apply against the states. In 1997, the Court in *City of Boerne v. Flores*[205] struck down RFRA's application to the states, concluding that Congress had exceeded its Fourteenth Amendment enforcement power. The Court's Enforcement Clause jurisprudence is discussed in Chapter 13 of this book. Despite *City of Boerne*, RFRA remains applicable to the federal government.[206]

After *City of Boerne* struck down RFRAs' applicability to the states, Congress enacted a more modest law, based on its spending power and its power to regulate interstate commerce.[207] The Religious Land Use and Institutionalized Persons Act (RLUIPA) restricts the ability of states to make land use decisions that infringe on free exercise rights or to infringe on institutionalized persons' religious conduct unless those infringements were necessary to further a compelling government interest. In *Cutter v. Wilkinson*,[208] the Court rejected a facial challenge asserting that RLUIPA's institutionalized persons provision violates the Establishment Clause.[209]

§ 12.04 The Relationship between the Establishment and Free Exercise Clauses

This book's discussions of the Establishment and Free Exercise Clauses make it clear that those two provisions relate to each other in important but complex ways. In recent years, the Court has explicitly examined the relationship between them. In particular, it has considered the circumstances under which a state can defeat a free exercise claim by asserting its interest in maintaining its distance from religion, in conformance with the anti-establishment principle, if not the Establishment Clause itself. To be sure, in earlier cases, the Court has considered such claims.[210] In several cases from the twenty-first century, the Court elaborated on the relationship between these two principles.

---

203. 42 U.S.C. § 2000bb-1(b).

204. *See, e.g.*, O'Bryan v. Bureau of Prisons, 349 U.S. 399, 401 (7th Cir. 2003) (upholding RFRA's applicability to the federal government under the Necessary and Proper Clause).

205. 521 U.S. 507 (1997).

206. *See, e.g.*, Burwell v. Hobby Lobby Stores, 573 U.S. 682 (2014) (applying RFRA to the federal law mandate that employers provide contraception coverage to their employees).

207. Congress's commerce and spending powers are discussed, respectively, in Chapters 6 and 5.

208. 544 U.S. 709 (2005).

209. *Cutter* is discussed in Section 12.02[7].

210. *See, e.g.*, Rosenberger v. University of Virginia, 515 U.S. 819 (1995) (holding that the need to comply with the Establishment Clause did not excuse a state university's constitutional obligation to provide equal funding for a student group that wished to express a religious viewpoint).

In *Locke v. Davey*,[211] the Court rejected a free exercise challenge to a Washington State college scholarship program that denied funds to students majoring in devotional theology. Under the program, qualifying Washington State high school graduates were given grants to attend schools located within the state. Consistent with the Washington Constitution, the grant could be used for any degree program except devotional theology. A qualifying student sued when he was prohibited from using the funds to pursue a double major in pastoral ministries and business management at a Christian college.

Writing for seven justices, Chief Justice Rehnquist noted that "the Establishment Clause and the Free Exercise Clause are frequently in tension," since conduct designed to avoid violating one provision risks violating the other. To alleviate that tension, he wrote that there is "'room for play in the joints' between them" so that "some state actions permitted by the Establishment Clause [are] not required by the Free Exercise Clause."[212] Thus, while an earlier case had held that there was no Establishment Clause violation when a state funded a student's pursuit of a devotional theology degree,[213] the Free Exercise Clause did not *require* such funding.

In essence, then, the concept of "play in the joints" means that simply because particular assistance to religion does not violate the Establishment Clause does not mean it is thereby required by the Free Exercise Clause. The Court rejected the plaintiff's argument that the state's refusal to fund his program of study thereby discriminated against religion, observing that the program had accommodated religion in many ways (for example, by allowing the scholarships to be used at religious schools) and concluding that devotional study was simply a different category of study that the state was not required to fund just because it funded secular studies.

In his dissent, Justice Scalia, joined by Justice Thomas, argued that the restriction was unconstitutional on its face because it withheld a generally available benefit on the basis of religion. In response to the "play in the joints" idea, Justice Scalia instead took the position that the two religion clauses "abut"[214] each other—that is, they demarcate a line in which any conduct assisting religion that was allowed by the Establishment Clause (such as funding devotional studies) was thereby required by the Free Exercise Clause in order to place the religious conduct on an equal footing with analogous secular conduct.

The Court refused to extend *Locke*'s idea of "play in the joints" in *Trinity Lutheran Church of Columbia v. Comer*.[215] *Trinity Lutheran* struck down a Missouri decision denying a church playground the ability to share in a state fund established to finance playground improvements because the playground was affiliated with a church. The

---

211. 540 U.S. 712 (2004).

212. *Id.* at 719 (citing Walz v. Tax Comm'n, 397 U.S. 664, 669 (1970)). *Walz*, a case dealing with an Establishment Clause challenge to a state tax exemption extended to religious organizations, is discussed in Section 12.01.

213. Witters v. Wash. Dep't of Servs. for the Blind, 474 U.S. 481 (1986).

214. 540 U.S. at 728 (Scalia, J., dissenting).

215. 137 S. Ct. 2012 (2017).

state defended its decision as mandated by the state constitution, which imposed stringent limits on state funding of religious institutions.

So posed, *Trinity Lutheran* might be seen as presenting the same "play in the joints" situation as *Locke v. Davey*: Missouri, just like Washington, was not compelled to deny funding for the religious purpose by the Establishment Clause, but the Free Exercise Clause did not require the state to provide it. The Court, however, concluded that Missouri's actions discriminated against religion in a way that violated the Free Exercise Clause. Writing for six justices of a seven-justice majority,[216] Chief Justice Roberts distinguished *Locke*, explaining that Missouri's decision discriminated against the status of being a religious institution, while in *Locke*, Washington State had simply prohibited the use of state funds to study to become a minister. Thus, according to the Court, the plaintiff in *Locke* was not forced to choose between his religious beliefs and a government benefit, while that was the situation faced by the plaintiff in *Trinity Lutheran*. The Court also distinguished *Locke* based on Washington State's strong anti-establishment interest in not using state money to pay for the training of clergy. The Court characterized the expenditure in *Trinity Lutheran* (to pay for playground improvements) as implicating anti-establishment concerns to a much lesser degree.

Importantly, Chief Justice Roberts added a footnote that all but limited the decision in *Trinity Lutheran* to its precise facts.[217] Justices Thomas and Gorsuch, who joined the rest of Chief Justice Roberts's opinion, refused to join in that footnote, reducing it to the status of a statement by a four-justice plurality. Justice Gorsuch's explanation for refusing to join that footnote, an explanation endorsed by Justice Thomas, strongly suggests that at least those two justices are ready to apply the case's principles more broadly.[218] On the other hand, Justice Breyer concurred only in the judgment, but, in the spirit of that footnote, similarly insisted on deciding the case on very narrow grounds. Justice Sotomayor, joined by Justice Ginsburg, dissented. She noted that the church used the playground for instruction in religious principles, and expressed concern that the Court for the first time had mandated government payments to a church.

In 2020, the Court expanded on *Trinity Lutheran*, and found a Free Exercise Clause violation in the application of a state constitutional provision limiting funding of religion. In *Espinoza v. Montana Department of Revenue*,[219] the Court considered a Montana program that provided tax credits to persons who donated to organizations that award scholarships to students to attend private schools. To comply with the state constitution's rule against funding church-sponsored schools, the state promulgated a rule construing that program to prohibit use of those tax-subsidized schol-

---

216. Justice Breyer concurred only in the judgment. Justice Sotomayor, joined by Justice Ginsburg, dissented.

217. *See id.* at 2024 n.3 ("This case involves express discrimination based on religious identity with respect to playground resurfacing. We do not address religious uses of funding or other forms of discrimination.").

218. *See id.* at 2026 (Gorsuch, J., concurring in part); *id.* at 2025 (Thomas, J., concurring in part).

219. 140 S. Ct. 2246 (2020).

arships at religious schools. When challenged, the state lower court enjoined that rule. On appeal, the Montana Supreme Court held that, without the rule in place, the program violated the state constitution and struck down the entire program.

The Supreme Court, on a 5–4 vote, reversed. Writing for that majority, Chief Justice Roberts concluded that the case was governed by *Trinity Lutheran*, in that it made a benefit unavailable based on the religious status of the organizations in question. On that ground—that is, the state's discrimination based on religious status rather than religious conduct—the Court distinguished *Locke v. Davey* just as *Trinity Lutheran* had. Applying strict scrutiny, the Court rejected the state's argument that complying with the state constitution's strict non-establishment principle constituted a compelling government interest, given the free exercise impairment the Court identified. The four dissenters argued that the case was closer to *Locke*, in that it involved a state decision not to fund religious education. They also worried that the decision compelled the state to fund religious education.

Clearly, *Espinoza* reduces the scope of *Locke*'s "play in the joints" idea. How much it reduces it remains an open question. For example, Justice Gorsuch's concurrence suggested that even discrimination that was tied to religious *conduct*, not just *status* (the distinction the majority relied on), was unconstitutional. This might suggest a much more robust free exercise right, with little room for "play in the joints" to accommodate any state's anti-establishment policy that extended beyond the limits of the Establishment Clause itself.

Chapter 13

Civil Rights Enforcement

Congress possesses important powers to enforce the Thirteenth,[1] Fourteenth[2] and Fifteenth[3] Amendments, the three Reconstruction era Amendments ratified after the Civil War. Each Amendment specifically empowers Congress to enforce its provisions with "appropriate" legislation. This Chapter discusses the Court's understanding of Congress's power to enforce each of the Civil War Amendments, focusing on the period starting in the 1960s.

The immediate post-Civil War period was marked by aggressive use of the enforcement power by Congress, as part of its Reconstruction program. Among a variety of other enforcement statutes, Congress enacted important civil rights legislation in 1866 and 1875. But as Reconstruction continued into the 1870s and the nation's interest in that project waned, the Court, perhaps reflecting the nation's mood, moved to limit and sometimes strike down those laws. Congress did not return to the civil rights field in a meaningful way until the 1960s, thus setting the stage for the Court to consider anew the scope of the enforcement powers these amendments provided. The three sections in this chapter (Sections 13.01–13.03) consider, in turn, Congress's power to enforce each of these amendments.

§ 13.01 Congressional Enforcement of the Thirteenth Amendment

The Thirteenth Amendment prohibition on slavery or involuntary servitude except as punishment for a crime is closely connected with the right to equal protection. Its purpose was to end slavery and to establish a system of completely voluntary labor.

---

1. The Thirteenth Amendment (1865) bans slavery and involuntary servitude except as a criminal punishment.

2. The Fourteenth Amendment (1868) confers citizenship on all persons born or naturalized in the United States, precludes a state from denying a citizen the privileges and immunities of United States citizens or denying any person life, liberty, or property without due process of laws, or denying any person the equal protection of the laws. Other provisions of the Fourteenth Amendment provide for reducing a state's congressional representation if it disenfranchises persons otherwise qualified to vote and address matters growing out of the confederate war debt and the status of former high confederate officials.

3. The Fifteenth Amendment (1870) provides that neither the federal nor state government may deny any American citizen the right to vote based on race, color, or prior servitude.

The Amendment has an enforcement provision identical to that in Section 5 of the Fourteenth Amendment.[4]

In addition to outlawing slavery and forced labor, the Thirteenth Amendment allows Congress to enact laws to abolish all incidents of slavery. Although the Court had long construed Congress's powers under the Thirteenth Amendment restrictively,[5] it drastically revised its approach in 1968 in *Jones v. Alfred H. Mayer Co.*[6] In *Jones*, private sellers had refused to sell real estate to an African-American couple. The prospective purchasers challenged that private race discrimination under a provision of the Civil Rights Act of 1866 giving persons equal rights to hold real estate regardless of race. The Court upheld that statute as legislation enforcing the Thirteenth Amendment. The Court explained that "Congress has the power ... rationally to determine what are the badges and the incidents of slavery, and the authority to translate that determination into effective legislation."[7]

As suggested by *Jones*, congressional power to enforce the Thirteenth Amendment extends far beyond cases involving the actual imposition of slavery or involuntary servitude, to allow Congress to attack what both *Jones* and an early case called "the badges and incidents of slavery."[8] For example, Congress may create a statutory cause of action for Black victims of a conspiratorial, racially-motivated assault to deprive them of the basic rights the law secures.[9] As these cases illustrate, that power reaches private conspiracies and other private conduct, as well as official conduct, because the Thirteenth Amendment is not limited to "state action."

The Court has applied *Jones* to uphold other statutes regulating private conduct under Congress' power to enforce the Thirteenth Amendment. Thus, in *Runyon v. McCrary*,[10] the Court held that a different provision of the Civil Rights Act of 1866—one giving all persons equal rights to contract regardless of race—prohibited a private school from excluding qualified students based on race and that the statute was within Congress's Thirteenth Amendment enforcement power. That law's reach also prohibits racial discrimination in employment.[11]

Congressional power under the Thirteenth Amendment is not limited to protection of any particular race.[12] The civil rights statute that bars racial discrimination in con-

---

4. U.S. Const. amend. XIII, § 2.

5. *See, e.g.,* The Civil Rights Cases, 109 U.S. 3 (1883).

6. 392 U.S. 409 (1968).

7. *Id.* at 440.

8. *Ibid.* (quoting The Civil Rights Cases, 109 U.S. 3, 20 (1883)).

9. *See* Griffin v. Breckenridge, 403 U.S. 88 (1971).

10. 427 U.S. 160 (1976).

11. *See* McDonald v. Santa Fe Trail Transp. Co., 427 U.S. 273 (1976).

12. *See, e.g.,* The Peonage Abolition Act of 1867, 42 U.S.C. § 1994 (statute, based on the Thirteenth Amendment enforcement power, banning peonage of any sort without any reference to race); McDonald v. Santa Fe Trail Transp. Co., *supra* (holding that whites as well as non-whites are protected from racial discrimination in employment by the equal contract rights provision of the Civil Rights Act of 1866).

tracts protects whites as well as non-whites.[13] Indeed, in recent years Congress has grounded at least some legislation on the Thirteenth Amendment when the legislation does not specifically reference race at all.[14] More generally, the modern era's broader construction of Congress's power to enforce the Thirteenth Amendment reflects an understanding that the Amendment is not properly understood only as a prohibition on the specific practice of chattel slavery, but instead as a far-reaching guarantee of slavery's opposite—freedom, whatever that term might be construed to mean.

§ 13.02 Congressional Enforcement of the Fourteenth Amendment

The provisions of Section 1 of the Fourteenth Amendment (*i.e.*, the Citizenship, Privileges and Immunities, Due Process, and Equal Protection Clauses) are self-executing—that is, they state constitutional norms which courts enforce. But the Amendment also provides, in Section 5, that "Congress shall have power to enforce, by appropriate legislation, the provisions of this article." Although the Court interpreted this provision broadly during the 1960s to authorize Congress "to exercise its discretion in determining whether and what legislation is needed to secure the guarantees of the Fourteenth Amendment,"[15] in a series of more recent cases the Court has constricted the scope of Congress's enforcement power (which is sometimes referred to as "the Section 5 power").

In *Katzenbach v. Morgan*,[16] the Court interpreted Congress's Section 5 power broadly. *Morgan* involved Section 4(e) of the Voting Rights Act of 1965, which provides that a literacy test could not be used to disqualify from voting anyone who had completed sixth grade in an American school where the predominant language was not English. The provision was clearly designed to allow Puerto Rican Americans living on the U.S. mainland to vote. (It had particular impact on New York, where most mainland residents of Puerto Rican descent lived at the time.) Section 4(e) overrode a New York law which required English literacy in order to vote. In so doing, Congress confronted an earlier Supreme Court decision[17] that held that literacy tests did not automatically violate the Equal Protection Clause.

The Court upheld Section 4(e) in part on two distinct grounds. First, the Court suggested that the provision, by granting voting rights to the Puerto Rican community, helped ensure that that community was represented in government and received its

---

13. *See McDonald*, 427 U.S. at 289.

14. *See, e.g.*, Matthew Shepard and James Byrd, Jr. Hate Crimes Prevention Act, 123 Stat. 2835 (2009) (codified as amended in scattered sections of 18, 28, and 42 U.S.C.) (amending a previously-enacted federal hate crimes law to add hate crimes based on gender, sexual orientation, gender identity, and disability).

15. Katzenbach v. Morgan, 384 U.S. 641, 651 (1966).

16. 384 U.S. 641 (1966).

17. *See* Lassiter v. Northampton County Bd. of Elections, 360 U.S. 45 (1959).

fair share of attention from elected officials. This was perhaps the most modest ground for upholding Section 4(e), as it did not directly implicate the Court's earlier holding refusing to strike down literacy tests on their own ground.

However, the Court also concluded that Section 4(e) could be upheld on the ground that Congress might reasonably have concluded that New York's literacy requirement reflected invidious discrimination. The Court then determined that it could perceive a basis under which Congress may have concluded that the New York law was based on racial prejudice, thereby validating the federal enforcement statute. This latter standard for evaluating federal enforcement legislation was generous. Indeed, the Court held that the enforcement power was as broad as Congress's power under Article I's Necessary and Proper Clause.[18] Writing for the Court, Justice Brennan wrote: "Correctly viewed, Section 5 is a positive grant of legislative power authorizing Congress to exercise its discretion in determining whether and what legislation is needed to secure the guarantees of the Fourteenth Amendment."[19] Applying that standard, the Court held that Congress might have concluded that Section 4(e) was an appropriate measure to enforce the Equal Protection Clause, even if Congress's conclusion led it to disagree with the Court's own understanding of what equal protection required.

Dissenting, Justice Harlan (joined by Justice Stewart) thought the Court's decision was irreconcilable with our system of separated powers, to the extent it held that Congress could enact legislation reflecting its own interpretation of the Constitution, even if that interpretation conflicted with the Court's. It was for the Court, not Congress, to define the substantive reach of the Equal Protection Clause, he urged. He warned that, if Congress could define constitutional norms, it could contract, as well as expand, them. In response to that warning, Justice Brennan replied by suggesting that Congress could expand rights beyond those found by the Court, but could not constrict them.[20]

After *Morgan*, the Court continued for a time to adhere to a generally broad understanding of the enforcement power. To be sure, in 1970, the Court struck down an attempt by Congress to use its Fourteenth Amendment enforcement power to lower the voting age in state elections to eighteen.[21] However, in 1980, it held that, in order to deter violations of judicially-recognized rights, Congress could cast a broader liability net, prohibiting conduct that was not itself unconstitutional, in order to ensure that evidentiary difficulties did not prevent the identification and punishment of conduct that was in fact unconstitutional.[22]

---

18. The breadth of Congress's power under the Necessary and Proper Clause is discussed in Section 5.03.

19. 384 U.S. at 651.

20. *See id.* at 651, n. 10. This theory became known as the "one-way ratchet," since it meant that Congress could re-interpret constitutional rights in only one direction — that is, toward increasing, but not decreasing, them.

21. *See* Oregon v. Mitchell, 400 U.S. 112 (1970).

22. *See* City of Rome v. United States, 446 U.S. 156 (1980). *City of Rome* was a case where the Court considered Congress's power to enforce the *Fifteenth* Amendment. That topic is addressed in the next section. During this period, however, the Court was generally thought to apply the same generous standard to legislation enforcing both the Fourteenth and the Fifteenth Amendments.

In 1997, however, the Court retreated from this broad interpretation of the enforcement power. *City of Boerne v. Flores*[23] involved a statute, the Religious Freedom Restoration Act (RFRA),[24] which expanded upon the Court's interpretation of the First Amendment right to free religious exercise. In *Employment Division v. Smith*,[25] decided three years before RFRA, the Court had held that neutral laws that imposed only incidental burdens on free religious exercise did not violate the Free Exercise Clause.[26] By contrast, RFRA required that even such neutral laws be subject to the strict scrutiny standard. Indeed, under RFRA, strict scrutiny is required even if the law did not have a disparate *impact* on religion; any time a law had a substantial impact on religious exercise, RFRA required strict scrutiny, regardless of whether the law had an equal impact on non-religious activity. In enacting RFRA, Congress made clear that it was seeking to reimpose the more plaintiff-friendly Free Exercise Clause standard the Court had severely curtailed in *Smith*. Congress made RFRA applicable to both the federal government and the states — the latter, through its power to enforce the Fourteenth Amendment.

Boerne held that RFRA's application to the states exceeded Congress's enforcement power.[27] The Court stated that Congress's enforcement power was remedial and preventive, not substantive — that is, Congress lacked the power to determine what conduct violates the Constitution. In stating that rule, *Boerne* severely limited the more aggressive aspects of the Court's holding in *Morgan*, even though it distinguished rather than overruled that case.

In place of *Morgan*'s broad understanding of congressional power, *Boerne* required that there be "a congruence and proportionality between the injury to be prevented or remedied and the means adopted to that end."[28] In essence, *Boerne* limited Congress's power under Section 5 to addressing "conduct transgressing the Fourteenth Amendment's substantive provisions," and required that Congress "tailor its legislative scheme to remedying or preventing such conduct."[29] This did not mean that Congress was limited simply to prescribing remedies for constitutional violations uncovered by courts in the normal course of litigation. Rather, as the Court explained three years after *Boerne*, Congress retained "the authority both to remedy and to deter violation of rights guaranteed [under the Fourteenth Amendment] by prohibiting a somewhat broader swath of conduct, including that which is not itself forbidden by

---

23. 521 U.S. 507 (1997).

24. 42 U.S.C. § 2000bb (2000).

25. 494 U.S. 872 (1990).

26. *Smith* is discussed in Section 12.03[2][c].

27. RFRA remains enforceable against the federal government, since that application of the law rests on different constitutional foundations. *See, e.g.* Burwell v. Hobby Lobby Stores, 573 U.S. 682 (2014) (applying RFRA to a federal statutory requirement that employers provide health care coverage for contraceptive services).

28. *Boerne*, 521 U.S. at 520.

29. Florida Prepaid Postsecondary Educ. Expense Bd. v. College Sav. Bank, 527 U.S. 627, 639 (1999).

the Amendment's text."[30] But it did mean that Congress needed to justify any such broader regulation by reference to actual constitutional violations as identified in judicial doctrine.

Applying the new, more restrictive "congruence and proportionality" test, the *Boerne* Court struck down RFRA's application to the states. The Court conceded that, in earlier cases, it had upheld enforcement legislation that prohibited acts that had disparate impact on a constitutionally-protected right (for example, racial equality), even when judicial doctrine required proof not just of impact but of discriminatory intent.[31] However, the Court concluded that Congress had not created a legislative record showing numerous violations of the underling free exercise right (as interpreted by the Court) that would justify broad prophylactic legislation of that sort in the religion field. Indeed, the Court also noted that RFRA regulated even state action that did not have a disparate impact on religious exercise rights—rather, RFRA imposed strict scrutiny anytime a law substantially impacted religious exercise, even when the law's impact was not primarily focused on religious conduct. The Court also commented on RFRA's breadth, noting the severity of the strict scrutiny test it required and, again, the fact that that test was triggered anytime a state government action impaired free religious exercise, even if that action did not have a disparate impact on religious exercise. For these reasons, it concluded that RFRA was simply too out of proportion to the underlying constitutional right it sought to vindicate.

The Court further restrained Congress's Section 5 power in two companion cases it decided on the same day in 1999 by identical 5–4 votes.[32] In one case the federal enforcement legislation failed to fall within the Amendment's "substantive" reach; in the other, Congress failed to show that its legislative scheme was commensurate with the unconstitutional conduct it addressed.

In *College Savings Bank v. Florida Prepaid Postsecondary Education Expense Board*,[33] the Court held that Section 5 did not empower Congress to enact the Trademark Remedy Clarification Act (TRCA), which subjected states to lawsuits for false and misleading advertising under federal trademark law.[34] The TRCA allegedly protected against state deprivations of two types of rights—freedom from a competitor's false advertising about its products and "a more generalized right to be secure in one's

---

30. Kimel v. Board of Regents, 528 U.S. 62, 81 (2000).

31. The discriminatory intent requirement in equal protection doctrine is discussed in Section 10.05.

32. The majorities in these cases consisted of Chief Justice Rehnquist and Justices O'Connor, Scalia, Kennedy, and Thomas; Justices Stevens, Souter, Ginsburg, and Breyer dissented in both.

33. 527 U.S. 666 (1999).

34. The enforcement power issue arose in *College Savings Bank*, because the statute in question authorized lawsuits against states seeking damages and other retrospective relief, which the Court had previously held was not available when Congress legislated under the Commerce Clause, because of states' sovereign immunity. Seminole Tribe of Florida v. Florida, 517 U.S. 44 (1996). However, the enforcement power does allow Congress to impose such liability, *Fitzpatrick v. Bitzer*, 427 U.S. 445 (1976), but only if the law is valid enforcement legislation. State sovereign immunity of the sort imposed by *Seminole Tribe* is discussed in Section 8.06[2].

business interests."[35] The majority held that neither was a property right under the Due Process Clause of the Fourteenth Amendment; accordingly, Congress could enforce neither under Section 5.

In *Florida Prepaid Postsecondary Education Expense Board v. College Savings Bank*,[36] the Court held that Section 5 did not allow Congress to enact the Patent Remedy Act (PRA), which subjected states to lawsuits in federal court for patent infringement. Although patents are "property," the deprivation of which Congress could protect against under Section 5, the Court found insufficient evidence that the PRA remedied Fourteenth Amendment violations. The Court found the legislative record inadequate to document "a history of widespread and persisting deprivation of constitutional rights"[37] that would justify Section 5 enforcement legislation.

The four dissenters criticized the Court's scrutiny of the legislative record as inappropriate and novel. They argued that the Court had not previously required a showing of "widespread and persisting" constitutional deprivations as a prerequisite for Section 5 legislation. Unlike the RFRA statute struck down in *Boerne*, the PRA did not impact substantive law, but instead simply sought to prevent states from asserting sovereign immunity to deny patentees property rights without any recourse. That legislative approach, the dissenters argued, was both congruent and proportional as *Boerne* required.

Florida Prepaid inaugurated a series of cases in which the Court split on the question of how rigorously it should review Congress's evidence of unconstitutional conduct justifying enforcement legislation. The next year, in *Kimel v. Florida Board of Regents*, the Court held that the Age Discrimination in Employment Act (ADEA) failed the congruence and proportionality test, because the substantive requirements the ADEA imposed on states regarding age discrimination were "disproportionate to any unconstitutional conduct that conceivably could be targeted" by the law.[38] In addition to the alleged lack of evidence documenting constitutional violations the statute sought to remedy, the Court also noted that age discrimination—the topic of the law—received only rational basis equal protection scrutiny. For the five-justice majority in *Kimel*—and, indeed, over the course of several subsequent enforcement power cases—the underlying status of the equality right Congress sought to enforce became critical to the law's ultimate fate.[39] In *Kimel*, for example, age discrimination's lack of suspectness means that Congress faced a tougher task in justifying legislation attacking that sort of discrimination. As Justice O'Connor wrote for the majority in *Kimel*, Congress' application of the ADEA to states "was an unwarranted response to a perhaps inconsequential problem."[40]

---

35. *College Savings Bank*, 527 U.S. at 672.

36. 527 U.S. 627 (1999).

37. *Id.* at 645.

38. 528 U.S. 62, 83 (2000).

39. The Court's equal protection jurisprudence according particular levels of scrutiny to particular types of discrimination is discussed in Sections 10.02–10.04.

40. 528 U.S. at 89.

The following year, in *Board of Trustees v. Garrett*,[41] the Court again limited Congress's ability to subject states to private suits for money damages under Section 5's enforcement authority. In a 5–4 decision, reflecting the same line-up as in the previous post-*Boerne* enforcement power cases, the Court held state governments immune from such damage suits for employment discrimination that violated Title I of the Americans With Disabilities Act (ADA). Unlike in *Kimel*, the ADA's legislative record included extensive documentation of state discrimination against the disabled. However, the majority found the record insufficient to demonstrate "the pattern of unconstitutional discrimination on which Section 5 legislation must be based."[42] In other words, after *Garrett*, Congress would have to create an extensive record not only of the relevant type of discrimination (here, for example, disability-based employment discrimination by states), but would have to create a record of incidents of such discrimination that would fail the relevant judicial standard if those incidents were litigated in court.[43]

The Court's analyses in *Kimel* and *Garrett* clearly imply that enforcement legislation that benefits non-suspect classes or protects non-fundamental rights will be reviewed skeptically by the Court.[44] Indeed, the Court itself suggested as much when it *upheld* an enforcement statute aimed at sex discrimination, a quasi-suspect classification. In *Nevada Department of Human Resources v. Hibbs*,[45] the Court held that the family-care leave provision of the Family and Medical Leave Act of 1993 (FMLA) was valid enforcement legislation; thus, it allowed a lawsuit to go forward seeking relief that would otherwise be barred by state sovereign immunity.[46]

In the FMLA, Congress sought to remedy sex discrimination. Since state action which classifies on that basis triggers heightened scrutiny,[47] the Court appeared to apply more lenient review to the legislative record Congress compiled when enacting the FMLA. The six-justice majority, speaking through Chief Justice Rehnquist,[48] ex-

---

41. 531 U.S. 356 (2001).

42. *Id.* at 370.

43. *See id.* at 370 ("Several of these incidents [identified in the plaintiffs' brief] undoubtedly evidence an unwillingness on the part of state officials to make the sort of accommodations for the disabled required by the ADA. Whether they were irrational [and thus failed the rational basis standard applicable in litigation challenging such discrimination] is more debatable.... But even if it were to be determined that each incident upon fuller examination showed unconstitutional action on the part of the State, these incidents taken together fall far short of even suggesting the pattern of unconstitutional discrimination on which §5 legislation must be based."). *See also id.* at 374 (Kennedy, J., concurring) (remarking on the relative lack of court cases finding unconstitutional disability discrimination).

44. *See, e.g.*, Larry Kramer, *The Supreme Court 2000 Term: Forward: We the Court*, 115 Harv. L. Rev. 4, 147–48 (2001) (suggesting that those cases limited the Court's equal protection enforcement power to enacting statutes targeting race or sex discrimination).

45. 538 U.S. 721 (2003).

46. *See* note 34, *supra* (explaining the relationship between state sovereign immunity and the enforcement power).

47. The Court's sex equality jurisprudence is discussed in Section 10.02.

48. The majority in *Hibbs* included the four justices who would have upheld the legislation struck down in *College Savings Bank, Florida Prepaid, Kimel,* and *Garrett*, plus Chief Justice Rehnquist and Justice O'Connor.

plained the difference between its approach to the FMLA and its approach to the ADEA in *Kimel* and the ADA in *Garrett*: "Because the standard for demonstrating the constitutionality of a gender-based classification is more difficult to meet than our rational-basis test ... it was easier for Congress to show a pattern of state constitutional violations"[49] that justified the enforcement legislation.

Moreover, the Court's opinion suggested that it found more convincing the evidence of unconstitutional state discrimination in *Hibbs* than the analogous evidence it examined in *Kimel* and *Garrett*. In addition, the Court was more willing to find a connection between that unconstitutional state discrimination and the family leave rights the FMLA provision provided. The Court commented that that provision of the FMLA was "narrowly targeted at the fault line between work and family—precisely where sex-based overgeneralization has been and remains strongest—and affects only one aspect of the employment relationship."[50] The majority rejected Justice Scalia's argument that, before FMLA could apply to a particular state, Congress needed to demonstrate that that state had itself discriminated, not simply that states generally had done so. Indeed, the Court, quoting language from *Kimel* and *Garrett*, reiterated that Congress could "prohibit 'a somewhat broader swath of conduct, including that which is not itself forbidden by the Amendment's text'"[51] in remedying discrimination.

The following year, the Court, in a 5–4 decision in *Tennessee v. Lane*,[52] held that Title II of the Americans with Disabilities Act, as applied in that case, was valid enforcement legislation.[53] *Lane* arose from complaints by two wheelchair users—a court reporter and a litigant—that several Tennessee state courthouses' lack of wheelchair accessibility denied them access to the state judicial system. In allowing their lawsuits for damages to go forward, a five-justice majority[54] speaking through Justice Stevens analyzed the Section 5 issue as applied to the particular application of Title II to courthouses. This narrowing allowed him to identify the relevant constitutional right as the due process right to access the judicial process—a right previous decisions had held was fundamental. In turn, and following the template established by the *Kimel* line of cases, the fundamental nature of the right the statute sought to enforce allowed the Court to be more relaxed in its review of the ADA. Moreover, the Court noted the standard used to judge violations of the underlying right to access to the judicial system, and concluded that Title II's "reasonable accommodation" requirement tracked that constitutional standard closely, thus rendering the statute congruent and proportional to the underlying right.

---

49. *Id.* at 736.

50. *Id.* at 738.

51. *Id.* at 727 (quoting *Garrett*, 531 U.S. at 365 (in turn quoting *Kimel*, 528 U.S. at 81)).

52. 541 U.S. 509 (2004).

53. The 2001 *Garrett* case, discussed earlier, dealt with Title I of the ADA—its employment provisions. *Lane* dealt with Title II of that statute—its provision restricting disability discrimination in the provision of public services.

54. This majority included the members of the *Hibbs* majority, except for Chief Justice Rehnquist.

The template set by *Kimel* encountered a setback in 2012, in *Coleman v. Court of Appeals of Maryland*.[55] *Coleman*, like *Hibbs*, dealt with the FMLA, but it considered a different provision of that statute. The provision at issue in *Coleman* was known as the FMLA's self-care leave provision, and gives persons leave time for self-care (for example, if the employee is ill). It was defended on the ground that it complimented the *family*-leave care provision upheld in *Hibbs*. The argument was that the family-leave provision would likely be seen by state government employers as providing a women's benefit, on the impression that women were the persons primarily responsible for caring for ill family members. Thus, the argument went, the family-care leave provision might, at least in the short run, make things worse for women in the workplace, as they would now be seen as likely to have to leave work for family reasons, but would now have a federally-granted right to such leave. The self-care leave provision was designed, its defenders said, to equalize the amount of FMLA leave time men and women took, and thus to make the statute as a whole seem less like something that would be mainly used by women. The hope was to counteract the impression that the FMLA had made women seem more costly and hence less desirable employees.

The Court rejected this argument, calling it "overly complicated" and "unconvincing."[56] Notably, even though the self-care provision was defended as a sex equality measure, the Court did not cite *Hibbs*' statement about the relatively easier task Congress supposedly faced when enacting sex equality enforcement legislation. *Coleman* might simply be an unusual case where the Court was not willing to make the logical connection between the statute and the underlying constitutional violation.[57] Or it could be seen as the case that broke the template that started with *Kimel*. If that ends up being the case, then the Court's application of congruence and proportionality review may be in for a period of instability. Indeed, in *Tennessee v. Lane*, Justice Scalia renounced the congruence and proportionality test, pronouncing it to be too subjective. If the template the Court has followed from *Kimel* through *Lane* really is broken, that subjectivity may become all the more prevalent, along with doctrinal instability.[58]

§ 13.03 Congressional Enforcement of the Fifteenth Amendment

The Fifteenth Amendment prohibits racial discrimination in voting, and, like the other Civil War Amendments, it authorizes congressional enforcement.[59] The path

---

55. 566 U.S. 30 (2012).

56. *Id.* at 40.

57. Indeed, another argument in favor of the self-care leave provision's constitutionality as enforcement legislation was that it attempted to make it easier for pregnant women to take medical leave. The Court rejected that argument as well.

58. *See* William D. Araiza, *The Enforcement Power in Crisis*, 18 U. Pa. J. Con. Law Online 1 (2015) (suggesting this possibility).

59. U.S. Const. amend. XV, § 2.

of the Court's Fifteenth Amendment enforcement power jurisprudence has largely followed that of the analogous power in the Fourteenth Amendment: early restrictive readings[60] followed by much more expansive interpretations in the 1960s and 1970s, followed in turn by more recent cutbacks.

By the 1960s, the Court had become willing to uphold aggressive voting rights legislation. In *South Carolina v. Katzenbach*,[61] the Court upheld all the challenged provisions of the 1965 Voting Rights Act. Some of those provisions, such as the requirement that certain states and other jurisdictions get advance federal approval of (or "preclear") changes in their voting rules, cut deeply into state prerogatives. But the Court cited a long history of voting rights discrimination, particularly in the South, where most (although not all) of the jurisdictions subject to the preclearance requirement were located. It thus concluded that the preclearance requirement prevented covered jurisdictions from simply switching to other discriminatory mechanisms when earlier ones were struck down, and thus continuing to deny voting rights pending litigation that would always be one step behind the forces of discrimination. More generally, in *South Carolina*, the Court applied an extremely deferential standard to Fifteenth Amendment enforcement legislation, stating: "As against the reserved powers of the States, Congress may use any rational means to effectuate the constitutional prohibition of racial discrimination in voting."[62]

This hospitable reception to voting rights legislation continued into the next decade and beyond. For example, in *City of Rome v. United States*,[63] the Court upheld, as valid Fifteenth Amendment enforcement legislation, a provision of the Voting Rights Act requiring federal preclearance of any state law that had either the purpose or effect of diluting minority voting rights. The Court reached this conclusion even though the Fifteenth Amendment itself prohibited only intentional discrimination. The Court, speaking through Justice Marshall, reasoned that states were subject to the preclearance requirement because they had had a history of racial discrimination in voting. Thus, he argued, Congress might have reasonably concluded that laws in those state that disparately *impacted* minority voting rights were at risk of having been *intended* to achieve that result. A slightly different way to think about this reasoning is that the restriction on laws that "merely" had a discriminatory impact assisted plaintiffs who might well have been the victim of intentional discrimination but found themselves unable to prove that intent due to evidentiary difficulties.

In more recent years, this deference has eroded. Most notably, in *Shelby County v. Holder*,[64] the Court struck down the formula governing the most recent reenactment of the preclearance requirement originally included in the original Voting Rights Act,

---

60. *See, e.g.*, United States v. Reese, 92 U.S. 214 (1875) (holding that a law defended as enforcing the Fifteenth Amendment exceeded that power by not confining its provisions to cases of racial discrimination in voting).

61. 383 U.S. 301 (1966).

62. *Id.* at 324.

63. 446 U.S. 156 (1980).

64. 570 U.S. 529 (2013).

enacted in 1965. That original law provided that the preclearance requirement would expire in five years, and in the years after 1965, Congress renewed the requirement and its coverage formula several times, most recently in 2006, when it renewed both the requirement and the formula for an additional twenty-five years. In doing so, it retained, as it had in previous renewals, the same formula for determining which jurisdictions would be subject to the preclearance requirement.

The Court struck down that coverage formula. It expressed concern that that formula — which Congress had not altered since 1965 — had fallen out of date, and that social changes in the covered jurisdictions (and in particular the South) had rendered the preclearance requirement unnecessary. Essentially, the Court concluded, the preclearance requirement had succeeded, with the result that it was no longer needed. But the Court clearly did not defer to Congress' judgments to the extent it had in *South Carolina*. Instead, the Court offered its own interpretation of the registration and voting statistics used to justify the coverage formula. Moreover, the Court cited a principle of "equal [state] sovereignty" that "requires a showing that a statute's disparate geographic coverage is sufficiently related to the problem that it targets."[65]

The Court's cut-back on congressional discretion when enforcing the Fifteenth Amendment appears, at least at first glance, analogous to the cut-back in the Fourteenth Amendment context begun in *City of Boerne v. Flores*,[66] discussed in the previous sub-section. Both developments reflect a concern for federalism, and, in particular, with the burdens enforcement legislation imposes on states given the broad restrictions on state conduct imposed by the Due Process and Equal Protection Clauses. But because Fifteenth Amendment legislation focuses specifically on race and voting, one might also conclude that the Court is simply less tolerant of aggressive federal measures designed to ensure equality along those two axes. If a future Congress enacts significant voting rights legislation, the Court will have an opportunity to decide whether *Shelby County* was simply the result of Congress not updating the coverage formula for the preclearance requirement, or whether, by contrast, that opinion was the harbinger of a less welcoming attitude to voting rights legislation more generally.

---

65. *Id.* at 542.
66. 521 U.S. 507 (1997).

Chapter 14

The State Action Requirement

The Fourteenth Amendment's Privileges or Immunities, Due Process, and Equal Protection Clauses all prohibit a "state" from infringing on those rights. This feature means that plaintiffs in Fourteenth Amendment cases must show "state action"— *i.e.*, they must show that the state has acted in a way that constitutes a deprivation of their Fourteenth Amendment rights.[1] Despite its name, the "state action" requirement also applies to Bill of Rights provisions in their original textual form—that is, plaintiffs challenging *federal* action for violating, say, the Fourth Amendment's prohibition on unreasonable searches and seizures must show that the federal government, rather than a private party, is responsible for the violation.

Often, state action is easy to show. If a city police officer or an FBI agent is the one who conducted an unreasonable search, then the state action requirement has been satisfied. But sometimes the connection between the government and the allegedly unconstitutional conduct is not as obvious. In such cases, courts must engage in a sensitive inquiry into the conduct in which the government *has* engaged, to determine whether that conduct violates the Fourteenth Amendment.

The important assumption lurking in that last sentence is that, in a fundamental way, government is *always* acting in some way, even if that government action lurks in the background of the complained-of conduct. Consider, for example, a private landowner who excludes someone from her property based on the other person's race. As private conduct, one might immediately conclude that the excluded person could not bring a Fourteenth Amendment equal protection claim against the landowner, since the landowner is a private person. But think again. What if the landowner called the local police to eject the undesired person? What if the landowner (with or without police assistance) was acting on the authority of a state law that allowed (or even required[2]) racial segregation on that particular piece of property?[3] Or

---

1. This requirement applies to most constitutional rights provisions. The notable exception is the Thirteenth Amendment, which prohibits the institution of slavery, whoever (public or private) might practice it.

2. *See, e.g.*, Plessy v. Ferguson, 163 U.S. 537 (1896) (upholding a Louisiana law that required private railroads to segregate their passengers based on race).

3. For example, *Pennsylvania v. Board of Trusts*, 353 U.S. 230 (1957), involved an equal protection challenge to exclusion of Blacks from a school established under a testamentary trust limiting enrollment to "poor white male orphans." The City of Philadelphia was the trustee and, by state statute, the trust was administered, and the school was operated, by the "Board of Directors of City Trusts of the City of Philadelphia." The school was private, but the Court found state action since a state agency was trustee.

what if the landowner was simply acting on the authority of a statute (or even a common law rule) that gave landowners absolute control over who could enter onto their property? In all these cases, the "state" is "acting" in some way. Does that "action" constitute the "state action" the Fourteenth Amendment requires?

Given the near-impossibility of deciding many state action questions by simply asking if the state is literally acting, courts often consider the larger policy issues implicit in a given state action issue. The state action requirement demarcates the boundary between public conduct that is subject to the Constitution's restraints and private conduct that is not. That demarcation creates a realm of private liberty—a realm in which, for example, a private party does not have to allow speech with which he disagrees or people he would prefer to exclude, and thus a realm that allows society to develop free of the strictures that bind government. Of course, that realm may allow undesirable conduct: for example, concluding that the Equal Protection Clause does not apply to a private gathering opens the door for that gathering to discriminate on whatever grounds it chooses, subject only to whatever laws Congress or the state legislature may enact.[4] Nevertheless, it is generally thought that maintaining some private realm, free of government or constitutional limitations, is critical to the maintenance of a free society.

As this chapter explains, while courts have developed a set of general categories of state action, judicial answers to those questions are often highly fact-intensive. This chapter examines those categories and the major cases that developed them. Section 14.01 considers the set of cases where a private party was held to be a state actor by performing a public or sovereign function. Section 14.02 considers the special case when judicial approval or enforcement of private action converts that action into "state action." Section 14.03 considers cases where a plaintiff claims that the government has so entangled itself with a private party that that private action should be understood as state action.[5] Section 14.04 examines more recent state action cases. Those more recent cases reinforce the deeply fact-intensive nature of most state action cases.

The state action requirement was first announced in the *Civil Rights Cases*.[6] Those cases invalidated the Civil Rights Act of 1875, which prohibited racial discrimination in inns, public conveyances, and places of amusement. The Court concluded that the statute exceeded Congress' power to enforce the Fourteenth Amendment, because it addressed wholly private discriminatory action (that is, the actions of the owners

---

4. Of course, many such state and federal laws do restrict and regulate private conduct. *See, e.g.*, Roberts v. Jaycees, 469 U.S. 609 (1984) (upholding the application to the Jaycees of a law prohibiting sex discrimination and thus requiring the Jaycees to admit women as full members, against their will); PruneYard Shopping Center v. Robins, 447 U.S. 74 (1980) (upholding a state law requiring a shopping center owner to tolerate speech on its property that it would have preferred to exclude).

5. One of the cases discussed in this section, *Jackson v. Metropolitan Edison Co.*, 419 U.S. 345 (1974), also alludes to what has sometimes been described as yet another category of state action cases, involving legislative or administrative approval of the private conduct.

6. 109 U.S. 3 (1883).

of those types of businesses). According to the Court, Congress was limited to remedying state action.[7]

§ 14.01 Performance of a Public Function

One obvious way a private party acts as "the state" is if that party performs a public or governmental function, by exercising powers the State traditionally performs. *Smith v. Allwright*[8] illustrates this approach. Previous to *Smith*, the Court had struck down Texas statutes precluding African-Americans from voting in political parties' primary elections.[9] Texas then delegated power to the state's political parties, which were non-state entities, to establish rules for their primary elections.[10] The Court held that a primary election involved state action because a political party, though not a state entity, performed the public function of conducting elections. Thus, Texas could not circumvent its equal protection duties by delegating control over an election to a private actor.

Two years after *Smith*, the Court in *Marsh v. Alabama* found that a private property owner was subject to the Fourteenth Amendment (*i.e.*, there was "state action") when the owner, a corporation, owned what used to be known as a "company town"— privately-owned property near a remote worksite that had all the hallmarks of a municipality.[11] The Court held that the town's owner could not deny the exercise of constitutionally protected rights (in this case, First Amendment rights) on the town's streets, simply because the owner was a private party.

Thus, in both *Smith* and *Marsh*, the private parties were performing a public function (respectively, operating an election and operating what to all appearances was a municipality). These cases also share the feature of exclusivity: in *Smith*, the Court observed that, in Texas in 1944, the Democratic Party primary was the only meaningful election in Texas, and in *Marsh*, the company owned the only streets in its town.[12]

---

7. *Id.* at 11. Congress's power to enforce the Fourteenth Amendment is discussed more generally in Chapter 13.02.

8. 321 U.S. 649 (1944).

9. *See* Nixon v. Herndon, 273 U.S. 536 (1927); Nixon v. Condon, 286 U.S. 73 (1932).

10. One of the earlier cases, *Nixon v. Condon*, involved a statute that had delegated power to discriminate to the executive committees of the parties. In *Smith*, the general membership of the Democratic Party made the discriminatory choice, a distinction the Court found sufficient to distinguish *Condon*.

11. Marsh v. Alabama, 326 U.S. 501 (1946). The Court gave a lengthy description of the town in question, noting its physical layout (with sidewalks and streets), the location of businesses, including a U.S. Post Office, along the streets, and the presence of a local sheriff's official, paid for by the town, as the town's police officer. *See id.* at 502–03.

12. On this point, one can compare *Flagg Bros., Inc. v. Brooks*, 436 U.S. 149 (1978). *Flagg Brothers* characterized *Smith* and *Marsh* in terms of this exclusivity idea but failed to find that same exclusivity on its own facts. *Flagg Brothers* involved a storage facility's sale of goods stored there, after nonpayment of rent on the storage space. The Court refused to find state action in that decision, even though the sale was authorized by state law, because the relationship between the parties was char-

The Court expanded the company town theory in *Amalgamated Food Employees Union v. Logan Valley Plaza, Inc.*, where it held a private shopping center could not preclude striking workers from picketing because the Fourteenth (and thus the First) Amendment applied to the shopping center's conduct.[13] *Logan Valley* was limited four years later in *Lloyd Corp. v. Tanner*,[14] where a shopping center's conduct halting distribution of anti-war material was ruled not state action. The tension between these two cases is clear — indeed, the Court later overruled *Logan Valley*, concluding that it could not be harmonized with *Lloyd*.[15]

To be sure, *Lloyd* attempted to distinguish *Logan Valley* on the ground that the speech interests at stake in *Logan Valley* (picketing of one of the mall's stores) was sufficiently closely connected with the shopping center that the First Amendment claim outweighed the property owner's normal right to exclude unwelcome visitors.[16] By contrast, the anti-war speech in *Lloyd* did not have to be conducted on the premises in order for it to be effective. This attempt to harmonize the cases may not sound convincing; indeed, as noted above, the Court soon overruled *Logan Valley* as inconsistent with *Lloyd*. But it does suggest that the state action inquiry can be a subtle one. In particular, it suggests that, at least sometimes, the conceptually preliminary state action question — "is it really the state that is acting?" — becomes embroiled in the ultimate merits question — "what is the conduct in question, and should it be considered unconstitutional?" Regardless of these intricacies, today a shopping center, even a large self-contained one, is not considered the functional equivalent of a municipality and its action can no longer be considered "state action" for Fourteenth Amendment purposes, regardless of how critical it is that would-be speakers be able to access it in order to make their speech effective.

§ 14.02 Judicial Action

"State action" exists most obviously when a person or agency formally identified as a state instrumentality takes action. State action includes legislative measures, whether a statute, ordinance, administrative rule or regulation,[17] executive action,

---

acterized by the availability of private remedies, and hence the involuntary sale did not reflect the performance of an exclusively sovereign duty.

13. 391 U.S. 308 (1968).

14. 407 U.S. 551 (1972).

15. *See* Hudgens v. NLRB, 424 U.S. 507, 518 (1976).

16. *See Lloyd*, 407 U.S. at 563 ("The opinion [in *Logan Valley*] was carefully phrased to limit its holding to the picketing involved, where the picketing was 'directly related in its purpose to the use to which the shopping center property was being put,' and where the store was located in the center of a large private enclave with the consequence that no other reasonable opportunities for the pickets to convey their message to their intended audience were available.") (quoting *Logan Valley*, 391 U.S. at 320 n.9).

17. *See* Moose Lodge No. 107 v. Irvis, 407 U.S. 163, 179 (1972).

and judicial action. As briefly explained earlier, as straightforward as this statement appears, the myriad ways in which government "acts" quickly raise complex questions. Consider *Shelley v. Kraemer*.[18] In *Shelley*, a private party sued to block a pending sale of a neighboring parcel of land to an African-American, seeking to enforce a real estate covenant restricting sale of the parcel to whites. The party seeking enforcement denied the Fourteenth Amendment was implicated in the private dispute. The Court held, however, that judicial enforcement of the racially restrictive covenant constituted state action under the Fourteenth Amendment.

At one level, *Shelley*'s holding is completely unexceptional. After all, the plaintiff in *Shelley* was seeking a court order preventing the sale of the real estate to a person of the excluded race. As the Court noted, judicial action is "state action" every bit as much as is the action of a police officer or a legislature. Yet if judicial enforcement constitutes state action, as it clearly does, the Constitution's distinction between the public and private realms experiences considerable erosion. Private contracts — perhaps the quintessential example of private action — are valuable mainly because a victim of a breach can seek judicial assistance in either enforcing the contract's terms or seeking damages. If a court order of either sort constitutes state action (which *Shelley* suggested it would), then enforcement of any contractual term becomes a matter of state action. Hence, judicial enforcement of any such private contractual term (such as a racially-discriminatory one) that would be unconstitutional if performed by government would, as in *Shelley*, constitute unconstitutional state action. What this means is that, as a realistic matter, private party contracts must be made consistent with the Fourteenth Amendment, unless the parties are content with not relying on judicial enforcement of any terms that would be constitutionally problematic if performed by a state.

One way out of this paradox, at least in *Shelley*, lay in the facts of the case. *Shelley* involved a willing (African-American) buyer of property contracting with a willing (white) seller of the property. The plaintiff in the case was a neighbor who wished to see the neighborhood remain all white. Thus, *Shelley* did not actually involve a situation in which two contracting parties had a dispute and one of them sought judicial redress, with that redress being subject to constitutional standards. Instead, *Shelley* more closely resembled a situation in which the state (here, the court, acting at the behest of a third party) insisted that two private parties act in a racially discriminatory way. So understood, one can analogize *Shelley* to equal protection cases where Jim Crow laws forced persons of different races to remain apart from each other. That structure of the case presents a much stronger argument for finding unconstitutional state action, and obviates the problem described above that would flow from a broader reading of the case. But regardless of how one analyzes issues like this, "judicial enforcement" has sometimes been identified as a category of state action cases.

---

18. 334 U.S. 1 (1948).

§ 14.03 Entanglement

State action is also found where the government is sufficiently entangled with private conduct so as to make it appropriate to attribute that private behavior to the state. As one can imagine, applications of the entanglement theory turn largely on the facts of each case.

In *Burton v. Wilmington Parking Authority*,[19] the Court found state action by virtue of the government's entanglement with a racially discriminatory restaurant that rented space from a public parking authority. The restaurant was located on the premises of a state-owned parking garage, above which flew the state flag, and paid the state rent. Its customers used the parking garage, and thus the restaurant furnished a supply of customers to the state, just as the availability of easy government-provided parking benefited the restaurant. Moreover, the Court observed that the state-run parking garage depended on the rent from the private restaurant in order to meet its debt repayment obligations. As if to tighten the connection between the state and not just the restaurant but the restaurant's actual discriminatory policy, the Court also took note of the restaurant's statement that the only way it could stay in business was if it excluded African-Americans. Thus, the Court concluded, the state was dependent not just on the restaurant *per se*, but on the restaurant's continuation of its discriminatory policy.

Burton suggested a potentially sweeping expansion of the state action concept. However, a decade later, the Court substantially narrowed the entanglement theory in *Moose Lodge No. 107 v. Irvis*.[20] *Moose Lodge* involved a private club that had refused to serve an African-American. He argued that that refusal constituted state action since the Pennsylvania Liquor Control Board, a state entity, had granted the club a liquor license. In response, the Court insisted that "[w]here the impetus for the discrimination is private, the State must have significantly involved itself with invidious discrimination" in order for that private conduct to constitute state action.[21] The lodge's building was located on private property, and it portrayed itself as a private, rather than public, establishment. Thus, the Court concluded that, unlike in *Burton*, the surroundings did not imply a state operation.

Moose Lodge also made clear that discrimination by a private party does not violate the Equal Protection Clause simply because the private party receives some state benefit, such as a liquor license. However, the Court did leave open a narrow path for finding state action in the lodge's discrimination. It observed that, under state law, a club seeking a liquor license must comply with its own by-laws. Moose Lodge's by-laws required racial exclusion. The Court then suggested that, if the state had compelled Moose Lodge to comply with that exclusionary provision as a condition of

---

19. 365 U.S. 715 (1961).
20. 407 U.S. 163 (1972).
21. *Id.* at 173.

receiving the liquor license, then the state would be responsible for the ensuing discrimination. This theory parallels the explanation given earlier of *Shelley v. Kraemer*, as involving a case where a court was being asked to compel a seller to comply with a racially exclusionary real estate covenant that the seller wished to ignore by selling to an African-American. Situations like those—where the government is compelling an otherwise-unwilling person to discriminate[22]—clearly present stronger cases for "state action."

Dissenting in *Moose Lodge*, Justice Douglas argued that state action embraced the discriminatory behavior of any business subject to governmental regulation, particularly one operating under a state-granted license. Applying his approach to the private club in question, he observed that, unlike with marriage and driver's licenses, the state imposed a quota on the number of liquor licenses it would issue. Justice Douglas noted that the area where Moose Lodge was located had been at its maximum number for years, with the effect that the club's discrimination had the effect of limiting the ability of African-Americans to procure alcohol in a bar. Justice Brennan, joined by Justice Marshall, also dissented. Like Justice Douglas, he stressed the intensity of the state's regulation of liquor sales, which he argued entangled the state with liquor licensees to a much greater extent than with other businesses operating under a state license.

The dissenters' views have not prevailed. For example, two years later in *Jackson v. Metropolitan Edison Co.*,[23] the Court refused to attribute to the state a privately-owned utility's allegedly-unconstitutional procedure for cutting off persons' electric service for non-payment. The Court first rejected the argument that the provision of basic utilities constitutes state action either because the utility enjoyed a state-granted monopoly or because provision of electric service is a traditional government function. Addressing the entanglement theory, the Court, speaking through Justice Rehnquist, stated that "the inquiry must be whether there is a sufficiently close nexus between the State and the challenged action of the regulated entity so that the action of the latter may be fairly treated as that of the State itself."[24] It rejected the claim that the state had entangled itself with the utility by approving the utility's tariff filings with the state's public utility board, including those filings that set forth the utility's allegedly inadequate procedures for cutting off customers for non-payment.[25]

---

22. The use of the word "discriminate" in these examples should not mislead one into thinking that this type of state action analysis only applies in equal protection discrimination cases. The same analysis would apply if, for example, government sought to compel an unwilling private party to deny a right that, if the government directly denied it, would violate the Due Process Clause.

23. 419 U.S. 345 (1974).

24. *Id.* at 351.

25. The Court noted that the cut-off provisions were never the subject of a hearing and that the state had never objected to or questioned the cut-off provisions. This theory of state action is sometimes identified as resting on legislative or (as in *Jackson*) administrative approval of private conduct. One

Plaintiffs have invoked the entanglement theory in cases involving in-court conduct by private parties. One notable context where this has occurred is when a private litigant discriminates based on race when using its peremptory challenges in jury selection. Peremptory challenges are a feature of the jury selection process in which a litigant is entitled to reject a potential juror without having to offer a reason. In *Edmonson v. Leesville Concrete Co.*,[26] the Court found state action in the behavior of a private litigant in a civil suit in striking persons from a jury pool based on race. The Court noted that federal law authorized peremptory challenges, the litigant raised those challenges when implementing a government procedure (the trial process), and that the jury resulting in part from those peremptory challenges performs a traditional government function. Justice O'Connor, joined by Chief Justice Rehnquist and Justice Scalia, dissented, arguing that some of what goes on in a courtroom is nevertheless purely private conduct. Justice Scalia also wrote a separate dissent, to warn of the consequences of the Court's decision.

The next year, in *Georgia v. McCollum*,[27] the Court extended the state action concept to a criminal defendant's use of peremptory challenges. This may sound odd, given the obvious fact that a criminal defendant is deeply adverse to the state; thus, one would not normally think that the defendant's actions should be attributable to the state. Nevertheless, the Court based its conclusion on the fact that the defendant's conduct during jury selection helps determine the composition of a governmental entity—the jury—and thus should be subject to constitutional standards. Chief Justice Rehnquist and Justice Thomas both joined Justice Blackmun's majority opinion, concluding that it followed from the Court's decision in *Edmonson*. Justice Scalia also thought the majority decision followed from *Edmonson*, but he refused to take that step, given his unwillingness to agree that a criminal defendant's conduct in a trial constitutes state action. Justice O'Connor also dissented, but attempted to distinguish the actions of criminal defendants from those of civil litigants.

The peremptory challenge cases are fascinating and important, because they highlight the cross-cutting and sometimes contradictory factors and impulses in state action analysis. One can understand how racial discrimination occurring in a courtroom, in

---

can understand other cases discussed in this chapter as also implicating this theory. For example, when the *Moose Lodge* Court explained that there might be state action in that case if the liquor board had compelled the lodge to adhere to its discriminatory by-laws, one could understand that entanglement as taking the form of a particular stringent form of administrative approval, indeed, one verging on government compulsion rather than simply approval.

As Justice Marshall noted in dissent, the majority's analysis in *Jackson* created a paradox for the plaintiff claiming state action: "The majority's test puts potential plaintiffs in a difficult position: if the [State] Commission approves the tariff without argument or a hearing, the State has not sufficiently demonstrated its approval and support for the company's practices. If, on the other hand, the State challenges the tariff provision on the ground, for example, that the 'reasonable notice' does not meet the standards of fairness that it expects of the utility, then the State has not put its weight behind the termination procedure employed by the company, and again there is no state action." 419 U.S. at 370 (Marshall, J., dissenting).

26. 500 U.S. 614 (1991).
27. 505 U.S. 42 (1992).

the course of selecting a body such as a jury that is charged with power over persons' property, liberty, and even life, should be subject to constitutional standards, while still wondering about a rule attributing to the state the actions of a criminal defendant.

§ 14.04 The Continued Fact-Intensiveness of the State Action Doctrine

Complexities and paradoxes such as those marking the jury cases reveal, yet again, the fact- and policy-intensiveness of state action decisions. Writing in a state action case from 2001, Justice Souter recognized this. That case, *Brentwood Academy v. Tennessee Secondary School Athletic Association*,[28] considered whether an interscholastic association responsible for athletic competitions between schools in Tennessee was a state actor when it penalized a school for a recruiting violation. In the course of deciding that the association was indeed a state actor for that purpose, the Court, speaking through Justice Souter, recognized that:

> What [conduct] is fairly attributable [to the State] is a matter of normative judgment, and the criteria lack rigid simplicity. From the range of circumstances that could point toward the State behind an individual face, no one fact can function as a necessary condition across the board for finding state action; nor is any set of circumstances absolutely sufficient, for there may be some countervailing reason against attributing activity to the government.[29]

He continued that state action could be found where a private organization exercises a governmental function or is coerced to act by the state, or where there was "pervasive entwinement"[30] of state officials in the private organization's structure. Given the variety of ways in which a court might find state action and "the necessarily fact-bound inquiry" state action questions entail, it is unsurprising that Justice Souter suggested reliance on precedent to answer those questions. As he observed: "Our cases have identified a host of facts that can bear on the fairness of [a finding of state action] .... Amidst such variety, examples may be the best teachers."[31]

A more recent example of state action analysis is *Manhattan Community Access Corp. v. Halleck*.[32] *Manhattan Community* involved a privately-owned cable television company (MNN) that produced locally-generated content for transmission on the cable system. MNN excluded from its facilities persons based on those persons' speech. Writing for the Court, Justice Kavanaugh rejected the traditional public functions

---

28. 531 U.S. 288 (2001).

29. *Id.* at 295.

30. Whether the relatively new "entwinement" idea is the same as, or a variant of, the older "entanglement" idea as exemplified in cases such as *Burton v. Wilmington Parking Authority* is unclear. *See* Christopher Schmidt, *On Doctrinal Confusion: The Case of the State Action Doctrine*, 2016 BYU L. Rev. 575, 589 n. 47 (discussing this confusion).

31. 531 U.S. at 298, 296.

32. 139 S. Ct. 1921 (2019).

theory for finding state action, observing that "very few functions fall into that category"[33] and that cable television operations did not. The Court noted that state law required cities giving cable franchises to make locally-produced content available on the cable system selected, and that the city in this case had selected MNN to fulfill that function. But the Court concluded that this fact simply made MNN analogous to any other contractor that provides goods or services to a government entity. The Court also rejected the argument that the city owned the public access channels on which MNN transmitted its content.

Implicitly recognizing the fact-intensive nature of state action questions, Justice Sotomayor, dissenting for herself and three other justices, began her opinion as follows:

> The Court tells a very reasonable story about a case that is not before us. I write to address the one that is.
>
> This is a case about an organization [MNN] appointed by the government to administer a constitutional public [speech] forum. (It is not, as the Court suggests, about a private property owner that simply opened up its property to others.) New York City (the City) secured a property interest in public-access television channels when it granted a cable franchise to a cable company. State regulations require those public-access channels to be made open to the public on terms that render them a public forum. The City contracted out the administration of that forum to a private organization, petitioner Manhattan Community Access Corporation (MNN). By accepting that agency relationship, MNN stepped into the City's shoes and thus qualifies as a state actor, subject to the First Amendment like any other.[34]

Manhattan Community, like the cases that came before it, should make clear the exceptional fact- and policy-intensiveness of state action cases. Justice Sotomayor's disagreement with Justice Kavanaugh's description of the situation in *Manhattan Community* reflects the importance of facts—and characterizations of facts—in state action cases. More generally, the difficult reality is that "the State" is always "acting" in our lives, even if its actions take the form of background rules of law. Determining when such action becomes "state action" will always turn on a sensitive understanding of what the state is really doing, and the policy implications of a state action finding. For example, Justice Kavanaugh ended his opinion in *Manhattan Community* by reminding readers of the importance of maintaining a divide between public and private:

> Consistent with the text of the Constitution, the state-action doctrine enforces a critical boundary between the government and the individual, and thereby protects a robust sphere of individual liberty. Expanding the state-action

---

33. *Id.* at 1929.
34. *Id.* at 1934 (Sotomayor, J., dissenting).

doctrine beyond its traditional boundaries would expand governmental control while restricting individual liberty and private enterprise. We decline to do so in this case.[35]

Responding, Justice Sotomayor concluded her dissent as follows:

> This is not a case about bigger governments and smaller individuals; it is a case about principals and agents. New York City opened up a public forum on public-access channels in which it has a property interest. It asked MNN to run that public forum, and MNN accepted the job. That makes MNN subject to the First Amendment, just as if the City had decided to run the public forum itself.

> While the majority emphasizes that its decision is narrow and factbound, that does not make it any less misguided. It is crucial that the Court does not continue to ignore the reality, fully recognized by our precedents, that private actors who have been delegated constitutional responsibilities like this one should be accountable to the Constitution's demands.[36]

One can fully expect future state action cases to continue to be decided based on both factual distinctions and on larger judicial concerns about the proper boundary between government and the private realm. Such difficult distinctions cannot hope to be definitively or objectively discoverable simply by recourse to the vague term "state action."

---

35. *Ibid.* (majority opinion).
36. *Id.* at 1945 (Sotomayor, J., dissenting).

Constitution of the United States

We the People of the United States, in Order to form a more perfect Union, establish Justice, insure domestic Tranquility, provide for the common defence, promote the general Welfare, and secure the Blessings of Liberty to ourselves and our Posterity, do ordain and establish this Constitution for the United States of America.

Article I

Section 1. All legislative Powers herein granted shall be vested in a Congress of the United States, which shall consist of a Senate and House of Representatives.

Section 2. The House of Representatives shall be composed of Members chosen every second Year by the People of the several States, and the Electors in each State shall have the Qualifications requisite for Electors of the most numerous Branch of the State Legislature.

No Person shall be a Representative who shall not have attained to the age of twenty five Years, and been seven Years a Citizen of the United States, and who shall not, when elected, be an Inhabitant of that State in which he shall be chosen.

Representatives and direct Taxes shall be apportioned among the several States which may be included within this Union, according to their respective Numbers, which shall be determined by adding to the whole Number of free Persons, including those bound to Service for a Term of Years, and excluding Indians not taxed, three fifths of all other Persons. The actual Enumeration shall be made within three Years after the first Meeting of the Congress of the United States, and within every subsequent Term of ten Years, in such Manner as they shall by Law direct. The Number of Representatives shall not exceed one for every thirty Thousand, but each State shall have at Least one Representative; and until such enumeration shall be made, the State of New Hampshire shall be entitled to chuse three, Massachusetts eight, Rhode-Island and Providence Plantations one, Connecticut five, New-York six, New Jersey four, Pennsylvania eight, Delaware one, Maryland six, Virginia ten, North Carolina five, South Carolina five, and Georgia three.

When vacancies happen in the Representation from any State, the Executive Authority thereof shall issue Writs of Election to fill such Vacancies.

The House of Representatives shall chuse their Speaker and other Officers; and shall have the sole Power of Impeachment.

Section 3. The Senate of the United States shall be composed of two Senators from each State, chosen by the Legislature thereof, for six Years; and each Senator shall have one Vote.

Immediately after they shall be assembled in Consequence of the first Election, they shall be divided as equally as may be into three Classes. The Seats of the Senators of the first Class shall be vacated at the Expiration of the second Year, of the second Class at the Expiration of the fourth Year, and of the third Class at the Expiration of the sixth Year, so that one third may be chosen every second Year; and if Vacancies happen by Resignation, or otherwise, during the Recess of the Legislature of any State, the Executive thereof may make temporary Appointments until the next Meeting of the Legislature, which shall then fill such Vacancies.

No Person shall be a Senator who shall not have attained to the Age of thirty Years, and been nine Years a Citizen of the United States, and who shall not, when elected, be an Inhabitant of that State for which he shall be chosen.

The Vice President of the United States shall be President of the Senate but shall have no Vote, unless they be equally divided.

The Senate shall chuse their other Officers, and also a President pro tempore, in the Absence of the Vice President, or when he shall exercise the Office of President of the United States.

The Senate shall have the sole Power to try all Impeachments. When sitting for that Purpose, they shall be on Oath or Affirmation. When the President of the United States is tried the Chief Justice shall preside: And no Person shall be convicted without the Concurrence of two thirds of the Members present.

Judgment in Cases of Impeachment shall not extend further than to removal from Office, and disqualification to hold and enjoy any Office of honor, Trust or Profit under the United States: but the Party convicted shall nevertheless be liable and subject to Indictment, Trial, Judgment and Punishment, according to Law.

Section 4. The Times, Places and Manner of holding Elections for Senators and Representatives, shall be prescribed in each State by the Legislature thereof; but the Congress may at any time by Law make or alter such Regulations, except as to the Places of chusing Senators.

The Congress shall assemble at least once in every Year, and such Meeting shall be on the first Monday in December, unless they shall by Law appoint a different Day.

Section 5. Each House shall be the Judge of the Elections, Returns and Qualifications of its own Members, and a Majority of each shall constitute a Quorum to do Business; but a smaller Number may adjourn from day to day, and may be authorized to compel the Attendance of absent Members, in such Manner, and under such Penalties as each House may provide.

Each House may determine the Rules of its Proceedings, punish its Members for disorderly Behaviour, and, with the Concurrence of two thirds, expel a Member.

Each House shall keep a Journal of its Proceedings, and from time to time publish the same, excepting such Parts as may in their Judgment require Secrecy; and the Yeas and Nays of the Members of either House on any question shall, at the Desire of one fifth of those Present, be entered on the Journal.

Neither House, during the Session of Congress, shall, without the Consent of the other, adjourn for more than three days, nor to any other Place than that in which the two Houses shall be sitting.

Section 6. The Senators and Representatives shall receive a Compensation for their Services, to be ascertained by Law, and paid out of the Treasury of the United States. They shall in all Cases, except Treason, Felony and Breach of the Peace, be privileged from Arrest during their Attendance at the Session of their respective Houses, and in going to and returning from the same; and for any Speech or Debate in either House, they shall not be questioned in any other Place.

No Senator or Representative shall, during the Time for which he was elected, be appointed to any civil Office under the Authority of the United States, which shall have been created, or the Emoluments whereof shall have been encreased during such time; and no Person holding any Office under the United States, shall be a Member of either House during his Continuance in Office.

Section 7. All Bills for raising Revenue shall originate in the House of Representatives; but the Senate may propose or concur with amendments as on other Bills.

Every Bill which shall have passed the House of Representatives and the Senate, shall, before it become a Law, be presented to the President of the United States: If he approve he shall sign it, but if not he shall return it, with his Objections to that House in which it shall have originated, who shall enter the Objections at large on their Journal, and proceed to reconsider it. If after such Reconsideration two thirds of that House shall agree to pass the Bill, it shall be sent, together with the Objections, to the other House, by which it shall likewise be reconsidered, and if approved by two thirds of that House, it shall become a Law. But in all such Cases the Votes of both Houses shall be determined by Yeas and Nays, and the Names of the Persons voting for and against the Bill shall be entered on the Journal of each House respectively. If any Bill shall not be returned by the President within ten Days (Sundays excepted) after it shall have been presented to him, the Same shall be a Law, in like Manner as if he had signed it, unless the Congress by their Adjournment prevent its Return, in which Case it shall not be a Law.

Every Order, Resolution, or Vote to which the Concurrence of the Senate and House of Representatives may be necessary (except on a question of Adjournment) shall be presented to the President of the United States; and before the Same shall take Effect, shall be approved by him, or being disapproved by him, shall be repassed by two thirds of the Senate and House of Representatives, according to the Rules and Limitations prescribed in the Case of a Bill.

Section 8. The Congress shall have Power To lay and collect Taxes, Duties, Imposts and Excises, to pay the Debts and provide for the common Defence and general Wel-

624 CONSTITUTION OF THE UNITED STATES

fare of the United States; but all Duties, Imposts and Excises shall be uniform throughout the United States;

To borrow Money on the credit of the United States;

To regulate Commerce with foreign Nations, and among the several States, and with the Indian Tribes;

To establish an uniform Rule of Naturalization, and uniform Laws on the subject of Bankruptcies throughout the United States;

To coin Money, regulate the Value thereof, and of foreign Coin, and fix the Standard of Weights and Measures;

To provide for the Punishment of counterfeiting the Securities and current Coin of the United States;

To establish Post Offices and post Roads;

To promote the Progress of Science and useful Arts, by securing for limited Times to Authors and Inventors the exclusive Right to their respective Writings and Discoveries;

To constitute Tribunals inferior to the supreme Court;

To define and punish Piracies and Felonies committed on the high Seas, and Offences against the Law of Nations;

To declare War, grant Letters of Marque and Reprisal, and make Rules concerning Captures on Land and Water;

To raise and support Armies, but no Appropriation of Money to that Use shall be for a longer Term than two Years;

To provide and maintain a Navy;

To make Rules for the Government and Regulation of the land and naval Forces;

To provide for calling forth the Militia to execute the Laws of the Union, suppress Insurrections and repel Invasions;

To provide for organizing, arming, and disciplining, the Militia, and for governing such Part of them as may be employed in the Service of the United States, reserving to the States respectively, the Appointment of the Officers, and the Authority of training the Militia according to the discipline prescribed by Congress;

To exercise exclusive Legislation in all Cases whatsoever, over such District (not exceeding ten Miles square) as may, by Cession of Particular States, and the Acceptance of Congress, become the Seat of the Government of the United States, and to exercise like Authority over all Places purchased by the Consent of the Legislature of the State in which the Same shall be, for the Erection of Forts, Magazines, Arsenals, dock-Yards, and other needful Buildings;—And

To make all Laws which shall be necessary and proper for carrying into Execution the foregoing Powers, and all other Powers vested by this Constitution in the Government of the United States, or in any Department or Officer thereof.

Section 9. The Migration or Importation of such Persons as any of the States now existing shall think proper to admit, shall not be prohibited by the Congress prior to the Year one thousand eight hundred and eight, but a Tax or duty may be imposed on such Importation, not exceeding ten dollars for each Person.

The Privilege of the Writ of Habeas Corpus shall not be suspended, unless when in Cases of Rebellion or Invasion the public Safety may require it.

No Bill of Attainder or ex post facto Law shall be passed.

No Capitation, or other direct, Tax shall be laid, unless in Proportion to the Census or Enumeration herein before directed to be taken.

No Tax or Duty shall be laid on Articles exported from any State.

No Preference shall be given by any Regulation of Commerce or Revenue to the Ports of one State over those of another: nor shall Vessels bound to, or from, one State, be obliged to enter, clear or pay Duties in another.

No Money shall be drawn from the Treasury, but in Consequence of Appropriations made by Law; and a regular Statement and Account of the Receipts and Expenditures of all public Money shall be published from time to time.

No Title of Nobility shall be granted by the United States: And no Person holding any Office of Profit or Trust under them, shall, without the Consent of the Congress, accept of any present, Emolument, Office, or Title, of any kind whatever, from any King, Prince or foreign State.

Section 10. No State shall enter into any Treaty, Alliance, or Confederation; grant Letters of Marque and Reprisal; coin Money; emit Bills of Credit; make any Thing but gold and silver Coin a Tender in Payment of Debts; pass any Bill of Attainder, ex post facto Law, or Law impairing the Obligation of Contracts, or grant any Title of Nobility.

No State shall, without the Consent of the Congress, lay any Imposts or Duties on Imports or Exports, except what may be absolutely necessary for executing it's [sic] inspection Laws: and the net Produce of all Duties and Imposts, laid by any State on Imports or Exports, shall be for the Use of the Treasury of the United States; and all such Laws shall be subject to the Revision and Controul of the Congress.

No State shall, without the Consent of Congress, lay any Duty of Tonnage, keep Troops, or Ships of War in time of Peace, enter into any Agreement or Compact with another State, or with a foreign Power, or engage in War, unless actually invaded, or in such imminent Danger as will not admit of delay.

Article II

Section 1. The executive Power shall be vested in a President of the United States of America. He shall hold his Office during the Term of four Years, and, together with the Vice President, chosen for the same Term, be elected, as follows:

Each State shall appoint, in such Manner as the Legislature thereof may direct, a Number of Electors, equal to the whole Number of Senators and Representatives to which the State may be entitled in the Congress: but no Senator or Representative, or Person holding an Office of Trust or Profit under the United States, shall be appointed an Elector.

The Electors shall meet in their respective States, and vote by Ballot for two Persons, of whom one at least shall not be an Inhabitant of the same State with themselves. And they shall make a List of all the Persons voted for, and of the Number of Votes for each; which List they shall sign and certify, and transmit sealed to the Seat of the Government of the United States, directed to the President of the Senate. The President of the Senate shall, in the Presence of the Senate and House of Representatives, open all the Certificates, and the Votes shall then be counted. The Person having the greatest Number of Votes shall be the President, if such Number be a Majority of the whole Number of Electors appointed; and if there be more than one who have such Majority, and have an equal Number of Votes, then the House of Representatives shall immediately chuse by Ballot one of them for President; and if no Person have a Majority, then from the five highest on the List the said House shall in like Manner chuse the President. But in chusing the President, the Votes shall be taken by States, the representation from each State having one Vote; a quorum for this Purpose shall consist of a Member or Members from two thirds of the States, and a Majority of all the States shall be necessary to a Choice. In every Case, after the Choice of the President, the Person having the greatest Number of Votes of the Electors shall be the Vice President. But if there should remain two or more who have equal Votes, the Senate shall chuse from them by Ballot the Vice President.

The Congress may determine the Time of chusing the Electors, and the Day on which they shall give their Votes; which Day shall be the same throughout the United States.

No Person except a natural born Citizen, or a Citizen of the United States, at the time of the Adoption of this Constitution, shall be eligible to the Office of President; neither shall any person be eligible to that Office who shall not have attained to the Age of thirty five Years, and been fourteen Years a Resident within the United States.

In Case of the Removal of the President from Office, or of his Death, Resignation, or Inability to discharge the Powers and Duties of the said Office, the Same shall devolve on the Vice President, and the Congress may by Law provide for the Case of Removal, Death, Resignation or Inability, both of the President and Vice President, declaring what Officer shall then act as President, and such Officer shall act accordingly, until the Disability be removed, or a President shall be elected.

The President shall, at stated Times, receive for his Services, a Compensation, which shall neither be encreased nor diminished during the Period for which he shall have been elected, and he shall not receive within that Period any other Emolument from the United States, or any of them.

Before he enter on the Execution of his Office, he shall take the following Oath or Affirmation: — "I do solemnly swear (or affirm) that I will faithfully execute the Office of President of the United States, and will to the best of my Ability, preserve, protect and defend the Constitution of the United States."

Section 2. The President shall be Commander in Chief of the Army and Navy of the United States, and of the Militia of the several States, when called into the actual Service of the United States; he may require the Opinion, in writing, of the principal Officer in each of the executive Departments, upon any Subject relating to the Duties of their respective Offices, and he shall have Power to Grant Reprieves and Pardons for Offences against the United States, except in Cases of Impeachment.

He shall have Power, by and with the Advice and Consent of the Senate, to make Treaties, provided two thirds of the Senators present concur; and he shall nominate, and by and with the Advice and Consent of the Senate, shall appoint Ambassadors, other public Ministers and Consuls, Judges of the supreme Court, and all other Officers of the United States, whose Appointments are not herein otherwise provided for, and which shall be established by Law: but the Congress may by Law vest the Appointment of such inferior Officers, as they think proper, in the President alone, in the Courts of Law, or in the Heads of Departments.

The President shall have Power to fill up all Vacancies that may happen during the Recess of the Senate, by granting Commissions which shall expire at the End of their next Session.

Section 3. He shall from time to time give to the Congress Information of the State of the Union, and recommend to their Consideration such Measures as he shall judge necessary and expedient; he may, on extraordinary Occasions, convene both Houses, or either of them, and in Case of Disagreement between them, with Respect to the Time of Adjournment, he may adjourn them to such Time as he shall think proper; he shall receive Ambassadors and other public Ministers; he shall take Care that the Laws be faithfully executed, and shall Commission all the Officers of the United States.

Section 4. The President, Vice President and all civil Officers of the United States, shall be removed from Office on Impeachment for, and Conviction of, Treason, Bribery, or other high Crimes and Misdemeanors.

Article III

Section 1. The judicial Power of the United States, shall be vested in one supreme Court, and in such inferior Courts as the Congress may from time to time ordain and establish. The Judges, both of the supreme and inferior Courts, shall hold their Offices during good Behaviour, and shall, at stated Times, receive for their Services, a Compensation, which shall not be diminished during their Continuance in Office.

Section 2. The judicial Power shall extend to all Cases, in Law and Equity, arising under this Constitution, the Laws of the United States, and Treaties made, or which shall be made, under their Authority;—to all Cases affecting Ambassadors, other public ministers and Consuls;—to all Cases of admiralty and maritime Jurisdiction;—to Controversies to which the United States shall be a Party;—to Controversies between two or more States;—between a State and Citizens of another State;—between Citizens of different States;—between Citizens of the same State claiming

Lands under Grants of different States, and between a State, or the Citizens thereof, and foreign States, Citizens or Subjects.

In all Cases affecting Ambassadors, other public Ministers and Consuls, and those in which a State shall be Party, the supreme Court shall have original Jurisdiction. In all the other Cases before mentioned, the supreme Court shall have appellate Jurisdiction, both as to Law and Fact, with such Exceptions, and under such Regulations as the Congress shall make.

The Trial of all Crimes, except in Cases of Impeachment, shall be by Jury; and such Trial shall be held in the State where the said Crimes shall have been committed; but when not committed within any State, the Trial shall be at such Place or Places as the Congress may by Law have directed.

Section 3. Treason against the United States, shall consist only in levying War against them, or in adhering to their Enemies, giving them Aid and Comfort. No Person shall be convicted of Treason unless on the Testimony of two Witnesses to the same overt Act, or on Confession in open Court.

The Congress shall have Power to declare the Punishment of Treason, but no Attainder of Treason shall work Corruption of Blood, or Forfeiture except during the Life of the Person attainted.

Article IV

Section 1. Full Faith and Credit shall be given in each State to the public Acts, Records, and judicial Proceedings of every other State. And the Congress may by general Laws prescribe the Manner in which such Acts, Records and Proceedings shall be proved, and the Effect thereof.

Section 2. The Citizens of each State shall be entitled to all Privileges and Immunities of Citizens in the several States.

A Person charged in any State with Treason, Felony, or other Crime, who shall flee from Justice, and be found in another State, shall on Demand of the executive Authority of the State from which he fled, be delivered up, to be removed to the State having Jurisdiction of the Crime.

No Person held to Service or Labour in one State, under the Laws thereof, escaping into another, shall, in Consequence of any Law or Regulation therein, be discharged from such Service or Labour, but shall be delivered up on Claim of the Party to whom such Service or Labour may be due.

Section 3. New States may be admitted by the Congress into this Union; but no new State shall be formed or erected within the Jurisdiction of any other State; nor any State be formed by the Junction of two or more States, or Parts of States, without the Consent of the Legislatures of the States concerned as well as of the Congress.

The Congress shall have Power to dispose of and make all needful Rules and Regulations respecting the Territory or other Property belonging to the United States; and nothing in this Constitution shall be so construed as to Prejudice any Claims of the United States, or of any particular State.

Section 4. The United States shall guarantee to every State in this Union a Republican Form of Government, and shall protect each of them against Invasion; and on Application of the Legislature, or of the Executive (when the Legislature cannot be convened) against domestic Violence.

Article V

The Congress, whenever two thirds of both Houses shall deem it necessary, shall propose Amendments to this Constitution, or, on the Application of the Legislatures of two thirds of the several States, shall call a Convention for proposing Amendments, which, in either Case, shall be valid to all Intents and Purposes, as Part of this Constitution, when ratified by the Legislatures of three fourths of the several States, or by Conventions in three fourths thereof, as the one or the other Mode of Ratification may be proposed by the Congress; Provided that no Amendment which may be made prior to the Year One thousand eight hundred and eight shall in any Manner affect the first and fourth Clauses in the Ninth Section of the first Article; and that no State, without its Consent, shall be deprived of its equal Suffrage in the Senate.

Article VI

All Debts contracted and Engagements entered into, before the Adoption of this Constitution, shall be as valid against the United States under this Constitution, as under the Confederation.

This Constitution, and the Laws of the United States which shall be made in Pursuance thereof; and all Treaties made, or which shall be made, under the Authority of the United States, shall be the supreme Law of the Land; and the Judges in every State shall be bound thereby, any Thing in the Constitution or Laws of any state to the Contrary notwithstanding.

The Senators and Representatives before mentioned, and the Members of the several State Legislatures, and all executive and judicial Officers, both of the United States and of the several States, shall be bound by Oath or Affirmation, to support this Constitution; but no religious Test shall ever be required as a Qualification to any Office or public Trust under the United States.

Article VII

The Ratification of the Conventions of nine States, shall be sufficient for the Establishment of this Constitution between the States so ratifying the same.

Amendment 1 [1791]

Congress shall make no law respecting an establishment of religion, or prohibiting the free exercise thereof; or abridging the freedom of speech, or of the press; or the right of the people peaceably to assemble, and to petition the Government for a redress of grievances.

Amendment 2 [1791]

A well regulated Militia, being necessary to the security of a free State, the right of the people to keep and bear Arms, shall not be infringed.

Amendment 3 [1791]

No Soldier shall, in time of peace be quartered in any house, without the consent of the Owner, nor in time of war, but in a manner to be prescribed by law.

Amendment 4 [1791]

The right of the people to be secure in their persons, houses, papers, and effects, against unreasonable searches and seizures, shall not be violated, and no Warrants shall issue, but upon probable cause, supported by Oath or affirmation, and particularly describing the place to be searched, and the persons or things to be seized.

Amendment 5 [1791]

No person shall be held to answer for a capital, or otherwise infamous crime, unless on a presentment or indictment of a Grand Jury, except in cases arising in the land or naval forces, or in the Militia, when in actual service in time of War or public danger; nor shall any person be subject for the same offence to be twice put in jeopardy of life or limb; nor shall be compelled in any criminal case to be a witness against himself, nor be deprived of life, liberty, or property, without due process of law; nor shall private property be taken for public use, without just compensation.

Amendment 6 [1791]

In all criminal prosecutions, the accused shall enjoy the right to a speedy and public trial, by an impartial jury of the State and district wherein the crime shall have been committed, which district shall have been previously ascertained by law, and to be informed of the nature and cause of the accusation; to be confronted with the witnesses against him; to have compulsory process for obtaining witnesses in his favor, and to have the Assistance of Counsel for his defence.

Amendment 7 [1791]

In Suits at common law, where the value in controversy shall exceed twenty dollars, the right of trial by jury shall be preserved, and no fact tried by a jury, shall be otherwise re-examined in any Court of the United States, than according to the rules of the common law.

Amendment 8 [1791]

Excessive bail shall not be required, nor excessive fines imposed, nor cruel and unusual punishments inflicted.

Amendment 9 [1791]

The enumeration in the Constitution, of certain rights, shall not be construed to deny or disparage others retained by the people.

Amendment 10 [1791]

The powers not delegated to the United States by the Constitution, nor prohibited by it to the States, are reserved to the States respectively, or to the people.

Amendment 11 [1795]

The Judicial power of the United States shall not be construed to extend to any suit in law or equity, commenced or prosecuted against one of the United States by Citizens of another State, or by Citizens or Subjects of any Foreign State.

Amendment 12 [1804]

The Electors shall meet in their respective states and vote by ballot for President and Vice-President, one of whom, at least, shall not be an inhabitant of the same state with themselves; they shall name in their ballots the person voted for as President, and in distinct ballots the person voted for as Vice-President, and they shall make distinct lists of all persons voted for as President, and of all persons voted for as Vice-President, and of the number of votes for each, which lists they shall sign and certify, and transmit sealed to the seat of the government of the United States, directed to the President of the Senate; — The President of the Senate shall, in the presence of the Senate and House of Representatives, open all the certificates and the votes shall then be counted; — The person having the greatest Number of votes for President, shall be the President, if such number be a majority of the whole number of Electors appointed; and if no person have such majority, then from the persons having the highest numbers not exceeding three on the list of those voted for as President, the House of Representatives shall choose immediately, by ballot, the President. But in choosing the President, the votes shall be taken by states, the representation from each state having one vote; a quorum for this purpose shall consist of a member or members from two-thirds of the states, and a majority of all the states shall be necessary to a choice. And if the House of Representatives shall not choose a President whenever the right of choice shall devolve upon them, before the fourth day of March next following, then the Vice-President shall act as President, as in the case of the death or other constitutional disability of the President — The person having the greatest number of votes as Vice-President, shall be the Vice-President, if such number be a majority of the whole number of Electors appointed, and if no person have a majority, then from the two highest numbers on the list, the Senate shall choose the Vice-President; a quorum for the purpose shall consist of two-thirds of the whole number of Senators, and a majority of the whole number shall be necessary to a choice. But no person constitutionally ineligible to the office of President shall be eligible to that of Vice-President of the United States.

Amendment 13 [1865]

Section 1. Neither slavery nor involuntary servitude, except as a punishment for crime whereof the party shall have been duly convicted, shall exist within the United States, or any place subject to their jurisdiction.

Section 2. Congress shall have power to enforce this article by appropriate legislation.

Amendment 14 [1868]

Section 1. All persons born or naturalized in the United States and subject to the jurisdiction thereof, are citizens of the United States and of the State wherein they reside. No State shall make or enforce any law which shall abridge the privileges or immunities of citizens of the United States; nor shall any State deprive any person of life, liberty, or property, without due process of law; nor deny to any person within its jurisdiction the equal protection of the laws.

Section 2. Representatives shall be apportioned among the several States according to their respective numbers, counting the whole number of persons in each State, excluding Indians not taxed. But when the right to vote at any election for the choice of electors for President and Vice President of the United States, Representatives in Congress, the Executive and Judicial officers of a State, or the members of the Legislature thereof, is denied to any of the male inhabitants of such State, being twenty-one years of age, and citizens of the United States, or in any way abridged, except for participation in rebellion, or other crime, the basis of representation therein shall be reduced in the proportion which the number of such male citizens shall bear to the whole number of male citizens twenty-one years of age in such State.

Section 3. No person shall be a Senator or Representative in Congress, or elector of President and Vice President, or hold any office, civil or military, under the United States, or under any State, who, having previously taken an oath, as a member of Congress, or as an officer of the United States, or as a member of any State legislature, or as an executive or judicial officer of any State, to support the Constitution of the United States, shall have engaged in insurrection or rebellion against the same, or given aid or comfort to the enemies thereof. But Congress may by a vote of two-thirds of each House, remove such disability.

Section 4. The validity of the public debt of the United States, authorized by law, including debts incurred for payment of pensions and bounties for services in suppressing insurrection or rebellion, shall not be questioned. But neither the United States nor any State shall assume or pay any debt or obligation incurred in aid of insurrection or rebellion against the United States, or any claim for the loss or emancipation of any slave; but all such debts, obligations and claims shall be held illegal and void.

Section 5. The Congress shall have power to enforce, by appropriate legislation, the provisions of this article.

Amendment 15 [1870]

Section 1. The right of citizens of the United States to vote shall not be denied or abridged by the United States or by any State on account of race, color, or previous condition of servitude.

Section 2. The Congress shall have the power to enforce this article by appropriate legislation.

Amendment 16 [1913]

The Congress shall have power to lay and collect taxes on incomes, from whatever source derived, without apportionment among the several States, and without regard to any census or enumeration.

Amendment 17 [1913]

The Senate of the United States shall be composed of two Senators from each State, elected by the people thereof, for six years; and each Senator shall have one vote. The electors in each State shall have the qualifications requisite for electors of the most numerous branch of the State legislatures.

When vacancies happen in the representation of any State in the Senate, the executive authority of such State shall issue writs of election to fill such vacancies: Provided, That the legislature of any State may empower the executive thereof to make temporary appointments until the people fill the vacancies by election as the legislature may direct.

This amendment shall not be so construed as to affect the election or term of any Senator chosen before it becomes valid as part of the Constitution.

Amendment 18 [1919]

Section 1. After one year from the ratification of this article the manufacture, sale, or transportation of intoxicating liquors within, the importation thereof into, or the exportation thereof from the United States and all territory subject to the jurisdiction thereof for beverage purposes is hereby prohibited.

Section 2. The Congress and the several States shall have concurrent power to enforce this article by appropriate legislation.

Section 3. This article shall be inoperative unless it shall have been ratified as an amendment to the Constitution by the legislatures of the several States, as provided in the Constitution, within seven years from the date of the submission hereof to the States by the Congress.

Amendment 19 [1920]

The right of citizens of the United States to vote shall not be denied or abridged by the United States or by any State on account of sex.

Congress shall have power to enforce this article by appropriate legislation.

Amendment 20 [1933]

Section 1. The terms of the President and Vice President shall end at noon on the 20th day of January, and the terms of Senators and Representatives at noon on the 3d day of January, of the years in which such terms would have ended if this article had not been ratified; and the terms of their successors shall then begin.

Section 2. The Congress shall assemble at least once in every year, and such meeting shall begin at noon on the 3d day of January, unless they shall by law appoint a different day.

Section 3. If, at the time fixed for the beginning of the term of the President, the President elect shall have died, the Vice President elect shall become President. If a President shall not have been chosen before the time fixed for the beginning of his term, or if the President elect shall have failed to qualify, then the Vice President elect shall act as President until a President shall have qualified; and the Congress may by law provide for the case wherein neither a President elect nor a Vice President elect shall have qualified, declaring who shall then act as President, or the manner in which one who is to act shall be selected, and such person shall act accordingly until a President or Vice President shall have qualified.

Section 4. The Congress may by law provide for the case of the death of any of the persons from whom the House of Representatives may choose a President whenever the right of choice shall have devolved upon them, and for the case of the death of any of the persons from whom the Senate may choose a Vice President whenever the right of choice shall have devolved upon them.

Section 5. Sections 1 and 2 shall take effect on the 15th day of October following the ratification of this article.

Section 6. This article shall be inoperative unless it shall have been ratified as an amendment to the Constitution by the legislatures of three-fourths of the several States within seven years from the date of its submission.

Amendment 21 [1933]

Section 1. The eighteenth article of amendment to the Constitution of the United States is hereby repealed.

Section 2. The transportation or importation into any State, Territory, or possession of the United States for delivery or use therein of intoxicating liquors, in violation of the laws thereof, is hereby prohibited.

Section 3. This article shall be inoperative unless it shall have been ratified as an amendment to the Constitution by conventions in the several States, as provided in the Constitution, within seven years from the date of the submission hereof to the States by the Congress.

Amendment 22 [1951]

Section 1. No person shall be elected to the office of the President more than twice, and no person who has held the office of President, or acted as President, for more than two years of a term to which some other person was elected President shall be elected to the office of the President more than once. But this Article shall not apply to any person holding the office of President, when this Article was proposed by the Congress, and shall not prevent any person who may be holding the office of President, or acting as President, during the term within which this Article becomes operative from holding the office of President or acting as President during the remainder of such term.

Section 2. This article shall be inoperative unless it shall have been ratified as an amendment to the Constitution by the legislatures of three-fourths of the several States within seven years from the date of its submission to the States by the Congress.

Amendment 23 [1961]

Section 1. The District constituting the seat of Government of the United States shall appoint in such manner as the Congress may direct: A number of electors of President and Vice President equal to the whole number of Senators and Representatives in Congress to which the District would be entitled if it were a State, but in no event more than the least populous State; they shall be in addition to those appointed by the States, but shall be considered, for the purposes of the election of President and Vice President, to be electors appointed by a State; and they shall meet in the District and perform such duties as provided by the twelfth article of amendment.

Section 2. The Congress shall have power to enforce this article by appropriate legislation.

Amendment 24 [1964]

Section 1. The right of citizens of the United States to vote in any primary or other election for President or Vice President, for electors for President or Vice President, or for Senator or Representative in Congress, shall not be denied or abridged by the United States or any State by reason of failure to pay any poll tax or other tax.

Section 2. The Congress shall have power to enforce this article by appropriate legislation.

Amendment 25 [1967]

Section 1. In case of the removal of the President from office or of his death or resignation, the Vice President shall become President.

Section 2. Whenever there is a vacancy in the office of the Vice President, the President shall nominate a Vice President who shall take office upon confirmation by a majority vote of both Houses of Congress.

Section 3. Whenever the President transmits to the President pro tempore of the Senate and the Speaker of the House of Representatives his written declaration that he is unable to discharge the powers and duties of his office, and until he transmits to them a written declaration to the contrary, such powers and duties shall be discharged by the Vice President as Acting President.

Section 4. Whenever the Vice President and a majority of either the principal officers of the executive departments or of such other body as Congress may by law provide, transmit to the President pro tempore of the Senate and the Speaker of the House of Representatives their written declaration that the President is unable to discharge the powers and duties of his office, the Vice President shall immediately assume the powers and duties of the office as Acting President.

Thereafter, when the President transmits to the President pro tempore of the Senate and the Speaker of the House of Representatives his written declaration that no inability exists, he shall resume the powers and duties of his office unless the Vice President and a majority of either the principal officers of the executive department or of such other body as Congress may by law provide, transmit within four days to the President pro tempore of the Senate and the Speaker of the House of Representatives their written declaration that the President is unable to discharge the powers and duties of his office. Thereupon Congress shall decide the issue, assembling within forty-eight hours for that purpose if not in session. If the Congress, within twenty-one days after receipt of the latter written declaration, or, if Congress is not in session, within twenty-one days after Congress is required to assemble, determines by two-thirds vote of both Houses that the President is unable to discharge the powers and duties of his office, the Vice President shall continue to discharge the same as Acting President; otherwise, the President shall resume the powers and duties of his office.

Amendment 26 [1971]

Section 1. The right of citizens of the United States, who are eighteen years of age or older, to vote shall not be denied or abridged by the United States or by any State on account of age.

Section 2. The Congress shall have power to enforce this article by appropriate legislation.

Amendment 27 [1992]

No law varying the compensation for the services of the Senators and Representatives shall take effect, until an election of Representatives shall have intervened.

Table of Cases

Index